PRINT AND THE PEOPLE 1819-1851

Edited, with an Introduction and Commentary, by LOUIS JAMES

Allen Lane

FOR MICHAEL TURNER,
JENNY TONKIN
AND THE LIBRARIANS
AT THE JOHN JOHNSON COLLECTION,
BODLEIAN LIBRARY, OXFORD,
IN GRATITUDE
FOR THEIR KIND, PATIENT
AND EXPERT HELP.

CONTENTS

III. ADMONITORY

IV. FABLES

ACKNOWLEDGEMENTS

My greatest debts have been to Michael Turner, Jenny Tonkin and the tireless librarians of the John Johnson Collection, Oxford. I have also been helped by librarians elsewhere as I have sorted through largely uncatalogued material. Mr Jim Styles and his helpers at the University of Kent have developed many hundreds of prints, of which only some have been used, but all of which shared the same expertise and care. My thanks to them. I have asked for, and received, help from many in the field; in particular from Brian Harrison, who gave crucial help at an early stage, and Martha Vicinus, whose own work has been a challenge and a stimulus. A. L. Lloyd has given of his expertise in folk song as part of the life of the people; Donald Read, Berthold Wolpe, and Hugh Cunningham have provided historical information; Victor Neuberg and Michael Hughes have advised on street literature. I hope these and many others who have given help will accept this grateful acknowledgement.

My first thanks must go to the Librarian of the Bodleian Library, Oxford, for permission to reproduce most of the facsimile material here; I also gratefully acknowledge permission given by the following: Berthold Wolpe (p. 16); Manchester Public Library (p. 63); United Society of Brushmakers (p. 66); Independent Order of Oddfellows, Manchester Unity (p. 67); Public Record Office, London (pp. 78, 169, 246, 342); Manchester Public Library (p. 229); Epworth Society Archives (p. 159); University of Kent (pp. 82, 226).

ABOUT THIS BOOK

This anthology makes available a range of popular literature of interest to both scholars and the general reader, although of a type generally inaccessible and often neglected. It covers the years between Peterloo (1819) and the Great Exhibition (1851), as significant watersheds in the life of the English people. These dates have been kept to, except for a few earlier items that were still being often reprinted.

The items have been chosen and arranged to show on one hand the development of popular literature with cheaper publishing methods and increased literacy; on the other, the ways this literature reflected the life of its readers. I have been concerned not only with direct statement, but with the communication that comes through style and the way in which a piece is written. An account of a murder, for instance, may be about ideas of Providence or Class as much as about a particular crime. Because print is a visual medium, facsimile reproductions have been used wherever possible.

It proved impossible to deal adequately with the major political and social movements, such as Chartism or the Corn Law agitation, so these have been largely omitted. Directly historical material is that most frequently reprinted elsewhere, and is to be found in such excellent anthologies as Dorothy Thompson's *The Early Chartists* (1971). This and other material is listed in the select annotated bibliography, which is arranged by topics, and is intended as an integral part of the book.

The introductory chapters offer a framework for the anthology, but are also an examination of aspects of popular culture in their own right. Many of the facts may be familiar – I have been indebted in particular to the work of E. P. Thompson, E. J. Hobsbawm, J. F. C. Harrison and Richard Altick – but the way the facts are used I hope is fresh. The study examines movements in the history of publishing and education, and the significance of the reading experience, before exploring such diverse topics as almanacks, Millenarianism and melodrama, to show ways in which popular literature took its place in the evolving culture of the people.

HISTORY AND PERSPECTIVES

Between the mother, with her fast-perishing
lumber of superstitions, folk-lore dialect,
and orally transmitted ballads, and the
daughter, with her trained National teachings
and Standard knowledge under the infinitely
revised Code, there was a gap of two hundred
years as ordinarily understood. When they
were together the Jacobean and the
Victorian ages were juxtaposed.

Thomas Hardy, *Tess of the d'Urbervilles*

COMMEMORATION OF THE ENACTMENT
OF
Parliamentary Reform,

DERBY, AUGUST 7, 1832.

THE REFORM BILL FOR ENGLAND RECEIVED THE ROYAL ASSENT, JUNE 7;
SCOTLAND, PASSED JULY 17; IRELAND, AUGUST 2.

Intellect and Justice have triumphed over Ignorance, Corruption, and misused Power. The Reform Bills have passed. The Land rejoices. In that joy the Printers of Derby—the men who exercise the glorious art of the PRESS—the art by which man communicates with man, and by which political truths, the strength and wealth of the public mind, the force of public opinion, are at once diffused and concentrated—unite with unreserved transport.—By the sword, the spear, ʌnd the cannon, nations were enslaved. By the PRESS, nations are delivered from their enslavers. In the days of ignorance, when men could not give utterance to the wrongs they felt—when the solitary truths that sometimes flashed across their reflexions were extinguished in their isolated miseries—mankind were delivered over, in chains and in unavailing sorrows, to superstition and tyranny. But, the PRESS appeared, and the clouds of ignorance gradually dispersed. The opinions of men were called forth and united. Millions knew what millions thought; and Truth, irradiate with the mutual knowledge, interchanged and confirmed among those who received and imparted it, constituted the mental strength of millions; at every movement of which tyranny trembles, and its armies turn pale. Nothing can resist this mental strength. Once combined it can never be broken: once brought into action, it will never cease from its labours; but, to the end of the world, it will go on, increasing the harmony, the liberty and the happiness of the human race.

THE GREAT ORGAN OF THIS MENTAL STRENGTH IS
The Press.

Do tyrants—whether EMPERORS, or KINGS, or ARISTOCRATS—still hope to restrain the mighty efforts of the PRESS?—Do they still presume to pronounce their penal statutes against it?—Do they imagine that their edicts—the miserable effusions of their greedy courtiers and interested counsellors—can preclude the millions from conceiving and combining those mental energies to which the labours of the PRESS have imparted a never-dying existence? FOOLS! MADMEN!

THE PRESS,

which they would subjugate, has broken their pretended authority, and turned into ridicule their imposing splendours—splendours which are bright only in proportion to the corruption and dissolution of the people's prosperity!

THE PRESS

has shown the world that governments have no basis, except as they are founded upon

Popular Representation in the Legislature.

Without that basis such Governments are but the *unaccredited few* usurping illegitimate authority over the *many*.

These Governments have been great in the obedience of ignorance. To the obedience, the servile and wretched obedience of ignorance, they owe their wealthy Priesthoods, their extravagant state expenditure, and all their other greedy and debasing establishments! To the obedience of ignorance they are indebted for the means they have so long enjoyed, of setting up vice and folly and of tricking them out in their licentious festivities, at the expense of the labouring poor! The obedience of ignorance has enabled the false splendour and the real misery of the Country to go hand in hand. But, THANKS TO THE PRESS, Ignorance itself hath fallen, and the obedience of ignorance will henceforth be sought for in vain. THE PRESS hath cleared the path for the advance of GREY, BROUGHAM, RUSSELL and ALTHORP. THE PRESS hath sustained the efforts of these patriotic Ministers against all the deceitful machinations of a Wellington, a Lyndhurst, a Croker, a Peel, and a Wetherell.

PARLIAMENTARY REFORM

Is the first of the blessings which this abused People owes to the downfal of the obedience of ignorance, and to the combination of popular opinion, effected by THE PRESS.

An Ode,
WRITTEN BY THOMAS NOBLE.
Set to Music by Mr. Gover.

Bring forth the PRESS!	Forth came the PRESS !	Th' eternal PRESS !
When first that mighty shout was heard,	Forth then that mighty engine came,	Corruption's worms shall ne'er destroy,
Truth rose, in radiant light emspher'd,	The power of knowledge to proclaim,	But patriots shall its powers enjoy,
The Nations to address.	And man with power to bless;	In peace and happiness.
Then Tyrants startled, with dismay,	And where its leaves of thought were	And, see th' eternal PRESS advance,
Call'd forth their armies in array,—	spread,	With freedom over eager France—
And Priestcraft, gaoler of the mind,	There Superstition, trembling, fled ;	With freedom o'er each German tribe—
In louder tones, blasphemed mankind :	And Tyrants, in their pride, confest	REFORM on Britain's flag inscribe—
But Truth, indignant, cried,	Dread of the people they oppress'd—	BROUGHAM, RUSSELL, ALTHORP,
While suffering man replied,	And courtiers, priests and peers,	GREY,
Bring forth the PRESS !	Shriek'd out amid their fears,	'Are names bright in the ray
	Destroy the PRESS !	Of the eternal PRESS !

(PRINTED DURING THE PROCESSION.)

1. MAGIC INTO PRINT

In August 1832, during the celebrations for the passing of the first Reform Act, a hand printing press was drawn on a cart by four horses through the streets of Manchester and Salford. Before it marched a pageant representing printing in the times of Caxton and of Elizabeth I, under banners bearing the slogans 'PRESS' and 'TERROR OF BAD GOVERNMENT'. The press itself was covered by a large canopy, festooned with more phrases, such as 'THE LIBERTY OF THE PRESS' and 'ENLIGHTENER OF MANKIND'. It was working. Three men were busy printing elaborate pamphlets celebrating ' "the PRESS", so eminently distinguished as a means of expanding knowledge and the most essential to the best interests of society, and wonderfully effective in giving utterance to the irresistible power of the public voice'. Still wet, the leaflets were passed down to the watching crowds.

The Manchester pageant was not an exception. Printers in London, Derby, Bungay, Hertford, and Nottingham mounted their own. In Sheffield, Ebenezer Elliott wrote a long ode to 'The Press', of which the final lines were

'The Press!' all lands shall sing;
  The Press, the Press we bring,
    All lands to bless:
O pallid Want! O Labour stark!
Behold we bring the second ark!
    The Press! The Press! The Press!

Behind this enthusiasm lay two main factors. The first was the rapid increase in literacy and printing in the early decades of the nineteenth century. In 1785 there were 124 letterpress printers in London; by 1824 there were some 316, and by mid-century there were 500. Moreover, in the eighteenth century each (wooden) printing press produced at most a hundred impressions an hour, but in the early nineteenth, the new iron-frame presses more than doubled this, printing a larger sheet, and by 1848 the power press could print 12,000 sheets of *The Times* in an hour.[1] Between 1801 and 1831, when heavy taxation on newspapers held production back, the production of officially stamped copies alone more than trebled from 16,085,000 to 54,769,000 a year.[2]

At the same time there was a rapid expansion in the reading public. There are no reliable statistics for this at this time: those that exist have no precise definition of what 'literacy' means, and too often equate reading with writing although, partly because many Sunday Schools taught only reading, this is not an accurate guide.[3] But mass education was increasing. The mechanical spirit of the Industrial Revolution was applied to school teaching, with the 'monitorial' system by which the top group of scholars taught those under them, 'turning out' a large number of pupils with little staffing or expense. Sunday Schools, Church of England and Nonconformist day schools (generally run on this system), Ragged Schools, adult education classes, Mechanics Institutes, mutual instruction groups and the like, all joined the considerable number of private schools in supplying a demand for reading skills.

Urbanization itself, which bombarded town-dwellers with print in the form of posters, periodicals and leaflets, helped educate, as did the more technical forms of factory work.[4] M. J. Quinlan has estimated that between 1780 and 1830, while the population of England doubled from about seven to some fourteen million, readers quintupled from one and a half to between seven and eight million.[5] By the latter date, R. K. Webb has stated, taking an average from many widely divergent areas, between two thirds and three quarters of the working classes in England could read, inclining towards the higher proportion.[6]

As an observer told an S.P.C.K. (Society for the Promotion of Christian Knowledge) committee in 1832, 'the population of this country [was] for the first time becoming a *reading* population, actuated by tastes and habits unknown to preceding generations, and particularly susceptible to such an influence as that of the press'.[7] There must be a note of caution here. There had always been a popular readership for broadsheet and chapbook literature,[8] and, most important, such literature accommodated the old superstitions and beliefs that reading is often assumed to exorcise. We are dealing here not only with a growth in literacy, but with a change in the type of literature available, and a new climate of rational inquiry within which the ability to read assumed a different meaning. Nevertheless, it is broadly true to say that the increase of the reading habit did in this context disrupt the traditions of the 'pre-industrial' world, and introduce new patterns of thinking and sensibility.

The earlier popular consciousness is peculiarly difficult to establish. The dramatic manifestations of popular superstition, such as trials for witchcraft, had ended some time before the laws against sorcery were repealed in 1736. The best witnesses, the early nineteenth-century working-class writers such as Samuel Bamford, tended to look unsympathetically at this time as an era of ignorance from which they had been liberated by 'the March of Intellect'. Yet most accounts are consistent in describing a rural world pervaded by spirits and charms.

'But a few of the lonely, out-of-the-way places,' wrote Bamford of the country around his childhood Middleton, ' – the wells, the bye-paths, the dark old lanes, the solitary houses – escaped the reputation of being haunted. "Boggarts", "fyerin", "fairees", "clap-can" and the like beings of terror, were supposed to be lurking in almost every retired corner, whence they came forth at their permitted hours, to enjoy their permitted freedom.'[9] 'The whole atmosphere

was supposed to be full of ghosts and spirits,' wrote Joseph Lawson of Pudsey.[10] In Gainsborough in Lincolnshire Thomas Miller declared 'of course they were firm believers in ghosts, from the highest to the lowest'.[11] Although none were prosecuted, in the early nineteenth century some form of witch was to be found in 'every village and town' of the East Riding;[12] and in Ashburton, Staffordshire, where Richard Carlile went to school, there were two. One, 'Cherry Chalk', ran the dame school he attended.[13]

The same was true of East Anglia. In July 1825 in Wickham Skeith in Suffolk, Isaac Stebbings, a huckster, aged sixty-seven, was suspected by the villagers of using witchcraft to derange the mind of a thatcher in a neighbouring cottage. An occult seance was held to detect Stebbings and, as it was in progress, Stebbings knocked at the door. Stebbings claimed that he was making an early round selling mackerel, although it was four in the morning. Other evidence was discovered against Stebbings. The village shoemaker found that he could not mix his cobbler's wax, looked up, and saw the huckster standing beside him.

At this point Stebbings offered to stand trial by the 'good old' ordeal by water; for some reason the usual test was reversed and, in this case, if he sank he was a wizard, if he floated, not. Before an audience of several hundred villagers he was immersed in the village pond, and floated like a cork. He was ducked, shifted round, and 'tried out' for three quarters of an hour before, half dead with cold and inhaling water, he was allowed to escape. But the villagers were not so easily convinced. A man of a similar weight and height from a neighbouring village was chosen to take the ordeal alongside Stebbings the following week so a comparison could be made. At this point the clergy got together to stop the proceedings. But as Stebbings's story disappears from view, we hear of a 'cunning man' providing (for a reputed three pounds) the oracle that Stebbings was indeed a wizard, and should be 'killed by inches'.[14]

While in this case the Anglican clergy intervened, it is important to realize that, for the majority of the lower-class, sectarian Christians and for many Anglicans, spirits and witchcraft were accepted as being authorized by the Bible – in particular Saul consulting the witch of Endor and calling up the spirit of Samuel (1 Samuel xxviii) – and by such authorities as John Wesley himself. When William Lovett doubted in a particular apparition, he was sharply told that he could not then believe the Scriptures, and when Samuel Bamford thrilled by the dying embers to 'An Account of the Apparition of the Laird of Cool', he was reading the Methodist *Arminian Magazine*.[15]

So horseshoes were nailed over doors, where the iron attracted the forces of evil, and their shape broke its circle. Sprigs of rowan, rabbits' paws, and 'witch stones' (circular pebbles) were kept in the pocket to defeat evil spells. The future was read in a flight of magpies, a guttering candle, or a random opening of the Bible. Among many rituals practised in East Yorkshire, John Nicholson describes 'chaff-riddling' on St Mark's Eve. 'The barn doors were set wide open, and at midnight the prying ones were to commence riddling the chaff. Should the riddler be doomed to die within the year, two persons would pass by the open door, carrying a coffin.'[16]

This superstitious consciousness was to continue in rural areas through the century, and to some extent has never died out. In 1841 Tremenheere, researching in Norfolk for a Parliamentary paper on education, reported 'here [was] a Wizard terrifying his Neighbours, by the Power of Inflicting Injuries by his Charms, there supernatural Appearances; in another Neighbourhood, a quack curing all Diseases by his knowledge of the Stars'.[17] A supposed wizard died after ducking in Essex in 1863, and twelve years later in Warwickshire one Ann Turner was murdered by a man who claimed that she had bewitched him.[18] This rural world of

magic could erupt into the world of the middle-class novel – that of Emily Brontë's *Wuthering Heights*, Dickens's haunted Chesney Wold and the Wessex of Hardy.

The more overt forms of superstition and witchcraft, however, declined rapidly with industrialism and urbanism from the eighteenth century on. The physical appearance of whole tracts of England was changing. Forests were cut down to make way for factories and roads, to provide charcoal for smelting or firewood for the rapidly increasing population. Places with centuries of superstitious tradition were covered up as if they had never been. From the 1820s gas-light, first introduced on a large scale to break down the natural cycle of day and night in the factories where a new generation of workers was chained to the steam engine, was used increasingly in streets and in houses, banishing the shadows and all that haunted them. Urbanism also broke down the old close-knit communities in which magical beliefs flourished, bringing a new materialist cynicism to the supernatural. So did the rapid growth of education and reading we have already noticed.

Besides these factors there was a pervasive 'spirit of the age' expressed by Samuel Bailey of Sheffield in 1821: 'there is a silent march of thought, which no power can arrest, and which it is not difficult to foresee will be marked by important events.'[19] Its clearest philosophical basis was laid by Jeremy Bentham and the Utilitarians who believed that the only block to progress was human ignorance, and that through education the ills of society could be done away with. This had widespread impact, in particular through its influence on Robert Owen (1771–1858), northern mill-owner and father of English socialism. The first of the Owenite *Social Hymns* (2nd ed. 1840) celebrated the power of education and reason that was to affect many working-class movements:

Joy to the earth! the light is come!
  The only lawful king:
Let every heart prepare it room,
  And moral nature sing.

Joy to the earth! now Reason reigns;
  Let men their songs employ;
While fields and floods, rocks, hills and plains
  Repeat the sounding joy.

It is impossible, however, to identify the faith in progress through the spread of education with any particular philosophical group. It united political, rationalist and religious groups, including the religious societies that provided the basis for nineteenth-century popular education. It motivated the Sunday School Union (1785), the National Society (1811) and the British Foreign School Society (1813). In 1827 the Utilitarians challenged the Society for the Promotion of Christian Knowledge by founding the Society for the Diffusion of Useful Knowledge, producing a large range of cheap 'useful knowledge' literature. The Society also encouraged the Mechanics Institutes, which had spread rapidly from their inception in Glasgow in 1823 'for the diffusion of useful knowledge among mechanics'.

At grass-roots, while the Mechanics Institute came to be largely taken over by the middle classes, small groups of working-class men were coming together for mutual education. Joseph Lawson describes one such class in Pudsey at the beginning of the century, meeting between five and six in the morning before work, to discuss 'grammar, history, geography and theology'.[20] William Lovett attended another in Gerrard Street, Newport Market, when he started as a cabinet-maker in London, and declared 'my mind seemed awakened to a new mental existence; new feelings, hopes and aspirations sprang up within me, and every spare moment was devoted to the acquisition of some kind of useful knowledge.'[21] A worker in the potteries was so moved by his experience of a group that he set up a study in a tiny room set over an alley. 'I know that when I entered that little room at night,' he wrote, 'I was in another world . . . I felt as if I had entered into converse with presences which were living and breathing in that room.'[22]

Sketches by Seymour.

Nº 16.—Vol. 3.

Have you read the Leader in this paper, Mr Brisket?
No I never touch a newspaper, they are all so werry
wenal and woid of sentiment.

Published by G. S. Tregear. 96. Cheapside. London

By the early 1830s the 'March of Intellect' had become a topic of the day. 'God bless my soul, sir!' exclaimed the Reverend Dr Folliott in Peacock's *Crotchet Castle* (1831), 'I am out of all patience with this march of mind. Here has my house been nearly burnt down, by my cook taking it into her head to study hydrostatics, in a sixpenny tract, published by the Steam Intellect Society . . . '[23] Literary dustmen and novel-reading butchers became the butt of cartoons and comic songs, though the ridicule was edged with apprehension as to the social consequences of educating the labouring classes.

> But worse of all, our lab'ring folks,
>   that toiled in their vocations
> 'Thro all the week contentedly,
>   as did become their stations,
> Distracted now with *learned things*,
>   home, wife and work neglect Sir,
> And slyly call their laziness,
>   this march of intellect Sir.[24]

It is important not to overestimate the numbers of 'worker scholars'. They were a minority who came to notice because they were articulate, and formed part of the group that were politically and socially active. Yet besides their importance in working-class movements, they are indicative of the way print was changing cultural perspectives across the wider spectrum. At the most basic level, as J. D. Burn has noted, print broke down the oral traditions by which communal beliefs were transmitted. Once 'a great portion of the legendary lore of the country was transmitted from father to son'; now the 'superstitions of the last century, with their train of supernatural agencies, have been substituted by the vilest trash imaginable'.[25]

Dimensions of reality were changed. Previously, the popular mind selected what was important to its world-view, dismissing what was irrelevant by a process of selective amnesia, and giving what was retained a mythical authority. With a written culture, all facts are present by the mere virtue of having been recorded: the authority of tradition gives way to the authority of print. Reality becomes essentially rational and secular, although for reasons we shall be examining, this was not wholly true in England. Print brought awareness of the wider situation, and so a new self-consciousness. The concept 'working class', linking a huge range of diverse occupations, was itself partly the result of literacy.[26] It was cemented by radical journalism.

Print also brought division. The great majority of working people spoke some form of dialect: in general they read and wrote in standard English. There was some important eighteenth-century dialect writing, such as John Collier's *A View of the Lancashire Dialect* (1746), and this was reprinted and

imitated in chapbook form for a century. In particular, with the growth of northern music hall, dialect songs and narratives were increasingly printed. But this only indicated the vitality of the dialect tradition bypassed by most reading matter.

There was also division within the working classes between those for whom reading was only for entertainment, and those for whom reading was part of a changing pattern of cultural expectation. Writing of the Continental experience, David Riesman has written that at such times the ability to read and write 'becomes identified with the urban world of progress and enlightenment, of ideology and utopia . . . the identification had many of the elements of

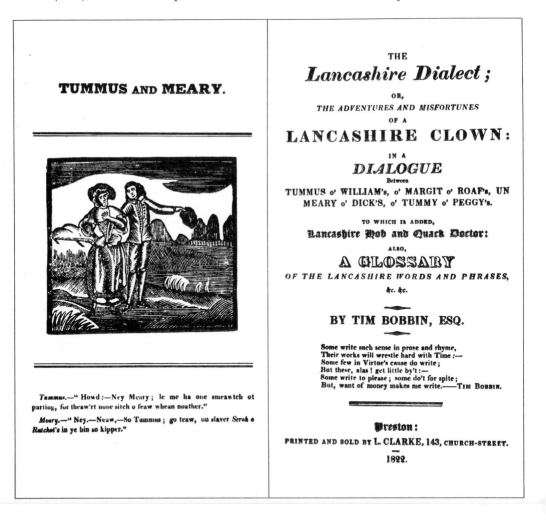

TUMMUS AND MEARY.

Tummus.—" Howd :—Ney Meary ; le me ha one smeawtch ot parting, for theaw'rt none sitch o feaw whean noather."

Meary.—" Ney.—Neaw,—So Tummus ; go teaw, on slaver *Scroh o Ratchot's* in ye bin so kipper."

THE
Lancashire Dialect ;
OR,
THE ADVENTURES AND MISFORTUNES
OF A
LANCASHIRE CLOWN:
IN A
DIALOGUE
Between
TUMMUS o' WILLIAM's, o' MARGIT o' ROAF's, UN MEARY o' DICK'S, o' TUMMY o' PEGGY's.

TO WHICH IS ADDED,
Lancashire Hob and Quack Doctor:
ALSO,
A GLOSSARY
OF THE LANCASHIRE WORDS AND PHRASES,
&c. &c.

BY TIM BOBBIN, ESQ.

Some write such sense in prose and rhyme,
Their works will wrestle hard with Time :—
Some few in Virtue's cause do write ;
But these, alas ! get little by't :—
Some write to please ; some do't for spite ;
But, want of money makes me write.——TIM BOBBIN.

Preston:
PRINTED AND SOLD BY L. CLARKE, 143, CHURCH-STREET.
1822.

conversion, print itself and the world it opened up being a kind of gospel'.[27]

From this we can understand at least one aspect of the profound psychological experience provided by reading and writing for men like Lovett. And if this experience approximates to evangelical conversion, print did become a form of faith in itself. When Richard Carlile started selling political pamphlets he 'knew nothing of political principles', 'I had a complete conviction that there was something wrong somewhere, and that the right application of the printing press was its remedy'.[28] Hone and Cruikshank portrayed the printing press surrounded with light, or with a snake, its tail in its mouth, round it, symbolizing eternity. Hetherington

The iron-frame press, of which the first was patented by Lord Stanhope in 1800, could be bought new for about thirty pounds, and could be used by anyone with a modicum of skill and determination. It provided a remarkably effective means of producing print that could fit into the variety of social life. Looking back, one is startled by the haphazard way it evolved. Almost all printers were small – until the fifties under twenty per cent of the London printers employed more than three men – and effective standardization of rates and labour conditions only came late in the century. John Soulby, an important printer in Ulveston, also sold a wide variety of goods from patent medicines to 'Gold and Silver

placed it as an ikon at the head of each issue of *The Poor Man's Guardian*, enclosed in a scroll with the slogan 'Knowledge is Power'.

Paradoxically, however, it was not the massive steam presses that made the biggest social impact. By the time they came into wide use, a new era in printing had largely been opened, and it was a hand press that swayed down the Manchester streets under its canopy.

Tooth Picks, with Silver Cases', and ran a circulating library.

Presses were rarely installed in specially built premises: printers moved into whatever rooms they could find in vacant shops and premises, reinforced where necessary to bear the weight of the machines. They were therefore in close physical contact with other activities, even sometimes those of household

THE PRESS, invented much about the same time with the *Reformation*, hath done more mischief to the discipline of our Church, than all the doctrine can make amends for. 'Twas an happy time, when all learning was in manuscript, and some little officer did keep the keys of the library! Now, since PRINTING came into the world, such is the mischief, that *a man cannot write a book but presently he is answered!* There have been ways found out to *fine* not the people, but even the *grounds and fields where they assembled:* but no art yet could prevent these SEDITIOUS MEETINGS OF LETTERS! Two or three brawny fellows in a corner, with meer ink and elbow-grease, do more harm than an *hundred systematic divines.* Their ugly printing *letters,* that look but like so many rotten teeth, how oft have they been pulled out by the public tooth-drawers! And yet these rascally operators of the press have got a trick to fasten them again in a few minutes, that they grow as firm a set, and as biting and talkative as ever! O PRINTING! how hast thou " *disturbed the peace!*" Lead, when moulded into bullets, is not so mortal as when founded into *letters!* There was a mistake sure in the story of Cadmus; and the *serpent's teeth* which he sowed, were nothing else but the *letters* which he invented.

Marvell's Rehearsal transprosed, 4to, 1672.

Being marked only with *four and twenty letters,—variously transposed* by the help of a PRINTING PRESS,—PAPER works miracles. The Devil dares no more come near a *Stationer's* heap, or a *Printer's Office,* than *Rats* dare put their noses into a Cheesemonger's Shop. *A Whip for the Devil,* 1669. p. 92.

William Hone and George Cruikshank, from The Political Showman – At Home!, *1821.*

life. When the officers came to take the printing press of the Radical printer Richard Carlile in 1819, they caused great inconvenience to Mrs Carlile lying in labour in the room above.

As presses moved in physically to take their place in economic and social life, so did print. Printing became more adaptable as a medium. While looking at the expansion in reading matter, it is important not to underestimate the visual aspect. This came largely from the development of wood engraving, a technique pioneered by the Newcastle artist Thomas Bewick (1753–1828). This method of working across the grain of the boxwood enabled the cutter to reproduce tone and texture in even small blocks, which

could then be set up in the type. While Bewick used it for book illustrations, wood engravings were used in newspapers from the early part of the century, and they quickly became an important feature of a wide range of popular literature from religious tracts and instructional material to the political cartoons, cheap fiction and the theatrical cuts that came to decorate working-class homes and public houses. Mary Merryweather found in teaching mill-girls to read how important was the appeal of the picture,[29] and in a rural area G. J. Holyoake found copies of the richly illustrated *Penny Magazine* 'as valuable as glass beads in

dealing with Indians', when settling with an inn-keeper.[30]

Typefaces too were changing. One problem with the older wood press was the low pressure possible, limiting the use of dense black areas of print. With the new, stronger, iron press new 'fat face' types were invented, notably by Robert Thorne in 1803, and Vincent Figgins (with seriffed 'Egyptian') in 1815. These styles seemed to shout at the reader from the page, gave to print some of the rhetorical devices of tone and emphasis natural to speaking, and led to a huge expansion of poster and pamphlet literature. They were called 'the circulating libraries of the poor' and 'the language of the walls!' 'In fact', wrote a 'Literary Policeman' in *Howitt's Journal* of wall posters, 'the enormous cost which is daily incurred for public amusement by private individuals, in painting and decorating the dead walls of our cities, is one of the wonders of the age. It is a fresco painting of an hour; a phantasmagoria of scenes as rapid in their progression as they are brilliant in their character; an ever changing kaleidoscope of the day's combinations.' Harriet Martineau described a boy learning to read from them.[31] No town dweller could escape their impact.

Posters and leaflets therefore played a central part in all the social, political and religious movements of the time. They were produced often within hours of each other, as answer and reply. As J. D. Burn noted, 'the walls afford an excellent battle field for polemical combatants, whereon they frequently wage war to the death for their respective dogma'.[32] Nor can this use of print be separated from the quasi-mystical sense of the power of printed matter we noted in the celebrations for the 1832 Reform Act. It was used with touching faith in its effectiveness.

On Sunday 30 October 1832, in Bristol, with the Mansion House sacked and angry crowds roaming the streets about to commence further violence, we find men going their rounds pasting up posters. One was from the Mayor declaring 'All persons found tumultuously assembling are Guilty of capital Felony', one from the Vice President

PUBLIC Caution.

To prevent as much as possible any fatal Results, under the present Circumstances, the

Boroughreeve & Constables
Of Manchester,

Feel it their Duty to issue the following Friendly

CAUTION:

WHEN

Stones are thrown from a Crowd,
(A practice by which the *Lives of the Peace Officers and Military, on Duty,* are continually endangered,)

The Persons offending must be *immediately SEIZED,* and given up by those about them, or such as did not actually throw a Stone *may suffer from the FIRING of the Military.*

In the Event of Stones being thrown, the *PERSONS CONCERNED,* who are flying from the Pursuit of the Civil or Military Authorities, *should be REFUSED ADMITTANCE into Houses or Cellars.* which may otherwise be Fired into.

The OCCUPIERS of HOUSES, from the *Windows* or *Roofs* of which *Stones are Thrown,* must consider themselves **RESPONSIBLE** for all the Consequences.

. It is earnestly requested, that Individuals will

AVOID COLLECTING IN
GROUPS or PARTIES,
In the Streets.

ASTON, PRINTER, MANCHESTER,

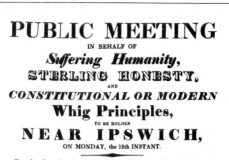

PUBLIC MEETING.

A PUBLIC MEETING OF THE
Inhabitants of Ipswich and its Vicinity
WILL BE HELD
On MONDAY next, the 15th Instant,
In the Field adjoining the DUKE OF YORK, on the Woodbridge Road,
To take into consideration the late melancholy
Transactions at Manchester,
And the propriety of Addressing the PRINCE REGENT thereon.

The COMMITTEE feel it unnecessary to invite the Friends of Liberty and Humanity on the present occasion, as the bare mention of the subject is of itself sufficient to ensure a numerous attendance.

At this time of the year, unfavourable weather may be expected, but we trust such a circumstance will not operate to weaken the meeting; the inconvenience of a wet coat must not be compared with the importance and interest which attach to the object of the Meeting.

A Subscription will be entered into, for the benefit of those who suffered at Manchester on the 16th of August last—He who cannot afford more than one penny, let him contribute thus much. It is desirable that a small sum should be raised, as a proof of the existence of that feeling, which every man would be ashamed to disavow, were he put to the test.

The following Regulations are submitted by the Committee and their Friends, to be observed on the Day of Meeting.

I. No Banners, or Placards bearing any inscription, nor any Ensign, or Flag of a colour emblematical of Revolutionary Principles will be allowed, but NATIONAL Colours of a different description may be exhibited.

II. Any person who may wish to address the Meeting, must not introduce the subject of Parliamentary Reform, as it is foreign to the object of the Meeting.

III. It is also requested, that Persons attending, will not bring sticks, or any kind of weapon whatever with them; and that even walking sticks which might be convenient for those who live at a distance from the place of meeting, will on this occasion be dispensed with.

By order of the Committee,
FRANCIS FISK.
THE CHAIR TO BE TAKEN AT ONE O'CLOCK.
A Dinner will be provided at the Unicorn, to be upon the Table at 4 o'Clock.—Tickets 2s. 6d. each.
Nov. 9th, 1819

COWELL, PRINTER, IPSWICH.

PUBLIC MEETING
IN BEHALF OF
Suffering Humanity,
STERLING HONESTY,
AND
CONSTITUTIONAL OR MODERN
Whig Principles,
TO BE HOLDEN
NEAR IPSWICH,
ON MONDAY, the 15th INSTANT.

Question 1st. Is the Person who called the above Meeting the identical *Bricklayer* who was tried and convicted at our Borough Sessions for a BRUTAL ASSAULT on a *Child?* the very recital of which excited HORROR in the breast of every individual present in Court.

Question 2nd. Is another *Radical* of the same name who signed the Requisition, which was so justly rejected by the Chief Magistrates, cousin to the above person, and the actual individual who was tried and convicted at our Sessions, some time since, for Manslaughter?

Question 3d. Is the Public House at which the *Radicals* are invited to dine on Monday the very same house in which a large quantity of Malt was found secreted, with a view to evade the new Malt Duty, and which Malt became forfeited, by an award of the Magistrates of this Town?

Question 4th. Is it certain that the *Pence* to be collected on this occasion will find their way to Manchester? or is it not more certain they will be found necessary to satisfy the wants of the *Radical Landlord?*

Question 5th. Which of the *two worthies* in this glorious cause, namely, CAUSIDICUS or ADVOCATUS, is to be called upon to preside on Monday, to explain the objects of the Meeting, by a forcible and happy illustration of *Modern Whig Principles?*

An answer to the above Questions left at the Post-office, and addressed to *Timothy Lawrance, Esq.* will meet with immediate attention.

November 13th, 1819.

DECK, PRINTER, IPSWICH.

of the Bristol Union asking the crowd to disperse, as 'outrages only injure the cause of Reform', and another asking inhabitants to assemble at the Guildhall. The Mayor's poster man had his pot of paste jammed over his head, and the burning of Bristol began. This was not an isolated example. Print was used massively both by the Establishment and reformers, even in such situations as the Captain Swing agricultural riots of the 1830s, where a large proportion of those involved were notably unable to read.

We are left, therefore, with a paradox. The spread of literacy and cheap literature was widely associated with the demystification of the universe, and the substitution of a world of reason and objectivity. Yet both developments could assume dimensions as magical as the old beliefs they displaced.

2. THE BATTLE FOR THE MIND

When Thomas Cooper's mother, widowed, gathered together a few possessions and journeyed across England from Exeter to Gainsborough in Lincolnshire, she carried with her the family Bible. Her son, later to become a Chartist leader and a poet, first experienced print in its pages, opened for him on Sunday afternoons by his mother.[1] While chapbooks and broadsheets were the common reading of the poor, in the eighteenth and early nineteenth centuries, the Bible stood at the centre of their serious literature, by its status and familiarity affecting the whole spectrum of print. It was the most commonly recorded book in poorer cottages and households, and formed a prosperous branch of the serial bookselling trade conducted by such publishers as Thomas Kelly, George Virtue and James Cooke – Kelly sold 40,000 of his huge folio Bible alone.[2] They had many rivals.

The scriptures were the basis of all forms of school education, studied and learnt by rote. The experience was that of D. H. Lawrence at the end of the century, who declared, 'I was brought up on the Bible, and have it in my bones . . . [its] language has the power of echoing and re-echoing in my unconscious mind.'[3] The book of Revelation permeated the popular view of history, the rhythms of the King James version permeated all forms of popular culture from melodrama to Radical protest: a worker in the Potteries noted that the more earnest trade unionists became, the closer they approximated to biblical prose.[4]

Religious literature also dominated the field. William Howitt, writing of northern country districts, noted that where a cottage held 'about half a dozen books', they were likely to include Hervey's *Meditations among the Tombs*, Baxter's *Saint's Everlasting Rest*, and similar works.[5] In London, 'there is not a stall in London where the passenger may not learn of its proprietor that the religious department is his most extensive and profitable business, *The Whole Duty of Man*, the *Pilgrims, The Holy Living and Dying*, and the *Book of Martyrs* are to be found in every alley in London.'[6] The most popular single religious work after the Bible was undoubtedly Bunyan's *Pilgrim's Progress*, Cooper's 'Book of Books'. Bunyan's allegory, as E. P. Thompson has noted,[7] mediated between the biblical dimension and the common life of the people, and was second only to the Bible in its impact on the popular culture.

The roots of education and reading matter in religion reinforced the attitudes, noticed in the preceding chapter, towards literacy as part of the march of the intellect towards Utopia. It also helps to explain the context in which literature developed at the turn of the century. What emerged was a struggle for control of the new media, waged between Church and State on one side, by Radical reformers on the other, while a third factor, commercial enterprise, was quietly making the biggest inroad of all.

The first shot in this war was Thomas Paine's *The Rights of Man*, part one of which appeared in 1791. The attack on Edmund Burke's evolutionary conservatism, *Reflections on the French Revolution* (1790), and statement of the relevance of the French Revolution for England, could not have come at a more opportune moment. The fall of the Bastille was fresh in the public memory, and the Reign of Terror still two years away. English sympathies with the Revolution were at their height. Aided by the London Constitutional Society, which gave it free distribution among the workers, the three-shilling edition sold 50,000 copies in a few weeks, and a sixpenny reprint of parts one and two sold 32,000 in a month.

Paine said little that was new, but wrote in a simple, direct style with which the common man could identify, skilfully played off against the refulgent rhetoric of Burke. And although Paine was attacked as the arch enemy of Christianity, he did in fact argue largely in religious terms. He compared the Bastille to Bunyan's Doubting Castle and Giant Despair. He countered Burke's account of a structure of society authorized by the 'Glorious Revolution' of 1688, with the Book of Genesis. 'In all the vocabulary of Adam there is no such an animal as a duke or a count.' For 'every child that is born into the world must be considered as deriving its existence from God. The world is as new to him as it was to the first man that existed, and his natural right to it is of the same kind.' Diderot had written 'there once existed a natural man; there has been introduced within this man artificial man'. Paine made this both political and biblical: 'Mr Burke has set up a sort of political Adam, in whom all posterity is bound for ever.' This Adam must be rejected in favour of the true free man.[8]

Yet Paine, while appealing to a generation nurtured, as he himself had been, on the Bible, also fused it with a Benthamite pragmatism. While in *The Age of Reason* (1794–5) Paine argued against the illogicalities of the Bible, in the two parts of *The Rights of Man* he attacked the irrational in government. Traditional abuses must be swept away, and be substituted for by a system that brings the greatest justice to the greatest number of people. His proposals included equal representation, the abolition of the Poor Law, direct taxation on estates and revenues above £22,000 a year, the establishment of grants for those under fourteen and over fifty, state aid for the unemployed and a national system of education. Which points to a further paradox. Condemned as a revolutionary, Paine's all-pervasive influence in fact helped to channel political activity in England away from revolution along lines that were to emerge in the establishment of the Labour Party in 1900.

Paine's work precipitated a flood of 'anti-infidel' literature. His biblical criticism was answered by William Paley's *A View of the Evidences of Christianity* (1794) and Bishop Watson's *Apology for the Bible* (1795). Other broadsheets detailed Paine's death as an agonized penitent, or gave such fearful examples as 'Terrors of the Lord! or the Last Hours of a Radical Reformer who BURNT HIS BIBLE'.

Significantly, much of the literature published against Paine approached his politics from a religious angle: politics and religion were on both sides closely interwoven. The most notable venture was Hannah More's *Cheap Repository Tracts*, begun in 1795 – tales and verses with catchy titles and the format of popular broadsheets and chapbooks. In circulation they swamped even the works of Paine: the extraordinary number of two million were sold in two years.[9]

From this point religious tracts became a major feature of the cheap publishing field. They were used indiscriminately against every social ill from prostitution and play-going to starvation and cholera. In particular they were directed against Radicalism. As the tensions built up in Manchester in the years preceding Peterloo, in moved the Auxiliary Bible Society, the Religious Tract Society, the Church Tract Association and the Ladies' Bible Society. Tracts were scattered in public houses, thrown through coach and (later) train windows, and carefully distributed, street by street, through most cities and villages by local groups. The Religious Tract Society, which augmented the various denominational societies also publishing tracts, in 1838 alone published over eighteen million, some of which, however, went abroad.[10]

Their reception varied considerably. They were sometimes given to those who could not read – frequently to those that resented them. 'No I ain't read the little book wot you left,' snarled the brickmaker at Mrs Pardiggle in Dickens's *Bleak House* (1852–3), 'There ain't anybody here as knows how to read it, and if there wos, it wouldn't be suitable to me. It's a book fit for a babby, and I'm not a babby.' But it is important also to see their appeal to

The Horrors of
A Dying Infidel.

THE following fact is related on the best authority. It serves to shew how awful and dangerous a thing it is to read *profane books*, and what misery and despair shall overtake the scorner and blasphemer in a *dying hour.*

"I was lately, observes the narrator, called to attend the DEATH-BED of a young man at HOXTON. On my entering the room, I found him in the greatest *horror of mind.* Thinking that it might, perhaps, arise from that deep remorse sometimes attending the DEATH-BED of a sinner, I began to point out to him Jesus Christ, as the only friend of sinful man, and to direct him to the promises of the gospel. He replied with a look of *agony* and *despair,* 'Ah! 'sir, but I have rejected the gospel.—Some years ago I unhappily 'read *PAINE's Age of Reason*; it suited my corrupt taste; I 'embraced its principles: after this, wherever I went, I did all that 'lay in my power to hold up the HOLY SCRIPTURES to contempt; by 'this means I led others into the fatal snare, and made converts to 'INFIDELITY. Thus, sir, I rejected GOD, and *now he rejects* 'me, *and will have no mercy on me.*' I offered to pray by him, (continues the gentleman) but he replied, 'Oh! no—it is all in 'vain to pray for me.' Then, with a dismal groan, he cried out 'PAINE'S AGE OF REASON HAS RUINED MY SOUL!' And with those words in his mouth, he instantly expired.

Oh! Reader, be wise in time. Let such a dreadful example prove a warning to *you.* The man that reads a *bad book*, or gives ear to *profane words*, does it at the *peril of his soul.*—He is like a person that swallows a poisonous draught. It is just possible, perhaps that he may be saved, but THE CHANCES ARE ONE HUNDRED TO ONE AGAINST HIM.

January 7th, 1820.   James Patrick, Printer, Manchester.

The *RIOT*;

Or, HALF a LOAF is better than no BREAD.

In a DIALOGUE between *Jack Anvil* and *Tom Hod*.

To the Tune of " A Cobler there was," &c.

TOM.

COME neighbours, no longer be patient and
    quiet,
Come let us go kick up a bit of a riot;
I am hungry, my lads, but I've little to eat,
So we'll pull down the mills, and seize all the meat:
I'll give you good sport, boys, as ever you saw,
So a fig for the Justice, a fig for the law.
    Derry down.

Then his pitchfork Tom seized—Hold a moment
    says Jack,
I'll shew thee thy blunder, brave boy, in a crack,
And if I don't prove we had better be still,
I'll assist thee straitway to pull down every mill;
I'll shew thee how passion thy reason does cheat,
Or I'll join thee in plunder for bread and for meat.
    Derry down.

What a whimsey to think thus our bellies to fill,
For we stop all the grinding by breaking the mill!
What a whimsey to think we shall get more to eat
By abusing the butchers who get us the meat!
What a whimsey to think we shall mend our spare
    diet
By breeding disturbance, by murder and riot!
    Derry down.

Because I am dry 'twould be foolish, I think
To pull out my tap and to spill all my drink;
Because I am hungry and want to be fed,
That is sure no wise reason for wasting my bread;
And just such wise reasons for mending their diet
Are us'd by those blockheads who rush into riot.
    Derry down.

I would not take comfort from others distresses,
But still I would mark how God our land blesses;
For tho' in Old England the times are but sad,
Abroad I'm told they are ten times as bad;
In the land of the Pope there is scarce any grain,
And 'tis still worse, they say, both in Holland and
    Spain.
    Derry down.

Let us look to the harvest our wants to beguile,
See the lands with rich crops how they every
    where smile!
Mean time to assist us, by each Western breeze,
Some corn is brought daily acrofs the salt seas,
Of tea we'll drink little, of gin none at all,
And we'll patiently wait and the prices will fall.
    Derry down.

But if we're not quiet, then let us not wonder
If things grow much worse by our riot and plunder;
And let us remember whenever we meet,
The more Ale we drink, boys, the less we shall eat.
On those days spent in riot no bread you brought home,
Had you spent them in labour you must have had some.
    Derry down.

A dinner of herbs, says the wise man, with quiet
Is better than beef amid discord and riot.
If the thing can't be help'd I'm a foe to all strife,
And I pray for a peace every night of my life;
But in matters of state not an inch will I budge,
Because I conceive I'm no very good judge.
    Derry down.

But tho' poor I can work, my brave boy, with
    the best,
Let the King and the Parliament manage the rest;
I lament both the War and the Taxes together,
Tho' I verily think they don't alter the weather.
The King, as I take it, with very good reason,
May prevent a bad law, but can't help a bad season.
    Derry down.

The Parliament-men, altho' great is their power,
Yet they cannot contrive us a bit of a shower;
And I never yet heard; tho' our Rulers are wise;
That they know very well how to manage the skies;
For the best of them all, as they found to their cost,
Were not able to hinder last winter's hard frost.
    Derry down.

Besides I must share in the wants of the times,
Because I have had my full share in it's crimes;
And I'm apt to believe the distress which is sent,
Is to punish and cure us of all discontent.
—But harvest is coming—Potatoes are come!
Our prospect clears up; Ye complainers be dumb!
    Derry down.

And tho' I're no money, and tho' I've no lands,
I've a head on my shoulders, and a pair of good
    hands;
So I'll work the whole day, and on Sundays I'll seek
At church how to bear all the wants of the week.
The Gentlefolks too will afford us supplies;
They'll subscribe—and they'll give up their puddings
    and pies.
    Derry down.

Then before I'm indue'd to take part in a Riot,
I'll ask this short question—What shall I get by it?
So I'll e'en wait a little till cheaper the bread,
For a mittimus hangs o'er each Rioter's head;
And when of two evils I'm ask'd which is best,
I'd rather be hungry than hang'd, I protest.
    Derry down.

Quoth Tom, thou art right; If I rise, I'm a Turk,
So he threw down his pitchfork, and went to his work.

    Z.

[*Entered at Stationers Hall.*]

Sold by J. MARSHALL,
(PRINTER to the CHEAP REPOSITORY for Moral and Religious Tracts) No. 17, Queen-Street, Cheapside, and
No. 4, Aldermary Church-Yard ; and R. WHITE, Piccadilly, LONDON.
By S. HAZARD,
(PRINTER to the CHEAP REPOSITORY,) at BATH; and by all Booksellers, Newsmen, and Hawkers in Town
and Country.

☞ Great Allowance will be made to Shopkeepers and Hawkers.
Price an Halfpenny, or 2s. 3d. per 100.—1s 3d. for 50.—9d. for 25.

those who could not afford other reading, and to the large popular public for religious literature. Many tracts were political pamphlets in pious dress, reactionary in content and patronizing in tone. But most were the same pious biographies, death-bed scenes and devout thoughts that dominated sectarian magazines, and provided for the various denominations that flourished in the early nineteenth century. Methodism alone increased its numbers from 107,000 in 1805 to 600,000 by 1851, significantly with the most rapid growth at periods of social tension, such as 1818 and 1831–4, when an increase of atheistic Radicalism might have been expected.[11]

At this point we must note a figure who had a greater impact on nineteenth-century popular literature than any other single person, but who remains outside any easy classification – even that of popular literature. William Cobbett (1763–1835) was born the son of a small farmer and inn-keeper among the Surrey hopfields at Farnham.[12] Memories of this idyllic childhood dominated his life and thought. His greatest anger was reserved for the new sprawling cities – 'wens' or sores poisoning the countryside – his strongest ideals were associated with a feudal world of farming communities that had largely passed. His father taught him the elements of reading, writing and arithmetic, and he dated 'the birth of [his] intellect' from the day on which he read Swift's *Tale of a Tub*, bought with a last threepence he had saved for food, and read until with darkness he fell asleep against a hay stack. His independent schooling gave him a suspicion of current schemes for popular education. They were designed 'to bend the minds of children towards passive obedience and slavery'. Tracts were 'gingerbread dolls'.[13] Cobbett set out to educate the people on his own.

In 1818 he published his *Grammar of the English Language*, to give in particular 'Soldiers, Sailors, Apprentices and Plough boys' all they needed in order to write well. But he was concerned with more than syntax. 'True learning,' he declared, 'is in the *mind* and not in the *tongue*.' Corrupt style is therefore corrupt thought and corrupt thought is bad politics. Confronted with a particularly confused knot of syntax, he stormed 'this sentence is a disgrace even to a Ministry selected by the grovelling borough tyrants'. Latin and Greek are called 'learned languages because those who teach them have, in consequence of their teaching, *very large estates of land*'. Instead he turns to the direct force of Anglo-Saxon prose.[14]

Cobbett's *Grammar* sold 100,000 copies. He also wrote books on French, geography, on emigration and *Cobbett's Religious Tracts* (1821–2). His advice on household and small farm management, *Cottage Economy* (1822), remained a standard work for a century. He played an important part in the movement for Catholic emancipation with his *History of the Protestant Reformation* (1824–6), and accurate reporting of Parliament begins with *Cobbett's Parliamentary Debates* (1804–12), taken over by Hansard in 1812. Without much consistent political theory beyond a hatred of Parliamentary corruption, Cobbett's vigorous style made politics personal and vital, setting the tone for political journalism for half a century, and taking the debate of public issues into market place, tavern and household sitting room.

Cobbett's finest achievement was his *Political Register* (1802–35), a weekly journal combining vigorous commentary with news of books, theatre, home and foreign affairs. It was here that he published his articles, later issued as *Rural Rides* (1830), describing his travels on horseback across southern England. The 'rides' brought together all the best qualities of Cobbett as a writer. Written in tavern rooms while Cobbett was still aglow with a long day in the open, they radiate the peculiar physical gusto that comes through his writing, his countryman's sensitive awareness of weather and conditions of the earth. At the same time they show Cobbett's political imagination, that can without strain make common details matters of government.

His *Political Register* also had an impact on popular literature as important in its way as that of Paine's *Rights of Man*. Paine's work was originally expensive; Cobbett characteristically published his works in sixpenny numbers. On 2 November 1816, Cobbett devoted the entire issue of his *Register* to an address 'To the Journeymen and Labourers of England, Scotland and Ireland', issuing it as an open sheet, costing 2d. or 12s. 6d. a hundred, instead of 1s. 1½d. each. 200,000 copies were sold. From 12 October 1816, week by week, Cobbett laid his plans for reform before his readers, and they 'were read on nearly every cottage hearth in the manufacturing districts'. A political journal had appeared that was cheap enough to be bought and kept by the people. Although Cobbett fled to the United States in 1817 when the Habeas Corpus Act was suspended, a new era in journalism had opened up.

With Cobbett out of England, more extreme Radical figures took over. The Yorkshire-born printer Jonathan Wooler published his heavily satirical *Black Dwarf* (1817–23). John Wade, an ex-woolsorter, who emerged as one of the finest Radical intellectuals of the era, published his Benthamite *The Gorgon* (1818–19). Richard Carlile, once a journeyman tin-plate worker converted by Paine to Republicanism and the cause of free speech, published a series of periodicals running from the Peterloo agitation to the 1830s, of which the most important was *The Republican* (1819–26).

The government was at first dilatory. In 1817 they had prosecuted a retiring London bookseller and antiquarian, William Hone, on charges of blasphemy for parodies he had published on the Litany, the Catechism and the Creed. The tone of the whole can be judged by five of the Commandments from his 'Parody on John Wilkes' Catechism'.

V. Honour the Regent and the helmets of the Life Guards that thy stay may be long in the Place which the Lord the Minister giveth thee.

VI. Thou shalt not call starving to death murder.

VII. Thou shalt not call Royal gallivanting adultery.

VIII. Thou shalt not say, that to rob the Public is to steal.

X. Thou shalt bear false witness against the people.

The government misjudged their man. Hone was one of the most widely, if not the most deeply, read men of his time. In three successive trials, conducted himself with speeches of up to six hours, he proved that parodies had been made on Holy Scripture with impunity by a large number of eminent people, including Canning, Martin Luther, the Chairman of the Association for Preserving Liberty and Property against Republicans and Levellers and Milton. In each trial the jury returned a verdict of 'not guilty', a decision that made Hone a national hero, and broke the sick and tired Lord Ellenborough who had presided.[15]

In 1819 the Government used a more direct attack. The Peterloo Massacre of thirteen unarmed civilians by the Manchester yeomanry had sparked off a wave of unrest throughout England on which the Radical papers were swept to new heights of influence – the Home Office estimated *The Black Dwarf* to be selling 12,000[16] – and scores of new ones were established. In December the Seditious Publications Act imposed a fourpenny tax on any periodicals containing news or comment, published more frequently than every twenty-eight days, and costing less than sixpence. Publishers also had to deposit bonds that were confiscated if they were convicted of 'seditious or blasphemous libel'. Political journals the working classes could afford to buy were illegal.

For over ten years the Act proved generally successful. Middle-class movements continued to use print, and in particular periodicals, intensively. 'Every little sect among us,' wrote Thomas Carlyle in 'Signs of the Times' in 1829, 'Unitarians, Utilitarians, Anabaptists, Phrenologists, each has its monthly or quarterly magazine . . . at no former era has literature, the printed communication of thought, been of such importance as it is now.' Yet the cheap weekly publications most valuable in working-class organizations were stifled.

The first effective reaction came against a background of industrial unrest, rick-burning in the country, and widespread agitation for factory legislation and parliamentary reform. On 6 March 1830, John Doherty, the Irish

THE
POOR MAN'S GUARDIAN.
A Weekly Newspaper
FOR THE PEOPLE.

PUBLISHED, CONTRARY TO "LAW," TO TRY THE POWER OF "MIGHT" AGAINST "RIGHT."

No. 3. · *Saturday, July 23, 1831.* · [Price 1*d.*

Friends, Brethren, and Fellow-Countrymen,

OUR tyrants have summoned us to Bow-street, to act over again the farce of *the " Law,'* before " their worships" Birnie and Halls.

Our course is adopted, nor shall we waste any more of our valuable time in striving to *evade* the power of *tyranny;* we have raised our standard of *defiance,* and we will stand by it, or fall by it—if so it must be—if you desert us in the good fight which we undertake for your sakes,—but which you will not do; yes, we depend upon your support, and *fearless* and confident as the unarmed David, will we grapple with our giant foe!

So; our masters are not content with the convictions already obtained; they will not enforce *them*, but will obtain so many others, until they have sufficient to make our imprisonment perpetual, and beyond all ransom. Merciful masters!—Do you not see their policy—their deadly policy? all that they know of virtue, is the empty name; and they know no more of honesty or moral courage; they cannot imagine to themselves a man who could hold himself more happy and more free in the dungeon of a tyrant, and with the fetters of despotism around his limbs, than in the enjoyment of personal liberty and domestic luxury, purchased by the compromise of all his natural rights, and by tame submission to the will—or "THE LAW" —of a self-elected and arbitrary POWER:—but they shall find themselves mistaken; there are many such men, we trust, and of them, we equally trust, we are the very least determined and most unworthy. Are they not mistaken, fellow-countrymen? are there not among you thousands, and hundreds of thousands, who envy us the proud post which fortune has assigned to us; are there not millions among you ready to support us even to loss of liberty—to loss of life (if so it must be!) in our struggle for common *justice* against brute MIGHT? Need we ask you? OUR FULLEST TRUST IS IN YOU!—But—to return to whence we digressed --knowing no more of human nature than their own narrow and self-acquaintance teaches them, our tyrants *mercifully* restrain their present means of persecution, until they have completely hemmed us in on all sides, and shut out the possibility of escape: the humbuggery of " *the law*" is getting more and more into contempt, and requires some terrible proof

of its dangerous omnipotence; to enforce, therefore, two paltry convictions of five pounds each would, as they think, be a mere timely notice of which we should of course avail ourselves, nor continue our offending; but they require a victim—" *to guilty* minds a terrible example,"—and they, therefore, suspend their present powers, in order to lull us into indolent security, until their operations for our destruction are complete. Fools! they little think that we would resist the penalty of a single penny, as much as we would one of a million or tens of millions! the question with us is not one of pounds, shillings, and pence, but one of right--indisputable right--not " *legal*" right, but *moral* right—not of " law," but of justice—not of individual interest, but general principle,—and we cannot—will not—surrender one inch of ground! we may be vanquished—beaten down—enchained—imprisoned—murdered—but we shall be so overcome only by the no longer disguised " virtue" of BRUTE FORCE.

Again, let us firmly declare that we dispute the power of any one man, or any set of men, however small or however great their number, to make " laws" affecting life and liberty, without any other authority than their own pleasure: they make " law" for themselves, or for so many as please to sanction them, but though we were the only man in this kingdom who objects to their power, they can have no *moral right* to subject an unwilling and adverse party to rules which suit their own interests: we object to, and dispute all their " laws;" and we shall equally object and dispute the " laws" of any " *reformed*" legislature, which shall *not* be specially authorized by ourselves: what! do not they themselves declare by their own " laws," that nothing—no every day— trifling transaction, done on our behalf by any third party, is binding on us, without our specific warrant of attorney, or special appointment of agency? and must we then be bound against our will—against all principles of *right, morality,* and equity, in matters of life, and freedom, and happiness, by the independent " law" of perfect strangers? no, their own " laws" find them *guilty* of oppression and injustice —their own " laws" justify our resistance and defiance! numbers, either on one side or the other, cannot, in a moral point of view, alter the case: whether there be only one tyrant and millions of

WANTED

SOME HUNDREDS OF

POOR MEN

Out of employ, *who have* NOTHING TO RISK---some of those persons to whom DISTRESS, occasioned by *tyrannical government*, has made a PRISON a desirable HOME.

An honest, patriotic, and moral way of procuring *bread* and *shelter*, and moreover of earning the thanks of their fellow-countrymen, now presents itself to such patriotic Englishmen as will, in *defiance of the most* ODIOUS "LAWS" *of a most odious, self-elected Tyranny,* imposed upon an *Enslaved and Oppressed People*, sell to the poor and the ignorant The

"POOR MAN'S GUARDIAN" AND "REPUBLICAN,"

Weekly "Papers" for the People,

Published in defiance of "Law," to try the power of "*Might*" against "*Right.*"

N. B. *A Subscription* is opened for the *relief, support, encouragement,* and *reward* of such persons as may be Imprisoned by the WHIG TYRANTS.

HETHERINGTON, *Printer, 13, Kingsate Street, Holborn.*

organizer of the northern cotton operatives, began his unstamped, militant *United Trades Co-operative Journal*. In London, Henry Hetherington published the *Penny Papers for the People* (1830–31) that were to become the most celebrated of the unstamped papers as *The Poor Man's Guardian* (1831–5). Hetherington was three times put in prison, three times fined, and once had his press confiscated. When his newsvendors were imprisoned, in a famous pamphlet he advertised for sellers 'to whom DISTRESS, occasioned by *tyrannical government*, has made a PRISON a desirable HOME'.

Copies were circulated by hand, given away on the sale of straws, and transported in a coffin, a practice said to have been followed by William Milner when later he used a hearse to carry the (stamped) Radical newspaper *The Northern Star*. In 1833 the circulation reached as high as twelve to fifteen thousand, with a readership of up to twenty times this number.[17] The success began a landslide in unstamped periodicals. Between 1830 and 1836, when the newspaper tax was reduced to a penny, over 560 unstamped periodicals appeared.

We return to the importance of the hand press, still at this time the dominant method of printing. It was possible to start a periodical for as little as ten pounds, with a sympathetic printer, if one organized the sales. With determination one could get together a second-hand press and some type, and print a periodical oneself. Joshua Hobson, a Leeds Radical, with particular concern for factory legislation, even built his own in wood, thereby evading the 'arbitrary yet petty censorship' of middle-class printers when he printed his influential *Voice of the West Riding* (1833–4).[18] At times Richard E. Lee wrote, printed and published much of the important serial *The Man* (1833). Against work on this scale the Home Office and police officials were impotent. Operating from unobtrusive premises, selling outside the normal bookselling channels through a separate sales network, Radicals with few resources could take on the might of the Establishment. It provided an 'alternative press' that operated largely outside the knowledge of the 'respectable' public, a forum in which the largely Owenite philosophies of the nascent working-class movements of the thirties could be argued out.

Yet the Radical press was quickly challenged by other contenders in the 'battle for the mind' of the new reading public. The Society for the Diffusion of Useful Knowledge, from 1832, published the unstamped *Penny Magazine*. The fine quality of the woodcuts was startling and helped it to reach sales in 1833 and 1834 of 200,000 an issue.[19] The S.D.U.K. philosophy – the dispelling of ignorance and fostering a healthful association of ideas through non-political scientific information – was not so successful with working-class readers. '*Useful* knowledge indeed,' declared a correspondent to *The Poor Man's Guardian*, 'would it be to those who live idly on our skills and industry, who would cajole us into apathetic resignation to their iron sway.'[20] The S.P.C.K. competed with *The Penny Magazine* with its Christian and reactionary *Saturday Magazine*, which reached a weekly circulation of 70,000.[21] *The Penny Lancet* prepared every man to be his own doctor. *The Probe* (1833) investigated assaults on servants. The *National Omnibus* (1831) crammed in 'Literature, Science, Music, Theatricals and the Fine Arts'. *The Ghost* (1833) offered ghosts. The Radical press was being forced out by the popularity of the very cheap literature it had helped to establish.

But the political scene, too, was changing. The passing of the Reform Bill in 1832 was followed by a period of political disillusionment. With the reduction of the stamp tax to a penny, severely enforced, the battle of the unstamped was virtually over. The printing scene had changed. Presses were becoming larger and more vulnerable. In 1835 Hetherington began using an expensive Napier rotary press capable of printing 2,500 impressions an hour. Larger circulations were required: the great Chartist periodical of the next Radical phase was the stamped newspaper *The Northern Star* (1837–48), using all the channels open to it. The 'battle for the mind' was increasingly dominated not only by politics and by religion, but by economics.

THE PENNY MAGAZINE

OF THE

Society for the Diffusion of Useful Knowledge.

36.]   PUBLISHED EVERY SATURDAY.   [OCTOBER 27, 1832.

THE BOA CONSTRICTOR.

[The Boa Constrictor about to strike a Rabbit.]

ONE of the most interesting objects in the fine collection of animals at the Surrey Zoological Gardens, is the Boa Constrictor. Curled up in a large box, through the upper grating of which it may be conveniently examined, this enormous reptile lies for weeks in a quiet and almost torpid state. The capacity which this class of animals possess of requiring food only at very long intervals, accounts for the inactive condition in which they principally live; but when the feeling of hunger becomes strong they rouse themselves from their long repose, and the voracity of their appetite is then as remarkable as their previous indifference. In a state of confinement the boa takes food at intervals of a month or six weeks; but he then swallows an entire rabbit or fowl, which is put in his cage. The artist who made the drawing for the above wood-cut, saw the boa at the Surrey Zoological Gardens precisely in the attitude which he has represented. The time having arrived when he was expected to require food, a live rabbit was put into his box. The poor little quadruped remained uninjured for several days, till he became familiar with his terrible enemy. On a sudden, while the artist was observing the ill-sorted pair, the reptile suddenly rose up, and, opening his fearful jaws, made a stroke at the rabbit, who was climbing up the end of the box; but, as if his appetite was not sufficiently eager, he suddenly drew back, when within an inch of his prey, and sunk into his wonted lethargy. The rabbit, unconscious of the danger which was passed for a short season, began to play about the scaly folds of his companion; but the keeper said that his respite would be brief, and that he would be swallowed the next day without any qualms.

All the tribe of serpents are sustained by animal food. The smaller species devour insects, lizards, frogs, and snails; but the larger species, and especially the boa, not unfrequently attack very large quadrupeds. In seizing upon so small a victim as a rabbit, the boa constrictor would swallow it without much difficulty; because the peculiar construction of the mouth and throat of this species enables them to expand, so as to receive within

3. THE FICTION TRAP AND THE GROWTH OF POPULAR PERIODICALS

'A habit of reading [novels] breeds a dislike to history, and all the substantial parts of knowledge; withdraws attention from nature, and truth; and fills the mind with extravagant thoughts, and too often with criminal propensities.'[1] James Beattie's blast against the novel in 1783 stated the position of many concerned with popular education well into the early decades of the nineteenth century. Most Nonconformists, and some Anglicans, avoided 'light reading', studying in the main the Bible and hymn book, together with Bunyan and a few other religious 'classics'. Bunyan was defended on the ground that he 'always dreams of *realities*, and *sees* things beyond the ken of carnal eyes';[2] but tract societies carefully considered whether their contributions were acceptably 'true'. Those supporting the 'March of Intellect' were also suspicious of fiction. Mechanics Institutes were divided over whether to take novels into their libraries, and such periodicals as *The Penny Magazine* eschewed all fiction. Its acceptance was eased first by Scott, whose historical realism and impeccable morality answered the two basic criticisms of the novel, fantasy and impurity; and then by the social engagement of Dickens. But as late as 1843, while noting that 'many hundreds of new-born intellectuals of modern improvement and enlightenment look out for novels with avidity', a reviewer in *The Northern Star* affirmed that 'we think novel-reading, at its best, only an indifferent substitute for a worse occupation of time'.[3] It is to 'entertaining' reading that we must now turn.

Broadsheets were the traditional 'non-serious' reading of the poor. In the 1750s Thomas Holcroft could find no other cheap literature in the country areas than the sheets pinned up in taverns and in cottages,[4] and a century later Charles Manby Smith wrote that criminal broadsheet circulation

alone 'far exceeds that of any other production of the press throughout the world'.[5] In the years immediately following the Napoleonic wars, broadsheets increased in volume along with other forms of printed literature. In London the scene was dominated by John Pitts (1765–1844) and James Catnach (1792–1842); but every provincial town of any size also had its chapbook and broadsheet publishers. The major centre outside London was Newcastle-upon-Tyne, where the largest publishers were John Marshall and the brothers William and Thomas Fordyce. Ballad sellers adapted their trade to the bustling streets of the cities, some carrying gauze squares fluttering with their songs, or posters painted with sensational pictures. Some dressed up, or performed in pairs; others hung their sheets on walls or railings, sold them on their stalls like Dickens's Silas Wegg, or took refuge from dust and rain in street corners, awaiting buyers.

Broadsheets have been blamed for the degeneration of the traditional oral ballad. Their verse was carelessly transcribed and printed. As commercial broadsheet printing grew, songs were composed and bought for their sensational value, instead of coming from the folk tradition – although this had always to some extent been the case. Most important, as David Buchan has convincingly shown, the printed ballad became something different in *kind* from that of popular song.

Where the nonliterate ballad-singer learned both a method of ballad composition and a number of ballad stories and thereby created ballad-texts, the literate singer merely learns ballad-texts. In the oral period the process of

THE COSTER'S SING SONG.

ST. LEONARD'S HALL, SHOREDITCH.

reproduction involved creative composition; in the modern period it involves only memorisation.[6]

Yet print also had its positive effects. It preserved and disseminated popular song. Lucy E. Broadwood, for example, has declared that 'the spread of ballads in England was of course due to the pedlars, who sold ballad-sheets with their other wares'.[7] Even at its most commercial, broadsheet ballads kept their link with performance – Catnach was said to have kept a fiddler on hand to hear how a ballad sounded before buying it to print.[8] The broadsheet ballad changed in character in the early nineteenth century, becoming realistic rather than romantic, concerned with common people and everyday affairs rather than noble life, and the purity of the ballad stanza and diction became largely lost.[9] But this is due not only to the increased use of print, as has been claimed, but to changes in the social life and the singing habits of the people.

The ballad in fact proved itself to be infinitely flexible. It adapted itself to urban and industrial life. It expressed the frustrations and injustices of the class struggle – a hand was said to have been punished for merely *whistling* the tune to a song by Joseph Mather (1737–1804), the Radical Sheffield factory poet. It embodied the love and hate of man's relation to his work, in songs such as 'The Bury New Loom'. It also reflected the violence and materialism of street life. 'Cocks' or spoof broadsheets were always a favourite genre. But while Shakespeare's Autolycus sold a tale of the 'fish that appeared upon the coast on Wednesday the four-score of April, forty fathom above water, and sang this ballad against the hard hearts of maids', James Catnach early in his career was imprisoned for a 'cock', published in 1818, suggesting that Mr Pizzey, a prominent Drury Lane butcher, made his sausages from human flesh.[10]

Crime was the best seller. From 1820, when by law there was a period between sentence and execution, to 1868, when public executions were stopped, ballad singers stood under the gallows as the drop thudded open, and began shouting the deceased's 'Last Dying Will and Testament', scooping the papers, which were printed after the the event. 'Many's the penny I've turned away when I've been asked for an account of the whole business *before* it happened,' a seller told Mayhew.[11] A 'stunning good murder' provided all the known highest-circulation broadsheets – two and a half million sheets were said to have been sold, 1848–9, on the occasion of the murder of the two Jermys by James Bloomfield Rush.[12] 'Fires are our best friends, next to murders, if they are *good* fires,' Mayhew was also told; but sellers exploited whatever sensation was going. 'My shoes I call Pope Pius; my trowsers and braces, Calcraft; my waistcoat and shirt, Jael Denny; and my coat, Love Letters. A man must show his gratitude in the best way he can'.[13]

The streets were only one place in which the urban masses heard and joined in song. They invaded the once fashionable pleasure gardens, such as Vauxhall (1661–1859) and White Conduit Gardens (1745–1849). Public houses had long been the centre for 'free-and-easy' and 'cock-and-hen' song evenings; a little up the social ladder were such song saloons as the Cyder Cellars, Maiden Lane and Evans's Supper Rooms, drawn on by Thackeray for the Cave of Harmony in *The Newcomes* (1853–5) and the Back Kitchen in *Pendennis* (1848–50). An increasing number of public houses provided entertainment, both professional and amateur, against a small entry fee refundable in drink. In *Sybil; or, The Two Nations* (1845), Disraeli described 'The Temple of the Muses' attached to the Cat and Fiddle Inn, in a northern industrial town. It was a tall, narrow room painted from floor to ceiling with literary tableaux, packed with three or four hundred working people seated at separate tables, drinking and listening to a lady who sang 'a favourite ballad' or a gentleman in 'a farmer's costume of the old comedy' offering 'a melancholy effusion called a comic song'. Other professional entertainers included 'the

principal harpiste of the King of Saxony and his first fiddler', but the most popular items were the 'Thespian recitations' by amateurs or novices who wished to become professional.[14] It was an indigenous part of popular culture.

From 1832, when music halls were opened in Bolton and Manchester, and the Grecian Saloon opened off the City Road in London, such places spread across England, in particular after Charles Morton in 1852, the year following the Great Exhibition, opened the Canterbury Hall, Lambeth. This initiated a charge made for entry rather than as a token against drink.

In this context popular song became at once more sensational, and more sentimental. It also produced hundreds of songbooks and the successors to earlier 'Garland' collections, such magazines as *The London Singer's Magazine* (1838–40) and *The Coal Hole Companion* (c. 1840). By the 1860s the songbooks were edging out the ballads, for they offered a dozen songs for the price of one broadside ballad. Broadsheets were also losing to another rival. About this time Charles Hindley pursued a street-seller shouting broadsheets and was offered the *Brighton Daily News*. While ballad street cries still drew attention, 'the days of cocks, sir, is gone by – cheap newspapers 'as done 'em up'.[15]

One step from broadsheets were chapbooks. These were sheets folded into sixteens, with generally a coarse, coloured cover, aspiring to the format of books. Mr Victor Neuberg has considered them 'the most important and numerically the most considerable element in the printed popular literature of the eighteenth century'.[16] If the broadsheet was the printed form of ballad, chapbooks took over the longer metrical romance, and standard titles such as *The Seven Champions of Christendom* were published well into the nineteenth century. By this period, however, they had become predominantly children's reading.

Towards the end of the eighteenth century the growth of circulating libraries throughout the country reflected the expanding reading public among the middle

No. I

Price 6d. each.

THE
GIPSEY GIRL:

OR

THE HEIR OF HAZEL DELL,

A ROMANTIC TALE

Embellished with highly Engraved Plates.

By HANNAH MARIA JONES,

AUTHORESS OF VILLAGE SCANDAL—CHILD OF MYSTERY—GIPSEY MOTHER—PRIDE OF THE VILLAGE—EMILY MORELAND—GRETNA GREEN—ROSALINE WOODBRIDGE—SCOTTISH CHIEFTAINS, &c. &c. &c.

LADYE, throw back thy raven hair,
Lay thy white brow in the moonlight bare,
I will look on the stars, and look on thee,
And read the page of thy destiny.

Little thanks shall I have for my tale,
Even in youth thy cheek will be pale,
By thy side is a red rose tree,   [be.
One lone rose droops withered, so thou wilt

Mark yon star,—it shone at thy birth ;
Look again,—it has fallen to earth,

Its glory has pass'd like a thought away,
So, or yet sooner, will thou decay.

I may not read in thy hazel eyes,
For the long dark lash that over them lies,
So in my art I can but see
One shadow of night on thy destiny.

I can give thee but dark revealings,
Of passionate hopes and wasted feelings,
Of love that past like the lava wave,
Of a broken heart and an early grave.

ANON.

" THE deep and powerful interest of this story, surpasses even any thing that has hitherto appeared from the pen of this highly talented authoress. The fate of the injured Eva and her child, and the miseries that are heaped upon the innocent and well meaning Mrs. Walsingham, by the discovery of her husband's heartless perfidy, are painted with a pathos and simplicity which must even touch the heart of the most thoughtless and unreflecting. The character of Herbert Walsingham is well and skilfully drawn and the struggle in his bosom between the worldly pride which goads him on to desert the victim of his falsehood, and the stings of conscience as well as the lingering remains of affection for the beloved Eva are most vigorously depicted ; while from these darker pictures of human nature we turn with delight to the sweet unassuming portrait of Elizabeth and the generous high-souled Clifford. In fact character, interest, eloquence, traits of feeling that melt, and flashes of humour that enliven the heart, together with the most accurate delineation of human nature, render the GIPSEY GIRL one of the most delightful novels that it has been our fortune to meet with for a long time."
London Review.

London:

PUBLISHED BY WILLIAM EMANS, 31, CLOTH FAIR.

1836.

PRINTED BY J. LRISCOE, 23, BANNER STREET, ST. LUKE'S LONDON

and lower middle classes, and in particular among women. By 1800 they were estimated at a thousand.[17] For the popular reader their gothic style of fiction was offered, abbreviated, in 'blue books' – chunky chapbooks published in particular by Dean and Munday and by Thomas Tegg, costing sixpence for thirty-six pages, a shilling for seventy-two.[18] For those wanting the novels in a longer form, there was also a growing trade in tales sold at sixpence a number, again following the Minerva Press style, though with emphasis on the domestic and rural. The queen of the sixpenny-issue novel industry was Hannah Maria Jones, with such titles as *The Gipsey Girl; or, the Heir of Hazel Dell*, and *The Child of Mystery, a Tale of Fashionable Life*, both offered by William Emans in 1836.

Also important were reprint libraries in serial form. These had been pioneered by John Harrison with *The Novelist's Library* (1780–88). In 1823 John Limbird began an even larger project with his twopenny *British Novelist*, offering everything from Johnson's *Rasselas* to the Minerva Press bestseller Mrs Regina Roche's *The Children of the Abbey*. Many similar projects run right through the century. The Cottage Library, started in 1837 by William Milner of Halifax, offered complete volume reprints for as little as a shilling.[19]

Meanwhile as the working-class, urban, reading public expanded, it was served by a wide variety of cheap libraries, often attached to coffee houses or tobacconists; educational establishments, such as Mechanics Institutes, and many Sunday Schools also had them.[20] The sixpenny 'number' novel became the penny 'blood', published weekly instead of monthly, eight pages instead of twenty-four or thirty-two, with a woodcut on the first page instead of a separate steel engraving. The first was a plagiarism of Dickens, *The Penny Pickwick*, written probably by Thomas Peckett Prest, calling himself 'Bos'. Its claimed circulation of 50,000 is quite possible. Then Prest adapted Hannah Maria Jones's *The Gipsey Girl* as *Ela the Outcast* (1838), again successful, and the penny-

issue novel became the dominant form of popular fiction until the late 1840s, when it was superseded by other types of fiction.

From the Napoleonic wars, newspapers, at first available to less affluent readers only in the public house or coffee house or hired by the hour,[21] became increasingly important as working-class reading. This was particularly true of the Sunday press. Sold by newsboys blowing their tin trumpets down the Sunday morning streets, they scandalized many 'respectable' readers, but provided news for those who had neither the time nor the money for a daily paper. They were begun by Mrs E. Johnson of Ludgate Hill in 1779 with *The British Gazette and Sunday Monitor*. In 1796 John Bell, typefounder, circulating library proprietor and one of the leading journalists and publishers of his day, began *Bell's Weekly Messenger*. His colourful editor, Bondini, was deported as a suspected French spy, but the paper was decorous family reading, with advertisements left out lest they offend lady readers. From about 1815 the rival publication of an Irish barrister, Robert Bell, *Bell's Weekly Dispatch* (founded 1801), became radical in politics, and gave wide coverage to crime and to sport, employing Pierce Egan, the leading sports writer of the day. This was the pattern followed by other Sunday papers, including *Bell's Life in London* (1822–86), founded by another Robert Bell, the *Observer* (founded 1791), revitalized by William Clements in the 1820s, and the *Sunday Times* (founded 1838).

Bell's Weekly Messenger remained the one conservative exception. In 1831 Bell died, disinheriting his journalist son, John Browne Bell. This may have been because of the son's political views, for he immediately brought out the radical *Bell's New Weekly Messenger*, giving sixty-four columns for $8\frac{1}{2}$d., and containing pull-out supplements, 'The Reviewer' and 'The Commercialist'. John Browne Bell is chiefly remembered for creating the *News of the World*, a double sheet the size of *The Times* yet costing only 3d., and providing detailed coverage of crime. By 1854 it sold 109,000 copies a week, the world's largest newspaper

BELL'S
LIFE IN LONDON,
AND
Sporting Chronicle;
COMBINING,
WITH THE NEWS OF THE WEEK,
A RICH REPOSITORY
OF
FASHION
WIT
and
HUMOUR
And the Interesting Incidents of
REAL LIFE.

"Then there's LIFE in't."—SHAKSPEARE.

PUBLISHED AT FOUR O'CLOCK EVERY SATURDAY AFTERNOON,
BY MESSRS. SMITH'S, 192, STRAND, LONDON.

PRICE ONLY SEVEN PENCE.

MR BARNES, BOOKSELLER,

Sends to all parts of the Kingdom, English, Scotch, Irish and Continental Newspapers, free of Postage at their respective
Prices.—Sunday's London Prints delivered in Shields on the Tuesday Mornings.

LLOYD'S

PENNY

Sunday

Times

AND PEOPLES'

POLICE GAZETTE.

No. 248.   LONDON: SUNDAY, DECEMBER 29, 1844   **Vol. 5.**

'ALL'S *RIGHT* THAT'S *LEFT.*

Behold this valiant man of war,
Stumping along with all his might;
His looks and voice assure us that
All that is *left* with him is *right.*

POLICE.

BOW-STREET.

"LARKING," &c., a SERIO COMIC JESTE ON WATERLOO BRIDGE.—On Thursday morning, three very dashing young bucks, who gave their names Augustus Frederick Hicks, George Hull, and Stanley Irving, were brought from the station house, where they had been immured since first o'clock the same morning, charged by one of the toll-takers on Waterloo-bridge, with committing an outrageous breach of the peace, and with attempting to "rob" the gate!

APPEAL ON BEHALF OF THE NATIVES.

If you swallow the oyster, pay for the *shell*,
We've but little doubt is your motto;
To prevent all dispute respecting the fact,
You instantly set up a grotto.

THE TWO FRIENDS DISCOVERING CLARA DI CAVALHO IN THE RUINS.

THE RUINS;

A SPANISH ADVENTURE.

THE BEQUEST.

A DISCIPLE OF PLATE-O (PLATO).

At peace with Cains you must be
(A thing most heartily wished),
O drink down sure you'll have,
And then you'll be nicely *dish'd.*

FAMILY HERALD

A Domestic Magazine of

Useful Information and Amusement.

DO NOT IN PROSPERITY WHAT MAY BE REPENTED OF
IN ADVERSITY.

HE THAT SWELLS IN PROSPERITY WILL BE SURE TO
SHRINK IN ADVERSITY.

No. 228.—VOL. V.]　　　FOR THE WEEK ENDING SEPTEMBER 18, 1847.　　　[PRICE ONE PENNY.

MARGARETTA.

When I was in my teens
I loved dear Margaretta;
I know not what it means—
I cannot now forget her.
That vision of the past
My head is ever crazing;
Yet when I saw her last
I could not speak for gazing.
Oh! lingering rose of May!
Dear when first I met her:
Worn in my heart alway,
Life-cherish'd Margaretta!

We parted near the stile,
Just as the morn was breaking;
For many a weary mile
Oh! how my heart was aching!
But distance, time, and change
Have lost me Margaretta;

And yet 'tis sadly strange
That I cannot forget her.
Oh! queen of rural maids,
Dear dove-eyed Margaretta!
The heart the mind upbraids
That struggles to forget her.

My love, I know, will seem
A wayward, boyish folly;
But, ah! it was a dream
Most sweet—most melancholy.
Were mine the world's domain,
To me 'twere fortune better
To be a boy again,
And dream of Margaretta.
Oh! memory of the past,
Why linger to regret her?
My first love is my last;
For that is Margaretta.　　G. P. M.

THE STORY-TELLER.

SAYING AND DOING.

The post-house of Oberhausberg had just been thrown into a flurry by a travelling-carriage arriving from Saverne, on its way to Strasbury. Master Topfer, the innkeeper, was running backwards and forwards, giving instructions to his domestics and postillions; whilst the carriage, standing unhorsed before the great gateway, was surrounded by children and idlers, making remarks and observations to each other. Among the latter was an individual with a lively eye and swarthy complexion, whose sharp, jerking accent formed a singular contrast with the Teutonic language of the other spectators. Master Bardanou was, in truth, born in the south of France; chance had directed his steps to Oberhausberg, where, facing the post-house, he had opened a barber's shop, the blue window-shutters of which bore the double inscription:

Hair cut and Beards   *Shaving done in the*
Dressed at all prices.   *Marseilles style.*

Mixed up with the crowd of gapers who thronged Topfer's gateway, the barber took part in the general conversation, in a kind of German, an idea of which may be formed from the circumstance that it was Alsacian spoken by a native of Provence.

"Have you seen the traveller, Master Bardanou?" inquired an old woman, who carried on her arm one of those baskets, filled with thread, pins, and stay-laces, which indicate the female pedlar.

"Doubtless, Dame Hartmann," replied the barber; "he is a stout personage, with an appearance of possessing more belly than brains."

It is to be remarked that Master Bardanou had a turn for the epigrammatic; and passed at Oberhausberg for a wit of no ordinary stamp and promise.

Those who heard his joke at the expense of the traveller replied to it by a horse laugh, in which Dame Hartmann began by taking part; then, shaking her head in a sage-like fashion, "Money is worth more than wit, neighbour," said she, looking the barber full in the face; "for with wit one walks a-foot; while money enables one to ride in a carriage."

"What you say there is the perfect truth, Dame Hartmann," replied the Provençal, with a profound air. "And yet heaven knows where wealth often goes! I should like to learn, for instance, what this stranger has done to merit travelling with an equipage."

"Be quiet, Bardanou; he is a baron," interrupted, all at once, a youthful and laughing voice.

Bardanou turned round, and perceived the god-daughter of Master Topfer, who had just made her appearance at the inn-door. "A baron!" he repeated. "Who told you that, Nicette?"

"The tall valet who accompanies him," replied the young woman. "He said that the baron could not be served in the public room, and that everything was to be carried into the grand saloon with the balcony."

The crowd looked upwards. The saloon of which Nicette spoke was situated immediately above the spot on which the gapers stood; and the window was open; but the blind being let down, permitted nothing to be seen within.

"So it is there you have served his dinner?" asked Dame Hartmann, indicating by a look the saloon.

"Not I," said the young woman. "The baron would neither make use of our porcelain nor of our crystal glasses. He always carries with him a dinner-service in silver; and I saw the valet take it out of a large ebony box."

A murmur of surprise and admiration rose from the crowd; the Provençal barber shrugged his shoulders. "That is to say, the baron can neither eat nor drink like other Christians," observed he, ironically. "He must have a chamber to himself, and eat out of silver-plate! The great King Solomon said, with reason, 'Vanity of vanities, all is vanity!'"

"Get along with you, Bardanou; you are going to speak ill of your neighbour," interrupted Nicette, laughingly.

"Of my neighbour!" echoed the barber. "Is a baron my neighbour? Let me alone. I know the stout gentleman already; he resembles all the nobles whom we see pass this way. Did you hear in what a tone he called his servant, who had stopped to say a word with Master Topfer?—'I am waiting for you, Germain—I am waiting for you!' just as if the poor fellow had no right to speak with any one for a moment. This same baron must be a real tyrant."

"Ah! what are you saying there, Bardanou?" cried Nicette. "Please heaven, you deceive yourself! Are you aware for what reason he is proceeding to the duchy of Baden?"

"Not I, indeed."

"His valet told me," continued the young woman, letting her voice drop, "that he is on his way to get married."

"To get married!"

"With the richest heiress of the country—a widow, whom——"

"Whom, without a doubt, he does not know?"

"I cannot answer that."

"It is not necessary he should know her. These people marry much in the way that commerce is carried on; that is, by correspondence. They think only of satisfying their avarice."

"Hold your tongue, Bardanou," again interrupted the lively Nicette. "You are too ready to judge ill of others, without knowing them."

"And I judge worse of them when I do know them," added the barber.

"You nevertheless know that everybody does not marry for riches," replied the young woman, slightly blushing, and throwing a look askance at him. "There are people who consult only their affection——"

"Like me, for instance," gaily continued Bardanou, who seized Nicette's hands, and forced her to look him in the face.

"That is not the affair at present," said the young woman, hurriedly.

"Pardon me," exclaimed the Provençal. "You are well aware that I do not run after wealth, and that I do not find you less beautiful, because Father Topfer has declared that he would give you no marriage portion. But I am an original, my charmer—a philosopher, as your godfather says. On these matters I entertain ideas different from those of other people. That is why my blood boils when I see men like your baron, for whom riches are only a means of vanity, tyranny, and avarice; and I cannot help thinking that, were I in his place, I would do more credit to the choice of Providence."

"That remains to be seen, Master Bardanou," observed the old female pedlar. "Riches produce strange effects on the character of man."

"Ay, that is when one is divested of principle," sharply chimed in the Provençal, "when one turns like a weathercock with every wind that blows. But I know what I mean, and what ought to be, Dame Hartmann. I possess some philosophy. Were I suddenly to become rich, do you see, I should no more change than our old church steeple. You would always find me as just, disinterested, and as good a fellow as I am now."

Distrust of himself, it would seem, formed no part of Bardanou's character. All that he disallowed in point of morals and good sense to his neighbours he ascribed to himself with a scrupulous exactness. As satisfied with his own person as he was dissatisfied with that of others, he would willingly have reproached Providence with having made man after his own image rather than after the image of Bardanou. Once engaged on this favourite topic, he suffered his tongue to run into an improvisation out of all bounds. He set forth the great and useful things he would accomplish, were chance suddenly to send him one of those rich Indian uncles who are no longer found even on the stage. He passed in review all the virtues he would display—the various kinds of merit of which he would give proof; he was, in short, about to accord himself an apotheosis, when the traveller, who had given rise to this self-gratulation, presented himself at the inn-door. He circulation at that time.[22] However much the Sunday press offended sections of the conservative and church-going public, nevertheless it must be stressed that in tone and format it remained restrained. In 1840 the *Sunday Times* experimented with an illustrated fiction serial: the woodcuts soon stopped, and after two years the venture ended. It was not 'respectable'.

On the other side of the 'quality' barrier, the penny imitations of the Sunday papers such as Edward Lloyd's *Penny Sunday Times and People's Police Gazette* carried fiction, general items but no news. The same was true of *The Novel Newspaper* (1838-c. 1848), *Chambers's Historical Newspaper* (1832–5) and *Clarke's Weekly Dispatch* (1841). This was to evade the newspaper tax – but why then appear as a newspaper? At this point cheap periodical literature was thought of as a 'newspaper' whatever the content: it kept the newspaper form in the way that early train carriages kept the shape of the horsedrawn coach.

The transition from this to the popular magazine can be seen in *The Family Herald*, begun on 13 May 1843 by John Biggs. For the first twenty-two numbers it took a four-page newspaper format, with no news. (It claimed to be the first paper ever to be produced, from newsprint to mechanical typesetting, by machine.)[23] It then changed to a quarto format for easy reading at home. It made a planned attempt to cater for working-class needs, advertising for 'an experienced female hand, who could from practical knowledge, add information peculiarly adapted to the humbler classes of her own sex'. It included fashions, articles on working-class conditions, fiction and a correspondence column.

Correspondence columns were not new, beginning at least as early as Eliza Haywood's *Female Spectator* (1744–6),[24] but with the new popular journalism they were to provide an increasingly important link between journal and reading public. In *The Family Herald* letters were received from male and female readers on a wide variety of subjects, taking up four densely printed columns at the centre of the magazine.

However, as the mildly radical image of the first numbers gave way to one of non-political domesticity, the correspondence became predominantly that of lower-middle-class girls and young women. Kate is warned against asking a young man to go for a walk with her, however innocent the circumstances; but 'Evelyn', at twenty-two still dominated by her mother, is told this could stunt her mind. 'Ada Grey', faced with a young man's ardour, is told to 'send him a copy of "Man will ever Deceive"', or, if he is very sensitive, some even more delicate hint'.

Such delicacy is foreign to the correspondence columns of *The London Journal* (1845–1912), which catered for a less genteel type of working-class reader. Its first editor was G. W. M. Reynolds (1814–79), a journalist with an upper-middle-class background who, after losing his inheritance on journalistic ventures in France, and making an indifferent success writing for English magazines, wrote a well-received 'continuation' of Dickens's novel, *Pickwick Abroad* (1839) for *The Old Monthly Magazine*, which he was editing. This drew his attention to the popular reading public that was buying the penny-issue fiction of Edward Lloyd. The first issue of *The London Journal* shows him experimenting with the popular taste. He included woodcuts and articles on geography, architecture and popular science – imitating 'useful knowledge' periodicals such as *The Penny Magazine* – alongside sensational items reminiscent of *The Terrific Magazine* and the like. The correspondence columns included information on how to apply for jobs, and on rent payment and emigration, showing the needs existing among the urban working-class public. Answers to personal problems were forthright, sometimes brutal – 'There is no cure for bow legs at your age' – and Reynolds brusquely told those who wrote in asking for help outside the scope of the column that their letters would be destroyed and the stamps sent for return postage consigned to 'the nearest police-station poor box'. There is no evidence that he had to make up letters to

THE
LONDON JOURNAL;
And Weekly Record of Literature Science, and Art.

No 9. Vol. I. FOR THE WEEK ENDING APRIL 26, 1845. [Price One Penny.

THE MYSTERIES OF THE INQUISITION.

CHAPTER III.
DOLOREZ.

We must now introduce the reader to one of those spacious and commodious Andalusian houses, lighted only by glass doors and windows opening upon a large court perfumed with flowers.

On one side of the upper storeys of this house, which served generally as the winter-residence, and adjacent to a large saloon in which the family partook of their repasts, was a small chamber furnished like the cell of a nun. A bed, white as snow, but of no downy and luxurious material,—two chairs of black wood beautifully sculptured,—a praying-desk in the same style, and surmounted by an ivory crucifix,—and a figure of the Madonna in a niche, with an ever-burning lamp suspended before it,—these were the characteristics of this unpretending little chamber.

The house to which we have alluded was the palace of Count Manuel Argoso, governor of Seville. the little chamber was that of his only daughter, the Donna Dolorez.

This young lady, who had lost her mother at an early age, was the darling of her father's heart. She was now seventeen years old, and was very far from resembling the other women of Andalusia. Of a loveliness at once simple and noble,—of a firm and elevated disposition, Dolorez had not passed her time in that mysterious indolence which has so baneful an effect upon the naturally ardent imaginations and voluptuous passions of the Spanish women.

Her preceptor was an uncle—a learned and enlightened man, who had travelled much in France and Germany, and had fortified his naturally powerful intellect by the aid of a sound and liberal philosophy. He had not sown in a sterile soil: Dolorez would even at the present day have been deemed a very remarkable woman.

Possessed of the most correct notions of probity, —loving virtue for virtue's sake,—and enthusiastic in her admiration of everything generous, noble, and good, Dolorez was imbued with the pure faith of the fathers of the church. Her indulgent charity revolted against all the errors, hypocrisies, and crimes of fanaticism. She was pious as was Isabella the catholic—that great queen whose faith taught her to struggle long, though timidly, against the establishment of the Inquisition, and always to counteract its most enormous crimes. The governor's daughter followed the true spirit and morality of the gospel—a most dangerous proceeding at that time, when, in order to live in peace, it was necessary not only to be the disciple of Christ, but the creature of the Inquisition.

Nevertheless, in spite of a philosophy so enlightened for her age and especially for the epoch in which she lived, Dolorez, faithful to the observance of external ceremonials, had endeavoured to avoid the suspicions of the terrible tribunal.

The Grand Inquisitor of Seville, Peter Arbuez, —who was even more dreaded than the Cardinal Archbishop of Seville, the Grand Inquisidor of the province,—seemed to extend his all-powerful protection over the mansion of the lord governor.

Received at all hours into the family,—in his quality of priest and as the chief of the inquisitorial tribunal of the city,—Arbuez, who was then in the prime of life, and was a prey to all the fiery passions of the tropics, had not beheld that pure and saint-like virgin, without becoming deeply enamoured of her beauty. Nor had he perceived without feelings of horrible jealousy, that the young Stephen de Vargas was the object of the charming creature's tenderest affections.

Vainly had he endeavoured, beneath the veil of a holy and paternal friendship, to instil into the reply to, as did some later editors, although he later used the popularity of the correspondence column to give prominence to pieces on social problems in his own *Reynolds's Miscellany* (1847–69).

These two periodicals, with *The Family Herald*, were pivotal publications for the development of popular journalism. They bring together the main trends of the 1820s and 1830s that we have looked at, including elements of radicalism, 'useful knowledge', and fiction, in a style adapted to the new urban reader. Their circulation was huge for this period. By 1850 *The London Journal* sold half a million copies.[25]

Their success appeared to middle-class observers to show the triumph of sensationalism over moral and political improvement. Charles Kingsley, in 1848, visited a working-class newsagent and was disgusted to find that beside the *People's Charter* and Lamartine's *Address to the Irish Deputies*, there was 'hardly anything' but 'Flash Songsters', 'Swell's Guides', 'Tales of Horror', and dirty milksop French novels. Moreover, advertisements for Voltaire's Tales, Tom Paine and 'the same French dirt which lay on the counter' was to be found 'in the People's Charter itself'.[26]

Kingsley's coupling of Paine and 'French dirt', however, points to inconsistencies in the opposition between 'serious' and 'entertaining' reading. These can be found at all levels. The young Samuel Bamford had asked 'innocently enough' why chapbook tales such as 'St George and the Dragon' 'could not be true', while 'it were a sin to disbelieve' equally extraordinary accounts in the Bible and in religious literature.[27] Again, the conventions of fiction and melodrama, unreal to those outside, could be the accepted rhetoric for those within the popular culture.

The Factory Lad (1839), an anonymous penny-issue novel, is an impassioned attack on factory conditions. Its intention is to describe an actual social situation, and it appeals to documentation. Yet the plot and style are the conventional ones of melodrama, and when the author wishes to show the wickedness of the mill-owner, he uses the cliché of the rape of a country girl at a country ball. To the middle-class reader, the realism is marred by the stereotypes; but it is unlikely that the reader for whom it was intended would have felt this unease. The melodramatic heightening was a natural way to focus the emotional content of the story. Indeed, the question of the author using two planes of 'reality' would probably not have arisen. As D. W. Harding has shown,[28] the distinction between 'truth' and 'fiction' is itself relative and socially learnt. 'Reality' depends on patterns of perception and cultural conventions of rhetoric. It is to these popular rhetorics that we must now turn.

4. TIME AND THE POPULAR ALMANACK

In 1837 navvies working on the Birmingham and London railroad at Fenny Stratford uncovered an ancient burial site.[1] A popular broadsheet published in Coventry recorded

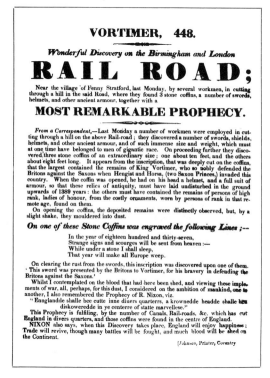

VORTIMER, 448.

Wonderful Discovery on the Birmingham and London

RAIL ROAD;

Near the village of Fenny Stratford, last Monday, by several workmen, in cutting through a hill in the said Road, where they found 3 stone coffins, a number of swords, helmets, and other ancient armour, together with a

MOST REMARKABLE PROPHECY.

From a Correspondent,—Last Monday a number of workmen were employed in cutting through a hill on the above Rail-road ; they discovered a number of swords, shields, helmets, and other ancient armour, and of such immense size and weight, which must at one time have belonged to men of gigantic race. On proceeding further they discovered three stone coffins of an extraordinary size ; one about ten feet, and the others about eight feet long. It appears from the inscription, that was deeply cut on the coffins, that the largest contained the remains of King Vortimer, who so nobly defended the Britons against the Saxons when Hengist and Horsa, (two Saxon Princes,) invaded this country. When the coffin was opened, he had on his head a helmet, and a full suit of armour, so that these relics of antiquity, must have laid undisturbed in the ground upwards of 1389 years : the others must have contained the remains of persons of high rank, ladies of honour, from the costly ornaments, worn by persons of rank in that remote age, found on them.
On opening the coffins, the deposited remains were distinctly observed, but, by a slight shake, they mouldered into dust.

On one of these Stone Coffins was engraved the following Lines ;—

In the year of eighteen hundred and thirty-seven,
Strange signs and scourges will be sent from heaven :—
While under a stone I shall sleep,
That year will make all Europe weep.

On clearing the rust from the swords, this inscription was discovered upon one of them.
' This sword was presented by the Britons to Vortimer, for his bravery in defending the Britons against the Saxons.'
Whilst I contemplated on the blood that had here been shed, and viewing these implements of war, all, perhaps, for this dust, I considered on the ambition of mankind, one to another, I also remembered the Prophecy of R. Nixon, viz.
" Englandde shalle bee cutte inne diuers quarterrs, a krownedde headde shalle bee diskowveredde in ye centerre of statte marvellese."
This Prophecy is fulfiling, by the number of Canals, Rail-roads, &c. which has cut England in divers quarters, and those coffins were found in the centre of England.
NIXON also says, when this Discovery takes place, England will enjoy happiness ; Trade will revive, though many battles will be fought, and much blood will be shed on the Continent.

[Johnson, Printer, Coventry]

the excavation under the heading 'Vortimer, 448'. According to the sheet, the following lines were found on a coffin which contained the sword of one Vortimer, who had defended the Britons against the Saxons.

In the year of eighteen hundred and thirty-seven,
Strange signs and scourges will be sent from heaven:–
While under a stone I shall sleep,
That year will make all Europe weep.

The writer coupled this inscription with a prophecy by the Cheshire astrologer Robert Nixon that ' "Englandde shalle bee cutte inne diuers quarterrs". This prophecy is fulfiling, by the number of Canals, Rail-roads. &c. which has cut England in divers quarters, and those coffins were found in the centre of England'. 'Vortimer, 448' is not the usual kind of hoax broadsheet. Railways, like cholera, civil disturbance and other public events, were part of a destiny ruled by God and the stars in the popular imagination of the early years of the nineteenth century.

The French Revolution intensified the social upheavals caused in England by the Industrial Revolution and awakened a new fever of speculation that the end of the world was approaching. 'At such a time,' wrote Carlyle in 1829, 'it was to be expected that the rage for prophecy should be more than usually excited.'[2] In 1794 a Devonshire domestic worker and upholsterer, Joanna Southcott, heard voices telling her that she was the Bride of the Lamb (Revelation xiv) and calling on her to seal the names of the saved for the imminent Day of Judgement. Soon she had 100,000 converts in London and the neighbourhood, and chapels, in particular, in the West Country, Lancashire and Yorkshire. She was closely associated with Richard Brothers, who declared himself King of the Hebrews and Nephew of God. In 1821 Joanna underwent a hysterical pregnancy, which was to have been the birth of Shiloh, the Promised One, and died broken.

Yet the Southcottians continued to spread. One leader was James Wroe, particularly strong in Newcastle-under-Lyme, Bradford and the West Riding, until he was arrested in 1830 for his secular attentions

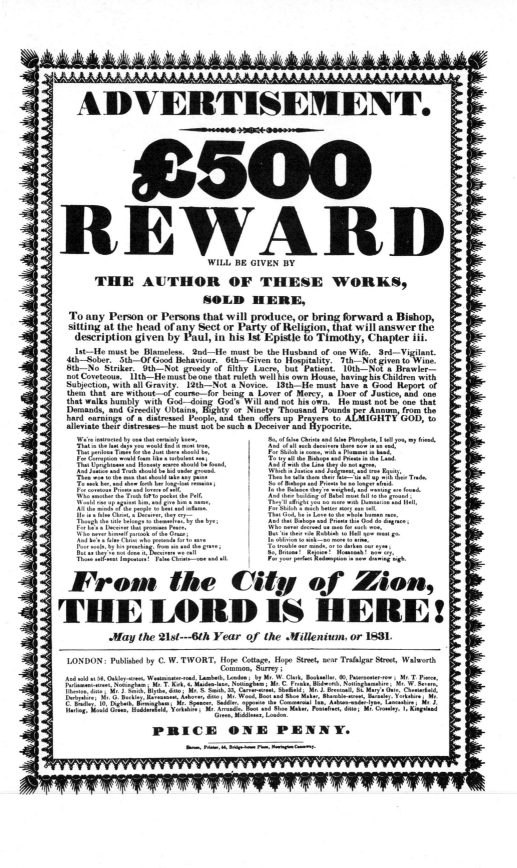

ADVERTISEMENT.

£500
REWARD

WILL BE GIVEN BY

THE AUTHOR OF THESE WORKS,

SOLD HERE,

To any Person or Persons that will produce, or bring forward a Bishop, sitting at the head of any Sect or Party of Religion, that will answer the description given by Paul, in his 1st Epistle to Timothy, Chapter iii.

1st—He must be Blameless. 2nd—He must be the Husband of one Wife. 3rd—Vigilant. 4th—Sober. 5th—Of Good Behaviour. 6th—Given to Hospitality. 7th—Not given to Wine. 8th—No Striker. 9th—Not greedy of filthy Lucre, but Patient. 10th—Not a Brawler—not Coveteous. 11th—He must be one that ruleth well his own House, having his Children with Subjection, with all Gravity. 12th—Not a Novice. 13th—He must have a Good Report of them that are without—of course—for being a Lover of Mercy, a Doer of Justice, and one that walks humbly with God—doing God's Will and not his own. He must not be one that Demands, and Greedily Obtains, Eighty or Ninety Thousand Pounds per Annum, from the hard earnings of a distressed People, and then offers up Prayers to ALMIGHTY GOD, to alleviate their distresses—he must not be such a Deceiver and Hypocrite.

We're instructed by one that certainly knew,
That in the last days you would find it most true,
That perilous Times for the Just there should be,
For Corruption would foam like a turbulent sea;
That Uprightness and Honesty scarce should be found,
And Justice and Truth should be hid under ground.
Then woe to the man that should take any pains
To seek her, and shew forth her long-lost remains;
For covetous Priests and lovers of self,
Who smother the Truth for to pocket the Pelf,
Would rise up against him, and give him a name,
All the minds of the people to heat and inflame.
He is a false Christ, a Deceiver, they cry—
Though the title belongs to themselves, by the bye;
For he's a Deceiver that promises Peace,
Who never himself partook of the Grace;
And he's a false Christ who pretends for to save
Poor souls, by his preaching, from sin and the grave;
But as they've not done it, Deceivers we call
Those self-sent Impostors! False Christs—one and all.

So, of false Christs and false Phrophets, I tell you, my friend,
And of all such deceivers there now is an end,
For Shiloh is come, with a Plummet in hand,
To try all the Bishops and Priests in the Land.
And if with the Line they do not agree,
Which is Justice and Judgment, and true Equity,
Then he tells them their fate—'tis all up with their Trade,
So of Bishops and Priests be no longer afraid.
In the Balance they're weighed, and wanting are found,
And their building of Babel must fall to the ground;
They'll affright you no more with Damnation and Hell,
For Shiloh a much better story can tell.
That God, he is Love to the whole human race,
And that Bishops and Priests this God do disgrace;
Who never decreed us men for such woe,
But 'tis their vile Rubbish to Hell now must go.
In oblivion to sink—no more to arise,
To trouble our minds, or to darken our eyes;
So, Britons! Rejoice! Hosannah! now cry,
For your perfect Redemption is now drawing nigh.

From the City of Zion,
THE LORD IS HERE!

May the 21st---6th Year of the Millenium, or 1831.

LONDON: Published by C. W. TWORT, Hope Cottage, Hope Street, near Trafalgar Street, Walworth Common, Surrey;

And sold at 56, Oakley-street, Westminster-road, Lambeth, London; by Mr. W. Clark, Bookseller, 60, Paternoster-row; Mr. T. Pierce, Parliament-street, Nottingham; Mr. T. Kirk, 4, Maiden-lane, Nottingham; Mr. C. Franks, Blidworth, Nottinghamshire; Mr. W. Severn, Ilheston, ditto; Mr. J. Smith, Blythe, ditto; Mr. S. Smith, 33, Carver-street, Sheffield; Mr. J. Brentnall, St. Mary's Gate, Chesterfield, Derbyshire; Mr. G. Buckley, Ravensnest, Ashover, ditto; Mr. Wood, Boot and Shoe Maker, Shamble-street, Barnsley, Yorkshire; Mr. C. Bradley, 10, Digbeth, Birmingham; Mr. Spencer, Saddler, opposite the Commercial Inn, Ashton-under-lyne, Lancashire; Mr. J. Harling, Mould Green, Huddersfield, Yorkshire; Mr. Arrundle, Boot and Shoe Maker, Pontefract, ditto; Mr. Crossley, 1, Kingsland Green, Middlesex, London.

PRICE ONE PENNY.

Barnes, Printer, 44, Bridge-house Place, Newington Causeway.

to girls in his pastoral care. Zion Ward, a Methodist shoemaker, toured the country preaching that he was Christ himself, denouncing the established churches, and drawing a mixed but at times enthusiastic response. In 1832, after a year in which he preached in the Rotunda, Blackfriars, London, he was convicted of blasphemy in Derby.[3]

About the same time 'Sir William Courtenay' appeared in Canterbury dressed as a Crusader, with crimson and gold velvet tunic embroidered with a Maltese cross, a cloak, cap, silk stockings and Turkish slippers. In reality J. N. Tom, a spirit merchant and maltster of Truro, with two stolen titles conflated, he quickly built up a following among all classes in the city. When he stood for the first Reformed Parliament he polled over a quarter of the votes, after only a brief campaign and the expenditure of £27. Shortly after this he was only saved from imprisonment for perjury by confinement for insanity in a local asylum.

Released in 1838, he assumed the smock and cap of a rustic. He rode the country on a grey horse that he compared, with transfiguring zeal, to the white horse of the apocalypse, befriending the labourers suffering a period of intense agricultural depression. He gave peppermints to the children. He discovered he was Christ. When he began promising labourers twenty-five-acre lots when he should come into his Kingdom, the authorities became increasingly uneasy.

In 1838 he brutally murdered a man sent to arrest him, and gathered together a band of followers in Bossenden Wood near Canterbury. On being told to follow 'in the flesh', one, Alexander Froad, cried out 'Oh be joyful! Oh, be joyful! The Saviour has accepted me. Go on! Go on! Till I drop, I'll follow thee.' Tom gave his disciples the Sacrament, promising them that bullets would not hurt them, and that his Kingdom was at hand. When surrounded by a large band of soldiers, he shot an officer before himself being killed. His followers, armed only with staves and pitch-forks, fell on the

rifles and bayonets of the militia like dervishes. Eleven or twelve died. As E. P. Thompson has noted, it was in all a higher death toll than Peterloo.[4]

The story of Sir William Courtenay is a minor incident in the history of the times, yet it is significant in that it could happen at all. Tom at first had support from tradesmen, clergymen and doctors in Canterbury, and was put up for Parliament by a respectable clockmaker. His persona of medieval crusader, complete with dress, symbolized at once loyalty to the Crown, the defence of the Church, and a nostalgic era of 'Merie England', for the depressed labourer. In the *Lion of Freedom* (1833), which he published from Canterbury gaol, he cloudily advocated a wide range of reform from universal suffrage to the removal of tithes and making the rich pay the national debt. Zion Ward, again, focused latent religious zeal in the direction of reform. But in all the prophetic movements, the urgency came from their insistence on the imminent approach of the end of the world, and their ability to draw on deep reserves of popular religious fervour.

Millenarianism, it is important to note, was a perfectly orthodox reading of the Bible. Study of Revelation to discover the date of the return of Christ to reign for a thousand years occupied the devout both in the sectarian bodies and in the Church of England itself. Joanna Southcott considered herself an Anglican to the day of her death, and included Church dignitaries among her supporters. In the fashionable Regent Square Chapel in London the Scots Presbyterian clergyman Edward Irving declared that the first of the six phials of divine wrath had been poured out in 1826, and that the Battle of Armageddon was

W. MARTIN'S INVENTION OF THE HIGH LEVEL BRIDGE;

HEIGHT, FROM HIGH WATER TO THE RAILWAY LEVEL, 108 FEET 6 INCHES.

He is also the original Designer of the Arch over the Side; Metallic Railways; high Wheels for Speed, and the wide Guage for Safety, not risking People's Lives.

Five lions on each side will make it look very noble, majestic, and grand ;
One in the centre, a ball under his foot, challenges the world where he doth stand.
The arch over the Side I must give a princely, noble, grand stater,
To stand on each side a fierce figure of a Roman muscular gladiator.

Alarming all the world's adventures, and also Great Britain's false schools,
Teaching lies in colleges, not knowing air to be God's spirit and of nature's rules.
Take notice, our Saviour's parable, good people like to a field of wheat;
The devil has now raised Dr. Pusey to sow tares amongst them, God's people to cheat.
Queen and ministers allow none to lecture without they bring in air to be the first cause,
One true religion, the apostolic church, will soon reach all nations without any flaws.
That will be a great blessing from God, his divine truth clearly to display;
Then the disciples of false philosophers can lead wise people no longer astray.
That will bring on the Millennium, our Saviour's words will divinely prove,
Will set all crowned heads at rest, and make great harmony and love.
An exploder for all college professors, as they are disciples of base false pretenders;
February, 1848, queen and ministers of state must be the mighty God's faith defenders.

WM. MARTIN, Philosophical Conqueror of all Nations.

[Printed by M. Ross, Pilgrim Street, Newcastle.]

approaching. In 1831 his congregation began speaking with tongues. He was expelled from the Chapel, but took with him over eight hundred followers to found the Catholic Apostolic Church.[5] Millenarian doctrines played a part in the many sects that flourished particularly in the towns, such as Assemblies of God, Plymouth Brethren, Elim Church, the Walworth 'Jumpers' and the disciples of God. The Mormons, who landed at Liverpool from the United States in 1838, shortly afterwards baptized their first converts in the Ribble outside Preston.[6]

Yet if Millenarians had a religious basis for expecting the end of the world, the sense of an imminent ending was equally proclaimed by the rationalist Utilitarians who rejected religion as superstition.

As Carlyle noted, 'the Fifth-monarchy men prophesy from the Bible, and the Utilitarians from Bentham. The one announces that the last of the seals is to be opened, positively, in the year 1860; the other assures us that the greatest-happiness principle is to make a heaven of earth, in a still shorter time.'[7] This aspect of utilitarianism affected the beginning of socialism, in particular through Robert Owen, industrialist and friend of Mill and the Edinburgh intellectual circle. In 1816 Owen declared that

... whatever ideas individuals may attach to the term Millenarianism, I know not, but I know that society can be formed to exist without crime, without property, with health greatly improved, with little, if any, misery, and with intelligence and happiness increased an hundred fold; and no obstacle whatever intervenes at this moment, except ignorance, to prevent such a state of society becoming universal.[8]

Owen attempted to create utopian communities freed from the capitalist system. The most important of several groups were in New Lanark in Scotland, and New Harmony in Indiana, in the United States. Socialist Millenarianism percolated through the whole fabric of evolving working-class ideology, including the thought of the young Karl Marx.

The division between religious and socialist movements indeed can be indistinct. 'Shepherd Smith' the Universalist was both a follower of Southcott and, at one time, editor of Owen's periodical *The Crisis* (1832–4). James Pierrepoint Greaves, the 'Sacred Socialist', was a disciple of both Owen and Zion Ward. The Owenite settlements used hymns and religious rhetoric, and were themselves antedated by the successful Moravian settlements such as that founded in 1746 at Fulneck near Bradford.[9] Both were a response to the religious milieu of thought and the acute pressures for social change. Later, Chartism was also to have complex associations with religious movements.[10]

'Men owe to [religion],' wrote Émile Durkheim, 'not only a good part of the substance of their knowledge, but also the form in which this knowledge has been elaborated.'[11] This is true also of that basic mental framework, that of time. Millenarianism, like the annual cycle of festivals and rituals that was losing its appeal over this period, was one way in which the endless progression of time was given a social pattern and meaning through a religious concept.[12] In its strict form, it is essential to note, it was believed in by a minority. As a generalized perspective it is reflected in the way the early nineteenth century looked at the advances of science and industry, at politics, or the claims of a patent medicine. It probably helped determine the dominant mode of melodrama, which will be looked at below, which also has the pattern of absolute conflict between Good and Evil, culminating in final judgement and the triumph of Good. It is important to an understanding of the literature in the anthology.

Concepts of time found their clearest illustration in print, however, in the popular almanack. Almanacks were at once the most widely diffused and the least known type of printed ephemera during our period. Even cottages without a broadsheet or chapbook would be likely to have a sheet almanack pinned to the wall. But as they were discarded when the year was through, even the most popular series have sometimes perished without trace. They might appear to break down old recurrent or Millennial concepts by indicating the scientific progress of time. Ian Watt, for example, writes of the almanack as 'that symbol of an objective sense of time by the printing press',[13] and considers that Fielding's use of them in constructing *Tom Jones* exemplifies the impact of modern time concepts on the novel. The popular almanack, however, at least until the coming of the Society for the Diffusion of Useful Knowledge's *British Almanack* in 1826, tended to be conservative in concept, if radical in politics.

Almanacks emerged from the medieval manuscript calendar of ecclesiastical and astronomical information. The original use of blackletter is still continued for indicating religious festivals today.[14] In the seventeenth century, significantly at another period of social upheaval, they became associated with prophecy. William Lilly (1602–81) published his prophetic almanack *Merlinus Anglicus Junior* from 1644, and this was the model for scores of rivals, notably Francis Moore's *Vox Stellarum, or, a Loyal Almanack* (1697–), which still sells over a million copies annually as *Old Moore's Almanack*. These overlapped with a large sub-literature of prognostications and dream books, such as *The Prophecy at Large of Robert Nixon, the Cheshire Poet* (1714–94), and many later versions. Lilly generally supported the Parliamentarians during the civil war, rendering such services as encouraging Cromwell's troops at the siege of Colchester with his arts, and at the Restoration he was briefly imprisoned under suspicion of helping in the King's execution. However he was also thrice consulted by Charles I when he was imprisoned in Hampton Court, and narrowly escaped, by the trick of rapidly printing an amended version, serious punishment for prophesying that 'Parliament stood on a tottering foundation'.[15] It was partly because of their political power that almanacks were kept the monopoly of the Stationer's Company and the Universities of Oxford and Cambridge presses until 1775.

The Stationer's Company almanacks, however, were expensive. They bore heavy taxes – between 1816 and 1835, as high as 1s. 3d. The common people therefore turned to the cheaper publications that were sold at fairs and from cottage to cottage by hawkers. There are no statistics for sales. Most were sold in the country. In 1835 the S.D.U.K. attempted a survey in certain towns, and estimated sales in Plymouth and Devonport to be from six to eight thousand, and in Nottingham to be only about a thousand.[16]

There is little standardization. Some are imitations of *Old Moore's* and *Raphael's;* others have perhaps nonce-titles, *Orion, Babel*. Some, such as the popular *Paddy's Watch*, had no 'prophecies'; others had nothing prophetic beyond the woodcut. In size, some were a single sheet; others were syndicated, bound by local printers and contained news of markets, parochial events and advertisements. They accreted articles and sometimes, as with *Poor Robin* (1664–1827) which formed two volumes, verse and short stories. Because of their regional relevance, almanacks were the natural outlet for the northern dialect literature which emerged in the 1850s and 1860s. The most famous dialect almanack, John Hartley's *Halifax Original Illuminated Clock Almanack* (1865–1956), sold 5,000 copies of the first number. But this lies outside our period.

Almanacks became a focus for ideological debate. In 1828 the S.D.U.K. led their attack on popular superstition with *The British Almanack*, patiently explaining how the movements of the stars indicated nothing but the laws of science. It was supported with a *Companion to the British Almanack*, and by 1830 was selling 40,000 copies a year.[17] The Religious Tract Society *Almanack* (from 1836) showed the Christian meaning of each day, with appropriate texts. Most religious denominations had their almanacks, as did the Corn Law Movement, and the various Radical bodies. *The People's Almanack for 1850*, for instance, included monthly articles on the conditions and prospects of the working classes. Almanacks became drawn into the battle against the 'taxes on knowledge'. B. D. Cousins's *A Political Pocket Handkerchief, a Duster for the Whigs* (1831) was one that attempted to evade the taxes by being printed on cloth: Cousins was prosecuted. However, James Watson's *Working Man's Almanack* (1832), published from Finsbury under the imprint of 'John Doyle, Liberty Street, New York', even deceived *The Times* into favourable notice of a good American import.[18]

It is therefore too simple to see almanacks as only 'prophetic'. Yet prophetic almanacks remained the most interesting, and probably the most widely circulated, of the many genres well into the century. Has the situation changed? In the 1970s *Old Moore's Almanack* sells over one million copies a

WONDERFUL PREDICTIONS.

And Remarkable Prophecies for the Year 1825.

London: Printed by J. Catnach,
No. 2, Monmouth-Court, 7 Dials.

Just Published—A variety of Scripture Sheets, Christmas
Carols, and Twelfth Night Characters, embellished with
Wood Engravings, superior to any of the
kind Printed in England.

Sold by Thos. Robbins,
Licensed Hawker.

PRICE TWOPENCE.

JANUARY.

" LET there be Light."—Thus spoke the Great First
Then Light appeared,—the Universe arose, (Cause ;
And Suns and Worlds their existence came,
Which loudly their Creator's power proclaim :
Our Sun, 'midst numerous Spheres, a centre found,
With planetary Worlds revolving round.

FEBRUARY.

The Earth is one of these ye the forms the year,
Its moving round the Sun's resplendent sphere ;
Her poles' obliquity the season's gives,
By turning on her axis day receives :
Attended by the Moon, whose silver light
Dispels the gloom, and beautifies the night.

MARCH.

The vegetable world, at its behest
th' th' Almighty rose, in beauty drest ;
White beasts, birds, fishes, serpents, insects, all
Sprung into life, at the Creator's call :
Next Man was made,—an animated clod ;
His soul—a striking image of its God !

WE see by the Laws of an ever-ruling Power, arrived in the Year
1825, which it is to be hoped may prove a more prosperous period than...

APRIL.

M... is with several agency endow'd,
Therefore, was capable of cheating proud ;
Yet evil chuode, although favour'd by Heaven,
And for his crime from Paradise was driven :
But God deni'd a plan, that man, in pain,
Might be brought back to happiness again.

MAY.

The Sacred Pages clearly shew the way,
That leads to bliss, and everlasting day ;
In them we find Jehovah's wond'rous plain,
And see our duty towards God and man :
God we must love, our neighbours too, else we
Celestial happiness can never see.

Russia and Sweden, or some other State in that quarter these shrike...

JUNE.

Many, alas ! we see amongst mankind,
Whose works declare, they ne'er their duty mind ;
Yet, there are some, whose conduct manifests,
That true Philanthropy inflames their breasts :
Is this were general,—what a happy life,
Would Britain be !—bless'd with her Maker's smile.

A Wolf in disguise gains his point. The gilded bait
wounds inclusively. Appearances in this month are of a
prosperous nature.

JULY.

The Poor would from impatient mourning cease,
Would look to God for help, and live in peace ;
The Rich with them would freely sympathize,
Relieve their wants, and wipe their weeping eyes :
Then trade and commerce would their wings expand,
And peace and plenty triumph in our land.

From the general complexion of the signs, gambling,
criminal voluptuousness, and those horrible sensual rites...

AUGUST.

Britannia long has been exalted high ;
And, as a beauteous Comet in the sky,
t: from a distance seen, and much removed.
So is Britannia by the nations lov'd :
For none with her can vie for Liberty,
Religious Knowledge, and Philosophy.

A Marriage, likely to supply the gossips with a rich fund
of prattle, is prefigured ; and a fatal duel is likely to take
place. Beware of such as whesstle for Election.

SEPTEMBER.

But for our numerous sins we punished are,
The proud, Jehovah fees them from afar ;
Now some in lofty stations are brought down ;
Some in obscurity rise to renown :
The haughty, and the vain, shall be deprest,
The meek, and humble, shall be rais'd, and blest'd.

OCTOBER.

Loud blow autumnal winds, and toss the main ;
And drive the yellow leaves along the plain,
That two months since appeared in lively green,
Decking the trees,—we view'd the pleasing scene :
True emblem of mankind !—the hand of time
Changes those hues that deck't us in our prime.

NOVEMBER.

All is not well, I fear, in France and Spain,
The people by oppression still complain ;
Some new's unpleasant cometh from afar,
In distant climes is heard the din of war :
Hasten, O God ! the time, when wars shall cease,
And bless all nations with a lasting peace.

DECEMBER.

O may Jehovah Royal George befriend,
Grant him long life, and then a peaceful end :
Bless those who do important nations fill,
That they may act according to Thy will :
May Knowledge and Religion wing their way,
Till all the world shall own their joyful sway !

Happy England ! know your privileges, rejoice in them, and preserve them !

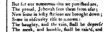

The Voice of the Seasons is the Voice of God.—We thereby read in all
the Changes of the Seasons, and of the Times.

A Winter Piece.

BLEAK November bids prepare
For coming winter with due care ;
See the woodman lop the boughs,
And each luxuriant branch that grows.

WINTER.

THE leaves have lost their vivid hue,
No flow'rets bloom, no landskies bleak...

SUMMER.

WELCOME kind and verdant show'rs,
Harbingers of birds and flow'rs...

THE PROPHETIC *Herein the Aspects of the Heavens learn / And of the times the mystic Signs discern* MESSENGER 1832.

HIEROGLYPHIC, *FOR THE EVENTFUL YEAR 1832*

year, and the role of popular astrologer has passed to the 'Your Stars and You' columns of weekly journals and the newspaper press. Yet a comparison of early nineteenth-century astrological literature with the petty and egocentric modern equivalent indicates that while superstitious instincts have continued, the dimension of imagery in which they exist has radically altered. In the nineteenth century this was rooted in the intimate sense of the Bible, in particular of the Book of Revelation. The most articulate expression of this comes in D. H. Lawrence, who, as we have noted, looked back to a working-class background with the cadences and imagery of the Bible.

From early childhood I have been familiar with Apocalyptic language and Apocalyptic image; . . . And so the sound of Revelation had registered in me very early, and I was used to: 'I was in the Spirit of the Lord's day, and heard behind me a great voice, as of a trumpet, saying: I am the Alpha and Omega' – as I was to a nursery rhyme like 'Little Bo-Peep'! I didn't know the meaning, but then children so often prefer sound to sense.[19]

To this was added the poetic appeal of the Zodiac, not only creating a prediction of events but, perhaps most important, investing history with mystical meaning. Writing on the 'Queen's Ominous Marriage' in 1840, the astrologer of *The Penny Satirist* wrote of his art as 'the symbolical language of destiny'.[20] 'The poetic mind reads and understands this language, the prosaic mind does not.' D. H. Lawrence will

MOORE's ALMANACK FOR 1843.

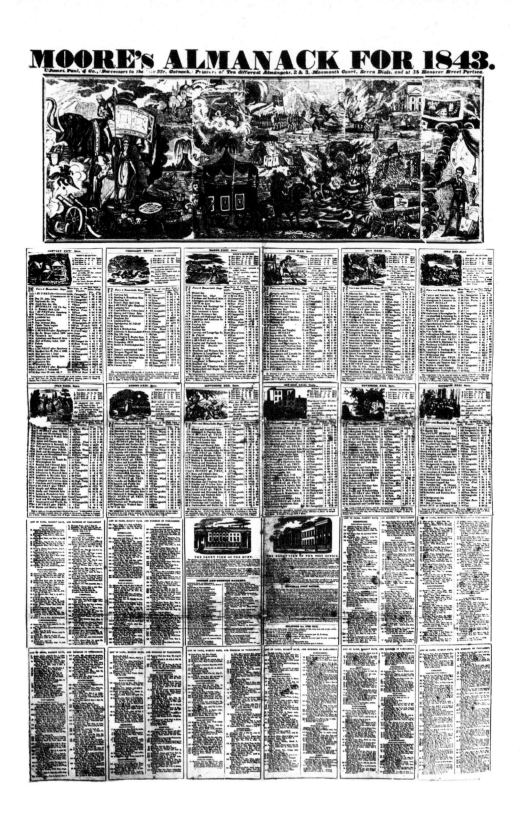

THE CELESTIAL AND HISTORICAL ALMANACK, 1843.

DESTRUCTION OF THE WONDERFUL CITY OF

BABEL

J. Paul, and Co. (Successor's to the late Mr. Catnach.) Printers, of Ten different Almanacks 2, & 3, Monmouth Court, 7 Dials, & at 35 Hanover Street Portsea.

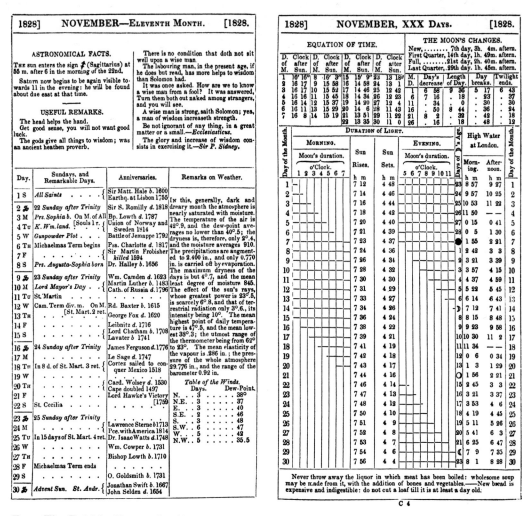

From The British Almanack, *1828.*

bear quoting again. 'To enter the astrological sky of the zodiac and the living, roving planets is another experience, another kind of experience; it is truly imaginative, and, to me, more valuable.'[21]

Any study of the way in which this imaginative dimension was also part of middle-class English culture is beyond our scope. The possibilities of such an approach, however, may be seen by comparing the prophetic broadsheet 'Vortimer, 448' with two brief examples. John Martin (1789–1854), born within a few miles of Newcastle in a mining area, was both an artist and an industrial engineer. His apocalyptic imagination combined biblical imagery with the landscapes and artefacts of the Industrial Revolution. His published collections, in particular *The Paradise Lost of John Milton* (1827) and *Illustrations of the Bible* (1837), were widely circulated, and his work entered the consciousness of his age.

His illustration to Book X of *Paradise Lost*, where Sin and Death create a bridge across Chaos to Earth, changes Milton's text, Francis Klingender suggests, to use his startling experience of venturing into Mark Brunel's gas-lit tunnel under the Thames.[22]

John Martin, from The Paradise Lost of John Milton, *1827.*

It shows a great viaduct sweeping down a vast vault. One writer who knew Martin personally, and who could have hardly failed to know this celebrated illustration, was Charles Dickens.

In Dickens's *Dombey and Son* (1846–8) a muted but important theme is the place of the new mercantile interests, represented by Dombey and his firm, as the false gods of nineteenth-century England.

The earth was made for Dombey and Son to trade in, and the sun and moon were made to give them light. Rivers and seas were formed to float their ships . . . stars and planets circled in their orbits, to preserve inviolate a system of which they were the centre . . . A.D. had no concern with anno domini, but stood for Anno Dombei . . . and Son.

In the strange undersea light of Dombey's city office sits Dombey, circled by his faithful servant Perch whose actions say reverently, 'You are the light of my eyes. You are the Breath of my Soul.'

Out from London, in the decade of the railway mania, the new lines stride in every direction across England. It is here that we recall Martin's illustration. Like Milton's Chaos, their workings were an uncreating confusion 'of Neither Sea, nor Shore, nor Aire, nor Fire'. Thinking of the Camden cutting, Dickens wrote that 'there were a hundred thousand shapes and substances of incompleteness, wildly mingled out of their places, upside down, burrowing in the earth, aspiring in the air, mouldering in the water, and unintelligible as any dream'. Waiting to pass the iron highways are 'tame dragons, bubbling and trembling, making the walls quake, as if they were dilating with the secret knowledge of great powers yet unsuspected in them'.

Their powers become more explicit in the account of Dombey's railway journey: 'away

with a shriek and a roar and a rattle, and
no trace to leave behind but dust and
vapour: like as in the track of the remorse-
less monster, Death!' But it is Carker,
who has arrogated Dombey's commercial
power and who attempts to take also his
wife, who finally faces the Franken-
stein's monster commerce has created. He

. . . felt the earth tremble – knew in a moment
that the rush was come – uttered a shriek –
looked round – saw the red eyes, bleared and
dim, in the daylight, close behind him – was
beaten down, caught up, and whirled away
upon a jagged mill, that spun him round and
round and struck him limb from limb, and
licked his stream of life up with its fiery heat.[23]

Dickens's imagery is sophisticated and
complex. The railways in *Dombey and Son*
also bring progress and employment for such
paragons as Mr Toodles the engine-driver.
Nevertheless Dickens and Martin at one end
of the spectrum, and the anonymous author
of 'Vortimer, 448' at the other, were both
drawing on the popular imaginative
dimension to be found in the apocalyptic
almanack.

*Hablôt K. Browne, detail from frontispiece
to* Dombey and Son, *1848.*

Detail from Moore's Prophetic Almanack
for 1837.

5. POPULAR ICONOGRAPHY: A CHAPTER ON HATS

No single event in modern British history made such an impact as 'Peterloo' at the time that it occurred, or has aroused such continuous attention since. This notice has seemed excessive to some. Donald Read, for instance, suggests that 'the successful designation of Peterloo as a "massacre" represents another piece of successful propaganda. Perhaps only in peace-loving England could a death-roll of only eleven persons have been so described'.[1] E. P. Thompson, however, who has written that 'it really was massacre', notes that by the end of 1819, 421 claims for relief for injuries sustained had been authenticated and 150 further cases awaited investigation.[2]

But there are other ways to explain its importance. Humphrey House[3] has suggested that it has the quality of a Shakespearean tragedy, with voices from every class and type contributing to the drama. A newspaper account in fact was advertised as 'THE DRAMA OF DEATH'. It had a curtain-raiser – a skirmish between reformers and police at Windy Brow outside Manchester – and advance handbills that read like a classical prologue. 'Our enemies will seek every opportunity by means of their sanguinary agents to excite a RIOT, that they may have pretence for SPILLING OUR BLOOD'.[4] To drama must be added ritual. For if history took place in the shadow of the apocalypse, its events took the nature of symbol.

On 16 August 1819, a crowd of between fifteen and twenty thousand had assembled in St Peter's Fields, Manchester, to hear the Radical orator Henry Hunt. It was an oppressively hot, midsummer day, with gusts of dry wind. When the local reform clubs and unions approached, they marched by hundreds in ordered ranks, with marshalls wearing a sprig of oak in their hats. Bands were playing. The groups carried banners embroidered with emblems and slogans. The Lees and Saddleworth Union, for example, carried a black flag bearing, in white, the letters 'love' under two hands joined together and a heart. The most elaborate banner belonged to the Oldham Club of Female Reformers. Their white silk banner was embroidered with 'Major Cartwight's Bill', 'Annual Parliaments', 'Universal Suffrage' and 'Vote by Ballot', under justice holding scales and sword, and a huge eye, signifying 'God Sees All'. The other side showed two draped women's arms, hands clasped: the text has not been recorded. 'Caps of Liberty' were attached to banners or carried separately: the Rochdale and Middleton Reformers carried one held between two green banners, on a red pole crowned with laurel and placarded 'Hunt and Liberty'.

As each troop marched into the square, it received three cheers from the crowd. It then paraded round before presenting its colours before the two carts lashed together that were to form the rostrum. As this was done, three more cheers were given. When Hunt arrived – late – there were sixteen standards and nine Caps of Liberty ranged below him. Before him went a procession with a band playing, a placard painted on both sides 'Order, Order', and flags. One was Hunt's personal flag, bearing on one side 'Universal Suffrage', with round the border and on the reverse 'Hunt and Liberty'. It was surmounted by a Cap of Liberty. Behind Hunt, with the standard of the Manchester Women's Reform Committee, sat a woman, Mary Feldes: to at least one observer she was a reminder of Joan of Arc.[5] Hunt sat in the barouche wearing a high white hat, an emblem of liberty.

The killing of civilians that ensued will be tragically familiar to a century that has seen the killings at Sharpeville, Kent State and Derry. But the ceremonial surrounding the event is not. There was also a confirming

The ordered processions and emblematic banners became increasingly important in working-class movements as the century advanced. A characteristic procession was that held in Manchester to welcome Peter McDouall and John Collins on their release from gaol on 15 August 1840. Six unions and associations processed with seven banners, five flags and a painting. The Wigan Chartist Association banner on one side

emblematic stroke, a linguistic one. Wellington, four years earlier victor at Waterloo, had just joined the Cabinet. On 21 August *The Manchester Observer* put together Wellington's triumph abroad and the death of unarmed civilians in St Peter's Fields, and coined the word 'Peterloo'. An event became a concept.

showed an enlarged portrait of Feargus O'Connor against a perspective of Henry Hunt's monument, tricolour flying, the whole surmounted with the slogan 'O'Connor: Hunt's Successor'. On the reverse, according to the enthusiastic *Northern Star* reporter, who described the scene in detail, there appeared

THE PIONEER;
OR, GRAND NATIONAL CONSOLIDATED
TRADES' UNION MAGAZINE.

" THE DAY OF OUR REDEMPTION DRAWETH NIGH."

No. 34.

SATURDAY, APRIL 26, 1834.
Printed by B. D. Cousins, 18, Duke Street, Lincoln's Inn Fields, London.

[PRICE 2d.

GREAT PUBLIC MEETING OF THE LONDON MEMBERS OF THE GRAND NATIONAL TRADES' UNION, ON MONDAY, APRIL 21, 1834.

The above View was taken by a Member of the Miscellaneous Lodge, from the upper part of Copenhagen-fields.
The Procession consisted of from forty to fifty thousand Unionists, was between six and seven miles in length ; and it is estimated that no less than four hundred thousand persons were assembled on the occasion.

Last Monday was a day in Britain's history which long will be remembered ; for labour put its hat upon its head and walked towards the throne. Labour has been a thing of late which politicians thought possessed no soul ; a thing of nerves and muscle without morality, and void of intellect. But wherefore did its footsteps shake the judgment-seat ? and why did warriors put their bucklers on awaiting its approach ? Its heavy tread made statesmen tremble, and as it shook its locks, ferocious scribes grew tremulous. Law held its jaws aghast and showed its teeth, but offered not to bite. Doubt, wonder, and suspense made many hearts uneasy, and far and near an anxious people awaited the result. The sun cast down its eyelids for an hour while labour gathered up its strength, then looked upon its majesty in full magnificence.

Ah, who can tell the mixed emotions which nerved each artizan that lovely morning ! The crimson badge

Working class procession, 1834.

the British Lion, rampant, is trampling
Under foot 'Starvation Bastiles, Debts, Funds,
Jew Jobbers, Aristocracy, Shopocracy, White
    Slavery, and State Paupers'.
A Mitre is seen falling. The Lion holds in his left
Paw a flaming Dagger, from which is suspended
    A Black Scarf, with the inscription,
'Down, Down to hell; and say I sent you there!'
    On a scroll, over all, the words:–
      'Tremble! Tyrants, Tremble!'
        Operatives, six abreast.[6]

Everything was done with the dignity of
ceremony. The petition against the
deportation of the Tolpuddle Martyrs at the
Copenhagen Fields demonstration on
Monday 21 April 1834 was presented as
scrolled parchment on an iron frame,
carried atop an oblong car festooned with
red calico over blue, quilted cloth. It was
preceded by horsemen, and carried by
fourteen Radical leaders, including the
Reverend Dr Wade, Chaplain to the
Executive Council, in full canonicals.[7]

This ceremonial had roots in the everyday
life of the people. Working-class culture
grew amid a network of social organizations
– chapel classes, educational and political
discussion cells, and work groups within
shop and factory. Friendly societies of all
kinds existed, from small-savings and
mutual-aid circles to national organizations
such as Oddfellows. They grew as the
century progressed, especially among the
better-off artisans in the north. In 1815
their membership was estimated as a
million; by 1870, four million. Craft unions
went back to the medieval guilds, which
regulated individual trades on a national
and sometimes international level. They also
formed a freemasonry for their members,
who in journeyman trades could present
their card at any branch, and receive
hospitality. The trade unions grew out of
these, but more directly out of the friendly
societies, especially among the textile
workers in the Midlands and the West of
England.

These organizations were governed
through elaborate and often secret rules,
initiation rites and emblems. Friendly
societies sometimes included regulations for
the private lives of their members. The early
trade unions practised elaborate initiation
ceremonies complete with blindfolding,
surplices, hymns, painted skeletons and other
memento mori, besides battle-axes, swords
and ritual stage properties from the gothic
past. Even after the Tolpuddle Martyrs had
been transported for taking part in such a
ceremony, the Order of Friendly
Boilermakers on their foundation in 1834
required an oath not to reveal society
secrets.

These rituals, as Dr Gwyn Williams has
written, focused group solidarity at a time
of intense repression. 'The fearsome oath
and darkly ominous initiation, tempered by
fraternal and alcoholic conviviality,
buttressed by any and every sanction men
could dredge up from the experience of
community, fellowship, popular religion,
theatre, carnival, broke a man from a cruel
and corrupt society and bound him into
brotherhood.'[8] But it was also the natural
expression of the working-class love of
ritual. Daily transactions, and moments
such as apprenticeship or a new job, all had
their little ceremonies, usually accompanied
by drink. Music halls and song clubs were
conducted with a chairman and a prescribed
routine. Radical meetings attacked
Parliament, but kept strict parliamentary
order in their proceedings.

Objects were given emblematic significance.
Political figures were given a dignified place
in the home as portraits, pottery statuettes
or medals. One correspondent to the
Northern Star suggested that an O'Connor
medal should be as 'sacred' as the
'principal household god!' and asked for a
Chartist tricolour ribbon to be designed and
worn over the left breast.[9] Even ordinary
items such as hats could have meaning. At
Peterloo, the first action of the officers
arresting Hunt was to smash his provocative
white 'Radical' hat about his eyes. Richard
Carlile, slipping away between the carts in
the mêlée, worried about recovering his
beaver – not because it was personally
valuable, but because it was the badge of
respectability, and without it he invited
arrest. Prints of working-class

demonstrations show a sea of stove-pipe hats. They were worn in the most inconvenient situations, by the new police on duty, or by cricketers in action on the field. The Southcottians showed their separateness by wearing tall whitey-brown, fluffy hats. In 1851 Kossuth arrived in England wearing a soft Hungarian hat, which the young Radicals imitated; by this

triangular, indicating that freedom rests on the broad base of the people, and a pyramid, symbolizing eternity. It is simple, because 'liberty is, in itself, the most shining ornament of man', it is woollen, for 'freedom belongs to the shepherd as well as the senator', and it is undyed white, signifying purity.[11] Few who carried Caps of Liberty would be aware of just this interpretation;

Member's passbook, 1851.

time conventions were beginning to relax, although W. E. Adams was hooted at in the seventies in Lancashire for wearing the wrong type of headgear.[10]

Purely symbolic hats also appeared in Radical parades. White Caps of Liberty were to be distinguished from the 'bonnet rouge' of the French revolutionaries (which also went back to the Roman 'pileus' of the freed slave), as indicating constitutional reform rather than revolt. An article in *The Manchester Observer* explained its significance. The cap had become the symbol of the free man in classical times because it was worn by the venerable. The cap is

nevertheless the piece represents a general love of elaborate symbol.

Individual groups had private emblems. These emerged into the open when, at Whitsun, friendly societies paraded through villages with their staffs and emblems, and when, in the years following Peterloo, unions increasingly emerged from necessary secrecy to march in parade behind the banners that were to become part of working-class art. Some of their symbolism went back to medieval heraldic traditions – for example, the beehive of industry, the spindle of life, the keys of knowledge[12] – although modified by Freemasonry,

Oddfellow's certificate, based on 1837 original.

Rosicrucianism and hermetic philosophy. The strongest underlying impulse was however biblical explication and the popular emblem book.

Bunyan, who had influenced Freemasonry through his *Soloman's Temple Spiritualised* (1688), is again central. His *Divine Emblems*, printed for children in 1701 and reprinted through the nineteenth century, is a fair guide to the reading of early nineteenth-century popular iconography. Bunyan wrote verse commentary on pictorial emblems, usually in two parts. Thus the text to Emblem 30, 'On the Going Down of the Sun', first requests the sun not to leave the watchers in darkness; the 'Comparison' sees the sun as the gospel, careless of which we 'with each other wrangle'.[13] Bunyan is not necessarily affirming an established image, but using everyday instances as the starting point for meditation. This can be metaphysically 'witty'. Thus 'Upon the Sight of a Pound of Candles Falling to the Ground' signifies 'the bulk of God's elect in their lapsed state'. It is not all that far from Zion Ward's explication of the word 'wick-ed' as signifying the extinguished 'wicks' of those without God's light.[14]

Popular iconography therefore is a combination of the traditional and open-ended interpretation. In May 1828, *The Oddfellows' Magazine* included a 'Lecture on Emblems', explicating the Oddfellow insignia.[15] It began with the 'eye', which signifies, in the language of sixteenth-century emblems, divine power and vision, and is sometimes associated with the sun and with virtue. The Oddfellow correspondent related it, sometimes impenetrably, to the nature and limitation of man's sight in God's creation, the Eye of Providence, Light and Darkness, and finally to our need to act as 'under the inspecting eye of the Great Judge of heaven and earth'. The explication, symbol by symbol, became increasingly rhetorical and involved until it ended unfinished, and the promised continuation never appeared.

The power of the image on this showing appealed more to the sense of the numinous than the intellect. It also indicates that earlier allegorical traditions were failing. From the thirties, trade-union emblems increasingly rely on portraits, and use scenes of industrial life depicted with realism (while, as it happened, interest in emblems increased among middle-class readers). The popular consciousness was changing before urban scepticism and the influence of such media as the newspapers.

Peterloo achieved its instant and profound impact because of its ritual and symbolic significance, but also because of the new power of the press. As the meeting had been once postponed, the newspapers had time to arrange the fullest coverage. Four of the small band on the carts beside Hunt were reporters. Moreover their political allegiance ranged from the ultra-Radical Richard Carlile to Richard Tyas of *The Times*. As the Radical press would be expected to attack the authorities, the witness of Tyas was particularly important. Not only did he come uncomfortably close to the sabres of the yeomanry, but also in the mêlée he was arrested and thrown into the New Bailey Gaol. There in a fever of excited indignation he wrote much of his report. Parliament was not sitting, and it did not escape notice that a nation was stirred to widespread anger exclusively on the witness of that growing power, the fourth estate of the press.

The 'Massacre' was celebrated by sensational broadsheets, and in particular in a fine large print emphasizing the dramatic qualities of the scene. In it the heads of the defenceless people, reaching into the distant perspective, part like a wheatfield before the poised swords of the reaping yeomanry. *The Manchester Observer*, however, illustrated its account with a map. Here the scene appears to be different. The square is comparatively narrow, and arrows pointing down the various approaches indicate the various troop movements that contributed to a tragedy of confusion. With the growing use of representational illustration in the forties, and the increasing influence of press reporting, popular history moves into a new dimension.

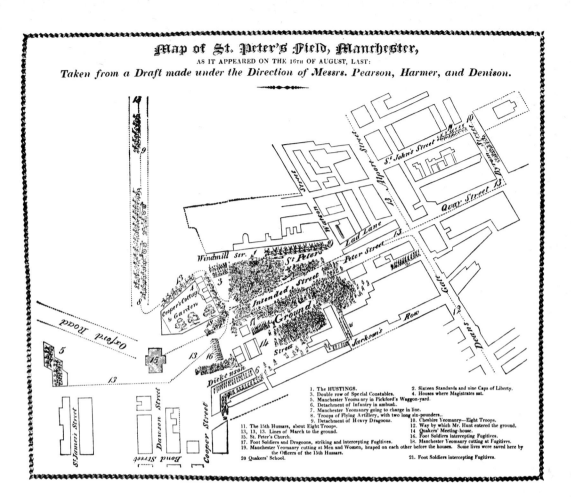

Map of St. Peter's Field, Manchester,

AS IT APPEARED ON THE 16TH OF AUGUST, LAST:

Taken from a Draft made under the Direction of Messrs. Pearson, Harmer, and Denison.

1. The HUSTINGS.
2. Sixteen Standards and nine Caps of Liberty.
3. Double row of Special Constables.
4. Houses where Magistrates sat.
5. Manchester Yeomanry in Pickford's Waggon-yard.
6. Detachment of Infantry in ambush.
7. Manchester Yeomanry going to charge in line.
8. Troops of Flying Artillery, with two long six-pounders.
9. Detachment of Heavy Dragoons.
10. Cheshire Yeomanry—Eight Troops.
11. The 15th Hussars, about Eight Troops.
12. Way by which Mr. Hunt entered the ground.
13, 13, 13. Lines of March to the ground.
14 Quakers' Meeting-house.
15. St. Peter's Church.
16. Foot Soldiers intercepting Fugitives.
17. Foot Soldiers and Dragoons, striking and intercepting Fugitives.
18. Manchester Yeomanry cutting at Fugitives.
19. Manchester Yeomanry cutting at Men and Women, heaped on each other before the houses. Some lives were saved here by the Officers of the 15th Hussars.
20 Quakers' School.
21. Foot Soldiers intercepting Fugitives.

70

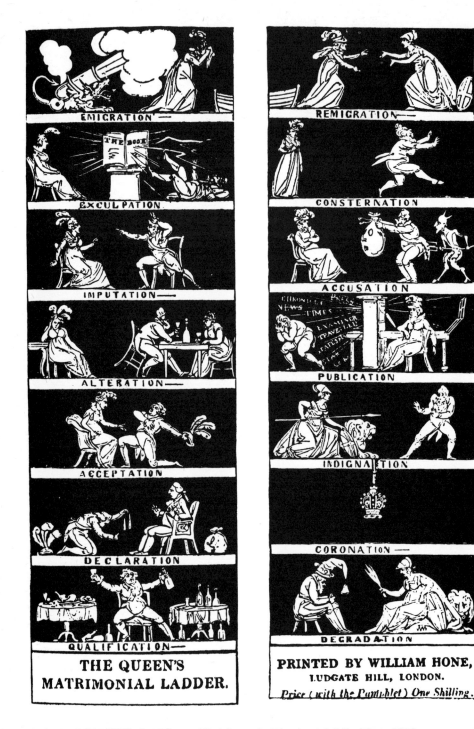

Hone and Cruikshank, insert to The Queen's Matrimonial Ladder, *1819.*

6. THE IMAGES OF GRAPHIC SATIRE

From the work of Hogarth (1697–1764) in the eighteenth century to that of George Cruikshank (1792–1878) in the early nineteenth, graphic satire played an important part in shaping the images through which the public understood social reality. Although only the better-off could afford political cartoons, bought or rented in collections for the evening, until towards the end of this period, they could be seen by most levels of society. They were pinned up in shop-windows and public houses, and Thackeray has described the crowd around a print-shop, ogling the latest designs while one person read out the text to the others.[1] The work produced in collaboration between George Cruikshank and William Hone (1780–1842) is one example of the way in which this visual art could both use popular concepts and to some extent create them anew.

Hone, who has been noticed earlier as the author of political parodies of the Litany, appears at first to be an unlikely political figure. A bookseller with an omnivorous passion for anything in print from incunabula to wrapping papers, possessing a photographic memory, his most lasting works are his antiquarian collections of English popular culture, *The Every Day Book* (1826–7), *The Table Book* (1827–8) and *The Year Book* (1832). He was so nervously sensitive that agitation could bring on seizures and, once, partial paralysis. He was totally incapable of managing money. Yet his sensitivity pricked him into becoming the most effective political satirist of the Regency.

At the age of fifteen he came to London, and reacted against an obsessively religious and loyalist home by attending Radical lectures at the London Corresponding Society, and exploring freethinking ideas. After a return to home at Chatham, in 1815 he opened a tiny lock-up shop, with a three-foot-square window, in Fleet Street. From here, and later from a larger shop on Ludgate Hill, he published a steady stream of broadsides and pamphlets, largely written by himself and illustrated by George Cruikshank. He also wrote and edited *The Reformists' Register* (1816–17). A friend of Charles Lamb and of Leigh Hunt, and one of the first admirers of Keats's poetry, he took his place on the periphery of the second phase of the English Romantic movement.

His first success characterizes both man and method. In 1815 he found himself trapped in a crowd outside Newgate watching the execution of one Elizabeth Fenning, a servant girl executed for the alleged murder of a family for which she worked. Convinced by a bookselling friend of her innocence, he lived for three weeks in a fever of agitation, rejecting even his wife and children who were living in a state of near-starvation in a single room in the Old Bailey. At this point he was released by inspiration. He borrowed four pounds in order to buy food for his family, then spent part of one going to see Pixérécourt's melodrama *The Maid and the Magpie*, which was enjoying a sensational success at the Lyceum Theatre. Hurrying home he called for George Cruikshank, and by six the next morning they had devised a pamphlet posthumously defending Elizabeth Fenning, headed with the print of a magpie hung on a gallows. The success was great enough to provide for the family for four weeks.

Hone had made an instinctive discovery. Direct statements of Elizabeth's innocence had produced no effect; an appeal using a popular conceptual framework – in this case melodrama – was effective. Repeatedly Hone achieved success not through literary brilliance – his style is undistinguished and relied on illustrations executed by Cruikshank – but through an unerring sense of where to kick his public on its nervous reflex. His parodies on the Litany, for example, caught popular religious sentiment, and became a sub-genre of political pamphleteering for the following three decades. Mayhew's informant told of broadsheet sellers who specialized in them, and at the time of Hone's trial would give suitably liturgical performances behind the locked doors of saloons and public houses. Hone conceived the iconography of the printing press, a rallying image in the 'war of the unstamped'. He published a pamphlet called 'The Age of Intellect' in 1819 before the phrase had become current.

Hone was also a multi-media artist. He printed imitation five pound notes displaying figures on a gibbet and signed 'J. Ketch', to bring notice to executions for forgery. The design Cruikshank made for him of the triumph of Queen Caroline was first done on stained glass, and hung in his shop so the light shone through the Queen's face. He printed from an idea by Cruikshank a mock copy of *The New Times*, complete with advertisements, to parody the reactionary sentiments of its editor, John Stoddart. He published a 'toy' in cardboard printed with a stepladder on which the rungs told the rise and fall of George IV's marriage relations with Queen Caroline, and published together with an explanatory leaflet attacking the King's behaviour, ending with a design showing him in a wheelbarrow, sold by a cupid for 'cat's meat'.

It was however *The Political House that Jack Built*, published in December 1819 when the Peterloo agitation was at its height, that caught the public imagination most. Its form exploited the appeal of the popular chapbook. Its nursery-rhyme parody may have been suggested by *The Manchester Observer* of 28 August, which included the lines, 'These are the poor reformers who met,

THE TRANSPARENCY, of which this is a copy, was exhibited by WILLIAM HONE during the ILLUMINATION commencing on the 11th, and ending on the 15th of November, 1820, in celebration of the VICTORY *obtained by* THE PRESS *for the* LIBERTIES OF THE PEOPLE, which had been assailed in the Person of *The Queen:* the words "TRIUMPH OF THE PRESS," being displayed in variegated lamps as a motto above it. On the 29th, when *The Queen* went to St. Paul's, it was again exhibited, with Lord Bacon's immortal words, "KNOWLEDGE IS POWER," displayed in like manner. — The Transparency was painted by Mr. GEORGE CRUIKSHANK.

A SLAP AT SLOP
AND THE BRIDGE-STREET GANG.

PRICE ONE SHILLING.

THE POLITICAL

HOUSE

THAT

JACK BUILT.

" A straw—thrown up to show which way the wind blows."

WITH THIRTEEN CUTS.

The Pen and the Sword.

𝕿𝖍𝖎𝖗𝖙𝖎𝖊𝖙𝖍 𝕰𝖉𝖎𝖙𝖎𝖔𝖓.

LONDON:
PRINTED BY AND FOR WILLIAM HONE, LUDGATE HILL.
1819.

ONE SHILLING.

on the state of affairs to debate, in the field of Peterloo . . . These are the butchers, blood thirsty and bold, who cut, slash'd and maim'd young defenceless and old . . . ' Hone's pamphlet, illustrated by George Cruikshank, begins with the House of England that contains the 'WEALTH' of Human Rights. The 'VERMIN' infesting the house are the law, clergy, tax officers, army and flunkeys to the aristocracy. These will be destroyed by the 'THING', a printing press. 'Thing' was a common term for penis, and was used in political squibs, for instance in C. Williams' design of the mortar sent by Ferdinand of Spain to the Prince Regent, described as 'A Representation of the Regent's tremendous THING ERECTED in the Park' (1816).[2] Hone was indicating that the Press was a virile weapon.

The stanzas, with their accumulating refrains, set up a tension between the nursery-rhyme tone and the bitterness of the words – 'These are the people all tatter'd and torn, who curse the day wherein they were born'. Its logical statement of the rotten structure of the state made it a Radical parable. In one year it sold forty-seven editions; in three, 100,000 copies, and it stirred up a minor literature of imitation and riposte.[3]

The partnership of Cruikshank and Hone ended an era of English political satire. Even during their period, the scale of public life was becoming too large, the decorum of the age too strict, to allow the intimate scurrility that made politics personal and accessible to art in the Gillray tradition. Further, as Francis Klingender has suggested,[4] the tradition begun by Hogarth brought together both the popular and the classical upper-class cultures. All levels of society enjoyed Hogarth or Gillray. By the 1830s this common culture was breaking up. A working-class style was characterized by C. J. Grant, of whom nothing is known but who executed hundreds of cuts for periodicals such as *Cleave's Penny Gazette*. It has both the strength and the limitations of crude vigour. In the designs Seymour made for *Figaro in London* (1832), a middle-class tradition was evolving that was to find a

BLACK SLAVES VERSUS WHITE SLAVES.

C. J. Grant's caricature of Brougham, Penny Satirist, *10 February 1838.*

focus in *Punch* (founded 1841). This separation can be seen in other ways, within the use of imagery in the visual tradition. Consider, for instance, the image of the tree.

Hone and Cruikshank had little sense of class division or economics. In *The Political House that Jack Built*, the 'People' are shown as poor largely as a rhetorical device: notably absent from the 'VERMIN' are capitalist mill-owners and bourgeois merchants. In their *Political Showman* (1821), the Tree of State embodies the People, supported by the printing press, while King, Lords and Commons are the branches. In the same pamphlet, however, Hone quotes Southey's lines in *Joan of Arc* (1796), referring to the symbol of the American War of Independence, the Liberty Tree 'sown by your toil, and by your blood manured'.

In the ensuing decades awareness of the two 'trees' became stronger. In Catnach's 1831 broadsheet, 'The Reformer's Attack on the Old Rotten Tree', the Rotten Borough system is cut down by the champions of the Reform Bill, while the old incumbents try to shore it up. It is watched, however, by the loyal people of England on 'Constitution Hill', over which the sun is rising. Three years later R. E. Lee in *A Whisper to the Whigs* was to show the Tree of Monarchy propped up by bayonets and cannon, rooted in Ignorance, and rising in Despotism. Beside it, a ragged figure mourns by the tomb of Justice. To the right is the Tree of Republicanism, radiating light, rooted in knowledge, and with 'Liberty' as

76

The Tree of LIBERTY,—with, the Devil tempting John Bull.

Cartoon by James Gillray, 1798. The serpent is C. J. Fox.

The Reformers Attack on the Old Rotten Tree;
OR, THE
Foul Nests of the Cormorants in Danger.

A New Dialogue

John Bull.—Come friend "Dobbin" lay hold of the pew-ter and drink success to the Ministers, and their *Reform Bill Russell's* purge will physic the *Cormorants of corruption*, and clear out the bowels of a decay'd Old Constitution.

Farmer Dobbin.—I can hardly tell you what this bill means the best bill has been a regular purge for the stuff they now sell operates like a Jollop making *privy counsellors* of all who drink it, it since *Gaffer Grey* bid, my wife has *Reform'd* the back road way, instead of *making* my stirabout in a Sa-turday night she makes a stir on politics, pots drunk, and abuses the *Boroughmongers*, forgets to pay the chees mon-gers bill & when I meanders she says, "Dom thee, take and drink to *Russell's* bill which will pay us in plenty of every thing by, and bye."

Shopkeeper.—Dear knows, say *Reform* will do good in London with high rents, & taxes, we can scarce sup-port our children, we pay dear for the light of heaven, by day, and gas light by night, & our poor rates go to feed for-eigners and the *great little* men who condescend to live on the sweat of the poor man's brow, but when things come to the worst they must mend, we'll have coals cheap, the *Fire of Reform* is lighted up in every British bosom and is kindling into a flame that will consume the tree of *Corruption* and all other faggots who try to support it.

John Bull.—Old *Neavy* has got the *black jaundice*,—& his colleagues have the *yellow fever* in, their pockets, Lord R——— a begins to tremble for his rotten borough & his 10,000. a year, which he gets for doing nothing , a new *Broom* is sweeping clean the Courts of *Law* where the Bar-risters late are now put to a dirty purpose indeed, to wipe away their filthy sins behind, when they cannot rob their clients as they did before.

Long Life to *King William* the true British *Radiat*, who has arm'd the officers friends of the crew, with *boarding axes* that will soon level the Tree of Corruption, & bring the *Rookery* down. The *cormorants* will have no more *golden eggs* to hatch at our expence, we shall have a reduc-tion of the *tithes* which will be equally divided so as poor cu-rates may come in for a share. *Grab & Rob* will have a fall, so drink, and let's have another Pot, here's " may *Pride* fall, and *Poverty* rise by a regular *Reform*."

Farmer Dobbin.—I have good hopes we will be able to vote without fear of overgrown landlords turning us out of our farms, we can't be drove to the hustings like pigs to a bad market. *Gaffer Grey* has got the right over by the ear, it may great, and squeak, but it must be thrown out with all the old *Boars*, and the Rope be cleared out by a *broad broom*, that will sweep them all to the D——l.

John Bull.—Aye, Farmer have a little patience you will soon be able to till the ground for your own benefit & drive off the overgrow'd locusts. The Parson and servants will eat down together over their old October beef and pudding as their ancestors did. And after supper on a summers eve be-neath the shadow of an Oak Tree smoke your pipe in com-pany with the *Parish Priest*, *Clerk*, and your wife who turns her spinning wheel singing God save the King, whilst a toast goes round to *Lord Grey* and the advocates of *Constitutional Reform*.

Shopkeeper.—With Gods will *Cheapside* will cease to be a dear place. The *Brewer's* give us good strong beer & leave off brewing mischief in Parliament, Trade, and Commerce, will come, with a revived *Constitution*, and industry receive the first reward of its labour.—So here's a health to the men who have broken the back of corruption, broken down *Boroughbridges*, and *wallops'd* the pot swallopers of Old Sa-rum, and other *old sores*; down in disgrace to the d——l from which they sprung.

John Bull.—The Tree of corruption will be destroyed root & branch, and the *Tree of Liberty* flourish in its place, bringing forth wholesome fruit for all loyal Britons to feed upon, come my friends with *Three Cheers* let's have a bum-per toast.—Here's the health of a *Free King*, over a *Free People*, & an honest Ministry in whom we all confide for a lasting *Constitutional Reform.*

REFORM!
A New Red Hot Radical Stave—by Mr. Ford.

THE Reformists are coming, oh ! dear ; oh ! dear ;
Boroughmongers are all very queer; very queer;
From a kick in the breech they cannot recover
A breech in Corruption has done them over.
Reform has struck in the root of the Tree,
The Axe will make all the *Rookery* fee,

The Cormorant's nests will all be brought low,
The state of *Corruption* have had their last crow.

The Reformists are coming, oh ! dear ; oh ! dear ;
And Money looks very queer, very queer,
The cormorant's nests will all be laid low,
Cocks & hens of Corruption have ceased to crow.

The *Axe of Reform*, has got in full play,
A blow has been pitch'd in by *Old Gaffer Grey*,
A *Broom* of *sharp birch* laid hard on the rump,
Rakish *placemen* away to the D—— all jump.
The *Chancery* broom *sick*, has eat up the webb,
Knock'd down *lying Lawyers*, and all their *Black Jobs*,
Hissing Serpents depriv'd of their venomous sting,
Are trampled in dust, by the people and King.

Reformation will render all darkness clear,
Provisions will fall that are dear, so dear,
The *Rats* may all now go and lick up, *curbing*,
Their legs, and their tails, are caught in a trap,
Then *Charley* and *Swine*, lay your raving aside,
In *Hunt's caravan* take yourselves a last ride,
Or, be shown as baboons at Bartholomew fair,
With the *laughing Hyena*, and *Russian Bear.*

Borough members, may now cupider their *false* costs,
Or to save more expences, cut all their own throats,
Their roguery now there is nothing conceals
To sink people pitch them head over heels,
Poor *Old Neavy*, has got a kick'd jaw
And looks like a live *Lion* stuff'd with straw,
Dandy R——— a now can't bite, only grin
The rogues are drumm'd out, and the honest men in.

Proud Peers, and *plenep* puppies are gone to decay
Dirty Dogs have at last had their dirty day,
Old Bags, on the Bench sits no longer at ease,
And a *Broom* has swept off all the *Chancery* fees.
Bis Derry down now set's Old Londonderry,
For the Fate of Corruption they're none sad or sorry,
The anti-*refor* since their death made may sing,
Like *felons* all go to old Nick in a sting.

John Bull will no longer be made a Cat's paw,
Be stick to the Church, in the King, and the Law.
Lord Russell's strong purge has soot'n'd the gripes
Borough blackguards, are twisting about with the gripes
Corruption it works in a summary way,
And the *back door root* and *bar backers* away,
The *Rats*, and the *Rooks*, to the D——l may fall,
Gaffer Grey is the dog that will physic them all.

Reformation will bring us oh ! dear , dear ;
Cheap candles and coals, and good beer ; good beer ;
The price of men's labour, will now be their own
The price of *Corruption* at nothing knock'd down.
By a blow that will scatter its rascally brains,
To fatten the hogs upon Salisbury plains,
All base greedy dogs, will run howling away,
Cut up by the broad *Axe* of *Old Gaffer Grey.*

The King's a Reformer, that's clear ; that's clear ;
Which makes him to all Britons dear; Oh ! dear ;
Old *Neavy*'s a noodle, not worthy his care,
Only fitting to carry rank guts to a bear.
For keeping bad company now Booby P——l
With *Croaker* has now got the right about wheel,
In future John Bull won't be dup'd by their slang
Fair Truth has broke up the whole of the gang.

The Parliament Purge, has well work'd its way,
And a good Constitution arised from decay
The *Tree of Corruption* comes down in a storm
That of Freedom now flourishes under *Reform*.
Hunt, and others are now jolly fellows well met,
With honest *Joe* 'Hume, and Sir Franky Burdet,
At close as the clue , a native with the sterple,
United are now all the friends of the people.

Out and outers have now got the helm of the ship,
And Billy the Brave with *Reform* takes a trip
To the D——l needs false Pilots in a fresh gale
And lubbers off to old Nick in full sail.
Their rudder set by our friend *Gaffer Grey*,
The people at last have *Reform* and fair play,
Equal rights, equal laws, Truth and Justice will sing,
The *Reform Bill* will serve both the people, and King.

J. Catnach, Printer, 2, Monmouth-Court, 7 Dials.

MONARCHIES and REPUBLICS.

"Look on this picture,   and on this."—*Hamlet.*

A Monarchy.

"The mischiefs of monarchy are, tyranny, expense, exaction, military domination; unnecessary wars, waged to gratify the passions of an individual; a want of constancy and uniformity in the rules of government. and, proceeding from thence, insecurity of person and property."—*Paley.*

"Government by kings was first introduced into the world by the heathens, from whom the children of Israel copied the custom. It was the most prosperous invention the devil ever set on foot for the promotion of idolatry."—*Paine.*

A Republic.

"In republics, the sovereign power, or the power over which there is no control, and which controls all others, remains where nature placed it, in the people. In a country under a despotic form of government, the sovereign is the only free man in it. In a republic, the people retaining the sovereignty themselves, naturally and necessarily retain freedom with it; for wheresoever the sovereignty is, there must the freedom be; the one cannot be in one place, and the other in another."—*Paine.*

---

its trunk. It is the 'Liberty Tree'. A decently clad man stands beside it, elevated on the grave of 'Tyranny'.

Lee's Republicanism put him in an extreme position, but a shift in consciousness takes place in other representations, too. 'The Tree of Taxation', for instance, reprinted from *The Northern Liberator* of 13

August, 1838, again shows the corrupt Tree of State. But its destruction is not being watched from 'Constitution Hill'; it stands above four ranks of society, with only the upper class untouched, the extreme poor being eaten alive by the tree's roots. The sense was that taken up about 1850 by an anonymous Chartist in a Blakean poem:

THE TREE OF TAXATION.

(FROM THE NORTHERN LIBERATOR OF AUGUST 11, 1838.)

THE above Engraving will give a visible representation of the manner in which the Taxing System works.

The Community may be divided into FOUR classes. The pockets of the FIRST, or Highest Class, escape from the Roots of the Tax Tree altogether—they get back, in the shape of Windfalls, more than they pay. The pockets of the SECOND Class the Roots touch but lightly. The THIRD, or Labouring Class, is the source of the whole nourishment drawn up by the Tax Tree. The FOURTH Class, the very Poor, it touches but to destroy.

NEWCASTLE UPON TYNE: PRINTED AT THE NORTHERN LIBERATOR OFFICE, 40 SIDE, BY JOHN BELL.

UPAS TREE

Tell not, how Java's Upas-Tree
Spreads poison far and near:
Of all the poison-trees on earth
The deadliest is here!

Fix'd firmly in the British Soil,
Though old, yet undecayed,
Its baneful vapours stunt the growth
Of life within its shade.

Oh Heaven! may yet thy lightnings strike
And cleave it to the root:
While Man shall rear fair Freedom's tree,
And all partake its fruit.[5]

Behind this change lies the whole evolution of Radical thought, in particular the statistical documentation of John Wade in his *Black Book* (1820–22) and his *Extraordinary Black Book* (1832) of the economic inequalities of rich and poor.[6] A standard form of working-class cartoon in the thirties is divided into two, with a situation (say the Lord Mayor's Banquet) as it appears to the rich on one side, the poor on the other. To trace the development of this concept in working-class journals would be to examine the roots of the socialist movement.

Yet this division is not only political. From 1820 to 1821 Pierce Egan published his widely popular *Life in London*, illustrated by George and Isaac Robert Cruikshank. It had over a hundred imitations; in various stage versions it dominated the theatre of the 1820s. By placing the new urban life in fictional perspective, it helped prepare the way for the urban realism of the Victorian novel that followed.

Egan's approach can again be summarized in the visual emblem of the frontispiece. This shows London society as a 'Corinthian' column – 'Corinthian' also meaning 'Man about town'. At the top are George IV and 'the Flowers of Society'. Immediately below are the higher orders, the nobility and the merchant classes. At the bottom are the miscellaneous workers, from 'mechanicals' to ballad singers, while at the base, in a cellar,

is the London underworld. At first this appears to reflect cohesion in society, but the groups are in fact islands. At the centre, the only focus of the various levels, a tableau portrays the trio of observers, Corinthian Tom, Jerry Hawthorne and Bob Logic, who in the book introduce the reader to the different aspects of the city. On either side of this 'eye' is the prophetically Dickensian image of the prison in which Jerry, like Mr Pickwick in a work that is indebted to Egan's, finds himself in the sequel, *The Finish . . . of Tom, Jerry and Logic* (1828).

Contrast is one of Egan's basic techniques. He pairs town and country, the moral and the immoral, the rich and the poor. 'EXTREMES, in every point of view, are daily to be met with in the Metropolis.'[7] In one chapter he shows 'All-Max', a lower-class dance saloon run by a Mr Mace (although both names are evidently authentic, 'Max' is slang for gin, 'Mace' for to steal). In the next he shows Almacks, the most exclusive upper-class club. But Egan's intention, beyond suggesting that the poor have more character and enjoy themselves better than the rich, is not one of socialist analysis. It is Egan's fascinated reaction to the phenomenon of the nineteenth-century city, and a way of organizing experience.

This mental structure had become a dominant one by the forties. Egan's method of counterpointing two social levels, and presenting a central figure who could move in both, appears successively in Eugène Sue's *Les Mystères de Paris* (1843), and in G. W. M. Reynolds' hugely popular *The Mysteries of London* (1845–7). But it was too widely diffused to make any generalizations of influence useful. It found perhaps its finest exposition in Dickens's *Bleak House* (1852–3) and *Our Mutual Friend* (1864–5). It was a central mental structure, created both by the facts of economic and social development, and by a network of changing images through which society explored its own reality.

CORINTHIAN CAPITAL.

ROSES, PINKS, AND TULIPS.

UPS
and

Noble   Respectable

INS &   OUTS

DOWNS

OF

Mechanical   Tag Rag & Bob tail

LIFE IN LONDON.

Bunches of Turn-ups   (THE BASE.)   Strings of Ingens

Here are we met three merry Boys,
Three merry boys I trow are we,
And many a night we're merry been,
And many more we hope to be   Burns

Drawn & Eng'd by Rob't Cruikshank

Pub'd by Sherwood, Neely, & Jones, July 15 1821.

BOWER SALOON.

Licensed by the Lord Chamberlain — Lessee and Manager, Mr J. Biddles, 71, Hercules Buildings, Lambeth.

Third and Last Week of Mr. S. ATKYNS

On MONDAY, FRIDAY, and SATURDAY, June 3rd, 7th., and 8th., 1850,

Will be performed an Historical and Romantic Drama, with novel and extraordinary effects, (written by Mr S. ATKYNS) entitled THE GREAT

FIRE OF LONDON!

Or, the MYSTERY AND THE MURDER!

The Earl of Raymond - Mr BURROUGHS	Barnaby Bounce - Mr WILSON	Vincent - Mr BOLTON
Thomas, a master Baker - Mr HALL	Robert Winter (his assistant, afterwards a Sailor)	- MR S. ATKYNS
Edward Montague - Mr SYMONDSON	Lord Mayor - Mr H. YOUNG	Ralph Marshall - Mr CRAUFORD
Stephen Sylvester (Host of the Lamb Tavern) - Mr MACKNEY	Jacob Brandon (his Partner in Trade and Crime)	Mr Stacy TEMPLETON
Solomon Eagle (an Enthusiast) - Mr R. DODSON	Simon Simpkins	Mr BIDDLES
Isabel Herbert - Miss Ellen GORDON	Eve Elliott - Miss WARDE	Margaret - Miss ADELAIDE
Mrs Herbert	Miss JEFFERSON	

View of Old London & the Southwark Side
The Incendiaries..the Plot to destroy the City..**Mrs Herbert's Apartment**..Mother & Daughter the escape from Danger..the Libertine

The Combat, Tavern & Baker's Shop in Pudding Lane
The Lamb and Wheatsheaf..a Wolf in Sheep's clothing...the Partner's in Crime..the Villain and the false Countryman

A STREET NEAR FINSBURY
The abduction..the Pursuit..the Assassination...Interior of the Baker's Shop..the Midnight Robber..the Murder..Burial of the Victim's Body..the Fire Bell

STREET NEAR LONDON BRIDGE
Consternation of the Citizen's at the Progress of the

GREAT FIRE OF LONDON!

A SPLENDID BALL ROOM!!
Wedded Bliss....Grand assemblage of Guests

☞ THE BALL!
Parlor in the Lamb Tavern, The Sailor & the Citizen
GLOOMY GARRET IN THE TAVERN.
The Maiden and the Ruffian....Perilous adventure....the Rescue..Terrific Struggle..the Knife

Dark Chamber and Vaults beneath the Tavern!
THE TRAP DOOR—APPALLING DISCOVERY.

THE UNHALLOWED GRAVE!
Discovery of the Skeleton—Seizure of the Murderer. Grand Tableau.

To be followed by

A LAUGHABLE FARCE!

Supported by the entire Strength of the Company.

The whole to conclude with the favorite Romantic Drama (written by Mr S. ATKYNS) of the

WANDERING JEW!

OR, THE
VETERAN, THE BRUTE TAMER

AND THE
ORPHAN GIRLS!

Marquis de Rosengel........ Mr BURROUGHS	Lord Lackwit.......... Mr MACKNEY	Jenkins, a Valet.......... Mr CRAUFORD	Maurice Flask..........Mr FORD
Morok....a Brute Tamer....Mr SYMONDSON	Karl ....his assistant .... Mr R. DODSON	Burgomaster of Mockeron....Mr BIDDLES	Old Boatman..........Mr JOHNS
Dagobert.....the Veteran, Protector of the Orphan Girls....Mr Stacy TEMPLETON	The Wandering Jew..........MR S. ATKYNS	Juan, a young Peasant..........Mr JONES
Claude and Paulo ....Messrs. H. YOUNG and BOLTON.	Gend-d'-armes........Messrs Wilks, James, Williams &c.	
Rose and Blanche...........the Orphan Girls...........Miss Ellen GORDON and Miss ADELAIDE	Jeanette.... Mrs BIDDLES	Widow..Miss WARDE	Lady Lackwit...Miss JEFFERSON

Watermill and distant View of Mockeron!
The Veteran Soldier and the Orphan's on their Journey .. a Veterans' grief..the Soldier of many Fights..the Orphan's Love for the Old Soldier

THE BRUTE TAMER'S LOFT.
Morok is seen to ascend..the surprise..the raised Pistol..the interview..they are coming..ah, sure the description

The Seizure. The Threat and the Robbery.
Murder, the House alarmed ..Morok, the Prophet..the proposal to trace the thieves..the capture the Property restored ..let him be confined to

THE DEN OF ANIMALS.
Pleasant reflections..the brand and the appointed spot..Dagobert's alarm at missing his Horse....the Beasts may be devouring him..the Old Soldier rushes to the rescue of his Horse

Court Yard of the Inn. The Brute Tamer
Sudden appearance of Dagobert..the Dead Horse..the Landlord and the Passport..there he goes no Horse, no Money, and no Papers

THE DESOLATE CHAMBER, the SLEEPING ORPHANS
The Window opens..an arm protruded through..the Soldier's Knapsack robbed of its contents..the alarm..the orphan's fears..the Orphan's tale..the Knapsack the search

The Discovery–The Lost Papers!
Arrival of the Burgomaster..the accuser and the accused..the Old Soldier demands justice for the loss of his companion..his favorite Horse..the

THE DYING MOTHER'S CHARGE. THE DEFENCE.
The whisper..one handed Justice..anger of Dagobert..the demand for the Passports..Triumph of the Brute Tamer..the Old Soldier of France..fear of the Burgomaster..the secret conference

The Soldier & the Orphans
The Exiled Mother..the prayer for Protection..the Hearts of Flint..the Arrest..the Struggle.. Bravery of Dagobert

Sudden Appearance of the Wandering JEW!
THE BANKS OF THE RHINE
The Soldier and his charge..the pursuit..we must fly..wither !..see the hand of providence is stretched for'h to save us..the Ferryman..the appeal..the Escape..the Partners

The Wandering Jew & the Brute Tamer
The revengeful Brute Tamer..the intended seizure..the sisters in danger..the Parchment and the Seal

Burning of the Palace. Destruction of Morok

Tuesday, for the Benefit of Mr Dean. Wednesday, the Benefit of Mr Williams Thursday, for the Benefit of Mr Templeton

On MONDAY, Next, will be Produced an entire

New Nautical Drama, in which Mr J. F. YOUNG will appear

Doors open at half-past Six, commence at Seven Precisely. Boxes - 6d. Pit - 4d. Gallery - 2d. Harley, Printer, 4, Gibson Street, Waterloo Road.

7. THE MODALITY OF MELODRAMA

Early nineteenth-century English drama presents us with a paradox. It is generally stated that, in terms of quality, it was at its lowest ebb. Yet at no time since Elizabeth's reign had theatre expanded so rapidly. In 1800 there were nine theatres in London; by 1832 there were fifteen; by 1843, twenty-three, and the increase was to continue. This does not include the multiplying saloons and song halls that offered forms of drama; nor the improvised 'penny gaffs', playhouses set up in any large room found available, which in 1838 James Grant estimated were entertaining some 140,000 of the younger working classes in any one night.[1] Partly through the business enterprise of men like Robert William Elliston, provincial theatre circuits also expanded. Companies toured the countryside and city fairs with large portable stages. The most important in the North was that of the versatile clown Willie Purvis; in the South, that of John Richardson, who for a time employed Edmund Kean, and, it is claimed, acted before George III at Windsor.[2]

This theatre was largely created by the rapidly increasing middle and lower classes of the towns. When William Kemble opened Covent Garden Theatre in September 1809, rebuilt in the style of the Greek Temple of Minerva, Leigh Hunt rapped the managers for their 'aristocratic impulse' in providing for the rich at the expense of humbler playgoers,[3] and an attempt to raise entrance fees led to over two months of rioting for 'Old Prices'. Kemble capitulated: it was a symbolic victory for the popular audience that only began to be reversed when, exactly twenty years later, Madame Vestris at the same theatre closed the shilling gallery. Frequent disturbances from the gallery, the presence of prostitutes, and the taste for either sensation or the broadest farce drove many respectable families from the theatre, although private theatricals flourished, and with the important exception of the strict nonconformists, members from all sections of the community supported drama.

'All the minor theatres in London, especially the lowest,' Dickens noted, 'constitute the centre of a little stage-struck community.'[4] They became the focus of community life, often with a large permanent company and a loyal following, and when at the height of the 1839 Chartist scare the Metropolitan Police Act had a special clause regulating 'illegitimate' theatres, they had an eye to their political significance.

'Legitimate' and 'illegitimate' theatre (or 'Patent' and 'Minor') provided a theatrical equivalent of the war against 'taxes on knowledge'. By the 1737 Licensing Act, not repealed until 1843, only the theatres of Drury Lane, Covent Garden and (in the summer) the Haymarket were allowed to perform straight drama; otherwise the performance had to be 'burletta' (by one definition, include five songs), 'melodrama' (mime to music), dumbshow. or some such evasion. In practice, the law was widely flouted, while the Patent theatres presented melodrama to draw the audiences from the Minor. Indeed, as working-class culture had a love of Shakespeare second only to that for the Bible and *Pilgrim's Progress*, there was a remarkable popularity for Shakespeare both in Minor theatres and even in fairground booths and 'penny gaffs' where, when the time was up, *Hamlet* or *Richard III* was rushed to its conclusion and the next audience let in. In 1831 the *Theatrical Observer* noted three Shakespeare performances at Minor theatres, including

Kean in *Othello*, while Drury Lane was offering the spectacle *Timour the Tartar* and Covent Garden, *The Life and Death of Buonaparte*.[5]

Playgoing, however, was a very different experience from that of today. Performances sometimes began at half past six, and ran until after midnight. There was little or no rehearsal (although Macready in the twenties began to change this) and the main play of the evening was a vehicle for the 'star'. The desire for variety and spectacle produced the genres of 'burlesque' (the comic 'takeoff' of a serious play), and the related 'extravaganza', in which fantasy and spectacle played a major part. An evening could alternate these with Shakespeare, melodrama, farce, song and dance, showing the promiscuity of a music-hall bill. With melodramas from France available for translation, authors were paid a pittance, and scene painters often received a larger billing. Literary talent turned elsewhere, leaving the field to fast-working journeymen such as W. T. Moncrieff and Edward Fitzball.

The touchstone was entertainment. From 1804 the Sadler's Wells theatre stage became a large water-tank and presented such nautical dramas as *The Siege of Gibraltar*, complete with ships and floating batteries. At 'Astley's' (Davis's Amphitheatre from 1817), Andrew Ducrow acted out whole plays while galloping round the ring on a horse, or led such spectaculars as *The Battle of Waterloo* (1829). In 1827 he took his company, including forty horses, a pack of hounds and a stag, by road to Edinburgh to act *Ivanhoe* before Sir Walter Scott. His successor William Cooke produced an equestrian version of *Richard III*, with Richard's horse taking a leading part.[6] The popularity of performing animals – including dogs, educated monkeys, an elephant and (probably trick) ravens and magpies – reflects French melodrama: Pixérécourt's *The Maid and the Magpie*, which inspired Hone, appeared in two English versions in 1814. But it also reinforced the links between drama and such related arts as circus and music hall.

Experiments in 'people's theatre' in the 1970s have indicated how what appears to be a low ebb of English drama was a period of exceptional vitality. Freed from academic concepts of what a play should be, theatre returned to the communal arts of illusion and entertainment. Dickens noted the engrossed audience participation of the Britannia audience; and the way 'penny gaff' actors would break off in the middle of a speech to answer back a spectator, then continue the part, indicated a (sometimes uncomfortably) intimate relationship between the performer and the entertained.[7]

The audience were experts, demanding that every gesture, every speech and fall, should be done correctly. At the high moments of a Shakespeare play every move of the main actor was noted to the accompaniment of sighs, cheers, or derision. The analogies are not with the modern playgoing experience, but with a bullfight, a football match, or, in terms of communal emotion, a pop festival. Its rhythmic conventions of words and action also link it with the traditional ballad dances Willa Muir has described, 'a primitive way of establishing a communal flow of feeling, which in turn released imaginative energies that need to take on shape'.[8] Outside the context of its social function, much nineteenth-century popular theatre is irrecoverably lost. To examine its 'aesthetic' academically is to explore a related but different dimension of meaning.

Yet some remarks can be made about what is loosely known as 'melodrama'. The first identifiable melodrama was Rousseau's 'scène lyrique', *Pygmalion* (1774). Here music alternates with monologue, intensifying Pygmalion's passion to the point at which it arouses Galatea to life. While it had little direct theatrical influence, it is emblematic of the melodramatic structure, which with the help of music culminates in a climax. At this climax, emotion serves as the quasi-religious milieu for the final resolution. In the work of Pixérécourt (1773–1844), the 'Corneille of melodrama', it became democratic. Pixérécourt, who had served in the

Succeeded by Splendid Entire Change and Brilliant

SCENES OF THE CIRCLE,

Introducing Unequalled **Feats of Horsemanship.**

Mons. VERDIE,

The Flying French Rider, will appear for the 7th time in England, **from Franconi's Cirque Olympique, Paris,** in his extraordinary Exercises

GYMNASTIC AND OLYMPIC EQUITATION !

Mons. MASSOTTA,

The Devil Rider, will appear with his Bounding Palfrey in his wonderful Scene, as the

EAGLE HORSEMAN

Mons. LOUIS TOURNIAIRE

The Great French Rider, will give his unparalleled Equestrian Scene, on

7, 8 & 9 HORSES,

as the

POST BOY OF MARSEILLES.

Mr. R. SMITH, and **Mr. BARRY,** the Hibernian Clown, in their Comic Extravaganza, with the Highly Trained Hanoverian Steed, Sable, and Diminutive Pony, Fire-fly, as the

COCKNEY SPORTSMAN

or the

FIRST OF SEPTEMBER.

Mr. STICKNEY,

THE CELEBRATED AMERICAN RIDER.

Will execute his Pantomimic Act of the

TROUBADOUR !

To vary the Exercises,

Mr. KEMP.

Will make his first appearance, in his Novel Evolutions with the

MAGIC POLE !

Clowns—Messrs. T. BARRY, TWIST, and **KEMP.**
Director of the Equestrian Arrangements, and Conductor of the Circle ....Mr. R. SMITH
Riding Masters ...... Messrs. SMITH and WIDDICOMB.

The Performances will conclude with, for the 2nd time, the admired Spectacle, in 5 Tableaux, of The

CHAMPION KNIGHT OF ORLEANS

OR, THE

WILD MAN OF THE WOODS.

Introducing the Beautiful Stud of Horses and Company of Equestrian, Gymnastic and Dramatic Artistes, to realize the Splendid Effects of the Popular Piece of

VALENTINE AND ORSON.

King Pepin .....Mr. CONRAD, Henry......Mr. PONISI, Haufray.........Mr. CROWTHER, Hugo.....Mr. T. BARRY,
Valentine......Mr. W. D. BROADFOOT, Orson......Mr. HARWOOD,
The Green Knight ......Mr. MATTHEWS,
Princess Eglantine....Mrs. PONISI, Agatha ...Mrs. MONTGOMERY, Princess Florimonda....Mddle. BERTHA.

Revolutionary army, wrote for the theatre audiences of the Paris Boulevard du Crime, providing simplified but sensational conflicts between good and evil 'for those who cannot read'.[9] After Holcroft's translation of his *Coelina* as *The Tale of Mystery* in 1802, French melodramas were translated into English as fast as they appeared.

Yet French melodrama only augmented English native traditions. Acting handbooks[10] indicate the presence of a stylized representation of emotions and

'hurries' unlike the music of the great composers. So do extremes meet; and there is some hopeful congeniality between what will excite MR WHELKS [Dickens's lower-class playgoer], and what will rouse a Duchess.[11]

The themes of melodrama are traditional. They are the medieval moral and religious conflicts of Good against Evil, humanized by Shakespeare, and given a bourgeois domestic context in the eighteenth century. A key play in this evolution is George Lillo's *The*

Gestures from Henry Siddons, Practical Illustrations, *1822. Woodcut from Anon., Adeline, 1842.*

moral attitudes which, accentuated by the need to be seen and heard in the new huge and badly lit theatres, edged the melodramatic style with its addition of thematic music towards ballet and opera. Dickens noted sword fighting stylized to the rhythm of the music, and remarked of a Britannia Theatre play:

. . . when the situations were very strong indeed, they were very like what some favourite situations in the Italian opera would be to a profoundly deaf spectator. The despair and madness at the end of the first act, the business of the long hair, and the struggle in the bridal chamber, was as like the conventional passion of the Italian singers as the orchestra was unlike the opera band, or its

London Merchant, first performed in 1731, and ritually given every Christmas in London until 1819. Lillo, writing as a Calvinist dissenter and a prosperous goldsmith and jeweller, transposed the ballad of Barnwell's seduction by the courtesan Milwood, and his subsequent robbery of his master and murder of his uncle, onto a socio-religious plane. Barnwell is made preternaturally good, the symbol of youth and innocence. At the same time he images the middle-class merchant ideal, working for his master Thoroughgood as part of an extended family, the business community. Milwood is motivated by a hatred of Barnwell's goodness and a Hobbesian scepticism towards all that

Thoroughgood stands for. When Barnwell falls, he is compared to the first Adam, to Cain, to Man at the seat of Judgement. Lillo's investment of the sexual ethic with socio-religious significance influenced Richardson in *Pamela* (1740), although the seducer there was male; and through Richardson, the pursued heroines and pursuing villains of nineteenth-century melodrama and fiction.

The religious significance remained close to the surface. Melodrama is concerned with emotion, and the psychic forces that underlie emotion. Fear, hatred, repressed memory – the will, the locket, the knock at the door from the long-forgotten enemy – are all, to use an advised phrase, in the blood of melodrama. But this is ritualized into the conflict between the ideal of Good, and the threat of Evil. The very gesture of the heroine to Heaven – which always answers – is quasi-theological; the villain's laughter and glaring eyes are 'of the very Devil'. Dickens, visiting the Britannia (to see *Lady Hatton's Tree*), noted the vision of Hell in which the heroine was invited to 'Be-old the tortures of the damned'.[12] The dislocated religious sense of the nineteenth-century town-dweller must have often found an answering echo in the dim-lit, smoky atmosphere, the chanted rhetoric and the ritualized action of the theatre.

Melodrama works through opposition and conflict. Indeed, it is this, Mr Wylie Sypher suggests, that makes it the central nineteenth-century mode. If the sonata reflected eighteenth-century order then melodrama is the expression of a culture for which reality wore the mask of crisis. Mr Sypher writes:

> To the nineteenth century mind the very iron laws of science operate with melodramatic fatalism – the pressure of population against subsistence, the dynamics of supply and demand and the wages fund, the struggle for existence in a nature red in tooth and claw, the unalterable majestic course of matter and force mythologised by Hardy and the biologist Haeckel . . . [13]

Melodrama then, with its roots in tradition and the sensibility of the people, but with its dynamic of emotional conflict and change, became a natural stylistic mode for the period. Its conventions can be found in areas from the popular sermon to the novel and painting, from the rituals of books of etiquette to the working-class love of ceremony we have looked at earlier. It is the key to the popular literature anthologized in this book.

NOTES TO THE INTRODUCTION

(Place of publication London unless otherwise noted)

Chapter 1: *Magic into Print*

1. Information on Reform Celebrations from Dr Berthold Wolpe. For printing developments see Michael Twyman, *Printing, 1770–1970*, 1970, pp. 50–66.

2. Arthur Aspinal, 'The Circulation of Newspapers in the Nineteenth Century', *Review of English Studies*, vol. XXII, January 1946, p. 29.

3. See R. S. Schofield, 'The Measurement of Literacy in Pre-Industrial England', in Jack Goody, ed., *Literacy in Traditional Society*, Cambridge, 1968.

4. See Carlo M. Cipolla, *Literacy and Development in the West*, Harmondsworth, 1969, chapter 3.

5. M. J. Quinlan, *Victorian Prelude*, New York, 1955, pp. 160–61.

6. R. K. Webb, *British Working Class Reader*, 1955, p. 22.

7. *S. P. C. K. Minutes*, 21 May 1832, pp. 284–5.

8. See Victor E. Neuberg, *Popular Education in Eighteenth Century England*, 1971.

9. Samuel Bamford, *Autobiography*, W. H. Challoner, ed., 1967, p. 34.

10. Joseph Lawson, *Letters to the Young on Progress in Pudsey*, Stanningley, 1887, p. 48.

11. Thomas Miller, *Our Old Town*, 1857, p. 246.

12. John Nicholson, *Folk Lore of East Yorkshire*, 1890, p. 90.

13. T. C. Campbell, *The Battle of the Press*, 1899, p. 9.

14. *The Times*, 19 July 1825.

15. William Lovett, *Life and Struggles*, with an introduction by R. H. Tawney, 1920, vol. I, p. 14; Bamford, op. cit., p. 110.

16. Nicholson, op. cit., p. 85.

17. *Parliamentary Reports, Mins. Cttee of Council for Education*, 1841–2, p. 206.

18. Christina Hole, *Witchcraft in England*, 1945, p. 157.

19. Samuel Bailey, *Essay on the Formation and Publication of Opinions*, pp. 163–7.

20. Lawson, op. cit., p. 44.

21. Lovett, op. cit., p. 36.

22. 'Old Potter', *When I was a Child*, 1903, pp. 221–9.

23. Peacock, *Crotchet Castle*, 1831, chapter 2.

24. W. T. Moncreiff, *The March of Intellect*, 1830, pp. 30–31.

25. J. D. Burn, *The Language of the Walls*, 1855, pp. 210–11.

26. Cf. McLuhan, *The Gutenburg Galaxy*, Toronto, 1962, pp. 263–6.

27. David Riesman, 'The Oral and Written Traditions', in Edward Carpenter and M. McLuhan, eds., *Explorations in Communications*, Boston, 1960, p. 113.

28. W. H. Wickwar, *The Struggle for the Freedom of the Press*, 1928, p. 75.

29. Mary Merryweather, *Experiences of Factory Life*, 3rd edition, 1862, p. 29.

30. G. J. Holyoake, *Sixty Years of an Agitator's Life*, 1892, p. 70.

31. 'A Literary Policeman', 'The Battle of the Posters', *Howitt's Journal*, 1847, pp. 54–5; Martineau, quoted in Webb, 'Working Class Readers in Early Victorian England', *English Historical Review*, LXV, 1950, p. 333.

32. Burn, op. cit., p. 12.

Chapter 2: *The Battle for the Mind*

1. Thomas Cooper, *Life of Thomas Cooper*, 1872, pp. 8, 22.

2. R. C. Fell, *Life of Alderman Kelly*, 1856, p. 138; on religious reading see Joseph Barker, *The Life of Joseph Barker*, J. T. Barker, ed., 1880, p. 53; 'Old Potter', op. cit., p. 3; Bamford, op. cit., vol. I, p. 40; William Heaton, *The Old Soldier*, 1872.

3. D. H. Lawrence, 'Introduction to *The Dragon of the Apocalypse*', *Phoenix*, 1936.

4. 'Old Potter', op. cit., p. 193.

5. William Howitt, *The Rural Life of England*, 1838, vol. I, p. 256.

6. *Vindicae Britannicae*, quoted in Quinlan, op. cit., pp. 160–61.

7. E. P. Thompson, *The Making of the English Working Class*, Harmondsworth, 1968, pp. 34–8.

8. Thomas Paine, *Selected Works*, Howard Fast, ed., 1940, pp. 110, 133, 122, 104, 124.

9. G. Spinney, 'Cheap Repository Tracts: Hazard and Marshall edition', *Library*, n. s. XX, 1939, pp. 295–340.

10. S. G. Green, *The Story of the Religious Tract Society*, 1899, p. 57.

11. E. J. Hobsbawm, *Primitive Rebels*, Manchester, 1959, p. 126.

12. The standard life of Cobbett is G. D. H. Cole, *The Life of William Cobbett*, rev. edition, 1947; see also Thompson, op. cit., pp. 820–37.

13. *Cobbett's Register*, LXXXVIII, 1835, pp. 370, 367.

14. Cobbett, *Grammar*, 1819, pp. 152, 180, 152.

15. The standard biography of Hone is F. W. Hackwood, *William Hone*, 1912.

16. Wickwar, op. cit., pp. 57, 64; Patricia Hollis declares this 'certainly exaggerated', Hollis, *The Pauper Press*, Oxford, 1970, p. 119.

17. Hollis, op. cit., p. 118.

18. Dorothy Thompson, 'La Presse de la classe ouvrière anglaise, 1830–40', in J. Godechot, ed., *La Presse ouvrière 1819–1850*, Paris, 1966, p. 18; *Voice of the West Riding*, 1 June 1833, p. 2.

19. Alice A. Clowes, *Charles Knight*, 1892, pp. 225–6.

20. *Poor Man's Guardian*, 23 August 1831, p. 18.

21. *S. P. C. K. Minutes*, 1832, p. 382.

Chapter 3: *The Fiction Trap and the Growth of Popular Periodicals*

1. James Beattie, 'On Fable and Romance', *Dissertations Moral and Critical*, 1783, p. 374; quoted in John Tinnon Taylor, *Early Opposition to the English Novel*, New York, 1943.

2. Advertisement for W. Gurney's *Lectures on the Pilgrim's Progress*, William Kelly, *Catalogue*, c. 1838.

3. *Northern Star*, 28 January 1843; see also 'Reading and Books', *Working Man's Friend*, vol. II, 1850, pp. 289–93.

4. Thomas Holcroft, *Memoirs*, 1816, vol. I, pp. 134–6; F. Kidson and M. Neal, *English Folk-Song and Dance*, Cambridge, 1915, pp. 79–80.

5. Charles Manby Smith, *The Little World of London*, 1857, pp. 257–8.

6. David Buchan, *The Ballad and the Folk*, 1972, p. 251.

7. Lucy E. Broadwood and J. A. Fuller Maitland, *English Country Songs*, quoted in Leslie Shepard, *John Pitts*, 1969, p. 45; Kidson, op. cit., pp. 85–6.

8. Charles Hindley, *The Catnach Press*, 1869, pp. 8–9.

9. G. Malcolm Laws, *The British Literary Ballad*, Carbondale, 1971, p. 13.

10. Shepard, op. cit., pp. 53–4.

11. Henry Mayhew, *London Labour and the London Poor*, 1851–64, vol. I, p. 237.

12. Smith, op. cit., p. 258.

13. Mayhew, op. cit., p. 238.

14. Benjamin Disraeli, *Sybil*, 1845, vol. II, chapter x.

15. Charles Hindley, *The History of the Catnach Press*, 1886.

16. Victor Neuburg, *The Penny Histories*, 1968, p. 3.

17. Taylor, op. cit., p. 27.

18. William W. Watt, *Shilling Shockers of the Gothic School*, Cambridge, Mass., 1832, *passim*.

19. W. E. Wroot, 'William Milner of Halifax', *The Bookman*, March 1897, pp. 169–75.

20. Louis James, *Fiction for the Working Man* (rev. edition), Harmondsworth, 1974, pp. 5–8.

21. William Hone, *Table Book*, 1827, p. 31.

22. Stanley Morison, *The English Newspaper*, Cambridge, 1932, chapter xiii; Morison, *A Catalogue of Books, Newspapers etc. Published by John Bell . . . and by John Browne Bell*, 1931.

23. 'Old Printer' [John Farlow Wilson], *A Few Personal Recollections*, 1896, pp. 18–21; W. Anderson Smith, *Shepherd Smith*, 1892, p. 219.

24. Alison Adburgham, *Women in Print*, 1972, pp. 99–102.

25. Henry Vizetelli, *Glances Back through Seventy Years*, 1893, vol. II, pp. 11–12.

26. *Politics for the People*, vol. I, 13 May 1848, p. 28.

27. Bamford, op. cit., pp. 90–91.

28. D. W. Harding, 'Psychological Processes in the Reading of Fiction', *British Journal of Aesthetics*, vol. II, 1962, pp. 133–47.

Chapter 4: *Time and the Popular Almanack*

1. Thomas Roscoe, *The London and Birmingham Railway*, 1847, pp. 80–81.

2. Thomas Carlyle, 'Signs of the Times', *Edinburgh Review*, XLIV, June 1829, p. 443.

3. See J. F. C. Harrison, *Robert Owen and the Owenites in Britain and America*, London, 1969; William Owen Chadwick, *The Victorian Church*, 2nd edition, London, 1970, pp. 33–6.

4. P. G. Rogers, *The Battle in Bossenden Wood*, Oxford, 1961; Thompson, op. cit., pp. 880–81; anon., *The Life and Extraordinary Adventures of Sir William Courtenay*, Canterbury, 1838.

5. Chadwick, op. cit., p. 36.

6. John D. Gay, *The Geography of Religion in England*, London, 1971, pp. 191–6.

7. Carlyle, loc. cit.

8. 'Address to the Inhabitants of New Lanark, 1816', in Owen, *A New View of Society*, 1927, p. 106.

9. See J. F. C. Harrison, *Robert Owen and the Owenites in Britain and America*, London, 1969.

10. See R. Wearmouth, *Methodism and the Working Class Movements of England 1800–1850*, 1934; H. U. Faulkner, *Chartism and the Churches*, 1916.

11. E. Durkheim, *The Elementary Forms of the Religious Life*, translated by J. W. Swain, 1915, p. 9. The whole of the 'Introduction' is relevant here.

12. See E. Leach, 'Two Essays Concerning the Symbolic Representation of Time', in *Rethinking Anthropology*, rev. edition, 1966, esp. pp. 125, 135.

13. Ian Watt, *The Rise of the Novel*, Harmondsworth, 1963, p. 26.

14. See A. Heywood Junior, *Three Papers on English Printed Almanacks*, Manchester, 1904.

15. ibid., p. 19.

16. Monica Grobel, *The Society for the Diffusion of Useful Knowledge*, University of London M. A. thesis, 1933, vol. II, app. vi, p. 1.

17. ibid.

18. Heywood, op. cit., pp. 22–5; quoted in Joel H. Wiener, *The War of the Unstamped*, Ithaca, 1969, p. 18.

19. Lawrence, op. cit., p. 302.

20. 25 January 1840, p. 1.

21. Lawrence, op. cit., p. 293.

22. Francis D. Klingender, *Art and the Industrial Revolution*, rev. edition, 1968, pp. 122–3.

23. See *Dombey and Son*, chaps. I, XII, VI, XX, LV.

Chapter 5: *Popular Iconography: A Chapter on Hats*

1. Donald Read, *Peterloo and its Background*, Manchester, 1958, p. vii.

2. E. P. Thompson, op. cit., pp. 752, 754.

3. Humphrey House, *All in Due Time*, 1955, pp. 46–57.
4. Quoted in Robert Walmsley, *Peterloo, The Case Reopened*, Manchester, 1969, p. 232.
5. Richard Carlile, quoted in Campbell, *The Battle of the Press*, 1899, p. 23.
6. 15 August 1840.
7. *Weekly Police Gazette*, 26 April 1834, pp. 3–4; see also Thompson, op. cit., pp. 456–69.
8. In John Gorman, *Banner Bright*, 1973, p. 4; for working-class ritual see also Thompson, op. cit., pp. 559–61; Read, op. cit., pp. 219–20; John Dunlop, *Artificial Drinking Usages*, 4th edition, 1836.
9. 8 January 1842, p. 7.
10. W. E. Adams, *Memoir of a Social Atom*, J. Savile, ed., 1968, p. 58; W. Scruton, *Pen and Pencil Sketches of Old Bradford*, Bradford, 1889, p. 245.
11. 'Origins and Properties of the Cap of Liberty', *Manchester Observer*, 25 September 1819, p. 726.
12. R. A. Leeson, *United We Stand*, Bath, 1971, pp. 7–8.
13. See Anon., *Sacred Emblems, with Miscellaneous Pieces Moral, Religious and Devotional in Verse*, 1828; Joseph E. Duncan, *The Revival of Metaphysical Poetry*, Minneapolis, 1959.
14. 'Zion' Ward, *Zion's Works*, H. B. Hollingsworth, ed., 1899, vol. V, p. 227.
15. *Oddfellows' Magazine*, n.s. (May 1828), 26–32.

Chapter 6: *The Images of Graphic Satire*

1. W. M. Thackeray, 'An Essay on the Genius of George Cruikshank', *Westminster Review*, June 1840, pp. 6–7.
2. Edgell Rickword, ed., *Radical Squibs and Loyal Ripostes*, Bath, 1971, p. 13.
3. F. W. Hackwood, *William Hone*, 1912, p. 194; James Routledge, *Chapters in the History of Popular Progress*, 1876, p. 482.
4. F. D. Klingender, *Hogarth and English Caricature*, 1944, p. xiii.
5. Quoted in Y. V. Kovalev, ed., *An Anthology of Chartist Literature*, Moscow, 1956, p. 43.
6. See Asa Briggs, 'The Language of "Class" in Early Victorian England' in Asa Briggs and John Saville, eds., *Essays in Labour History*, 1960, pp. 43–73.
7. Pierce Egan Sr, *Life in London*, 1821, pp. 22–3.

Chapter 7: *The Modality of Melodrama*

1. J. O. Bailey, *British Plays of the Nineteenth Century*, New York, 1966, p. 4.
2. James P. Robson, *The Life and Adventures of the Far-Famed Billy Purvis*, Newcastle upon Tyne, 1849; Pierce Egan Sr, *The Life of an Actor*, 1825, chapter V.
3. *Examiner*, 24 September 1809.
4. 'Private Theatricals', *Sketches by Boz*, 1837.
5. Quoted in Bailey, op. cit., pp. 4–5.
6. John M. Last, 'Andrew Ducrow', *Theatre Quarterly*, October–December 1971, pp. 37–9.
7. Dickens, 'The Amusements of the People', *Household Words*, I, 1850, pp. 13–15.
8. Willa Muir, *Living with Ballads*, 1965, p. 16.
9. 'Pixérécourt', in Phyllis Hartnoll, ed., *Oxford Companion to the Theatre*, 2nd edition, 1967, p. 616.
10. See Henry Siddons, *Practical Illustrations of Rhetorical Gestures*, 2nd edition, 1822, reissued New York, 1968.
11. *Household Words*, op. cit., p. 60.
12. ibid. p. 59.
13. Wylie Sypher, 'Aesthetic of Revolution: the Marxist Melodrama', *Kenyon Review*, X, Summer 1948, p. 435.

List of Illustrations used in the Introduction

Paul Pry, nos. 10 and 20, 1857. Both 18 x 12 cm; (41) Cover of a 'number' novel, 1836. 15 x 23 cm; (43) Window bill, 1822. 19 x 37 cm; (44) *Lloyd's Penny Sunday Times*, 29 December 1844. 39 x 49 cm; (45) *Family Herald*, 18 September 1847. 21 x 27 cm; (47) *The London Journal*, 26 April 1845. 21 x 27 cm; (49) *Vortimer*, broadsheet, 1837. 25 x 31 cm; (50) Zion Ward, Millenarian broadsheet, 1831. 25.5 x 31 cm; (51) Death of Courtenay, *Penny Satirist*, 9 June 1838. 20 x 12 cm; (52) Pamphlet by brother of John Martin, 1848. 21 x 17 cm; (55) *Wonderful Predictions*, 1825. 38 x 50 cm; (56) Folding frontispiece to *The Prophetic Messenger*, 1832. 29 x 24 cm; (57) *Moore's Almanack for 1843*. 39 x 50 cm; (58) *Babel*, 1843. 21 x 37 cm; (59) From *The British Almanack*, 1828. 10.5 x 18 cm; (60) John Martin, from *The Paradise Lost of John Milton*, 1827. 20 x 14.5 cm; (61, above) Hablôt K. Browne, detail from frontispiece to *Dombey and Son*, 1848. 4 x 5 cm; (61, below) Detail from *Moore's Prophetic Almanack for 1837*. 10 x 8 cm; (63) Contemporary print, Manchester Public Library, 1819. 51 x 58 cm; (64) Working-class procession, *The Pioneer*, 26 April 1834. 19 x 25 cm; (66) Member's passbook, 1851. 7 x 11 cm; (67) Oddfellow's certificate, based on 1837 original. 44 x 57 cm; (69) From *The Manchester Observer*, 23 October 1819. 22.5 x 27.5 cm; (70) Hone and Cruikshank, insert to *The Queen's Matrimonial Ladder*, 1819. 12.5 x 16 cm; (72) Hone and Cruikshank, from *The Political Showman – At Home!*, 1821. 14 x 23 cm; (73) Hone and Cruikshank, parody of *The New Times*, 1821. 13 x 20.5 cm; (74) Hone and Cruikshank, *The House that Jack Built*, 1819. 14 x 23 cm; (75) C. J. Grant's caricature of Brougham, *Penny Satirist*, 10 February 1838. 14 x 10.5 cm; (76) Cartoon by James Gillray, 1798. The serpent is C. J. Fox. 26 x 35 cm; (77) Reform bill agitation pamphlet, April 1831. 38 x 52 cm; (78) R. E. Lee, *A Whisper to the Whigs*, 1834. P.R.O., H.O.64.19. 14 x 22.5 cm; (79) From *The Northern Liberator*, 12 August 1838. 38 x 52 cm; (81) I. R. and G. Cruikshank, frontispiece to *Life in London*, 1821. 13.5 x 23 cm; (82) East End melodrama, 1850. 45 x 63 cm; (85) Playbill, Astley's Royal Amphitheatre, *c.* 1842. 19 x 22 cm; (86, left) Gestures from Henry Siddons, *Practical Illustrations*, 1822. Both 8 x 9 cm; (86, right) Woodcut from Anon., *Adeline*, 1842. 9.5 x 8 cm.

ANTHOLOGY

I. WORK AND ENTERTAINMENT

1. RURAL

COBBETT AND THE SAND-HILL

In quitting Tilford we came on to the land belonging to Waverly Abbey, and then, instead of going on to the town of Farnham veered away to the left towards *Wrecklesham*, in order to cross the Farnham and Alton turnpike-road, and to come on by the side of *Crondall* to *Odiham*. We went a little out of the way to go to a place called the *Bourne*, which lies in the heath at about a mile from Farnham. It is a winding narrow valley, down which, during the wet season of the year, there runs a stream, beginning at *Holt Forest*, and emptying itself into the *Wey*, just below Moor-Park, which was the seat of *Sir William Temple*, when *Swift* was residing with him. We went to this Bourne, in order that I might show my son the spot where I received the rudiments of my education. There is a little hop-garden in which I used to work when from eight to ten years' old; from which I have scores of times run to follow the hounds, leaving the hoe to do the best that it could to destroy the weeds; but, the most interesting thing was, a *sand-hill*, which goes from a part of the heath down to the rivulet. As a due mixture of pleasure with toil, I, with two brothers, used occasionally to *desport* ourselves, as the Lawyers call it, at this sand-hill. Our diversion was this: we used to go to the top of the hill, which was steeper than the roof of a house; one used to draw his arms out of the sleeves of his smock-frock, and lay himself down with his arms by his sides; and then the others, one at head and the other at feet, sent him rolling down the hill like a barrel or a log of wood. By the time he got to the bottom his hair, eyes, ears, nose and mouth, were all full of this loose sand; then the others took their turn, and at every roll, there was a monstrous spell of laughter. I had often told my sons of this while they were very little, and I now took one of them to see the spot. But, that was not all. This was the spot where I was receiving my *education*; and this was the sort of education; and I am perfectly satisfied that if I had not received such an education, or something very much like it; that, if I had been brought up a milksop, with a nursery-maid ever-lastingly at my heels; I should have been at this day as great a fool,

as inefficient a mortal, as any of those frivolous idiots that are turned out from Winchester and Westminster School, or from any of those dens of dunces called Colleges and Universities. It is impossible to say how much I owe to that sand-hill; and I went to return it my thanks for the ability which it probably gave me to be one of the greatest terrors, to one of the greatest and most powerful body of knaves and fools, that ever were permitted to afflict this or any other country.

From the Bourne we proceeded on to *Wrecklesham*, at the end of which, we crossed what is called the *river Wey*. Here we found a parcel of labourers at parish-work. Amongst them was an old playmate of mine. The account they gave of their situation was very dismal. The harvest was over early. The hop-picking is now over; and now they are employed *by the Parish;* that is to say, not absolutely digging holes one day and filling them up the next; but at the expense of half-ruined farmers and tradesmen and landlords, to break stones into very small pieces to make nice smooth roads lest the jolting in going along them, should create bile in the stomachs of the overfed tax-eaters. I call upon mankind to witness this scene; and to say, whether ever the like of this was heard of before. It is a state of things, where all is out of order; where self-preservation, that great law of nature, seems to be set at defiance; for here are farmers, *unable* to pay men for working for them, and yet compelled to pay them for working in doing that which is really of no use to any human being. There lie the hop-poles unstripped. You see a hundred things in the neighbouring fields that want doing. The fences are not nearly what they ought to be. The very meadows to our right and our left in crossing this little valley would occupy these men advantageously until the setting in of the frost; and here are they, not, as I said before, actually digging holes one day and filling them up the next; but to all intent and purposes, as uselessly employed. Is this Mr. Canning's *'Sun of Prosperity?'* Is this the way to increase or preserve a nation's wealth? Is this a sign of wise legislation and of good government? Does this thing *'work well,'* Mr.

Canning? Does it prove, that we want no change? True, you were born under a Kingly Government; and so was I as well as you; but I was not born under *Six-Acts;* nor was I born under a state of things like this. I was not born under it, and I do not wish to live under it; and, with God's help, I will change it if I can.

We left these poor fellows, after having given them, not *'religious Tracts,'* which would, if they could, make the labourer content with half starvation, but, something to get them some bread and cheese and beer, being firmly convinced, that it is the body that wants filling and not the mind. However, in speaking of their low wages, I told them, that the farmers and hop-planters were as much objects of compassion as themselves, which they acknowledged.

We immediately after this crossed the road, and went on towards Crondall upon a soil that soon became stiff loam and flint at top with a bed of chalk beneath. We did not go to Crondall; but kept along over *Slade-Heath*, and through a very pretty place called *Well*. We arrived at *Odiham* about half after eleven, at the end of a beautiful ride of about seventeen miles in a very fine and pleasant day.

THE LIFE OF SWING

In Kent I found myself still worse off than at home, for I could procure no employment whatever, and as I had no claim on the poor-rates, I was in danger of starving, and felt myself compelled to return home; before, however, I could do so, my poor wife fell ill of fever, and in order to prevent her perishing from want, I was obliged to go and beg – downright hunger having conquered my reluctance to ask charity. I proceeded along the road in order to do so, and saw a fat man, dressed in black, approaching me, to whom I applied for something to prevent my wife and children of dying of starvation. – 'I cannot *afford* to give you anything,' replied he; 'go to your parish.' His manner was so repulsive, that I considered it useless to make a second application, and passed on: when I had walked a few yards, I began to think I had

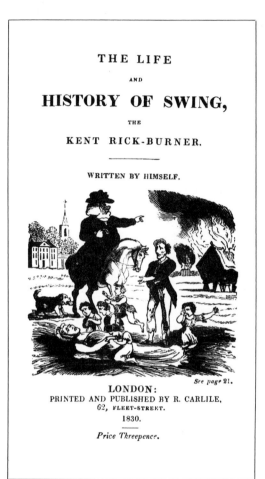

THE LIFE

AND

HISTORY OF SWING,

THE

KENT RICK-BURNER.

WRITTEN BY HIMSELF.

See page 21.

LONDON:
PRINTED AND PUBLISHED BY R. CARLILE,
62, FLEET-STREET.
1830.

Price Threepence.

somewhere before seen the gentleman in black, and, after a few minutes' recollection, remembered he was the Rev. Mr. Saint Paul, who had taken my cow in payment of his small tithes, and who afterwards took three-tenths of my crop for his tithe of my plot of ground: he was a pluralist; and, having five livings, seldom or never came to the parish I had lived in, except to receive his tithes, so that I did not at first recognise him. I walked on for some time longer, and not meeting any person, was obliged to return to the cottage that my wife was in, without anything to give her; as I could not bring myself to enter the cottage and behold my wife dying for want, I sat down on the road, a little distance from the door, and soon beheld the parson returning from his walk. He had a cake in his hand, which, as he had no inclination to eat, he threw to a large pampered dog that walked beside him. The dog, having no better appetite than his master, took the cake in his mouth, played with it for a moment, then tossed it in the dirt and left it there. A little child of mine beheld the scene from the cottage door, and ran and picked the cake out of the gutter, when the parson demanded how dare she take it from his dog? 'Oh, Sir!' said the little girl, 'the dog will not eat it, and I wish to bring it to my poor mother, who is starving.' – 'Your mother and yourself ought to be in the work-house,' said the parson; 'it is a shame for the parish officers to allow little naked vagabonds like you to be running about the roads.'

'Can this man,' thought I, 'be a descendant of the Apostles, who carried nothing with them but scrip and staff, and who preached that we should consider every man as our brother, and relieve the necessities of our fellow-creatures?' Such an impression did his conduct make on me, that I got a piece of paper, and wrote a few lines, cautioning him against the consequences of his cruelty, and having signed it with my real name, 'SWING,' I left it at his hall-door during the night, and the following day the village rung with the report of the parson's having received a threatening notice, and that if the author could be detected, he would certainly be transported. When writing the notice, I had not the most distant intention of making

£150 REWARD,

AND THE
King's Pardon.

WHEREAS,

Some evil-disposed Person or Persons did, on the Night of *April* the 12*th*, wilfully and maliciously *SET FIRE* to the Drying-house, Outhouses and Mills, GREAT MARLOW, *Bucks*, occupied *by* Mr. JOSEPH WRIGHT, *Paper-Maker*, with a View to *DESTROY* the same; and did on the SAME NIGHT place Fire-Brands with Pitched or Tarred Cloth *round them*, in the *PAPER-MILLS* of Mr. WM. WRIGHT (*adjoining* those of his Brother), *with intent to* Destroy *them also.*

The above Reward of £150 will be paid to any Person who will give such Information as shall bring the Perpetrators to Conviction, by applying to Mr. JAMES ILBERY, 1, Great Titchfield Street, *London*, or to the *West-of-England Assurance Office, Exeter,* or *Bridge Street, Blackfriars, London.*

And beyond the Reward offered above, His Majesty's Free Pardon will be extended to any Accomplice or Accomplices, who shall give Information as will lead to Conviction.

Signed — JOSEPH WRIGHT,
WILLIAM WRIGHT.

J. INNES, Printer, 61, Wells Street, Oxford Street, London. — *APRIL 22, 1826.*

myself the instrument of punishment to the parson; it was a mere ebullition of the moment, called forth by my suffering, and I thought no more about it. In a few days after the serving of the notice my wife died, and I was obliged to procure a coffin from the parish to bury her: no person attended her remains to the grave but a man who helped me to carry the coffin, and my five motherless children. It was late in the afternoon when we reached the churchyard, and as the man was obliged to leave me before the grave was entirely covered in, it became quite dark ere I could finish it, and I was obliged to procure a lantern to enable me to do so. When I completed it, I beheld my five children starving and shivering with cold beside the grave of their poor mother, without the smallest prospect of obtaining any food for them until morning; and in this condition I returned towards the cottage from whence I had that day carried my wife to be buried: the idea of passing the night on the straw on which she had expired was so repugnant to me, that I determined not to do so, and as the parson's haggard was only a short distance from me, I brought my children to pass the night on some loose straw that was lying on the ground. I was too much overwhelmed with grief and misery to attend to any thing, and I forgot to extinguish the light in the lantern which was carried by one of my children; the child incautiously placed the lantern close to a rick, which caught fire, and was in a few minutes in a blaze; frightened and confounded at the accident, I immediately left the place, and the next morning journeyed homewards, begging for subsistence along the road: every where I went I heard of fires and notices signed 'SWING.' 'How happens this,' thought I. 'I am not the author of those burnings! – What can have caused them?' A few minutes reflection on the history of my own life, which without any alteration may stand for that of thousands of others, enabled me to give myself a satisfactory answer. 'Those fires,' said I, 'are caused by farmers having been turned out of their lands to make room for foxes – peaceable people assembled to petition Parliament, massacred by the military, – peasants confined two years in prison for picking up a dead partridge, – English labourers set up to auction like slaves, and treated as beasts of burthen, – and pluralist parsons taking a poor man's only cow for the tithe of his cabbage-garden. These are the things that have caused the burnings, and not unfortunate "SWING!"'

I continued my route, reached home, and am again harnessed like a horse to the gravel cart. But I bear it, with patience, under the conviction that, in a very short time, Reform or Revolution must release me from it.

RURAL SPORTS AT NORTHFLEET

[*Pierce Egan Sr describes a country festival in Kent.*]

PUBLIC BREAKFAST. – Plates were laid for two hundred (in Mr Pitcher's long room, formerly used for ship-building), to be in readiness when the steamers discharged their cargoes – or rather, when the company disembarked, and the guns announced the arrival of the visitors from London. Never was '*cutting* and *coming* again' performed in better style upon any occasion – and the advantages of a trip by water was conspicuous in the extreme, respecting an increase of appetite. The visitors came to be happy, and they were happy; *etiquette* was out of the question, and 'helping one's self' was the order of the day; and it was a lucky thing for some of the party who could help themselves, as *niceties* were not stood upon – but there was no *grumbling* – the '*wisit*' was made pleasant – and scarcely was the breakfast finished when the Ball commenced, in order that digestion might go on quickly, – and that nothing like apoplectic fits might occur, or a coroner's inquest be necessary.

THE BALL – ASSEMBLY – DANCE – OR HOP; – call it what you please; or by any of the above names you may like best. The room was crowded to excess; but nevertheless it was a fine specimen of good-nature, pleasure, and happiness. It is true that a master of the ceremonies attended from the metropolis to keep good order; but the fact is, there was nothing like *ceremony* about it. Pride was out of the question; every man was as good as his neighbour; and the female part of the company were all alive and merry on the 'fantastic toe!' The assembly commenced with Quadrilles, but finished with Country Dances; and there was no time nor room for criticism respecting the *steps*; every one did their best – and hops, skips, and jumps were not noticed. Two or three songs from professionals, engaged by the proprietors of the Fete, not only afforded considerable pleasure to the lovers of harmony, but gave a variety to the scene; which was also enlivened by a celebrated ventriloquist from London, whose imitations of birds, and the inhabitants of a farm-yard, not only astonished the natives, but kept the *genteel* part of the company in roars of laughter. The dancing was kept up with great spirit until the announcement of cannon from the steamers that 'TIME and *tide* wait for no man, nor woman neither!'

CLIMBING UP A GREASY POLE FOR A LEG OF MUTTON. – The above feature, for fun, frolic, and laughter, beat all the other sports of the day, two to one. It was a *slippery* thing altogether, and the disappointments which occurred to the numerous candidates to *grapple* with the mutton, were of the most ludicrous description. All manner of *schemes* were resorted to obtain the delicious joint which was tied to the top of a long pole, about fifty feet from the ground. The country *hawbucks*

had not the slightest chance whatever, although some of them threw resin and sawdust on the pole as they climbed up, to reduce its *slipperiness;* but all attempts were useless, and they came down much faster than they got up – indeed they all came down with a *run*, without moving their legs, to the great amusement of a very large multitude of spectators, who had assembled together for miles round to enjoy the humours of a RUSTIC FETE. But a young son of Neptune, a dreadnought hero, offered himself for the prize, and ascended the pole like a seaman; but he had scarcely got up half the way to the mutton, when he came down like a shot; but little Jack, too *game* to be denied, and well knowing that *nothing venture, nothing win*, he made another trial of skill and courage, obtained a few paces nearer to the leg of mutton than before, but down he came again to the ground before you could say Jack Robinson. A pyramid was then formed by three or four men at the bottom of the pole, and another pyramid also on them, when Little Jack again had another trial, amidst the shouts of the multitude, trying a different scheme; having a piece of rope in his hand with a noose at the end of it, he fastened the rope round the pole, and pulled himself up so successfully by it, that he *touched* the mutton with his left hand, receiving the loudest tokens of approbation,

and several wagers were laid that the leg of mutton would soon be in his possession, but it was tied so tight to the pole that Jack could not remove it, therefore his knife was necessary to release the leg from its confined situation; but as many things happen between the 'cup and the lip,' Little Jack, in searching his pockets for the bit of steel, lost his hold, when he came down with a run, and also knocked both his pyramids to the ground, to the great laughter and shouts of the crowd. However, nothing dismayed by the disappointment, the pyramids were again formed, and little Jack ascended once more the pole, determined on victory. He tied the rope as before, twisted his legs round the pole, and worked well with his knees, and after making three or four slips, but never exactly loosing his situation, he firmly ascended the pole, and clapping his left hand on the top of it, the critical minute again arrived, when Jack felt for his knife – the eyes of the crowd were now in suspense, and doubts and fears were expressed upon the subject, when little Jack flourished his knife, put an end to all surmises, and separated the leg of mutton from the pole. He remained in this situation for about a minute, enjoying the plaudits of the multitude for his exertions – when he descended in quick time, holding the mutton fast in his hand. Several persons were so pleased with little Jack's exertions, that a subscription was entered into for him, and his cap was soon filled with halfpence, when little Jack exclaimed, 'the mutton would not go without *sauce* to it' – 'nor *capers* neither,' said an ould tar, who had been contemplating the Rustic scene.

Such were the humorous *features* displayed at one of the *Rustic Fetes* at NORTHFLEET – it was all happiness; – every body appeared pleased and satisfied; – and not the slightest disorder occurred: we therefore feel ourselves perfectly correct in asserting that no man can be viewed as a friend to his country, or a supporter of the government, who would endeavour in the slightest degree to *interfere* or *prevent* the people from enjoying *those* SPORTS which have been handed down to them from their forefathers, and which tend so much to lighten TOIL, and to promote HAPPINESS — *Amicus humani generis*

WREKINGTON HIRING

O lads an' lasses hither come,
To Wrekinton to see the fun,
An' mind ye bring yor Sunday shun.
   There'll be rare wark wi' dancin, O,
An' lasses now without a brag,
Bring pockets like a fiddle bag,
Ye'll get them cram'd wi' mony a whag,
   Of pepper-cyek an' scranchim O.

An' Bess put on that bonny gown,
Thy mother bought thou at the town,
That straw hat wi' the ribbons brown,
   They'll a' be buss'd that's comin' O;
Put that reed ribbon round thy waist,
It myeks thou luik se full of grace.
Then up the lonnen come in haste,
   They'll think thou's come frae Lunnun O.

Ned put on his Sunday coat,
His hat an' breeches cast a note,
With a new stiff'ner round his throat,
   He luikt the very dandy, O.
He thought that he was gaun to choke,
For he had to gyep before he spoke,
He met Bess at the Royal Oak,
   They had byeth yell and brandy, O.

Each lad was there with his sweetheart,
An' a' was ready for a start,
When in com Jack wi' Fanny Smart,
   An' brought a merry scraper, O.
Then Ned jumpt up upon his feet,
An' on the table myed a seat,
Then bounc'd the fiddler up a heet,
   Cryin, Play an' we will caper, O.

Now Ned an' Bess led off the ball,
'Play smash the windows', he did call,
'Keep in yor feet,' says hitchy Mall,
   'Learn'd dancers hae sic prancin O;'
Now Ned was nowther laith nor lyem,
An' faith he had baith bouk an' byen,
Ye wad thought his feet was myed of styen,
   He gav' sic thuds wi' dancin O.

Now Jackey Fanny's hand did seize,
Cryin, 'Fiddler get yor strings a' greas'd,
Play kiss her weel amang the trees,
   She is my darlin, bliss her O;'
Then away they set wi' sic a smack,
They myed the joists a' bend an' crack.

When duen he tuik her round the neck,
  An' faith he did'nt miss her O.

The fiddler's elbow wagg'd a' neet.
He thought he wad drop off his seet,
For deel a bit they'd let him eat,
  They were se keen of dancin O;
Some had to strip their coats fer heet,
An' shirts an' shifts were wet wi' sweat;
They cram'd their guts for want of meat,
  Wi ginger-bread an' scranchim O.

Now cocks had crawn an hour or more,
An' owr the yell pot some did snore,
But how they luikt to hear the roar,
  Of Matt the King pit caller O;
'Smash him' says Ned 'he mun be wrang,
'But he's callin through his sleep aw warm,'
Then shoutin to the door he ran,
  Thou's asleep thou rousty bawler O.'

Now they danc't agyen till it was day,
An' then went hyem, but by the way,
There was some had rare fun they say,
  An' found it nine months after O;
But dinna myek now sic a mouth,
It's nobbit just a trick o' youth,
It will be duen while in the south,
  Without mare noise or laughter O.

Suen Wrekinton will bear the sway,
Two members they'll put in they say,
Then wor taxes will be duen away,
  An' we'll a' sing now or never O;
Backey an' tea will be se cheap,
Wives will sit up when they sud sleep,
An' we'll float in yell at yor pay week,
  Then Wrekington for ever O.

TRIAL OF GEORGE LOVELESS, LEADER OF THE SIX DORSETSHIRE LABOURERS TRANSPORTED FOR TAKING AN ILLEGAL OATH TO A TRADE UNION

Directly after we were put back, a Mr Young, an attorney employed on our behalf, called me into the conversation room, and, among other things, inquired if I would promise the magistrates to have no more to do with the Union if they would let me go home to my wife and family? I said, 'I do not understand you.' – 'Why,' said he, 'give them information concerning the Union, who else belongs to it, and promise you will have no more to do with it.' – 'Do you mean to say I am to betray my companions?' – 'That is just it,' said he. 'No; I would rather undergo any punishment.'

The same day we were sent to the high jail, where we continued until the assizes. I had never seen the inside of a jail before, but now I began to feel it – disagreeable company, close confinement, bad bread, and what was worse, hard and cold lodging – a small straw bed on the flags, or else an iron bedstead – 'and this,' said I to my companions, 'is our fare for striving to live honest.' In this situation the chaplain of the prison paid us a visit, to pour a volley of instruction in our ears, mixed up, however, in the cup of abuse. After upbraiding and taunting us with being discontented and idle, and wishing to ruin our masters, he proceeded to tell us that we were better off than our masters, and that government had made use of every possible means for economy and retrenchment to make all comfortable. He inquired if I could point out any thing more that might be done to increase the comfort of the labourer. I told him I thought I could; and began to assure him our object was not to ruin the master, but that, for a long time, we had been looking for the head to begin, and relieve the various members down to the feet: but finding it was of no avail, we were thinking of making application to our masters, and for them to make application to their masters, and so up to the head; and as to their being worse off than ourselves, I could not believe it, while I saw them keep such a number of horses for no other purpose than to chase the hare and the fox. And, besides, I thought gentlemen wearing the clerical livery, like himself, might do with a little less salary. 'Is that how you mean to do it?' said he. 'That is one way I have been thinking of, Sir.' – 'I hope the Court will favour you, but I think they will not; for I believe they mean to make an example of you.' And saying this he left us.

On the 15th of March, we were taken to the County-hall to await our trial. As soon as we arrived we were ushered down some steps into a miserable dungeon, opened but twice a year, with only a glimmering light; and to make it more disagreeable, some wet and green brush-wood was served for firing. The smoke of this place, together with its natural dampness, amounted to nearly suffocation; and in this most dreadful situation we passed three whole days. As to the trial, I need mention but little; the whole proceedings were characterized by a shameful disregard of justice and decency; the most unfair means were resorted to in order to frame an indictment against us; the grand jury appeared to ransack heaven and earth to get some clue against us, but in vain; our characters were investigated from our infancy to the then present moment; our masters were inquired of to know if we were not idle, or attended public-houses, or some other fault in us; and much as they were opposed to us, they had common honesty enough to declare that we were good labouring servants, and that they never heard of any complaint against us; and when nothing whatever could be raked together, the unjust and cruel judge, John Williams, ordered us to be tried for mutiny and conspiracy, under an act 37 Geo. III., cap. 123, for the suppression of mutiny amongst the marines and seamen, several years ago, at the Nore. The greater part of the evidence against us, on our trial, was put into the mouths of the witnesses by the judge; and when he evidently wished them to say any particular thing, and the witness would say 'I cannot remember,' he would say, 'Now think; I will give you another minute to con-sider;' and he would then repeat over the words, and ask, 'Cannot you remember?' Sometimes, by charging them to be careful what they said, by way of intimidation, they would merely answer, 'yes;' and the judge would set the words down as proceeding from the witness. I shall not soon forget his address to the jury, in summing up the evidence: among other things, he told them, that if such Societies were allowed to exist, it would ruin masters, cause a stagnation in trade, destroy property, – and if *they should not find us guilty, he was certain they would forfeit the opinion of the grand jury.* I thought to myself, there is no danger but we shall be found guilty,

as we have a special jury for the purpose, selected from among those who are most unfriendly towards us – the grand jury, land-owners, the petty jury, land-renters. Under such a charge, from such a quarter, self-interest alone would induce them to say, 'Guilty.' The judge then inquired if we had any thing to say. I instantly forwarded the following short defence, in writing, to him: – 'My Lord, if we have violated any law, it was not done intentionally: we have injured no man's reputation, character, person, or pro-perty: we were uniting together to preserve ourselves, our wives, and our children, from utter degradation and starvation. We chal-lenge any man, or number of men, to prove that we have acted, or intend to act, different from the above statement.' The judge asked if I wished it to be read in Court. I answered, 'Yes.' It was then mumbled over to a part of the jury, in such an inaudible manner, that although I knew what was there, I could not comprehend it. And here one of the counsel prevented sentence being passed, by declaring that not one charge brought against any of the prisoners at the bar was proved, and that if we were found guilty a great number of persons would be dissatisfied; 'and I shall for one,' said he.

Two days after this we were again placed at the bar to receive sentence, when the judge (John Williams) told us, 'that not for any thing that we had done, or, as he could prove, we intended to do, but for an example to others, he considered it his duty to pass the sentence of seven years' transportation across his Majesty's high seas upon each and every one of us.' As soon as the sentence was passed, I got a pencil and a scrap of paper, and wrote the following lines:–

'God is our guide! from field, from wave,
From plough, from anvil, and from loom;
We come, our country's rights to save,
And speak a tyrant faction's doom:
    We raise the watch-word liberty;
    We will, we will, we will be free!

God is our guide! no swords we draw,
We kindle not war's battle fires;
By reason, union, justice, law,
We claim the birth-right of our sires:

We raise the watch-word, liberty,
We will, we will, we will be free!'

While we were being guarded back to prison, our hands locked together, I tossed the above lines to some people that we passed; the guard, however, seizing hold of them, they were instantly carried back to the judge; and by some this was considered a crime of no less magnitude than high treason.

Almost instantly after this I was taken ill, occasioned by being kept in the dungeon already spoken of, and two days after getting worse, requested to be allowed to see the doctor, and consequently was taken to the hospital. As soon as I entered I had to cope with a new antagonist, Dr Arden, surgeon of the hospital. I told him I was too ill for conversation, and requested him to allow me to go to bed; but he appeared so angry as not to regard what I said. At length, I threw myself on a bed and answered his questions, until he was very mild, and after this he manifested the greatest possible kindness and attention towards me until I left Dorchester Castle. I told him they could hang me with as much justice as transport me for what I had done.

THE PLOWMAN'S DITTY

BEING AN ANSWER
TO THAT FOOLISH QUESTION,

'WHAT HAVE THE POOR TO LOSE?'

To the Tune of – *He that has the best Wife*

Because I'm but poor,
And slender's my store,
    That I've nothing to lose, is the cry, Sir;
Let who will declare it,
I vow I can't bear it,
    I give all such praters the lie, Sir.

Tho' my house is but small,
I might have none at all,
    Should rebellion be brought into action;
Shall my garden, so sweet,
And my orchard, so neat,
    Be the prize of a jacobin faction?

On Saturday night
'Tis still my delight,
    With my wages to run home the faster;
But if riot rule here,
I may look far and near,
    But I never shall find a paymaster.

I've a dear little wife,
Whom I love as my life,
    To lose her I should not much like, Sir;
And 'twould make me run wild,
To see my sweet child,
    With its head on the point of a pike, Sir.

I've my church too to save,
And will go to my grave,
    In defence of a church that's the best, Sir;
I've my king too, (God bless him!)
Let no man oppress him,
    For none has he ever opprest, Sir.

British laws for my guard,
My cottage is barr'd,
    'Tis safe in the light or the dark, Sir;
If the Squire should oppress,
I get instant redress,
    My orchard's as safe as his park, Sir.

My cot is my throne,
What I have is my own,
    And what is my own I will keep, Sir;
Should riot ensue,
I may plow, it is true,
    But I'm sure that I never shall reap, Sir.

Now, do but reflect
What I have to protect,
    Then doubt if to rise I shall choose, Sir;
King, Church, Babes, and Wife,
Laws, Liberty, Life;
    Now tell me I've nothing to lose, Sir.

DAFT WATTY'S RAMBLE TO CARLISLE

If you ax me where I come frae, I say the
    fell syde,
Where fadder and mudder, and honest fwok
    beyde,
And my sweetheart, O bless her! she thought
    nyen like me,

For when she shuik hands, the tears gush'd
    frae her e'e,
Says I, 'I mun e'en get a spot if I can,
But whatever betide me, I'll think o' thee,
    Nan!'

Nan was a perfect beauty, wi' twee cheeks
like codlin blossoms; the verra seet on her
made my mouth a' water, 'Fares-te-weel,
Watty!' says she; tou's a wag amang lasses,
and I'll see thee nae mair!' – Nay, dunnet
growl, Nan, says I –

'Fur, mappen, er lang, I'se be maister
    mysel';'
Sae we buss'd, and I tuik a last luik at the
    fell;

On I whussl'd and wander'd: my bundle I
    flung
O'er my shoulder, when Cowley he efter me
    sprung
And howl'd, silly fellow! and fawn'd at my
    fit,
As if to say, Watty, we munnet part yet!
At Carel I stuid wi' a strae i' my mouth,
And they tuik me, nae doubt, for a promisin
    youth; –

The weyves com round me in clusters –
'What weage dus te ax, canny lad?' says yen.
'Wey, three pun and a crown; wunnet beate a
hair o' my beard.' 'What can te dui?' says
anudder. 'Dui – wey I cun plough, sow, mow,
shear, thresh, dike, milk, kurn, muck a byer,
sing a psalm, mend cargear, dance a whorn-
pype, nick a nag's tail, hunt a brock, or feight
iver a yen o' my weight in aw Croglin parish.'

An auld bearded hussy suin caw'd me her
    man;
But that day, I may say't, aw my sorrow
    began.

Furst, Cowley, peur fellow! they hang'd i'
    the street,
And skinn'd, God forgi'e them! for shoon to
    their feet;
I cry'd, and they caw'd me poor half-
    witted clown,
And banter'd and follow'd me all up and
    down;
Neist my deam she e'en starv'd me that
    ever liv'd weel,

Her hard words and luiks wad hae freeten'd
    the de'il.

She had a lang beard, for aw t'warl' like a
billy-goat, wi' a kiln-dried frosty face, and
then the smawest leg o' mutton in aw Carel
market sarved the cat, me and her for a week.
The bairns meade sec gam on us, and thun-
dered at the rapper, as if to waken a corp;
when I opened the duir, they threw flour i' my
e'en, and caw'd me daft Watty;

Sae I pack'd up my duds when my quarter
    was out,
And, wi' weage i' my pocket, I saunter'd
    about.

Suin my reet hand breek pocket they pick'd
    in a fray,
And wi' fifteen white shillings they slipp'd
    clean away,
Forby my twee letters frae mudder and Nan,
Where they said Carel lasses wad Watty
    trapan;
But 'twad take a lang day just to tell what
    I saw,
How I 'scap'd frae the gallows, the swodgers
    and aw.

Ay, there were some forgery chaps had me
just sign my neame. 'Nay,' says I, 'you've
getten a wrang pig by the lug, for I cannot
write!' Then a fellow like a lobster, aw leac'd
and feathered, ax't me, 'Watty, wull te list?
thou's either be a general or gomeral.' Nay, I
winnet, that's plain; I's content wi' a cwot o'
mudder's spinnin;'

Now, wi' twee groats and tuppence, I'll e'en
    toddle heame,
But ne'er be a swodger, while Watty's my
    neame,

Now my mudder'll gowel, and my fadder'll
    stare,
When I tell them poor Cowley they'll never
    see mair;
Then they'll bring me a stuil; as for Nan
    she'll be fain,
To see I'm return'd to my friends yence
    again; –
The barn and the byre, and the auld hollow
    tree,

Will just seem like cronies yen's fidgin to
see;

The sheep'll nit ken Watty's voice now! The
peat-stack we used to lake round 'ill be burnt
ere this! As for Nan, she'll be owther married
or broken-hearted. An' aw be weel, at Croglin
we'll hae sic fiddlin, dancing, drinkin, singin,
and smeukin, till aw's blue about us –
Amang aw our neybors sec wonders I'll tell,
And never mair leave my auld friends or the
fell.

2. MINING

THE COLLIER'S RANT

A very celebrated Northumberland ditty

As me and my marrow were ganning to wark,
We met with the devil, it was in the dark;

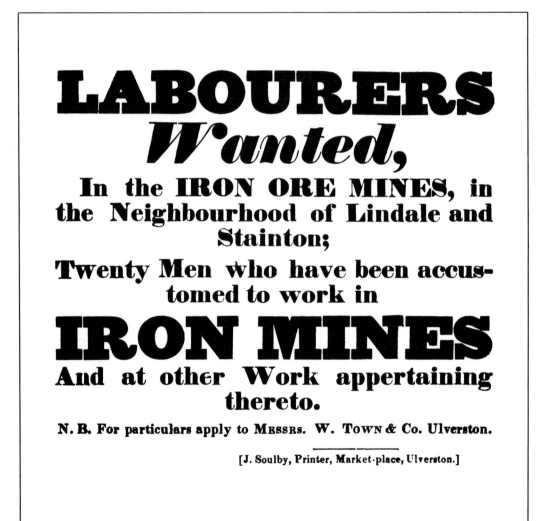

LABOURERS *Wanted,*

In the IRON ORE MINES, in the Neighbourhood of Lindale and Stainton;

Twenty Men who have been accustomed to work in

IRON MINES

And at other Work appertaining thereto.

N. B. For particulars apply to MESSRS. W. TOWN & Co. Ulverston.

[J. Soulby, Printer, Market-place, Ulverston.]

I up with my pick, it being in the neit,
And knock'd off his horns, likewise his club
feet.
    Follow the horses, Johnny, my lad, oh!
    Follow them through, my canny lad, oh!
    Follow the horses, Johnny, my lad, oh!
    Oh laddy away, canny lad, oh!
As me and my marrow was putting the tram,
The low it went out, and my marrow went
wrang;
You would have laughed had you seen the
gam –
The de'il gat my marrow, but I got the
tram.
          Follow the horses, &c.
Oh! marrow, oh! marrow, what dost thou
think?
I've broken my bottle, and spilt a' my
drink;
I lost a' my shin-splints amang the great
stanes;
Draw me t' the shaft, it's time to gang
hame.
          Follow the horses, &c.
Oh! marrow, oh! marrow, where hast thou
been?
Driving the drift from the low seam,
Driving the drift, &c.
Had up the low, lad, de'il stop out thy een!
          Follow the horses, &c.
Oh! marrow, oh! marrow, this wor pay week;
We'll get penny loaves and drink to our
beak,
And we'll fill up our bumper, and round it
shall go:
Follow the horses, Johnny, lad, oh!
          Follow the horses, &c.
There is my horse, and there is my tram;
Twee horns full of grease will make her to
gang!
There is my hoggars, likewise my half shoon.
And smash my heart, marrow, my putting's
a' done.
    Follow the horses, Johnny, my lad, oh!
    Follow them through, my canny lad, oh!
    Follow the horses, Johnny, my lad, oh!
    Oh, laddy away, canny lad, oh!

A BANG-UP
COLLIER'S
LETTER
TO HIS
SWEETHEART.

Dear Madam,

The light of your Beauty has been long confined in the CORF of my Affections in the very center of my Cabin, but now it is tumbled down the SHAFT of my Reason, and fixed itself to the TRAM of my Understanding, pushed forward with great velocity on the wheels of Desire, along the Mother-gate of Despair; and had it not been for the rise-hitch of Self-sufficiency, it would have run into the Dibboard of my Brains, and consequently knocked down the Pillar of my Senses, then the thready Roof of Distraction would have brought on a Thrust, which all the propping in the World could not support; and, sink my pit sark, would have happ'd up my Soul. Pray, Madam, to prevent the like Misfortunes, take me into your Colliery, let me curve in the Coal of your Pleasure with my curving Pick of Delight, sump you with the Hack of my Love, and full your Jud with the Mal of Desire and Wedge of Love; Lastly, when I am tired, send down the Rope of Good-nature, and the Hook of your Kindness, and draw me to Bank to the Settle Boards of Ease, there shall I rest on the Heap of Plenty.

WILL WATERCOURSE.

Collier Lass.

My name's Polly Parker, I'm come
    o'er from Worsley,
  My father and mother work in a
    coal mine:
Our family's large, we have got seven
    children,
  So I too am obliged to work in a
    mine.
And as this is my fortune, I know
    you'll feel sorry,
  That in such employment my days
    they should pass;
But I keep up my spirits, I sing and
    look merry,
  Although I am nought but a collier
    lass.

By the greatest of dangers, each day
    I'm surrounded,
  I hang in the air by a rope or a
    chain,
The mine may fall in, I may be killed
    or wounded,
  May perish by damp, or the fire of
    a train.
And what would you do, were it not
    for our labour?
  In wretched starvation your days
    they would pass
While we can provide you with life's
    greatest blessing,
  O do not despise a poor collier lass.

All the long day you may see we are
    buried,
  Deprived of the light and the
    warmth of the sun,
And often at night from our beds we
    are hurried,
  The water is in, and barefooted we
    run.
Although we go ragged, and black are
    our faces,
  As kind and as free as the best we
    are found;
And our hearts are as white as your
    lords in fine places,
  Although we're poor colliers that
    work under ground.

I am growing up fast, and somehow
    or other,
  There's a collier lad strangely runs
    into my mind,
And in spite of the talking of father
    and mother,
  I think I should marry if he was
    inclin'd;
But should he prove surly and will
    not befriend me,
  Perhaps a better chance will come
    to pass,
And my heart I know, will to him
    recommend me,
  And I will no longer be a collier lass.

BRAVE COLLIER LADS

As I walked forth one summer's morn, all in
the month of June –
The flowers they were springing, and the
birds were in full tune –
I overheard a lovely maid, and this was all
her theme: –
'Success attend the collier lads, for they are
lads of fame.'

I stepped up to her, and, bending on my
knee,
I asked her pardon for making with her so
free:
My pardon is granted, young collier, she
replies:
Pray do you belong to the Brave Union boys?

You may see I'm a collier as black as a sloe;
And all the night long I am working down
below:
Oh I do love a collier as I do love my life –
My father was a pitman all the days of his
life.

Come now, my young collier, and rest here
awhile,
And when I have done milking, I'll give you
a smile.
He kissed her sweet lips while milking her
cow;
And the lambs they were sporting all in the
morning dew.

Come all you noble gentlemen, wherever you
may be,
Do not pull down their wages, nor break
their unity;
You see they hold like brothers, like sailors
on the sea,
They do their best endeavours for their
wives and family.

Then she clapt her arms around him like
Venus round the vine;
You are my jolly collier lad: you've won
this heart of mine;
And if that you do win the day, as you have
won my heart,
I'll crown you with honour, and for ever
take your part.

The colliers are the best of boys, their work
lies under ground,
And when they to the alehouse go they
value not a crown;
They spend their money freely and pay
before they go;
They work under ground while the stormy
winds do blow.

So come all you pretty maidens wherever
you may be
A collier lad do not despise in any degree
For if that you do use them well they'll do
the same to thee;
There is none in this world like a pit-boy
for me.

THE COLLIERY UNION

by Elizabeth Gair, Collier's Wife

Come all ye noble colliery lads, wherever
you belong.
I pray you give attention and you shall hear
my song.
Tis concerning of our Union Lads, for they
have proved so true,
They have stood fast, man to man, we must
give them their due.
  So stick unto your Union and mind what
  Roberts say,
  If you be guided by his word, you'll surely
  win the day.

Little did the Masters think that you would
stand so fast.

They thought that hunger it would bite, you
 would give up at last.
But like the widow's crouse of meal that
 never did run out,
The Lord did send them fresh supplies that
 served them round about.

The Masters they devised a plan their Union
 for to break.
It only made the colliery lads the firmer for
 to stick.
For when they thought upon the time that
 they'd been bit before
Before that they would go to work they'd
 beg from door to door.

Then for to get the pits to work they have
 tried every plan.
Both Scotch and Irish they have brought,
 and every countryman.
But all the coals that they have got have
 cost them double pay.
Cheer up your heart, you colliery lads,
 you're sure to win the day.

Success to your commander, and Roberts is
 his name,
Since he has proved so loyal we'll spread
 about his fame.
Cheer up your hearts, ye colliery lads, he'll
 not leave you alone,
After he has eat the meat he will give them
 the bone.

Let's not forget young Beesley, a man of wit
 possessed.
He's gained the country's favour, for he has
 stood the test;
And let your day be e'er so dull, you'll see
 the rising sun,
For they will gain the victory without
 either sword or gun
  So stick etc.

HASWELL CAGES

Tune – *The Wedding of Ballyporeen*

Come all you good people and listen a while,
I will sing you a song that will cause you to
 smile,

It is about Haswell I mean for to sing,
Concerning the new plan we started last
 spring.
  And the very first thing I will mention,
  Without any evil intention,
  It is concerning this new invention,
   Of winding up coals in a cage.

It was in eighteen hundred and thirty eight,
We began to prepare to make the shaft
 right,
We put in the conductors from bottom to
 top,
The materials were ready prepar'd at the
 shop,
  From the top of the pit to the bottom,
  One hundred and fifty six fathom,
  And the distance you do think it
   nothing,
   You ride so quickly in the cage.

Now considering the depth its surprising to
 say,
The quantity of work we can draw in a day,
Five hundred and thirty tons of the best
 coal,
In the space of twelve hours we can win up
 this hole,
  About forty five tons in an hour,
  And viewers, overmen, and hewers,
  Our engines must have a great power,
   To run at such speed with the cage.

Then as soon as the tubs do come to the day,
To the weighing machine they are taken
 away
Where two men are appointed there to
 attend,
To see justice done between master and men.
  And when they leave the weighing
   machine, sir,
  Straightway they do go to the screen,
   sir,
  And the keeker does see that they're
   clean, sir,
   All the coals that come up in the
    cage.

I have wrought with the corves, I have
 wrought with the tubs,
I have wrought where the baskets came up
 by the lugs,

I have wrought by the dozen, I have
  wrought by the score,
But this curious contrivance, I never saw
  before.
    When we get in, they then pull the
      rapper,
    At the top it does make a great clatter,
    And the brakesman they know what's
      the matter,
      And bring us away in a cage.

And when the bell rings and the top we
  approach,
It oft puts me in mind of a new railway
  coach,
The number of passengers I cannot tell,
But she brings a great many I know very
  well.
    But I wish they may not overload her,
    And do some mischief on the road, sir,
    Too much charge makes a cannon
      explode, sir,
      And so will too much in the cage.

Now the young men and maids do sometimes
  take a trip
Out to sea in fine weather, on board a steam
  ship,
But if any be curious enough to engage,
For a trip down below, and a ride in our
  cage,
    It would be a fine recreation,
    For to go down and view the low
      station,
    I wish they may meet no temptation,
      When they take a trip in our cage.

3. WEAVING

JONE O'GRINFILT

I'm a poor cotton weaver as many one
  knows,
I've nowt to eat i'th house an I've worn out
  my cloas,
You'd hardly give sixpence for all I have on,
My clugs they are brossen and stockings
  I've none,
You'd think it wur hard to be sent into th'
  world,
    To clem and do th' best ot you con.

Our church parson kept telling us long,
We should have better times if we'd hold
  our tongues,
I've houden my tongue till I can hardly
  draw breath,
I think i' my heart he means to clem me to
  death;
I know he lives weel by backbiting the de'il,
    But he never picked o'er in his life.

I tarried six week an thought every day
  wur t' last,
I tarried and shifted till now I'm quite fast;
I lived on nettles while nettles were good,
An Waterloo porridge were best of my food;
I'm telling you true I can find folks enew,
    That are living no better than me.

Old Bill o' Dan's sent bailiffs one day,
For a shop score I owed him that I could
  not pay,

Cotton Spinners from Manchester.

FOR THE MASTER OR MISTRESS.

Good Lady or Gentleman,

We ask pardon for the liberty taken in calling upon you, and assure you that nothing but want of employment would have induced us thus to intrude. Machinery has so overstocked the market, that it is impossible to obtain employment; and the parish is so overburthened that we could get but little relief; we therefore trust that the lady or gentleman will purchase some of the best reels of cotton of two unfortunate cotton spinners: for it is the only support we have to depend upon until the Lord assists us with some employment.

COPY OF VERSES

We are cotton spinners by our trade;
  Employ we cannot find :
Hundreds are by want compell'd
  To leave their friends behind.

The oldest man now on the earth,
  Or living in the land,
Cannot remember trade so bad,
  Nor work at such a stand.

The mother, she sat weeping—
  She raves and tears her hair,
When she beholds her children dear,
  For they are all her care.

Their altered looks she does behold,
  Like death appears the view ;

With weeping eyes to heaven she cries,
  Good Lord, what shall we do.

Our visit now to you, kind friends,
  We hope you will excuse;
And as we have explain'd our cause,
  We hope you'll not refuse.

For when we saw one in distress,
  We join'd to help him through ;
But now we cannot help ourselves ;
  We have no work to do.

For he that giveth to the poor,
  But lendeth to the Lord ;
So now, kind friends, on us bestow
  Whate'er you can afford.

There are more than Four Hundred out of Employment at this time.

The person who will call for this bill will bring a sample of the very best reels of cotton for sale.

James Paul and Co., Printers, 2 & 3, Monmouth Court, Seven Dials.

But he wur too late for oud Bill o' Bent,
Had sent tit and cart and taen goods for
  rent,
We had nou bur a stoo, that wur a seat for
  two,
  And on it cowered Margit and me.

The bailiffs looked round assly as a mouse,
When they saw aw things were taen out ot
  house,
Says one to the other all's gone thou may
  see,
Aw sed lads never fret you're welcome to me;
They made no more ado, but nipp'd up th'
  owd stoo,
  And we both went wack upoth flags.

I geet howd of Margit for hoo wur strucken
  sick,
Hoo sed hoo ne'er had such a bang sin hoo
  wur wick.
The bailiffs scoured off with owd stoo on
  their backs,
They would not have cared had they brook
  our necks,
They're mad at owd Bent cos he's taen
  goods for rent,
  And wur ready to flee us alive.

I sed to our Margit as we lay upoth floor,
We shall never be lower in this world I'm
  sure,
But if we alter I'm sure we mun mend,
For I think in my heart we are both at far
  end,
For meat we have none nor looms to weave
  on,
  Egad they're as weel lost as found.

Then I geet up my piece and I took it em
  back
I scarcely dare speak mester looked so black,
He said you wur o'erpaid last time you
  coom,
I said if I wur 'twas for weaving bout loom;
In a mind as I'm in I'll ne'er pick o'er again,
  For I've woven mysel toth' fur end.

Then aw coom out and left him to chew
  that,
When aw thought again aw wur vext till aw
  sweat,

To think that we mun work to keep them
  and awth set,
All the day o' my life and still be in their
  debt;
So I'll give o'er trade an work with a spade,
  Or go and break stones upoth road.

Our Margit declared if hoo'd cloas to put on,
Hoo'd go up to Lundun an see the big mon
An if things didn't alter when hoo had been,
Hoo swears hoo'd feight blood up toth e'en,
Hoo's nought again th' Queen but likes a
  fair thing,
  An hoo says hoo can tell when hoo's
  hurt.

BURY NEW LOOM

As I walked between Bolton and Bury,
  'twas on a moonshiny night,
I met with a buxom young weaver whose
  company gave me delight.
She says: Young fellow, come tell me if your
  level and rule are in tune.
Come, give me an answer correct, can you
  get up and square my new loom?

I said: My dear lassie, believe me, I am a
  good joiner by trade,
And many a good loom and shuttle before
  me in my time I have made.
Your short lams and jacks and long lams I
  quickly can put in tune.
My rule is in good order to get up and
  square a new loom.

She took me and showed me her loom, the
  down on her warp did appear.
The lams, jacks and healds put in motion, I
  levelled her loom to a hair.
My shuttle run well in her lathe, my treadle
  it worked up and down,
My level stood close to her breast-bone, the
  time I was reiving her loom.

The cords of my lams, jacks and treadles at
  length they began to give way.
The bobbin I had in my shuttle, the weft in
  it no longer would stay.

Her lathe it went bang to and fro, my main
    treadle still kept in tune,
My pickers went nicketty-nack all the time
    I was squaring her loom.

My shuttle it still kept in motion, her lams
    she worked well up and down.
The weights in her rods they did tremble;
    she said she would weave a new gown.
My strength now began for to fail me. I
    said: It's now right to a hair.
She turned up her eyes and said: Tommy,
    my loom you have got pretty square.

But when her foreloom-post she let go, it
    flew out of order amain.
She cried: Bring your rule and your level
    and help me to square it again.
I said: My dear lassie, I'm sorry, at Bolton
    I must be by noon,
But when that I come back this way, I will
    square up your jerry hand-loom.

THE WEAVER
AND THE FACTORY MAID

I am a hand-weaver to my trade.
I fell in love with a factory maid,
And if I could but her favour win
I'd stand beside her and weave by steam.

My father to me scornful said:
How could you fancy a factory maid
When you could have girls fine and gay
And dressed like to the Queen of May?

As for your fine girls, I don't care,
And could I but enjoy my dear
I'd stand in the factory all the day
And she and I'd keep our shuttles in play.

I went to my love's bedroom door
Where oftentimes I had been before,
But I could not speak nor yet get in
To the pleasant bed my love laid in.

How can you say it's a pleasant bed
When nowt lies there but a factory maid?
A factory lass although she be,
Blest is the man that enjoys she.

Oh, pleasant thoughts come to my mind
As I turned down the sheets so fine

And I seen her two breasts standing so
Like two white hills all covered with snow.

Where are the girls? I'll tell you plain,
The girls have gone to weave by steam,
And if you'd find 'em you must rise at dawn
And trudge to the mill in the early morn.

4. MACHINERY

THE NEED FOR MACHINERY

[*From a widely circulated pamphlet designed
to combat machine-breaking. The author,
Harriet Martineau, argues the case for factories
with a worker.*]

'Yes, Sir: and it would be all the better if all
the power-looms were done away with.'

'Very well: we will suppose all the machinery
abolished, and you are employed with ninety-
nine more – that your employer sets on a
hundred hands. We will suppose him to begin
when trade is brisk, and times are good. For a
year or so he gives you constant work; the
engineers and carpenters are all gone, and you
hear no more of machinery: so you are quite
contented, and think all the mischief is over,
now that wood and iron no longer do the work
that men ought to do. After a while, however,
your employer's agents write him word that
he is undersold in the markets, and that he
must lower his prices if he means to keep his
trade. He looks round him to see how he can
make a reduction. The materials of his manufacture cannot be had at less cost; so the only
thing he can do is lower your wages. You say
you won't work for lower prices, so you apply
to another manufacturer; but you find he too
has reduced his prices, because he is undersold: and the same with the next you go to,
and the next, and the next. But if all are
undersold, who undersells them? Why, the
foreign manufacturers. "The foreign manufacturers!" you exclaim; "why, we used to
manufacture better than they." Ay, you *used*
to do so; but now they have made great

improvements in their machinery, and can manufacture goods cheaper than we can. How came they to improve the machinery? The English engineers are gone over, and have set up looms like those we pulled down. "O, if that be all," you say, "their prosperity won't last long: they will overstock the markets; and then they must stand still." You find, however, that you have to wait a long time for the turn of affairs. Your employer lowers your wages more and more, and at last turns off half his hands, because his trade falls off. You are more and more pinched by want, till you are also turned off, and your employer ruined. At length, however, you have the satisfaction of hearing that trade is very bad abroad; and you say, "I knew 'twould be so; I said they would overstock the market." Well, in course of time the market is cleared, and you hope your turn is coming at last. But no: when trade revives, the foreigners are just as able as they were before to undersell you; and you find you may wait in vain, for your trade is gone for ever.'

'That's a very bad state of things, Sir, to look forward to.'

'It's just what we have to expect, in my opinion, if we do away with our machinery.'

'But matters would be full as bad, Sir, if we keep up the machinery.'

'I think not. Trade is very bad indeed, at present. But when the market is cleared, the masters will begin to manufacture again, on a small scale. I will suppose you to be employed in a factory with fifty power-loom weavers. Your master's agents write him word that the foreigners cannot come up to us, in the excellence and cheapness of their goods. Your employer accordingly sells all he can make, and, on the whole, at a good profit. He sets on more hands, and increases his number of looms, and at the end of ten years he perhaps employs three or four hundred hands, where he began with only fifty. The other manufacturers get on by the same means, and at the same rate. More and more people are employed; money flows into the kingdom; population increases; commerce is extended; and trade placed on a sure footing. The foundations are laid of real and lasting national prosperity.'

A FACTORY VICTIM

Henry Wooley, the subject of the present engraving, is another victim who has been sacrificed on the altar of Mammon. He exhibits in his person a *beautiful* specimen of the 'fine fruits' of the factory system. Henry Wooley was born at a place called Bolsterstone, in Yorkshire, in the year 1804. At eight years old, he went to work in the factory of the late John and Edward Chadwick, at a place called Park Hall Clough, about half way between Ashton and Staley-bridge, Lancashire. He began as a piecer, and ultimately became a spinner. His hours of work were $14\frac{1}{2}$ a day, exclusive of over time.

For the first six years he stood the system pretty well. At the age of fourteen, his limbs began to grow crooked. They continued to get worse every succeeding year, until he had reached his eighteenth year. He had then become so feeble, from the deformity of his limbs, as to be unable to stand for any length of time; and as his occupation required constant standing, he was obliged to quit it altogether. At this time he was earning four and twenty shillings a week. He had then been ten years in the factory, and had thus served two moderate apprenticeships to a business which he found he was unable to follow, and had to seek a fresh employment, and to learn a new trade. He was, like too many of his class, extremely poor; and the only employment which he could procure was the unhappy one of cotton weaving. He exchanged his one pound four shillings per week for less than half that sum, in order to enable him to exist at all. Yet in the teeth of this and a thousand other similar facts there are men who affect to believe that working in the factory is a peculiarly delightful and refreshing occupation. But for the monstrous factory system, this man would have stood more than six feet high. Even as it is, he measures five feet nine inches. His arms, when extended, measure six feet three and a half inches; and his brother stands six feet four inches. Wooley is now in his 28th year, and at that age, as far as regards agility and strength, is an old man. Here is a man who was intended by nature to be a tall, robust, and athletic figure, converted into a miserable, deformed, and almost helpless cripple, even before he had attained his eighteenth year. Three years before the laws of his country consider him capable of providing for himself, he is rendered unable to do so for the remainder of his life. – And is there to be no inquiry, no atonement for injuries like these? Are men and women and children to be thus destroyed by wholesale, for the benefit of some greedy capitalist, who exultingly puts in his pocket the price of his fellow-creature's ruin, or for the gratification of the 'economists?' Are pensions from the public purse to be profusely heaped upon every bastard of an idle brood, who never touched work in their whole existence, and men like this, who have been sacrificed to the great Moloch of the age, be cast off to perish without pity? But more of this hereafter. Wooley now resides at No 18, Back Style Street, St George's Road, Manchester. – The above spirited engraving is by Mr W. KEELING.

THE FACTORY LAD

[*In this penny-issue novel, Simon Smike is an 'Oliver Twist' figure, abandoned into poverty, and forced to work in a factory. His sister has been raped by the mill-owner, Thorneycroft.*]

What a meeting was that of the two orphans! Years had flown since they last beheld each other; and how much had they both endured in the interim! Sally, for a long time, had lived upon parish mercy – which, at the best, doles out but a scanty pittance. She saw her mother wither and fade into the grave; and she had herself become the victim – the unyielding, resisting victim of a monster's lust. And as for Simon – his tale has already been told: his emaciated body – his sunken eyes – colourless cheeks, and wry limbs – were a sufficient narrative to show how heavily the hand of sorrow had pressed upon him.

There is joy so mingled with grief that one knows not whether to consider it as yielding more gladness than sorrow. It is a feeling which neither subdues nor excites; it places every kindlier impulse of Nature in action: but it so balances the operation of each as to give neither the mastery – until some trifling and apparently irrelevant incident occurs to do so. Such were the undefinable – the mysterious – and yet the oft experienced sensations which actuated the breasts of Sally and Simon at their unexpected meeting. The signal for the mastery of grief over joy was occasioned by the poor lad inquiring for his mother.

Sally's tears almost choked her words; but she contrived, through her sobs, to ask if he did not know she was dead.

No pen can describe what Simon felt: it must be, and it *can* be imagined by those who agree with Sir Anthony Carlisle in their estimate of the sympathies and affections of the needy sons of the soil.

'Suspicion ever haunt the guilty mind.'

Thorneycroft, at some distance from the stocks, discovered Sally and Simon engaged in their mournful interchange of heart-rending intelligence. He hastily returned to the meadow, and calling Tomlinson out of the crowd, directed him to proceed by a circuitous route, which would enable him, unobserved, to station himself near to the two orphans, and hear all that they said. Of course Tomlinson obeyed – and the approaching duskiness of the evening favoured his design.

Before Simon gave utterance to any expression touching his mother's death, Sally led him round to the gate which opened into the churchyard, which was used as a grazing-field for the curate's horse, whose salary was so stinted by the non-resident, plethoric rector, that he, of necessity, led a most abstemious – nay, even mortified – life. Often did the parishioners grumble at beholding the rising hillocks over the bodies of their friends trampled down by this unceremonious clerical Rosinante – for whose special ease, accommodation, and comfort, the various headstones seemed to have been erected as charitable substitutes for rubbing-posts.

Conducting Simon round the chancel Sally led him to the most remote corner of the churchyard, which was shaded by some large trees which hung over the wall from the rector's neglected garden.

That was the pauper's corner, in which neither a stone, nor even an osier-bound hillock, marked the last home of the wretched. ''Twas somewhere here,' said Sally, 'that they laid her.'

But it is not our intention to attempt to picture all that was said and done by the two orphans of whom we are speaking. They sauntered back to the stocks, and each leaned against one of the uprights.

As each narrated their wrongs to the other, both were urged to vengeance; nor were their threats either guarded or measured. Tomlinson was attentively listening to all that passed, and treasuring it up in his mind for repetition to Thorneycroft.

From Sally he heard the history of her violation; while Simon vowed that his hand should yet reap the vengeance due to the gallows.

From Simon, the spy overseer heard a recital of his factory sufferings; for which Sally, in her turn, uttered threats against the heartless cotton-lord.

Words also fell upon this subject from Simon, which showed that a scheme for vengeance had been laid; and that, if Thorneycroft escaped in person, disasters great, unexpected, and irremediable, were about to befall his property.

'Aye,' said Simon, with a malicious jeer, which was the more remarkable after the grief in which he had been plunged; 'and the beauty on it is, as when the job's done, nobody 'ull be up to who did't. There 'ull be the mill, and the big wheels, and all the great work as is in wood and in iron, but it woan't be worth nothin'. It 'ull be like a mill as is dead, and there woan't be no work in't: that's how we 'ull ha' vengeance for cut-heads, blackened bodies, bad grub, pigstye beds, and the worst o' all bad treatment. It 'ud be far better for us to be black *slavies* beyand the sea; we should not be so badly dealt by, nor half.'

[*Shortly afterwards, Simon confronts Thorneycroft at the factory.*]

Simon and Thorneycroft were now the only persons in that room; the seducer and the brother of the seduced. The callous-hearted Thorneycroft thought not of this, and took out his pocketbook to examine certain papers or memoranda. Judge of his surprise when he heard Simon exclaim 'Mr Thorneycroft!'

'Well, I am glad you've come to at last: go on: tell me all,' said the factory lord who expected that he was about to make disclosures. He was, however, quickly undeceived by Simon, who with fury in his countenance, and with an upraised arm, bounded towards him, exclaiming, 'You've ruined my sister – my only sister!'

Before either could utter another word, and at the moment in which Simon had assumed his menacing attitude, Tomlinson re-entered the room, accompanied with Nelson, another of the humane tribe of overseers.

By the time that has elapsed since Simon entered the factory, it will be evident that he was no longer a mere boy. Tis true he was emaciated, careworn, sickly, and warped from the fair form which nature gave him, but he had a noble and daring spirit. Tomlinson knew this, and whilst he would not have feared to heap any indignity or cruelty upon him in the factory when other overseers were at hand, or within call – still he was afraid to have recourse to violence towards him, when he had no one to aid him in resenting resistance. He knew too the hateful feelings which Simon cherished towards Thorneycroft, and that he would not spare any means to satiate his vengeance. Hence he had left the room to procure the aid of Nelson, whilst he resorted to a means most brutal, and yet not new, for extorting a confession from Simon.

'The wretch has threatened me whilst you were away,' said Thorneycroft.

'Oh, we 'ull soon stop that,' was the reply of Tomlinson. He gave a sign previously agreed upon, to Nelson, who instantly seized Simon by the arms and pinned him against the wall.

Tomlinson, in the mean time, used the most tantalising and irritating language towards the prisoner, whom Nelson held with a cruel grasp – and, drawing out of his pocket a small iron vice, he proceeded to screw it tightly on Simon's nose.

Simon made a desperate effort to escape; but so practised was Nelson in operations of such a character, that he could not wrench himself out of his hold.

Every method of cross-questioning and of perplexity was resorted to by the two overseers and their master, to drag a confession out of Simon, but he was proof against all their efforts.

'Well, any how,' said Tomlinson, 'I'll try if I canna screw it out o' thee,' and so saying, he drew out of his jacket pocket a small iron vice, such as are used in various mechanical operations. The weight of it was from two to three pounds, but the power of the *screw* was very great.

Tomlinson eyed Simon with an almost demoniac grin of hatred as he opened the lips or pressure parts of this vice, and held it tauntingly before him, whilst he exclaimed, 'Yes, yes, we 'ull see if we can't *screw* it out of him.'

At this moment a loud shout, as of many youthful voices, was heard in the adjoining yard of the factory. 'Damn 'em, there they go again; they are at it – what can be up wi' 'em now?' said Tomlinson; and then, turning to his master, he said, with a look of enviable self-complacency, 'You see, sir, there's lots o' trouble wi' these chaps. It's no slight work to ha' 'em all in order. Nelson,' continued he, 'step and come tell us what's afoot.'

The reader will no doubt have been puzzled to imagine for what the vice which Tomlinson had produced could be used. Even the explanation will appear scarcely credible. Unhappily, however, it is matter of history. Simon Smike was not the first to whom this instrument of torture was applied. It was used to the unfortunate Robert Blincoe, whose MEMOIR has already been noticed in the course of this narrative. He states therein, that his overseer, in the exuberance of his cruelty, more than once placed him in his frame to work with a small vice screwed on his nose, and to each of his ears. The combined torture of the pressure and the weight was dreadful, and he was left to endure it for hours, and cruelly beaten, if, notwithstanding, he did not pursue his work. When any new kind of cruelty is discovered by some inventive overseer, it seldom remains long confined to the factory in which it was first practised. They were the aristocrats of the thousands who fill the factories, and when they met at the tavern-taps in the evenings, to drink their ale, whilst their wretched sub-ordinates were on their beds of sorrow, each communicated to the other the new mode of torture, the fresh stimulus, or the novel cor-rective, which he might have discovered. There is little doubt that the utility of the *screw-vice*, as a means of compelling young operatives to do as they were desired, had been handed down traditionally among the overseers, from the time of him who applied its power to Robert Blincoe down to the wretch who applied it to Simon Smike. But wherever Tomlinson got the notion, he was well acquainted with the application of the instrument.

Though Nelson had left the room, he no longer feared to encounter Simon, because he was convinced that he would offer no resis-tance, inasmuch as he must be aware that Nelson and others as cruel, as subservient, and as strong, were within call.

He repeatedly put questions to Simon to elicit something from him, but each new effect failed. One *vice* was screwed to one of his ears, and another was located on his nose. When Tomlinson had tightly screwed on the first, and still as he held the jutting bit of iron between his finger and thumb, ready to give it another twitch, he asked Simon if he would 'open;' that is, if he would divulge anything, but Simon still refused. Another vice was placed upon his nose, and a similar course was taken by Tomlinson. Thus it was that the innocent martyrs of old were placed on the rack, and had each limb in succession dislo-cated, unless they would satisfy the curiosity of those who questioned them.

Tomlinson produced his third screw-vice. He was not reluctant to use it, for he saw that the excruciating novelty was welcome, if not amusing to Thorneycroft. That Nero of the factory gazed with savage joy upon the process. – As Tomlinson drew near to Simon to affix the third instrument of torture; whilst he was vehemently threatening him with other and worse punishment unless he made disclosures, and whilst Simon was declaring that he knew nothing and could therefore tell nothing, – Tomlinson and Thorneycroft were astonished at hearing a loud and somewhat peremptory knock at the door. They did not heed it, and it was promptly repeated with more decision than before. – It was still unheeded, and at length the door was opened, and there stood Mr Wartenby, the attorney who had previously interfered in behalf of Sally.

STEAM AT SHEFFIELD

[*In this extract from Ebenezer Elliott's poem blind Andrew Turner is used to convey the sense of energy beneath the vision of the working machinery.*]

Come, blind old Andrew Turner! link in mine
Thy time tried arm, and cross the town with
   me;
For there are wonders mightier far than
   thine;
Watt! and his million-feeding enginery!
Steam-miracles of demi-deity!
Thou can'st not see, unnumber'd chimneys
   o'er,
From chimneys tall the smoky cloud aspire;
But thou can'st hear the unwearied crash
   and roar
Of iron powers, that, urg'd by restless fire,
Toil ceaseless, day and night, yet never tire,
Or say to greedy man, 'Thou dost amiss.'

Oh, there is glorious harmony in this
Tempestuous music of the giant, Steam,
Commingling growl, and roar, and stamp,
   and hiss,
With flame and darkness! Like a Cyclop's
   dream,
It stuns our wondering souls, that start and
   scream
With joy and terror; while, like gold on snow
Is morning's beam on Andrew's hoary hair!
Like gold on pearl is morning on his brow!
His hat is in his hand, his head is bare;
And, rolling wide his sightless eyes, he
   stands
Before this metal god, that yet shall chase
The tyrant idols of remotest lands,
Preach science to the desert, and efface
The barren curse from every pathless place
Where virtues have not yet atoned for
   crimes.
He loves the thunder of machinery!

It is beneficient thunder, though, at time,
Like heaven's red bolt, it lightens fatally.
Poor blind old man! what would he give to
see
This bloodless Waterloo! this hell of wheels:
This dreadful speed, that seems to sleep and
snore,
And dream of earthquake! In his brain he
feels
The mighty arm of mist, that shakes the
shore
Along the throng'd canal, in ceaseless roar
Urging the heavy forge, the clanking mill,
The rapid tilt, and screaming, sparkling
stone.
Is this the spot where stoop'd the ash-crown'd
hill
To meet the vale, when bee-lov'd banks,
o'ergrown
With broom and woodbine, heard the cushat
lone
Coo for her absent love? – Oh, ne'er again
Will Andrew pluck the freckled foxglove
here!
How like a monster, with a league-long
mane,
Or Titan's rocket, in its high career,
Towers the dense smoke! The falcon,
wheeling near,
Turns, and the angry crow seeks purer
skies.

*

Engine of Watt! unrivall'd is thy sway.
Compared with thine, what is the tyrant's
power?
His might destroys, while thine creates and
saves.
Thy triumphs live and grow, like fruit and
flower;
But his are writ in blood, and read on
graves!
Let him yoke all his regimented slaves,
And bid them strive to wield thy tireless fly,
As thou canst wield it. Soon his baffled
bands
Would yield to thee, despite his wrathful
eye.
Lo! unto thee both Indies lift their hands!
Thy vapoury pulse is felt on farthest
strands!

Thou tirest not, complainest not – though
blind
As human pride (earth's lowest dust) art
thou.
Child of pale thought! dread masterpiece of
mind!
I read nor thought nor passion on thy brow!
To-morrow thou wilt labour, deaf as now!
And must we say 'that soul is wanting
here?'

No; there he moves, the thoughtful engineer,
The soul of all this motion; rule in hand,
And coarsely apron'd – simple, plain,
sincere –
An honest man; self-taught to understand
The useful wonders which he built and
plann'd.
Self-taught to read and write – a poor man's
son,
Though poor no more – how would he sit
alone,
When the hard labour of the day was done,
Bent o'er his table, silent as a stone,
To make the wisdom of the wise his own!
How oft of Brindley's deeds th' apprenticed
boy
Would speak delighted, long ere freedom
came!
And talk of Watt! while, shedding tears of
joy,
His widow'd mother heard, and hoped the
name
Of her poor boy, like theirs, would rise to
fame.

THE NEW LONDON RAILWAY

Now folks I will tell you, although I'm no
clown,
By steam you can ride with speed up and
down,
Now that's all the go, I'll tell you for why,
The people are eager to learn for to fly.

chorus

You may travel by steam as the folks say,
All the world over upon the railway.

On the 4th of July you all know well,
What a bustle there was in the morning, I'll tell,
With the lads and young lasses so buxom and gay,
Delighted and talking about the railway.

There's coaches and carts to accommodate all,
The lame and the lazy, the great and the small,
If you wish for a ride, to be sure you must pay,
To see all the fun upon the railway.

To view the railroad away they do go,
'Tis a great undertaking you very well know,
It surpasses all others, believe me its true,
There's tunnels for miles you'll have to go through.

The colliers from Hampton and Bilstos likewise,
And Wedgebury nailors were struck with surprise,
Dress'd up in their best, they cut a fine show,
To see the railroad away they did go.

There's Dumpling Bet, and Jack the Moonraker,
And buxom young Kit, with Butcher and Baker,
And Black Sal from Walsall, with two wooden legs,
To see the railroad how she trudged on her pegs.

What a treat for lovers to Gretna Green,
The blacksmith will tie the knot for them by steam,
With his hammer and anvil he'll make them obey,
Then pack them off snugly upon the railway.

In London I've heard there is a machine
Invented for making young children by steam,
Hatch dear little creatures full 30 per day,
For young engineers to supply the railway.

Talk of ships on the sea – that is all stuff,
By water or land you may ride far enough,

If you have got money your passage to pay,
You may ride far and near upon the railway.

So now my good fellows let us all be free,
Again fill our glasses, and merry we'll be,
Success to all trades in the reign of our Queen,
And the boiling hot water that travels by steam.

To see them come in how the people do flock,
To accommodate all there's lots of fine pop,
And the ladies dress'd up in their costumes so fine,
Partake of good ale, and whiskey so fine.

THE
PRODUCTIONS OF ALL NATIONS!!
ABOUT TO APPEAR AT THE
GREAT EXHIBITION OF 1851.

Specimen of English Home Production

Specimen from the Highlands.

Specimen of Irish Wall Fruit, with a real Native.

Specimen of Italian Manufactured Cardinals for Exportation

Specimen of French Manufactured Articles

Austria having exhibited this Specimen before, we therefore only give a slight sketch in place of the original, Haynau.

Nicholas the Great.

Turkish Preserves.

Specimen from Amsterdam.

Specimen from Hong Kong—a Mandarine.

Specimen from the Sandwich Islands.

London :—Printed and Published by H. ELLIOT, 475, New Oxford Street ; WINN, Holywell Street ; COLLINS, Fleet Street ; and Sold by all Booksellers in Town and Country—PRICE ONE PENNY.

" The Three Pillars of Popery," also, "Popery in Power," are still on sale, and can be had of all Booksellers. Just published, the " Anti-Popish Litany," to be said in all Protestant Churches and Chapels. May be had of all Booksellers, Price 1. Now Publishing, The Extraordinary Fight, between the Westminster Cardinal and Jack Cumming, of Crown Court, (alias, The Protestant Champion,) for an immense stake, with two beautiful Engravings. Price 1d.

Scene the First.

THE EXHIBITION OPENED

John Smith, in town,
to his cousin, in the country.

DEAR JESSIE, – I am glad that you were pleased with my last letter respecting the opening of the Great Exhibition; and, in accordance with your desire, I proceed to gossip on about it in another epistle. You wish to know what I saw after the Queen and her suite had left the place. Well, then, I will tell you; but you must expect nothing more than the most faint idea; for so vast and sublime is the building, and so many are the thoughts engendered by its magnificence and the beauty and variety of its contents, that I find it difficult to analyse and arrange my ideas respecting it. You know, of course, that it is 1,851 feet long, 458 feet wide, and 66 feet high at its greatest elevation – that is, under the transept; but how shall I convey to you the idea of its actual enormous dimensions? Well, then, you recollect, when you were in London last summer, we visited the Bank of England. Allowing for the difference of shape, the Bank of England might stand within the glass walls of the Crystal Palace! I walked from end to end of the principal avenue, and I found it just 719 of my steps; you, being a short, natty little body, may perhaps make about thirty more steps than I should: therefore, if you walk about 750 paces across the meadow at the back of the cottage, and look at the spot whence you started, you will get at the length of the building. But then, being entirely covered in, and having a double row of galleries, which increases the walking space by more than half, and being filled in every part with splendid specimens of the world's industry, it appears even larger than it actually is; and so great is the distance from one end to the other, that all pre-formed ideas of distance and perspective are quite at fault. Sound, too, is apparently lost and oblivionised in this giant building; for when, at six o'clock, the great bell at the western end of the palace tolled for the departure of the visitors, though it almost cracked your ears when standing beside it, the sound of its giant tongue was not heard at the other end of the

eastern gallery. In fact, the more I try to give you an idea of the appearance of the interior, the more am I perplexed, so totally is it unlike anything of which we have had previous knowledge or acquaintance. The lights, too, and the varied effects of sunshine and shade upon the covered glass roof and elegantly painted iron ribs which span and arch the fairy-like construction, are quite magical in their beauty and novelty. Never was Aladdin palace of Eastern story equal, in magnificence and variety of outline, to this great conservatory in Hyde Park.

But if I go on in this strain of praise, you will take me for a novel writer instead of a plain draper's shopman; so, putting aside all hyperbolical expressions, – two rather long words – I will endeavour to tell you a few of the things which I saw, in as plain prose as the nature of the subject will allow. And, for the matter of that, Jessie, I think there is more real, earnest, downright poetry in this meeting of the nations – in this peaceful contest of industry and pleasant rivalry of trade – in this neutral ground, where peer and peasant, prince and mechanic, Queen and people, meet and fraternise – than in all the love-verses which you and I have ever read together under the elm tree in the garden.

What with trees and flowers, fountains and statues, music, models, furniture, looking-glasses, groups of rare things in nature and art, incongruous yet accordant, in transept, nave, and galleries – what with bright colours and graceful forms, in iron, and wood, and stone, and silk and cotton, of many-shaped fancy and varied contour – what, too, with the gaiety which the thousand visitors throw upon the scene, enlivened by many a bright glance and laughter-loving face filled with curious, wondering expression – one is fairly in a waking dream of magnificence and grandeur. But don't be jealous, Jessie. I thought, in all this splendid show, how much more I should have enjoyed it had Somebody I know been leaning on my arm.

Entering the transept from the south door, opposite the Prince's Gate at Knightsbridge, you come at once upon the grandest sight conceivable. Right before you, overshadowed by giant trees at either end, are statues, and elegant iron gates, and palms and flowers in rich profusion; while in the centre of the whole, right in the front of the throne on which sat the Majesty of the empire on which the sun never sets, the great crystal fountain bubbles, and splashes, and shines, and glitters, and throws about and around it rays of living light, like nothing ever seen before in wildest dreams of night or phantasies of most luxuriant imagination. Turn which way you will, new wonders meet the eye, and newer forms of beauty greet the astonished senses. On the right are the treasures of the Celestial Empire, China, and Greece, and Turkey, and Persia, and Egypt, and Tunis. Further on, in the same direction, the industry of France, and Austria, and Italy, and Germany, and Russia, and Belgium, and the great nation of the West, the yet half-peopled New World of America, takes palpable shape and substance in a myriad strange and varied ways, – in natural productions and the fruits of national handiwork – in gorgeous statues and simple handicraft – in mineral treasures and striking contrasts; while on the left the great kingdom of India, and yet greater, because more civilised and powerful, home of the all-conquering Briton, shows forth in ten thousand forms the utility of labour and the triumph of mind.

As the eye is incapable of taking in the whole scene before it, so is the mind unable to grasp and comprehend the entire value and importance of the magnificent show within these walls. Contrasts accumulate – beauty grows more beautiful – rare sights and unfamiliar objects give new ideas to the mind – the hum and bustle of the moving throng – the sounds of music ever and anon floating through the air – the distant whirr of moving wheels and flying spindles, no more observable than the burr of the bees in the old garden at home – and the newness, freshness, activity, and order of all around contribute each in its own way to give to this great industrial hive a character and similitude never before witnessed perhaps in the whole world.

As you pass through the great central avenue, the stamp of the genius of the people of each country contributing is plainly visible. On the British side are articles of utility – great sections of trees, giant looking-glasses,

stone fountains, heaps of rich silk woven at Spitalfields, machines, models of towns, bridges, and tunnels, and the wonderful iron dome from Colebrook-dale; on the east, or foreign side, on the contrary, are to be seen beautiful statues, an elegant painted window, exquisite specimens of workmanship in gold and silver, and the great Indian diamond, called the Mountain of Light, enclosed in an iron-gilt cage, and secured by Chubbs' patent lock. This exquisite jewel is as large as a pigeon's egg, and is said to be worth a million of money. In the same cage are two others, about half the size, but quite as bright and sparkling. Oh, the eyes that twinkled round this spot – you can have no idea, Jessie!

As the eye gets accustomed to the wonders all around, it has leisure soon to examine more particularly the contents of certain compartments, and I will endeavour, ere I close my letter, to give a faint idea of one section of the building – the north western – that containing the carriages, railway trains, locomotives, and machines in motion. I know not whether you will be quite so interested as I was in this portion of the show; but as I shall write again on other things to be seen, you will not be uninterested in the description of some few of the wonders observable in this department.

Besides carriages of all descriptions, – from the aristocratic satin-lined chariot of a queen to the humble gig of the tradesman – there are here railway carriages on iron rails, steam-engines and boilers, and various working models of new and patent inventions in the useful arts. Here I saw what I have often read about, and once examined in a factory at Manchester – large machines for making cotton cloth. These are wonderful indeed, and serve to show what may be accomplished by the union of mind and industry. The whole process of cotton-spinning is here shown in motion; and though I despair of giving you a description of even one machine, I will endeavour to tell you something of the contents of this, to me, most interesting of all the sights in the Crystal Palace.

As soon as you enter the room, your ears are greeted with strange noises of whirling wheels, and for some minutes you are lost in wonder and amazement; but soon your attention is fixed on, perhaps, one machine. It is what is called a power-loom. This, you are aware, is used for the manufacture of cotton-yarn. Beside it is an old dirty-looking machine, made fifty years since; and the contrast between it and the plain though elegantly fitted machine of modern times is great indeed. And then in this end of the room are self-acting mules, carding engines, spindles and flyers, roving frames, looms for weaving, throstle frames, and, in fact, a number of machines used in the manufacture of cotton, with such curious names as would puzzle you if I were to give them. All these, and various other like instruments, are driven by machinery; the boiler for the numerous large and small steam-engines having its home in a building all to itself, outside the walls of the Exhibition Palace. You would be interested in observing the dexterity with which the little girls, imported from Manchester for the express purpose, join the broken ends of the cotton together, as they walk to and fro before the ever-twisting mules; but probably you like better to see the stocking-frame, and the stockinger from Nottingham at work before it; or the patent sewing-machine, which works with two threads, and bids fair to supersede in some measure the labours of the needlewoman.

Passing from the region of cotton-spinning, flax-preparing, weaving, winding, and throwing, I come to where the wonderful printing machine (invented by Applegarth for the proprietor of the *Times*), attracts its crowd of spectators. Differing from all the other machines exhibited for steam printing, in the fact of its being capable of throwing off ten thousand copies an hour, and in the more curious fact of the type being fixed round a vertical cylinder instead of lying on a horizontal metal bed, as in the others, this clever contrivance promises to supersede all other contrivances for rapid newspaper printing.

Then there is a machine for cutting card-boards into cards for printing, and another which cuts, prints, numbers, and packs tickets in an orderly and regular style quite pleasant to behold. You have heard, no doubt, of the envelope folding machine, invented by Mr. Hill, the brother of the Post-office Reformer. It is a clever contrivance, which folds and gums the sides of the envelopes as fast as a boy can place the paper in its proper position. But there is an even more clever contrivance still, in which the labour of the boy is superseded, for the machine only requires a heap of open envelopes to be placed in a certain position, and it feeds itself; and not only does it gum and fold the envelope, but it actually embosses the coloured die or stamp, so that nothing is left but to dry and pack them ready for use.

To give you an idea of the number of engines and tools, pumps and mills, lathes and cylinders, sugar-cane crushers, centrifugal pumps, planing, boring, drilling, and cutting apparatus, which cuts, smooths, bends, twists, and turns about iron and brass as though they were cheese; to talk to you of machines for making ropes, biscuits, and soda water; for roasting coffee, corking bottles, grinding corn, cutting blocks of stone, blasting mines, drawing water from mines, rolling iron and lead into thin plates, or dressing flour, would be sheer madness: you must come and see them for yourself. Neither can I explain to you the strength and magnificence of beam engines, hydraulic machines, disc and oscillating steam-engines, railway bars, sawing, paper-making, gas-measuring, and brick-making contrivances – much less convey to you a clear idea of the immensity and power exhibited in these varied and curious products of genius. You must come to London yourself. And besides, I am forgetting that you, like most other young ladies, will prefer the bright colour of flowers and the rustle of rich dresses, to the whirr and incessant buzz of a great machine-room like this – eight hundred feet long, and nearly two hundred wide; so I will, till next week, conclude by hoping I have not tired your patience.

By the way, I understand that there were thirty thousand persons in the Exhibition on the opening day: it looked as if it would hold four times as many, and not inconvenience a single person. At a later visit I was enabled to make, I was informed that the building would hold, in galleries and avenues, about eighty thousand people. London is full, folks say;

but I do not observe that the streets are more
crowded than usual in May, or that any one
is inconvenienced in the least. If any of our
friends in the country are coming to London
and want lodgings, I should advise them to
consult the classified list kept in the office of
No. 8, Exeter Change, in which they will not
only ascertain the situation of the best private
lodgings, but also discover the prices they
will have to pay. Believe me, yours,   J.S.

A REVERIE ABOUT
THE CRYSTAL PALACE

by the author of 'Proverbial Philosophy'

Dream of splendour, bright and gay,
  Disenchanted all too soon,
Dimly fading fast away
  Like a half remembered tune, –
Lo! my spirit's harp is sad
  For the end of earthly things,
And refuses to be glad
  While I touch these trembling strings.

Fountains, gushing silver light,
  Sculptures, soft and warm and fair,
Gems, that blind the dazzled sight,
  Silken trophies rich and rare,
Wondrous works of cunning skill,
  Precious miracles of art, –
How your crowding memories fill
  Mournfully my musing heart!

Fairy Giant! choicest birth
  Of the Beautiful Sublime,
Seeming like the Toy of earth
  Given to the dotard Time, –
Glacier-diamond, Alp of glass,
  Sindbad's cave, Aladdin's hall, –
Must it then be crush'd, alas;
  Must the Crystal Palace fall?

Yes; – as autumn's chequered hues
  Thus are tinted with – decay,
As the morn's prismatic dews
  Glittering – exhale away,
So, with thee; in beauty's pride
  All thy brightness must depart, –

Nature's fair consumptive bride,
  Fragile paragon of Art!

But, Not all of thee shall die;
  O not all shall perish thus!
Thy sweet spirit ever nigh
  Will remain to gladden us, –
Thy sweet spirit – *Brotherhood!*
  This was in thee like a Soul,
Every Part to gild with good,
  And to glorify the Whole!

5. DOMESTIC

THE PAWNSHOP BLEEZIN'

Wor Sall was kaimin' oot her hair,
  An' aw was turnin' dosy,
Whiles snot'rin' in wor easy chair,
  That myeks a chep sleep cosy,
When frae the street cam screams an' cries –
Wor Sall says 'Wheest!' aw rubs my eyes;
An' marcy! shoots o' 'Fire!' aw hears –
Aw myeks yen lowp doon a' wor stairs,
  An' smash, aw seed a queerish seet,
  Yel thousands crooded i' the Street –
  It was the Pawnshop bleezin'.

The wimmin folks 'twas sair to see
  Lamentin' their distresses;
For mony a goon, an' white shemee,
  Was burnt wi' bairns' dresses;
Peg Putty stamp'd an' cried, 'Oh, dear,
Wor Geordey's breeks is gyen, aw fear;
Maw bonny shawl an' Bella's frock –'
Says Betty Mills, 'An' there's wor clock,
  An' a' maw bits o' laddies' claes –
  My pillowslips an' pair o' stays –
  Is in the Pawnshop bleezin'.'

A dowpy wife wi' *borrow'd fat*,
  An' wiv a puggy beak, man,
Cam pushin' wiv her bonnet flat,
  And puffin oot her cheeks, man;
Ye niver seed sic bullet eyes –
Her screams aw thowt wad splet the skies;
'Oh Lord! maw babbie's things is gyen!
Maw unborn babe hes claes noo nyen!

A

Hint to Husbands & Wives

Or, an entertaining Dialogue between a Man & his Wife in this neighbourhood concerning Housekeeping.

Husband. BRING me my holiday clothes, and give me half-a-crown to put in my pocket that I may appear like another man, for I have got an invitation card to spend this evening at a Free and Easy.

Wife.—Why, Charles, I have but one sixpence in the world, and I wonder how you can expect me to have more, when you know I am paying weekly for the childrens' shoes, and you know I buy every thing to the best advantage

Husband.—What! only sixpence left, and I bring you twenty shillings a week whilst many of our neighbours bring home only fifteen; besides we have but five children, and the two youngest cannot destroy a great deal

Wife.—Well, my dear, I do not wish to contradict you, as it often brings on strife, but as I know you to be a man that will hear reason, I will reckon things up to you, that you may know what I have to pay.

Husband.—Well, Sally, it is what I never did do, but as it is your proposal, begin your reckoning, and I shall convince you that you have about five shillings to spare.

Wife.—Well, Charles, in the first place there is 8 quartern loaves, that is 4s. 8d.,—then there is 9lb. of meat which is 4s. 6d., that is only 1lb. per day, and 3lb. for Sunday.

Husband.—Well, my dear, that is not half of twenty shillings yet.

Wife.—Stop, Charles, you have not half the expences yet: There is 1s. 6d. per week at least for potatoes & greens, and 1¼d for pot-herbs, tea 1s., sugar 1s. 3d., candles 6d., soap 7d., starch and blue 1d., wood, 2d., herrings 2d., which you will have on a Sunday morning, and your tobacco 9¼d., and 2 half-pints of beer which is all I allow myself during the week.

Husband.—Well, Sally, I find all these articles amount to 15s. and 6d. it is as I expected, that you would have four shillings and sixpence to spare.

Wife.—But stop my dear, then there is 3s. for rent, and firing 1s. 6d., which makes just the money.

Husband.—Oh! the rent and firing, I had quite forgot.

Wife.—Now, Charles, let me ask you what is to cloathe us, and buy other little articles which I have not mentioned.

Husband.—Say no more, take back my holiday clothes, bring me pen, ink, and paper, that I may publish the house expences as a hint to others, being certain that no person knows what money it takes, except those that have the laying of it out.

—◄●►—

J. Catnach, Printer, 2, Monmouth-court, 7 Dials.

A COMICAL AND DIVERTING DIALOGUE,

Between a Farmer, a Butcher, a Miller, a Publican, a Tea-Dealer, a Cheesemonger, a Milkman, a Baker, a Brewer, a Churchwarden, and their old Friend the DEVIL.

THE other evening, as I walked by the market p'ace, I chanced to step into a public house, where I heard the following curious conversation:—

Farmer.

Welcome, brother, we are met to enjoy the benefit arising from the price of our markets. It is a pleasant prospect. Though my barns are breaking down with corn, I won't abate a farthing. Keep it up, what is the cry of the poor to us? Nonsense. Although we've had a good harvest I am the man that will stick to my price. How could I drink wine, my daughters wear silk pelisses, dandy bonnets, go to the French hobby-horse school, and learn French music, if that were not the case!

Brewer.

Well done! we are all in the same mess. Who would think that I put composition in my beer!

Miller.

My good friends I fear our reign will soon be over, though I have done all in my power to grind the poor. What shall I do with my flour, that is ready to run away with the maggots? The poor man must in a short time have a large loaf for sixpence, and I shall hang myself in my garters, and no one will cut me down.

Publican.

Upon my conscience you're all after my own heart; for when a company sits down, I generally take a snack, and chalk up two for one.

Baker.

Stop, brother, let me have a share with you. You praise yourselves for starving the poor, I play my part better; besides, I have a double advantage over you, I can mix my flour with potatoes, bean meal, bone dust, alum, and other things.

Grocer.

That's right, keep the game alive, I mix beans with coffee, and sloe leaves with tea.

Cheese-monger.

Talk as you like, gentlemen, you cannot out-do me in cheating the public: I make butter out of kitchen stuff, and new laid eggs come from over the water.

Milkman.

To call you, sir, a rogue, but who can beat me at deception! I milk my cows at night, and my pump in the morning; if it is too blue I put in plenty of chalk, as well as in my customers scores. There's a trick, my boys.

Butcher.

That's right, we have it in our own hands, who is to control us? Drop our prices indeed! When I go to a fair, I can spend my money like a king, and ride on a good horse; my wife has French lace in the tail of her gown, better than the squire's lady. What are the poor to us? let them go without meat, if they can't pay the price; potatoes and red herrings are good enough for them.

Church-warden.

We get several girls to swear themselves with child by their masters, whom we know to have plenty of rhino. To hide the matter from their wives, they give us 20l. So we share ten, and spend the other ten on a jolly good dinner.——But who is that strange gentleman in black, that has taken the chair?

The Old Man.

It is I, my darling prick-eared sons; it glads my heart to hear you play your parts so well. Though the barns and warehouses are breaking down with all kinds of grain, never mind. Grind the poor, starve the nation; I assist you all: teach your children the same lesson, and if they will not learn, knock about their dumpling skulls. Dear children, did you but know the joy you give me and my race, and others of your former friends and acquaintance, whom I have at home, you would participate in my good success, and I will try to make room for you all, though pretty full with Farmers, Graziers, Butchers, Bakers, Monopolizers, Forestallers, Grocers, Brewers, &c. I must try to make room for you all.

(Here the landlord came to say it was past 12 o'Clock. The chairman left the chair with promises of future support, & the company separated.)

An Excellent New SONG.

SUCH an age as we live in must needs be confest,
In the days of old Noll, was ne'er known such distress
The parishes they've so severe grown of late,
The poor won't relieve till almost dead at their gate.

If a man for relief to his parish should go,
Quite naked, distrest, and relate his sad woe,
Mr. Gripe, the churchwarden, cries prithee begone,
You are able to work, relief for you there's none.

If a poor woman to them for help should apply,
With her children lamenting for bread they do cry,
Tho' her goods are all siezed, her rent for to pay,
With her babes in the street she is forced straightway.

Mr. Dip, the overseer, blabbers again,
you're a hearty stout hussey, 'tis no use to complain,
To your back take your bastards, dismiss now I pray,
Or to bridewell we'll send you, without more delay.

So indiscriminate are these wretches, I vow,
To either sex or age any pity will shew,
But Old Nick he one day will pay off their old score,
A reward to those who grind the face of the poor.

To see these great dons, when together they meet,
Says Gripe unto Dip, now for a parish treat,
And Swill-tub he swears he'll not flinch in the least,
To shake hands with a bottle at a good parish feast.

Printed by J. Catnach, 2, Monmouth-court

An' when wor Billy finds it oot,
There'll murder be, aw hae nee doot;
 Oh dear! what garr'd me put them in?
 'Twas a' the races an' curs'd gin –
 That set my claes a-bleezin'.'

'Oh, marcy, aw'll be hammer'd tee;'
 Cries Orange Jinny, blairin';
'Aw popp'd Ned's suit te hae a spree,
 But suen aw'll get me fairin', –
He thinks, poor sowl, his claes is reet,
He'll want yen suit o' Friday neet –
What mun aw dee? aw wadent care,
But, hinnies, watch an' seal is there;
 An' warse an' warse; he'll quickly knaw,
 That earrings, weddin' ring an' a'
 Is in the Pawnshop bleezin'!'

Lang Skipper Jack, wi' mony a sweer,
 Cam laingerin' up the Side, man,
Says he, 'What's a' the matter, here?
 Noo, here's a bonny tide, man!
Why, marrows, sure it cannit be,
This isn't Trotter's place aw see?'
So oot his baccy fob he tuik,
Hawled oot some *tickets* frae a buik:
 'Why sink the sowls of a' the lot;
 Aye, d—n the yel scrape's gyen to pot,
 There's a' maw fortin bleezin'!'

The yells, an' blairs, an' curses lood,
 And cries o' stupefaction:
An' bits o' bairns amang the crood,
 Increased the mad distraction;
Aye, mony a wife will rue the day
She put her husband's things away;
An' men will groan wi' bitter grief –
(For Pawnshop law hes ne relief) –
 To find their labour, toil, an' pain,
 To 'pear like decent foaks is vain –
 There a' their goods is bleezin'!

The world was better far aw'm sure,
 When Pawnshops had ne neym, man:
When poor folks could their breed procure,
 Withoot a *deed o' shyem*, man!
Ther Boxes luik like cuddies' stalls;
There's hell-fire in ther hollow balls;
Their gains is large, wor chance is sma –
They often's get wor pledges a' –
 Just like the plagues ov Egypt sent,
 They banish peace an' calm content –
 Aw wish they a' were bleezin'.

PAUPER'S DRIVE

There's a grim horse hearse at a jolly round
 trot.
To the churchyard a pauper is going, I wot,
The road it is rough, the hearse has no
 springs,
And hark to the dirge the sad driver sings,
Rattle his bones over the stones,
He's only a pauper whom nobody owns.

Oh! where are the mourners? alas there are
 none,
He has left not a gap in the world now he's
 gone.
Not a tear in the eye of child, woman, or
 man,
To the grave with his carcase as fast as you
 can.
Rattle his bones, over the stones,
He's only a pauper whom nobody owns.

What a jolting and cracking and splashing
 and din,
The whip how it cracks, the wheels how they
 spin!
How the dirt right and left o'er the hedges
 is hurl'd
The pauper at length makes a noise in the
 world.
Rattle his bones over the stones,
He's only a pauper whom nobody owns.

But a truce to this strain, for my soul it is
 sad,
To think that a heart in humanity clad,
Should make, like the brute, such a desolate
 end
And depart from the world without leaving
 a friend.
Bear softly his bones over the stones,
Though a pauper, he's one whom his Maker
 yet owns.

THE WORKHOUSE AND THE RICH

Alas! that New Year's Day was one of strange
contrasts in the social sphere of London.
 And as London is the heart of this empire,
the disease which prevails in the core is conveyed through every vein and artery over the
entire national frame.

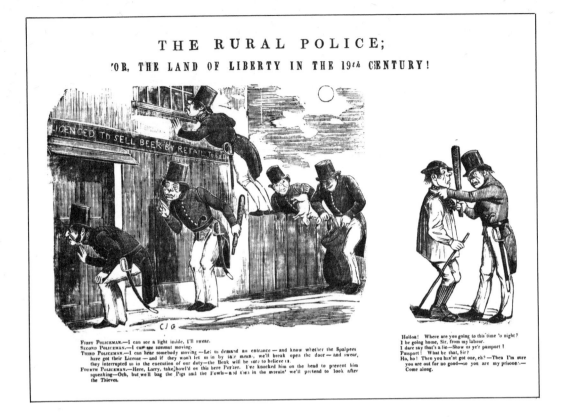

THE RURAL POLICE;
OR, THE LAND OF LIBERTY IN THE 19th CENTURY!

FIRST POLICEMAN.—I can see a light inside. I'll swear.
SECOND POLICEMAN.—I can see summut moving.
THIRD POLICEMAN.—I can hear somebody moving—Let us demand an entrance — and know whether the Spalpees have got their License — and if they won't let us in by fair means, we'll break open the door — and swear, they interrupted us in the execution of our duty—the Beak will be sure to believe us.
FOURTH POLICEMAN.—Here, Larry, take hould ov this here Per'zer. I've knocked him on the head to prevent him squeaking—Och, but we'll bag the Pigs and the Fowls—and then in the mornin' we'll pretend to look after the Thieves.

Holloa! Where are you going to this time 'o night?
I be going home, Sir, from my labour.
I dare say that's a lie—Show us ye'r passport!
Passport! What be that, Sir?
Ho, ho! Then you hav'nt got one, eh?—Then I'm sure you are out for no good—so you are my prisone:—Come along.

The country that contains the greatest wealth of all the territories of the universe, is that which also knows the greatest amount of hideous, revolting, heart-rending misery.

In England men and women die of starvation in the streets.

In England women murder their children to save them from a lingering death by famine.

In England the poor commit crimes to obtain an asylum in a gaol.

In England aged females die by their own hands, in order to avoid the workhouse.

There is one cause of all these miseries and horrors – one fatal scourge invented by the rich to torture the poor – one infernal principle of mischief and of woe, which has taken root in the land – one element of a cruelty so keen and so refined, that it outdoes the agonies endured in the Inquisition of the olden time.

And this fertile source of misery, and murder, and suicide, and crime, is –

THE TREATMENT OF THE WORKHOUSE.

Alas! when the bees have made the honey, the apiarist comes and takes all away, begrudging the industrious insects even a morsel of the wax!

Let us examine for a moment the social scale of these realms:

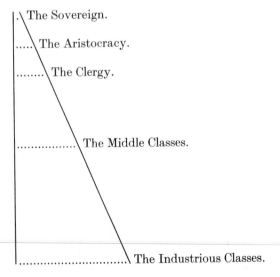

. The Sovereign.

..... The Aristocracy.

.... The Clergy.

.... The Middle Classes.

.... The Industrious Classes.

The lowest step in the ladder is occupied by that class which is the most numerous, the most useful, and which ought to be the most influential.

The average annual incomes of the individuals of each class are as follows:–

The Sovereign ....£500,000.
The member of the Aristocracy   £30,000.
The Priest............................. £7,500.
The member of the middle classes   £300.
The member of the industrious
classes................................   £20.

Is this reasonable? is this just? is this even consistent with common sense?

It was New Year's Day, 1839.

The rich man sat down to a table crowded with every luxury: the pauper in the workhouse had not enough to eat. The contrast may thus be represented:–

Turtle, venison, turkey, hare, pheasant, perigord-pie, plum-pudding, mince-pies, jellies, blanc-manger, trifle, preserves, cakes, fruits of all kinds, wines of every description.	½ lb. bread. 4 oz. bacon. ½lb. potatoes. 1½ pint of gruel.

And this was New Year's Day, 1839!

SONG

Tune – *Robin Adair*

Child, is thy father dead?
  Father is gone!
Why did they tax his bread?
  God's will be done!
Mother has sold her bed;
  Better to die than wed!
Where shall she lay her head?
  Home we have none!

Father clamm'd thrice a week –
  God's will be done!
Long for work did he seek,
  Work he found none.

Tears on his hollow cheek
Told what no tongue could speak:
Why did his master break?
  God's will be done!

Doctor said air was best –
  Food we had none;
Father, with panting breast,
  Groan'd to be gone:
Now he is with the blest –
Mother says death is best!
We have no place of rest –
  Yes, ye have one!

THE CHARTER

When thrones shall crumble and moulder to
    dust,
  And sceptres shall fall from the hands of
    the great,
And all the rich baubles a Monarch might
    boast,
  Shall vanish before the good sense of a
    state;
When Lords, (produced by the mandate of
    Kings),
  So proud and dominant, rampant with
    power,
Shall be spoken of only as by-gone things
  That shall blast this part of creation no
    more,
Based firm upon truth, the Charter shall
    stand
The land-mark of ages – sublimely grand!

When class-distinctions shall wither and die,
  And conscious merit shall modestly bear
The garlands wrought by its own industry,
  The proper rewards of labour and care;
When man shall rise to his station as man,
  To passion or vice no longer a slave;
When the *march of mind* already begun,
  Shall gathering roll like a vast mountain
    wave,
The Charter shall stand the text of the free,
Of a Nation's rights the sure guarantee.

So long as tyrannic oppression is found
  To come as a blight o'er the face of the
    earth;

THE
NEW POOR LAW BILL
IN FORCE.

All round the country there is a pretty piece of work
All round the country against poor people's will,
Feeble. and borne down with grief,
They ask the Parish for relief,   (Law Bill.
They tell you to go home and try to learn the Poor

CHORUS.

*Now, if a man has got a Wife and seven Children Starving, Distress
should only seize him, he his got no work to do, and if to the Overseers
go, Ground down with Sorrow, Grief, and Woe, they will tell you to go
home and try to learn the Poor Law Bill.*

SPOKEN.—Now, Mr. Blubberhead the Beadle,
fetch in the Overseers' and Churchwardens 12 bottles
of the best Port Wine, yes Sir, and Blubberhead, is
there any Vagrants outside wants examining? why,
Sir, there is a wonderful lot of people outside, and I
think they are all Bones, for there is very little flesh
upon them.---Now, Mr. Blubberhead, the Beadle,
let in one of those Rascals - -Who are you pray,
Why Sir, my name is John Pineway, who is been ill
Seventeen long months, I have a Wife Confined, and
eight Children Starving.---Well, what odds is that to
me? Go home and sell your bed   I have no bed;
I sleep upon straw. Well, poor man. I pity you.—
When had you any food? Last Saturday, Sir. Mr.
Blubberhead. Yes, Sir. Get a truck and put this
old man and his family into it, and have them removed to the New Workhouse. Put the man in 114
cell, and the woman in 395 ward; and take the children six miles from thence, and tell them not to let
them see each other for once in six months.

Now (if a man has got a Wife, &c.

SPOKEN.—Now, Mr. Blubberhead, let in another.
Who are you, pray? Why. Sir, my name is Bill
Fastamonth. Aye, and I expect you will have to fast
three months. How old are you? 122 next Friday
week. Where is your wife? She is dead, Sir And

why did not you die too, you good-for-nothing old
son of a rascal?-- because nobody would not kill me.
Mr. Blubberhead, yes Sir, get a barrow and tie this
old man to the legs of it. and tell Tom Sweatwell, to
drive him to the New Workhouse, sixteen miles off,
and tell him when he comes back he shall have a
basin of water Gruel for his trouble.

Now (if a man has got a Wife, &c.

Now Mr. Blubberhead, is there any likelihood of a
rest outside? why Sir, there is old Bellyskin a bones,
and old Peter Broken Back grumbling. Put them in
the Stocks side by side till to-morrow, at Eleven
o'Clock, and they shall have three months each at the
Treadmill. Let in another. Who are you ma'am?
why Sir, my name is Jenny Frolicksome, and you
appear in a Frolicksome way? yes Sir I am very
queer. so it seems, who is the Father of it? Blubberhead the Beadle, Sir, the deuce he is, is that true
Blubberhead? perhaps so Sir, then kick her out. and
how much is your pay One Pound per week. well
for the future it shall be Thirty Shillings, thank he Sir,
Let in another, who are you ma'am? Why Sir, my
name is Betsy Begenough, so it seems, have you the
dropsy, why, why, why, why the devil don't you
speak up, Sir, I am, I am, I am, What are you?
I am in the family way, Sir, the devil you are.
Are you not ashamed of yourself? No Sir, the
devil you are not. Who is the Father of it? Blubberhead, the beadle Sir, Where did he get it? Behind the tombstone in the church-yard, Sir. Kick
her out Blubberhead, and for the future your salary
shall be two guineas per week. Thankee, Sir.

Now (if a man has got a Wife &c.

SPOKEN.—Now. Mr. Blubberhead, let in another.
Who are you Ma'am? Why sir, my name is Mary
Neversweat. What the devil do you want? Why
sir, my husband is very ill, and I have nine children
starving. Who sent you here? The magistrate.
Mr. Blubberhead, send all the paupers and vagrants
home to their homes; and them that has got no
homes must go, to Farmer snuffnose's cart-house to
sleep; and take this old man and his wife in our dung
cart to the New Workhouse. Put the man in 116
cell, and the woman in 394 ward, and take the children to the barn twelve miles from there, and tell
them not to let them see each other for once in two
years, for we must enforce the rule of the New Poor
Law bill.

Sharp, Printer, 30, Kent Street, Borough.

To spread its devastating influence round,
  And nip 'patient merit' e'en in its birth;
So long as we see in meagre array,
  The demons of want and misery and woe,
In their direst forms stalk forth at noon-day,
  Spreading havoc and death in their track
    as they go!
The Charter shall shine the pole-star bright,
The hope of these victims of 'might against
  right'.

So long as Justice impartially spreads
  The savour of truth o'er discord and strife;
So long as kindly benevolence sheds
  Her halo divine on the dark path of life;
So long as the thrice-hallow'd sacred fires
  Of 'love of country' burns in the breast;
So long as the impulse virtue inspires
  Shall lead to relieve and support the
    oppress'd;
So long shall the Charter be deeply engrav'd
On the high-beating hearts of millions
  enslav'd!

TO THE WEST

To the West, to the West, to the land of the
  free,
  Where mighty Missouri rolls down to the
    sea,
Where a man is a man, if he is willing to
  toil,
  And the humblest may gather the fruits
    of the soil:
Where children are blessings, and he who
  has most,
  Has aid for his fortunes and riches to
    boast.
Where the young may exult and the aged
  may rest,
  Away, far away, to the land of the West.

chorus

To the west, to the west, to the land of the
  free,
  Where mighty Missouri rolls down to the
    sea,
Where the young may exult and the aged
  may rest,
  Away, far away, to the land of the West.

To the West, to the West, where the rivers
  that flow,
  Run thousands of miles spreading out as
    they go,
Where the green waving forest shall echo
  our call,
  As wide as old England and free for us
    all.
Where prairies like seas where the billows
  have rolled,
  As broad as the kingdoms and empires of
    old;
And the lakes are the oceans in storm and
  in rest,
  Away, far away, to the land of the west.

To the West, the West, there is wealth to
  be won,
  The forest to clear is the work to be done;
We'll try it – we'll do it – and never dispair!
  While there's life in the sunshine and
    breath in the air.
The bold independence that labour shall
  buy,
  Shall strengthen our hands and forbid us
    to sigh,
Away, far away, let us hope for the best,
  And build up a house in the land of the
    West.

6. SPORT

GREAT FIGHT FOR THE CHAMPIONSHIP BETWEEN SPRING AND LANGAN

*For Three Hundred Sovereigns a side,
at Worcester, on Wednesday last.*

The Grand Stand was filled to an overflow in
every part, with two additional wings or
scaffolds *erected* for the occasion. Ten shillings
each were paid for the admission of each
person. The masts of the vessels in the river
Severn, which flowed close behind, moored on
each side of the Stand, were overloaded with
persons; and even temporary scaffolds about

two stories high, outside of the waggons, were filled by anxious spectators, regardless of danger, so great was the public curiosity excited by this event. It was a beautiful sight, indeed: let the reader picture to himself a spacious amphitheatre, encircled by waggons; an outer roped-ring within for the *Padders* and *bluntless* lads, who stood up to their knees in mud. What is termed the P.C. Ring was raised about two feet from the ground, covered over with dry turf: and a cart-load of saw-dust dispersed all over it. The race-course was so intolerably bad and full of *slush* that all the scavengers and *mud larks* from the Metropolis could not have cleaned it in a week. Outside of the waggons the ground displayed one complete sheet of water; and several lads who were jolly enough to save a few yards of ground in jumping over ditches measured their lengths in the water, receiving a complete *ducking*, to the no small amusement of the country girls, who were putting the *blush* upon the *Cocknies* astray, by their loud laughter. – What will not curiosity do? Here the *Swells* were seen sitting down in the *mud* with as much *sang froid* as if they were lolling on a sofa *tete-a-tete* with some attractive, lovely, fair damsel. Not a place could be obtained in the Stand after ten o'clock. The City of Worcester was full of gaiety early in the day; the streets were filled with the arrival of coaches and four-post chaises, mails, and vehicles of every description, blowing of horns, and the bells ringing, in short, it was a perfect jubilee to the inhabitants. Spring rode through the town in a slap-up set out and four (Col. Berkeley's) about twelve o'clock. The postillions were in red, and every thing corresponding in *tip-top* style. He arrived on the ground by half past twelve, amidst the shouts of the spectators, and drove close up to the ropes in a post-chaise. He threw his hat into the Ring: accompanied by TOM CRIBB and NED PAINTER. He was dressed remarkably genteel. At this period all was anxious expectation and on the *look out* for LANGAN, but a *quarter* of an hour had elapsed and no LANGAN; *half* an hour gone and no Paddy; *three quarters* over and still no Irish Champion in sight. Spring pulled out his watch, and said, 'It is time.' In the midst of the hour, waiting for the arrival of LANGAN, the right wing belonging to the stand gave way; and fifteen hundred persons at least, were all thrown one upon another. It was an awful moment. To give anything like an outline of the feelings displayed by the spectators baffles every attempt. – Hundreds were in tears, loudly exclaiming, 'I have lost a father – a brother – a dear friend.' It was afflicting beyond every thing to behold a Noble Lord frantic with agony, as he had the moment before placed his brother on the scaffold as a place of safety, Spring turned pale, and said, 'how sorry I am for this accident.' In a few minutes cheerfulness was restored, it being ascertained that nothing material had occurred, excepting a few contusions, and some of the persons limping away from the spot. 'Thank God,' ejaculated Spring, 'I would not have had it happened while I was fighting for 100,000.'
[*Langan finally arrived and the contest was joined. Towards the end, the fight nearly ended in a riot.*]

71. The ring was now in one complete jostle, and the rank of the swell was lost sight of, opposed to the hardihood and strength of the commoners with whips and sticks in their hands. Yet some of the sharpest rounds were now fought. Spring received another severe fall, and was undermost.

72. The general opinion in the small *mob* (the 24 foot ring, which was nothing else but a crowd), appeared to be, that Spring would *win*, but nevertheless, the countenances of Spring's backers indicated, it was not quite *safe*. Spring had no room to get away; indeed, it was one of the most shameful things that the writer of this article ever witnessed, and Colonel Berkeley, the Referee, said, 'I am so disgusted with the treatment I have experienced that I will give up the watch. – Here is no ring. It is impossible to stand still half a second without being assailed with a cut from a whip or a blow from a stick; and no good done either.' In no fight whatever was there such a scene of confusion in the space allotted for the men to fight. The battle was now little more than pulling and hauling; and in closing, both down. During the time Spring was on Painter's knee, Sampson, Oliver, and Israel Belasco were giving advice 'Hallo!' said Josh,

Great Battle between Spring, & Langan
FOR THE
CHAMPIONSHIP OF ENGLAND.

JACKSON.

Molyneux, (the Black,)

SPRING.

Richmond, (the Black,)

CRIB.

BELCHER.

LANGAN.

MENDOZA,

THE disappointment created by the beak in removing the scene of action from the environs of Warwick caused the whole of the P. C to be in a state of unusual bustle, and rendered it necessary for them to use more than common diligence, in order to be at the newly appointed place in time. Early on Sunday morning the leaders of the pugilistic corps were off, and the roads from London to Chicester, presented a busier scene then they had done for many a long day. The building of the stage on which the great conflict did take place, commenced yesterday morning in a plough'd field situated direct south and about three miles from Chichester, near Delkey, and Appletown

At a quarter before one, Mr. Jackson the Commander in Chief, walked round the ring, and requested the Gentlemen would keep their places, and also not call, "out," "or arr," but leave it to the Umpires.

At five minutes to One, the men entered the ring. Spring first, with his backers, Crib and Painter; Langan followed, with Belcher and a countryman of Langan's. Langan took off his coat immediately, and Spring followed his example, The umpires and referee were placed at one corner of the stage on a platform erected for that purpose, even betting that Spring wins it in one hour two and three to one on the event. Both men looked well and pleasant at each other. At this time there could not be less than twenty thousand persons present, Spring's colour was blue, and Langan's black as in the last battle, which were both tyed to the rail of the stage

Langan won the toss. He then examined the belt and shook hands with Spring, Both stript and their appearance fine in the extreme

THE FIGHT;

At six minutes past One, they set to.

Round 1 Langan made play first, and tried to throw—A severe fibbing, and Langan got away, He shewed first marks, a feint made, and Spring got away, and Langan tried for an opening, but Spring was too strong, Heavy hitting, Langan tried again to throw, and went on his knees, This round lasted six minutes

2. Langan blowed somewhat, severe hitting a close, and Spring threw Langan from him. Langan tried to put in his right hand hit but was stopped by Spring, Severe hitting, a close, and desperate struggle; Spring down on his hands and knees, round three minutes

3, Langan piping a little from the effects of last round. Spring tried his left hand, but he stopped it well, Spring did the same, Spring got away from another well meant hit Spring put in a tremendous right handed hit, Langan missed a well aimed blow at the head Spring put in a good left handed facer, Langan tried to fib Spring at the ropes, Spring would not have it and threw Langan—this was a very long round,

4, Langan [illegible], two, three, four five, without success. Spring's left eye was swollen and [illegible]d, Spring nearly fell over the rail. Langan struggled hard, both fell, Spring under,

5, Langan's left ear appeared damaged, several beautiful stops, Spring put in a good left handed facer, and another, which drew the claret from the nose, Langan thrown over on his back. Claret flowing in all directions,

6, Sparring for some time, Spring got Langan to the corner of the stage and punished him on the back of the head, when both went down together,

7. Spring put in a right handed hit, on the ear of Langan which told; then a left handed facer,—the generalship of Spring beautiful. Spring put in another left handed hit, both bellows to mend. Spring put in several right hits; he received another on his ribs, and was all abroad,—he then rallyed manfully but with little chance, Langan received several hits and went down from weakness, An even guinea to nothing

8. Langan made first play but all was abroad, and again went down exhausted,

9. Spring walked to the scratch, Langan was led and received severe punishment, which made him stagger, and again went down,

10, Langan hit completely out of distance, (Bank of England to a nut shell,) Langan rallyed & threw Spring cleverly, Spring under.

11, Langan received on his lush trap, but appeared recovered, a severe struggle at the rails and Langan was thrown.

12 Langan endeavoured to put in a blow which Spring stopped, they closed and both fell, Spring under, both their heads hung over the stage,

13, Severe blows, given and received by both, Langan thrown,

14 Langan attempted a body blow without success, a close, and Langan again thrown

15, Langan put in a good left handed hit; both hugged at the rails and tried for a throw, Langan slipped thro' Spring's arms and received a hit,—(some murmurs)

16. Langan made a left handed hit, went in, and attempted to throw, both went down together

17, Several blows exchanged, a close, and Spring thrown heavily, his legs flying in the air, betting at a stand still.

18. Spring tried a left handed hit, but was cleverly stopped, Spring touched the nob, Spring very cautious, A close, took place, and both fell

19, Both cautious—a close, Langan received a severe fibbing and a desperate throw on his face

20, Langan came up the worse for the last round Langan put in a good right handed blow on Spring's face, and closed and both fell,

21. Spring put in a good right handed hit; after a severe struggle at the railings, Spring threw Langan heavily, Spring smiled.

22 Spring stopped an intended blow, Langan again thrown. Spring appeared to be blind with the right eye, both winded,

23 Spring got Langan against the rails, and fibbed him down,

24 Langan rushed in, received several hits in the wind and at length Spring fibbed him down, a good round.

2[illegible]. Langan received a hit on the side of the head and another on his nose, which brought him down on his hands.

25, Langan received a nobber and another, they closed, and Spring went down on the top of Langan

27, Langan very weak, and unable to rise; Belchel held his man rather too long; which Cribb took notice, and said, we want nothing but fair, Langan went down awkwardly

28. A severe struggle, Spring threw Langan heavily and fell on him,

29, A severe round, Langan received several heavy hits, and was thrown heavily. Spring on him

30 Langan extremely weak, and efforts very faint Langan put in a hit, both went down Langan under,

31, Langan made a lunging hit he received three right handed hits, which made him stagger, and fall backwards

32 Spring threw Langan heavily against the stage

33, Langan again went down

34. Langan got away from a right handed hit, This was the best round of the fight, but Langan was hit most severely and was obliged to go down

35, Langan game, but was hit all over the stage

36, Langan was knocked down,

37. Langan quite stupid, but still too game to say enough.

38 Langan came again received a hit which turned him round Shame shame, take him away,

39 Langan again knocked down,

40. Langan rushed in, received a hit, and fell upon his knees, "Take him away," was all the cry

41. This round reflected great credit on Spring, he laid his man down easy, and Langan patted him on the back for it, "What a game man he is," was the cry;

42 Langan down—Spring on him heavily,

43, Langan again thrown,

44, Some hitting, Langan got hold of Spring's drawers—(Cries of "Let go,") Langan down

45, A smart rally but both very weak, Langan again down very heavy.

46. Two severe blows from Spring, Langan again down,

47 Same as last,

48, Langan again thrown, he appeared quite blind betting twenty to one

49, Both staggering from weakness Langan thrown

50 Langan showed real game but was thrown

It is unnecessary for us to pursue the descriptive further, the contest was so well maintained by both, at one time and victory appeared so doubtful, that the bets were nearly reduced to a level, We may venture to say that a nobler display of science and skill, was never witnessed before. At the 77th round, Langan was unable to come to time, and Victory was declared in favour of

SPRING.

This Great Battle lasted One Hour and Fifty five Minutes.

Pitts Printer, Toy and marble warehouse
6 Great st Andrew street 7 dials

A NEW SONG.

COME all you gallant milling (blades
Wherever you may be
Attend awhile to what I've penn'd
And listen unto me,
Tis of a gallant hearts of oak
The truth I will unfold
Fought for one Thousand sovereigns
in bright and shining gold.

CHORUS

In bumpers fine of sparkling wine
We'll drink to gallant Spring
And long may Ireland rue the day
They Matched the British Ring

The one a brave Hibernian youth'
Young Langan is his name
The other was the Champion Spring
Of courage and great fame,
It was on June the 8th my boys
The truth I will declare
To a Field near Chichester,
These two Champions did repair

'Twas at the hour of one o'clock,
They entered the ring,
The bets in all directions flew

Sutton, (the Black,)

DONELLY.

In favour of bold Spring
The Irish blades their bets did make
In favour of Langan'
But Spring like lightning plac'd his (hits
Upon the Irishman,

O when the fighting did commence
Their courage for to try
Quick as lightning Spring soon (plac'd
A hit on Langan's eye,
The Irish bloods were all surpris'd,
To view such scene so rare
And wished within their hearts my (boys
They never had come there

From the 9th unto the 11th round
To Spring was added fame
The Irish Lads they one and all
Were sickning at the game
And when the twelfth was ended
Few marks on Spring were found
But in closing of the same
They both of them fell down

The 13th and 14th round
Were well maintained by Spring
Which plainly proved to all around
His title to the ring
Tho' Langan he fought manfully

GULLY.

His friends lost all their hopes
And in the 17th round my boys
They both fell near the ropes
Until the 77th round
The Champions kept the Field
When Spring severely punish'd him
And forced him to yield
Old Erin's sons cry'd one and all
We surely are undone
And so with empty purses boys
They all returned to London

So now the Fight is ended, and
And the contest is all o'er
The knowing ones of Paddy's land
Their loss they do deplore
If they again should make a march
All for the British Ring
Your Langan great in his retreat
Will always find a Spring

In bumpers fine of sparkling wine
We'll drink to Gallant Spring
The pride of British science
And the hero of the RING

RANDALL,

'do you call this fair play! How many seconds is Spring to have;' and snatching a whip out of a by-stander's hand, with the strength of a Lion, endeavoured, regardless of any person before him, to whip out the ring, followed by Oliver. Not a single person present in the above mob but received numerous blows, and was in great danger of having his nob cut to pieces. 'Only give us a chance,' cried Josh, 'and we can't lose it.' Nothing foul appeared to be attempted on the part of Spring, or on the side of Langan. – The Constables and their long poles were all mixed in the mob struggling for breath: the fighting men hoarse with calling out 'clear the ring,' and *dead beat* from the exertions they had made. Nothing less than a company of the Horse Guards could have made out a ring at this period, too closely jammed together were all the spectators.

73. The courage, confidence, and good spirits displayed by Langan excited the admiration of every beholder. He was too short in the arms for Spring: he could not reach his head without rushing in to *mill*. Langan left his second's knee rather weak; in closing, he was *fibbed* severely by Spring, who was well assured, he had not a minute to lose. The English Champion was cool, felt his situation, and from his knowledge and experience in the Prize Ring, gave him the advantage, when the *nicety* of the thing was required.

74. On Langan placing himself in attitude, 'Go and fight,' said Cribb to Spring; when the Champion went to work without delay, and Langan received a heavy blow in the middle of his head, and went down. 'Twenty to one,' said a *swell*, 'he'll not come again!'

75. The Irish Champion appeared rather the worse for the last round, and on his appearing at the scratch, Spring commenced the attack, when Langan returned with great spirit; but Spring had decidedly the best, and Langan was fibbed down, his face covered with claret. 'Take the brave fellow away.' 'I will not be taken away – who dare to say so?' urged Langan.

76. Spring was now determined to lose no time, and again went to work; but Langan showed fight, and he likewise struggled to obtain the throw: both down. 'Take him away!' Langan's head rested on his second's shoulder till time was called. The *Springites* roared out – 'It's now as right as the day. Ten Pounds to a Crown the battle is over in five minutes.'

77, and last. Langan came up rather *groggy*, but still full of *pluck*. Spring now administered heavy punishment with both of his hands, and Langan fell down quite exhausted. Reynolds had great difficulty in getting him off the ground – Langan was in a state of stupor, and his eye closed. Several gentlemen said, 'do not let the brave fellow fight any more.' Reynolds, 'take him away. It is impossible he can meet Spring any more at the *scratch*;' and when time was called, Langan was insensible to it – and Josh. Hudson *gave in* for him. In about half a minute after this circumstance had occurred, Langan opened his eyes, still sitting on the knee of his second, when he was told the fight was over. He said 'his second had no right to give in for him. He could fight for more than forty rounds.' 'Don't leave the ring, Spring,' several persons cried out. Cribb told Langan, 'the battle was over;' and Painter observed, 'don't let so good a man be killed, he does not know at the present moment what he is talking about!' The umpire was asked for his decision, who said 'Langan did not come to fight when time was called; and therefore he had lost the battle, according to the rules of Pugilism.' Upon this answer, and decision of the Umpire, Spring left the ring, amidst the shouts of the populace, Langan roaring out 'I am not beaten – clear out the ring – I can fight for four hours.' In the course of a few minutes, he left the ring; and as he approached the Grand Stand, he was received with thunders of applause, and jumped over some ropes in his way with great agility. The battle lasted two hours and twenty-nine minutes.

BOXING – ANOTHER VIEW

What, let us ask, are the superior recommendations of this wondrous paper? *Bell's Weekly Dispatch* is dearer than the others, though, to be sure, it copies out of the other papers a little more matter, – but we should hope that quantity is not its best merit: yet, what is its

merit? is it the upholding it affords to the barbarous system of prize fighting? – is it because it, with so much spirit and ability, relates the manner in which a human being has, for mere sport, bruised and cut a fellow-creature's face and body, and how long and how admirably the poor sufferer endured his 'punishment,' – and how much delighted thousands were with the brutal exhibition? – we hope to God that our fellow-countrymen are not so debased as to support such a paper for such a merit!

MR BAYLEY AND CLUB AGAINST MARY-LA-BONNE

A grand match was played at the Mary-la-bonne Ground, in July, 1828, between John Bayley, Esq. (a son of Judge Bayley) and his club, consisting principally of farmers in the immediate neighbourhood of his country residence (Updown House, near Sandwich, in Kent), with Mr. Knatchbull added, against twelve of the Mary-la-bonne Club.

*

On the first day the Kentish men had many disadvantages to cope with on account of the beautiful evenness of the ground, which made them unprepared for the ball in the field, and the different style of bowling lately brought into vogue (a fine specimen of which was given by Mr. Jenner), which, added to the very thought of playing with the Mary-la-bonne club, not a little daunted their confidence. These 'novelties' made them commit many blunders on the first day, which drew forth not a few jokes at their expense from their opponents. However, on the second day, having 231 runs to get, on going in for their second innings, they amply made up for all their past bad play, and gained for themselves fresh laurels to crown their manly brows, already thickly shaded, having gained last year eight matches in nine. As the *Dons* had many a laugh at the *Johns* on the first day, it is but justice to state that the tables were completely turned on the second – so confident were the *Great Club* of easy success, that they gave orders to Mr. Dark, at the stand on the ground, not to provide dinner for them on that day, as the match would be over so early they should not require it; and also ordered their servants to bring their horses, &c. for them at three o'clock; but, behold, the countrymen played so much superior to what was expected, that it was six o'clock before the last wicket went down. This nettled them much; however, it was *fine nuts* for the *awkwards*, and they made the most of it, as it was the source of many a laugh during the whole of the evening. It was remarked by many on the ground, that had Mr. Bayley's club shown as good play on the first, as they did on the second day, the Mary-la-bonne would have been beat.

NEW SONG IN FAVOUR OF

BLACKBURN

Mick.

You merry blades of England, one
    moment lend an ear,
It is of some splendid foot racing, that
    happened this year;
At Bellview on Monday last, there was
    running in grand style,
From one hundred yards to the length
    of a mile.

CHORUS.

So success to Lancashire,
The pride of England,
For Pedistrains in all the World,
Non with it could even stand.

On the first day of December eighteen
    hundred & forty-five,
Some thousands came to Bellview with
    hearts all fine,
To see those gallant heroes bold, come
    and strip unto the skin,
To try their best for fifty pounds,
    which of them could win.

Both heroes then did quickly peel, and
    come to the starting ground,
When Turner said, to Blackburn Mick,
    I am sure to win the sixty pounds;
But Mick said to Turner lad, for that
    I do not mind,
For if I do not run the first, I'll not
    be far behind.

The shot went off, away they went, and
    Turner took the lead
And then they both run half-a-mile,
    when Mick past his man with
    speed:
Then Turner said I must give in, for I
    can do no more
And the distance that bold Mick did
    win, was three hundred yards and
    three score.

There was Dee and Walker had a race,
    and Chip and brave Atkinson;
But Chip and Dee their races won,
    and took both prizes home;
There was Marlow and Smith and
    other two, who run that very day,
But none like Chip and Blackburn
    Mick, took so much gold away.

So now for to conclude and finish my
    song,
I must not forget the Clogger, who has
    proved himself a don,
He beat Cowper in November last,
    and bore the prize in gallant
    style;
So Clogger for two hundred yards, and
    Blackburn Mick a Mile.

BULLBAITING

'What's the matter?' said Mr. Everingham.

'Why. I gave a quarter's holiday to the work-people to-day,' answered Thorneycroft, 'and they are to have a bullbait. Fine recreation that! and I fear, sir, as neither you nor I are much inclined to go and enjoy their mirth. It is delightful to see them at their relaxation in such fine old English sports; and they are the sort of intellectual pleasures which I delight to propagate. No man, Mr. Everingham, is a greater friend than I am to education and learning, if they are kept in their proper place; but give me one bullbait, and I had rather have it than ten Mechanics' Institutes: and, thank God, I have brought my people pretty generally to the same way of thinking. There's some of them yet as will run after books, and hanker after newspapers; but give me a bullbait – that's the thing for me. There's something manly in a bullbaiting; and so there is in a boxing match: and I would encourage prize-fighting amongst my people, only they would bung up each others' eyes, and perhaps otherwise hurt each other, and then I should lose their work; and whilst they were getting better they would have time to talk politics, and that never does any good to working-people: a bullbait is the thing after all, Mr. Everingham. Many's the dog among my people that will *pin* the bull in fine style.'

THE BONNY GRAY

Come all you cock merchants far and near,
Did you hear of a cock battle that happened here?
Those Liverpool lads I have heard them say,
The Charcoal Black and Bonny Gray.

We went to Jim Ward's and called for a pot,
Where this cock battle was fought;
For twenty guineas a side these cocks did fight,
The Charcoal Black and the Bonny Gray.

Then Lord Derby he came swaggering down,
I'll bet Ten Guineas to a Crown,
If this Charcoal Black, it gets fair play,
He will rip the wing of the Bonny Gray,

O these two cocks came to the sod,
Cries the Liverpool Lads, how now? what odds,
The odds the Prescot Lads did say,
The Charcoal Black and the Bonny Gray.

The cock battle was fought,
While the Charcoal he lay dead at last;
The Liverpool Lads gave a loud huzza,
And carried away the Bonny Gray.

WEDNESBURY COCKING

At Wednesbury there was a cocking,
    A match between Newton and Scroggins,
The colliers and nailers left work,
    And all to Spittle's went jogging,
To see the noble sport,
    Many noblemen resorted,
And though they'd little money,
    Yet that they freely sported.

There was Jeffery and Colborn from Hampton,
    Ane Dusty from Bilston was there,
Plummery he came from Darlaston,
    And was as rude as a bear;
There was old Will from Walsall,
    And Smacker from Westbromwich came,
Blind Robin he came from Rowley,
    And staggering he went home.

Ralph Moody came hobbling along,
    As though he some cripple was mocking,
To join in the blackguard throng,
    That met at Wednesbury Cocking;

He borrowed a trifle off Doll,
   To back old Taverner's gray,
He laid fourpence halfpenny to fourpence,
   He lost and went broken away.

But soon he returned to the pit,
   For he borrowed a trifle more money,
And ventured another large bet
   Along with blubber mouth Coney.
When Coney demanded his money,
   As is common on all such occasions,
He cried blast thee, if thee don't hold thy
     peace
   I'll pay thee as Paul paid the Ephesians.

Scroggins's breeches were made of nankeen,
   And wore very thin in the groin,
In stooping to handle his cock,
   His b— burst out behind!
Besides his shirt tail was bes—t,
   Which caused among them much laughter,
Scroggins turned round in a pet,
   And cried, b— ye, what's the matter.

The morning's sport being over,
   Old Spittle a dinner proclaimed,
Each man he should dine for a groat,
   If he grumbled he ought to be d—
For there was plenty of beef,
   But Spittle he swore by his troth,
That never a man should dine,
   Till he ate his noggin of broth.

The beef it was old and tough,
   Of a bull that was baited to death,
Barney Hyde got a lump in his throat,
   That had liked to have stopp'd his breath;
The company all fell into confusion,
   At seeing poor Barney Hyde choke,
They took him into the kitchen,
   And held his head over the smoke.

They held him so close to the fire,
   He frizzled just like a beef steak
Then threw him down on the floor,
   Which had like to have broken his neck;
One gave him a kick in the stomach,
   Another a kick on the brow,
His wife said throw him into the stable,
   And he will be better just now.

Then they all returned to the pit,
   And the fighting went forward again,
Six battles were fought on each side,
   And the next was to decide the main;
For they were two famous cocks,
   As ever this country bred,
Scroggins's a duck-winged black,
   And Newton's a shift-winged red.

The conflict was hard on both sides.
   Till Brassy's duck-winged was choked,
The colliers were tarnationly vexed,
   And the nailers were sorely provoked;

Peter Stevens he swore a great oath,
    That Scroggins had played the cock foul,
Scroggins gave him a kick on the head,
    And cried, yea, God d—n thy soul.

The company then fell in discord,
    A bold fight did ensue,
Kick, b— and bite was the word,
    Till the Walsall men all were subdued;
Ralph Moody bit off a man's nose,
    And wished that he could have him slain,
So they trampled both cocks to death,
    And then made a draw of the main.

The cock pit was near to the church,
    An ornament unto the town,
On one side an old coal pit,
    The other well gors'd round;
Peter Hadly peep'd through the gorse,
    In order to see them fight,
Spittle jobbed out his eye with a fork,
    And said b— thee, it served thee right.

Some people may think this is strange,
    Who Wednesbury never knew,
But those who have ever been there,
    Won't have the least doubt it is true
For they are as savage by nature,
    And guilty of deeds the most shocking,
Jack Baker whacked his own father,
    And so ended Wednesbury Cocking.

THE DERBY FOOT-BALL PLAY

(*From a Correspondent*)

In a volume entitled 'Les derniers Bretons,' by M. Souvestre, published at Paris in 1836, a long account is given of a peculiar game which is played in Bretagne at Shrovetide. The following passage, quoted in the 'London and Westminster Review' for August last, p. 368, will give some idea of the sport; and for fuller particulars the reader is referred to the review itself, where a long extract on the subject, from M. Souvestre's work, is given in an English translation.

'The *soule* is an enormous ball of leather filled with air, which is thrown in the air, and fought for by the players, who are divided into two parties. The victory rests with the party that can carry off the soule into a different township from that where the game has commenced. This exercise is the last vestige of the worship which the Celts paid to the sun. . . . The very word is of Celtic origin, derived from *heaul* (soleil), in which the initial *h* is changed into *s*, as in all the foreign words adopted by the Romans.'

The description here given of the Bretagne game of the soule reminds us strongly of the Derby foot-ball play, peculiar, so far as our knowledge previously went, to the single town of Derby; played likewise at Shrove-tide; interesting in the fate of the game all ranks of the townsmen; and, in short, resembling in all essential particulars its French prototype. For the credit of our country however we must be allowed to say that though at Derby we have witnessed serious broils, arising from the heat engendered by the contest, they have never been known by any means to resemble the atrocities practised on these occasions by the Souleurs, – the malicious maimings, the murders committed through cherished revenge, and so effected as to appear accidental, – as described by M. Souvestre.

The town of Derby contains five parishes; All Saints, St. Michael's, St. Aulkmund's, St. Werburgh's, and St. Peter's. The last is so extensive, and furnishes so large a share of the foot-ball players, that it singly stands against the other four parishes together; and the rallying cry of the two parties thus becomes 'All Saints' and 'Peter's' respectively. The adjoining country parishes take part, more or less, with the side which approaches the nearest in position to their boundaries, and the fate of the game is frequently decided by the one party or the other bringing in an unusual influx of these outlying players; and from time to time there rise up reformers, who would cut off these out-voters (so to speak) from the glories and honours of the game, and limit the foot-ball play to the genuine townsmen of Derby.

The ball is made of very strong leather, about a foot in diameter, and stuffed hard with cork shavings. At two o'clock on Shrove-Tuesday begins the sport; and as the hour approaches, the whole town seems alive with expectation. It is a universal holiday, and all ranks and ages are seen streaming towards the market-place. Here the shops are found to be shut, and the houses all round filled with spectators, men, women, and children, crowding the windows and perched upon the house-tops. The players arrive by degrees from opposite sides of the market-place, coming generally in parties of a dozen or more, each greeted as it appears by the cheers of its respective side. The market-place is chosen as a central spot for the commencement of the game, and the goals are well known by long-standing agreement. That of the 'Peter's' is the gate of a nursery-ground, situated somewhat more than a mile off, in the direction of London; that of the 'All Saints,' the wheel of a watermill at a rather shorter distance on the road towards Manchester by Ashbourne. The object of the game is the goaling of the ball at the one or the other of these places, a process performed by striking it three times against the gate or the wheel respectively.

At the appointed hour arrives the ball, carried by the hero of the last year who was lucky enough to goal it then. The crowd of players opens to receive him; and, going into the middle of the market, he throws up the ball; all cluster round it, and the game begins. The thorough-going players, who know their business well, come unincumbered by unnecessary clothing, with trowsers tightly strapped round the loins; coat, and usually waistcoat too, removed, and arms bare. Their arms also they hold up above their heads on entering the fray, as they would be very apt to be broken from the extreme pressure of such a mass. On the outskirts of the throng hover others, whose standing in society will not suffer them to appear in the simple dishabille described above. Yet, eager as any for their party, they are there, encouraging, directing, vociferating; and ever and anon carried forward by their zeal; pushing, too, as hard as any, and often in the middle of the throng. We have indeed heard of townsmen of high standing and well deserved reputation losing their spectacles, unused to such hard labour, in the cause; and men who at any other time would be ashamed to appear, except in nicest dress may, after two o'clock

on Shrove-Tuesday, be seen without a hat, with half a coat, and yet without a blush.

Such then is the scene in the market-place; a dense central mass of uplifted arms; and around, a throng closely wedged together, pushing with all their might towards their distant goal. And ever and anon we see a fresh combatant entering the mass, with broad chest and brawny arms, and, like one of Homer's heroes, 'of stature far above the rest;' while others, tired and faint with their exertions, are coming out for a mouthful of fresh air, a glass of ale from the nearest public-house, or oranges, supplied in abundance by venders attendant on the game, and bought up with eagerness by the spectators for the refreshment of their own side.

The ball generally follows, as might be expected, the slope of the market-place, which is somewhat in favour of the 'Peter's' party; and it is their usual policy to get it as soon as possible into the river, which lies in the same direction. Not that the river leads directly towards their goal; but water-carriage is uniformly easy, and at any rate it takes the ball farther and farther from the opposite goal. The river being too deep for pushing as they do on land, one man swims down the stream with the ball, embracing it in his arms, and buoyed up by it as by a life-preserver. The rest of the players and such of the spectators as still keep up a sufficient interest in the protracted game, follow the course of the ball on the bank of the river on which lies the 'Peter's' goal. It is now the object of this party to land the ball at the nearest point to their own goal, if they be strong enough to carry it thither at once; or if not, to protract the game till darkness shall give them the opportunity of carrying it thither by stealth. The 'All Saints' party, on the other hand, have little chance except in the bold stroke of mastering the man in the river, and landing the ball on the opposite side, making off with it by three, four, or more miles of land conveyance to their goal. Such a struggle in the water is occasionally attended with danger; but this is rarely known to produce very serious effects. Whichever way the game ends, it is seldom over till late when once the ball has thus gone down the river. Sometimes indeed the course which the game takes is through the streets pretty directly to one of the goals; in which case its progress, or expected progress, is marked by the closing of the shops, especially in the closer built parts of the town. This however happens only when the 'All Saints' party are uncommonly strong and keep it by main force out of the river; or when the 'Peter's' are strong enough to attempt a direct course – a dangerous policy for them, as they must cross the brook on which their rivals' goal is situated, and thus enable them to put in practice their own aquatic tactics, though on a smaller scale. In such a case as this, the ball is sometimes goaled in two or three hours.

In the more usual instance related above, when the game is adjourned till darkness comes on, it is soon known at which side of the river the ball has been landed, and consequently at which goal it may be expected; and here the final struggle takes place. The unsuccessful party endeavour to surround their rivals' goal so as to prevent the possibility of bringing the ball up to it; and many are the tales mutually told, of stratagems for effecting this object. The most usual perhaps has been, to remove the cork-shavings, and smuggle in the cover, under a countryman's frock or a woman's gown, to the desired place. And tradition records that once, when the 'All Saints' were approaching their goal, the water-wheel, which we have mentioned as forming it, was set in motion by a device of the enemy.

Goaled however at length the ball is, by the one party or the other; and then the hero who effected the triumph is hoisted on his fellow-players' shoulders, and carried with the ball in his hands through the parish or parishes of the victorious party, soliciting and receiving pretty largely from the enthusiasm of their compatriots the hard-earned means of refreshment after their labours, and encouragement in their glorious toils.

The following day, Ash Wednesday, is called the 'Boys' day,' when a juvenile performance of the same kind takes place, on the principle of teaching a child the way he should go. And to say the truth, the young ones are very ready to learn, and give every promise of perpetuating the glorious game of their native town. This second day's sport is in one respect different from that of the previous one; the men of both sides attend to see fair play, and many doubtful cases arising, of great boys and little men, disputes are far more frequent than on the men's own day. Indeed, it is said, that such as do arise on the Tuesday are by mutual consent deferred to the Wednesday. Attempts have been made to put down the game as tending to foment quarrels and to endanger life; the fact is, however, that life is hardly ever lost and we do not think the quarrels are either very serious or very permanent. The practice has never been put down; but, we understand, continues to prevail to the present day.

The following anecdote, to doubt which appears unreasonable to a true *Darby* man (so the natives call their town), shows the peculiarity and provinciality of the game. Two English settlers in the back-woods of America, meeting by chance, began talking of the old England they had left. 'And where did you come from?' says the one. 'From Darby,' replies the other. 'Oi don't think thee looks loike a Darby mon; but oi'l troi thee . . . All Saints for ever!' 'Peter's for ever;' was the instant reply, and the rival foot-ball players, thus proved to be fellow-townsmen, shook hands, preferring their common town –'the pretty, clean, little Derby,' as travellers call it, to their hostile parishes of All Saints and Peter's.

SNOWBALL THE FASTEST GREYHOUND IN ENGLAND

To have capital coursing, a good dog is only one part of the business; it is not only necessary to have a good hare also, but a country where nothing but speed and power to continue it can save her, over the high wolds of Stackton Flixton, and Sherborne in Yorkshire, where hares are frequently found three or four miles from any covert or enclosure whatever; the ground the finest that can

possibly be conceived, consisting chiefly of sheep-walk, including every diversity of hill, plain, and valley by which the speed and strength of a dog can be fairly brought to the test; it will not require many words to convince the real sportsman, that such courses have been seen there, as no other part of the kingdom in its present enclosed state can possibly offer, and these necessarily require a dog to be in that high training, for which in coursing of much less severity there cannot be equal occasion. But the day is fast approaching when coursing of such description will no more be seen; in a very few years these wolds will be surrounded, and, variously intersected with fences, and thus equalized with other countries . . .

The excellence of Snowball, whose breed was Yorkshire on the side of the dam, and Norfolk on that of the sire, was acknowledged by the great number who had seen him run, and, perhaps, taken 'for all in all,' he was the best greyhound that ever ran in England. All countries were nearly alike to him, though bred where fences seldom occur; yet, when taken into the strongest enclosures, he topped hedges of any height, and in that respect equalled, if not surpassed, every dog in his own country. They who did not think

his speed so superior; all allowed, that for wind, and for powers in running up long hills without being distressed, they had never seen his equal.

On a public coursing day given to the township of Flixton, the continuance of his speed was once reduced to a certainty by the known distance, as well as the difficulty of the ground. From the bottom of Flixton Brow, where the village stands, to the top of the hill, where the wold begins, is a measured mile, and very steep in ascent the whole of the way. A hare was found midway, and there was started with Snowball, a sister of his, given to the Rev. Mr. Minithorpe, and a young dog about twelve months old, of another breed. The hare came immediately up the hill, and after repeated turns upon the wold, took down the hill again; but finding that in the sandy bottom she was less a match for the dogs, she returned, and in the middle of the hill the whelp gave in, Snowball and his sister being left with the hare: reaching the wold a second time, she was turned at least fifty times, where, forcibly feeling the certainty of approaching death, she again went down the hill, in descending which the bitch dropped, and by immediate bleeding was recovered. – Snowball afterwards ran the hare into the village, where he killed her . . . The inhabitants of Flixton talk of it to this day, and accustomed as they are to courses of the richest description in the annals of sporting, they reckon this amongst the most famous they have seen.

Snowball, Major, his brother, and Sylvia, were perhaps the three best, and most perfect greyhounds ever produced at one litter. They were never beaten.

7. LOW LIFE IN LONDON

LIFE IN LONDON

THE CONTRASTS OF LONDON

The EXTREMES, in every point of view, are daily to be met with in the Metropolis; from the most rigid, persevering, never-tiring industry, down to laziness, which, in its consequences, frequently operates far worse than idleness. The greatest love of and contempt for money are equally conspicuous; and in no place are pleasure and business so much united as in London. The highest veneration for and practice of religion distinguish the Metropolis, contrasted with the most horrid commission of crimes: and the *experience* of the oldest inhabitant scarcely renders him safe against the specious plans and artifices continually laid to entrap the most vigilant. The next-door neighbour of a man in London is generally as great a stranger to him as if he lived at the distance of York. And it is in the Metropolis that *prostitution* is so profitable a business, and conducted so openly, that hundreds of persons keep houses of ill fame for the reception of girls not more than *twelve* and *thirteen* years of age, without a blush upon their cheeks, and mix with society heedless of stigma or reproach; yet honour, integrity, and independence of soul, that nothing can remove from its basis, are to be found in every street in London. Hundreds of persons are always going to bed in the morning, besotted with dissipation and gaming, while thousands of his Majesty's liege subjects are quitting their pillows to pursue their useful occupations. The most bare-faced villains, swindlers, and thieves, walk about the streets in the daytime, committing their various depredations, with as much confidence as men of unblemished reputation and honesty. In short, the most vicious and abandoned wretches, who are lost to every friendly tie that binds man to man, are to be found in swarms in the Metropolis; and so depraved are they in principle, as to be considered, from their uncalled-for outrages upon the inhabitants, a *waste of wickedness*, operating as a complete terror, in spite of the *activity* of the police. Yet, notwithstanding this dark and melancholy part of the picture, there are some of the worthiest, most tender-hearted, liberal minds, and charitable dispositions, which ornament London, and render it the delight and happiness of society.

Indeed, the Metropolis is a complete CYCLOPAEDIA, where every man of the most religious or moral habits, attached to any sect, may find something to please his palate, regulate his taste, suit his pocket, enlarge his mind, and make himself happy and comfortable. If places of worship give any sort of character to the *goodness* of the Metropolis, between four and five hundred are opened for religious purposes on Sundays. In fact, every SQUARE in the Metropolis is a sort of *map* well worthy of exploring, if riches and titles operate as a source of curiosity to the visiter. There is not a *street* in London but what may be compared to a large or small volume of intelligence, abounding with anecdote, incident, and peculiarities. A *court* or *alley* must be obscure indeed, if it does not afford some remarks; and even the *poorest* cellar contains some *trait* or other, in unison with the manners and feelings of this great city, that may be put down in the note-book, and reviewed, at an after period, with much pleasure and satisfaction.

Then, the grand object of this work is an attempt to portray what is termed 'SEEING

LIFE,' in all its various bearings upon society, from the *high-mettled* CORINTHIAN of St James's, *swaddled* in luxury, down to the *needy* FLUE-FAKER of Wapping, *born without a shirt*, and not a *bit of scran* in his cup to allay his piteous cravings.

TOM AND JERRY VISIT ALL MAX

[Life in London (1820–21) *takes the form of a guided tour of the metropolis, in which Corinthian Tom, accompanied by Bob Logic, initiate Jerry Hawthorne, up from the country, into the mysteries of city life. Here they visit a low-life saloon in the East End. A glossary to the slang can be found in the notes (p.349).*]

ALL MAX was compared by the sailors, something after the old adage of 'any port in a storm.' It required no patronage; – a card of admission was not necessary; – no inquiries were made; – and every *cove* that put in his appearance was quite welcome: colour or country considered no obstacle; and *dress* and ADDRESS completely out of the question. *Ceremonies* were not in use, and, therefore, no struggle took place at ALL MAX for the master of them. The parties *paired off* according to *fancy*; the eye was pleased in the choice, and nothing thought of about birth and distinction. All was *happiness*,* – everybody free and easy, and freedom of expression allowed to the very echo. The group

motley indeed; – Lascars, blacks, jack tars, coalheavers, dustmen, women of colour, old and young, and a sprinkling of the remnants of once fine girls, &c. were all *jigging* together, provided the *teazer of the catgut* was not *bilked* of his *duce*. *Gloves* might have been laughed at, as dirty hands produced no *squeamishness* on the heroines in the dance, and the scene changed as often as a pantomime, from the continual introduction of new characters. *Heavy wet* was the cooling beverage, but frequently overtaken by *flashes of lightning*. The *covey* was no *scholard*, as he asserted, and, therefore, he held the pot in one hand and took the *blunt* with the other, to prevent the trouble of *chalking*, or making mistakes. *Cocker's* arithmetic in his bar was a dead letter, and the *publican's leger* only waste paper: *book-keeping* did not belong to his *consarn;* yet no one could *read* his customers better than Mr. *Mace*.* The attention he displayed towards any of his party, when Mr. *Lushington* had got the 'best of them,' showed his judgement; – he had a butt of *heavy wet* prepared for the occasion, and also a cask of liquor, which gave considerable proofs of his kindness, that his articles should not be too strong for their already-damaged heads. His motto was 'never to give a *chance* away'; and Mr. *Mace* had long been christened by the *downies*, the "*dashing covey*".' He was '*cut out*' for his company; and he could '*come it well*' upon all points. On the sudden appearance of our '*swell* TRIO,' and the CORINTHIAN'S friend, among these unsophisticated sons and daughters of Nature, their *ogles* were on the roll, under an apprehension that the *beaks* were out on the *nose*; but it was soon made 'all right,' by one of the *mollishers* whispering, loud enough to be heard by most of the party, 'that she understood *as how* the *gemmen* had only dropped in for to have a *bit of a spree*, and there was no doubt they *voud* stand a *drap* of *summut* to make them all *cumfurable*, and likewise prove good customers to the *crib*.' On the *office* being given, the *stand-still* was instantly removed; and the

*'It is,' said LOGIC to TOM, 'I am quite satisfied in my mind, the LOWER ORDERS of society who really ENJOY themselves. They eat with a good appetite, *hunger* being the sauce; they *drink* with a zest, in being *thirsty* from their exertions, and not *nice* in their beverage; and, as to *dress*, it is not an object of serious consideration with them. Their minds are daily occupied with work, which they quit with the intention of *enjoying* themselves, and ENJOYMENT is the result; not like the rich, who are out night after night to *kill* TIME, and, what is worse, dissatisfied with almost every thing that crosses their path from the dulness of *repetition*.' 'There is too much truth about your argument, I must admit,' replied the CORINTHIAN; and among all the scenes that we have witnessed together, where the LOWER ORDERS have been taking their *pleasure*, I confess they have appeared ALL HAPPINESS. I am sorry I cannot say as much for the higher ranks of society.'

*It is rather a curious coincidence, that the name of the proprietor of ALL MAX should be *Mace*, which is a slang term for *imposition* or *robbery!*

*Tom and Jerry "Masquerading it" among the Cadgers in the "Back Slums,"
in the Holy Land.*

kidwys and *kiddiesses* were footing the *double shuffle* against each other with as much *gig* as the '*We we-e-e-ps*' exert themselves on the first of May. The CORINTHIAN smiled to himself, as his eyes *glanced* round the room at the *characters*, and observed to LOGIC, in a low tone of voice, 'that it was quite a new scene to him, notwithstanding all his previous rambles throughout the Metropolis, but so exceedingly *rich*, that he would not have *missed* it for a hundred pounds.' As to JERRY, the GOLDEN ROOM at Carlton Palace, with all its *talismanic* touches, did not appear to have had more effect upon his feelings, when he entered it, than the group of figures, 'all alive O!' at ALL MAX seemed now to operate upon his mind. LOGIC, who was considered an *out-and-outer*, for continually scouring the *back-slums*, both in town and country, in search of something new, admitted the scene before him was one of the greatest novelties that he had ever witnessed in low life; and although the *Oxonian* was rather forward on the *bosky* suit, 'It is,' said he, tapping JERRY on the back, 'one of the invaluable mines of Nature: her

stores are inhaustible. What a fine subject would a sentimental stroll through London have afforded the pen of STERNE;' LOGIC's old complaint, the *hiccough*, was creeping fast upon him; and, after tossing off a glass of *max*, making up his comical face, in drinking the health of *Black-Moll*, – 'JERRY, my boy,

'Eye NATURE's walks, shoot folly as it flies,
And catch the *manners* living as they rise:
VIRTUOUS and *vicious* ev'ry man must be;
Few in the EXTREME, but all in the *degree:*
The ROGUE and FOOL by *fits* are fair and wise,
And e'en the BEST, by *fits*, what they despise.
Know NATURE's children shall divide her care,
The *fur* that *warms* a MONARCH *warm'd* a BEAR!'

The orders of the CORINTHIAN had been obeyed like *winking* by the *knowing* Mr. *Mace;* and the 'fair ones' had, without hesitation, *vetted* both eyes with a *drap* of the right sort, and many of them had, likewise, proved jolly enough to have *tossed off* a third and a fourth glass. Lots of MAX were also placed on the table, and the *coveys* were not *shy* or behind-hand in helping themselves. The *spree* and the *fun* were increasing every

minute, and the 'TRIO' made the most of it, with as much pleasure and satisfaction as the lowest *mud-lark* amongst the group. LOGIC (as the Plate represents) appeared as happy as a *sand-boy*, who had unexpectedly met with good luck in disposing of his hampers full of the above household commodity in a short time, which had given him a holiday, and was listening to the *jargon* of *Black* SALL, who was seated on his right knee, and very liberally treating the *Oxonian* with repeated *chaste* salutes; whilst *Flashy* NANCE (who had *gammoned* more seamen out of their *vills* and power than the ingenuity or palaver of twenty of the most knowing of the frail sisterhood could effect) was occupying LOGIC's left knee, with her arm round his neck, laughing at the *chaffing* of the '*lady in black*,' as she termed her, and also trying to engage the *attention* of LOGIC, who had just desired HAWTHORN to behold the '*Fields of Temptation*' by which he was surrounded, and *chaunting*, like a second Macheath,

How happy could I be with either,
　Were t'other dear charmer away,
But while you both *mug* me together,
　You'll make me a *spooney*, (hiccoughing,) I say.

JERRY, whose time had been employed in waiting upon the heroines generally, is seen *ginning* the *fiddler*, in order that the '*harmony*' might not cease for a single instant; but the black *slavey*, who is entering the room, is singing out, '*Massa*, you ought to be shamed; your fiddle is drunk; you no play at all!' TOM inquired of the *covess* of the *ken* (who, by-the-bye, was quite pleased with the CORINTHIAN, from the very liberal manner in which he had dropped his *blunt* at her house) the names of the dancers, of whom he had observed that –

Sure such a pair was never seen!

'*Vy*, Sir,' replied Mrs. *Mace*, 'that *are* black *voman*, who you *sees* dancing with *nasty Bob*, the *coal-vhipper*, is called *African Sall*, because she comes from foreign parts; and the little *mungo* in the corner, holding his arms out, is her child; yet I *doesn't* think *as how*, for all that, SALL has got any husband: but, *la!* sir, it's a poor heart that never rejoices,

THE LITERARY DUSTMAN.

an't it, sir?' Our heroes had kept it up so gaily in dancing, drinking, &c. that the friend of the CORINTHIAN thought it was time to be *missing;* but, on mustering the TRIO, LOGIC was not to be found. A jack tar, about *three sheets in the wind,* who had been keeping up the *shindy* the whole of the evening with them, laughing, asked if it was the gentleman in the *green barnacles* their honours wanted, as it was very likely he had taken a voyage to *Africa,* in the *Sally,* or else he was out on a cruise with the *Flashy Nance;* but he would have him beware of *squalls,* as they were not very *sound* in their *rigging!* It was considered useless to look after LOGIC, and a *rattler* was immediately ordered to the door; when JERRY, TOM, and his friend, bade adieu to ALL MAX. Our heroes only stopped to put down the friend of TOM, near the Tower, and they soon arrived safely at *Corinthian-House.*

THE LITERARY DUSTMAN

Some folks may boast of sense, egad;
    Vot holds a lofty station;
But tho' a dustman, I have had
    A lib'ral *hedication,*
And tho'f I never vent to school,
    Like many of my betters,
A turnpike-man, vot varn't no fool,
    He larnt me all my letters.
They calls me Adam Bell, 'tis clear,
    As Adam vos the fust man, –
And, by a co in-side-ance queer,
    Vy, I'm the fust of Dustmen,
        Vy I'm the fust of Dustmen!

At sartin schools they makes boys write,
    Their alphabet on sand, sirs,
So, I thought dust vould do as vell,
    And larnt it out of hand, sirs;

Took in the 'Penny Magazine,'
  And Johnson's *Dixionary;*
And all the Peri-o-di-calls,
  To make me *literary*.
                    They calls, &c.

My dawning genus fust did peep,
  Near Battle-bridge 'tis plain, sirs;
You recollect the cinder heap,
  Vot stood in Gray's-Inn Lane, sirs,
'Twas there I studied pic-turesque,
  Vhile I my bread vos yearnin';
And there inhalin' the fresh breeze,
  I *sifted out my larnin!*
                    They calls, &c.

Then Mrs. Bell 'twixt you and I,
  Vould melt a heart of stone, sirs,
To hear her pussy's wittals cry,
  In such a *barrow-tone*, sirs;
My darters all take arter her,
  In grace and figure easy;
They larns to sing, and as they're fat,
  I has 'em taught by *Grisi!*
                    They calls, &c.

Ve dines at four, and arter that,
  I smokes a mild *Awanna;*
Or gives a lesson to the lad,
  Upon the grand *pianna*.
Or vith the gals valk a *quod-rille,*
  Or takes a cup of cof-ee;
Or, if I feels fatig'd, or ill,
  I lounges on the *sophy!*
                    They calls, &c.

Or arter dinner read a page
  Of Valter Scott, or Byron;
Or, Mr. *Shikspur*, on the stage,
  Subjects none can tire on.
At night ve toddles to the play,
  But not to gallery attic;
Dury-Lane's the time o' day,
  And quite *aristocratic!*
                    They calls, &c.

I means to buy my eldest son
  A commission in the Lancers,
And make my darters every one,
  Accomplished Hopra dancers.
Great sculptors all conwarse wi' me.
  And call my taste diwine, sirs,
King George's *statty* at King's Cross
  Vas built from my design, sirs;
                    They calls, &c.

And ven I'm made a member on,
  For that I means to try, sirs,
Mr. Gully fought his vay,
  And verefore shouldn't I, sirs?
Yes, vhen I sits in Parli'ment,
  In old Sin Stephen's College,
I means to take, 'tis my intent,
  The 'Taxes off o' knowledge.'
They calls me Adam Bell, 'tis true,
  'Cause Adam vos the fust man,
I'm sure it's wery plain to you.
  I'm a *literary dustman!*

II. RELIGION

1. FAITH

BY COMMAND OF THE KING OF KINGS,[a]
And at the *Desire* of all who *love* HIS *Appearing*.[b]

Search the SCRIPTURES.

At the Theatre of the Universe,[c]
On the EVE of TIME,[d] will be performed,

THE GREAT ASSIZE;[e]
OR,
DAY of JUDGMENT.

THE SCENERY, which is now *actually* preparing, will not only surpass every thing that as yet been seen, but will infinitely exceed the utmost stretch of human Conception.[f] There will be a just Representation of ALL THE INHABITANTS OF THE WORLD, in their *various* and *proper Colours;* and their *Customs* and *Manners* will be so exactly and minutely delineated, that *the most secret* THOUGHT will be discovered.[g]
For God shall bring every Work into JUDGMENT, *with every secret Thing, whether it be Good, or whether it be Evil.* Eccles. xii. 14.

THIS THEATRE will be laid out after a new Plan, and will consist of PIT and GALLERY only; and, contrary to all others, the GALLERY is fitted up for the Reception of the People of high (or *heavenly*) Birth;[h] and the PIT for those of low (or *earthly*) Rank.[i]—N.B. The GALLERY is very *spacious,*[j] and the PIT *without Bottom.*[k]
To prevent Inconvenience, there are *separate* Doors for admitting the Company; and they are so different, that none can mistake that are not wilfully BLIND. The Door which opens into the GALLERY is very *narrow,* and the Steps up to it are somewhat difficult; for which reason there are seldom many People about it.[l] But the Door that gives Entrance into the PIT is very *wide,* and very commodious; which causes such numbers to flock to it, that it is generally crowded.[m]—N.B. The *strait* Door leads towards the Right Hand, and the *broad* one to the left.[n]
IT will be in vain for one in a tinselled Coat and borrowed Language, to personate one of high Birth, in order to get Admittance into the upper Places;[o] for there is One of wonderful and deep Penetration, who will search and examine every Individual;[p] and all who cannot pronounce *Shibboleth*[q] in the Language of *Canaan',* or have not received *a white Stone* or *New Name,*[r] or cannot prove a clear Title to a certain Portion of the Land of Promise,[s] must be turned in at the Left-Hand Door.[t]

The PRINCIPAL PERFORMERS
Are described in 1 *Thess.* iv. 16. 2 *Thess.* i. 7, 8, 9. *Matt.* xxiv. 30, 31. xxv. 31, 32. *Daniel* vii. 9, 10. *Jude,* 14, 15. *Rev.* xx. 12 to 15, &c. But as there are some People much better acquainted with the Contents of a *Play-Bill* than the Word of God, it may not be amiss to transcribe a verse or two for their Perusal.
" The Lord Jesus shall be revealed from Heaven with his Mighty Angels, in flaming Fire, taking Vengeance on them that obey
" not the Gospel," but " to be glorified in his Saints. *A fiery Stream issued and came forth from before him: A thousand thousand*
" ministered unto him, and ten thousand times ten thousand stood before him. *The Judgment was set, and the Books were opened;*
" and whoever was not found written in the Book of Life, was cast into the Lake of Fire."

ACT I. of this GRAND and SOLEMN PERFORMANCE
Will be opened by an ARCHANGEL, with the TRUMP of GOD.[x]
" *The Trumpet shall sound, and the Dead shall be raised.*" 1 Cor. xv. 52.

ACT II.
Will be a PROCESSION of SAINTS in *White,*[y] with *Golden* HARPS, accompanied with Shouts of Joy, and Songs of Praise.[z]

ACT III.
Will be an Assemblage of all the *Unregenerate.*[a] The Music will consist chiefly of Cries;[b] accompanied with Weeping, Wailing, Mourning, Lamentation, and Woe.[c]
To conclude with an ORATION, by The

SON OF GOD,

As it is written in the 25th of *Matthew,* from the 34th Verse to the end of the Chapter. But for the Sake of those who seldom read the Scriptures, I shall here transcribe two verses : " *Then shall the King say to*
" *them on his Right Hand, Come, ye blessed of my Father, inherit the Kingdom prepared for you from the*
" *Foundation of the World : Then shall he say also to them on the Left Hand, Depart from me, ye cursed,*
" *into everlasting Fire, prepared for the Devil and his Angels.*"

After which the CURTAIN will drop—
Then! O to tell!
Some rais'd on high, and others doom'd to hell!	*John* v. 28, 29.
These praise the Lamb, and sing redeeming Love,	*Rev.* v. 8, 9.—xiv. 3, 4.
Lodg'd in his Bosom, all his Goodness prove :	*Luke* xvi. 22, 23.
While those who trampled underfoot his Grace,	—xix 14, 27.
Are banish'd now for ever from his Face.	*Matt.* xxv. 30, 2 *Thess.* i. 9.
Divided thus, a Gulf is fix'd between,	*Luke* xvi. 29.
And (EVERLASTING) closes up the Scene.	*Matt.* xxv. 46.

Thus will I do unto thee, O Israel; and because I will do thus unto thee, prepare to meet thy God, O Israel. Amos. iv. 12.

TICKETS for the PIT, at the easy Purchase of *following the vain Pomps and Vanities of the fashionable World, and the Desires and Amusements of the Flesh.* To be had at every Flesh-pleasing Assembly.
If ye live after the Flesh ye shall die. Rom. viii. 13.
TICKETS for the GALLERY, at no less Rate than being *Converted,* Forsaking all,[f] *Denying self,* Taking *up the Cross,*[g] *and following* CHRIST *in the Regeneration.*[h] To be had no where but in the WORD of GOD, and where that WORD appoints.
He that hath Ears to hear let him hear. And be not deceived; God is not mocked : For whatsoever a Man soweth, that shall he also reap. Matt. xi. 15. Gal. vi. 7.
N.B. No Money will be taken at the Door;[i] nor will any Tickets give Admittance into the GALLERY. but those sealed by the Holy Ghost,[k] with IMMANUEL's Signet.[l]
Watch therefore; be ye also ready; for in such an Hour as ye think not, the Son of Man cometh. Matt. xxiv. 42, 44.
REVISED AND CORRECTED BY J. QUIGLEY.

Printed and sold by J. QUIGLEY, 15, Cable-Street, Whitechapel, London, at 1½d. each, or 10s. 6d. per Hundred; of whom may be had, The Lord's Prayer Illustrated, African's Glory, Lines for a Watch Case, &c.

Messenger
Or Life. and
of Mortality,
Death Contrasted.

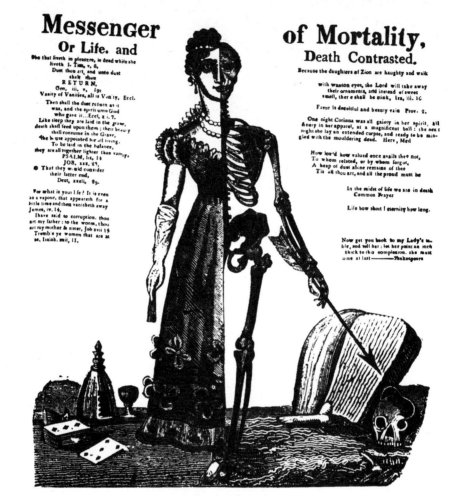

She that liveth in pleasure, is dead while she
liveth 1. Tim, v, 6,
Dust thou art, and unto dust
shalt thou
RETURN,
Gen, iii, v, 19:
Vanity of Vanities, all is Vanity, Eccl.

Then shall the dust return as it
was, and the spirit unto God
who gave it...Eccl, x i. 7.
Like sleep they are laid in the grave,
death shall feed upon them ; their beauty
shall consume in the Grave,
She is one appointed for all living,
To be laid in the balance,
they are all together lighter than vanity,
PSALM, lix, 14
That they would consider
their latter end,
Deut, xxxii, 29.

For what is your life? It is even
as a vapour, that appeareth for a
little time and then vanisheth away
James, iv. 14,

I have said to corruption, thou
art my father ; to the worm, thou
art my mother & sister, Job xvii 14
Tremble ye women that are at
se, Isaiah, xxii, 11,

Because the daughters of Zion are haughty and walk

with wanton eyes, the Lord will take away
their ornaments, and instead of sweet
smell, there shall be stink, Isa, iii, 16

Favor is deceitful and beauty vain Prov. 2.

One night Corinna was all gaiety in her spirit, all
finery in her apparel, at a magnificent ball ; the next
night she lay an extended corpse, and ready to be mingled with the mouldering dead. Herv, Med

How lov'd how valued once avails thee not,
To whom related, or by whom forgot,
A heap of dust alone remains of thee
Tis all thou art, and all the proud must be

In the midst of life we are in death
Common Prayer

Life how short! eternity how long.

Now get you back to my Lady's table, and tell her : let her paint an inch
thick to this complexion, she must
come at last———Shakespeare

A DIALOGUE,

DEATH, Fair Lady, lay your costly robes aside
No longer may you glory in your pride ;
Take leave of all your carnal vain delight ;
I'm come to summons you away this night,

Lady, What bold attempt is this ? pray let me know
From whence you come, and whither I must go,
Shall I who am a Lady, stoop or bow,
To such a pale fac'd visage? Who art thou !

D. Do you not know me ? I will tell thee then,
'Tis I that conquer all the sons of men,
No pitch of honour from my dart is free ;
My name is Death ; have you not heard of me ?

L. Yes ; I've heard of thee time after time
But being in the glory of my prime,
I did not think you would have come so soon,
Why must my morning sun go down at noon,

D. Talk not of noon ; you may as well be mute ;
This is no time at all for vain dispute ;
Your riches, garments, gold, and jewels bright
Your houses and lands must on new owners light,

L. My heart is cold ; I tremble at the news,
There's bags of gold if you will me excuse.
And seize on those (so finish thou the strife,]
Who wretched are and weary of their life

Are there not many bound in prison strong,
In bitter grief of soul who languish'd long,
Who could but find a grave a place of rest
From all the grief of which they are opp ess'd.

Beside there's many with a hoary head
and palsied joints from whom all joys are fled
Release thou them whose sorrows are so great
But spare my life to have a longer date.

D. Tho' thy vain heart to riches is inclined
Yet thou must die and leave them all behind
I come to none before their warrants sealed
And when it is they must submit and yield
tho some by age be full of grief and pain
Till their appointed time they must remain
I take no bribe believe me, this is true
Prepare yourself to go ; I'm come for you,

L. But if you were to me once obtain
My freedom and a longer life to reign;
Fain would I stay if thou my life would'st spare
I have a daughter beautiful and fair,
I'd live to see her wed whom I adore.
Grant me but this and I will ask no more

D. This is a slender frivolous excuse,
I have you fast and will not let you loose
L ave her to Providence, for you must go,
along with me, whether you will or no,
If Death commands the King to leave his crown
He at my feet must lay his sceptre down
Then if to Kings I don't this favor give.
But cut them off, can you expect to live,
Beyond the limit of your time and space
No ; I must send you to another place,

L, You learned doctors now express your
skill
and let nor Death of me obtain his will,
Prepare your cordials let me comfort find,
M gold shall fly chaff before the wind,

D. Forbear to ca l, their skill will never do,
Th y are but mortals here as well as you
I give the fatal wound my dart is sure
'T is far b yond the doctor's skill to cure

How freely can you let your riches fly,
To purchase life rather than yield to die
But while you flourish here with all your store
You would not give one penny to the poor
Tho' in God's name the suit to you they make
You would not spare one penny for his sake,
My Lord beheld wherein you did amuse,
And calls you hence to give account for this,

L. O heavy news ! I must I no longer stay
How shall I stand at the great judgment day,
Down from her eyes the chrystal tears did flow
She said none knows what I do undergo,
Upon my bed of sorow here I lie ;
My selfish life makes me afraid to die,
My sins are many, great and foul,
Lord Jesus Christ have mercy on my soul
And tho I do deserve thy righteous frown
Yet pardon Lord and pour a blessing down
Then with a dying sigh heart did break
and did the pleasures of this world forsake

Thus may we see the mighty rise and fall
For cruel Death shews no respect at all
To those of either high or low degree
The great submit to death as well as we
I no' they are gay their life is but a span
A lump of clay, so vile a creature's man
Then happy those whom Christ has made his
care
Who die in the Lord, and ever blessed are,
The grave's the market place where all men
meet
Both rich, and poor, both small and great
If life were merchandise that gold could buy
The rich would live the poor alone would die,

Pitts printer Wholesale Toy and Marble Warehouse 6, Great st Andrew street 7 dials

THE SUN OF RIGHTEOUSNESS.

Song of the Angels, at the Nativity of our Blessed Saviour. **Set to Music.**

Hark! the Herald Angels Sing.

HE DIED FOR OUR SINS.

HOSANNA;

PRINTED BY
J. CATNACH,
No. 2,
MONMOUTH-COURT,
SEVEN DIALS, LONDON.

THE STAGES OF LIFE

The various Ages and degrees of Human Life explained by these Twelve different Stages from our Birth to our Graves.

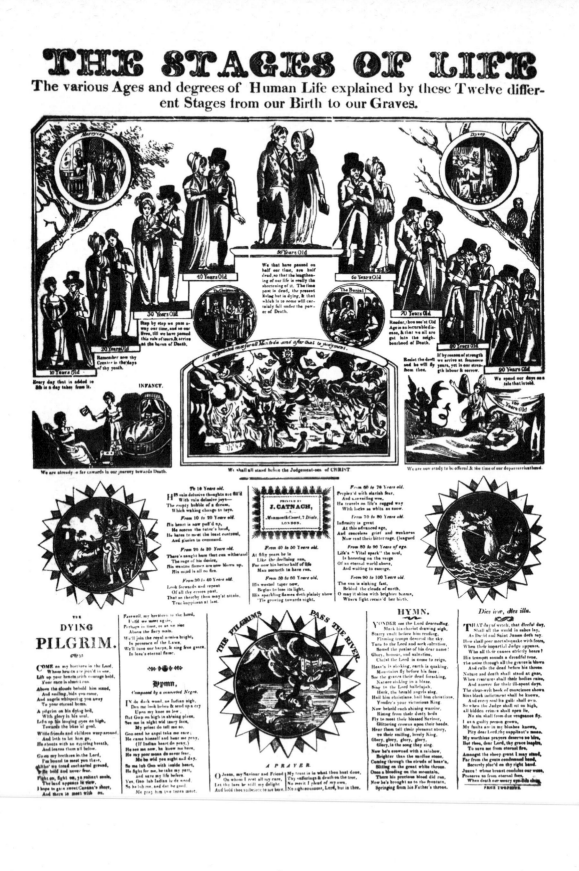

2. TRACTS

ON THE ADVANTAGES OF READING

Mrs. Trueman. In six days the Lord made the heavens and the earth, and rested on the seventh; he hallowed the day, and commanded us to do the same. And how can we hallow it (that is keep it holy) better than by getting up early, saying our prayers, washing ourselves, going to Church, and afterwards reading a portion of the Holy Scriptures? And in order to be able to read them, children, when they have an opportunity, should not fail to attend the Sunday School.

Mrs. Harris. This may be all very true Ma'am, but in my young days, and in the village I lived in before I came here, there was no such talk of learning to read, and I don't know but people were just as good then as they are now; there's my good man there, he can't read a letter, and there can't be a fonder husband, nor a better father, nor a kinder hearted man than he is.

Mrs. Trueman. Well, my good friend, I do not doubt your word, and I am glad you have got so good a husband: but do you not think he would be quite as good a man if he *could* read the Scriptures? In all ages there have been good as well as bad people, but have not those a better chance of being good who have the light of the Gospel? There were people living many years ago, called Heathens, and they lived before Christ was born, so they were not to blame for not being acquainted with his doctrines, but when he came upon earth, and preached his blessed Gospel, how happy were those who listened to him and followed his example! Those also who are able to read improve more, by going to Church, than those who cannot read: they can follow the Clergyman in the Prayer-Book, and therefore attend to him better, and they can read over the Lessons again in the Holy Scriptures to themselves, and what can be more delightful than to read the history of our blessed Saviour? How beautiful is the story of his birth; how pleasing his obedience to his parents, how mild was his temper, how kind

and benevolent were all his actions, how compassionate and charitable was his disposition! He indeed went about doing good; healing the sick, making the deaf to hear, the blind to see, and even raising the dead to life! To little children he speaks in the kindest and most affectionate manner. 'Suffer the little children to come unto me, and forbid them not, for of such is the kingdom of heaven.'

Eldest Boy. Oh pray Ma'am go on; I like the story so much.

Mrs. Trueman. I am glad it pleases you; you shall hear this and a great deal more at the Sunday School.

At this moment Mr. Trueman entered the cottage, and told his wife it was time to return home. Mrs. Trueman, on taking her leave, told Mrs. Harris that she would give a Prayer-Book and Testament to the first of her children who could read, and, wishing them good night, she gave them this friendly hint:

'Altho' you are all now in the enjoyment of high health, the time may come when you may be upon the bed of sickness; an accident may happen, which may deprive you of the use of your limbs; then what a comfort would it be, if one of your children could sit and read to you!'

Though not quite convinced by what Mrs. Trueman said, Joe Harris and his wife determined to try and follow her advice, so the next Sunday great bustle and preparations were made to send the boys, in good time, to the Sunday School; they were up with the lark, washed themselves very nicely, and put on a clean shirt, which their mother had washed on purpose for them, combed their hair, which was thin and short, so looked comfortable and clean, and arrived in very good time at the Church, where Mr. and Mrs. Trueman were ready to receive their little flock. On their first coming into the School, they were a little ashamed of finding themselves so far behind-hand with some of the younger boys, but Mrs. Trueman kindly desired them to come to her, and told a nice-looking clean boy to point out the letters to them. No proverb was ever more true than 'Where there's a will there's a way;' the boys got on very fast, and Mrs. Trueman was called upon much sooner than she expected, to perform her promise of giving them each a Prayer-Book and Testament. They soon learnt to repeat the Collect for the Sunday, and used to say it over to each other when they were at work; they likewise learnt some pretty hymns by heart, with which their father and mother could not fail to be very much pleased. Things went on in this way for a twelvemonth; the farmer with whom the boys worked found more and more reason to be pleased with them. They were so industrious, so civil in their manner, so clean in their appearance, so particular in never using any bad expressions, that he often spoke of Joe Harris's boys as promising to turn out as well as any boys in the parish. The whole family had indeed learnt that 'There is nought in sleep to charm the wise,' and, when any of their neighbours complained of want of time to learn to read and study the Scriptures, Harris and his wife were sure to recommend them not to lie in bed on the Sunday morning, but to get up as early as if they were going to work in the fields: by this means many hours were gained, which, when added together, gave them time to do a great deal.

THE TRACT DISTRIBUTOR

On an autumnal evening, I was musing near the turnpike-road, and had taken out my pocket-book to note down some of the fancies that had crossed my brain, when my attention was excited by a stranger at a distance. He was an old gentleman, dressed in black, mounted on a black horse; and, as he approached and passed me, I was struck with the benevolence of his features. He must have been upwards of threescore years of age, yet he appeared to possess all the life and freshness of youth. He had one of those benign and mercy-loving countenances that one never sees without being drawn by the bands of love towards them. I might be in error in supposing him to be a clergyman; but I could not be mistaken in believing him to be a merciful, pious, and good man. He wore high boots, and kept his horse up to that pace wherein old

people seek to unite the ease of walking with the speed of trotting. His elbows were squared almost as high as his shoulders; and in one hand he carried a large, long-lashed whip, which, like his spurs, appeared more for ornament than for use. A pair of saddlebags was thrown across his saddle; and every now and then he pulled from his coat-pocket a bundle of tracts, and scattered two or three in the road.

NATURE AND GRACE

Visited by Mr Davis, who came to exchange my tract.

NATURE	GRACE
Asked me how I liked the last tract. Replied, it gave very good advice; but, if the writer was tried as I was, he would not find it so easy to follow it. He shook his head, and handed me another tract, entitled, 'Temper is every thing.' On seeing which I was convinced that he had heard of my quarrel about the pig, and designed, in this sly way, to reprove my warmth. He bade me good day; but, feeling he had insulted me, I gave him no answer.	Much pleased to see the worthy Mr Davis come with another tract. Told him the one he left last clearly showed self denial to be the narrow path to heaven, and that it led me to pray for grace that I might steadily walk therein. Observing the title of the new tract was 'Temper is every thing,' I said, it was my constant desire to possess a larger measure of 'the mind of Christ,' which was the *best* temper. After some refreshing converse, he invoked the divine blessing upon myself and family, and proceeded on his errand of love.

THE BROKEN SABBATH

'REMEMBER the Sabbath-day, to keep it holy.' (Exod. xx. 8.). Such was the important subject of an exhortation by a worthy Clergyman, now no more, on the Sabbath morning following that most sad event which

I am about to relate. Not one of the congregation, I am persuaded, heard him with indifference, or closed their ears against his heart-touching appeals, as all were more or less interested in the awful fate of the individuals who, but the Sunday previous, had formed part of his audience.

It was a beautiful morning in September; the sun was shining in full autumnal splendour; the leaves yet lingered on the trees, and nature seemed reluctant to cast off the gay garb of summer, when rather a large congregation assembled in the parish church of Chepstow. The service had commenced, when a little commotion was made by the entrance of a large party into the pew belonging to the principal inn of the town. The appearance of the younger ladies of the party was particularly striking: they were in the bloom of youth and beauty, and life to them had doubtless a thousand charms; and hope told a flattering tale of years of health and happiness to come. The tallest was engaged; and on her return from a tour into Wales, was to be united to the object of her affections. The sermon that morning was on the brevity of human life, the uncertainty of all earthly pleasures, the languor that attends the ordinary occupations of life, the insipidity of its amusements, and the depression of spirits that follows after them, with the constant craving of the immortal soul for something higher and greater than what the common round of the world affords. The folly and madness of endeavouring to stifle the appeals of conscience in giddy dissipation, or to quench the thirst for immortal joys by drinking deeper of the impure stream of sensual pleasures, was also insisted upon: 'particularly,' added the Preacher, 'when eternity is in view, when even now many of my hearers may be on the very verge of it. Some here, it is but rational to conclude, will never again see the sun revolve; and with *this year* end their pleasures, cares, and anxieties, their appointed time of probation, and of preparing to meet their God. Nay,' he continued, in language unusually impressive and energetic, and as if inspired by a prophetic spirit, 'so brief, so uncertain is life, so frail the thread that unites us with it, that even in one little

No. 454.

THE BROKEN SABBATH.

LONDON:

PUBLISHED BY JOHN MASON, 14, CITY-ROAD

AND SOLD AT 66, PATERNOSTER-ROW.

month many that hear me now will possibly have passed away, and gone to their last account. A month!' he exclaimed: 'what do I say? one *week*, and some of you may be summoned to the bar of your offended Creator and Judge. Yes, one *day*, and your souls may be summoned to give an account of the deeds done in the body. Alas! alas!' he added, turning himself so as to face the window, through which the sun just then poured forth his rays in all the splendour of noon, 'there may be some here who will see that bright orb set never to rise again; for in the midst of life we are in death, and no mortal can boast he knows what the morrow may bring forth. Then let me urge you, let me beseech you, (as a dying man I speak to dying men,) to improve the present hour, the important now, and secure your salvation by casting yourselves at the foot of the cross in deep penitence and humble prayer. You cannot make sure of God's love, and of an interest in Christ, too soon; you cannot secure your soul too soon.' Thus he proceeded in solemn pathetic appeals, as if impressed with the forebodings of some awful and sudden death awaiting one or more of his hearers, and (as the Gloucester Journal afterwards remarked) in the language of prophetic inspiration warning and exhorting his congregation not to depend on the future, but to prepare for death without delay.

The service over, the pathway from the churchyard was a little impeded by the party of strangers, whose travelling-carriage had drawn up opposite to it: the elder branches of the family took their seats inside, and two of the younger ladies outside. One of these, a gay blooming girl of about fifteen, whose heart throbbed with joy, and who seemed to inhale pleasure with every passing breeze, exclaimed, 'O what a lovely view! See, sister, those hills, those pretty houses, those rocks; is it not lovely?' and she pointed to the varied landscape her elevated situation commanded. The other, a remarkably fine young woman, nodded assent; and the carriage drove off, whilst their eyes were gazing on a scene they were never more to behold.

The party proceeded to Tintern, to view the celebrated abbey, unrivalled in beauty, and majestic even in ruins. In the evening, as I was returning from a friend's house, I paused for an instant on the bridge at Chepstow. The tide was up; the moon shone in full splendour, so that the old castle was distinctly visible, appearing like a continuation of the rocks on which it is built, which, as they were washed by the silvery waters of the river Wye, and fantastically shaded by ivy and lichens, presented a scene of unrivalled beauty. A boat glided over the surface of the glassy river, and not a ripple disturbed its tranquil smoothness. There was a solemn stillness above and below, which was only disturbed by the wild notes of a bugle, which caused the rocks to reverberate to its sweet sounds. The boat glided on; and hundreds who were promenading the bridge hung listlessly over the rails, watching its swan-like advance to the shore, and listening in silence to the music. I passed on; though well I remember exclaiming in rapture, 'What a beautiful scene! How smoothly the boat glides along! How I wish I was one of the party!' A thoughtless wish, and proceeding from a blindness to the future, in which destruction was concealed. How many of our wishes, if realized, would prove equally foolish!

Ten minutes had scarcely elapsed after I left the spot before a frightful shriek assailed my ears: it was the shriek of agony from assembled hundreds. There succeeded to it a confused noise, that gradually died away as I went on; and lost in wonder at the cause, I arrived at home. An hour, or perhaps more, elapsed, when the housemaid came to me: she was pale with terror, and trembling with agitation. 'O!' she exclaimed, 'O! such a dreadful accident! such an awful thing has happened! The boat you saw, when passing the castle, in going under the bridge, upset; and nine persons are drowned. Only the old gentleman and one of his nieces are saved: the rest are all lost.'

It was too true! The gay party of the morning, that I had seen in buoyant spirits drive from the churchyard gates, were in eternity, together with two boatmen. One body after another was picked up; and in the old lady's pocket-book was written the text of the morning, and on the opposite page was a sketch of Tintern Abbey. The younger ladies consisted of her daughter and two nieces, the first was found clinging to the seat of the boat, which unfortunately was not turned up until the following morning. One of her nieces, a remarkably fine young woman, was not found until nine days afterwards; and then a fearful change had indeed taken place in her appearance. Her cheeks, so lately blooming in beauty, were consumed; her lips were gone; her eyes, so bright and sparkling, eaten from the sockets; and on her brow was stamped in fearful truth the dread impress of corruption. Her lover came to take a last look on one whom he had parted from in youth and loveliness. In vain was he urged to forego his intention: he would see her, and he was prepared for a change; but alas! the utmost stretch of his imagination could have conceived nothing so ghastly. He removed the covering from her face: one lengthened shriek of anguish escaped him, and he fell senseless beside the disfigured corpse. He was removed whilst insensible, and shortly after quitted the town. The agony of the survivers we cannot portray: the old gentleman by one stroke had lost a wife, an only child, and two nieces. The surviving young lady, – a beloved aunt, cousin, and sister; and for many months the bereaved sufferers were inconsolable. One spot in Chepstow churchyard marks this sad event. It is the grave of the coachman, who, on the fatal Sunday morning, was seen walking through the avenue of trees in the centre of the churchyard, with his master and mistress. His mistress observed him steadfastly gazing on one spot, and said, 'This is a very pretty churchyard, Thomas; is it not?' 'Yes, Madam,' he replied, 'and I was thinking I should like to be buried just there;' and he pointed to a particularly quiet-looking nook. Little did he think it would soon become his grave.

Again I heard the text, 'Remember the Sabbath-day, to keep it holy.' It was taken by the Rev. — —, Wesleyan Minister. The sermon was, in its plain and forcible appeals and exhortations, strikingly like to the one I had heard twenty-four years before. It brought very powerfully to my mind the sad consequences of disregarding the commandment,

as they are shown by the facts which I have narrated, and which I spoke of in our circle at home. By a strange coincidence, a few hours only had elapsed, when I heard that a boat was lost in crossing Aust Passage, scarcely three miles from Chepstow, and that all on board (eleven persons) were lost. Among them were many wealthy farmers, going to Bristol, to be in readiness for the fair, which commenced on the morrow; and also a gentleman of considerable property, in the morning of his days. One individual was providentially saved from a watery and sudden death. He arrived in breathless haste at the spot which the boat had just left: he hailed her, but she could not return, because the wind was so high; and so he stood disappointed on the shore, gazing on her as she receded further and further from him, and lamenting the three minutes too late, that kept him from pursuing his journey. As he gazed, he saw a slight movement of the boat to one side; and the next, both boat and crew had disappeared.

How do these events enforce the commandment of the text, 'Remember the Sabbath-day, to keep it holy!'

3. CONTROVERSY

WHO IS ABADDON?

You ask, Who is Abaddon? Mr Glas says (and I think he is correct), The Clergy are represented by locusts, having on their heads, as it were crowns of gold. – *Nahum* iii. 17. The fall of the Assyrian empire *may be* [It is] a type of the Anti-Christian. The description of these locusts in *Rev.* ix., and their qualities, answer to the character and conduct of the Clergy, and their dominion, supported by the kings of the earth; Civil and Ecclesiastical power being blended together in the Anti-Christian kingdom. – These locusts deny, and endeavour to extinguish the *power* of Christianity, with the subtilty and spite of the scorpion, and with all the violence of horses running to battle, and with the same deceit and violence, they keep

men under some *form* of Christianity, and by their power to torment, and the pain they inflict, live and reign and have their wealth and grandeur. Now these locusts have a king over them, whose name is Abaddon, even the *Dragon* that gave power to the Beast, ch. xiii. 4. His name signifies the *Destroyer*, and seems to be opposed to the name Jesus – the *Saviour* – as his kingdom is opposed to the kingdom of Christ. Abaddon and Satan are the same – the God of this world, and the Priests are his servants.

V. T.

THE DEXTEROUS FORNICATOR; AN ACCOUNT OF T. HEPPEL

A Methodist Preacher,
better known in the Northern Counties
by the name of Miss Jane Davison.

'We have a little sister, what shall we do for our
sister for she hath no breasts?'
SOLOMON'S SONG.

During the year 1793 and 4, a young woman travelled over the counties of Durham, Northumberland, Cumberland, and into Scotland; she professed to have a *call* from the Holy Ghost; and in truth she had a call of a very *natural* description. She preached in the Methodist Chapels, and having an impressive delivery and a handsome face, many were the hearers who attended her 'love feasts,' and her success in making female converts was deemed supernatural. A farmer's daughter, named Bowrie, near the Town of Morpeth, absolutely left her father's house on foot, to follow the Petticoat Minister; but Miss Bowrie had more of the spirit of grace instilled into her, than those who heard the truth with their ears in public.

The Grace of Godliness did not long attend Miss Bowrie, she was brought back to her parents: and actuated by the same *rambling spirit*, chose for her next travelling Minister, a grenadier, so little had she profited by the preacher's exhortations.

For two years Miss Davison laboured in her vocation through the north, when an awkward circumstance caused her 'to take up her bed and walk;' at Alnwick, she remained four months in the house of Mr Hastings, the Methodist Minister, where she was treated as 'an angel sent from heaven.' She did not, indeed, 'lie in his bosom, and be unto him as a daughter;' but she lived in the house with his two daughters, fine buxom lasses under twenty years of age; in process of time, they both proved 'great with child,' to the horror of their religious parent.

Miss Jane Davison was in fact a man in woman's garments, a real 'wolf in sheep's clothing,' 'seeking whom he might devour;' he persuaded both these girls, unknown to each other, to confide to him the care of their wardrobes, and agreed to meet them at different parts of the town, where he was to convey them away; he never kept his appointment, but went off with their little all and twenty guineas, of which he had robbed the father. This transaction gave a great shock to the Methodist Church in the North of England; and many of the sisterhood exhibited such *prominent* proofs of this man's power, that they became a 'bye word in Israel.' This man was soon afterwards taken up for stealing dead bodies at York, when Mr Hastings appeared against him, and he was transported for the robbery. Assuredly after such an example as this, the Church of Methodism, unless it aims to 'increase and multiply' by fornication, will not in future look for support to a *pillar* in petticoats.

THE GOSPEL ACCORDING TO RICHARD CARLILE

Jesus Christ not a real Person.

1. The Christian writings about Jesus Christ, which are here assumed to be so many fables, date his birth about seventy years before the destruction of Jerusalem by Titus, and his death at the age of thirty-three, or thirty-seven years before that period.

2. The objections to such an existence are:–

3. That no writer who wrote in the first century, or within one hundred years of the alleged birth, or within seventy years of the alleged death, has made any mention of such a person as Jesus Christ.

4. That such a birth, such a life, and such a death, could not have passed, without the notice of the provincial Roman authorities in Judea, and without the notices of contemporary historians, such as Philo, Josephus, Pliny, sen. and others.

5. That, as no mention was made of the alleged life and death of this Jesus Christ, by any persons in the first century, what good authority could writers of the second century have to make such mention?

6. That, no respectable historian of the first,

THE PROMOTION OF PRIESTIANITY.

" You know that by this craft we have our wealth."—THE MAKER OF DIANA'S SHRINES.

Thus they plunder and bleed in the name of believing,
While they practice, BY LAW, equal modes of deceiving;
And yet with assurance as bald as their pate,
Cry 'Heaven in mercy will soon mend the state';
Like Saints, with a look of serene admiration,
They recommend poverty, curse peculation,
While they laugh when they think of the wealth they procure—
The portion of orphans—the blood of the poor,—

And finally, strut off in royal parade,
Deriding the fools and the dupes they have made.
And this is religion ! and this is benign !
And this is the practice of theory divine !
And this is the manner in which it is given
To ride in a JUGGERNAUT CHARIOT to HEAVEN,
And present, as an off'ring on God's holy fane,
The life of the spoil'd, by their avarice slain !

THE CHURCH IS OUR GUIDE

Exult Catholics and praise the Redeemer,
For having been baptized in the saving
   creed,
The true church, you should ever esteem
She is pure from thorn or weed ;   [her,
She never is subject to error,
She stands quite unshaken whate'er betide
She is proof against hell and her terror,
The Church cannot fail with God for her
   guide

For century's our church has existed,
Her doctrine she spread round the earth-
   ly ball,
To convert the infidel she ever persisted,
And Paganism caused it to fall.
She laid the foundation of intolution,
And stands quite regardless of each revo-
   lution   (her guide.
The church cannot fail that has God for

Tho' Heresy oftimes made her to mourn,
And cut off branches from her spotless tree
she sighs for their speedy & pious return.
Well knowing the wages of apostacy.
The earth often smoked with the blood of
   Martyr's,
That suffered and gloriously died. (guide
The church cannot fail with God for her

Luther swore he'd tear her assunder(hard
And split the block that was knotty and

He roar'd in his rage like thunder,
But all his yelping's could not her retard,
And numberless renegades backed him
   beside,
But these silly fanatics see with vexation,
The church cannot fail with God for her
   guide,

The viper gavazzi, with Russell & Norfolk
Used their endeavour towork its downfall
but since Dr Wisemau is left to direct us
The pot bellied parsons must go to the
   wall
Hell's gates can't prevail tho' in motion,
St. Peter's pure ark will triumph o'er her
   foemen,   [guide.
The church cannot fail with god for her

So now my friends give thanks to your
   maker,   (ark,
For having been placed in the all saving
The Catholic church you must never forsake her
The glorious st. Peter's infailliable bark
she will steer you quite safe to the port of
   salvation,   (ation
Whilst every sectarian will sink to ruin
That will not take god's church for his
   guide.

Jones Printer, Drury Lane.

BEWARE OF THE POPE!!

BIRT, Printer, 39, Great St. Andrew Street,
Seven Dials.

Have you heard what a row & a rumpus, oh ! dear;
There is with the people now every-where,
Oh where shall we wander or where shall we stray,
The Pope is a coming get out of the way,
He his coming to England on Friday night sir,
With his Rubies, Crucifix. Sceptre and Mitre,
His Faggots and Fires. Mould Candles and rope,
Oh ! run and get out of the way of the Pope.

Wherever you wander, wherever you steer,
All old men and women are quaking with fear,
they are terribly frightened and cry out so queer,
The Pope is a coming, oh dear ! oh dear !

Jack Russell and Nosey upon Guy Faux day,
Sent the Pope a long letter Prince Albert did say
To say if he dared land on England's ground,
The policemen should flog him all over the town,
And the Bishop of London will licence the boys,
To carry his effigy—making a noise,
singing up by the ladder and down by the rope,
Will you give us a penny to burn the old Pope ?

If the Pope comes to London there'll be such a game
Archbishops of Shoreditch and Petticoat Lane,
Lord Bishops of Newgate mabe every day,
With Bishops of Wapping and Ratcliff Highway,
We will never be conquered come banish all pain,
We will never have fire or faggots again,
May this bother all end in a bottle of smoke,
Oh England for ever and down with the Pope.

Two Parsons was talking and said in a joke,
That the old Duke of Wellington wrote to the Pope
A tremendous long letter upon Guy Faux's day,
Saying, in Hyde Park on the seventh of May;
Where the people of England would play him a rig
And present to his Holiness such a big wig,
With a three farthing rushlight to stick in his coat
Won't that be a jolly flare up for the Pope ?

Oh Mother, cried Betty, the world's at an end,
Oh ! save me from Popery, Mother,—Amen.
I heard my old grandmother's grandmother say,
She saw old Queen Mary burn ninety a day,
In the middle of Smithfield, oh ! crikey, oh ! dear,
I must not go out for I feel very queer,
They'll kill us and drown us, and eat us I fear
for the Pope is a coming. oh, crikey ! oh, dear

Should the Pope come to England we'll pepper
      his nob,
And tell all the Policemen to send him to q
We'll hiss him, and hoot him, and pelt him
            eggs,
And send him to Rome upon his two wooden legs,
Why don't the old vagabond leave us alone ?
We neither want him or his subjects of Rome,
If we catch him we'll flog him to his heart's content
Thirteen times a day in the middle of Lent.

Come, cheer up old woman, in sorrow don't mope,
We don't care a pin for the tinker or Pope,
Times are different now and so are peoples' ways
To what they was in my old grandmother's days
God save Prince Albert and long live the Queen,
And all the young lasses of Bethnal Green,
Cheer up like a brick sing and banish all strife.
Since we don't care a fig for the Pope or his wife

WARNING.

BEWARE of a NEW SECT of PREACHERS, especially of one of this number, a tall stout man, who goes about entering into houses, and asking the people, "If they believe?" If they do not answer him in the affirmative, he will without any scruple tell them, that they are going to hell.—But if they should appear to be alarmed at his threatening, he will then address them in the most fawning and sycophantic manner, and tell them only to give him their hand and say that they believe, and they will then be safe; or in other words, they will go to HEAVEN.—If this is not Popery what is Popery? It is undoubtedly, the embryo of the Beast. It is generally if not universally believed in Whitburn, that he so deranged an inhabitant of that village, who became so furious, that the Heritors were obliged to send him to the Lunatic Asylum near Edinburgh, where he still remains, and for whose lodging and support they pay £26 yearly; And that he has acted in a similar manner to some people at and near West Calder. The above person has a female proxy, who goes about in like manner, endeavouring to delude the people.

second, third, fourth, or any of the eighteen centuries by which we date, has given us a history of the life and death of this Jesus Christ, upon any authority that will bear the least critical examination.

7. That no authority, such as we require for historical facts, is to be found in the Christian story of Jesus Christ.

8. That there is no better authority than is to be found in the story of Jack the Giant Killer, Don Quixote, Valentine and Orson, or any other fabulous and romantic story.

9. That the alleged birth, life, death, and resurrection of Jesus Christ are romantic and not in accordance with probability, or such matters of fact as we find in the present day, or in approved histories.

10. That the fabulousness or defect of the history of Jesus Christ is visible, in the defects of the system of religion founded upon it, throughout the seventeen centuries that it has existed.

11. That, when Gospels of the life and death of Jesus Christ began to appear in the second century, there was no agreement among them, each writer, in some measure, making his story according to his own invention.

12. That the writer of the Epistles called the Epistles of Paul clearly denounces all other Gospels but that which he preached, and what that is we do not now know, as it has not been preserved.

13. That the Gospels and Epistles of the book called the New Testament cannot be consistently received as according testimonies of the life and death of Jesus Christ.

PROTESTANTISM VERSUS SOCIALISM,
OR THE REVIVAL OF GOOD OLD TIMES.

4. POLITICAL

METHODIST CALL
TO RESIST SUBVERSION

As many of you to whom this measure of national suffering has been appointed reside in places where attempts are making by 'unreasonable and wicked men,' to render the privations of the poor the instruments of their own designs against the peace and the government of our beloved country, we are affectionately anxious to guard all of you against being led astray from your civil and religious duties by their dangerous artifices. Remember you are Christians, and are called by your profession to exemplify the power and influence of religion by your patience in suffering, and by *'living peaceably with all men.'* Remember that you belong to a Religious Society which has, from the beginning, explicitly recognized as high and essential parts of Christian duty, to *'Fear God and honour the King; to submit to magistrates for conscience' sake, and not to speak evil of dignities.'* You are surrounded with persons to whom these duties are the objects of contempt and ridicule: show your regard for them because they are the doctrines of your Saviour. Abhor those publications in which they are assailed, along with every other doctrine of your holy religion; and judge of the spirit and objects of those who would deceive you into political parties and associations, by the vices of their lives, and the infidel malignity of their words and writings. *'Who can bring a clean thing out of an unclean?'*

OWEN'S RELIGION

I ask you, my friends, whether you think men have more charity and love for each other now than they had four, five, or six thousand years ago?

For my own conscientious belief is that they have much less. Two days ago I was told in company of some very respectable conscientious religious persons, and a clergyman of the Evangelical persuasion or sect, and by a very good, humane, and worthy Christian, who I am sure felt a deep interest in my conversion to his faith, that if I did not believe as he did, or if I continued to believe, as I publicly declare to all men I do believe, that I should be eternally burned in hell flames, and for ever tormented by the devil and his angels.

So, I thought, this is Christian knowledge and Christian charity in the nineteenth century. A pretty specimen this, truly, of credulity, imbecility, and inconsistency. To imagine, for one moment, that an Existence, said to be infinitely wise, good, and powerful, should create a being called man, and give him an organization which compels him to believe according to the strongest conviction made upon his faculties, and which belief he, of himself, has no power to change; and yet, for that belief, and this all wise, all good, and all powerful Existence, who gives belief and disbelief, shall punish the work of his own hands by torments which shall have no end!!

Yet, my friends, while from my inmost feelings I pitied the mental weakness of my host, I loved the man the more for the warmth and honesty of his expression, and for the deep interest which he evidently felt in my welfare and eternal happiness.

This party were of the class of minds, No 1: they are amiable, possess the best intentions, will make many sacrifices to do good in their own way, and are what are called the best moral men in society; and this is the highest and best character that religion, as it has been hitherto taught, can create for man. And yet, my friends, you see it is full of the most glaring defects.

Now, if it be possible to make men love one another as they love themselves, and to imbue them from infancy with real charity, pure and genuine as it ought to exist in every created being, it must be effected through very different principles, and by a very different practice from any which the world has yet seen or known.

These heavenly results can be attained only through a knowledge of the religion of nature, the only religion that ever has been or can be true. And this religion, when it shall be developed to the world, and when it shall be fully understood, and when it shall be fairly and honestly applied to practice, will be found competent to make every man love his neighbour as himself, and to have like charity for others that he feels others, to be just, ought to have for him!!

When this religion, of high intelligence and perfect purity, shall be introduced, and not before, there will be 'peace on earth and goodwill to man;' then shall the lion lie down with the lamb, and war and famine and pestilence and poverty and evil speaking among men shall be known no more!

A CHARTIST SERMON

ZACHARIAH vii. 11, 12, 13, 14.

But they refused to harken, and pulled away the shoulder, and stopped their ears that they should not hear.

Yea, they made their hearts as an adamant stone, lest they should hear the law, and the words which the Lord of Hosts hath sent in his spirit by the former prophets: therefore came a great wrath from the Lord of hosts.

Therefore it is come to pass, that as he cried, and they would not hear; so they cried, and I would not hear, saith the Lord of hosts:

But I scattered them with a whirlwind among all the nations whom they knew not. Thus the land was desolate after them, that no man passed through nor returned; for they laid the pleasant land desolate.

Now it follows from this – nothing can be clearer; it needs not another word to make a deep and lasting impression of its truth and certainty upon your minds – it follows from this, that if a nation, by its laws and institutions, commits acts of injustice, tyranny

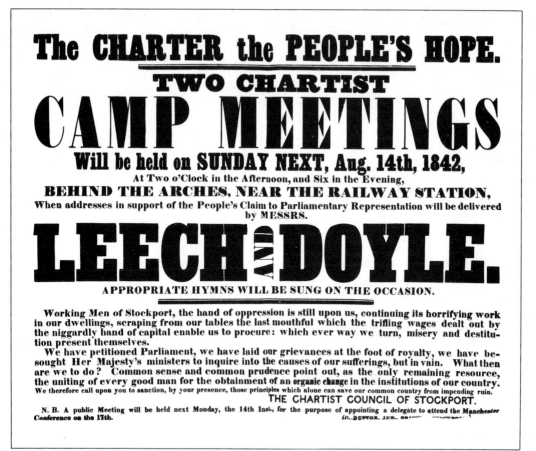

and oppression upon the poor, and especially upon the widow, the fatherless, and the stranger, that God's anger will be kindled against that nation; God's vengeance will be poured out upon that people; destruction from the hand of God, as he here declares, by the whirlwind; the whirlwind of his vengeance will blow upon that land and sweep them away from the face of the earth. If I have spoken, from time to time, here and elsewhere; if I have been plain and bold in what I have said; if I have said strange things, words which made the people shudder; words which made the land to shake and tremble; the words have not been mine. I have not spoken my own words; I have not said my own say; I have not invented my fables out of my own imagination; I have not addressed you in words calculated to excite your passions, and inflame

and throw into phrenzy and madness those feelings that are easiest harrowed up and soonest aroused by men who have the power of speech at their command. I have done nothing like this. I have only said to you time after time, 'The mouth of the Lord hath spoken it.' Have I been wrong in so doing? God is our judge. He is my witness and yours; and I leave it in his hands. I know that he has a controversy with England, because I know him to be a God of justice, and a God of truth; a God of righteousness and mercy. I know he has a controversy with England, because the laws and institutions of England are laws of violence and institutions of blood. If we had nothing in England but the factory system to curse us, that would destroy us as a nation. If there had never been a law passed against God and man in England since it was a country but the Poor Law Amendment Act, that Act, that Act alone would damn us a nation; as a nation it would destroy us; as a nation it would annihilate us, for there is more than enough in that law to make the sea open on either hand, and swallow England, leaving a wide waste of waters along the illimitable depths of ocean, out of which our lovely speck of earth had once appeared. And so surely as there is a God in heaven, who now looks down upon us, so surely will that destruction come which is mentioned in the chapter I have just read to you. I often think, my brethren, that all that has been done in England, of late years, to stop that day of vengeance, will have been done in vain. I recollect that when the question of the Emancipation of the Negroes of the West Indies was agitated in England, I said at that time that God would not allow us to emancipate those slaves and escape his vengeance. I always said that the deeds of blood which had been done by Englishmen towards their black brethren in the West Indies, would be answered by deeds of blood back again upon their own heads; and I believe it will be so yet; and, from all the tokens of the times – from all the appearances of things that can or may be gathered from what we see around us, I am often ready to think that this will be the end of England also. There is more blood upon the door steps of that parish office – more blood upon the door steps of every parish office in England, of every workhouse, and of every foundling hospital – there is more blood on the door steps of these houses, which ought to be houses of mercy, sanctuaries to which the poor and the destitute can fly for refuge – there is more blood on the door steps of these houses than ever was shed on the field of Waterloo – aye, than ever was shed during the whole of the last tremendous European war. There is more blood on the walls of yonder mills in Ashton – and in every other town where the factory system has reared its hateful head, and sent down its hellish smoke and fire upon the people – there is more blood upon these factories, than ever was shed in the time of the civil wars in England. God says, 'Whoever sheddeth man's blood, by man shall his blood be shed.' God's Word says that; and I believe, as it is the intention of God that the

murderer should, at the hands of the law, receive punishment for the taking away of life, so national sins – sins of murder committed by the law – I believe that these national sins, that those national murderers, will have to be visited by God with an awful retribution upon the nation. It is not for me to say, and God forbid that I should appear to you as if I had the power and the inclination to say, that the time of God's forbearance and mercy is utterly gone by. I can only tell you, that from the signs of the times, there is no hope for us. I am sure of one thing, there is no hope in England; there is no hope from England's Crown; there is no hope from England's Government; there is no hope from England's Parliament, or from England's Princes. There is no hope from the capitalists, the mill-owners, the manufacturers, the merchants, or the landlords. There is no hope from the rich, from the great, or from the mighty; and the people are like sheep without a shepherd, unless and until God himself comes down and leads the way. I believe in that God who has often aforetime led the way for his people: I believe in that God who came down to Moses at the burning bush: I believe in that God who went before Moses in the pillar of cloud by day, and in the pillar of fire by night: I believe in that God who sometimes shews his mercy and his majesty at one and the same moment; the majesty making the mercy more conspicuous, because the mercy was more imperatively required by the emergency and the extremity of those on whose behalf it was to be exercised. I believe that God sometimes shows his power and his love at one and the same time; that sometimes He shows his might, and mercy, and majesty together, lifting up the one, and putting down the other; lifting up the poor and the needy, and pulling down the lofty from the high seats they have usurped. If that be God's will to England, and I hope it is; if that be God's will to England, and I pray that it may be; I pray that it may be; if that be God's will to England, there are some that must come down. You have men that go about and among you from time to time, that tell you they don't want to bring anybody down. These men are either wilful imposters, trying to catch a fleeting popularity on the other hand, and to escape personal danger on the other, or they are ignorant, and know nothing at all about the business on which they profess to be sent. There are those who must come down. The mountains must be brought low, and the vallies must be raised. The poor, and the needy, the stranger, the fatherless and the widow must be lifted up.

III. ADMONITORY

1. DISEASE AND CLEANLINESS

THE CHOLERA

Last Lord's day, two strangers came into the meeting, at No 18, Aldermanbury; and having addressed themselves to me, I asked them whence they came? They said from Sunderland. I then asked them whether they belonged to the Church of Christ (not the Church of bullets) in that town? They replied in the affirmative. My next question was, how many members have you? The answer was, between seventy and eighty. I then enquired whether any of the Church had been affected by, or become victims to, the Cholera Morbus? Not one, nor any of their families, was the reply! I suppose, then, I continued, you often thought with confidence, as you now think with gratitude, of the 91st Psalm? – Indeed, we did, said the strangers.

The Christian witnesses the existence of the Cholera with awe, but without fear. The Boroughmongers and the higher orders are dreadfully alarmed. Their rotten boroughs and their ill gotten wealth will not stand them in the stead of the 91st Psalm; with which they have nothing to do, further than to read the 'recompence' which is coming, or rather is come, upon them. The Marquis (a high sounding title when Cholera is at the gate) of Stafford, who is one of the vile boroughmongers; who has an income of between three and four hundred thousand pounds a year; and who lives in the house built out of the public money for one of the 'so-help-me-Gods,' is barracading his house against the Cholera!

The NOBLE, I beg pardon, the MOST Noble, Marquis, cannot stand the Cholera! The postman is ordered to throw all the letters down the area, the tradespeople, in all cases where it is practicable, throw the things they take to the NOBLE Mansion, over a wall; ingress and egress are almost entirely prohibited, and the servants, when necessity compels them to go out, are enjoined, on pain of being discharged, not to go east of Charing-cross. What a horrible thing it is, if a man who has such an enormous income, has no hope towards God! Why the poorest Christian, whom Boroughmongers and Priests have brought to want and starvation, (for they enjoy all their riches at the expence of the poor) is happy in his God, while these wretches are miserable with their devil. The GREAT folks (who are mighty GREAT when the Cholera is at their heels)

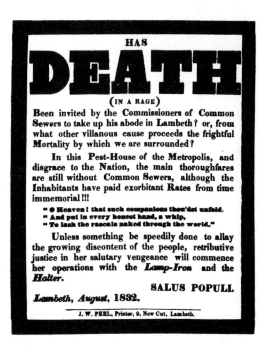

HAS

DEATH

(IN A RAGE)

Been invited by the Commissioners of Common Sewers to take up his abode in Lambeth? or, from what other villanous cause proceeds the frightful Mortality by which we are surrounded?

In this Pest-House of the Metropolis, and disgrace to the Nation, the main thoroughfares are still without Common Sewers, although the Inhabitants have paid exorbitant Rates from time immemorial !!!

" O Heaven! that such companions thou'dst unfold,
" And put in every honest hand, a whip,
" To lash the rascals naked through the world."

Unless something be speedily done to allay the growing discontent of the people, retributive justice in her salutary vengeance will commence her operations with the *Lamp-Iron* and the *Halter.*

SALUS POPULI.

Lambeth, August, 1832.

J. W. PEEL, Printer, 9, New Cut, Lambeth.

about Blackheath are evincing the same alarm and terror, and having recourse to the same means of safety, as the MOST NOBLE Marquis of Stafford. But what, perhaps, is more alarming to the Boroughmongers (who of course indulge in some hope of escaping) than all the rest, is the possibility of the Cholera visiting their friends the red-coats.

ALARMING VISITATION OF DIVINE PROVIDENCE

A pitman, at — , who had received his fort-night's wages, gave his wife twenty shillings of the money to maintain the family for an equal period and, with the rest, (amounting variously from ten to twenty shillings,) he set off to a public-house, with the declared inten-tion of spending it. While there, his wife obtained another shilling from him, for urgent purposes. He afterwards staggered his way home, found where the shilling was laid; re-turned and drank the whole. Having spent all, he again made his way home, – sat some hours on a cold stone at the door. The Cholera fol-lowed this bout, and he was presently in his grave! Some of his family were attacked, but recovered. The bed, bedding, &c. of the unhappy man, were drawn from his miserable abode, and committed to the flames!

A woman in Newcastle, whose habits were grossly intemperate and dissolute, was seen in a state of intoxication at a late hour on a cer-tain day. The next morning she was attacked by this disease, and died the same day!

Another woman in Newcastle, whose name was —, was drunk in the evening, attacked also next morning, and that day quitted this world!

A middle-aged person in the —, remarkable for nothing but gross profanity, lewdness, and excessive drinking, died of Cholera within 24 hours!

It is reported, at a village on the Tyne, one — was drinking to intoxication, and jovially sporting at the Cholera. Capering merrily, he called out 'Play us the Cholera,' and danced about to his own tuning. Then sprawling on the floor, he mimicked the agonies of spas-modic pain, and shouted, 'I've got the Cholera, bring me some brandy.' The derided Cholera, so to speak, marked him for its prey, soon after smote him, and he fell its victim! An awful warning to drunkards, and a dreadful proof that hardness of heart is a *sorry defence* against the arrows of death.*

Reader! are these sufficient? If not sufficient, the number may be DOUBLED! But surely these melancholy instances may suffice to con-vince you that the feet of the drunkard 'go down to death, and his steps take hold on hell.'

Should this Tract fall into the hands of any addicted to this crime, we entreat you by all that is dear to you in this world or the world to come, *to break off from this guilty practice before it is too late.* Multitudes of excessive dram-drinkers and drunkards are yet spared; they have not yet come under God's vindic-tive hand, and we pray they never may. But let us tell you, that if these awful warnings make no impression upon you; if you con-tinue by this crime to rebel against God, and dishonour his name and cause, *He will prepare for you a still worse fate.* God himself has reproved you in the most appalling and ter-rific manner, by suddenly removing many around you. Why has he spared you? No doubt it is to give you 'space of repentance.' But if you harden yourself against Him, *your ruin cannot be far distant.*

HINTS TO WORKING PEOPLE ABOUT CLOTHING

In a former Tract, (No 4,) it was said, that in order to ensure complete *personal cleanliness*, some attention should be paid to the state of your clothing. There can be no doubt that the cleanliness or otherwise of your clothes, especially of your under-clothes, – those worn next your skin, – has much to do with the cleanliness of the body.

*It appears that two of his friends and his wife have taken the warning and are likely to profit thereby, both to their present and eternal welfare.

But there are two other important purposes served by clothing, which demand attention; namely, –

1st. Its power of preserving the *warmth* of the body, and defending it from the changes of weather in our variable climate, on which subject errors seriously affecting health are frequently committed: and

2nd. The effect of clothes on the *shape* of the body; from the neglect of a due regard to which, so many are now suffering, or may probably hereafter suffer very greatly.

What has to be said, then, on the subject of Clothing, falls under the three heads of *Cleanliness*, *Warmth*, and *Shape*.

The present Tract will be confined to the first of these; namely, '*Clothing as it affects Cleanliness.*'

In Tract No 4, you were informed, that 'the quantity of matter perspired by an ordinary-sized man, in twenty-four hours, amounts to not less than between two and three pounds.' This consists chiefly of water, but it is not all water. Every hundred parts contain about one part of solid matter. In this there are some salts, but it mainly consists of animal matter already in a partially decomposed, or putrifying, state. The sweat which comes out on those parts of the body not covered by the clothing dries up, leaving its solid matter on the skin or in the pores.

But it is different with the parts of the body which are covered. The sweat given out from these is sucked up by the clothes, and its fluid portion gradually passing off from the outer surface, leaves the solid matter in the substance of the clothing itself.

But this is by no means all that the clothes get from the body. The skin gives out, not only sweat, but an oily fluid which is poured from innumerable little tubes, or outlets of what are called *oil glands:* and it is this oil which gives to a long unwashed face its peculiarly greasy appearance.

There is yet a third source of uncleanliness to the clothing. All of you must sometimes have remarked, if in pulling off your stockings you turn them inside out, that a cloud of fine dust falls from them. This dust consists of very small scales, and is the outer layer of the skin, called the *scarf-skin*, or *cuticle*, which is continually scaling off.

Consequently, after you have worn any garment next to the skin for a certain time, you are carrying about with you in your clothes a quantity of animal matter, which is rapidly becoming putrid, and as such, constitutes the most disgusting and poisonous filth.

Such clothing makes the wearers offensive to all with whom they come in contact, unless it be to those whose bad habits have accustomed them to the sickening smell which it occasions, and it becomes also a cause of disease. The bad smell is a hint from nature of the presence of something injurious to health. The effluvia arising from the waste particles of the body left in the clothes by the sweat and oil glands, even when they do not directly produce some of the diseases from which the working classes peculiarly suffer, greatly increase their liability to them, and give a malignant character to others, which are usually mild and simple.

The stench arising from foul clothes is not the only hint given by nature in the way of caution, to persons of dirty habits. Those who do not keep their persons clean, and regularly change their clothing, if they have naturally tender skins, soon begin to feel a troublesome itching and smarting. In a short time many little pimples break out, which sometimes inflame, and become festering sores. There is a

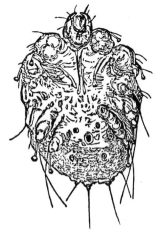

(A) *Magnified view of the Itch Insect.*

I care not for life's gaudy toys,
But love the homely fire-side joys;

The table spread with neatest care,
Tho' simple the repast that's there.

CLEANLINESS.

It is an old saying that Cleanliness is next to Godlines; and it cannot be reckoned one of the errors of catholicism, that they place Cleanliness among the cardinal virtues. That it is pleasing to God, may be known by the ablutions and changes of raiment, commanded in the Mosaic law; and it is pleasing to God, because it is a blessing to man: who can deny this, that has contemplated the wide difference in the aspect of everything, where the presiding spirit, alias, the wife, is a votary of Cleanliness, and the state of things where she is not. How ill-favoured the handsomest furniture looks, covered with dust and stains—the most beautiful carpet, by crumbs and shreds: on the contrary, the polished oak table, the well-rubbed floor, on which the light of heaven shines through the clear glass; the white hearth, and shining fire-irons; the bright fire, which blushes not for the ashes that lay scattered before it, but smiles because only its own clear face can be seen, render the poorest cabin an earthly paradise.—Take again the contrast between that pretty girl, on whom nature has been elaborate, and whom simplicity and neatness render more lovely, who is busy at her needle, while her little brother in his clean white frock is reading his lesson to her; and that equally lovely but thoughtless creature, who, with her showy silk dress, ornamented with dirty lace and faded bows, is lounging on a sofa, reading the last new Novel, her hair hanging in wild disorder on a neck that would be white but for neglect; whose little sister, left to riot about, has clambered on the table, upsetting the inkstand on her frock, and is now crying because there is no more mischief for her to do:—the last may make a good caricature, but the first forms a lovely picture; and it requires no conjurer to tell us which would make the best wife. And now we come to wives: how can the careless, untidy wife wonder that her husband is a truant, and seeks abroad for comforts he cannot find at home? What misery to a man of business whose time for meals is often short, to have to examine every mouthful lest he should swallow a caterpillar in his vegetables, or wipe the knife and fork with the corner of the table-cloth before he can use it, and to feel a shuddering consciousness that he could not have dined at all had he been present at the preparation.— But a word to the men who are so fortunate as to have made a happier choice; it is very disheartening, when everything is well ordered, to have all disarranged the moment you come home. Let not the industrious wife find that her labours fail to ensure the society of her husband—that her neat parlour is deserted for the smoky tap room; or you may have to bewail, when too late, the absence of those comforts you knew not how to appreciate.

G. E. PETTER, 102, CHEAPSIDE.

disgusting disease of the skin, which, if not directly produced by dirt, is much favoured by its presence. It is called the Itch, because of the troublesome irritation which it occasions, and consists in an eruption of the kind just described, caused by an insect (A) so small that it cannot be seen except by the help of a magnifying glass. This little animal burrows in the scarf-skin, and there lays a number of eggs from which other insects are produced, and which increase in like manner, until the surface of the body, in the parts preferred by the creature, is covered with the eruption thus produced.

Some of the motives which should lead you to attend to the cleanliness of your clothing, have already been named. It will improve your health, and render you less liable to disease. It will make you more agreeable to those who live with you, and to your neighbours; and may tend to remove one of those causes of separation which we all so much deplore.

Attention to cleanliness may be urged upon you from higher motives even than these. It may be regarded as a religious duty. In many passages in the Bible, physical purity is spoken of as in close connexion with moral purity; and it is certain that no really good man will, if he can help it, be a man of dirty habits.

In a future Tract, some Hints will be given on Clothing, as it affects the *warmth* and *shape* of the body.

SOAP

In 1791, the quantity of soap made in Great Britain was 43,123,578 lbs. of hard, and 3,842,136 of soft. In the year ending January 5, 1850, it was 179,984,542 lbs. of hard, and 17,447,581 lbs. of soft. The yearly consumption per head is estimated at from 7 lbs. to 9 lbs. The quantity exported of both kinds was nearly eleven millions of pounds, and the quantity imported, a little over a thousand hundredweight. The number of licenses granted to soap makers was – in England, 152; in Scotland, 23; in Ireland, 153. The charge for a license is £4. yearly.

Soap produces more than a million sterling annually to the revenue, and its manufacture consumes, also annually, 6,000,000 tons of tallow, 12,000 tons of palm oil, and 20,000 tons of resin, or coarse turpentine.

2. TEMPERANCE

A LABOURER'S HOME

On a sultry day of last summer, a little party entered one of the lanes branching off from the great thoroughfare of Whitechapel, and walking slowly forward, oppressed with the heat and the burdens they had to carry, stopped before the door of a small house of two stories. The party consisted of a man, his wife, and five children, the youngest being a baby in arms. They were evidently country people; and the wife's ruddy cheeks, and the children's bright complexions, were enough to remind every one that looked at them of green fields and fresh breezes. The husband carried a little girl in his arms, and a large bundle on the end of his stick over one shoulder. The wife carried the baby, and a basket so full of all manner of articles, that the lid gaped open. The three boys, who made the rest of the family, had each a pack, box, or bundle; and beside them was a man with a truck, on which were deposited a couple of small bedsteads, a cradle, and a chest, a table and three chairs, with two or three little stools. They had come up by the canal from their village, and had brought all their furniture and goods with them to settle in London, where the man had reason to expect to get into constant work; and work had become scarce down in the country. He was a bricklayer's labourer, and had a cousin in the same trade, now employed on the houses of a grand new street in course of building in the neighbourhood; and it was this cousin who had advised his move to London, and who had taken two rooms for him in this lane in Whitechapel.

The outer door stood open, and a crowd of little dirty children who were at play in the passage, ran off up the narrow, dark staircase as the new comers entered. They evidently ran to announce the arrival of the lodgers, as a pale, lame woman, with a crying infant in her arms, soon appeared with the keys of the two ground-floor rooms, which the landlord had left with her; and these being opened, our party from the country entered their new abode.

A close, stifling sensation struck them as they went in, but heat and fatigue had got the mastery for the time, and the first thought was rest; so they put down their burdens without a word, set about unlading the truck, paid the porter's hire, and when he was gone seated themselves on some of their goods.

'John, dear,' said the wife, after a minute's breathing time, 'there's a horrid smell, and it's dreadfully dark. I wish you would open the window.'

She had lost her bright colour, and looked faint and sick as she spoke. Her husband directly tried to comply with her wish, but it was no easy task. The window was thick with sooty dust, and splashed with mud, and seemed glued to the frame-work with dirt. He shook and pulled from top and bottom, and at last had to force it up with an iron tool which he took out of the bundle he had been carrying. It was not made to open from the top. The three boys began to look out and take their observations; and Peter, the eldest, declared that the nasty smell came in at the window from that black stuff in the gutter. The little girl was clinging to her mother's side as if frightened at the strange place, and now asked for a drink of water.

'I should like a draught of cold water, too, John,' said her mother, 'better than anything I can think of.'

'That you shall have, Sally,' he replied; and after searching out a clean jug from a basket of crockery, he set off in quest of water. He groped along the passage, and called to the woman up stairs, whose voice was heard trying to quiet two screaming children, to ask 'where the pump was?' Receiving for answer, that the water-butt was in the back yard, he groped his way farther along the passage, and stumbling down two steps came to a ricketty door, half broken off the hinges and without a

latch. Pushing it open, he went out into the yard.

What a place he had got into! Poor John's weatherbeaten face became livid with the sudden disgust. He had done plenty of hard work, and many a rough job, but such a place as this close to a human dwelling, he had never seen yet. The yard was one mass of the most offensive refuse, stagnating and putrefying in the burning sun. The water-butt he was looking for stood close beside the centre of these abominations. He had to remind himself of Sally, and her pale lips, or he would not have been able to make up his mind to pick his way up to it. He did it, however, but when he turned the cock no water came; it was empty.

'There's no water in the butt,' he called up the stairs.

'The water came in this morning, too,' answered the lame woman. 'Well I suppose my husband never told them to put the ball-cock right, and I know none came in last water day, neither.'

'And when will it come in again?' asked John.

'This is Friday; why next Monday,' she answered.

'What's to be done?' thought John to himself, struck dumb at the sudden experience of a new kind of hardship. Many a privation had he endured, but the denial of a drop of cold water had never happened to him before.

'Can you oblige us with a little water, neighbour?' he said, shutting the door upon the reeking yard, and returning towards the stairs.

'I have only a little left,' she replied, 'but you are welcome to it, if you will come upstairs and fetch it. It's hard work for me to carry it up or down, with my lame leg, and the child in my arms.'

John went up, and followed her into her room. It was so crowded and dark, that he hardly saw what was in it at first. On a bed in one corner lay a pale, consumptive girl, of about fifteen, whose cough sounded hollow and death-like. Beside her was a boy about twelve, whose head and throat were bandaged up, and much swelled. Besides these were six children of different ages, including the infant. The mother pulled a small wooden tub from

under the bed, and told him to take what water was there, adding that she 'wished there was more, for his sake.'

He took a little – not all – he could not bear to do that – and kindly thanking her, went back to Sally with it. She was nursing her baby, and eagerly put her lips to the jug; but in a moment she set it down again, and shook her head. John soon found out why. His senses had been deadened by the horrors of the yard, and the stifling air of the up-stairs room: but he now perceived the smell and colour of the water were equally odious.

'You shall have some beer in a minute, Sally,' he cried; and without listening to a caution as to spending their little stock of money, he set off to get it.

At the door he met a friendly face. It was his cousin Joe, who had come at his dinner hour to see after them all. The two went out together, and soon returned with a can of

beer, a supply of bread and cheese, and a hearty greeting to Sally from Joe. And now the comfort of rest after fatigue, and refreshment after thirst and hunger, drove away all care for the moment. They ate, and drank, and talked and laughed. They were used to hardships, and the wife especially was always ready to be cheerful and hopeful. Even the children all took good draughts of beer. If they had been used to such draughts, John would not have kept such a stock of the goods and furniture together that Sally's savings as a servant had bought on their marriage, nor have been able to move his family to London without help, and only by parting with the chest of drawers and looking-glass; but, without a drop of water to give them, what could he do?

When this pleasant meal was over, the present evils did come to mind a little, however; and Joe was asked whether he could not have found a better place for them. He answered, that since the improvements had been begun in the city, so many poor people's houses had been knocked down to make room for the new streets, that there was no getting lodgings anywhere. That they had told him he must not go beyond four shillings a week, and he could do no better. That as to the bad smell, and dirty yard, and want of water, it was as bad as everywhere about; and that a butt in the yard was something above the common, for numbers of lanes and alleys had only one stand-cock for all the houses. He and John sallied forth, and soon put the ball-cock to rights, and shovelled the worst of the horrible refuse that covered the yard into a heap in one corner. That was all they could do: nothing like a drain to carry any of it off could be found; there was none whatever. And so, with an agreement that John should go to work next morning at six, they parted. Work and good wages were sure: that seemed to make all smooth.

By ten o'clock at night, the labourer, and his wife and five children, were all in bed and asleep, in one room of their new home. It was true they had another; but Sally had declared at the first glance that her poor boys could not sleep there till she had scoured it. The wall near the window was green and damp, and smelt most offensively: they did not know why; but it was because it was saturated with the same disgusting matter which had overflowed into the yard, and which there was no drain to carry away. The window looked into the yard. They had done the best they could. John had brought a pail of fresh water from a pump several streets off, tired as he was; and they had coffee; and the little bit of fire seemed to sweeten the room; and they had put up the two beds, and arranged all as well as possible; and now they slept too soundly to feel the bites of noisome vermin, or to be conscious that they were drawing in poison at every breath. The sleep of toil is indeed a boon. Only the mother was roused from time to time by her infant's restlessness; never since he was born had he needed so much nursing in the night; but sleep came upon her again as soon as she had quieted him.

It was wonderful to see how much Sally did for the two rooms in the course of Saturday. All that could be done without water she did. The precious pailful, and the little that Peter had strength to fetch in, she had to husband with the greatest care, and only used a little to clean the windows. Everything was arranged as tidily as possible when John came home in the evening from his work. The back room was of great use, to hold all spare things, though Sally could never go into it without a shudder. She and Joe went out, and marketed for Sunday with the day's wages. She sighed as she put her children into bed without their Saturday night's good washing; but to put by a little water to cleanse the faces and hands of all the family was all she could do. Still she consoled herself, and said, 'The water will come in on Monday.'

During the night, however, an anxiety began to press upon her that she could not shake off. Her infant's restlessness increased; it cried and wailed unceasingly, and little Mary began to droop also, and often woke up crying. She got scarcely any sleep; and the hollow cough of the girl in the room above sounded very sadly in her ears. The heat, closeness, and bad smell, oppressed her, and she was fevered by the bites of vermin. The increasing illness of the two youngest children kept her employed all Sunday. She could not go to church with her husband, nor join his walk with Joe and the boys.

Monday morning came round. The wished for Monday, the day for the water to come in. But besides the continual attention required by the children, a new hindrance to the scrubbing she longed to begin now appeared. A heavy rain had fallen in the night, and out of a court close by the house there began to run a stream of abominations like that in the yard. This court contained about twenty houses, with four or five families in each, and it had neither drains, nor water, nor scavengers. There had been three weeks of dry, hot weather. No wonder that a 'stream of abominations' flowed out of it now. It flowed more and more; and the rain falling again, it spread and came into the room. Again and again did Sally stem this odious flood, and sweep it back into the gutter. Whenever she tried to get to work, this black, noisome enemy seemed to make its appearance. Once towards the afternoon, as she was labouring at her hopeless task, she observed a gentleman on the opposite pavement, who had stopped to look at her. There was something so sympathizing in his face, that she could not help expressing something of her troubles to him.

'Five times this very day, sir,' said she, 'have I swept this place as clean as I possibly could; but you see the state in which it is again. It is no use to try to keep it clean.' He gave her a look of pity, and passed on.

Besides this, another trouble had come upon her. The water she had so longed for was discoloured and offensive when she drew it, and a nasty black scum appeared on the top. A little which had been left in the bottom had tainted it all; and, besides, the butt was old and rotten, and enough to spoil the water had there been nothing else. Such as it was, however, it must be used; and first she set about washing up all the clothes that had been worn, meaning to finish and clear up before her husband came in. But what with the black stream, and the poor restless children, she got on very slowly; and the wet clothes were still about, and the floor still unscrubbed, when he appeared at the door. The bad water caused the steam and the clothes to smell very badly; the baby had cried for a long time, and was still evidently in too much suffering to be quieted; the supper was not laid; the passage was wet up to the door of the room, for the attempt to cleanse it had been given up in despair. Peter was nursing little Mary, who leaned her sick head on his shoulder, and Bill and Dick were complaining, in turn, of hunger, and fretting for their supper.

'Here's a pretty place for a man to come home to after his hard day's work,' cried John. 'I thought you were going to clean it all up, and you've got it worse than ever.' So saying, he flung himself on the bed, and soon fell fast asleep from utter exhaustion. The day had been close and hot, and he was tired to death.

Sally hid her face in her hands, and the tears dropped fast through her fingers: she did not hear even her baby's cries. She only heard her husband's harsh tones, and saw his angry

look. And all he had said was true: it was a wretched home for a tired man to come to; but he did not know all she had to contend with.

That night was but the beginning of troubles. Matters only grew worse and worse, and before the week was out John had found out how bright and comfortable a place the inside of a gin palace is, and never entered his miserable home till late at night.

Before the end of the week, too, the poor family above stairs had all left the house. The father came home one day from his work too ill to stand; next day he was prostrate with typhus fever, and was carried off to the hospital; and the same evening his wife and eight children all went into the Union workhouse. What could they do? They depended on his daily wages for support, and his illness left them paupers. Another family took possession of the room next day.

In the other room, up stairs, there lodged a poor Irishwoman, named Mary Miller, who was out all day selling apples in the streets. As she came in at night she would stop to say a kind word to Sally, or give some fruit to the boys: hers was the quietest corner of the house; but this week it also underwent a change. She had a married sister, with a large family, whose husband was seized with fever, and died. To save her helpless relations from starvation, she took them all into her one little room, which now became a scene of noise, confusion, and dirt. How few of the richer classes who exercise hospitality in their convenient houses, can estimate the virtue of this action:*

The first week was over and John's wages were paid, but part of them went to pay his score at the public-house. It was the first time in a long life of labour that this had ever happened, for he was a most temperate man. He could not bear his own reflections, but the dirt and wretchedness around him constantly stifled his better feelings. Sally had worked hard, but all she did seemed of no use, for the rainy weather made the yard worse than ever. Damps and overflowing refuse encroached from back and front; the children were all fret-

*It is a fact.

ful, and she herself seemed changed. She looked dull, and heavy, and untidy, and dirty, instead of being bright and clean as she used to be. John, however, set off on Monday evening after his work, to search for better lodgings. He could not believe but what he could find better. The wide streets were clean and airy; the houses and shops full of comfort and riches; but everything there was quite beyond his means. He was obliged to turn down the lanes and courts again, and there he found nothing but patterns of his own wretched home. Anything at all better was already full. Many were much worse. In some he saw scenes of misery that sickened his heart. In one room he saw a sick man lying by his dead wife, on a heap of straw, and their children were crying round them for food. In another a coffin stood among the living family, and a grave-like odour told the tale of how long it had stood there. He staggered off and went home. He had gone through toil, and suffering, and sorrow; but this was a form of evil he knew nothing of, and it bewildered him. There are many large towns and small towns also where such things are, and even in villages they may be found; but his village was particularly sweet and healthy, and a well of pure spring water was in the middle of it. There he had been full of care for want of work; here he had plenty of work, and good wages: but they were of no value to him. He could buy food, it was true; but the poisonous air seemed to taint it; and his sick children and pale wife seemed as if it did them harm instead of good.

He went in downcast and moody. Sally thought he had been drinking, and reproached him. He answered angrily, and words were uttered such as had never passed before between them. He took to the public-house again, next night. The week passed on drearily. Joe had gone off to the country to hay-making. He was a single man and could go where he liked. John half made up his mind to pay his rent when he got his wages, sell off all he had, and go back to his village. But when the wages were paid, they were all required for a mournful purpose – to buy a little coffin. Poor Sally laid her baby in it with choking tears, and John went out like a broken man to pawn his Sunday suit to buy bread. A few days more and little Mary was laid in her coffin too. The poor mother sat in the dark back room beside her lost treasures, and the father went to his daily toil to earn the means of burying them. Before he could earn it that back room had to be given up to save the rent, and he saw in his own family what had horrified him in another's – the coffins of the dead stand among the living. At last, by selling a bed, the cradle, the table, and pawning more clothes, the price of laying the little children in our common earth was got together, and on a Sunday morning the heartstricken parents followed them to the grave.

When they returned to their desolate room with the three boys crouching by them, and Peter's sobs for the little sister he had loved so much breaking the silence, John took his wife's hand, and in his plain homely way, asked her to forgive him. 'I have neglected you,' said he, 'I have left you in your wretchedness and gone to the ale-house; but look at me and say you forgive me, and it shall never happen again.'

She made no answer. Her hand was cold, and a shivering fit, followed by burning fever, came on. He put her into bed; he made some tea for her, but she could taste nothing, nor could she understand the words of affection he spoke. It was too late.

The physician came; he was the same who had stood with pitying looks when she had tried in vain to clean the doorway some time before. How changed was the fresh ruddy face now! There was no hope for her in such a tainted air as that which she breathed, and the fever hospital was full. Another week and she had escaped from this rough world, and before she died her little Dick lay by her a corpse. But she did not know it; she was mercifully insensible to all the woes around her.

And poor John, where was he? He had toiled through the weary days with aching heart, and nursed her through the night. But now his brain was bewildered; his head ached, his limbs seemed unable to support him. He leaned over his dead wife, and kissed her, and groaned aloud. On some straw in the corner lay the other two boys; the room was bare of

A SERMON

ON

Mr. Dodd, was a Gen- hola meet Mr. Do will ask him to preach
tleman li v ed with rs, wh dd, and us a Sermon So m
in a few m iles of C o thoug when th eot ing him the
a mbridge a nd had h t here ey saw y c omplim en
b een prea ching a f lected him at a t ed him w
g ainst dr uukenn o n them distance ith "Yo
c as for some t As they were hey said on ur Serv
i me.t his affr o n a Jour e to ano ther ant Sir,
o nte d some n ey one d here is fathe he repl
of the C ambridge Sc ay, the y happeu'd to r Dodd coming, we ied, "Your's,

Gentlemen; they said, we have a favour to ask which must be granted." He asked wha' it was; they replied it was to preach them a Sermon from a text they should choose; adding, "We hear you have been preaching against drunkenness for this half year past;" asking him if it was not so? He answered it was, 'and if you please,' said he, 'to appoint the time and place, I will preach you a Sermon' They told him the time was present, and the place 'that hollow tree,' pointing to one near them, the good man said it was an imposition, for

Be that he ought to have a little consideration Be
loved, before preaching; but they said if he re- loved,
let me cra fused, they would put him into the my text is
ve your atten- tree; he therefore went into it, Malt, I cannot
tion; I am a little asking them what was to be divide it into syll-
man, come at a short his text? so they told ables, it being but one,
warning, to preach a short him the word was therefore I must neces-
sermon, from a small MALT. He sarily divide it into
subject, to a thin then begun Letters; which I
congregation & as fol- find in my text
in an unwor lows to be four,
thy pul § M,A,L,
pit. T.

M, my beloved, is Moral.
A, is Allegorical.
L, is Literal.
T, is Thelogical.

The MORAL is set forth to teach you drunkards good manners, therefore,

M, my masters
A, all of you
L, listen,
T, to my text.

The ALLEGORICAL is when one thing is spoken, and another meant; the thing spoken MALT, the thing meant is the OIL OF MALT, which you rustics make

M, your meat,
A, your apparel,
L, your liberty,
T, your trust.

The LITERAL is according to the Letter.

M, much,
A, ale,
L, little,
T, thrift.

The THEOLOGICAL is according to the effects it works, and those I find to be of two kinds; the first in this World, and secondly, in the world to come.

The effect it works in this world are, in some

M, mischief & murder.
A, adultery.
L, in all looseness of life, and in some,
T, treason.

Secondly in the world to come.

M, misery.
A, anguish,
L, lamentation—and
T, torment, & so much for this time & text.

1st. I shall prove, by way of reflection; and,

M, my masters.
A, all of you.
L, leave off.
T, tipling.

2dly. by way of commination.

M, my masters,
A, all of you,
L, look for,
T, torment.

3rdly. By way of caution take this;

A drunkard is the annoyance of modesty---the spoiler of civility---the destroyer of nature and reason---the brewer's agent---the ale-house benefactor--his wife's sorrow--his children's trouble---his own shame---his neighbour's scoff---a walking swill tub--the picture of a beast---and the monster of a man.

Printed & Sold by T. Ruddock, Stationer, Brighton-place, Brighton.—Price 2d.

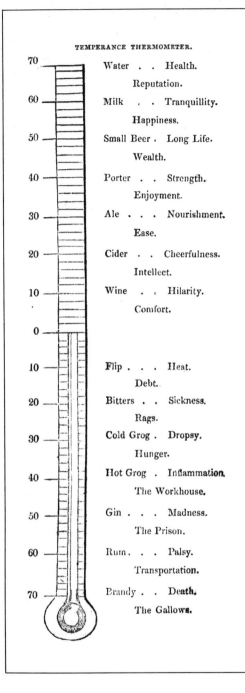

TEMPERANCE THERMOMETER.

70	Water . .	Health.
		Reputation.
60	Milk . .	Tranquillity.
		Happiness.
50	Small Beer .	Long Life.
		Wealth.
40	Porter . .	Strength.
		Enjoyment.
30	Ale . . .	Nourishment.
		Ease.
20	Cider . .	Cheerfulness.
		Intellect.
10	Wine . .	Hilarity.
		Comfort.
0		
10	Flip . . .	Heat.
		Debt.
20	Bitters . .	Sickness.
		Rags.
30	Cold Grog .	Dropsy.
		Hunger.
40	Hot Grog .	Inflammation.
		The Workhouse.
50	Gin . . .	Madness.
		The Prison.
60	Rum . . .	Palsy.
		Transportation.
70	Brandy . .	Death.
		The Gallows.

all else. Beside him stood the poor Irish-woman, Mary Miller, the tears streaming down her kind face.

Two gentlemen had entered without any one seeing them – it was the physician and a friend who visited these abodes of sorrow for the first time. Some exclamation of pity escaped him.

'These miseries will continue,' answered the physician, 'till the government will pass measures which shall remove the sources of poison and disease from these places. All this suffering might be averted. These poor people are victims that are sacrificed. The effect is the same as if twenty or thirty thousand of them were annually taken out of their wretched homes and put to death; the only difference being that they are left in them to die.'

The unhappy husband raised his head and gazed with a half inquiring look at the speaker. The physician took his hand, and then wrote an order on a slip of paper, which he gave to a man who waited without to deliver.

'You will stay here,' said he to Mary Miller, 'until they come from the Fever Hospital to carry away the father and the elder boy; the younger will not live that time.'

'Never!' shrieked John, in a frantic voice; 'no man on earth shall separate me from *her!*' and so saying he fell senseless on the floor.

'You will stay by them, as I have said,' repeated the physician to the sobbing Irish-woman; 'there is hope for him still.'

'I will stay,' replied she, 'and may the Lord bless you.'

The hospital received the sick, and the parish took charge of the dead; and so this labourer's home was once more vacant.

Let no one think there is exaggeration in this tale of misery; such wretched homes, and such harrowing scenes, exist by hundreds and by thousands in all our large towns. Let us arouse from our apathy, and demand from our legislature that it shall be so no longer.

PINS A-PIECE

Hie you! hie you! come with me,
And a curious sight you'll see;
Come without one *if* or *but*,
And inspect the drunkard's *hut*. –

Pins a-piece to look at a show,
Lots of nothing all in a row.

Bring your *bottles*, lest by chance
You should *faint* as you advance,
For as fame most soothly tells,
It is full of horrid smells. –
Pins a-piece to look at a show,
Spit and *pick-up* all in a row.

Look within, and look without,
Look straight on, and round about;
Isn't it supremely grand? –
Straw for a bed, and *grease* for sand! –
Pins a-piece to look at a show,
Tallow for carpets all in a row.

Torn with winds, and soaked with rains,
Paper bags for *window-panes*,
Which, when through the weather pops,
Are blocked up with sods and cops. –
Pins a-piece to look at a show,
Strange contrivements all in a row.

Snails are creeping up the wall,
Round the windows spiders crawl,
A long-legged and grisly throng,
Weaving muslin all day long. –
Pins a-piece to look at a show,
Cobweb curtains all in a row.

Where's the table? That old door,
In the middle of the floor,
Lashed with sundry hazel sticks,
Propped with legs composed of bricks. –
Pins a-piece to look at a show,
Family fixtures all in a row.

SAM WELLER SIGNS THE PLEDGE

Mr Pickwick. – And did you go to this meeting, Sam?

Sam. – Did I not – that's all! to be sure I did; an' a wery tidy one it wos too. Fust one feller vith a vooden leg gets up, and tells the people that he never knowed wot health and happiness wos till he signed a pledge-book, as they calls it. He seemed a wery nice kind of a man, and made a wery excellent speech. Then comed a calico-printer from Stratford; an' he drew a most afflictin' pickter of his case afore he wos reclaimed, for he'd been a terrible hard-drinker, sure-*ly*. Then comed three or four others; an' a wery great impression they made upon the audience, as Van Amburgh said ven all his lions and tigers jumped down into the pit o' the theaytre. An' then comed that young gen'leman vith spectacles on, as wrote the wery celebrated ac-count o' our adwentures, doin's, and sayin's in France, under the title o' *Pickwick Abroad*, you know, Sir. Wery much surprised I wos to see *him* there –

Mr Pickwick. – Why, Sam?

Sam. – 'Cos I thought all literary men wos lushing fellers. I heerd talk o' von o' them chaps as had a certain task given him to do, three hours to do it in, an' a bottle o' champagne to cheer his sperets while he *wos* a-doin' it. But when the person as give him the job, went to see if it wos done, he found that it wasn't begun, an' that the literary gen'leman wos so drunk under the table, he'd been sick upon the paper on which he ought to have wrote. – 'Vy, my eyes,' says the wisitor, 'blowed if you've ever touched that there little job as I give you at all' – 'Not touched it!' hiccups the literary gen'leman; 'vy, don't ye see that I've been *poring* over it?'

Mr Pickwick. – Not bad, Sam. But let me hear the result of the meeting.

Sam. – With wery great pleasure, Sir – as Jack Ketch said, ven the gen'leman asked him to make the rope long. Well, Sir – I see and heerd a good deal at that Teetotal meeting in Aldersgitt-street, to vich I'm alludin'; an' blessed if vonce or twice I didn't vipe away a tear, as the soldier said ven he turned upon the hill, you know, Sir. At last I could n't stand it no longer: I jumps up – starts out o' the pew vhere I was a-sittin' – bolts up the stairs to the platform – knocks two old vimen an' a rayther stout gen'leman down in the hurry and con-fusion o' the moment – snatched a pen out o' the hands o' von o' the fellers as wos sittin' on the platform, and writes the name o' *Samivel Veller* down in the pledge-book.

Mr Pickwick. – I cannot blame you, Sam, for the step you have taken. The Institution is doubtless a philanthropic and humane one, and must do much good.

Sam. – So them there immortal lines as I

wrote to my vife, and which the gen'leman in spectacles copied into his book, page 352, must be altered in a certain way.

Mr Pickwick. – How?

Sam. – I'll jist read them wery remarkable lines to you, Sir, vith the amendment. These is 'em:–

MR WELLER TO HIS WIFE.

There ai'nt no place, my dearest Mary,
    Vere I don't think of thee,
Ven you're lookin' up the kitchen airey
    Vith a hinfant on your knee.
Oh! when you're gazin' through the vinder
    To watch for my return,
My heart, vich your charms has made a
      cinder,
    To wery dust will burn.
Dear Mary, I'll ever think of you;–
Ve haven't a dearer friend than our wife,
As the gen'leman said as wos transported for life
    For havin' married two!

To Dulwich I shall haste so nimbly
    When Pickvick gives the word;
And, seated by the kitchen chimbley,
    I'll tell you all I've heard.
So, Mary, in a glass o' water
    I'll drink myself an' you;
For to you I'll stick like bricks and mortar,
    And I'll toast the babbies too.
But best friends must part, through some
      mishap;
As the mouse observed, vith a troubled mind,
When he was forced to leave half of his tail
      behind,
    As he escaped from the trap!

Mr Pickwick. – I approve of the alteration, Sam. You may leave me now. But – Sam!

Sam. – Yes, Sir.

Mr Pickwick. – When you lay the cloth for dinner to-day, don't put any wine or beer upon the table. I'll just try this Teetotal system for a week or two. I'll then tell you what I think of it.

3. THE ART OF LIFE

THE ART OF LIFE

But the Art of Life can be practised, and its best results obtained, with comparatively small money means. It is not wealth that gives the true zest to life, but appreciation, reflection, taste, and culture. Above all, a seeing eye and a feeling heart are indispensable. With these, the humblest lot may be made blest; labour and toil may be associated with the highest thoughts and purest tastes; and thus the lot of labour becomes elevated and ennobled. For 'all moral philosophy,' as Montaigne observes, 'is as applicable to a vulgar and private life as to the most splendid. Every man carries the entire form of the human condition within him.'

Even in material comfort, good taste is a real economist, besides being an enhancer of joy. Scarcely have you passed the door-step of your friend's house, when you can detect whether it presides within or not. There is an air of neatness, order, arrangement, grace, and refinement, wherever it exists, that gives a thrill of pleasure, though you cannot define it, or explain how it is. There is a statuette on a side-table, a picture against the wall, or a flower in the window, that marks the home of taste. A bird sings at the window-sill: books lie about; and the furniture, though common, is tidy, suitable, and it may be, even elegant. The Art extends to all the economies of the household. It selects wholesome food, and serves it up with taste. There is no profusion; the fare is perhaps very humble, but it has a savour about it; all is so clean and neat, the water so sparkles in the glass, that you do not desire any richer viands or more exciting beverage.

Look into another house, and you will see profusion enough, but without either taste or order. The expenditure is much larger, and yet you cannot feel at home; the very atmosphere seems to be full of discomfort. Books, hats, shawls, and stockings in course of repair, are strewn about. Two or three chairs are loaded with goods. The house is always in an

THE IMPORTANCE OF PUNCTUALITY.

METHOD is the very Hinge of Business; and there is no Method without Punctuality. Punctuality is important, because it subserves the Peace and good Temper of a Family: The want of it not only infringes on necessary Duty, but sometimes excludes this Duty. The Calmness of Mind which it produces, is another Advantage of Punctuality: a disorderly Man is always in a hurry; he has no Time to speak to you, because he is going elsewhere; and when he gets there, he is too late for his Business; or he must hurry away to another before he can finish it. Punctuality gives weight to Character. "Such a man has made an Appointment:—then I know he will keep it." And this generates Punctuality in you; for, like other Virtues, it propagates itself. Servants and Children must be punctual, where their Leader is so. Appointments, indeed, become Debts. I owe you Punctuality, if I have made an Appointment with you; and have no right to throw away your Time, if I do my own.

uproar, and the rooms are hugger-mugger. No matter how much money is spent, you cannot mend matters. Taste is wanting, for the manager of that household has not yet learnt the Art of Life.

And how different is the happiness of the inmates of these respective houses, we need scarcely say.

You see the same contrast in cottage life. Even the lot of poverty is sweetened by taste. It selects the healthiest, cleanest neighbourhood, where the air is pure and the streets are cleansed. You see, at a glance, by the sanded door-step, and the window-panes without a speck, perhaps blooming roses or geraniums shining through them, that the tenant within, however so poor, knows the art of making the best of his lot. How different from the foul cottage-dwellings you see elsewhere; the dirty children playing in the gutters; the slattern-like women lounging by the door-cheek, and

the air of sullen poverty which seems to pervade the place. And yet the weekly income of the former home may be no greater, perhaps even less, than that of the other. You see it, also, in the deportment of the respective husbands of the two humble women. The one goes to work merry as a lark, is always sober and cheerful, indulges in some happy thought while at his labour, is as willing to help others as to be helped himself, is cleanly clad as his toil will permit him to be, besides sending his children to school, and feeding them wholesomely; he is a member of a benefit club, and has something laid by in the savings' bank besides, as a stay in bad times, or a help in his old age: while the other issues from his home in the morning with a soured face and bleared eyes, telling of late hours spent at the public-house; he is unwashed and unshaven, and the mud penetrates his garments at various points; his children are left to grow up

A THERMOMETER,

NECESSARY FOR ALL FAMILIES.

Excessive heat, with thunder and lightning.		The Devil in the house, alias house in a flame.
	60	60
Very warm.		Blood boils. Face distorted.
	55	55
Warm.		Foul language. Disagreeable gestures.
	50	50
Inclining to heat.		Scolding commences.
	45	45
Cloudy and wet.		Passion begins to work.
	40	40
Somewhat Cloudy.		Now and then a Frown.
	35	35
Clear sky and sunshine		Perfect good humour.
	30	30
A little Cloudy		Rather disposed to Irony.
	25	25
Inclining to frost.		Impatient at trifles.
	20	20
Snow and rain.		Frequent disputes and contentions. Prov. 27, 15.
	15	15
Frost.		Severe looks. Hard words.
	10	10
Hard frost.		Now and then a sentence and that provoking.
	5	5
Excessive Cold.		Sullen, alias silence in the house.
	0	0

Printed and Sold by J. BARNES, Regent-Street, Great Yarmouth.

untrained and untaught, and he saves nothing, provides in no way against loss of work or advancing old age, and the only prospect before him is destitution or the workhouse. The difference between these two men is, that the one knows the Art of Life, and practises it, – the other knowing nothing, and caring nothing about it.

4. BE SOMETHING

BE SOMETHING

It is the duty of every one to take some active part as actor on the stage of life. Some seem to think that they can vegetate, as it were, without being any thing in particular. Man was not made to rust out his life. It is expected he should 'act well his part.' He must be something. He has a work to perform, which it is his duty to attend to. We are not placed here to grow up, pass through the various stages of life, and then die without having done any thing for the benefit of the human race. It is a principle in the creed of the Mahometans, that every one should have a trade. No Christian doctrine could be better than that. Is a man to be brought up in idleness? Is he to live upon the wealth which his ancestors have acquired by frugal industry? Is he placed here to pass through life like an automaton? Has he nothing to perform as a citizen of the world? A man who does nothing is useless to his country as an inhabitant. A man who does nothing is a mere cipher. He does not fulfil the obligations for which he was sent into the world; and when he dies, he has not finished the work that was given him to do. He is a mere blank in creation. Some are born with riches and honours upon their heads. But does it follow that they have nothing to do in their career through life? There are certain duties for every one to perform. *Be something.* Don't live like a hermit, and die unregretted.

THE CARPENTER'S BOY

'I wish to speak to Miss Lelia Vermont,' said a carpenter's boy, as he entered a stately mansion in a fashionable street in New York, in 1830.

'Help yourself to a seat in the entry; you will be attended to presently,' was the haughty reply. Then, turning to an individual with whom she had been conversing, and with a sneer (having noticed the lad to have some carpenter's tools in his hand) said, 'I have such a dislike to speak to a mechanic. I hate to encounter one.'

'Possibly he is on business,' said the individual.

'Oh, I never speak to one except on business,' was the reply. 'He has come, I presume, to erect an arbour. We applied to Mr Thomas this morning to have one built, and I take this to be his apprentice.'

Mr Vermont, the father of Lelia, for this

was the lady inquired for, was a merchant of good standing and owned considerable property; hence Lelia's haughty aristocratic pretensions to respectability. Had Mr Vermont been the father of the carpenter's boy, Albert had no doubt occupied as lofty, and perhaps a much more prominent position in society than did the infatuated Lelia. But, alas! Albert was an orphan boy – a desolate stranger in a strange land.

'Pity he is only a mechanic,' exclaimed Lelia, as she gazed with unspeakable delight on the green goose of a mechanic, as she deemed him. 'If he had been a lawyer, or a professor of some sort, he might have been.' –

'A noble soul,' interposed Mr Shrivy, who was a professor, though not an aristocrat.

'I was going to say, from his appearance he might have merited' –

'Be cautious, Lelia.'

'Allow me to express my sentiments; he might have merited the hand of one in the higher walks of life. A noble-looking lad he is, truly.'

'But were he a lawyer, doctor, or professor, and indulging the views he now doubtless cherishes, my word for it, he would aspire to something noble.'

'And where should he seek for noble spirits but among the respectable classes of society?'

'Ah, Lelia, many a noble heart has throbbed beneath the leathern apron of the mechanic, as ever swelled beneath the silken vestments of the lawyer, doctor, or professor.'

'Mr Shrivy, I am surprised to hear you uphold such a low, vulgar, set of blockheads, all of whom you know to be as ignorant of refinement as are the aborigines of the west.'

'Not at all, Lelia.'

'But who has ever heard of a mechanic being a great man?'

'I have. Name but Franklin, Fulton, Whitney, Watt, Arkwright, and a host of others I could mention – and where do you find their equals? The greatest men in the annals of the world, the men who have done the most to enlighten and advance the prosperity and liberties of the human race, have been mechanics.'

'It is a menial employment, and beneath the station of a gentleman.'

'Not so, Lelia; there never was a doctrine more untrue. They are almost the only professions that have subsistence, reality, and practical utility.'

'I am sorry, Mr Shrivy, to see you endeavour to elevate the mechanic to a level with respectable society.'

'Why, Lelia, to the wise they are floodgates of knowledge, and kings and queens are decorated with their handiwork.'

Here the conversation was interrupted by a gentle rap at the door. The lad had become impatient, knowing that his employer would require a certain amount of work to be done. With a modesty seldom to be found in one of his sex, he requested Miss Lelia to give him some necessary directions relative to the locality of the labour. The professor left, and Lelia attended Albert to the garden. The arbour was soon finished, and the 'carpenter's boy' was almost as soon forgotten.

About two years from the period of which we are speaking, Miss Lelia made a visit to Albany. The coach company, and those constituting her travelling companions, she was informed by the proprietor were to consist of Dr W. P., Professor M., and a young mechanic, all of the city of New York. Lelia, while viewing the select company, was thrown into consternation by a wild shriek from the driver. 'Leap, leap, leap for your lives!' resounded through the coach.

The horses had taken fright. They were descending a long hill. The driver, having lost all control over the noble animals, saw that it would be death to remain where he was, it could be but death to leap for life: he leaped. The gentlemen put open the door and threw themselves out in confusion, leaving Lelia, the only female in the coach, and the young mechanic to shift for themselves. Seeing this, the young man, who had previously attracted Lelia's attention, being the only male remaining in the coach, proffered her assistance, which was most gladly accepted. Taking her in his arms, and placing his foot firmly against the side of the coach, he bounded so clearly upon the bank as to be entirely beyond the reach of danger: they escaped unhurt. The next moment the coach was dashed to atoms against a tree; the horses were caught soon after by some labourers on the road. Lelia was melted to tears by the unparalleled kindness of the stranger, who had proved himself a genuine friend in risking his life to save hers. Such disinterested friendship was beyond conception. She inquired his name.

'The carpenter's boy who built your arbour,' replied he.

'Take this as the reward of your valour,' said Lelia, tendering to him her own splendid gold watch.

'I have my reward,' said he, respectfully declining the rich and valuable present.

'I pray you, then, not to decline accepting my address,' placing her card in his hand, 'that should you need a friend you may know where to find one.'

They were within a short distance of Albany, and concluded to walk the remainder of the road. Lelia and Albert were the only passengers who were able to walk.

In a few days after this event, Lelia returned to New York, and Albert, as soon as he could arrange matters, established himself in business at Albany. His efforts were attended with success far beyond his most sanguine expectations. In all his dealings and associations with men, he had a single eye to the promotion of one principle, that 'all men are born equal,' and that inequality of respect should be awarded to men in proportion to their amount of virtue and intelligence.

Seven years had elapsed when Mr Vermont's name was found among the list of applicants for the benefit of the insolvent law. This circumstance for a few days produced a slight change in the conduct of Lelia; but it was like the early dew which soon passed away. While she had fine apparel and plenty of money, she was not so circumscribed in the usual routine of pleasure. Retrenchment is, perhaps, the most difficult part with those who are reduced in circumstances, at least it appeared to be the most difficult part of the way to Mr Vermont. How to descend from the lofty eminence of wealth and fashion, and to retire to obscurity and seclusion, he knew not. He had been too long the child of prosperity to bear adversity with fortitude. He had no profession: dig he could not, and to beg he was ashamed.

'Would to heaven,' said he, in perplexity of soul – 'would to heaven I had been a mechanic!'

'La, pa!' said Lelia, 'what has come over you? I have frequently heard you say that you would as soon be a boot-black as a mechanic of any sort; that it was a menial employment.'

'I grant it, Lelia, but it was one of my fashionable errors. Were I a mechanic, now that my fortune is gone, that my riches have taken to themselves wings, my trade would be a resource.'

'Have you forgotten having spoken of mechanics as a presuming set of blockheads, who you said stalked about the streets with their tools with as much *sang froid* as a lawyer with his books, or a doctor with his instruments?'

'No, I have not forgotten, but I have abandoned, totally abandoned, my former erroneous sentiments. I have very recently discovered that there exists no difference between the books of a lawyer and the tools of a mechanic, save that the latter requires the exertion of the hands, and the former that of the head; they equally promote the operator's design, though I believe the mechanic contributes more to the public good and the public prosperity.'

It was deemed expedient by Mr Vermont to retire with his family from the fashionable street and mansion in which they resided. Every vestige of splendour being now gone, it was with a feeling of relief that the husband and wife sat down together to lay plans for the future. They determined to, and eventually did, take lodgings in a respectable boarding-house, where there was a single transient boarder besides themselves. This gentleman, they were informed, was from Albany, and would remain but a week or ten days at most, having come to the city to purchase some articles of merchandise which were not to be found at Albany.

The dinner-bell rang, and the little group assembled in the diminutive dining-room, the new comers were introduced collectively to Mr Albert Orville, who at once recognised Lelia. Dinner passed in a very agreeable manner. Mr Vermont, having just retired from mercantile life, could speak of the turmoil attendant thereon, the losses through failure and fluctuations of the market, of the restless anxiety, of the tortured state of mind incident to such as engaged in it – all of which Mr Orville was a perfect stranger to; consequently to him it was an interesting subject, inasmuch as he was preparing to embark in a mercantile career.

To Lelia 'twas a luxury to gaze upon this self-made nobleman of nature, rather than to feast upon the choicest viands before her. His light but elegant frame, evidently spirit worn, a pale, intellectual face, ever beaming with the beauty of an ardent soul, a forehead singularly fair and high, a well-formed head, a calm and graceful address; all were objects of admiration to the wondering Lelia.

The limits we have allocated to this narrative will not admit of minute detail of circumstances; let it suffice that Mr Orville's stay was protracted some four or five weeks beyond the appointed time for his departure, in consequence of a growing attachment between himself and Lelia. Duty, however, called him to dash away for a time the cup of happiness he longed to drain to the bottom.

Six months after this period, Mr Orville returned to replenish his store; but more especially to suggest the following propositions to Mr Vermont.

First, the union of himself and Lelia (having obtained her consent by letter).

Second, to offer Mr Vermont the management of his store, having learned his difficulties.

The first of these the old man acceded to with evident pleasure, but when Orville commenced and said,

'Now, my purpose is, if you will accept of it without attributing to me a selfish motive, to remove your entire family to Albany, where you shall during life lack none of your comforts, if they can be obtained by honest industry – '

This astonishing intelligence was more than the good man was prepared to receive, and he was completely overwhelmed in a flood of tears – tears of unspeakable gratitude. The old lady, rubbing her hands, with an occasional ejaculation of 'Heaven be praised!' while Lelia sat motionless, too full to utter a word.

'What! oh say!' exclaimed the old man, 'who can this generous benefactor be?'

'Possibly, my fond, my faithful Lelia can tell,' said Mr Orville, as he handed Lelia her own card.

A glance was sufficient. 'Is it possible!' exclaimed Lelia. 'Is it the Carpenter's boy?'

'Yes,' he answered, in accents of love, as he pressed her to his bosom, 'it is the Carpenter's boy.'

'And the preserver of my life,' she added.

'May he be the sweetener of it too,' continued the old man.

The scene that followed the above may possibly be vaguely imagined by the reader, for I shall not attempt to describe it, lest I do it injustice.

The latest accounts from Albany are highly favourable. Everything goes swimmingly under the new arrangement. The old gentleman is in the store; Albert superintends an extensive business; and Lelia's firstborn, although called after her father, seldom goes by any other name than 'THE CARPENTER'S BOY.'

GERALD MASSEY

When the self-risen and self-educated man speaks and writes now-a-days, it is of the subjects nearest to his heart. Literature is not a mere intelligent epicurism with men who have suffered and grown wise, but a real, earnest, passionate, vehement, living thing – a power to move others, a means to elevate themselves and to emancipate their order. This is a marked peculiarity of our times: knowledge is now more than ever regarded as a power to elevate, not merely individuals, but classes. Hence the most intelligent of working-men at this day are intensely political: we merely state this as *a fact* not to be disputed. In former times, when literature was regarded mainly in the light of a rich man's luxury, poets who rose out of the working-class sung as their patrons wished. Bloomfield and Clare sang of the quiet beauty of rural life, and painted pictures of evening skies, purling brooks and grassy meads. Burns could with difficulty repress the 'Jacobin' spirit which burned within him; and yet even he was rarely if ever political in his tone. His strongest verses having a political bearing were those addressed to the Scotch Representatives in reference to the Excise regulations as to the distillation of whiskey. But come down to our own day, and mark the difference: Elliott, Nicoll, Bamford, the author of 'Ernest,' the Chartist Epic, Davis, the 'Belfast Man,' De Jean, Massey, and many others, are intensely political; and they defend themselves for their selection of subjects as Elliott did when he said, 'Poetry is impassioned truth; and why should we not utter it in the shape that touches our condition the most closely – the political?' But how it happens that the writings of working-men now-a-days so generally assume the political tone, will be best ascertained from the following sketch of the life of Gerald Massey:–

He was born in May, 1828, and is, therefore, barely twenty-three years of age. He first saw the light in a little stone hut near Tring, in Herts, one of those miserable abodes in which so many of our happy peasantry – their country's pride! – are condemned to live and die. Ninepence a week was the rent of this hovel, the roof of which was so low that a man could not stand upright in it. Massey's father was, and still is, a canal boatman, earning the wage of ten shillings a week. Like most other peasants in this 'highly-favoured Christian country,' he has had no opportunities of education, and never could write his own name. But Gerald Massey was blessed in his mother, from whom he derived a finely organized brain and a susceptible temperament. Though quite illiterate like her husband, she had a firm, free spirit – it's broken now! – a tender yet courageous heart, and a pride of honest poverty which she never ceased to cherish. But she needed all her strength and courage to bear up under the privations of her lot. Sometimes the husband fell out of work; and there was no bread in the cupboard except what was purchased by the labour of the elder children, some of whom were early sent to work in the neighbouring silk-mill. One week, when bread was much dearer than now, and the father out of work, all the income of the household was 5s. 9d.; but with this the thrifty mother man-

aged to provide for the family – and there were not fewer than six children to feed – without incurring a penny of debt. Disease, too, often fell upon the family, cooped up in that unwholesome hovel; indeed, the wonder is, not that our peasantry should be diseased, and grow old and haggard before their time, but that they should exist at all in such lazarhouses and cesspools.

None of the children of this poor family were educated, in the common acceptance of the term. Several of them were sent for a short time to a penny school, where the teacher and the taught were about on a par; but so soon as they were of age to work, the children were sent to the silk mill. The poor cannot afford to keep their children at school, if they are of an age to work and earn money. They must help to eke out the parents' slender gains, even though it be only a few pence weekly. So, at eight years of age, Gerald Massey went into the silk-manufactory, rising at five o'clock in the morning, and toiling there till half-past six in the evening; up in the grey dawn, or in the winter before the daylight, and trudging to the factory through the wind or in the snow; seeing the sun only through the factory windows; breathing an atmosphere laden with rank oily vapour, his ears deafened by the roar of incessant wheels,

'Still, all day the iron wheels go onward,
  Grinding life down from its mark;
And the children's souls which God is calling
    sunward
  Spin on blindly in the dark.'

What a life for a child! What a substitute for tender prattle, for childish glee, for youthful playtime! Then home shivering under the cold, starless sky, on Saturday nights, with 9d., 1s., or 1s. 3d., for the whole week's work; for such were the respective amounts of the wages earned by the child labour of Gerald Massey.

But the mill was burned down, and the children held jubilee over it. The boy stood for twelve hours in the wind, and sleet, and mud, rejoicing in the conflagration which thus liberated him. Who can wonder at this? Then he went to straw-plaiting – as toilsome, and perhaps more unwholesome than factory-work. Without exercise, in a marshy district, the plaiters were constantly having racking attacks of ague. The boy had the disease for three years, ending with tertian ague. Sometimes four of the family and the mother, lay ill of the disease at one time, all crying with thirst, with no one to give them drink, and each too weak to help the other. How little do we know of the sufferings endured by the poor and struggling classes of our population, especially in our rural districts! No press echoes their wants or records their sufferings; and they live almost as unknown to us as if they were the inhabitants of some undiscovered country.

And now, take as an illustration of this vivid picture, the child-life of Gerald Massey. 'Having had to earn my own dear bread,' he says, 'by the eternal cheapening of flesh and blood thus early, I never knew what childhood meant. I had no childhood. Ever since I can remember, I have had the aching fear of want, throbbing in heart and brow. The currents of my life were early poisoned, and few, methinks, would pass unscathed through the scenes and circumstances in which I have lived; none if they were as curious and precocious as I was. The child comes into the world like a new coin with the stamp of God upon it, and in like manner as the Jews sweat down sovereigns by hustling them in a bag to get gold-dust out of them, so is the poor man's child hustled and sweated down in this bag of society to get wealth out of it; and even as the impress of the Queen is effaced by the Jewish process, so is the image of God worn from heart and brow, and day-by-day the child recedes devil-ward. I look back now with wonder, not that so few escape, but that any escape at all, to win a nobler growth for their humanity. So blighting are the influences which surround thousands in early life, to which I can bear such bitter testimony.'

And how fared the growth of this child's mind the while? Thanks to the care of his mother, who had sent him to the penny school, he had learnt to read, and the desire to read had been awakened. Books, however, were very scarce. The Bible and Bunyan were the principal; he committed many chapters of the former to memory, and accepted all Bunyan's

allegory as *bona fide* history. Afterwards he obtained access to 'Robinson Crusoe' and a few Wesleyan tracts left at the cottage. These constituted his sole reading, until he came up to London at the age of fifteen, as an errand boy; and now for the first time in his life he met with plenty of books, reading all that came in his way, from *Lloyd's Penny Times*, to Cobbett's works, 'French without a Master,' together with English, Roman, and Grecian history. A ravishing awakenment ensued – the delightful sense of growing knowledge – the charm of new thought – the wonders of a new world. 'Till then,' he says, 'I had often wondered why I lived at all – whether,

> It was not better not to be
> I was so full of misery.

Now I began to think that the crown of all desire, and the sum of all existence, was to read and get knowledge. Read! read! read! I used to read at all possible times, and in all possible places; up in bed till two or three in the morning – nothing daunted by once setting the bed on fire. Greatly indebted was I also to the bookstalls, where I have read a great deal, often folding a leaf in a book and returning the next day to continue the subject; but sometimes the book was gone, and then great was my grief! When out of a situation, I have often gone without a meal to purchase a book. Until I fell in love, and began to rhyme as a matter of consequence, I never had the least predilection for poetry. In fact, I always eschewed it; if I ever met with any, I instantly skipped it over, and passed on as one does with the description of scenery, &c., in a novel. I always loved the birds and flowers, the woods and the stars; I felt delight in being alone in a summer-wood, with song like a spirit in the trees, and the golden sun-bursts glinting through the verdurous roof, and was conscious of a mysterious creeping of the blood and tingling of the nerves, when standing alone in the starry midnight, as in God's own presence-chamber. But until I began to rhyme, I cared nothing for written poetry; the first verses I ever made were upon 'Hope,' when I was utterly hopeless; and after I had begun, I never ceased for about four years, at the end of which time I rushed into print.'

There was, of course, crudeness both of thought and expression in the first verses of the poet, which were published in a provincial paper. But there was nerve, rhythm, and poetry; the burthen of the song was 'At even-time it shall be light.' The leading idea of the poem was the power of knowledge, virtue, and temperance, to elevate the condition of the poor – a noble idea truly. Shortly after he was encouraged to print a shilling volume of 'Poems and Chansons' in his native town of Tring, of which some 250 copies were sold. Of his later poems we shall afterwards speak.

But a new power was now working upon his nature, as might have been expected – the power of opinion as expressed in books, and in the discussions of his fellow workers.

'As an errand boy,' he says, 'I had of course many hardships to undergo, and to bear with much tyranny; and that led me into reasoning upon men and things, the causes of misery, the anomalies of our societary state, politics, &c.; and the circle of my being rapidly out-surged! New power came to me with all that I saw, and thought, and read. I studied political works – such as Paine, Volney, Howitt, Louis Blanc, &c., which gave me another element to mould into my verse, though I am convinced that a poet must sacrifice much if he write party political poetry. His politics must be above the pinnacle of party-zeal; the politics of eternal truth, right, and justice. He must not waste a life on what to-morrow may prove

to have been merely the question of a day. The French Revolution of 1848 had the greatest effect on me of any circumstance connected with my own life. It was scarred and blood-burnt into the very core of my being. This little volume of mine is the fruit thereof.'

But meanwhile, he had been engaged in other literary work. Full of new thoughts, and bursting with aspirations for freedom, he started, in April, 1849, a cheap journal, written entirely by working men, entitled 'The Spirit of Freedom:' it was full of fiery earnestness, and half of its weekly contents were supplied by Gerald Massey himself, who acted as editor. It cost him five situations during a period of eleven months, – twice because he was detected burning candle far on into the night, and three times because of the tone of the opinions to which he gave utterance. The French Revolution of 1848 having amongst its other issues, kindled the zeal of the working men in this country in the cause of association, Gerald Massey eagerly joined them, and he has been recently instrumental in giving some impetus to that praiseworthy movement, – the object of which is to permanently elevate the condition of the producing classes, by advancing them to the status of capitalists as well as labourers. He is now the Secretary to the Working Tailors' Association, at 34, Castle Street East, Oxford Street, an association of which we have already given some account in this journal.

IV. FABLES

1. TALES

WONDERFUL ADVENTURES OF THE SEVEN CHAMPIONS OF CHRISTENDOM

In former times, a very great while since, when there were giants, enchanters, and magicians, who had the power to do wicked actions, it was foretold, that seven worthy champions would arise in Christendom, whose renown for good and valiant deeds should be spread through the whole earth. – The first of these heroes was to be St Denis of France, the second St James of Spain, the third St Anthony of Italy, the fourth St Andrew of Scotland, the fifth St Patrick of Ireland, the sixth St David of Wales, and the seventh, and most famous of all, the valiant St George of England.

Calyba, a great and most wicked enchantress, now trembled for the downfall of her power, so she sent the evil spirits under her command to steal six of these heroes while they were yet in their cradles, and bring them to her brazen castle. But she thought she would herself make sure of St George, who was born in Coventry, and son to the lord high steward of England; for she was much more afraid of him than of the others, as George had at the time of his birth the marks of a green dragon on his breast, a red cross on his right arm, and a golden garter on his left leg. Calyba then made herself invisible, entered the nursery of the lord high steward, and bore away the lovely sleeping babe, leaving his parents to die of grief for the loss of him.

Calyba kept all these youths in her castle till they grew to be men; and then the beauty of St George's person, his manly figure, and pleasing manners, won the heart of Calyba and she used all her arts to make him marry her.

One day she led him into a lofty stable, almost grand enough to be taken for a palace, where seven of the finest horses that ever were seen, stood in seven stalls made of cedar wood, inlaid with silver; one of them was even finer and larger than the rest; his hoofs were of pure gold, and his saddle and bridle were adorned with precious stones. Calyba led this from the stall, and gave it to St George: its name was Bucephalus. She then led St George into an armoury, where she buckled a noble breastplate upon him, placed a helmet, with a lofty plume of waving feathers, upon his head, and gave him a fine sharp sword. When the young

champion was thus armed for battle, he looked so very handsome, that Calyba could set no bounds to her love for him: so at last she put into his hand the silver wand which gave him all her power, and told him to use it just as he pleased.

St George knew, and hated the wicked actions of Calyba, so he took the wand with a pleasure which he could hardly conceal. It was then about the hour that Calyba used to retire to a cave dug in the solid rock, to feast upon the bodies of children that she had killed. St George watched her, and when he saw her enter the cave, he waved the wand three times, and the rock shut upon the wicked wretch for ever.

He then set out for Coventry along with the other six champions; and in that time he built a grand monument to the memory of his beloved parents.

Early in the next spring, the seven heroes bade each other farewell, and they all took different roads in search of adventures; and St George of England, after some tiresome voyages and travels, came into Egypt. That country was then in a most wretched state, on account of a dreadful fiery dragon, which tainted the air with his breath in such a manner, that a plague raged through all the land, and there were hardly people enough left alive to bury the dead. For this reason the king had made it known, that if any valiant knight would come forward to fight with the fiery dragon, he should receive the hand of the princess royal in marriage, and on the king's death should reign over Egypt.

When St George heard this, he declared that he would himself fight the dragon, for the sake of the princess and the whole kingdom.

Early the next morning St George set out to find the fiery dragon. He had not gone far before he saw the princess Sabra, with some of her women, who were loudly weeping for the cruel state of the country. Our hero rode up to them, and told them he was resolved either to kill the dragon, or to perish in the trial. The fair Sabra was struck with surprise on finding that a stranger would engage in an attempt of so much danger, which the stoutest of the Egyptian champions had shrunk from with fear: but she thanked him in a proper manner, and, by St George's advice, she went back to her palace, to wait for the issue of the great event.

As soon as our hero had reached the cave, the dragon sent forth such a dreadful roaring as seemed to shake the earth; and at the first onset St George's spear was broken to pieces, and he himself was thrown from his horse. He then boldly drew his sword, and though almost stifled by the monster's noisome breath, he fought with such fury, that he soon felled his enemy beneath his feet. At this moment the dragon spread his wings in order to take flight: but by so doing, he showed a soft part of his skin, and St George at once stabbed him to the heart. The monster died with a horrid groan, and St George, having cut off his head, rode back in triumph towards the palace.

He had hardly reached the city, when he was basely set upon by twelve armed men, whom the king of Morocco (who courted the princess Sabra) had hired to kill him. St George soon put these villains to flight; and when he came to the court, he was treated with all sorts of honours, and the lovely Sabra gave him a diamond ring, as a small mark of her esteem.

In spite of this failure, the Moorish prince still vowed to destroy or ruin St George. For this purpose he asked a private audience of the king, and told him, that St George was an open foe to the religion of Egypt, and had tried to make the Princess a Christian. The king was so angry when he heard this, that he declared St George should not live any longer; but as it might not have been safe to put him to death in Egypt, where he had done such a great service to the people in killing the dragon, he wrote a letter to the sultan of Persia, begging him to put the bearer, St George, to death, as he was an enemy to the religion of Persia and Egypt.

St George little thought of this deceit, so he took this letter to the sultan; but as soon as he came into Persia he was taken up, and brought before the sultan, who had him thrown into a deep dungeon till a day should be fixed for his death.

At the end of three days, two fierce and hungry lions were put into the dungeon; but St George having prayed to heaven for strength, burst the cords which he was bound with, and finding an old broken rusty sword in a corner of the dungeon, he laid both the lions dead at his feet.

The sultan of Persia was amazed at this; and was afraid to put to death in public the noble champion, so he kept him in prison, where we will leave him at present, to look after the other champions.

[*Then follow the adventures of the other six champions.*]

While the other champions were doing these great exploits, St George of England, after being kept seven years in prison, found means one night to break out of his dungeon, and then went onward till he arrived at the garden of Ormandine, where St David had at that time slept seven years. When St George saw the enchanted sword, he seized it, and pulled it up: the castle then sunk into the ground, and the wicked enchanter was carried away with it. After this, St David went back to the court of Tartary, and St George went to Barbary.

St George heard on his journey, that the king of Morocco and his nobles were gone to enjoy the pleasure of hunting. He then put on a hermit's gown, made haste to the palace, where a number of beggars were waiting to receive alms from the fair Sabra. St George mixed with the crowd; and when he saw the princess, he slipped the diamond ring, which she had given him, into her hand: she then led him into the hall, and gladly agreed to escape before the tyrant should come back, who had long tried to force her to marry him. Towards the evening of the same day, the princess and a Moorish servant contrived to meet St George at the hermit's cave, where our champion put on his armour. Then taking the fair Sabra behind him, and being attended by the Moor, he gallopped off as quickly as he could, till he had got quite out of the kingdom of Barbary.

After a tiresome journey, they found themselves near a large forest; and as they were faint with hunger, St George left his lady with the Moor, and went boldly into the forest to procure some food. He had the good fortune to kill a deer, and returned with a haunch of venison; but how greatly was he shocked to find the Moor torn in pieces by two lions, and the creatures asleep on Sabra's lap! After getting the better of his first alarm, he ran them through with his sword, and gave thanks to Heaven for the safety of his beloved princess.

St George and his lady at length came to Constantinople, where a great feast was held in honour of the emperor's marriage. In this city they had the good fortune to meet the other six champions, who, after many strange adventures, had also arrived at Constantinople with their ladies. Here the Christian champions showed wonders of courage in warlike games, with the knights of Greece, Hungary, and Bohemia. On the last day of these sports, St George of England came into the field on a beautiful black steed; while the lovely Sabra sat in a car of triumph, to be a witness of his noble exploits. There was hardly any knight who would engage against the hero of England; and when at last some of them made trial of his strength, he threw down men and horses with such ease, that the field was soon cleared. The heralds crowned him with the garland of victory, and Sabra felt the highest pleasure in hearing the shouts of all the people.

But while the Christian champions were happy in the friendship of the emperor, and the enjoyment of their charming brides, the king of Morocco and the pagan princes, whose daughters had followed these champions, declared war against Christendom. On this the emperor of Constantinople made peace with his other foes, and then begged the champions to depart from his country. The Christian heroes and their ladies now left Constantinople; and agreed that every one should repair to his own land, and raise forces to subdue their enemies.

When the cause of their return was known, such numbers of people flocked to join them, that by the next spring they had an army of five hundred thousand men; who chose St George to be their leader.

The pagans got together an army still greater than that of the Christians; but when they came to choose a general, they could not agree among themselves, and the dispute rose to such a height, that the kings of Persia,

Egypt, and Jerusalem, soon drew off their armies, and went back into their own countries. Those who staid with the king of Morocco, split into parties, and fought a dreadful battle among themselves, with such fury, that the fields were covered with dead bodies, and the rivers stained with blood.

The Christian army at last came to the borders of Egypt; and when they marched into the inner parts of that country, they found the villages and most of the towns empty. St George was fearful that this was only a plan laid to deceive him; so he told his soldiers to remain in their ranks, and to have their arms ready in case of a sudden attack. They then marched to the capital in perfect order, till they came near the palace, when the gates were thrown open on a sudden; and the king of Egypt, in deep mourning, walked forth at the head of his nobles, and the great officers of the kingdom, with broken swords and lances. On their coming near the Christian champions, they all fell upon their knees, while the king in humble terms begged for peace.

St George said he would freely forgive him, if he and all his nobles should become Christians. The king gladly agreed to this, and made a promise of his own free-will, that the crown of Egypt should belong to St George and Sabra after his death.

An English knight now arrived, and told St George that his Sabra, who had been left in England, was condemned to be burnt, unless some champion should appear to take her part against her false accuser.

When St George heard this, he set out for England, where he arrived on the very day fixed for Sabra's death.

The king of England caused the heralds to summon the accuser, who came forward on a proud steed, adorned with gold and precious stones. The lady's champion was then called, and St George rushed through the crowd, demanding that he might fight in her defence.

The heralds sounded a charge, and the two knights engaged. At the first onset, their spears were broken into pieces, and men and horses were thrown to the ground. The accuser leaped up, and struck so fiercely, that he cleft his enemy's shield in two. St George then put forth his strength, and smote off the accuser's right arm, so that he sank to the earth, and died.

St George now set sail with his beloved Sabra for Persia, which on reaching, he found the other six champions had conquered. After completing their conquest, the seven champions took shipping for England, where they were received with every mark of joy.

The six champions then embraced St George; and then set out together to return to their native countries, where they lived honoured and beloved, and after their deaths their names were enrolled among the saints of Christendom.

LETTERS OF THE BLACK DWARF

From the Black Dwarf in Warwick Gaol, to the Yellow Bonze at Japan.

> I CAN'T GET OUT! I CAN'T GET OUT!
> *Sterne's Starling.*

> Every island's but a prison,
>   Strongly guarded by the sea;
> King's and princes, for that reason,
>   Prisoners are, as well as we!
> *Alexander Stevens.*

RESPECTED FRIEND,

I have at last, after a laborious, and lengthened political journey of nearly four years and a half, reached a *resting-place*, in *safety;* – on the heights of which I may sit down in quietude, and calmly survey the rugged region through which my footsteps have passed. And, in truth, when I remember the difficulties and dangers of the way – what monsters I have encountered, what giants, what griffins, from the man who carried his ears in his hands, (as we are told, in some half-discovered region, men carry their heads under their arms,) down to the Dragon of Wantley, and the city-gogs, – it is amazing that I have not long since been swallowed up, as the renowned Tom Thumb was by the dun cow, and buried in the sepulchre of the capacious bowels of the sturdy tax-eater! It has been 'how little distant dangers seem!' but I am satisfied, that the more environed a MAN is with perils, the less he sees of them. A poor *dwarf* like me may be permitted to look round him with more anxiety than a *man* is expected to do; and, in a natural wish 'to keep his limbs, and to preserve his sight,' to take as much care as he can, lest some of the magogs among whom he is compelled to move, may not trample under foot, and crush his little bones to pieces. Yet I, with all my care to walk steadily, and to keep out of the way of madmen, knaves, fools, and mischievous imps, saw not half the dangers to which I have been exposed, until I reached my present elevation, and took a general view of the 'valley of death,' through which my *rash indiscretion* had tempted me to urge my luckless way! It is from sheer good fortune, that I have not been killed, and eaten up, a great while ago. I was indeed taught to believe that I was prepared for a defence – that I was 'arm'd at all points, exactly cap-a-pee!' with a certain *imaginary shield* which it is here pretended is thrown alike over all, who have need of its protection. This shield is composed of *parchment* and *paper*, with a multitudinous assemblage of *magical words* written thereon; and is called the *shield of law!* As soon as *a stranger* arrives here, they *tell* him he is invested with it, and that upon certain constant *payments*, he may assuredly have recourse in all times of need, by summoning to his aid one of the genii of this magical shield, of which there are several degrees, and who are known by the names of judges, counsel, attorneys, &c. The superiors are clothed in black gowns, and white wigs; and on stated days assemble at particular places, waiting for the summons of any imagined possessor of this *shield*, to do their duty. An inferior race, who are called attorneys, solicitors, have various establishments, to direct enquirers to the principal genii; and a still more inferior race run about the streets under the names of tip-staves and bailiffs, to lay hold of those who are accused of any offence towards the *shield-bearers*. In other establishments the *charm* of the shield is *prepared*, and *renewed*, when by any accident the spell is broken; and a sage wizard, much given to melancholy and tears, sits over all,

KING DEATH.

J. CATNACH, Printer, 2, & 3, Monmouth-court, 7 Dials.

KING DEATH was a rare old fellow,
   He sat where no sun can shine;
And he lifted his hand so yellow,
   And pour'd out his coal black wine.
        Hurrah for the coal black wine

There came to him many a maiden,
   Whose eyes had forgot to shine,
And widows with grief o'erladen
   For a draught of his coal black wine.
        Hurrah,&c

The scholar left all his learning,
   The poet his fancied woes,
And the beauty her bloom returning,
   Like life to the fading rose.   Hurrah, &c;

All came to the rare old fellow,
   Who laugh'd till his eyes dropp'd brine,
And he gave them his hand so yellow,
   And pledg'd them in Death's black wine'.
        Hurrah'

The Knight
OF THE
SILVER SHIELD.

SPLENDOUR blaz'd in the castle hall
   As they danc'd the gallied measure,
No thought of the past did grief recall,
   The soul was wrapp'd in pleasure.
There was but one heart in the castle grand
   That to sorrow's force did yield,
'Twas the Lady's, who had promis'd her hand
To him who had fought in the holy land,
   The Knight of the Silver Shield.

All but one were with joy elate,
   Eyes beam'd with pleasure bright,
When the bugle's sound at the castle gate
   Announced the return of a knight.
The lady's heart 'gainst her breast did beat
   Her eyes true joy reveal'd,
When a throbbing bosom hers did meet,
And she view'd kneeling at her feet,
   The Knight ohlver e Stif h c8ld'

to regulate the prices at which the charms shall be retailed to the shield-bearers. When you have purchased this *shield*, you are told to consider yourself perfectly safe, and only to take care you do not perform any act which is forbidden in the cabalistic jargon, which is inscribed upon its surface. If you do not violate these precepts, say these islanders, you need fear neither man nor devil. The king himself, say they, nor any of his ministers dare not attempt to touch this shield. It is more invulnerable than the shield of Achilles. The spear of Pelides would shiver in pieces, ere it could penetrate this safeguard.

I have been, thou art aware, in my days, a piece of a soldier: and, notwithstanding my disposition to believe all the simple islanders told me, I could not so far forget my military lessons, as to think a shield of so much use without a sword as with one. It might be a very good shield; and all might be true that was said in its behalf; but yet I wished to have a little additional security. I said a brave man ought not to be content, in a contest for an honest cause, with the means of self-defence, or the security of his personal safety. He should be armed for attack, as well as shielded for defence, that he might assist his fellow-soldiers, and contribute his share to the glories of the day. This was strongly opposed by these simpletons, who had been taught to place all their reliance upon this *legal shield*, though there are many instances in which it had been broken to pieces before their faces, while the guardian genii stood petrified and dumb, under the superior influence of a very powerful *imp* called self-interest: who sometimes visible, and sometimes invisible, laughs at the hieroglyphics of the paper-shield, and changes them at his pleasure.

*

For some time, it served me much better than I dare have ventured to suppose; – but this I attribute rather to a sort of lance, which I borrowed from the armoury of the *liberty of the press* – a weapon which I was told it was *forbidden to use;* but I could not be persuaded I should be more easily conquered in an offensive, than in a defensive warfare. And I am satisfied, if I had trusted only to the shield of law, I should have been knocked down in the first three months of my pilgrimage, and my *shield* would only have served me for a tomb-stone, on which might have been written, in fair characters, to warn other adventurers: –

Under this broken and useless buckler,
Lies, fairly destroyed,
By due process of our admirable law,
The Body
Of the BLACK DWARF,
Who fell
In the Reign of Sir Samuel Shepherd, Knt
In
A rash attack,
On the corruptions of the day.

Reader, beware – and mark his fate!
Be wise, and *silent*, ere too late!

I wonder, even with the assistance of my lance, that I escaped. I had, it is true, nothing to fear from *open* enemies, or fair fighting; but here pits were dug under my feet, and precipices on either hand. The torrents of Castlereagh's eloquence, and Eldon's tears, were continually roaring across my path; and I was exorcised as an evil spirit by the dignitaries of the church.

RICHARD THE LION KING MEETS A LION

[*Richard has fallen into the power of the King of Almaine when returning to England in disguise after a shipwreck. He is provoked into a duel of buffets by Armour, the King of Almaine's son, and kills him.*]

'Now, what sayst thou?' cried the enraged monarch of Almaine, to his faithful councillor, Ritsal Gobertz. 'Shall this base king who has slaughtered my only son, and dishonoured my daughter, be allowed to live?'

'By no means,' replied Gobertz; 'but the messenger from Leopold of Austria has arrived, and would fain speak with you, sire.'

'Admit him,' said the king.

Gobertz motioned an attendant, and the messenger from the Arch-Duke was instantly admitted into the presence of the King of Almaine.

'Now, then, thine errand,' said the king.

'Leopold of Austria greets you well, King of Almaine,' replied the messenger, 'and is right glad to hear you have in safe keeping King Richard of England. In two days the Arch-Duke will be here in person to decide upon his fate, until when he requires that your prisoner should be carefully looked to.'

'I will carefully look to him, doubt it not,' said the king. 'See,' continued he, 'that the messenger be attended to,' and so saying he dismissed the Envoy of the Arch-Duke.

'By heaven!' cried the king, when he found himself once more alone with his councillor, 'but he shall not escape me; if he get alive in Austria's power he will exact a ransom large enough to purchase a kingdom; and too well I know the greedy duke will satiate his revenge with wealth rung from the proud Islanders. The blood of my son calls for vengeance – the honour of my daughter for satisfaction – all induce me to act with firmness; none but thou and I will know the truth; and when Richard of England is dead, it shall seem he met his fate by accident.'

'How mean you, sire?' asked Gobertz.

'I will tell thee, my faithful friend,' answered the fierce vindictive king, his whole frame convulsed with agitation, 'thou knowest the Nubian lion that is caged, next to the dungeon of the prisoner?'

'Ah!' cried Gobertz, with astonishment not unmixed with alarm.

'He shall be turned into his prison as if by accident,' said the monarch, 'and we will gaze upon the meeting of the Lion King and his forest rival.'

''Tis too horrible to think of,' replied the councillor; 'reflect I pray you; some other death if he must die.'

'It shall be as I say. It was but a careless guard, and unbarred door; and I am free from the vengeance of Austria,' cried the king.

'At least give the prisoner intimation of his doom,' said Gobertz, 'and let him be prepared.'

'I will do so,' shouted the king fiercely: 'I will glad my sight with the view of his blanched cheek and shrinking eye, when he shall hear his doom. This instant let him be conducted before us.'

In a few minutes, Richard, heavily fettered, was brought into the presence of the king; Gobertz alone remaining with him.

'I told thee,' said the King of Almaine, 'that thou shouldst die; art thou prepared to meet thy fate?'

'Monarch of Almaine! first hear me,' replied Richard, haughtily. 'Thy son met his fate by his own seeking; thy daughter is, for me, pure and innocent; and did but like the daughter of a monarch, compassionate the sufferings of a king. If thou dost doom me to death, think not thou wilt do it with impunity; my faithful subjects will revenge my death; and within three months from the murder of Richard Plantagenet thou wilt be the last of thy race, and no stone shall attest where stood the city of Almaine.'

'Indeed!' replied the king, with a bitter sneer; 'but how if thy death be attributed to accident?'

'Cowardly slave!' cried Richard, forgetting himself in his rage; 'wouldst thou murder me in cold blood?'

'Thy blood shall be warm enough ere thou diest,' replied the king.

'Do thy worst,' said Richard. 'It ill becomes one of my race to parley with such a monarch as thee. Let thy headsman do his office.'

'Thou shalt not fall by the headsman's blow,' answered the king; 'thou shalt battle for thy life.'

'Ah!' cried Richard; 'give me lance and sword, and head thou six of thy chosen followers – give a fair field to Plantagenet, and he will win his freedom.'

'Thou shalt have neither lance nor sword,' replied the king, in a tone of bitter mockery; 'and thou shalt combat but with one.'

'I care not then,' said Richard, 'whatever be the advantage of arms in my antagonist, I will not shrink from the combat.'

'Thy antagonist shall have no other arms than thyself,' replied the king, in the same calm tone of irony; 'the arms nature alone has provided him with.'

'Ah! what mean you?' cried Richard, astonished; 'and who is to be my opponent?'

'Thou hast not yet seen him,' said the king;

but thou hast heard his voice.'

'Ah!' exclaimed Richard, 'thou meanest –'

'*The Nubian Lion!*' answered the king. 'What!' continued he, 'have I found a way to touch thee, mighty champion? Thou little deservest the name thou hast gained if thou shrinkest from the encounter with thy namesake.'

'Art thou a man?' said Richard, calmly.

'Art thou a *Lion* King?' replied the monarch of Almaine, smiling. 'What ho!' added he, 'my guard!' and the chamber was instantly filled with armed men.

It was well the King of Almaine had taken the precaution of placing his guard near the chamber where his conference with Richard was taking place, for the Lion King had gathered up his fetters with both hands, and was about to rush upon him, when he was seized by numbers, who threw themselves upon him.

'Hear me,' shouted Richard, still undismayed; 'thou wilt, at least, order the removal of my fetters?'

'No!' said the King of Almaine; 'but now thou proved to me thou art not safe without them.'

'Wilt thou allow me a weapon?' demanded Richard.

'None! save those nature has given thee,' answered the King. 'I will give thee a night's repose; but neither food, or even water, and at daybreak, look, thou Lion King, for the roaring of the lion.'

'And look, thou inhuman beast,' said Richard, 'for a bloody grave and an extinguished name, ere three short months expire. Stain on manhood, blot on the creation, thus I spit at and defy thee!' And, so saying, the Lion King was hurried from the presence of the Monarch of Almaine to his dungeon, denominated the Lion's Den.

*

In the meanwhile, the Princess Priscilla, who had been consigned to the care of her attendants, sat alone within her chamber.

'I will yet save the good King,' ejaculated she, 'for to-morrow will, I know, consign him to a shameful death.' She listened – all was still – her attendants slept. Taking a bunch of keys and a dagger from out a secret drawer

in a cabinet she lifted the arras in her apartment, and passed out from her chamber through a private door; she silently wended her way towards the dungeon of Richard, when she was stayed by a guard.

'You cannot pass,' said the soldier.

'Knowest thou me, slave?' asked the princess.

'Full well, lady,' replied the soldier; 'but my orders are precise.'

'Ah!' cried Priscilla, 'what red light gleams yonder?'

The guard turned for an instant in the direction to which she pointed, and, quick as lightning, the princess plunged her dagger to his heart.

To tear off his cloak was, with the undaunted princess, but the work of a moment, and dragging the body of the murdered soldier into a deep recess in the passage, she, covered with his garment, continued for some moment to pace the vaulted passage, all was still.

'Now, then, for my prisoner!' cried she, and she rushed along the corridor to reach the dungeon of Richard.

The long passage down which the princess passed, terminated in two much narrower, one of which led to the dungeon of Richard. The keys she held were the master keys of all the tower apartments; and with a hand trembling with agitation she undid the fastening, which enabled her to remove the massive bars and bolts of iron which secured the door; she opened it cautiously.

'Richard,' she cried, 'dost thou sleep?'

No answer was returned.

She entered the dungeon, and was almost overpowered by a strong and offensive effluvia.

'I am mistaken,' she cried in terror, and raising the lamp she bore in her hand, threw its faint light over the dungeon.

'God!' she cried, 'I am in the *Lion's Den!*' Crouched in the far corner of the dungeon lay the king of beasts, and stretched at his full length, and fast asleep, she gazed for a moment, petrified with horror, and then cautiously retreating, closed the massive door after her; but without replacing any of the fastenings, and retracing her steps, gained the passage which, in her agitation and terror, she had mistaken. She found no difficulty in removing the fastenings, and was soon clasped in the arms of Richard.

'No time is to be lost!' she cried; 'quick, let me undo thy fetters!' and, applying a key she held in her hand, the iron shackles fell from the galled limbs of the Lion King.

'I have the key of the inner portal,' said she; 'and you must swim the moat, and climb the outer wall.'

'And what will become of you, my gentle girl,' replied Richard.

'Fear not for me, noble Richard,' answered she, 'you will be safe, and I can die content.'

'But my brave companions, I cannot leave them in peril,' said Richard. 'Know you where they are confined?'

'In the upper tower of the northern turret,' replied Priscilla; 'and I have no means to rescue them.'

'Then I will not leave them for your cruel father to wreak his spite on them,' said Richard. 'It shall never be said that Richard Plantagenet left those in jeopardy whom his own imprudence led into danger.'

'Then you will perish!' exclaimed the princess.

'Fear not for me,' cried Richard. 'Ah!' continued he, as his eye fell on the blood-stained weapon which Priscilla still retained, 'what do I see – a dagger! – give it me.'

Priscilla proffered it to his grasp.

''Tis a good weapon,' he exclaimed, as he examined its point and edge; 'and, by God's help, and good St. George, with it *I will fight the Lion!*'

Richard now urged Priscilla to retire lest she should be missed. It was in vain she begged him to escape. The hero was immovable.

'Go!' he cried, 'my best, my only friend. Should you be discovered it would but endanger us both. I should be again in fetters, and my weapon would be lost to me. 'Tis my only resource. I have combatted with men fiercer and wilder than beasts. Why should I dread the noble forest monarch?'

'Ah!' cried Priscilla, 'I see the gleams of early day. Farewell, noble King; may heaven nerve your heart and arm for the unequal contest.' And so saying, she embraced Richard, and wept for a few moments on his arms, and then, tearing herself suddenly away, she sought her distant chamber, which she gained undiscovered.

The Lion King placed his fetters so as to deceive his jailors should they enter the dungeon, and, securing the weapon given him by the princess, waited, with a beating heart, for the approach of the morning.

*

The dungeon in which Richard was confined was a lofty vaulted apartment excavated in the solid rock. Along one side ran a gallery, communicating with the ground floor apartment of the castle, and an iron door led to another dungeon, now used as a den for the Nubian lion. Often during the night had Richard listened to the roar of the imprisoned beast, who was now to be loosed upon him in all its rage and fury; and, brave as he was, it was not without considerable fear and apprehension that he awaited the approach of morning. The morning at length broke, dull and heavily, and the King of Almaine entered the gallery which looked down upon the dungeon. He was attended by guards, two of whom bore lighted torches. Richard stood calm and collected, with his eye fixed upon the door through which the lion would pass into his dungeon. Soon the massive bolts were removed, and the door thrown wide open, and he saw the bright flash of the lion's eye, who was evidently aroused by some means from without – and now he had caught sight of his prey – and with a roar which struck a temporary panic, even on the heart of Richard, he passed through the aperture.

At the moment the beast entered the dungeon, Richard, who had gathered up his heavy fetters with both hands so as to deceive his jailors, dashed them suddenly to the ground, and stood with his right hand upraised, and with his eye fixed upon that of the lion, ready for the encounter. The noise made by the chains falling on the stones of the dungeon appeared to startle and surprise the forest monarch, who stopped and stood as if uncertain whether to advance or retreat. Richard, who remained in the same attitude he had at first assumed, had caught the eye

of the beast, on which he still continued, with a firm and unshrinking gaze, to rivet his own. Gradually the lion sank down upon his knees, and then inclining his head close to the ground, crawled slowly along, and words cannot express the astonishment of the King of Almaine and his attendants, when they saw the huge, and hitherto fierce monster, extend himself at his full length at the feet of the Lion King!

Placing his foot upon the lion's neck, but still keeping his bright eye fixed upon him, Richard exclaimed –

'Now, King of Almaine, thou seest I have tamed thy lion.'

'There has been some treachery here,' cried the king; 'how didst thou remove thy fetters? But even now thou shalt not escape me, the lion may be aroused; bring more torches,' he continued, 'and throw them down upon him.'

The attendants instantly obeyed the orders of the king, and several lighted brands were thrown upon the lion. Aroused by this annoyance, the animal turned upon Richard, who, still cool and collected, had been prepared for the worst. The dagger given him by the princess he had carefully preserved; and, as the beast rushed open-mouthed towards him, he thrust his right arm into its throat and fixed the weapon firmly in the tongue of the lion.

A tremendous struggle now commenced; but the king still retained the hold of his weapon, and all the struggles of the monster were futile; who, soon overcome by loss of blood, sunk powerless at the feet of his antagonist.

Richard, madly excited by the furious encounter, and bathed in the blood of the animal which he had conquered, cried out exultingly to the king –

'Now art thou satisfied, King of Almaine? I have conquered the lion! Come down, thou and thy guards, and let me offer thee a fitting hecatomb to the manes of the Forest King!'

'Call hither a bowman,' said the King of Almaine, 'and we will – '

At this moment the loud blast of a trumpet rang through the dungeon, and a servant entered hastily, and announced the arrival of the Archduke Leopold of Austria.

'Follow me, Gobertz,' said the king; and he left the dungeon to attend the summons of his liege lord Leopold of Austria.

'Noble beast,' said Richard, looking on the prostrate lion; 'thou hadst spared me but for thy more brutal master. Ah!' continued he, on seeing the jailor hesitate at the door of the dungeon; 'thou mayst enter; the lion is dead, and the Lion King too wearied to harm thee.'

In a few minutes the jailor ordered his attendants to bring water for Richard to wash himself, and also food and wine; and after performing his ablutions and making a hearty meal, he was removed into a more comfortable apartment of the castle.

*

On the evening of the same day in which Richard had encountered the lion, he was conveyed, by the orders of the Archduke of Austria, to a strong fortress on the Danube. His companions, Sir Fulk D'Oyley and Sir Thomas Multon, were liberated, and returned safely to England, to tell that Richard of England was a prisoner in Germany.

HERMAN IS INITIATED INTO THE 'ORDER OF BENEVOLENCE'

[*Set in eleventh-century England,* The Red Cross Warrior *is concerned with Saxon resistance to marauding Danes in the Isle of Thanet. The initiation rites of the resistance organization are interestingly close to trade union and freemason ritual. This emphasizes the connection between the popularity of historical romance and ceremonial of working-class movements.*]

But it is time for us to return to the subterranean cavern, which formed the principal retreat of the warrior and his devoted followers.

As Herman was rapidly approaching to a state of convalescence, he had expressed his desire to be admitted into the armed but benevolent association of his friend.

Three hours after sunset, Bernulph came to the vaulted chamber of his friend, and informed him that the members of the Order of Benevolence had assembled, and that he was at liberty to offer himself for admission. It was not usual, he observed, to receive any one into their number without a certain period of probation; but, on the present occasion, the esteem and regard which his conduct had produced, had induced them to suspend this regulation.

'During the forms of initiation,' Bernulph observed, 'it is necessary that you place implicit confidence on me, in return for that which this morning I reposed on your friendship. As a soldier, guided by the principles of honour, but still more as a Christian, influenced by the dictates of truth, I require this of you. In consequence of your wounds, you are still, my dear Herman, weak; and as I am precluded from the privilege of attending you myself, I have appointed one of my worthy associates to support and conduct you through the ordeal, which has been deemed necessary previous to admission into our society. You will be perfectly silent, except when you are required to speak in answer to questions which may be proposed, and you will carefully attend to the directions which may be given to you.'

After Herman had professed his readiness to comply with these regulations, Bernulph clapped his hands loudly together, and as he quitted the arched apartment at one door, a tall stout figure in a black robe, and masked, entered at another on the opposite side, which, inclining its head, advanced towards the Saxon chief. Herman, for a moment hesitated, and was about to step back.

'Fear not,' said the stranger, who observed the light movement, 'only rely confidently on the word of your tried and noble friend, be assured he can deceive no one.' He then advanced his arm, upon which Herman seized, and they both quitted the apartment. The passage into which they entered, was narrow, long, and arched. A single lamp in the distance, struggled with the subterranean gloom. Towards it they advanced. It was suspended over a low gothic door of iron, on either side of which stood a figure clothed like the conductor, and bearing a glittering sword.

'Is it peace?' said the one on the right.

'It is peace!' answered the conductor of the chief.

'What wilt thou here?' asked the figure on the left.

'I demand admittance to the abode of virtue and peace,' replied the guide, 'for myself and my friend.'

'By what authority?' rejoined the first.

'By this,' replied the conductor, making a sign, 'which ye will not dispute.'

'It is well,' was the answer; 'but remember, *humility* is the first step to virtue.'

Immediately the iron door ascended slowly, after the manner of a portcullis, and discovered a very low arched passage, not more than three feet in height. 'Imitate me,' said the guide, as he stooped down upon his hands and knees. Herman followed his example. The heavy iron door descended harshly through its gratings behind, and cut off all retreat. After proceeding some way in this uncomfortable manner, and in complete darkness, Herman could not avoid expressing some degree of inquietude.

'*Patience*,' said his guide, 'is the second step to virtue.'

The passage soon became sufficiently high for them to advance in an erect posture; but it was exceedingly incommoded with large and small stones, so that it was difficult to go forward, especially in total darkness; but at length, by the assistance of the guide, this difficulty was also surmounted.

'Courage!' said the conductor. 'Perseverance is the third step to virtue.'

They now suddenly turned round a corner in the dark passage, and a faint light appeared suspended over a small portico at a distance. As they approached nearer, Herman discovered, written upon it, in large letters of silver, the word TRUTH.

'Through that portal,' said the guide, 'it is necessary for us to pass, if we can obtain ability to do so.' He then took from underneath his long cloak, a large and thick woollen cap, which he directed Herman to draw over his face, and added, that it was

THE
Fatal Book Opened!

AN AUTHENTIC ACCOUNT OF
JOHN ALBERT, A YOUNG GENTLEMAN IN HAMBURGH,
WHO BY THE CONSTANT STUDY OF
The Works of Friar Bacon and Doctor Faustus,
AND OTHER BOOKS OF MAGIC AND ASTROLOGY.
HAD ACQUIRED AN AWFUL KNOWLEDGE OF CABALISTICS,
NECROMANCY, and the BLACK ART;

Shewing how he obtained access to the Study of Anthony Cornel, a noted **Professor of the Black Art**, and having locked himself in, began to read a most Horrible Book, which lay open upon the Table, the Letters of which were written in Human Blood, and the Leaves of Dead Men's Skins; when a dreadful clap of Thunder alarmed him, the door was broken open with great violence, and in came the **TERRIBLE ONE**, the Chief of the Powers of Darkness, attended by a host of Griffins and other Monsters of most hideous appearance, vomiting Sulphur and Fire!— "What wouldst thou with me?" cried the Demon: and on his repeating it the third time, struck the affrighted Youth with his dreadful Claws, and killed him on the spot!

ONCE a famed necromancer, one Cornel of old;
Had long made the Black Art his study, we're told;
He the stars and the planets pretended to rule;
No doubt he was learned, at least not a fool.

He was gloomy, morose, and was ne'er known to smile;
Like his deeds, most mishapen, he bent as with toil;
Whomsoever approached him, were stricken with fear;
His wife only spoke to him once in the year,

And that was each year, on the eve of St. Mark,
Then he hied from his studio, at sun-set, when dark,
With pale haggard look! and the dew on his cheek
Spoke plainly,—the countenance plainly can speak.

His wife heard his usual terrible charge,
As he from his closet at night did emerge :
Observe well my words, but approach not the door;
Behold ! here's the key—and of this be you sure :

'Twas wrought in a cavern, 'midst sulphurous flame !
'Tis spell-bound, by magical, mystical name !
Therefore, mark well my words, nor speak 'bove your
breath;
To neglect them, were awful and horrible death !

Should man dare to ask you my chamber to see,
Their life's of no value, scarce worth a pin's fee !
Whomsoever may beg, or entreat, or implore,
Let no living creature e'er enter that door !
She faithfully swore his command to obey,
When forth to the church-yard he wended his way,

Saying, dare not look back, neither left nor the right,
And expect my return when the bell tolls midnight.

She follow'd in order the portal to close,
When she felt that resistance did strongly oppose ;
For in rush'd a youth quite determined to see
The magical room, who wrench'd from her the key.

Then the magical key he applied to the lock,—
The door open'd wide with a terrible shock !
And such sights met the eye, (protect us from evil !)
Only known to the wretch who's enslaved to the devil !

'Mongst horrible relics of dead men's bleach'd bones,
'Midst terrible visions, 'midst shrieks, and 'midst groans;
Gaping skulls, grinning skeletons, ghosts at their
gambols,
Aye, this and much more,—'tis not my muse rambles.

There lay on a tombstone a magical book,
On which none but Cornel had e'er dared to look,
Inscribed full of blood-written symbols within,
And the leaves were all made of a murderer's skin ;

Except those of magic inserted between,
On which strange hieroglyphics unnumber'd were seen.
Which would horror-strike all who were doom'd to
behold
Such sights so unearthly, not fit to be told.

Impell'd by his fate, the youth view'd it again ;
He scarce could proceed, yet he could not refrain :

Once entangled in sin, 'tis most hard to retreat,
He'd have given all the world to have been in the street.

He opened the book, when the magical spell
Was broken, and heard was a horrible yell !
A fierce fiend-like form, quite enveloped in flame,
Rush'd into the chamber, and bellow'd his name !

Two hideous horns he beheld on his head,
Like two bars of iron when heated to red ;
The breath of his nostrils was brimstone and fire,
And his serpent-like tail he lash'd round him with ire.

With hideous laugh, he cried out " Thou art mine!
I am come at thy call—thou art mine—I am thine !"
His hair like the porcupine's quills stood upright,
While the poor trembling youth shook with fear and
affright.

" What wouldst thou with me ?" cried the author of
ill ;
The poor wretch was silent and powerless still :
" What wouldst thou with me ?" again the fiend cries,
And a flame of blue lightning flashed in his eyes !

" I come at thy will, from the pit of despair ;"
He lifted his griffin-like claw in the air,
Then he tore out his heart, which he seiz'd for his
prey,
And in thunder and lightning vanished away !

CERTAIN authors on Conjuration, account it next to death for an illiterate person to raise an Evil Spirit; for by reason of his ignorance he knoweth not how to dismiss it : and they give many cautious against attempts to force a Goblin to appear. If the incantation be imperfect, so much the better for him that doeth it, for then he shall only have trouble for his pains ; because such creatures obey not but upon compulsion of a real enchanter, or through his art stolen by a pretender, who may have pains for his trouble ; as Eucratus had with the Goblin, (as hereafter,) which he could not have enchanted if he had not privily discovered so much of the enchantment as would make the Goblin appear, but which he could not lay again, because he knew not the form.

The learned in the Black Art say, if you raise an Evil Spirit, and do not dismiss him quickly, or fully employ him till you can lay him again, he will be your master instead of your servant, and do you bodily harm or slay you. Yet if my readers require information from my own knowledge, or experience herein, I have none to give them ; except that passion hath sometimes become my master, and so I have been under the dominion of an Evil Spirit, and suffered accordingly; so that every one who submitteth is lorded by that which he ought to control.

There is a wonderful narrative of a Goblin by a celebrated thor who lived some years ago He saith that one Eucratus

became acquainted in Egypt with an enchanter named Pancrates, who had resided twenty years in the subterranean recesses, where he learned the Art Magic. And one day he persuaded Eucratus to leave all his servants at Memphis, and follow him alone, telling him that they should not be in want of attendance to wait upon them: and so it happened. For when they came to any inn, Pancrates would take a wooden pin, or latch, or a bolt, or any such like thing, and clothe it ; and then he would repeat a verse over it, and so, by enchantment, it would walk, and appear a man to every one. And this creature would go about as a servant, and prepare their supper, and lay the cloth, and wait upon them right courteously, and always do as they desired. And when they had not occasion for such services, then Pancrates would repeat another verse, and it would become a pin, a latch, or a bolt, or whatever it was before it had been enchanted. 'Eucrates, seeing this, desired to perform the like wonder, but Pancrates would not acquaint him with the verses, nor again make enchantment in his presence. And so Eucrates remained ignorant until, one day, he hid himself in a dark place, while Pancrates, thinking himself alone, said the verse over a pin, which thereupon became a serving man. And the next day, when Pancrates had gone to the market-place, Eucrates remembered the words, and repeated them over a stick which he dressed up ; and thereby he enchanted the stick into

a like creature, which, to keep it employed in the enchantment required, he was obliged to find in work, and therefore he ordered it to fetch some water, and when it had brought a full jar, he cried " Stop! draw no more water, but be a stick again." But it heeded him not, and, instead of obeying him, it went on and on! drawing and bringing in water till it almost filled the house. Then Eucrates feared the return of Pancrates, lest he should be displeased ; and he was also alarmed at the coming in of so much water, and tried to prevail on the goblin to leave off, but to no end; for, as though he had been deaf, he kept swiftly going from the house to the well, drawing jars full of water and bringing them, so that Eucrates felt great fear, and being suddenly angered by the disobedience of this mere walking-stick which he had made, he suddenly seized a hatchet, and split it ; but instead of its being destroyed, the two pieces forthwith became two goblins, and each taking a jar ran and drew water, so that Eucrates had two servants instead of one, and he was ready beswoon with terror, when Pancrates happily returned, and understanding the matter, he presently stayed the goblins, by repeating a verse that dismissed them both into one piece of wood again, as they were before the incantation. This is the narration of a Latin writer called Lucian, whose works you may lawfully read ; and if you understand them, and be of a right mind, the perusal shall stand you in good stead.

COPYRIGHT.—PRINTED BY WILLIAM WALKER, OTLEY ; AND SOLD, WHOLESALE, BY HIM, ON THE MOST LIBERAL TERMS requisite he should submit, for a short time, to have his hands bound, and to wait till he could obtain an entrance through the portal of truth. His guide now left him, and Herman distinguished the sound of footsteps, as they seemed gradually to recede to a great distance, through the vaulted passages. At length they ceased to reverberate. A stillness, the most profound, succeeded, and the helpless Saxon, hoodwinked and bound, began to feel all the loneliness of his situation. But for the confidence which he felt in Bernulph, he would have imagined himself betrayed into a situation, where defence and escape were alike impossible, only to be destroyed more easily.

He was not suffered to remain long in a state of suspense. The sound of footsteps, close at hand, were heard, and he felt himself firmly grasped on either side.

'Who art thou?' said a voice, which was not that of his guide.

'I am a Saxon soldier,' answered Herman.

'What dost thou here?' rejoined the other.

'I am a candidate for admission into the Order of Benevolence,' replied the chief.

'And how dost thou expect to obtain the privilege?' demanded the unknown.

'By passing through the portal of Truth.' said Herman.

'Advance, then, and make the attempt,' said the stranger.

Thus saying, they led him up the steps.

'It is written,' said one of those who held him, 'Ask, and ye shall receive; seek, and ye shall find; knock, and the door shall be opened unto you.'

'But my hands are tied, and I cannot knock,' said the chief.

The bands were then removed, and he felt around for the door, though in vain; he grasped only the air.

'Unless the covering be removed from my eyes,' added he, 'I shall not be able to find the entrance.'

The cap was then taken from his head.

'Thus helpless, and thus blind are we,' said his conductor, who now stood before him; 'even when we are arrived at the door of truth, unless ability be given us to pass the threshhold.'

Herman was now requested to close his eyes for a moment, and when he opened them, that side of the room in front of him discovered, as by magic, a beautiful transparency representing the world with a bright light shining upon it, while the figure of a dove, with an olive branch in its mouth, was seen hovering over. Above, in letters of gold, the following extract from the sacred writings was conspicuous: –

PEACE ON EARTH
AND
GOOD-WILL TOWARDS MEN

While he contemplated the pleasing picture, a low strain of sweet and solemn music was heard. He turned to his guide, and began to express the surprise and delight with which his almost bewildered mind was filled. No reply was made, but the masked being to whom he addressed himself, extended his arm, and pointed significantly forward. Herman again directed his attention towards the transparency, but it had vanished; and through the opening which its removal had left, appeared, to his astonished view, the spacious hall of the order, brilliantly illuminated by two rows of candelabres. On either side, on elevated seats, sat the associates of the order, clothed in crimson robes, with purple sashes crossing the body from the right shoulder to the left side, and each wearing a large silver medal upon his breast. At the end of the passage, formed by the rows of candelabres, appeared the chief associate of the order, clothed in a robe of rich purple silk, and seated upon a highly ornamented canopy. On each side of the chief, but on the floor of the hall, sat one of the associates, who acted as a secretary.

Herman was now conducted forwards. As he entered the hall, all except the chief associate rose from their seats, and stood till he arrived at the foot of the throne, on which sat his friend the noble Bernulph. The floor of the room was of a dark green colour, and as he passed to the upper end, he observed on it, in large white characters, the same words which had been so forcibly impressed upon his mind during the whole of his initiation.

Arrived at the foot of the throne, he beheld the benign countenance of him whom he regarded as his rightful sovereign, sitting in almost regal pomp and splendour. With a most engaging smile, he said –

'My dear friend and brother; will you, before me and my companions, repeat the answers which you have already given to our brother-associate, by whom you were interrogated?'

This having been done, Bernulph descended from his seat, and taking from the hands of one of the attendants a crimson robe, he put it over the shoulders of Herman, and placing the purple sash, with the medal and its collar over his neck, he said aloud, 'This attire will never be dishonoured by its wearer.' Then tenderly embracing his friend, he resumed his seat, and Herman was conducted to one appointed for him on the right.

After a short space, during which the several associates who had any thing to communicate, or any directions to receive, came to the front of the throne, and then retired to their seats, the chief rose to dissolve the assembly.

'Brethren! Associates of the Order of Benevolence! we have, through the good providence of God, enjoyed the pleasure of once more meeting in tranquillity. The cruel invaders are gone, and peace again smiles upon the simple inhabitants of these shores. You well know, my brave companions in arms, the exalted pleasure with which we lay aside the weapons and the practices of war, and assume those of peace. Go, my beloved friends, be humble, patient, and persevering, in your endeavours to obtain truth, knowledge, and virtue, and strive to imitate your .divine Master, whose life was spent in efforts to diffuse peace on earth, and good will towards men.'

The assembly now broke up, the dresses were laid aside, and Herman, leaning on the arm of his friend, withdrew to his apartment.

'Farewell, my dear Herman,' said Bernulph, at parting, 'you have seen me to-night upon the only throne I am ambitious to occupy, and here my elevation is elective.'

THE DEMON OF SICILY

[*Sir Ugo De Tracy went away on a pilgrimage; while he was away, his wife ill-advisedly let the knight Leonardi into the castle.*
This account is set as a flash-back in the story, at the point where Sir Ugo, returning, has been beckoned into the castle dungeon by a shadowy figure.]

Restless was the soul of Leonardi as he strode through the halls of the Castle of De Tracy, revolving in his mind dark and horrible deeds.

Passing by the portals which led to the chapel, he thought he heard a voice within; he listened again; the voice sweetly sounded in his ear, it was like music to the bite of the deadly tarantula, it charmed his senses to a forgetfulness of all beside, for it was that of Isabella.

On her knees, before the altar, he beheld the lovely wife of De Tracy; with impatience and dissatisfaction he heard her petition the saints for his safe return. At that moment he stood by her side, she turned around, and overcome by a sudden emotion of fear, she shrieked aloud.

Echo alone heard her. Thrice she repeated the exclamation along the vaulted roofs and dreary corridors where she held her reign; but it reached not the ears of other mortal than those of the gloomy Leonardi.

On the step of the altar, seizing the trembling hand of Isabella, he bent his knee, while through his grated visor, by the light of the bright clouds which tinged with the glories of the sun, who was then fast retiring from other worlds, cast a crimson radiance into the chapel through the twisted panes of the large altar window, she beheld his darkly-rolling eyes.

'Fair Isabella,' said the Knight, 'why petition Heaven to bring thee thy husband? Listen to the suit of Leonardi; he loves, he adores thee; thy beauties dwell in his heart; all night he has thought on them; behold him a suppliant who never knelt before.'

'And of little use, Sir Knight,' said the fearstruck Isabella, 'is that lowly posture now. Suffer me, Signor Leonardi, to use my own discretion in retiring from this place, nor longer detain my hand.'

'Say not so, beauteous Isabella, suffer me to hope that time and my unceasing attentions may' –

'May what, Signor?' said Isabella, her lofty soul swelling high with indignation. 'Know you not that I am the wife of Ugo De Tracy, who, if he were here, would well chastise thee for this insolence. Like him, I spurn whatever is base and dishonourable, and such I hold thee, Signor Leonardi.'

The Knight rose from his bended knee, in a transport of rage he flung from his grasp the arm of Isabella; he laid his hand on his faulchion, suddenly he withdrew, while he gnashed his teeth, and inwardly muttered curses deep and horrid.

Isabella, with a dignified firmness, walked towards the portals of the chapel. Soon her elegant form was lost to the view of the deep-plotting Vicensio; who, when he heard the closing of the distant portals, laid his right hand on the altar, and solemnly swore to be revenged of Isabella De Tracy.

The statue of the Holy Mother started at his horrid oath, while from each marble tomb in the chapel burst a melancholy groan, which deep sounded in the ears of Leonardi.

'Groan on, and start,' he furiously exclaimed, 'portends and prodigies are lost on me, use your arts, ye mouldering bones, and you, inanimate represenative of the Immaculate Virgin, may raise your arms again, and look with horror on me, I fear not all that you can do.'

Dark grew the chapel; a murky cloud hung before the large casement; but by the still small glimmering of light Leonardi beheld himself surrounded by tall skeletons, who waved their fleshless arms for him to depart.

It was then that cold drops of water stood on the forebead of Leonardi – 'Tremble!' said a voice over the altar. He raised his eyes, the statue of the Virgin again appeared animated; its gaze was fixed on him.

Leonardi fled, he was unable to endure the horror of the moment. With him fled the shadow of night, the murky cloud disappeared, and the frail remains of mortality sought their silent tombs.

Hastily he proceeded to the stables, where snorted his coal-black steed; quickly he saddled him, and vaulting on his back, was soon far from the ken of the tower of De Tracy's castle.

In the bosom of a dark forest, where the beams of day in their meridian lustre faintly glimmered, Leonardi reined in his steed; there he alighted; and there his memory recalled the horrible prodigies he had witnessed; but his memory likewise retained the charms of Isabella, his dreadful oath, and her insulting expressions.

'And I will be revenged,' said he, as unlacing his helmet shaded with black plumes he cast it on the verdant grass, 'let but the sun descend, let but the gloomy shade of night be unfurled from the battlements of Heaven, and I will bear away the haughty, lovely Isabella.'

*

Ryno, the black steed of the savage Vicensio, was cropping the herbage, while the Knight, with arms folded, leaned against the stem of a large tree. The increasing shade shewed the sun to be declining from his meridian altitude. – Gloomy was his soul, and far more black his thoughts than the fabled river which rolls its sable waves into the vast Tartarean gulph.

The Knight prepared to depart: he stooped to take from the ground his helmet, when he hastily drew back on perceiving that a snake had made it his abode.

He had not as yet armed his hands with the ponderous gauntlet. Sullenly he drew them on. Approaching the snake which had twisted its scaly folds in the hollow of its casque, he suddenly seized on its head which rested in the midst.

The poisonous reptile twisted its speckled form round the body of the Knight, but its efforts were vain, for the head was soon crushed in the gauntlet, and it for ever ceased to dart its deadly tongue.

Leonardi smiled horribly. 'What other men,' said he, 'would have converted into an omen of bad import, I construe into success. Scaly wretch, thou shall adorn my helm with the bright colors of thy variegated skin.'

This said, he bound around his casque the long body of the snake, unmindful of the black gore which dropped from the lacerated head, and then called to Ryno his steed.

The sable courser at the well-known voice of his master threw up his head in the air, and neighed aloud. In an instant he came up to the place where stood the vindictive Knight.

Leonardi was on his saddle in a moment; the steed measured back his swift paces, and soon arrived at the skirts of the forest.

A gloomy horror presided over Nature. The sun had sunk to other worlds; the crimson of the clouds had disappeared: a misty vapour enveloped the face of creation; a mournful silence reigned around, save that at a distance was heard the unceasing roaring of Etna in her fiery caverns.

Leonardi looked toward the place where the mountain rose, but the flames were obscured by the gloomy vapour.

This opaque mist, thought Leonardi, favours my design; under its kind couvert I can, unseen, approach the castle of the peerless Isabella, and, if fortune·will befriend me, bear her away.

He now drew near its lofty walls. Ryno he placed in the concealing recess of a buttress while he strode into the hall with cautious pace, his hand grasping his glaive.

Unseen he crossed it; and entering the chapel, leaned against the column which was nearest to the portals, for his soul had not yet forgot the terrific omens of the morning.

The storm that had been long gathering in the gloomy clouds now burst forth in awful fury, blue lightnings darted around the chapel which vibrated at the tremendous peals of thunder that roared unceasing in the arch of Heaven. The rain poured down in torrents, and, driven by the blast, dashed against the painted casements of the chapel. At times he heard the wild shrieks of the spirits of the mountains between the pauses of the angry gusts of wind; but he derided the utmost fury of the storm, and waited impatiently in the hope of seeing Isabella enter the chapel.

Nor long did he hope in vain; the unfortunate wife of De Tracy, alarmed by the storm, left her chamber to supplicate at the altar for the safety of her husband.

With a cautious, trembling hand, she opened the portal; she raised her lamp to illuminate the dusky aisle, but its feeble rays pierced the surrounding gloom but a few paces before her.

Leonardi concealed his gigantic form behind a column, and as the Signora advanced he rushed forward, and caught her in his arms.

She rent the air with her shrieks, but her exclamations were lost in the wild howling of the storm; and soon her senses forsook her, and she lay inanimate in his iron grasp.

Hastily he bore her through the hall, and coming to the buttress looked in vain for Ryno; scared by the peals of thunder and vivid flashes of lightening, he had wandered from the place. Loudly he called on him, and soon the faithful steed appeared through the dull gloom.

The sound of his voice awoke the hapless Isabella from her insensate state to a knowledge of the extent of her misery. She was placed on the steed; Leonardi held her in one arm, while the other grasped the reins; and swiftly as the arrow from the bow of the hunter they darted through the stormy vapors which clustered around.

*

Their course lay by the base of Etna: as they approached toward it, the flames lighted them on their way, Isabella trembled when she beheld the fiery torrents which descended the mountain sides, but she trembled more at being in the power of the unprincipled Leonardi.

Swiftly the steed proceeded obedient to his master's will the whole of that night. When gloomily the morning dawned the turrets of a dismantled castle rose to view.

At the decayed bridge Leonardi alighted, he conducted the trembling form of Isabella through the broken portals. Well knew the Knight the subterraneous recesses of the castle; within its tottering walls his own arm had perpetrated dark deeds of horror.

Down many a step which seemed to be a passage to the bowels of the earth, he forced the wretched Isabella, till at length they entered a dungeon.

'Now, lady,' said he in harsh accents, ''tis like thou mayest repent of the deep insult you have offered me. No longer a suitor, I command thee to yield to my wishes; dreadful indeed will be the punishment of disobedience, for my soul yet burns with the remembrance of the injury I have received.'

The soul of Isabella rose above the horrors of her situation; she seized the dagger that glittered in the girdle of the gloomy Leonardi.'

'Barbarian,' said she, 'I fear thee not; in a moment I can put myself beyond thy infamous design. Powers of mercy, receive my soul!'

The dagger she had directed to her bosom here interrupted her; she fell to the ground, her pure blood dyed her garments.

Furious grew Leonardi at being disappointed of his expected prey; he looked blackly on the prostrate Isabella; she still lived, for the wound was not mortal.

'Since not my desires, I can however yet satiate my revenge; the pangs of death from my hand shall torture thee.'

Thus said, he drew his glaive; he divided the lovely head of Isabella from the convulsed body; he caught it by the beautiful long black tresses, and strode away with it to another chamber; he set it on a piece of a broken column, and contemplated with a demoniac satisfaction the features once so lovely, so interesting, but now ghastly with the agonies of death. 'Those eyes,' said he, 'will no longer look indignant on me; neither will that mouth

further insult me. Would I could have increased the torture of death; gladly would I have done it; for her groans were comfort to my soul.'

Some days he continued indulging his black revenge; at length a new thought struck him; 'I will go,' said he, 'to the cell where her body lies, and take from it her proud heart; I shall find pleasure in trampling on it.'

He was going; when strange terrors shook his soul; on a sudden his imagination hears the complaining spectre of the murdered Isabella groan, his hair stiffens, he starts, the headless shade seems to pursue him through the gloom – his blood chilled, he stood leaning on his faulchion, while with a pale, disordered, countenance, he questioned thus himself:

'What! shall Leonardi become the slave of superstitious terrors? shall his mighty soul yield to the fever of imagination? perish the thought, perish myself first! No, I am resolved I will tear out the heart of Isabella!'

*

Mournful was the soul of Ugo de Tracy when the supernatural appearance faded from his view; and the blue light ceasing to illumine the dreary cell left him in the murky shades of night: left him too with the murdered, headless body, which he was told was that of his beloved Isabella.

Suddenly he heard a heavy step sounding through the subterraneous caverns of the castle; the clank of armour accompanied the echoing paces.

Bearing a torch, entered a gigantic figure clothed in sable armour; round his helmet, shaded with black plumes, was twisted a large snake, the poisonous head hung loosely in the air; in his left hand he bore the head of a female, as appeared by the dark flowing locks, in his right and unsheathed faulchion and torch.

His vizor was up. Dark as the shades of night when the lightnings fly and thunder is heard, was his countenance. His eyes rolled gloomily dreadful.

De Tracy, anxious to know the purport of his coming, drew back into the gloom of the cell. Nor long staid he there.

'Thus,' said the sable, black-hearted Knight, 'do I seek my last revenge. I will find

'Thou, then,' said he 'art the husband of that Isabella who lies between us. There lies her head, this sword separated it from her body; it has the like office to perform on thee.'

Gloriously rushed the knights to combat. Leonardi flung his torch to the earth; dreadful was the contest, for the fierce power of just passion swelled the soul of Ugo de Tracy, black malice and revenge the heart of Leonardi de Vicensio.

The combat long hung in doubtful balance, till at length Ugo pierced the throat of his dire opponent; dreadful he fell, the clash of his armour rung through the vaulted caverns of the castle, a black torrent of blood rolled out his soul, the attendant fiends of hell, in anxious expectation, stood awaiting its escape from its mortal coil, they seized it in their sharp talons, grinning horribly they darted through the bosom of rifted earth, and plunged it deep in red oceans of unextinguishable flames.

Sadly mourned Ugo de Tracy over the body of his beloved Isabella; he kissed the wan lips, he raised the earth over the once so much adored form; but the body of her savage murderer he left uncovered.

Such was the face of the fair Isabella; such was the punishment of Leonardi de Vicensio. The avenging Deity who surveys the sinful actions of men at last brought on him the retributive arm of justice.

Pray for his soul, ye who read these pages, for it endures horrible torments. His bones yet lay unbruised, the left wing of the monastery covers the dragon's cell, where it is said his spectre on the first of every moon is compelled to come and view them whitening through time, while the attendant furies lash him with their whips formed of scorpions' deadly stings. Such is the punishment destined for the murderer, and which Leonardi de Vicensio will endure to the end of time.

that heart, that proud, vaunting heart of Isabella, which made her defy me, which made her resist the desires of my bosom.'

Thus having spoke, he flung to the earth the head; it rolled toward De Tracy, the light of the torch gleamed on the sunken features, he beheld in them the mortal remains of his adored wife. Rage, bloody rage, strung his nerves; he drew his glaive, and as the Knight was tearing away the garments that once concealed the swelling beauties of Isabella's bosom, he strode from his murky recess.

'Fiend of Hell!' in accents hoarse, with rage he exclaimed, 'my eyes have seen thy deed, my ears have heard thy speech, look up, before thee stands Ugo de Tracy!'

Leonardi stopped his dreadful employment; he rolled his eyes on Ugo.

Wonderful Adventures of

MR. O'FLYNN IN SEARCH OF

OLD MOTHER CLIFTON.

Understanding that old Mother Clifton's house was blown 336 miles above the moon, I went in search of her. I was searching nine days, running as hard as I could with my two shin bones in my pocket, and my head under my arm, by order of Old Joe Buck, the pensioner, who lost his middle eye at the battle of Waterloo, chewing half-boiled stirabout. I then got upon a buck-flea's back, which carried me over large hills of skillogolee and bogholes of buttermilk, till I met Jarvis the coachman, driving two dead horses under an empty post-chaise loaded with eighteen milliners, two tambour workers, two loads of apples, a roasted millstone, and half-a-dozen grenadier cock magpies, belonging to the French Flying Artillery, drinking tea till they were black in the face. I asked Mr. Jarvis if he had any account of the old Woman of Radcliffe Highway, who was drowned in a shower of feathers last night, about a fortnight ago, and he told me he had no account of her whatever, but if I went to John Ironsides I'd get some intelligence; and where John Ironsides lived, he told me was two miles beyond all parts in the parish, up and down a street where a mad dog bit a hatchet next week, and pigs wrestle for treacle. I thanked him for his information, bid him good night. I then began to run as fast as I could sit down by the side of a ditch, with my two shin bones and my head in my pocket, till I met with a gentleman with the Custom-house of Dublin on his back, the Manchester Exchange in his pocket, and Lord Nelson's Pillar in London stuck in his hand for a walking-stick. The Lord help you, poor man, said I, I am sorry for you, and the devil skewer you, why had you not better luck. I asked him what was the matter, and he told me he was bad with the gravel in the eye, the daddy wrumble in the guts, and the worm cholic in his toe. I then put him into a coach and drove him into a druggist's shop, and ordered him two pennyworth of pigeons' milk, three ounces of the blood of a grasshopper, a pint of self-basting, the head and pluck of a buck flea, the ribs of a roasted chew of tobacco, and the lights and liver of a cobbler's lap-stone, boiled seperately altogether in a leathern iron pot.

Immediately after taking the mixture, he was delivered of a pair of blacksmith's bellows and a small tombstone a ton weight.

Then proceeding on to Johnny Goola's house, said I to him, John did you get any account of Mother Clifton's house, that was blown 336 miles above the moon by a gale of wind from a sow gelder's horn. I got no account says Johnny, only I wrote a letter to her to-morrow night, when I was snoring fast asleep, with my eyes open, knowing her father to be a smith, and farrier to a pack of wild geese, and her mother nurse to a nest of young monkies that was held in the said parish of Up-and-down, where pigs wrestle for stirabout. But John told me I should not go till I had dined with them, we then sat down, and what should be brought up but a dish of stewed paving stones, mixed with the oil and ribs of a chew of tobacco, and two quarts of the blood of a lamplighter's snuff box. The next wonder she showed me, she brought me into a fine garden and placed me by a cabbage stalk which only covered 52 acres of ground, and where I saw ten regiments of artillery firing a royal salute of 21 guns. The next great wonder she showed me, was a big man standing on a small table of heath, dressed in a scarlet black cloak, who made a very great sermon, but a north buck-flea bit him in the pole of the neck and made him roar murder. The next wonder I saw a small boy only a thousand years old, thrashing tobacco into peas; one of the peas started through a wall eighteen feet thick, and killed a dead boy on the other side. Then there was the London Privateer and the Channel Royal Mail Coach in a desperate engagement, firing boiled oyster shells, stewed lapstones, and roasted wigs one at the other; one of the lapstones struck Mother Clifton over the right eye, and delivered her of the Old Woman of Radcliffe Highway, who was sister to Mother Clifton, who had nine rows of bees'-wax teeth, and a three-cocked hat made of the right side of a crab's nostril. I then took the old hag and made a short leap from Liverpool to Nass in the North of Ireland, where I saw a French frigate coming with Nelson's monument at the top of her mainmast. So now to bring my story to an end, this old woman and me stepping out of the vessel into the port-hole, I made my escape, but the Old Woman was always tipsy with drinking Chandler's tobacco, so she sunk to the bottom, and if you go there you will find her making straw hats of deal boards.

(HARKNESS, PRINTER, PRESTON.)

VARNEY, THE VAMPYRE;

OR,

THE FEAST OF BLOOD

𝔄 Romance.

‒ ‒ 'How graves give up their dead,
And how the night air hideous grows
With shrieks!'

MIDNIGHT. ‒ THE HAIL-STORM. ‒ THE DREADFUL VISITOR. ‒ THE VAMPYRE.

The solemn tones of an old cathedral clock have announced midnight – the air is thick and heavy – a strange, death-like stillness pervades all nature. Like the ominous calm which precedes some more than usually terrific outbreak of the elements, they seem to have paused even in their ordinary fluctuations, to gather a terrific strength for the great effort. A faint peal of thunder now comes from far off. Like a signal gun for the battle of the winds to begin, it appeared to awaken them from their lethargy, and one awful, warring hurricane swept over a whole city, producing more devastation in the four or five minutes it lasted, than would a half century of ordinary phenomena.

It was as if some giant had blown upon some toy town, and scattered many of the buildings before the hot blast of his terrific breath; for as suddenly as that blast of wind had come did it cease, and all was as still and calm as before.

Sleepers awakened, and thought that what they had heard must be the confused chimera of a dream. They trembled and turned to sleep again.

All is still – still as the very grave. Not a sound breaks the magic of repose. What is that – a strange, pattering noise, as of a million of fairy feet? It is hail – yes, a hail-storm has burst over the city. Leaves are dashed from the trees, mingled with small boughs; windows that lie most opposed to the direct fury of the pelting particles of ice are broken, and the rapt repose that before was so remarkable in its intensity, is exchanged for a noise which, in its accumulation, drowns every cry of surprise or consternation which here and there arose from persons who found their houses invaded by the storm.

Now and then, too, there would come a sudden gust of wind that in its strength, as it blew laterally, would, for a moment, hold millions of the hailstones suspended in mid air, but it was only to dash them with redoubled force in some new direction, where more mischief was to be done.

Oh, how the storm raged! Hail – rain – wind. It was, in very truth, an awful night.

*

There is an antique chamber in an ancient house. Curious and quaint carvings adorn the walls, and the large chimney-piece is a curiosity of itself. The ceiling is low, and a large bay window, from roof to floor, looks to the west. The window is latticed, and filled with curiously painted glass and rich stained pieces, which send in a strange, yet beautiful light, when sun or moon shines into the apartment. There is but one portrait in that room, although the walls seem panelled for the express purpose of containing a series of pictures. That portrait is of a young man, with a pale face, a stately brow, and a strange expression about the eyes, which no one cared to look on twice.

There is a stately bed in that chamber, of carved walnut-wood is it made, rich in design and elaborate in execution; one of those works of art which owe their existence to the Elizabethan era. It is hung with heavy silken and damask furnishing; nodding feathers are at its corners – covered with dust are they, and they lend a funereal aspect to the room. The floor is of polished oak.

God! how the hail dashes on the old bay window! Like an occasional discharge of mimic musketry, it comes clashing, beating, and cracking upon the small panes; but they resist it – their small size saves them; the wind, the hail, the rain, expend their fury in vain.

The bed in that old chamber is occupied. A creature formed in all fashions of loveliness lies in a half sleep upon that ancient couch – a girl young and beautiful as a spring morning. Her long hair has escaped from its confinement and streams over the blackened coverings of the bedstead; she has been restless in her sleep, for the clothing of the bed is in much confusion. One arm is over her head, the other hangs nearly off the side of the bed near to which she lies. A neck and bosom that would have formed a study for the rarest sculptor that ever Providence gave genius to, were half disclosed. She moaned slightly in her sleep, and once or twice the lips moved as if in prayer – at least one might judge so, for the name of Him who suffered for all came once faintly from them.

She has endured much fatigue, and the storm does not awaken her; but it can disturb the slumbers it does not possess the power to destroy entirely. The turmoil of the elements wakes the senses, although it cannot entirely break the repose they have lapsed into.

Oh, what a world of witchery was in that mouth, slightly parted, and exhibiting within the pearly teeth that glistened even in the faint light that came from that bay window. How sweetly the long silken eyelashes lay upon the cheek. Now she moves, and one shoulder is entirely visible – whiter, fairer than the spotless clothing of the bed on which she lies, is the smooth skin of that fair creature, just budding into womanhood, and in that transition state which presents to us all the charms of the girl – almost of the child, with the more matured beauty and gentleness of advancing years.

Was that lightning? Yes – an awful, vivid, terrifying flash – then a roaring peal of thunder, as if a thousand mountains were rolling one over the other in the blue vault of Heaven! Who sleeps now in that ancient city? Not one living soul. The dread trumpet of eternity could not more effectually have awakened any one.

The hail continues. The wind continues. The uproar of the elements seems at its height. Now she wakens – that beautiful girl on the antique bed; she opens those eyes of celestial blue, and a faint cry of alarm bursts from her lips. At least it is a cry which, amid the noise and turmoil without, sounds but faint and weak. She sits upon the bed and presses her hands upon her eyes. Heavens! what a wild torrent of wind, and rain, and hail! The thunder likewise seems intent upon awakening sufficient echoes to last until the next flash of forked lightning should again produce the wild concussion of the air. She murmurs a prayer – a prayer for those she loves best; the names of those dear to her gentle heart come from her lips; she weeps and prays; she thinks then of what devastation the storm must surely produce, and to the great God of Heaven she prays for all living things. Another flash – a wild, blue, bewildering flash of lightning streams across that bay window, for an instant bringing out every colour in it with terrible distinctness. A shriek bursts from the lips of the young girl, and then, with eyes fixed upon that window, which, in another moment, is all darkness, and with such an expression of terror upon her face as it had never before known, she trembled, and the perspiration of intense fear stood upon her brow.

'What – what was it?' she gasped; 'real, or a delusion? Oh, God, what was it? A figure tall and gaunt, endeavouring from the outside to unclasp the window. I saw it. That flash of lightning revealed it to me. It stood the whole length of the window.'

There was a lull of the wind. The hail was not falling so thickly – moreover, it now fell, what there was of it, straight, and yet a strange clattering sound came upon the glass of that long window. It could not be a delusion – she is awake, and she hears it. What can produce it? Another flash of lightning – another shriek – there could be now no delusion.

A tall figure is standing on the ledge immediately outside the long window. It is its finger-nails upon the glass that produces the sound so like the hail, now that the hail has ceased. Intense fear paralysed the limbs of that beautiful girl. That one shriek is all she can utter – with hands clasped, a face of marble, a heart beating so wildly in her bosom, that each moment it seems as if it would break its confines, eyes distended and fixed upon the window, she waits, froze with horror. The pattering and clattering of the nails continue. No word is spoken, and now she fancies she can trace the darker form of that figure against the window, and she can see the long arms moving to and fro, feeling for some mode of entrance. What strange light is that which now gradually creeps up into the air? red and terrible – brighter and brighter it grows. The lightning has set fire to a mill, and the reflection of the rapidly consuming building falls upon that long window. There can be no mistake. The figure is there, still feeling for an entrance, and clattering against the glass with its long nails, that appear as if the growth of many years had been untouched. She tries to scream again but a choking sensation comes over her, and she cannot. It is too dreadful – she tries to move – each limb seems weighed down by tons of lead – she can but in a hoarse faint whisper cry, –

'Help – help – help – help!'

And that one word she repeats like a person in a dream. The red glare of the fire continues. It throws up the tall gaunt figure in hideous relief against the long window. It shows, too, upon the one portrait that is in the chamber, and that portrait appears to fix its eyes upon the attempting intruder, while the flickering light from the fire makes it look fearfully life-like. A small pane of glass is broken, and the form from without introduces a long gaunt hand, which seems utterly destitute of flesh.

The fastening is removed, and one-half of the window, which opens like folding doors, is swung wide open upon its hinges.

And yet now she could not scream – she could not move. 'Help! – help! – help!' was all she could say. But, oh, that look of terror that sat upon her face, it was dreadful – a look to haunt the memory for a life-time – a look to obtrude itself upon the happiest moments, and turn them to bitterness.

The figure turns half round, and the light falls upon the face. It is perfectly white – perfectly bloodless. The eyes look like polished tin; the lips are drawn back, and the principal feature next to those dreadful eyes is the teeth – the fearful looking teeth – projecting like those of some wild animal, hideously, glaringly white, and fang-like. It approaches the bed with a strange, gliding movement. It clashes together the long nails that literally appear to hang from the finger ends. No sound comes from its lips. Is she going mad – that young and beautiful girl exposed to so much terror? she has drawn up all her limbs; she cannot even now say help. The power of articulation is gone, but the power of movement has returned to her; she can draw herself slowly along to the other side of the bed from that towards which the hideous appearance is coming.

But her eyes are fascinated. The glance of a serpent could not have produced a greater effect upon her than did the fixed gaze of those awful, metallic-looking eyes that were bent on her face. Crouching down so that the gigantic height was lost, and the horrible, protruding, white face was the most prominent object, came on the figure. What was it? – what did it want there? – what made it look so hideous – so unlike an inhabitant of the earth, and yet to be on it?

Now she has got to the verge of the bed, and the figure pauses. It seemed as if when it paused she lost the power to proceed. The clothing of the bed was now clutched in her hands with unconscious power. She drew her breath short and thick. Her bosom heaves, and her limbs tremble, yet she cannot withdraw her eyes from that marble-looking face. He holds her with his glittering eye.

The storm has ceased – all is still. The winds are hushed; the church clock proclaims the hour of one: a hissing sound comes from the throat of the hideous being, and he raises his long, gaunt arms – the lips move. He advances. The girl places one small foot from the bed on to the floor. She is unconsciously dragging the clothing with her. The door of the room is in that direction – can she reach it? Has she power to walk? – can she withdraw her eyes from the face of the intruder, and so break the hideous charm? God of Heaven! is it real, or some dream so like reality as to nearly overturn the judgment for ever?

The figure has paused again, and half on the bed and half out of it that young girl lies trembling. Her long hair streams across the entire width of the bed. As she has slowly moved along she has left it streaming across the pillows. The pause lasted about a minute – oh, what an age of agony. That minute was, indeed, enough for madness to do its full work in.

With a sudden rush that could not be foreseen – with a strange howling cry that was enough to awaken terror in every breast, the figure seized the long tresses of her hair, and twining them round his bony hands he held

her to the bed. Then she screamed – Heaven granted her then power to scream. Shriek followed shriek in rapid succession. The bed-clothes fell in a heap by the side of the bed – she was dragged by her long silken hair completely on to it again. Her beautifully rounded limbs quivered with the agony of her soul. The glassy, horrible eyes of the figure ran over that angelic form with a hideous satisfaction – horrible profanation. He drags her head to the bed's edge. He forces it back by the long hair still entwined in his grasp. With a plunge he seizes her neck in his fang-like teeth – a gush of blood, and a hideous sucking noise follows. *The girl has swooned, and the vampyre is at his hideous repast!*

THE ALARM. – THE PISTOL SHOT. – THE PURSUIT AND ITS CONSEQUENCES.

Lights flashed about the building, and various room doors opened; voices called one to the other. There was an universal stir and commotion among the inhabitants.

'Did you hear a scream, Harry?' asked a young man, half-dressed, as he walked into the chamber of another about his own age.

'I did – where was it?'

'God knows. I dressed myself directly.'

'All is still now.'

'Yes; but unless I was dreaming there was a scream.'

'We could not both dream there was. Where did you think it came from?'

'It burst so suddenly upon my ears that I cannot say.'

There was a tap now at the door of the room where these young men were, and a female voice said, –

'For God's sake, get up!'

'We are up,' said both the young men; appearing.

'Did you hear anything?'

'Yes, a scream.'

'Oh, search the house – search the house; where did it come from – can you tell?'

'Indeed we cannot, mother.'

Another person now joined the party. He was a man of middle age, and, as he came up to them, he said, –

'Good God! what is the matter?'

Scarcely had the words passed his lips, than such a rapid succession of shrieks came upon their ears, that they felt absolutely stunned by them. The elderly lady, whom one of the young men had called mother, fainted, and would have fallen to the floor of the corridor in which they all stood, had she not been promptly supported by the last comer, who himself staggered, as those piercing cries came upon the night air. He, however, was the first to recover, for the young men seemed paralysed.

'Henry,' he cried, 'for God's sake support your mother. Can you doubt that these cries come from Flora's room?'

The young man mechanically supported his mother, and then the man who had just spoken darted back to his own bed-room, from whence he returned in a moment with a pair of pistols, and shouting, –

'Follow me, who can!' he bounded across the corridor in the direction of the antique apartment, from whence the cries proceeded, but which were now hushed.

That house was built for strength, and the doors were all of oak, and of considerable thickness. Unhappily, they had fastenings within, so that when the man reached the chamber of her who so much required help, he was helpless, for the door was fast.

'Flora! Flora!' he cried; 'Flora, speak!'

All was still.

'Good God!' he added; 'we must force the door.'

'I hear a strange noise within,' said the young man, who trembled violently.

'And so do I. What does it sound like?'

'I scarcely know; but it nearest resembles some animal eating, or sucking some liquid.'

'What on earth can it be? Have you no weapon that will force the door? I shall go mad if I am kept here.'

'I have,' said the young man. 'Wait here a moment.'

He ran down the staircase, and presently returned with a small, but powerful, iron crow-bar.

'This will do,' he said.

'It will, it will. – Give it to me.'

'Has she not spoken?'

'Not a word. My mind misgives me that something very dreadful must have happened to her.'

'And that odd noise!'

'Still goes on. Somehow, it curdles the very blood in my veins to hear it.'

The man took the crow-bar, and with some difficulty succeeded in introducing it between the door and the side of the wall – still it required great strength to move it, but it did move, with a harsh, crackling sound.

'Push it!' cried he who was using the bar, 'push the door at the same time.'

The younger man did so. For a few moments the massive door resisted. Then, suddenly, something gave way with a loud snap – it was a part of the lock, – and the door at once swung wide open.

How true it is that we measure time by the events which happen within a given space of it, rather than by its actual duration.

To those who were engaged in forcing open the door of the antique chamber, where slept the young girl whom they named Flora, each moment was swelled into an hour of agony; but, in reality, from the first moment of the alarm to that when the loud cracking noise heralded the destruction of the fastenings of the door, there had elapsed but very few minutes indeed.

'It opens – it opens,' cried the young man.

'Another moment,' said the stranger, as he still plied the crowbar – 'another moment, and we shall have free ingress to the chamber. Be patient.'

This stranger's name was Marchdale; and even as he spoke, he succeeded in throwing the massive door wide open, and clearing the passage to the chamber.

To rush in with light in his hand was the work of a moment to the young man named Henry; but the very rapid progress he made into the apartment prevented him from observing accurately what it contained, for the wind that came in from the open window caught the flame of the candle, and although it did not actually extinguish it, it blew it so much on one side, that it was comparatively useless as a light.

'Flora – Flora!' he cried.

Then with a sudden bound something dashed from off the bed. The concussion against him was so sudden and so utterly unexpected, as well as so tremendously violent, that he was thrown down, and, in his fall, the light was fairly extinguished.

All was darkness, save a dull, reddish kind of light that now and then, from the nearly consumed mill in the immediate vicinity, came into the room. But by that light, dim, uncertain, and flickering as it was, some one was seen to make for the window.

Henry, although nearly stunned by his fall, saw a figure, gigantic in height, which nearly reached from the floor to the ceiling. The other young man, George, saw it, and Mr Marchdale likewise saw it, as did the lady who had spoken to the young men in the corridor when first the screams of the young girl awakened alarm in the breasts of all the inhabitants of that house.

The figure was about to pass out at the window which led to a kind of balcony, from whence there was an easy descent to a garden.

Before it passed out they each and all caught a glance of the side-face, and they saw that the lower part of it and the lips were dabbled in blood. They saw, too, one of those fearful-looking, shining, metallic eyes which presented so terrible an appearance of unearthly ferocity.

No wonder that for a moment a panic seized them all, which paralysed any exertions they might otherwise have made to detain that hideous form.

But Mr Marchdale was a man of mature years; he had seen much of life, both in this and in foreign lands; and he, although astonished to the extent of being frightened, was much more likely to recover sooner than his younger companions, which, indeed, he did, and acted promptly enough.

'Don't rise, Henry,' he cried. 'Lie still.'

Almost at the moment he uttered these words, he fired at the figure, which then occupied the window, as if it were a gigantic figure set in a frame.

The report was tremendous in that chamber, for the pistol was no toy weapon, but one made for actual service, and of sufficient length and bore of barrel to carry destruction along with the bullets that came from it.

'If that has missed its aim,' said Mr Marchdale, 'I'll never pull a trigger again.'

As he spoke he dashed forward, and made a clutch at the figure he felt convinced he had shot.

The tall form turned upon him, and when he got a full view of the face, which he did at that moment, from the opportune circumstance of the lady returning at the instant with a light she had been to her own chamber to procure, even he, Marchdale, with all his courage, and that was great, and all his nervous energy, recoiled a step or two, and uttered the exclamation of, 'Great God!'

That face was never to be forgotten. It was hideously flushed with colour – the colour of fresh blood; the eyes had a savage and remarkable lustre; whereas, before, they had looked like polished tin – they now wore a ten times brighter aspect, and flashes of light seemed to dart from them. The mouth was open, as if, from the natural formation of the countenance, the lips receded much from the large canine looking teeth.

A strange howling noise came from the throat of this monstrous figure, and it seemed upon the point of rushing upon Mr Marchdale. Suddenly, then, as if some impulse had seized upon it, it uttered a wild and terrible shrieking kind of laugh; and then turning, dashed through the window, and in one instant disappeared from before the eyes of those who felt nearly annihilated by its fearful presence.

'God help us!' ejaculated Henry.

Mr Marchdale drew a long breath, and then, giving a stamp on the floor, as if to recover himself from the state of agitation into which he was thrown, he cried, –

'Be it what or who it may, I'll follow it.'

'No – no – do not,' cried the lady.

'I must, I will. Let who will come with me – I follow that dreadful form.'

As he spoke, he took the road it took, and dashed through the window into the balcony.

'And we, too, George,' exclaimed Henry; 'we will follow Mr Marchdale. This dreadful affair concerns us more nearly than it does him.'

The lady who was the mother of these young men, and of the beautiful girl who had been so awfully visited, screamed aloud, and implored of them to stay. But the voice of Mr Marchdale was heard exclaiming aloud, –

'I see it – I see it; it makes for the wall.'

They hesitated no longer, but at once rushed into the balcony, and from thence dropped into the garden.

The mother approached the bed-side of the insensible, perhaps the murdered girl; she saw her, to all appearance, weltering in blood, and, overcome by her emotions, she fainted on the floor of the room.

When the two young men reached the garden, they found it much lighter than might have been fairly expected; for not only was the morning rapidly approaching, but the mill was still burning, and those mingled lights made almost every object plainly visible, except when deep shadows were thrown from some gigantic trees that had stood for centuries in that sweetly wooded spot. They heard the voice of Mr Marchdale, as he cried, –

'There – there – towards the wall. There – there – God! how it bounds along.'

The young men hastily dashed through a thicket in the direction from whence his voice sounded, and then they found him looking wild and terrified, and with something in his hand which looked like a portion of clothing.

'Which way, which way?' they both cried.

He leant heavily on the arm of George, as he pointed along a vista of trees, and said in a low voice, –

'God help us all. It is not human. Look there – look there – do you not see it?'

They looked in the direction he indicated. At the end of this vista was the wall of the garden. At that point it was full twelve feet in height, and as they looked, they saw the hideous, monstrous form they had traced from the chamber of their sister, making frantic efforts to clear the obstacle.

Then they saw it bound from the ground to the top of the wall, which it very nearly reached, and then each time it fell back again into the garden with such a dull, heavy sound, that the earth seemed to shake again with the concussion. They trembled – well indeed they might, and for some minutes they watched the figure making its fruitless efforts to leave the place.

'What – what is it?' whispered Henry, in hoarse accents. 'God, what can it possibly be?'

'I know not,' replied Mr Marchdale. 'I did seize it. It was cold and clammy like a corpse. It cannot be human.'

'Not human?'

'Look at it now. It will surely escape now.'

'No, no – we will not be terrified thus – there is Heaven above us. Come on, and, for dear Flora's sake, let us make an effort yet to seize this bold intruder.'

'Take this pistol,' said Marchdale. 'It is the

fellow of the one I fired. Try its efficacy.'

'He will be gone,' exclaimed Henry, as at this moment after many repeated attempts and fearful falls, the figure reached the top of the wall, and then hung by its long arms a moment or two, previous to dragging itself completely up.

The idea of the appearance, be it what it might, entirely escaping, seemed to nerve again Mr Marchdale, and he, as well as the two young men, ran forward towards the wall. They got so close to the figure before it sprang on the outer side of the wall, that to miss killing it with the bullet from the pistol was a matter of utter impossibility, unless wilfully.

Henry had the weapon, and he pointed it full at the tall form with a steady aim. He pulled the trigger – the explosion followed, and that the bullet did its office there could be no manner of doubt, for the figure gave a howling shriek, and fell headlong from the wall on the outside.

'I have shot him,' cried Henry, 'I have shot him.'

THE DISAPPEARANCE OF THE BODY.

'He is human!' cried Henry. 'I have surely killed him.'

'It would seem so,' said Mr Marchdale. 'Let us now hurry round to the outside of the wall, and see where he lies.'

This was at once agreed to, and the whole three of them made what expedition they could towards a gate which led into a paddock, across which they hurried, and soon found themselves clear of the garden wall, so that they could make way towards where they fully expected to find the body of him who had worn so unearthly an aspect, but who it would be an excessive relief to find was human.

So hurried was the progress they made, that it was scarcely possible to exchange many words as they went; a kind of breathless anxiety was upon them, and in the speed they disregarded every obstacle, which would, at any other time, have probably prevented them from taking the direct road they sought.

It was difficult on the outside of the wall to say exactly which was the precise spot which it might be supposed the body had fallen on; but, by following the wall in its entire length, surely they would come upon it.

They did so; but, to their surprise, they got from its commencement to its further extremity without finding any dead body, or even any symptoms of one having lain there.

At some parts close to the wall there grew a kind of heath, and, consequently, the traces of blood would be lost among it, if it so happened that at the precise spot at which the strange being had seemed to topple over, such vegetation had existed. This was to be ascertained; but now, after traversing the whole length of the wall twice, they came to a halt, and looked wonderingly in each other's faces.

'There is nothing here,' said Harry.

'Nothing,' added his brother.

'It could not have been a delusion,' at length said Mr Marchdale, with a shudder.

'A delusion?' exclaimed the brothers. 'That is not possible; we all saw it.'

'Then what terrible explanation can we give?'

'By heavens! I know not,' exclaimed Henry. 'This adventure surpasses all belief, and but for the great interest we have in it, I should regard it with a world of curiosity.'

'It is too dreadful,' said George; 'for God's sake, Henry, let us return to ascertain if poor Flora is killed.'

'My senses,' said Henry, 'were all so much absorbed in gazing at the horrible form, that I never once looked towards her further than to see that she was, to appearance, dead. God help her! poor – poor, beautiful Flora. This is, indeed, a sad, sad fate for you to come to. Flora – Flora – '

'Do not weep, Henry,' said George. 'Rather let us now hasten home, where we may find that tears are premature. She may yet be living and restored to us.'

'And,' said Mr Marchdale, 'she may be able to give us some account of this dreadful visitation.'

'True – true,' exclaimed Henry; 'we will hasten home.'

They now turned their steps homewards, and as they went they much blamed themselves for all leaving home together, and with terror pictured what might occur in their absence to those who were now totally unprotected.

'It was a rash impulse of us all to come in pursuit of this dreadful figure,' remarked Mr Marchdale; 'but do not torment yourself, Henry. There may be no reason for your fears.'

At the pace they went, they very soon reached the ancient house, and when they came in sight of it, they saw lights flashing from the windows, and the shadows of faces moving to and fro, indicating that the whole household was up, and in a state of alarm.

Henry, after some trouble, got the hall door opened by a terrified servant, who was trembling so much that she could scarcely hold the light she had with her.

'Speak at once, Martha,' said Henry. 'Is Flora living?'

'Yes; but – '

'Enough – enough! Thank God she lives; where is she now?'

'In her own room, Master Henry. Oh, dear – oh, dear, what will become of us all?'

Henry rushed up the staircase, followed by George and Mr Marchdale, nor paused he once until he reached the room of his sister.

'Mother,' he said, before he crossed the threshold, 'are you here?'

'I am, my dear – I am. Come in, pray come in, and speak to poor Flora.'

'Come in, Mr Marchdale,' said Henry – 'come in; we make no stranger of you.'

They all then entered the room.

Several lights had now been brought into that antique chamber, and, in addition to the mother of the beautiful girl who had been so fearfully visited, there were two female domestics, who appeared to be in the greatest possible fright, for they could render no assistance whatever to anybody.

The tears were streaming down the mother's face, and the moment she saw Mr Marchdale, she clung to his arm, evidently unconscious of what she was about, and exclaimed, –

'Oh, what is this that has happened – what is this? Tell me, Marchdale! Robert Marchdale, you whom I have known even from my childhood, you will not deceive me. Tell me the meaning of all this?'

'I cannot,' he said, in a tone of much emotion. 'As God is my judge, I am as much puzzled and amazed at the scene that has taken place here to-night as you can be.'

The mother wrung her hands and wept.

'It was the storm that first awakened me,' added Marchdale; 'and then I heard a scream.'

The brothers tremblingly approached the bed. Flora was placed in a sitting, half-reclining posture, propped up by pillows. She was quite insensible, and her face was fearfully pale; while that she breathed at all could be but very faintly seen. On some of her clothing, about the neck, were spots of blood, and she looked more like one who had suffered some long and grievous illness, than a young girl in the prime of life and in the most robust health, as she had been on the day previous to the strange scene we have recorded.

'Does she sleep?' said Henry, as a tear fell from his eyes upon her pallid cheek.

'No,' replied Mr Marchdale. 'This is a swoon, from which we must recover her.'

Active measures were now adopted to restore the languid circulation, and, after persevering in them for some time, they had the satisfaction of seeing her open her eyes.

Her first act upon consciousness returning, however, was to utter a loud shriek, and it was not until Henry implored her to look around her, and see that she was surrounded by none but friendly faces, that she would venture again to open her eyes, and look timidly from one to the other. Then she shuddered, and burst into tears as she said, –

'Oh, Heaven, have mercy upon me – Heaven, have mercy upon me, and save me from that dreadful form.'

'There is no one here, Flora,' said Mr Marchdale, 'but those who love you, and who, in defence of you, if needs were would lay down their lives.'

'Oh, God! Oh, God!'

'You have been terrified. But tell us distinctly what has happened? You are quite safe now.'

She trembled so violently that Mr Marchdale recommended that some stimulant should be given to her, and she was persuaded, although not without considerable difficulty, to swallow a small portion of some wine from a cup. There could be no doubt but that the stimulating effect of the wine was beneficial, for a slight accession of colour visited her cheeks, and she spoke in a firmer tone as she said, –

'Do not leave me. Oh, do not leave me, any of you. I shall die if left alone now. Oh, save me – save me. That horrible form! That fearful face!'

'Tell us how it happened, dear Flora?' said Henry.

'Or would you rather endeavour to get some sleep first?' suggested Mr Marchdale.

'No – no – no,' she said, 'I do not think I shall ever sleep again.'

'Say not so; you will be more composed in a few hours, and then you can tell us what has occurred.'

'I will tell you now. I will tell you now.'

She placed her hands over her face for a moment, as if to collect her scattered thoughts, and then she added, –

'I was awakened by the storm, and I saw that terrible apparition at the window. I think I screamed, but I could not fly. Oh, God! I could not fly. It came – it seized me by the hair. I know no more. I know no more.'

She passed her hand across her neck several times, and Mr Marchdale said, in an anxious voice, –

'You seem, Flora, to have hurt your neck – there is a wound.'

'A wound!' said the mother, and she brought a light close to the bed, where all saw on the side of Flora's neck a small punctured wound; or, rather two, for there was one a little distance from the other.

It was from these wounds the blood had come which was observable upon her night clothing.

'How came these wounds?' said Henry.

'I do not know,' she replied. 'I feel very faint and weak, as if I had almost bled to death.'

'You cannot have done so, dear Flora, for there are not above half-a-dozen spots of blood to be seen at all.'

Mr Marchdale leaned against the carved head of the bed for support, and he uttered a deep groan. All eyes were turned upon him, and Henry said, in a voice of the most anxious inquiry, –

'You have something to say, Mr Marchdale, which will throw some light upon this affair.'

'No, no, no, nothing!' cried Mr Marchdale, rousing himself at once from the appearance of depression that had come over him. 'I have nothing to say, but that I think Flora had better get some sleep if she can.'

'No sleep – no sleep for me,' again screamed Flora. 'Dare I be alone to sleep?'

'But you shall not be alone, dear Flora,' said Henry. 'I will sit by your bedside and watch you.'

She took his hand in both hers, and while the tears chased each other down her cheeks, she said, –

'Promise me, Henry, by all your hopes of Heaven, you will not leave me.'

'I promise!'

She gently laid herself down, with a deep sigh, and closed her eyes.

'She is weak, and will sleep long,' said Mr Marchdale.

'You sigh,' said Henry. 'Some fearful thoughts, I feel certain, oppress your heart.'

'Hush – hush!' said Mr Marchdale, as he pointed to Flora. 'Hush! not here – not here.'

'I understand,' said Henry.

'Let her sleep.'

There was a silence of some few minutes' duration. Flora had dropped into a deep slumber. That silence was first broken by George, who said, –

'Mr Marchdale, look at that portrait.'

He pointed to the portrait in the frame to which we have alluded, and the moment Marchdale looked at it he sunk into a chair as he exclaimed, –

'Gracious Heaven, how like!'

'It is – it is,' said Henry. 'Those eyes – '

'And see the contour of the countenance, and the strange shape of the mouth.'

'Exact – exact.'

'That picture shall be moved from here. The sight of it is at once sufficient to awaken all her former terrors in poor Flora's brain if she should chance to awaken and cast her eyes suddenly upon it.'

'And is it so like him who came here?' said the mother.

'It is the very man himself,' said Mr Marchdale. 'I have not been in this house long enough to ask any of you whose portrait that may be?'

'It is,' said Henry, 'the portrait of Sir Runnagate Bannerworth, an ancestor of ours, who first, by his vices, gave the great blow to the family prosperity.'

'Indeed. How long ago?'

'About ninety years.'

'Ninety years. 'Tis a long while – ninety years.'

'You muse upon it.'

'No, no. I do wish, and yet I dread – '

'What?'

'To say something to you all. But not here – not here. We will hold a consultation on this matter to-morrow. Not now – not now.'

'The daylight is coming quickly on,' said

Henry; 'I shall keep my sacred promise of not moving from this room until Flora awakens; but there can be no occasion for the detention of any of you. One is sufficient here. Go all of you, and endeavour to procure what rest you can.'

'I will fetch you my powder-flask and bullets,' said Mr Marchdale; 'and you can, if you please, reload the pistols. In about two hours more it will be broad daylight.'

This arrangement was adopted. Henry did reload the pistols, and placed them on a table by the side of the bed, ready for immediate action, and then, as Flora was sleeping soundly, all left the room but himself.

Mrs Bannerworth was the last to do so. She would have remained, but for the earnest solicitation of Henry, that she would endeavour to get some sleep to make up for her broken night's repose, and she was indeed so broken down by her alarm on Flora's account, that she had not the power to resist, but with tears flowing from her eyes, she sought her own chamber.

And now the calmness of the night resumed its sway in that evil-fated mansion; and

although no one really slept but Flora, all were still. Busy thought kept every one else wakeful. It was a mockery to lie down at all, and Henry, full of strange and painful feelings as he was, preferred his present position to the anxiety and apprehension on Flora's account which he knew he should feel if she were not within the sphere of his own observation, and she slept as soundly as some gentle infant tired of its playmates and its sports.

NOVELS AND ROMANCES

In giving a little advice to our working friends on this subject, we observe:

That *novels* and *romances consist*, to a wide extent, *of light reading*. They often undertake to exhibit what never has been, and never can be, so that there is little that is real; and the morsel which is so, is generally exaggerated or caricatured to such a degree, that the substantial part is nearly concealed. An individual who has read nothing but works of fiction, would have very few correct ideas of the real world, and would be neither fit for heaven nor earth. The great design of reading should be, not only to obtain thoughts, but to store the mind with such as are great, good, and correct. Those who read but little, will have contracted minds; and those who peruse hardly anything but works of fancy, will be almost as ignorant as those who do not read at all. Novelists do not teach astronomy, nor mathematics, nor chemistry, nor natural history, nor real biography. They would not be read if they led us out into God's real world. They create a universe of their own. It is true, they borrow their materials from ours, but then they unmake, or new-make, everything; so that you read as a sceptic, and as you go along, you are continually saying, 'This is not true.' You have fairies, nymphs, dryads, oreads, sylphs, giants, &c., but not real men and women. Now we ask our working friends, if it is at all likely that their minds should ever become enlightened or strong by perusing nothing but this description of literature? What if we fed a labourer, a quarryman, or a miner, on pastry and sugar-plums! Would he be able to follow his arduous employment?

Every one says 'No! he would be only fit for a saloon and a sofa.' So the mind, which is fed and filled with nothing but fiction, will be as light and visionary as the fanciful sentimentalism on which it feeds. We have known many who read hardly anything but tales, novels, and romances; but we never found a deep-thinker among them.

2. WONDERS

The Mermaid.

This eighth 'wonder of the world;' this 'frightful monster which the world ne'er saw,' until the present year, is now the great source of attraction in the British metropolis; and three to four hundred people every day pay their shilling each to see a disgusting sort of a compound animal, which contains in itself every thing that is odious and disagreeable. But the curiosity to see a *real* Mermaid, after all the fictions that have been related respecting it, is natural enough – the only point is, whether it is a real one or not; and even on this professional men disagree.

This singular creature, which it is reported was brought to Batavia, in the East Indies, from some of the neighbouring islands, is in a state of high preservation, and appears to have been so for many years. It is nearly three feet in length. Its head is nearly round, about the size of that of a child two or three years old – its forehead somewhat depressed, and chin projecting similar to the negro. Its teeth perfect, and beautifully set in circular rows; but the canine teeth, as they are called, being longer, project much beyond the others. The cheeks of the face project a little, which, together with the eyes, eye-brows, chin, mouth, tongue, ears, throat, &c. exactly resemble those of the human species. Its head is somewhat bent forward. The spinous processes of the cervical and dorsal vertebræ project in that distinct and regular order, down to the lower part of the breast, that we find in the human subject; when they gradually lose themselves on entering the natural form of the lower portion of the body of a fish. The scapula and arms – the latter of which are of great length – hands, thumbs, fingers, and nails, furnish us with an exact representation of those of a delicate female; the breast bone, clavicles, and ribs of the chest are perfectly distinct, and the breasts, which are now of some size, and appear to have been very large – and nipples, are a tolerable model of those in the human species. Its body appears to be muscular above the chest, and covered with cuticle and hair, dispersed as in the human skin.

The one side of the head is covered with black human hair, about half an inch or an inch in length; but on the other side it appears to have been worn or rubbed off.

When examining this singular phenomenon, what excited astonishment was, the external covering from the chest upwards to be such a near representation of that of a human being, whilst the whole body below was enveloped with the scaly covering of a fish.

Immediately under the breasts, the fishy form commences, by two large fins on its belly, on which it has been represented by those who have seen it at sea to rest the upper part of its body above water; it then tapers off and terminates in the tail of a fish, not unlike that of a salmon.

The engraving we give in our present number is a very correct delineation of the appearance of the Mermaid which has been brought from one of the Molucca Islands. But, positive as some persons are, as to its really being that long-deemed fabulous creature, the Mermaid, we must beg leave to express our doubts – we may say firm conviction – that it is an imposture – certainly not the first that has been practised on the credulity of honest John Bull. The fact is, that the lower part is a real fish, of a species found in the rivers of China and Japan, the head and shoulders being cut off, and replaced by the bust of a baboon.

*

But while we doubt the reality of the disgusting looking Mermaid (as it is called) now exhibiting, we are compelled to acknowledge that there is a host of evidence in favour of the existence of such a creature, both in ancient and modern times. Pliny says, that 'the Ambassadors to Augustus from Gaul declared that sea-women were often seen in their neighbourhood.' Solinus and Aulus Gellius also speak of their existence.

It is related in the Histoire d'Angleterre, part 1, page 403, that in the year 1187, a Merman was 'fished up' in the county of Suffolk, and kept by the governor for six months; it was exactly like a man *in every respect*, and wanted nothing but speech. He never could be brought to any understanding of his nature or situation, and at length made his escape, and was seen to plunge into the sea, from whence he returned no more.

In 1430, in the great tempests which destroyed the dykes in Holland, some women at Edam, in West-Freezeland, saw a Mermaid who had been driven by the waters into the meadows which were overflowed. They took it, and (as it is said) *dressed it in female attire,*

WONDERFUL!!

What no one can believe without Seeing;

What none can see without believing;—and what all are astonished at when they do see:

THE THREE BEAUTIFUL ALBINI

Children,

THE GREATEST

Phenomena  of Nature

ever Exhibited.

The Nobility, Gentry, and Public in general, are most respectfully informed, that those three beautiful ALBINIS are just arrived, and to be seen in

A Commodious Pavilion,
DURING THE RACES.

They are peculiarly worthy the attention of all who delight in viewing such parts of the Creation as display the marvellous Productions of Nature: their Beauty cannot be credited but on sight. They have been viewed with admiration, and particularly by the Faculty, who have pronounced them to be truly the only HUMAN LIVING PHENOMENA ever exhibited to the public.

To the Ladies in particular this Exhibition is recommended, as nothing can display more innocence and beauty.— THEIR SKIN IS SUPERIOR TO WAX-WORK, almost transparent; their Hair nearly as White as Snow; their Eyes have a surprising sparkling Lustre, quite different, far superior, and more brilliant than any Eyes ever beheld. which with the Phenomena, must shew to the Spectator the surprising and extraordinary Works of Nature, as the like was never seen before. Miss Crawly is eleven, one Boy nine, and the other seven years old. The Mother of the Albinis attends them.

———

Admittance to Ladies and Gentlemen, 1s. each—Servants and Children, 6d.

SEDDON, PRINTER.

MIRACULOUS
Circumstance,

Being a full and particular Account of John Macintire, who was buried alive, in Edinburgh, on the 15th day of April, 1824, while in a Trance, and who was taken up by the Resurrection Men, and sold to the Doctors to be dissected, with a full Account of the many strange and wonderful Things which he saw and felt while he was in that state, the whole being taken from his own words.

I had been some time ill of a low and lingering fever. My strength gradually wasted and I could see by the Doctor that I had nothing to hope. One day towards evening, I was seized with strange and indescribable quivering. I saw around my bed, innumerable strange faces; they were bright and visionary, and without bodies. There was light and solemnity, and I tried to move, but could not, I could recollect with perfectness, but the power of motion had departed. I heard the sound of weeping at my pillow,—and the voice of the nurse say, "He is Dead." I cannot describe what I felt at these words. I exerted my utmost power to stir myself, but I could not move even an eyelid. My father drew his hand over my face, and closed my eyelids. The world was then darkened, but I could still hear, and feel and suffer. For three days a number of friends called to see me, I heard them in low accents speak of what I was; and more than one touched me with his finger. The coffin was then procured, and I was laid in it. I felt the coffin lifted and borne away. I heard and felt it placed in the hearse,—it halted, the coffin was taken out— I felt myself carried on the shoulders of men, I heard the cords of the coffin moved, I felt it swing as dependent by them. It was lowered and rested upon the bottom of the grave. Dreadful was the effort I then made to exert the power of Action, but my whole frame was immoveable. The sound of the rattling mould as it covered me, was far more tremendous than thunder. This also ceased and all was silent. This is death, thought I, and soon the worms will be crawling about my flesh. In the contemplation of this hedious thought, I heard a low sound in the earth over me, and I fancied that the worms and reptiles were coming. The sound continued to grow louder and and nearer. Can it be possible thought I, that my friends suspect they have buried me too soon. The hope was truly like light bursting through the gloom of death. The sound ceased. They dragged me out of the coffin by the head, and carried me swiftly away. When borne to some distance I was thrown down like a clod, and by the interchange of one or two brief sentences, I discovered that I was in the hands of two of those robbers, who live by plundering the grave, and selling the bodies of parents, and children, and friends.

Being rudely stripped of my shroud, I was placed naked on a table. In a short time I heard by the bustle in the room, that the doctors and students were assembling. When all was ready the Demonstrator took his knife, and pierced my bosom. I felt a dreadful crackling, as it were, throughout my whole frame, a convulsive shudder instantly followed, and a shriek of horror rose from all present.— The ice of death was broken up—my trance was ended. The utmost exertions were made to restore me, and in the course of an hour I was in full possession of all my faculties.

Stephenson, Printer, Gateshead.

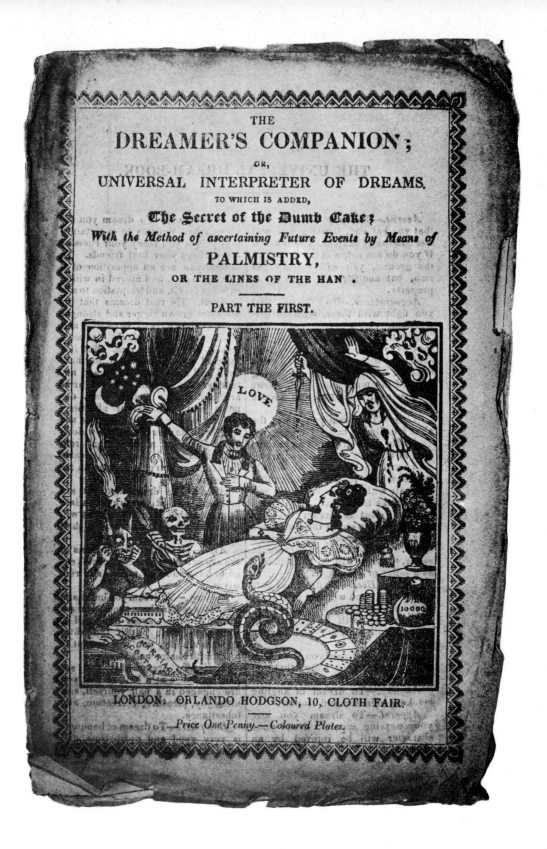

THE
DREAMER'S COMPANION;
OR,
UNIVERSAL INTERPRETER OF DREAMS.
TO WHICH IS ADDED,

The Secret of the Dumb Cake;

With the Method of ascertaining Future Events by Means of
PALMISTRY,
OR THE LINES OF THE HAND.

—

PART THE FIRST.

LOVE

LONDON: ORLANDO HODGSON, 10, CLOTH FAIR.

Price One Penny.—Coloured Plates.

For the Good of the Public!!

ON MONDAY, ~~29th~~ of ~~AUGUST~~, 1825,

AT MR. RIMMER'S, SHAKSPEARE TAVERN,

WILLIAMSON SQUARE, LIVERPOOL,

A LECTURE

WILL BE DELIVERED UPON

Natural Philosophy & Disease

Which will show a victory is gained over that inveterate enemy Disease. A victory which will pull down the fabric of confusion and uncertainty, and erect upon its ruins the glorious edifice of truth of what will preserve health better and prolong life, and fill the kingdom full of health and riches. Then there will be very few poor sick people; so that will save some thousand pounds a-year in each hospital. Health is the source of riches in all countries; disease is the source of idleness, misery, and destruction. A fixed gout; dim eyes; asthma; the bile; the piles; a pain in the bowels; the scurvy; bad sore eyes; all are easily cured, and the small-pox prevented. Mr. Pedley, who will show the source and cause of disease, and how the several disorders originate, will explain a new experiment made on perspiration, by which you see at once what state of health you are in, and how to prevent untimely death. And Mr. P. will endeavour to establish a new system in the practice of physic, with six vegetable medicines, which will easily cure the disorders in children up to old age, directed by the English language, then every Briton will know what he takes. A Latin thesis, I know, by ancient and reverend custom, is made the passport to doctorial dignity, a custom I will not depreciate, yet, I will show a substitute in the English tongue which will far excel that dignity, because it will prevent mistake and completely supersede the painful operation for dropsy, cupping, drawing the tooth, blistering, salivation, &c.

THE FEVER AND PLAGUE ARE A DROPSY.
THE GOUT IS A DROPSY.

A cure for the Gout, in my letter to His Majesty the King of the greatest of all nations, will be read at each lecture. The late French King had an erysipelas in his legs and thighs that he could not walk. That disorder I can also cure.

It did not want superior learning to make this discovery. No. I will show you what it wanted in my lecture, which will be a high treat to ladies and gentlemen.

Of Homer the Poet it has been said,—

"A thousand cities vied for Homer dead,
"Through which, when living, Homer beg'd his bread."

Now I am free to say I have done more good for the world than all the poets and prose writers in the world have done: for this reason; I have found and proved what will preserve health better, and prolong life.

I am, with true respect, the public's very humble servant,

TIMOTHY PEDLEY.

N. B. My medicines will keep the body cool, and prevent those epidemical disorders in hot climates.

TO COMMENCE AT ELEVEN O'CLOCK IN THE MORNING, AND FOUR O'CLOCK
IN THE AFTERNOON PRECISELY.

Admission—Front Seats 2s.   Back Seats 1s.

and taught it to spin. It fed on cooked meat, but all efforts to teach it to speak proved ineffectual, though Parival says, 'it had some notion of a deity, and *made its reverences very devoutly* when it passed a crucifix.' It was taken to Haerlem, where it lived some years, but it ever retained an inclination for the water. At its death it was allowed christian burial.

THE SIGNIFICANCE OF DREAMS

Apes. – To dream of apes forbodes no good, they are a sign of wicked and secret enemies who will seek, by many devices, to injure you; be, therefore upon your guard, for some one who pretends to be your friend, is about to deceive you and you are very near losing your liberty – if you are in love do not attempt to marry, for he or she will prove unfaithful, and involve you in much trouble.

Apparel. – To dream that your apparel is proper and suitable to the season of the year, denotes prosperity and happiness.

White. – To dream you are dressed in white is a sure token of success in the first object you undertake; and that you will be successful in love, and your sweetheart is of a good temper.

Green. – Denotes that you are about to take a journey to your advantage, and that your sweetheart prefers you to all lovers.

Black. – is unlucky: some quarrel is about to happen between you and a relation or friend; sickness is likely to attend you or your family, and death will deprive you of some person who is very dear to you. Beware of law-suits, lest you get involved in difficulties; and undertake no journey, for it will not prove successful. If you are in love, it denotes the person on whom you have placed your affection is very unhappy, and that sickness and various other trouble are about to attend him or her.

THE ORIGINS OF HOLLOWAY'S OINTMENT

[*Mr Holloway is serving as medical officer in Algeria when plague attacks.*]

Three times did the plague attack, and each time he was saved, and such was the conviction found in the minds of the multitudes, that they deemed his life a charmed one, and though taught by their religion to treat the infidel with scorn and contumely, yet many who approached his bed, as they thought, of death, and visited the Christian dog merely 'to scoff, remained to pray'. They knew not how he could emancipate himself from the grasp of the plague; but it was evident that he had done so, and they afterwards viewed him as being under the especial care of the prophet. [*Holloway disappeared into Algiers for three weeks. He is given up for lost, but emerges well and with his secret formula.*]

His first experiments were upon the wounded in the hospital, and so fortunate were his exertions that the medical staff at Algiers presented him with a superb piece of plate at a public dinner, just previous to his departure for England.

On his arrival home he was determined to give his fellow-creatures the benefit of his knowledge, and now the world is acquainted with the wonder-working properties of 'Holloway's Universal Ointment'.

SONNET

To the memory of OLD PARR, written on the discovery of his last Will and Testament, in which is contained the medium of preparing his infallible Medicine, for conquering disease, and prolonging human life.

O, venerable Parr, lo trumpet fame
Again calls forth thy long-forgotten name;
Mortal of many years' how blessed the plan
Thy might secret does reveal to man.
From this auspicious hour will evil cease,
Mourning to joy will turn, – discord to peace.

Thy benign remedy to man gives power
To lengthen out on earth his 'little hour,'
Desease to conquer, anguish drive away,
And sickly sorrow turn to joyous day;
Despair to banish from the dying man
A God-like gift! O do not lightly scan
A boon so great, nor wisdom's purpose mar:
God gave the power – his instrument was
Parr.

3. SPECTACLE

MR PICKWICK
AND THE BLOOD-STAINED BANDIT

Upon entering the parlour, the chubby lad left him, and Mr Warner found himself in the presence of a man about thirty, with a complaisant pale countenance, long curly hair, a very seedy green coat, with carved buttons, fastened close up to his chin, and nearly concealing an old black stock, a pair of tight, and very short black trowsers, drawn with much difficulty over the tops of a pair of boots, highly polished, very much worn down at the heels, and considerably decayed at the toes; his hand held what had once been a silk hat, curled up at the brim like a butter-boat. The seedy man advanced two steps, and bowed obsequiously to Mr Warner, and that gentleman returned the compliment by bowing almost to his boot tops, to the seedy man. 'Mr Warner, I presume,' said the seedy man with a smile, and again bowing.

'True,' replied Mr Warner, also bowing, 'may I inquire who I have the honour of addressing?'

'Ahem! hem!' replied the seedy man, 'certainly, sir, my name's Snooks!'

'Snooks, Mr Snooks!' ejaculated Warner, 'really I have not the pleasure of knowing you.'

'Probably not, sir,' said the seedy man, 'and yet 'tis wonderful, too; nearly all the world MUST have heard of me! – I'm a professional gentleman – Mr Snooks, the gentleman who caused such a wonderful sensation at the Theatres Royal, London, last season!' Mr Warner evinced his ignorance, and the seedy man proceeded: 'I have been induced to come down here, sir, with a very excellent company of comedians; all first-rate stars, I assure you; scenery, dresses, all new; machinery on the most expensive scale; pieces written by the most celebrated authors – slap – capital – out-and-out, I can assure you.'

Mr Warner remained in a blessed state of ignorance as to the wishes of Mr Snooks, and was obliged to make another inquiry, ere he elicited the following explanation:

'Knowing you to be a most liberal patron of genius, and hearing that those wonderful and learned gentlemen, the members of the Pickwick Club, are visiting you, I have taken the liberty of calling upon you to solicit your attendance at the Theatre, Redford's Barn, just outside the town! Have had several bespeaks, all the first gentlemen of the place have honoured us with their presence – highly delighted, I assure you – fine pieces – admirable treat – extraordinary novelty – Mr

THE FIENDS FRYING PAN or Annual Festival of Tom Foolery & Vice.
Under the Sanction of the LORD MAYOR and the Worshipful Court of ALDERMEN! — IN THE AGE OF INTELLECT

Guff, the first actor in the world, engaged for a limited number of nights, at an enormous salary, all native talent, no foreign importations; shall I do myself the honour of making use of the names of yourself and learned friends? – "Great novelty, for this night only under the patronage of Mr Warner, of Mushroom Hall, and the members of the Pickwick Society, who will honour the Theatre with their presence!" Great draw – house crowded – no orders admitted – you MUST do me the honour!'

The good Mr Warner could not resist this opportunity of supporting native talent; he knew his friends would be delighted; he therefore signified something like an assent, and the sunshine of pleasure illumined the pallid features of the seedy man.

'How many private boxes shall I say?' he inquired, 'a private box to contain eight, one

guinea only; one to hold a dozen, one pound ten; – say three boxes at one pound ten!'

Mr Warner agreed, the next night was fixed, and the seedy man bowed his way out of the Hall; Mr Warner returned to his friends, and apprized them of what he had done; they were pleased, and they all agreed to go to the theatre, with the exception of Mr Dreary, who was fearful that the laughter might throw him into convulsions.

The next morning, long before the break of day, large placards graced every wall, paling, and trunks of trees, in and for miles round Uxbridge, with the names of Mr Warner and his learned friends shining in large capitals, printed in red, black, and blue ink. The names of the pieces were astounding, and the novelty surpassing everything of the kind that had ever before been attempted. The title of the first piece was:

Circus agent's advance publicity (cover, and letter opposite).

I beg with great respect to inform you, that Mr Hughes Great Mammoth Establishment with the first Continental talent (including Italian, French and British Male and Female Artistes) will perform in this place positively for One day only. This immense Establishment will form in grand procession at Eleven o Clock, which will be signalled by hoisting the British Standard at the Pavilion, when you will have an opportunity of witnessing one of the most magnificent Cavalcades ever exhibited in Europe headed by The Rath or Burmese State Carriage and Throne drawn by The Royal Male & Female Elephants. The idea was taken from the one at the Egyptian Hall, the estimated cost of which is £12,500, and was captured on the 9th of Septr 1824 at Tavoy, an important maritime town of the Burman Empire, by a detachment of the British Army, under the command of Lieut. Colonel Miles, C. B. a gallant and distinguished officer, in his Majesty's service, The first impression upon this Splendid effort at Eastern Magnificence entering the Town, will be surprise that a people almost unknown to us, & imagined to be in a state of rudeness scarcely removed from barbarism, should out of their own means & resources have been capable of executing a work possessing so many of the properties of taste & refinement—so elegant in its construction and correct in its proportions — so grand in its design & above all so rich and elaborate in the execution of its carving & gilding. The length of the Carriage is 13 ft. 6 in. and its height to the summit of the Peasath, or Royal Canopy, with which it is surmounted is 15 feet. The Caparisons for the Elephants are of the most exquisite Workmanship, and sheeted with Crimson Silk Velvet and Gold. and the celebrated band of the Establishment in a most splendid Carriage upon the ornaments of which the first Heraldry Artists were employed by Messrs Bourne & Hartley. This Carriage will be drawn by 14 Horses driven in hand followed by three other Carriages all finished in the same costly style & every horse in Royal State harness, next will follow those prodigies of Animals the Splendid black Mat Beda" and the graceful & highly trained Male "Victoria" both in sumptuous Trappings after which will follow the Juveniles of the Troop mounted on their fancy Palfreys and Pigmy Ponies. The Cavalcade will be brought to a close by the principal Italian, French & British Male & Female Artistes mounted on their trained Chargers The Pavilion is conveyed on Nine highly finished Vans built by Mr Shatton of Bristol. On the behalf of the Establishment I beg very respectfully to solicit the honor of your support. and remain

Your obedt Servant

J Sheffield
Agent

'THE BLOOD-STAINED BANDIT,
OR THE
CRUEL CUT-THROAT OF THE LION'S GLEN!
STABANDO BRUTALDOS,
(THE BLOOD-STAINED BANDIT,) BY
MR. HORATIO BRUTUS GUFF!!!
TO BE FOLLOWED BY
VARIETY OF SINGING AND DANCING,
BY THE
MOST EMINENT ARTISTES;
THE WHOLE TO CONCLUDE WITH THE
LAUGHABLE FARCE
OF
THE DEVIL TO PAY!!!'

The interest excited was immense; at an early hour the doors of the barn were thronged with anxious joskins, and as soon as they opened, Mr Warner and his friends appeared, and were politely bowed by Mr Snooks, the manager, into the theatre! They found themselves in a very delapidated, but certainly extensive barn, thronged with a number of rude seats, formed out of rough unplained boards, and elegantly parted off into pit and gallery by a long pole. The boxes were divided from the pit by a long strip of canvass, ornamented with numerous harps, Apollos' heads, lyres, and other exquisite decorations. The stage was about six feet six inches wide, and the artistes were hid from the view by a beautiful green curtain of the finest glazed calico. A wooden chandelier depended from a beam by a cord, supporting four dazzling halves of eights, and the same quantity illumined the front of the orchestra; in one corner of which was a very thin dirty-faced man, something like death on board wages, his cheeks puffed out in an unnatural manner by blowing a trumpet, and at the other end was a large drum, and a very small boy to beat it. They commenced their music directly the distinguished audience made their appearance, and certainly made up in noise what they wanted in harmony. In the second row in the pit were seated John White and the chubby lad, the former opening his huge mouth with expectation, and the latter snoring most musically, in unison with the blasts on the trumpet by the thin man, and the blows on the big drum by the little boy. Ever and anon a meagre face peeped out from a hole in the green curtain. It rained, and the roof of the theatre being rather in a ruinous state, the drops that descended upon the heads of the audience in the pit, somewhat damped the spirit of this animated scene. After about sixteen overtures by the thin man and the little boy, and about twenty-four apologies by Mr Snooks, the curtain rose, a dark wood presented itself to the eyes of the delighted spectators, full two feet deep! A blast on the trumpet, a blow on the drum, a clap of thunder, a burst of applause, several flashes of lightning, red, blue, and white fire, and 'THE BLOOD-STAINED BANDIT,' appeared R. H. Tremendous applause, which the bandit acknowledged. He was a very little man with bow legs; and was attired in a terrific tunic, awful black tights, ghastly russets, fearful cloak, murderous slouch hat, ferocious whiskers and mustachoes, appalling belt, three sanguinary pistols, and one very long dagger!

The bandit spoke – a burst of astonishment from the Pickwickians, and a scream of terror from Widow Dupps, followed the well-known tones of the bandit's voice, in the much, though ill-starred Mr Guff; they recognised in a moment the identical straight-haired man who had BORROWED the clothes and the ten pound note from Mr Snodgreen, danced with Widow Dupps, and drawn Captain Julius Cæsar in to fight his cause with Sir Flummery Flutter! Widow Dupps fainted in the arms of her brother, and Mr Pickwick and Mr Snodgreen both at the same time jumped ferociously upon the stage, and grasping the collar of the astonished bandit, exclaimed together, 'Villain, villain! we've got you now!'

A dreadful scene of confusion followed: actors, half undressed, rushed on the stage, and loud cries of 'Shame!' 'Turn 'em out,' burst from the audience; but still Mr Pickwick and his friend retained their hold of Shirk, till the latter GENTLEMAN recovering himself, vociferated melodramatically: 'Off, off, damned reptiles!' and hoisting Mr Pickwick two or three feet in the air, precipitated him into the big drum, and caused him to smash the nose of the little boy behind it with his elbow!

The consternation now became greater; the Pickwickians rushed to the help of their friends; the audience followed them, and a

ASTLEY'S

ROYAL AMPHITHEATRE OF ARTS.
Proprietor & Manager, Mr. WILLIAM BATTY, Bridge Road, Lambeth, Surrey
LICENSED BY THE LORD HIGH CHAMBERLAIN.

GRAND

SPECTACLE

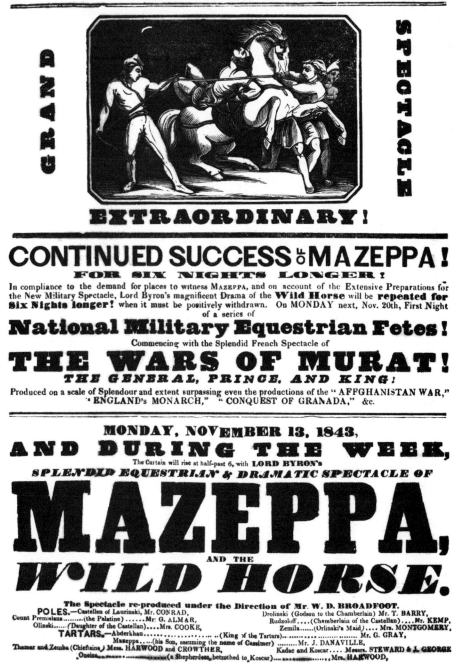

EXTRAORDINARY!

CONTINUED SUCCESS OF MAZEPPA!

FOR SIX NIGHTS LONGER!

In compliance to the demand for places to witness MAZEPPA, and on account of the Extensive Preparations for the New Military Spectacle, Lord Byron's magnificent Drama of the **Wild Horse** will be **repeated for Six Nights longer!** when it must be positively withdrawn. On MONDAY next, Nov. 20th, First Night of a series of

National Military Equestrian Fetes!

Commencing with the Splendid French Spectacle of

THE WARS OF MURAT!

THE GENERAL, PRINCE, AND KING!

Produced on a scale of Splendour and extent surpassing even the productions of the "AFFGHANISTAN WAR," "ENGLAND's MONARCH," "CONQUEST OF GRANADA," &c.

MONDAY, NOVEMBER 13, 1843,

AND DURING THE WEEK,

The Curtain will rise at half-past 6, with LORD BYRON's

SPLENDID EQUESTRIAN & DRAMATIC SPECTACLE OF

MAZEPPA,

AND THE

WILD HORSE.

The Spectacle re-produced under the Direction of Mr. W. D. BROADFOOT.

POLES.—Castellan of Laurinski, Mr. CONRAD,
Count Premislaus..........(the Palatine) ......Mr. G. ALMAR,
Olinski......(Daughter of the Castellan)....Mrs. COOKE,

Drolinski (Godson to the Chamberlain) Mr. T. BARRY,
Rudzoloff....(Chamberlain of the Castellan)....Mr. KEMP,
Zemila......(Orlinski's Maid)....Mrs. MONTGOMERY,

TARTARS.—Abderkhan.................... (King of the Tartars)........................ Mr. G. GRAY,
Mazeppa.....(his Son, assuming the name of Cassimer) ....Mr. J. DANAVILLE,
Thamar and Zeuba (Chieftains) Mess. HARWOOD and CROWTHER,   Kadac and Koscar.. Messrs. STEWARD & J. GEORGE
Oneiza........................(a Shepherdess, betrothed to Koscar)....................Mrs. HARWOOD,

general battle ensued – Widow Dupps' shrieks being heard above the shouts of the combatants! The scenes were torn down, the seats torn up, the thin musician was buried under the body of a huge farmer, John White was pummeled by three sweeps, the chubby lad got a blow in the stomach and went to sleep; and in the midst of it all, the wicked cause of it, Mr Shirk, alias, the straight-haired man, alias, Mr Horatio Brutus Guff, alias, 'The blood-stained Bandit!!!' vanished no one knew how or whither!

DE ORIGINAL JIM CROW

Sung by the celebrated Tom Rice.

Oh, Jim Crow's cum again, as you must all
    know,   [just so,
For he wheel about, he jump about, he do
And ebery time he jump about, he jump Jim
    Crow,
    So I wheel about, I turn about,
    I do just so,
    And ebery time I wheel about,
    I jump Jim Crow.
I kneel to de buzzard, and I bow to de crow,
And ebery time I wheel about, I jump Jim
    Crow.
           So I wheel about, &c.
I stopt at Washington City, as I came from
    de West

An went for to see de great President.
           So I wheel about, &c.
I met ole Andy at de corner ob de street.
Says he, Jim Crow, an't you gwan for to
    treat.
           So I wheel about, &c.
So I pull'd out my pocket-book, I didn't
    mind expense,
An went in an got a horn ob good stone fence.
           So I wheel about, &c.
An arter I had treated him to a smaller ob
    de best,   [quarter left.
I went to count my money, and found but a
           So I wheel about, &c.
Den, says he, Jim Crow, I know what you
    are at,   [shoe black.
You cum for an office, and I'll make you my
           So I wheel about, &c.

BAGGY NANNY; OR, THE PITMAN'S FROLIC

Tune – *The Kebbuckstane Wedding*

Come lay up your lugs, and aw'll sing ye a
    sang,
    It's nyen o' the best, but it's braw new
      and funny;
In these weary times, when we're not varry
    thrang,
    A stave cheers wor hearts, tho' it brings us
      ne money.
Aw left Shiney Raw, – for Newcassel did
    steer,
    Wi' three or four mair of our neighbours
      se canny,
Determin'd to gan to the play-house to hear
    The king o' the fiddlers, the great Baggy
      Nanny.
           Right fal, etc.

We reach'd the Arcade, rather drouthy and
    sair –
    It's a house full o' pastry-cooks, bankers,
      an' drapers;
At the fine fancy fair, hoo my marrows did
    stare,
    On the muffs, hats, an' beavers, se fam'd
      i' the papers.

If " Brother Jonathan" had not sent over Mr. T. D. RICE to shew us the antics of " JIM CROW," we much question whether " John Bull" would have gathered the humour from the words or the melody. However suiting the action to the word, as the song gives a portrait with the attitude, which somebody says, " Is every thing," we can understand the

" Vheel about, and turn about, and do jis so, Eb'ry time I vheel about, I jump Jim Crow."

At Beasley's, where liquor's se cheap an' se
    prime,
  A bottle aw purchas'd for maw sweetheart
    Fanny,
We drank nowt but brandy – and when it
    was time
  We stagger'd away to see great Baggy
  Nanny.

               Right fal, etc.

We gat t' the door, 'mang the crowd we did
    crush,
  Half-way up the stairs aw was carried se
    handy –
The lassie ahint us cried 'Push, hinny! push' –
  Till they squeez'd me as sma' an' as smart
    as a dandy.

We reach'd the stair-heed, nearly smuther'd
    indeed; –
  The gas-letters glitter'd, the paintin's
    look'd canny;
Aw clapt mysel doon 'side a lass o' reet
    breed,
  Maw hinny! says aw, hae ye seen Baggy
  Nanny?

               Right fal, etc.

The lassie she twitter'd, and look'd rather
    queer,
  And said, in this house there is mony a
    dozen,
They're planted se thick that there's ne
    sittin' here,
  They smell so confounded o' cat-gut an'
    rosin.

The curtain flew up, and a lady did squall,
　To fine music play'd by a Cockney bit
　manny,
Then frae the front seats aw seun heard my
　frinds bawl,
　Hats off, smash yor brains! here comes
　greet Baggy Nanny.

　　　　　　　　　　Right fal, etc.

An ootlandish chep seun appear'd on the
　stage,
　An' cut as odd capers as wor maister's
　flonkey,
He skipp'd and he fiddled as if in a rage –
　If he had but a tail he might pass for a
　monkey!
Deil smash a gud teun could this bowdykite
　play –
　His fiddle wad hardly e'en please my aud
　granny, –
So aw seun joined maw marrows, and
　toddled away,
　And wish'd a gud neet te the greet Baggy
　Nanny.

　　　　　　　　　　Right fal, etc.

On crossin Tyne Brig, hoo wor lads ran the
　rig,
　At being se silly deun oot o' thor money!
Odd bother maw wig! had he played us a
　jig,
　We might tell'd them at hyem we'd seen
　something quite funny;
But, law be it spoke, and depend it's ne
　joke,
　Yen and a' did agree he was something
　uncanny –
Tho, dark ower each tree, he before us did
　flee,
　And fiddled us hyem, did the greet Baggy
　Nanny.

　　　　　　　　　　Right fal, etc.

4. POLITICAL SHOWMAN

THE BOA DESOLATOR, OR LEGITIMATE VAMPIRE

It overlays the continent like an ugly Incubus sucking the blood and stopping up the breath of man's life. It claims Mankind as its property, and allows human nature to exist only upon sufferance; it haunts the understanding like a frightful spectre, and oppresses the very air with a weight that is not to be borne.
Hazlitt's Political Essays and Characters, p. 91.

This hideous Beast, not having at any time put forth all his *members*, cannot be accurately described. Every *dark* Century has added to his frightful bulk. More disgusting than the

filthiest reptile, his strength exceeds all other *brute force*.

His enormous, bloated, toad-like body is *ferruginous*:* the under surface appears of *polished steel*.† His cavern-like mouth is always open to devour; 'his teeth are as *swords*, and his jaw-teeth as knives' – as millions of *bristling bayonets* intermingled with

* Shaw's Zoology. Art. Boa, iii. 344.　† ibid. 366.

black fangs containing mortal venom. His roar is a voice from the sepulchre. He is marked '*in form of a cross,*'* with a series of *chains*, intersected by the TRIANGLE,† and glittering colours, variegated with *red*.

His aspect is cruel and terrible. He loves the *dark*, but never sleeps. Wherever he makes his lair, nature sickens, and man is brutified. His presence is 'plague, pestilence, and famine, battle, and murder, and sudden death.' His bite rapidly *undermines the strongest* CONSTITUTION, and dissolves the whole into an entire mass of CORRUPTION. He has no *brain*, but the *walls* of the skull emit a *tinkling* sound, that attracts his victims, and lulls them into *passive obedience*. In this state he clutches them in his coils, and *screws* and *squeezes* them to destruction – *slavering* them over, and sucking in their *substance* at leisure. It is difficult to witness the half-stifled cries of his harmless prey, or to behold its anxiety and trepidation, while the monster writhes hideously around it, without imagining *what our own case would be in the same dreadful situation.*‡

His rapacity is increased by *indulgence*. He grinds, cranches, and devours whole multitudes without being satisfied. His blood is cold. His ravening maw does not digest: it is an ever-yawning grave that *engulphs* – a 'bottomless pit' continually crying '*give, give!*' Sometimes he 'rests from his labors,' to admire his loathsome *limbs*, and *slime* them over. He has no affections: yet he appears charmed by the *hum* of the INSECTS that follow him, and pleased by the *tickling crawl* of the MEANEST REPTILES – permitting them to hang upon his lips and partake of his leavings. But his real pleasure is in listening to the cries of his captives, the wail of the broken hearted, and the groans of the dying.

* Linnaeus's Nat. Hist, by Gmelin, 8vo. (Jones) 1816. Art. Boa Consctor, xii. 437. † Shaw's Zoology, iii. 339. ‡ Macleod's Wreck of the Alceste, 291, 295.

GRAND POLITICAL PANTOMIME

All the word's a stage,
And each one in his time plays many parts.
SHAKESPEARE

While the theatrical pantomimes are at present the rage *in town*, we call the attention of our readers to a Grand Political Pantomime now acting *in the country*. It abounds with tricks and changes of every kind, most of which, owing to good management, have been got up – we are happy to say, without the usual ruinous expense to the treasury. The most eminent actors have been employed in it, and even those noted personages, Lord Eldon and Sir Charles Wetherell, each of them, on this occasion, actually *support a character!*

The scene of the prelude is laid in a place of public resort, called the Crown, a well known house of call for Cabinet Makers, of which William is the proprietor. He pays great attention to the numerous supporters of his house, but is, himself, annoyed by several noisy vagabonds, who try to bring the Crown into disrepute, two of the most desperate having formerly held confidential situations at the *bar*, before the concern came into William's hands; but even the former host, who was not over particular in those matters, was compelled to put them out of their situations for gross misbehaviour to the customers. Finding themselves *out of place*, these worthies fall to annoying their master as much as they can, and, by way of extreme revenge, ally themselves to one Hunt for the purpose of supporting *republican* instead of *publican* principles! Wharncliffe personates an individual who *wants a place* in the Crown establishment, but is detected in diluting the new invigorating drink, called *Grey* (not *brown*) stout, which is being loudly called for every minute, and which William had determined on presenting in a new and much approved *reform measure*. The lover always introduced in the latter scenes of a Pantomime is represented by Earl Howe, who, in the prelude, appears as a pot boy, and being a bit of a favourite with his mistress, endeavours to dissuade her from acquiescing in her husband's resolution to serve out the Grey Stout,

Columbine.
Sure there is none who'd basely try to win,
The heart of Columbine from Harlequin

Lover.
Behold the lover, who, with smile and bow,
Courts graceful Columbine—we all know Howe.

Harlequin.
Here is a Harlequin changing the Nation,
Giving a very "fair representation."

Pantaloon.
Were Pataloons like this to us but will'd,
The stuff that makes them, should be double mill'd.

Good Genius.
Genius, like his, has power to impart,
"A grace," indeed, "beyond the reach of art."

Clown.
See here the very prince of all buffoons,
Good in clown's part, but bad in Pantaloons.

which is now so much in demand. The pot boy is supposed to be in conspiracy with Wharncliffe, to endeavour to palm off the filthy mixture which the latter has prepared under the pretence that the healthy liquor beforementioned will be too strong for the *constitution* of his master's customers. Things are going on in this way when Lord Brougham enters as a good genius, and instantly converts Eldon and Wetherell into Clown and Pantaloon, in which characters they have full scope for the display of that folly and knavery for which they had shown themselves so admirably fitted by the parts they had taken in the prelude. William, the landlord, is changed into Harlequin, and presented by the good genius with a magic wand, which he uses for turning from evil into good whatever he can find in need of the wholesome metamorphosis. Among the most singular of these transformations, is that of an old shattered and decayed fabric, which has almost fallen into pieces from corruption, though still bearing the ostentatious name of the Constitution, which is magically restored to its original beauty in spite of the opposition of Clown and Pantaloon, who have for a long time been living on the ruins. On the first attempt this change was not accomplished as speedily as could have been desired, but the machinery has since been made complete, and it will doubtless be effected, on a future occasion, with ease and rapidity. The hostess is changed into Columbine, and the pot boy into the Lover, in which character he still continues his insolent attempts to create a breach between Harlequin and Columbine, though the rebuffs he meets with from both are numerous and indubitable. He is ultimately prevented from offering further annoyance at the instigation of the good genius, who continues to perform some miraculous changes. He turns the Court of Chancery into the *Dispatch Office*, and, with surprising energy, leaps at one effort through an enormous quantity of very ponderous *cases*, Pantaloon having previously tried the same experiment, and stuck in the middle of one overcome with extreme doubt and imbecility. Each change appeared to give the most complete satisfaction, with the exception of the conversion of Bucking-

ham Palace into an old picture shop; – a very expensive trick, and apparently got up for the sole benefit of the inventor.

It would be needless to proceed further with the description of the Political Pantomime; we shall therefore content ourselves with giving the portraits of the principal characters!

REPUBLICS AND MONARCHIES.

"The official Report of the Finances of the United States is a paper which ought to become the manual of every English statesman. Here is a country, second only to Great Britain in power amongst maritime states, overflowing with prosperity and happiness—one which knows not the meaning of internal tumult; —one of which all the citizens, with scarcely an exception, can command the necessaries of life, meat, drink, clothing, and shelter from the elements in abundance; one in which labour is sure of its reward; yet, where Members of Parliament are chosen by Universal Suffrage,—where neither tithes nor game-laws are to be found, and where the chief magistrate lives with dignity on an income from the public of about £5000 per annum. See how the country is taxed, a country of 12,000,000 of inhabitants. The revenue raised upon the United States last year, has been about six millions and a quarter sterling, and yet the government has contrived to devote to the liquidation of the Public debt within the same period, no less than £3,300,000 sterling, more than double what the managers of English finance have been able to bestow upon the same object, out of a revenue of £46,000,000."—From "The Times" of Friday, Jan. 6, 1832.

SCENE,

His Majesty's ship BRITANNIA, with all her pendants flying—the American frigate CONSTITUTION approaching—JOHN BULL in an Admiral's uniform on board the Britannia.

John. Hoy! Captain! what ship's that a-head?

Captain. The American Constitution—a trim, tight, well-built frigate, by George.

John. See that she pays due respect to the British flag, and hail her.

Captain. [Through his speaking trumpet.]—Whose ship, my hearties?

American Captain. The States' Constitution, President Yankee on board—wants to have a "TALK" with John Bull!

John. Damn the unmannerly boor! it might be the "Right Honourable John Bull" in his plebian mouth.

Captain. The fellow knows no better.

John. We must not offend him, however; low-bred though he be, the Yankee is a spiteful customer when vexed. Invite their rum President on board.

Captain. [Through his speaking trumpet.] The Right Hon. John Bull, K.C.B. Sovereign of the Ocean, &c. invites President Yankee on board the Britannia.

American Captain. He will be with you in the turning of a handspike.

John. How vulgar!

Captain. Hush! hush! for Heaven's sake—here is the President.

[Enter President Yankee, attended by a few athletic sailors, in plain check dresses. President Yankee himself in a homely, snuff-coloured suit, wearing his broad-leafed hat in "the presence."]

John Bull. How d'do! How d'do! Yankee! how goes fear and sad barrelled flour?

Pres. Yankee. Why, tarnation well, John; trade is progressing slick with us; but talking of trade, how go on tea, taxes, and colonies with you, old chap?

John Bull. [aside]Curse your impudence, scoundrel! thus to talk of "tea, taxes, and colonies," knowing how sore I am on these matters since I lost my whip-hand and reins over you! [to Pres. Yankee aloud.] Why, look ye, Master President, "the embarrassments of commerce, and the consequent interruption of the pursuits of industry, have occasioned want of employment —for removing the causes and mitigating the effects of which, my Representatives always find me ready and anxious to assist."——

*King's speech, third paragraph.

[remaining body text continues in multiple columns, largely a satirical dialogue between John Bull and President Yankee]

. The Wood Cuts on this sheet have been kindly lent by the proprietor of THE POLITICAL ALPHABET; of which the Morning Advertiser said—" This pamphlet, with its notes and pungent graphic illustrations, is even more dangerous and powerful than the lord chancellor himself, to all who deal in boroughs, pensions, or sinecures."

‡‡ This article is reprinted from a valuable weekly newspaper, THE DUBLIN COMET, sold at sixpence, and containing more original writing than any other paper published.

TAXES ON KNOWLEDGE.

Common Sense. By Thomas Paine. Price Eightpence.
Agrarian Justice. Same author. Twopence.
Dissertation on First Principles of Government. By the same author. Threepence.
Volney's Lectures on History. 1s. 6d.—in extra cloth bds. 2s
Volney's Life, with a sketch of his Writings. Twopence.

The following cheap and useful publications are earnestly recommended to The People's Most Excellent Majesty.

An Address on the Necessity of an Extension of Moral and Political Insurrection among the Working Classes. By Rowland Detrosier. Twopence.
Cain, a Poem. By Lord Byron. Beautifully printed. 6d.
The Poor Man's Book of the Church. Nat by Dr. Southey. This little Work is Illustrated with Twelve Engravings 2d.

The Trial of William Cobbett, Esq, with all the Documents. 6d.
Lectures by W. Cobbett, Esq, on Church Property, Standing Army, &c. Threepence each.
Anecdotes of the Second French Revolution. By William Carpenter. In 16 Nos. at 2d each, or complete, 3s.
Carpenter's Political Magazine, (Monthly) Eightpence.

The Article on—The Ballot," from the Westminster Review 1d
The People's Book. By W. Carpenter. In nos. at 2d or complete 3s 6d
The Political Alphabet. 22 engravings after G. Cruikshank. 6d
A Slap at the Church (weekly). With engravings One Penny

The friends of liberty will render a service to the cause of cheap government by aiding to circulate this Dialogue.

Printed and Published by J. WATSON, 33, Windmill Street, Finsbury, and sold by all Booksellers.

PRICE ONE PENNY

Manchester and Salford Elections.----No, 1.

Billy Tory Wooing Sally-Ford.

O, fam'd Lark Hill there lives a Swain,
BILL "SHALLOW" is his name,
A "Justice" vain, who strives to gain
A Senatorial fame;
He oft has tried, as oft denied,
Yet thus bespeaks his will—
"I'd 'crowns' resign, M.P. to shine,
For SAL-FORD at Lark Hill."

Within his view, there dwells in state,
This dame whom he adored,
With power a Statesman to create,
They call her name SAL-FORD;
And Billy sigh'd, " My Love," he cried,
" I prithee grant my will,
" My jewels thine to call thee mine,
" A GARNETT at Lark Hill."

Now Sally was a wily lass,
And gammon'd would not be,
With gin and beer quite free;
But ogle-eyed, sweet Sally shy'd,
And thus made known her will—
" For jewels fine, I'd ne'er be thine,
" No Garnett, or Lark Hill."

Then Billy warm, thus press'd his suit—
" I'll find thee night and morn,
" Garnett's Elixir,' free to boot,
" And Brown Stout Barleycorn ;

A great Struggle between a Man and his Wife, in Market-street, on the Present Election, about who he should vote for.

"My color true, is scarlet hue—
" Thy green's a bitter pill—
" I'd give thee wine to call thee mine,
" Sweet SAL-FORD at Lark Hill."

Quoth Sal, "My choice thou'rt not to be ;
" Old Billy,'—'tis no go ;
" So long as Joe is true to me,
" Joe Brotherton's my Jo.
" No scarlet mien—my color's green—
" Unalter'd is my will,
" For all thy wine, I'd ne'er be thine,
" No, not for thy Lark Hill.

Then Billy said to Sally-Ford,
" Alas ! my fate I see,
" Thou art too bad, upon my word,
" In thus rejecting me ;
" If ' Lot and Will,' and ' Billy Ill,'
" Would not have made a row
" With Bunting P. and Redhead T.
" I'd ne'er have tried thee now.

" Adieu ! adieu ! my dear SAL-FORD,
" For thou wilt not, I see,
" Be gull'd by gin, or beer, or tea,
" Or bought by bribery ;
" Adieu ! adieu ! it will not do,
" Again, I ne'er will try,
" Abroad I'll go, like '32,
" And shun a Scrutiny."

Entry List of all the Can't-i-Cheats, for Manchester and Salford.

MURRAIN, by Tory, (lately nick-named Conservative) has been a good fighter in the service of old Nosey, but length of days has worn out the poor old horse, and made him unfit to run for Whig plates of these modern times. His backers and trainers however are determined to run the aged animal once more. The old dose of has got instructions to run under the sliding scale, but to suit his running, snorts out a fixed plan, in order to catch fish; but the knowing coves do not like his breed, and are shy at booking him, as he is much given to the sliding race, and is very likely to throw his jock, being guilty of very slippery tricks, having deceived his Scotch trainers in a late race, who would nae more back him for a babees worth. He is rather greedy over his own corn, and does not like foreign corn, and exempt all others from eating from the same manger. Colour BLUE.

HENYHISTLE, by Slaughter, a green horn colt, own brother to Murrain, trained by Ratcatcher, likes Conservative corn, has neverstarted for any Plate, not in good condition, short of training, too rough & blunt in his running, short of shuffling kind of gammon, and not up to the tricks of the course. It is expected he will bolt, having but a slight chance in this great race. Colour BLUE-TAILED FLY.

MARKER, by Little John, the winner of the Reform Stakes in 1832, a very promising nag, he is not over nice about his corn, likes any corn, very fleet, it is expected he will come off first best in the race. His performances has been very good in St. Stephen's arena. His backers have taken him against the field. Colour RED.

GIBSONIAN, got by Tory, trained and fed on graball corn, first started at Ipswich, won the Prize there, was backed by the Waterloo Charger and Bobby the Ratcatcher, and entered St. Stephen's full of Conservative corn ; but having bolted over the course, he broke down and was compelled to go to grass. The pasture we are informed turned out to be Whig growth, which has produced in him a full crop of the Melbourne swath ; but it is intended that he shall again re-enter St. Stephen's, as a cc. Whig feeding. Should he prove reative this time, he will be sent t Radical mares, to breed Destructives. He is now under the special training of the Anti-Corn Blacklegs, who are confident of his running well for this Plate and coming first to the winning post many lengths.

JOE BROTH-URTON, of Sallyford, got by swedenburgh, hater of good beef, and mutton, has run, and beat Garnisher, alias Lushington, twice, starts under Whig sneaking, dislikes running after time in St. Stephen's breaks down at an early hour, and is very restless to go to the stable. His breed retrenchment, economy, and no union bastiles ; has proved a good goer for the last two races, and is pretty freely backed for the third ; but strong doubts are entertained of his coming in first for this Plate. His backers must be well spurred, otherwise the heavy wets will be ahead in the race, dry mouths and chaff must be on the alert, or the Lark Hill birds will sing sweetly over Sallyford. Colour, GREEN

GARNISHER, aged, by Peelite, out of Conservative; he was broke in as a hunter, his temper seems more inclined for racing. His owner has thought proper on entering for the Salford Stakes. He was getting very fat, having been laid up in a stable for a long time. His backers have oftimes been drenched with a quantity of Hodge's best, to make them merry for his approaching contest. His trainers are very cautious, as he has been out of order a long time for racing. By care and good Jockeying, he might be placed in an eminent position on the turf. RED.

JOE BROTHERTON, MY JO.

Joe Brotherton, my Jo, Joe,
When first we were acquent
Your heart was true as steel, Joe,
On good you were intent,
And now we know it well, Joe,
To oppression you're the foe,
And blessings on your trusty heart,
Joe Brotherton, my Jo.

Joe Brotherton, my Jo, Joe,
Your duty you have done,
And now we will do ou's, Joe,
And make old Garnett run ;
Corruption we'll withstand, Joe,
In gin we will not roll,
But nobly will we make our stand,
And head you on the poll.

Joe Brotherton, my Jo, Joe,
Our true unshaunted friend,
Think not to paltry bribes, Joe,
That we will basely bend,
We'll be as true as you, Joe,
Our gratitude we'll show,
And make the tyrant faction quake,
Joe Brotherton, my Jo.

Representation of the Great Battle which took place between Mrs. Botherum and Mrs. Garflint, in Salford, last night, in which Mrs. Botherum proved victorious, after a very severe contest of 3 hours and 103 minutes, during which time they fought elevenfeen rounds.

KIERNAN, Printer, Garden-street, Manchester.

THE LIGHT OF TORY DAYS.

The light of Tory days is faded,
And the plunder game is nearly past ;
Repeal's bright arguments hath shaded
The rent law—too vile to last.
The land, with tax-fed idlers crowded,
Emitteth learning's rays ;
And our hearts now feel in sorrow shrouded
The light of Tory days,

Estates the corn law tempests wither ;
The steeple chase—the ball takes wing—
Fox hunts and tournaments together ;
And our spears must turn to ploughshares
in spring.
Our very rent roll on the ruin,
An altered face displays ;
But in common-sense there's no renewing
The light of Tory days.

A. WILSON.

Just Published—the whole Partculars of a most

CRUEL MURDER,

Committed by Charles Young, a Grazier, upon the Body of his Sweetheart Mary Ann Walmsley.

Shewing, how under pretence of Marriage, the Villain Seduced her, and how she became Pregnant by him; after which he gave her a deleterious drug, which threw her into a deep sleep, when the Monster stabbed her to the heart with a knife, and threw her Body into a Lake, which was wonderfully discovered by a Shepherd's dog. Also, the Committal of the Murderer.

Mary Anne Wansley.

A shepherd driving forth his flock,
  To feed by dawn of day,
By chance he came unto the lake
  Where th' murder'd damsel lay.

And while upon its banks he stood
  His dog with sudden spring,
Div'd into the chrystal flood,
  And out her corpse did bring.

A Very interesting and amiable female, the daughter of a highly respectable individual in the West Riding of Yorkshire, and who is steward to a nobleman, became attached, owing to repeated solicitations, to a young grazier, whose family connexions were co-equal with her own. Their walks, in the evening, were frequent, and the attachment on the part of Mary Ann's lover, apparently increased at each succeeding interview.

About a fortnight since, they were seen together, for the last time, by some villagers crossing a stile, which leads to a lonely spot in that neighbourhood. Her ruin having been previously effected, she paid him her last visit with a determination of putting his honour to the test, as her destruction otherwise would be complete. He appeared, with his usual duplicity, to hold out the most sincere promises of marriage, which he pledged himself, most solemnly to fulfill. They had strayed to a considerable distance when they seated themselves on a green shady bank, at the back of which was a pond of considerable depth, and here the traitorous wretch put his diabolical plan into execution. Wine, it is supposed, from a flasket, was proffered to her to quench her thirst, into which the villain had infused a deleterious drug, for the purpose of throwing her into a deep sleep in order that he

might dispatch her. In a few minutes she sunk back asleep, when the villain plunged a knife into her breast, and she expired upon the spot. He endeavoured to conceal the two-fold murder by plunging his body into the adjoining pond; but "murder will out" in nine cases out of ten, and the following circumstance proves that an all-seeing Providence directs the most miraculous means of bringing such miscreants as the one before us to the bar of retributive justice.

A few mornings after the perpetration of this horrid deed, a shepherd was passing over the field with his dog and crook, when his attention was suddenly drawn to the pond by the moanings of his faithful companion, who dived into the water, and, in a few minutes brought to the margin of the bank the lifeless body of the unfortunate Mary Ann, A rigid enquiry immediately took place, and the result was, the instant apprehension of the supposed murderer, who was examined and finally committed to prison upon the capital charge, where his reflections ought to be of the most agonizing description, and at the ensuing Assizes he will doubtless forfeit his worthless life as a partial atonement for the heinous offence he has committed against the laws of God and man.

The following letter, which she evidently intended for her base seducer and murderer, was found, amongst others, in one of he private drawers :—

Dear Charles,
Unless you perform your often repeated promise of marriage, I shall become a mother under the most wretched circumstances, My loving and affectionate parents are at this moment totally unconscious of the disgrace which I am hourly advancing upon them and myself. Do, for God's sake, meet me this evening at the usual spot, and may that meeting prove the sincerity of your intentions, and our future mutual hap piness. Oh, do not—do not deceive
  Your loving, though desponding,
    Mary Ann.

J. Catnach, Printer, 2, Monmouth-court
7 Dials.

MELANCHOLY VERSES.

O, all ye maidens fair, beware
  Of this my wretched fate;
Nor e'er be led in treach'rous snare,
  Or you'll repent too late.

For man's deceptive, you all know,
  Till once his end he gains;
Then leaves you, sad disgrace to show,
  For all his amorous pains.

A maiden, chaste, I once was deem'd
  By all---the village pride;
For virtue none was more esteem'd,
  It was my constant guide.

The villain plunges a knife into her breast.

Till faithless Charles entwin'd my arms,
  And vow'd he'd constant be;
'Twas then I lost a virgin's charms,---
  And thus he's ruin'd me.

But who would e'er suppose a fiend,
  Could to your bosom creep;
Then from you suddenly be wean'd
  To plunge you in the deep

A murder, base, lurk'd in his breast,
  As youv'e the story read;
But whilst my soul does calmly rest,
  To dungeons he'll be led.

V. CRIME

1. MURDER GALLERY

JOHN THURTELL, EXECUTED FOR THE MURDER OF WEARE, 9 JANUARY 1824

A Newspaper Report.

THE LAST SAD CEREMONY!

The Under-Sheriff now led the way to the fatal spot, followed by Thurtell, the Chaplain, Mr Wilson, and the Turnkey. Thurtell having arrived at the foot of the steps by which he was to ascend to the drop, shook hands with the Chaplain and one or two persons who were standing by. There was a good deal of affection in his manner, and to each he said in an emphatic manner, 'God bless you!' The unhappy convict then slowly ascended the steps, the clanking of his chains, which he still wore, very considerably heightening the effect of the scene. He was dressed in an olive surtout, close buttoned about his neck, light trowsers, and gaiters. He wore his hat, and had on a pair of black kid gloves. His hands, which were still restrained by handcuffs, appeared as if they were crossed in the meek attitude of resignation. His aspect was that of one who had already encountered and passed the agony of a final separation from earthly partialities, and gained the tranquillity that is the result of that struggle. He stood firmly the universal gaze to which he was exposed. He surveyed with calmness the immense congregation which was collected before him — moving his eyes slowly from one quarter to the other, and recognized in the crowd two or three persons, to whom he made an inclination of his head. He had already declared that he would not utter a word to the people, and entreated that the duration of the fatal ceremony might be as short as possible. His hat, stock, and collar were removed, and the cap was placed on his head. The rope was previously adjusted. He observed to the executioner, casting his eyes up to measure the rope, that he feared there would not be fall enough. The executioner assured him there would. But not satisfied with his assurance, Thurtell turned to Mr Wilson and appealed to him. Mr Wilson having satisfied him that there was no ground for the fears he expressed, he calmly yielded to his fate. – The Under-Sheriff, Mr Wilson, and the turnkey, then shook hands with him. To each he said, and in an emphatic manner to Mr Wilson, 'May God bless you!' In a few moments he was launched into eternity. His demeanour at this trying crisis was admirable, decent, and, we trust, bespoke the existence of a fortitude within, which could have its foundation only in a strong religious confidence. All who beheld him in these moments felt pity for his fate; and there were many who felt it necessary to recur to the atrocious crime, in order to get relief from the bitterness of their sympathy, so bravely and so calmly did he meet death. It was soon seen that he had no reason to fear that the process would not be effectual. The fall was full two feet and a half, and when his own weight, added to that of the chains which were still attached to him are considered, it is scarcely necessary to state that the struggle was very short. Bundles of straw were placed under the drop, in order that no noise might be made by the fall. The body remained a full hour suspended, and then the executioner re-appeared, and after untying the rope from the beam, lowered the body into the arms of two of the javelin men. It was then carried into the Chapel, where it was stripped by order of the Under-Sheriff. Shortly before the execution, the Chapel bell of the adjoining school (the Blue Coat School,) began to toll, and afterwards the bell of All Saints Church was tolled for a few minutes. The unfortunate man had been merely hand-cuffed and not pinioned, though the execu-tioner requested it might be done. The body, when brought into the chapel, was laid on a table, the head being supported by a Bible. It was stripped and the limbs were composed. The fine proportions and muscular strength of Thurtell were very striking. It was found that the vertebrae of the neck had been dislocated, in which case it is to be supposed the Sufferer was speedily put out of pain. The Under-Sheriff ordered that the clothes should be sent to Thurtell's brother, and, if necessary, that a compensation in money should be given to the executioner, who claimed the clothes as his property by custom. The Worthy Under-Sheriff with good feeling, likewise ordered that the rope should be burned, for even the rope had become an object of interest, and some pounds were offered for it in the course of the day. The body was then put into the care of Mr Colbeck, the surgeon, who went through the form prescribed by the law.

MARIA MARTEN

Act I, Scene 3

Red Barn: Flats across: window L.C. Door L.3. oblique: [*Agit:* WILLIAM *delving half down trap up C: then comes up spade in hand*].

WILLIAM: All is ready: the grave but awaits the coming of its victim; will she come? I think so – I fancy she loves me sufficiently to trust me so far, besides the anticipation of becoming my wife will urge her to come! [*at window*] Yes, I see her form now entering the gateway; not a moment too soon. [*closes window, leans spade against flat L.C. goes to D.*] Now I hear her footfall upon the gravel path: she little thinks she comes to meet her fate.

[*Agit:* MARIA *enters D.L.3.* WILLIAM *be-hind D. She X's C.R.* WILLIAM *locks D.*]

MARIA: What a fearful place this is; I was seized with an unaccountable awe as I crossed its threshold: where can William be, surely he does not intend to keep me waiting here alone: [*turns*] ah William you gave me such a fright, but I am glad you are here. Why have you locked the door? Oh let us leave this horrid place at once.

WILLIAM: Not yet Maria, I have business to transact before you leave here.

MARIA: Oh quick then William for I have a horror of this barn, even with you by my side: oh let us go.

WILLIAM: Not yet: there are one or two ques-tions I want to ask you first.

MARIA: Why how strangely you say this, and what cruel harsh look is in your eye, one I have never seen before; oh my Darling, you frighten me, what does it mean?

WILLIAM: It means I must speak to you and set matters right.

MARIA: You can do so on the journey William, oh do take me from here at once.

WILLIAM: Listen! Some little time back while crossing the meadows leading from our farm to Polestead, I was almost on the heels of Farmers Matthew and Eyres, they knew not I was close behind them, so near I could hear every word of their conversation, I heard your name which caused me to listen more attentively; I heard Eyres say that he had heard from you that you sus-pected your child had met its death by foul play and that you thought I was the cause of its demise, and that unless I kept my promise to you, you would shield me no longer, but make known your suspicions to the whole world: now Maria I want to know what those men meant, and how came they to speak such words?

MARIA: I don't know William: but surely this is not the place for such enquiries. Cannot you see I am trembling like an aspen leaf, oh I beg of you take me away from here.

WILLIAM: Not until you have answered my question.

MARIA: Oh, how can I answer? What can I say? You know I have suffered terribly, and cannot be held responsible if people will

A Horrible MURDER,
A Father Cutting his Child's Head off!

A MOST horrid Murder was committed on Thursday night at Whitechapel, by a Father, upon his Child, an Infant about four months old. The man whose name is Sheen, resides at No. 1, Christopher-Alley, Lambeth-street, near the Police Office, and obtained his living by selling wood about the streets. It appears that on several occasions when he had returned home intoxicated, and quarrelled with his wife, he had threatened to murder the child, by cutting its head off, but it is most singular that there appears to exist no cause which could induce the wretch to commit such a diabolical act. It was his only child, and from enquiries that have been made it does not seem that he entertained any jealousy respecting his wife. About seven o'clock last evening he returned home intoxicated, and said to his wife that he would cut the child's head off. She did not pay the slightest attention to his threat, and about an hour afterwards he sent her out to procure some tea, in her absence he cut the child's head from the body, he then threw the body under the bed, and placed the head on the table, where it was found by the Mother on entering the room. Sheen has absconded, but Dalton, an Officer of Lambeth-street, is in search of him. Sheen is about 30 years of age, and his wife is about the same age.

It appears that immediately after he committed the murder, he went to the residence of his father and brother, in White's-yard, Rosemary-lane, and told them that he had been playing at skittles, had quarrelled with an Irishman, and had stabbed him in the back with a knife, which he then produced. He was afraid, he said, of being apprehended for the outrage, and therefore begged them to assist him with the means of making his escape. Neither father nor brother had any money to give him, but the father took him to a Mr. Pugh, a carpenter, in Carnaby-market, who had known the family when they resided in Radnorshire and he advanced Sheen, 18 shillings, and also lent him a coat as he declared he had left his own in the skittle ground, whereas he left it in the room, after he had committed the murder, and where it was found covered with blood, Mr Pugh declared, if he had for a moment suspected he had committed so foul a crime, he would have seized him, and brought him to justice.

It appears that the murderer and his wife had cohabited together for some time before their marriage, that having burthened the parish with several children, the parish Officers caused him to be apprehended, and he had his choice either to give security for the maintainence of the children or to marry the woman, and as is usual in such cases to receive a reward from the parish of 5l sheen accepted the 5l, and only 12 weeks ago they were married.

tThe mother of the unfortunate child said that on Thursday evening, when sheen, came home he was intoxicated, and requested her to make him some tea; that she went out for the ingredients, and left him in the room lying on the bed where the child was also lying asleep, she was gone about a quarter of an hour, when on her return, and opening the room door, her feelings of horror can be more easily conceived than described, when she beheld the head of her child on the table, with its eyes fixed towards the door, and the body on the bed. sheen had, on several occasions, declared he would murder the child, since the birth of the infant he hated it so much, that he has frequently struck it on its mother's knee. Last Sunday week he struck it such a violent blow, that the lump is now visible on its head. The Jury returned a verdict of Wilful Murder against the Father, who has not yet been taken.

A Copy of Verses.

YE tender loving mothers all,
  Who love your offspring dear,
Fast from your eyes the tears will fall,
  When this sad tale you hear.
A frightful and a horrid deed,
  I quickly shall unfold,
This most appalling fact to read,
  Will make your blood run cold.

The murderers' name is William Sheen,
  O horrible to write,
The wicked wretch did often swear
  He'd take his infants life.
On Thursday night he bade his wife
  To go and buy some tea,
That he, the monster might complete
  The horrid tragedy.

His wife had scarcely left the room
  when he did grasp the babe,
So sweetly smil'd the harmless child,
  Mercy it seem'd to crave.
His deadly knife the monster drew,
  And hacked off its head,
And then the bleeding body threw
  All underneath the bed.

The mother shortly did return
  And grief her heart did wring,
On the table stood her baby's head,
  Its lips still quivering.
The floor with blood was dyed red,
  Most frightful for to see,
And the cruel father gone and fled,
  But taken he soon will be.

The wretched mother shriek'd and cried,
  In agony and distress,
No language surely could describe
  The sorrows of her breast.
Inhuman man, thy infan'ts blood,
  Loud to the LORD doth cry,
Vengeance will recompense the deed,
  From it thou can'st not fly.

Cards and Bills Printed very Cheapby J. Catnach, 2 Monmouth-court, 7 Dials.

talk. Besides if I have said anything concerning the death of my babe, the words were doubtless spoken in anger, when I feared being abandoned by you, but think no more of it I beg of you! oh let us go!

WILLIAM: In anger? the woman who is anxious to bear my name, the woman who would have me believe she loves me, speaks such words in anger that would place the rope around my neck and meet the fate of a murderer.

MARIA: Oh no, no William! God knows I love you too well, too fondly to cause you one moment's pain, ah believe me, believe me.

WILLIAM: You lie, too much have I already suffered at your hands, nights of agony, days of misery, have been my portion accelerated by your hypocritical woman's tongue.

MARIA: William I –

WILLIAM: Hear me still further, you can never be my wife; even now there is a wealthy Heiress of my Parents' choice awaiting me to conduct her to the Holy Altar, but this cannot be while you live.

MARIA: William you mean –

WILLIAM: That I have lured you here with the one intent, and that is, of ridding myself of you for ever.

MARIA: Rid of me; how?

WILLIAM: There is only one way open to me and that is – death!

MARIA: Surely you would not murder me? You only say this to frighten me, you are jesting with me, 'tis a cruel jest William.

WILLIAM: Let your eyes rest upon mine and read the jest upon them; should that not convince you, gaze there: [*points to trap*] let them rest upon the grave ready for the coming of its victim.

MARIA: Oh God! tis true then! Yes I can read it in your eyes; ah fool that I was; yes, yes; the gipsy's words are now ringing in mine ears, oh William see on my knees, I beg, I crave, I implore you to let me go: let me return home to my aged grey haired Mother and Father and I swear never to divulge one word of this or of the past, let me go, oh, let me go!

WILLIAM: No! I re-iterate my words, too long have I suffered at woman's lying deceitful tongue to forego my purpose now! [*folds arms and stands facing her, as she kneels pleading with arms outstretched. First picture.*] If you have ought to say, if you would make peace with your Maker, say it now, say it now.

MARIA: I can read your determination: [*rises*] and your cruel words give me courage: So William Corder, if I am to die, at least it shall not be without a struggle. [*flings coat and cap off. Chord*]

WILLIAM: Not for long, for your puny strength will not cope with mine.

MARIA: Then Heaven will aid me and grant me courage to outwit your brutal power. [*hurry*]

WILLIAM: We shall see!

[*Struggle, she throws him off R. seizes spade, uplifts it, he shrinks from it. Second picture*]

MARIA: Back I warn you!

[*Chord: he seizes her – struggle is renewed – spade is dropped well up: she breaks from him and runs to Door: he seizes her by the hair from behind. Third picture. She turns, resumes struggle and throws him R. He stumbles and falls. She runs to D. tries to open it, he recovers, draws revolver as she turns, he fires, she staggers forward and falls C. bleeding from forehead.*]

MARIA: William you have kept your word – you have murdered me! give me your hand! [*he at window, comes down and reluctantly gives* MARIA *hand*] You have done me to death, but I loved you so, I forgive you! my sufferings will soon be over, but not so – yours – fa – re – well Wil— [*falls back dead:* WILLIAM *runs to D. listens, then to window*]

WILLIAM: Not a soul about! oh, what have I done? I have killed her: the only woman who really truly loved me; loved me sufficiently to trust her very life in my hands, and how have I requited that love? The world would I now give could I but recall this one mad and cruel act of mine; could I but once more hear the sound of her voice; how I prate, too late, too late: oh may this murder ever stand accursed, the last of murders as it is the worst.

[*Stands shielding sight of body from his eyes with outstretched hands. Fourth picture.*]

GOD'S
REVENGE AGAINST MURDER.

"WHOSO SHEDDETH MAN'S BLOOD, BY MAN SHALL HIS BLOOD BE SHED."

No. 6.   SATURDAY, JUNE 1, 1833.   PRICE ONE PENNY.

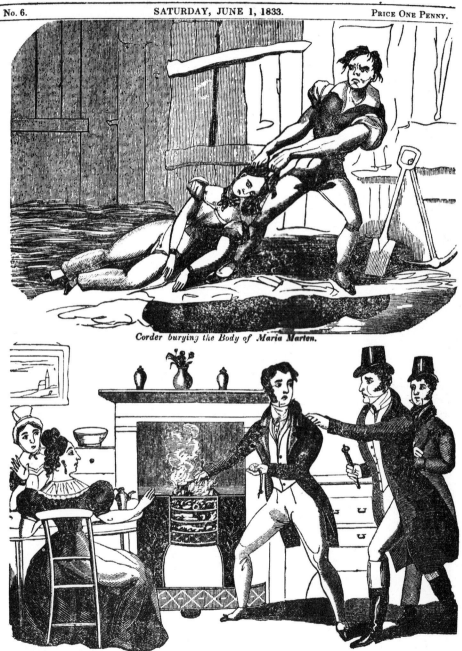

Corder burying the Body of Maria Marten.

The Arrest of Corder.

Act II, Scene 1

Front chamber: one chair R:
Mad: MRS MARTEN *Enters R.I.*

MRS MARTEN: How very strange, 10 days have now passed and no tidings of our child, beyond the letter we received from William Corder on the 3rd day, saying Maria had injured her right hand in alighting from the train so could not write, but he hoped in a few days she would recover sufficiently to do so: and no news since, I watch the Postman every time he comes this way, but in vain! I should have thought Maria would have got someone to write for her knowing how anxious we shall be; what with my sleepless nights and uneasy mind, to say nothing of the shocking dreams I have when I do dose off: tis surely enough to unnerve the strongest: [*sits R.*] poor Maria, I do hope she is happy, if not she surely would have let me know: but if I hear nothing by tomorrow's post, I shall certainly go to Corder farm and ask for William's address. [*sleepily*] For – I – am – so – weary – of – this silence. [*sleeps*]

> [*Visions as marked pictures in Act 1 scene 3: at end of fourth vision, she screams and rises:* ANN *runs on R.1.*]

ANN: Whatever is the matter Mother dear?

MRS MARTEN: Oh Annie, Annie dear, where is your Father?

ANN: In the garden Mother, why? Do you want him?

MRS MARTEN: Yes, yes, bid him come to me at once for the love of Heaven don't delay child.

ANN: Very well Mother; why whatever can be the matter with her? [*exit R.1.*]

MRS MARTEN: Just Heaven, this is the third dream I have had that my poor dear child has fallen a victim to foul play: but neither of the dreams was so vivid.

> [MARTEN *and* ANN *enter R.1.*]

MARTEN: Why Dame, what can have happened? No bad news I hope. I watched the Postman, but I thought he passed without calling here.

MRS MARTEN: So he did Father, it is not that, I've had no bad news, in fact none at all.

MARTEN: Why then be disturbed, remember no news is good news as the proverb says.

MRS MARTEN: Ah Father, I've had such a terrible dream. This is the third in succession, but the worst of all: I saw our poor Maria struggling for her life with William Corder: and at last she fell a victim to his murderous hands.

MARTEN: Come come Dame, compose yourself, for you know dreams always come by contraries, and depend upon it we shall yet hear of our child being happy with the man she loves.

MRS MARTEN: Heaven grant it may be so, but ah Father, do pray get assistance and go to the Red Barn, and search it carefully, for t'was there I dreamed our child had been murdered.

JAMES GREENACRE, EXECUTED FOR THE MURDER OF HANNAH BROWN, 2 MAY 1837

[*Hannah Brown disappeared shortly after introducing Greenacre to some friends, the Davises, as her future husband. At this time Greenacre also abandoned another woman, Gale, by whom he had had a child.*]

On the 28th of December a circumstance took place, which excited an extraordinary sensation throughout the metropolis and its neighbourhood, in consequence of the discovery of a human body tied up in a sack, which had been found near the Pine-apple Gate, Edgeware-Road. This discovery was made by a labouring man, who was passing by on his way to work. The sack was tied at the mouth; curiosity led him to open it, and, on viewing its horrible contents, he immediately gave the alarm to a policeman, who came and carried it to the workhouse. A coroner's jury was summoned, and, after a minute investigation, a verdict of wilful murder was returned; and the parish, as well as his majesty's government, offered each a reward for the apprehension of the offender or offenders.

The utmost vigilance was exercised by the police in their endeavours to trace out the murderer; but it continued to baffle their efforts, and it remained for some days without any fresh light thrown upon it. At length, on the 6th of January, as a barge was passing down the Regent's Canal, near Stepney, one of the eastern environs of London, the bargeman found that some substance obstructed him in his endeavours to close the lock gates; he, therefore, acquainted the lock-keeper, who went with him, and with an implement called a hitcher, which is a long pole with a hook at the end of it, after several attempts, he succeeded in drawing up the substance, which, to his unspeakable horror, proved to be a human head. The jawbone had been dreadfully fractured, one of the eyes appeared to have been knocked out, and one of the ears was slit, as if an ear-ring had been torn out. Proper notice of this circumstance was forwarded to the police, meanwhile the head was deposited in the bone-house. It was now very generally supposed, that it would prove to belong to the body found in Edgeware Road, although at the distance of nearly five miles, and this conjecture proved to be correct.

On the 2nd of February, as a young man, named Page, was working in an osier ground, near Cold-harbour Lane, Camberwell, he saw an old sack laying on the ground, having a hole in it, through which projected the knee of a human leg; another man, who was engaged in the same employ, opened the sack, and they then saw the entire thighs, legs, and feet. They left it, and hastened to inform the police, and a party of those officers fetched it away, and conveyed it to Paddington, where the head was preserved in spirits, and the body remained deposited, until some unforeseen event might render it necessary to refer to them as a means of convicting the parties who had been guilty of such an atrocious deed.

These mutilated remains were carefully matched together, and no doubt existed of their being the dissevered parts of some unhappy being who had been horribly murdered; but still the bloody transaction remained enveloped in darkness and mystery. At length one of those extraordinary impulses of the mind, which human reason cannot account for, and which shows, that in the discovery of murder the interference of an offended Deity is often conspicuously manifested, tended to fix the eye of suspicion upon the true author of the hellish deed. From the first discovery of the trunk, and pending those discoveries which followed, Mrs. Gay felt an unusually strong presentiment, that the mutilated body was that of her husband's sister; and so strong at length did this impression become, that she would not be satisfied until he consented to go to view the head, which had been carefully preserved in spirits, in order that it might at some time be identified. William Gay accordingly went to see the head, and in a moment recognised the features of his sister. Mr. and Mrs. Davis, and other friends of the unfortunate victim, repaired to see it, and were satisfied as to its identity.

On whom could suspicion fall so justly as upon Greenacre? His conduct was reviewed by those who best knew the particulars of his connexion with Mrs. Brown, and his behaviour had borne an appearance so equivocal that they became satisfied that he was the guilty individual. On the 26th of March, a warrant for his apprehension was placed in the hands of Feltham, a police-officer, who had shown himself laudibly active in this affair; and, after some trouble and research, he learned that he lived in St. Alban's-Street, Lambeth Road. He, attended by another policeman, proceeded there, and, having obtained admittance, was told by the landlord, that the person he sought lived in the parlour. He, accordingly, knocked at the door, and called 'Greenacre!' – 'Well, what do you want?' answered he. – 'I want to speak with you,' said Feltham. – 'Wait till I find the tinder-box' replied Greenacre, and was heard to get out of bed and walk about the room. The officer, not choosing to run any risk by delay, applied his hand to the latch, and the door opened; when he told him that he had a warrant to apprehend him, on a charge of murdering Mrs. Hannah Brown. – 'I know no Hannah Brown,' said Greenacre. – 'What!' said Feltham, 'were you never asked in church with Hannah Brown?' – He now acknow-

Trial of Good

For the MURDER of JANE JONES, at Putney.

Daniel Good, as he appeared in the Cell previous to his Trial.

Central Criminal Court.

Yesterday being fixed for the trial of Daniel Good, for the murder of Jane Jones, alias Good, the Court and all the avenues to it were besieged by numbers of the curious at an early hour. The doors of the Court were opened at eight o'clock, and before nine nearly every seat, both in the body of the Court and on the Bench was occupied, although no person was admitted without an order from one of the sheriffs.

The counsel for the prosecution were the Attorney-General, Mr. Waddington, Mr. Adolphus, and Mr. Russell Gurney. The prisoner's counsel was Mr. Doane.

At a few minutes before ten o'clock the Duke of Sussex entered the Court and took his seat on the judges' bench.

At ten o'clock Lord Denman, Mr. Baron Alderson, and Mr. Justice Coltman, took their seats on the Bench. The prisoners Daniel Good and Mary Good were then brought in and placed in the dock to plead to the indictment. As soon as Good came to the front of the dock, he put his hand to his forehead, and respectfully bowed to the judges. The prisoner Mary Good, looked much better than before her imprisonment.

Mr. Street having read the indictment, called upon the prisoner, "What say you, Daniel Good, are you guilty or not guilty?"

The prisoner in a low tone of voice replied, " Not guilty."

The indictment against Mary Good, for feloniously harbouring and succouring the prisoner, was then read, and to the question " What say you, Mary Good, are you guilty or not guilty?" she replied in a strong Irish accent " No, sir."

Mr. Doane said he appeared to defend the prisoner Daniel Good, and had an application to make to the Court to allow that there should be separate trials of the two prisoners.

The prisoner Daniel Good was then arraigned on the coroner's inquisition, to which he also pleaded " Not guilty."

The jury having been then sworn, the trial proceeded.

The Attorney-General rose, and said it was his duty to state the circumstances under which the prisoner at the bar was charged with the crime of murder. The learned gentleman then described the stables, and their relative position, and detailed the circumstances attending the discovery of the body in one of the stalls of the stable, and the absconding of the prisoner.

Mr. Adolphus then called the first witness, Wm. Gardiner, the constable, who deposed to the circumstances attending the finding of the mutilated trunk of the murdered woman.

Thomas Houghton was the next witness examined by Mr. Russel Gurney—He was the gardener to Mr. Shiell, and went into the stable with the witness

already examined. He stated that on the night of Wednesday he examined the fire-place, and found therein fuel three times as much in quantity as was necessary for an ordinary fire.

The next witness examined (by the Attorney-General) was Samuel Palmer, policeman V 6, who was at the stable a little before eleven the night Good escaped. This witness deposed to finding a fire, consisting of wood, coal, and straw, laid in the harness-room ; and that under it he found the portions of calcined bones produced. He also produced the keys found in the same room.

Robert Tee, parish constable of Putney, examined by the Attorney-General, deposed to finding other keys (produced) on the top of the corn-bin in the stable opposite that in which the body was lying.

Josiah Tighe, constable, 190 V, deposed to finding in the cinders two pieces of bone on the Wednesday night, and on the Tuesday after, a small piece of flesh on the edge of the lid of the seat-box.

Inspector Busain (V) gave evidence of his having found some linen and books in a box in the harness-room, which he broke open, as well as a knife in the drawer of a table, which had blood marks on the handle and blade, the latter of which appeared to have been rusty and subsequently sharpened. On the 8th, assisted by Dr. Ridge, he sifted the cinders, and found more bones (now produced).

John Houghton, son of Mr. Shiell's gardener, examined by Mr. Gurney—This witness slept in a room over the stables, to which, however, he had no access, as the prisoner Good kept the key, and had it always locked. He deposed to observing on the Tuesday before the body was found a very unpleasant smell, like the singeing of horses. He remarked it to the prisoner, who told him he had been in liquor the overnight, and had been toasting some cheese to refresh himself. He had seen the youth named Daniel Good with the prisoner, and also a woman whom he had lately told witness was his sister ; the last time he saw her was on Easter Monday.

The next witnesses called were the medical gentlemen, who deposed to the appearance of the body, and from which the deductions they made were, that it was that of a female, that the person did not appear to have died from apoplexy, that she had not been dead when found more than five days, that the marks on the axe were those of blood, that the fragments of bone found in the cinders were those of a human being ; that the incisions by which the head been removed were made after death ; that the heart and lungs were highly healthy ; that death was not occasioned by disease, but from violence from the sudden loss (while in health and the muscular powers in action) of blood ; and that deceased was pregnant.

The Lord Chief Justice having summed up the evidence, the jury immediately returned a verdict

of " GUILTY," and sentence of death was then passed. The prisoner then made the following confession :—

My Lord,—Butcher was the cause of the death of the unfortunate Jane Jones. We went to Mrs. Hester's, from there we went to the stable. I wished Jones to remain in the stable all night, but she said she would go and commit suicide. I locked her in the stable, and when I returned at night I found her a corpse. A sharp pen-knife lay by her side, with which she had killed herself. The next morning a man called at the stables. I told him what had happened, when he advised me to conceal the body. I said I would give him a sovereign if he would do it for me, to which he agreed. He cut off the head, and then asked me to light a fire in the harness-room ; but on my refusing to do so, he made a fire himself, and then commenced burning part of the body. Ann Butcher has been the cause of all.

COPY OF VERSES.

Tune—" The Gallant Poachers."

Good people all, both young and old.
A dreadful tale I will unfold,
Will make your warm life blood run cold,
When you the same shall hear.
Of Good I'll tell,
That wretch so fell,
Who a cruel deed has done,
As e'er was witness'd 'neath the sun.
But his career of crime is done,
His end is drawing near.

He helpless woman did betray,
His victim afterwards did slay ;
To hide his guilt from open day,
The body hacked and hew'd,
No mercy show'd,
For none he knew'd.
From pity he disdainful turns,
Compunction and remorse he spurns,
The quivering limbs with fire he burns,—
Thou monster, Daniel Good.

Her tender limbs he sawed and tore,
The entrails, reeking in their gore,
He gave the flames for to devour—
O?, what a deed of blood !
Could no one speed,
And stop the deed ?
Was there no one to save ther nigh,
When thou for succour loud did cry ?
No ; no one saw thy parting sigh,
But cruel Daniel Good.

A scaffold soon thy end will be,
And hissing thousands flock to see,
For none will cheer or pity thee,
Not mourn the murderer's fair.
Youth and age
Will curse thy rage,
And ages yet unborn will tell,
And on thy crimes with anguish dwell,
And mourn thy cruel deed so fell,
Deserving scorn and hate !   J. HUGHES.

Printed by E. LLOYD, 231, Shoreditch.

ledged such to have been the case, but added, 'What right have you to ask me such questions? you have no right to do so.' – 'I shall ask you no more,' replied the officer, 'but you are my prisoner, and must go with me.' As soon as a light was brought in, the officer perceived a woman in the bed: 'What woman is that?' inquired he. – 'She is a woman that I have to sleep with me,' said Greenacre. At that moment he observed that she had something in her hand, which she was attempting to conceal: 'What have you in your hand?' said he; 'give it to me, and dress yourself, for you are my prisoner also.' She then handed him a watch, and seeing on her fingers two rings, he took them from her, also her pockets in which he found a pair of ear-drops and a duplicate. A coach being sent for, the woman said she had a child sleeping in the next room, and she could not go away without it; she was allowed to fetch it; and all being in readiness for going, Greenacre requested to have a great-coat, which Feltham gave him from a trunk that was in the same room. They then were driven to the station-house at Paddington.

The gradual manner in which this diabolical deed had been brought to light, had excited in the public mind a deeply-rooted interest, while it raised a moral and honest indignation; and, therefore, when it was first rumoured, that the author of the atrocious deed had been discovered, an immense multitude assembled to see the delinquent, and they gave vent to their indignation by the only means in their power. When his examination was to take place, thousands of people were congregated, to obtain a view of the man who had thus signalized himself among the list of the most sanguinary murderers. But the object of their curiosity had determined to disappoint their eager desire to see him; for, when left in his cell, he made an attempt to defeat the ends of justice: fastening his neck-handkerchief and pocket-handkerchief together, and making a slip-knot around his neck at one end, and fastening the other end to his foot, he had nearly completed the process of strangulation, when the attention of one of the policemen was attracted by an unusual noise issuing from the cell in which he was confined, and, on opening the door, he was dicovered in a state of complete insensibility, and to all appearance dead. A surgeon, Mr. Girdwood, was sent for, who resorted to every means for his resuscitation, which, after a considerable time, proved successful. On his recovery he said to that gentleman, 'I don't thank you for this – I had rather have gone off.' This incident in itself exhibits a mind of no ordinary stamp, and leads us to imagine, that in an emergency he would shrink from no deed that would administer to the completion of any purpose that he meditated to effect, however violent might be the means necessary to its attainment.

THE SORROWFUL LAMENTATION OF JAMES BLOOMFIELD RUSH

Now lying under Sentence of Death
in Norwich Castle, for the horrid Murders
at Stanfield Hall

Kind Christians hear this doleful tale,
  Whilst I for mercy cry,
And plead unto the Lord for me,
  A wretch condemned to die.
'Twas horrid murder's dreadful crime –
  That crime for which I'm tried,
It fires my brain with agony.
  To think, by me they died.

The Father was by me shot dead,
  And afterwards his Son,
My revenge it was not satisfied,
  The dreadful crime's begun.
My murd'ring hand then did attempt
  Still further to proceed,
And woman's innocence had no effect
  To deter me from the deed.

But Mercy here did step between,
  Those victims for to shield;
The Maid and Mistress they were shot,
  And wounded, but not kill'd.
At the Lent Assizes I was tried,
  Such facts did then come out;
I was declared the murderer,
  For there remained no doubt.

And for the space of six long days,
  My trial it did last;
The sentence then of Death on me,
  By the learned Judge was pass'd,
What agony my mind is in,
  All in this dismal cell;
The horrors of my dreadful thoughts,
  No mortal tongue can tell.

For mercy do I try to pray,
  At the awful throne of God;
But mercy how can I expect,
  Stained with my victims blood.
Oh! give me death I loudly cry,
  And ease my burning brains,
No answer in this lonely cell,
  But the rattling of my chains.

Again I try to call on God,
  Have mercy blessed Lord;
O may the cross of Jesus Christ
  Wash out my deeds of blood,
I know that Christ my Saviour died
  All on Mount Calvery;
To save the worst of sinners then,
  A guilty wretch like me.

Now do I clasp my murd'ring hands,
  With horror weep aloud;
I think I see each murdered form,
  Wrap't in their deadly shroud.
Remorse now tears my troubled soul,
  When I think on my guilt,
That through revenge alas! it was,
  My victim's blood I spilt.

But soon alas! the time will come,
  When I shall yield my breath,
And suffer for these crimes of blood,
  An ignominious death.
No hopes on earth are now for me,
  For crimes so black and foul;
My only hope must be in Christ,
  For mercy on my soul.

2. ATTITUDES

LICENTIOUSNESS OF THE PRESS

The extensive circulation of newspapers is a sure criterion of the *mental* activity of the people of this country, but by no means of the advancement of moral principles and virtuous habits. This is certain from the circumstance, that the most licentious papers usually command the largest sale. The 'Life in London,' an abominable print, has an amazing circulation, whilst others of a similar character are sought after in proportion as they publish anything that is vile and destructive to virtue and religion. The press is degraded by adventurers, who constantly prostitute their talents for gain. Knowing the depraved taste of our immoral population, they suit their article to their readers, and are thus openly, and with an unsparing hand, sowing and watering the seeds of moral deformity. Rapes and every obscenity are published to pander to the corrupt tastes of their readers. A bit of a paper in Manchester, called 'The Squib,' not worth a farthing, I was told, circulated 2,000 copies at the charge of 2d. The slang style and the vitiated taste exhibited in the following extract from the Morning Chronicle, which happens to be before me, is a specimen of what we constantly meet with, and which cannot be too strongly condemned.

THAMES POLICE. – INNOCENT AMUSEMENT. – Yesterday, Maria Anderson, a little stout built female, was charged with biting off part of the right ear of Sarah Creed. Both parties are yoked to dustmen, and a grudge has long subsisted between them, in consequence of Mrs. Creed entertaining 'a mutual jealousy of Mrs. Anderson.' They quarrelled at a public-house at Shadwell, when they 'agreed to have a turn up.' Mrs. Anderson being a 'dab at milling,' pounced on her rival, and having 'floored' her, she stepped upon her stomach, and 'danced a hornpipe in good *earnest,*' so as not 'to leave a *breadth* of *hare* in her.' – Mrs. Creed at length got up, and she seized hold of her antagonist's 'harm' with her teeth, so as to make her 'beller;' but

The Life, Trial, and Execution of

MARY WHITE.

Aged 19, who was executed at Exeter, on Saturday last, for the murder of her Master and Mistress ; giving an account of

Her Innocence being Proved, and the Real Murderer Discovered.

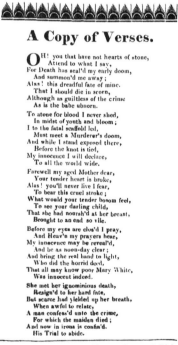

THE master and mistress of the above female was most inhumanly butchered by having their throats cut from ear to ear. This young woman had lived servant with these aged and unfortunate people upwards of seven years, and was much esteemed by all who knew her; and by her general good conduct had gained the confidence of those with whom she lived, who entrusted her with the management of their affairs, and placed the greatest reliance on her honesty. They had kept the large Inn at Exeter for a number of years, but had a short time since retired to a small pot-house, to pass the remainder of their days in greater quietude than the bustle of an Inn permitted. It was the practice of the old couple to retire to rest about nine o'clock at night, and rise about the same hour in the morning, leaving every thing to the servant's care, not having any child of their own, it was generally believed that her master would behave handsomely to her, providing she married according to his wishes. This brought the girl a number of lovers and among them a young man the name of Smith was most assiduous in his attention towards her, who, behaving always with the greatest propriety, became a great favourite with the old couple.

On Saturday, Smith went as usual to the house, and when the company had left, and the old couple retired to rest, the servant sat with him by the kitchen fire. She had occasion to leave the kitchen a short time, and on her return she missed him. On hearing a noise, she ran up stairs to her mistress's room, where to her great terror, she found the drawers plundered, and her master and mistress lying with their throats cut, and the blood gushing in torrents from the wounds. She immediately threw up a front window and gave the alarm, and the neighbours entering no one being found in the house besides her, suspicion fell upon her, and from constancy to her lover, she permitted herself to be fully committed to trial. At the late assizes she was arraigned, convicted, and sentenced to be hung and dissected.

At the place of execution she addressed the numerous by-standers as follows :—

'Good People.---You ere now come to see the latter end of a poor unfortunate young woman, 19 years of age, who is brought to an ignominious death for murder ; I say there is a just God that sitteth in the judgment seat of Heaven, before whom I must shortly appear to answer for all my sins. I most solemnly declare before God and the world, that I am innocent of the murder as the child unborn'. She burst into tears.

After this she prayed with the Minister, and sung a penitential psalm, she went down upon her knees, and prayed that the Almighty would convince the multitude assembled of her innocency or guilty by shewing them the following miracles—that if she was guilty it might be one of the finest days that could come from heaven ; but if she were innocent that the darkness might overspread the town during the time she was suspended. Her supplication reached the throne of grace for immediately on her being turned off, a dark thick cloud covered the country for many miles, attended with thunder, lightning, and rain. Smith, who was a spectator, stung with guilt and horror. rushed through the crowd, exclaiming ' I AM THE MURDERER!' and delivered himself into the hands of justice. He fully confessed his guilt, but declared that the deed was not premeditated, but he was struck with a desire to gain their riches, and he intended to have murdered his sweetheart also. He is fully committed for trial at the next Assizes.

A Copy of Verses.

OH! you that have not hearts of stone,
　Attend to what I say,
For Death has seal'd my early doom,
　And summon'd me away ;
Alas! this dreadful fate of mine.
　That I should die in scorn,
Although as guiltless of the crime
　As is the babe unborn.

To atone for blood I never shed,
　In midst of youth and bloom ;
I to the fatal scaffold led,
　Must meet a Murderer's doom,
And while I stand exposed there,
　Before the knot is tied,
My innocence I will declare,
　To all the world wide.

Farewell my aged Mother dear,
　Your tender heart is broke,
Alas! you'll never live I fear,
　To bear this cruel stroke ;
What would your tender bosom feel,
　To see your darling child,
That she had nonrsh'd at her breast,
　Brought to an end so vile.

Before my eyes are clos'd I pray,
　And Heav'n my prayers hear,
My innocence may be reveal'd,
　And be as noon-day clear ;
And bring the real hand to light,
　Who did the horrid deed,
That all may know poor Mary White,
　Was innocent indeed.

She met her ignominious death,
　Resign'd to her hard fate,
But scarce had yielded up her breath,
　When awful to relate;
A man confess'd unto the crime,
　For which the maiden died ;
And now in irons is confin'd.
　His Trial to abide.

J. Catnach, Printer, 2, & 3, Monmouth-court, 7 Dials.

Missus Anderson recovered her 'pleasure of mind,' and she speedily inserted her teeth in Mrs. Creed's ear, and shook it like a terrier. One of the witnesses said poor Mrs. Creed was 'terribly slaughtered,' and they thought Mrs. Anderson 'had bolted part of her right *here*.' – Mr. Broderip fined the defendant five shillings, but not being able to pay it, she was committed to prison. She was taken out of the office exclaiming, 'I'll serve her out when I catch her; I'll bit t'other ear off, she may take her davy.'

ON THE PURSUIT, APPREHENSION AND EXECUTION OF GOOD

It would be good for all if they would ask themselves the question, 'Did the thought of the well-being of society animate my sympathy with the pursuers? and does the same thought cause the satisfaction with which I look forward to the approaching catastrophe [of execution]? or does it arise from a blind predominance of that very propensity which led to the perpetration of the crime – the propensity to *destroy*, without consideration, all things the existence of which can be distasteful to our feelings?'

SAVED BY CASTLEREAGH

The door opened again to admit a man of middle age, whose habiliments merited the description of 'shabby-looking,' given of them by the clerk, and whose countenance, unless it greatly belied him, indicated him as deserving the character of scoundrel given him by the Home Secretary. The low, receding forehead, the small restless eyes, the thin lips, and the short thick neck, would have tempted any beholder the least acquainted with the system of Lavater, to exclaim, as Foote said of Macklin, 'If God writes a legible hand, that man must be a villain!'

'Mornin', my lords,' said he, in a tone of assurance. 'You see I am punctual to a minute.'

'The placards are ready,' said the Earl of Sidmouth, opening a drawer, and taking out a roll of large printed bills, which he gave to the shabby individual. 'See that they are all posted; their object,' he added, turning to Lord Castlereagh, 'is to throw odium upon the intended radical meeting to-morrow night, and to deter respectable men from attending.'

'Bread or blood!' said the shabby individual

DANIEL GOOD, THE MONSTER MURDERER! !!!

THE MURDER AND MUTILATION.
"Go, murderer. Hide thy deeds in the blackest night, yet will the Almighty God pierce them like a noon-tide sun."

BURNING OF THE MANGLED LIMBS.
"Can fire wash guilt from the Murderer's soul? No! Can it dry up the victim's blood? No! far rather will it make that blood arise to the altars of Heaven."

reading the words printed in large letters, and with red ink upon the placards. 'I think I deserve some credit, my lord, for suggesting such an excellent means of running the radicals down, and causing respectable people to look upon them with suspicion. Harry Hunt, and Cartwright, and young Wooler will be as mad as March hares, and swear it's all the doing of the gover'ment, but who'll believe them? They will be scouted henceforth by every respectable person in the country.'

'As they ought to be!' exclaimed Lord Castlereagh, emphatically.

'Your lordship is quite right,' said the fellow, bowing. 'There is a perfect coincidence of opinion between your lordship and myself.'

'You will post these bills this afternoon,' said the Home Secretary, 'and to-morrow night you must attend the meeting, observe who are there, cheer all the most violent portions of the speeches, and when you find the people getting excited, raise a shout of *"Down with the ministers! Death to Sidmouth and Castlereagh!"* The execution of the Cato-street conspirators has not destroyed the hopes of the radicals, nor damped their ardour; we must have the Manchester affair re-enacted in London, and this meeting may afford us a pretext for it. There is nothing more, Wilson.'

The shabby-looking individual bowed and withdrew, with the placards under his arm, and Lord Castlereagh, who had taken up the memorial in favour of Paul Copsley, while his colleague was speaking, now recalled the latter's attention to it.

'This memorial, I see, is signed by the magistrate whose gamekeeper was shot, by another magistrate of the district, and by nearly all the resident gentry and professional men,' he observed.

'Indeed!' returned the Earl of Sidmouth.

'That is strange, but it materially alters the aspect of the case, and I suppose the fellow must have a reprieve. Let me see the memorial again; it is not worth while to read the reasons advanced in support of the prayer of the memorialists, but the signatures, aye – the magistrates are Stapleton and Broadfield, who own nearly all the land in that part of Somerset, the signatures deserve considera-tion. We must not lose the support of the memorialists at the next election, my lord; therefore the fellow's sentence must be commuted.'

'The time is short,' observed Lord Castlereagh, looking significantly at his colleague. 'A little delay, and the bearer of the reprieve would arrive too late, and your lordship would still have credit of intending to spare him.'

'It would not be safe,' returned the Home Secretary, shaking his head. 'The memorial arrived last night; no – I must despatch a messenger immediately.'

He instantly wrote an order to the governor of Taunton Gaol to defer the execution of Paul Copsley, until the receipt of further instructions, and summoning a messenger, sent it off immediately.

*

The day dawned on which the life of Paul Copsley was to be sacrificed to the offended majesty of the laws, to use a phrase with which judges and lawyers gloss over the guilt of legal homicide; in other words, on which he was to suffer death to conceal the inefficiency of the laws to prevent crime. Powerless for positive good, the laws revenge themselves by destroying the individual whom they cannot reform; they can make, and do make, criminals by thousands in this highly civilised and Christian land, ironically called 'Merry England,' but they cannot unmake them, therefore they destroy them. It is so much more easy to destroy the body than to regenerate the mind; up, then, with the scaffold; live the wisdom of our ancestors. Penal law amelioration may accord with Russian barbarism, and national education with Prussian rationalism, but we are a civi-lised and an eminently Christian people, and cannot be expected to follow in the steps of semi-savages and disguised infidels.

Knowing that there was no time for them to receive an answer from the Home Office, before the hour appointed for Copsley's execution, and anxious as to the result of the memorial, George Stapleton and Valentine Crossingham set off for Taunton on the morning of the day on which the condemned homicide was to suffer, and found the pre-parations for the tragedy completed, and a dense crowd assembled in front of the goal. The scene struck a chill to the heart of George Stapleton, for it showed that no communication, the effect of which would be to stay the proceedings, had reached the authorities, and only the space of an hour was between the prisoner and death.

The two young men retired to an inn nearly opposite the prison, not to gaze, as many were doing, on the horrible scene to be enacted on the platform raised in front of the prison, but to seclude themselves in a private room, and there await in anxiety the passing of the supreme moment. At the front windows of the inn, well dressed men, and – we are sorry to add – women were waiting for the noontide hour, with as much eagerness and impatience as if they were waiting for the rising of the curtain at a theatre on the first night of a new piece; in that little private room at the back, those two young men sat, silent and thoughtful, or if they spoke, it was in a tone little above a whisper, as if a feeling of awe was upon them, and ever and anon they looked at their watches, and sighed as they counted the minutes which the condemned homicide had yet to live.

'Five minutes!' observed George Stapleton, looking at his watch for the tenth time, and speaking in a low and solemn tone, as he glanced uneasily at his cousin.

'There is no hope,' said Valentine, moving nervously upon his seat, and speaking in the same subdued tone.

'I am afraid not!' returned George, with a deep sigh; and then they relapsed into silence.

Presently the clock began to strike the hour of twelve; never had it seemed so long in striking as it then did to the minds of George Stapleton and his cousin; its metallic tones sounded not sharp or musical, but loud, sonorous, and solemn, like the tolling of the passing bell.

'Let us pray for the soul that is passing from time into eternity!' said Valentine, as he knelt down in that room in which a prayer had probably never been offered before, and George Stapleton followed his example.

But he could not pray; for it was not so easy for him to concentrate his thoughts as for Valentine, and the scaffold, the condemned,

the hangman, the oscillating throng, were before his mind's eye, though walls shut out the horrible reality.

Precisely as the clock struck, the death procession filed through the gloomy passages of the prison, and emerged upon the scaffold. The pale and pinioned victim, the officers whose duties compelled them to be present at the consummation of the sacrifice, the chaplain reading words of love and truth to the unhappy victim of class hatred and social error, all the *dramatis personae* of the exciting drama of legal homicide were there; and thousands, to whom the spectacle served all the purposes of the amphitheatre to the ancient Romans, or the bull-fight to the modern Spaniards, gazed eagerly upon the scene, jostled and elbowed one another to obtain a better view, and admired the *pluck* of the condemned, as the Romans would have done that of the gladiator, or the populace of Madrid that of the matador.

The hangman placed Copsley upon the fatal plank, drew over his countenance the cap designed to conceal from the spectators the horrible distortions of the victim's features in the agony of strangulation, and attached to his neck the cord that was to deprive him of existence. This was a moment of terrible suspense to the mob below; every eye was

fixed, as if by a species of fascination, upon the condemned, and every voice was hushed. All fighting, squabbling, swearing, and jesting had ceased; but pickpockets were busy among the crowd, this being the moment when the harvest of watches, breast-pins, and silk handkerchiefs is gathered by the light-fingered *chevaliers d'industrie*, and peripatetic vendors of cheap literature for the million, waited with anxiety and impatience for the falling of the drop, to begin bawling 'The full, true, and particular account of the life, trial, and execution of Paul Copsley.'

The hangman went below the platform of death to draw the fatal bolt, and the excitement of the gazing thousands increased in its horrid intensity; the disappearance of the degraded functionary acted upon their morbid feelings in precisely the same manner as the repeated exits and entrances, the frequent looking up at the clock, the minute hand of which seems to move so slowly, and then the placing of the meat before the cages, by the keeper of the carnivora, does upon the curiosity of the visitors to zoological collections, at the hour of feeding. At that moment, when the feelings of all were wrought up to the greatest tension, a voice was heard from a distance shouting 'Hold!' but though many turned their heads in the direction from whence it came, no one could see who it was that had raised the cry, and on the scaffold it seemed to be quite unheeded.

'In the midst of life we are in death,' said the chaplain, proceeding with the solemn service, but as he uttered the last word he looked up, for again the cry of 'Hold!' fell upon every ear, and this time louder, and in more piercing accents.

'Hold!' repeated the sheriff, and the cry stayed the hangman's hand, at the moment when it had grasped the bolt beneath the fatal plank on which stood the condemned.

A third time the cry of 'hold!' was raised, and then a horseman was seen endeavouring to push his way through the crowd, and holding up a paper.

'A reprieve! a reprieve!' exclaimed those who were nearest to the horseman, and the word passed rapidly from mouth to mouth, from one end of the dense throng to the other;

and the revulsion of feeling which the shouts excited in the mind of Paul Copsley was so overpowering that he would have fallen, had he not been supported by the sheriff.

Then a loud shout of 'Hurrah!' rose from the crowd, for many of the spectators were agricultural labourers, and by that class the condemned was regarded as a victim to aristocratic privilege.

KILLING NO MURDER

AGRARIUS TO THE KING-GULLED, PRIEST-GULLED ARISTOCRAT AND PROPERTY-GULLED PEOPLE OF BRITAIN AND IRELAND

There are no terrors, Cassius, in your words,
For I am armed so strong in honesty,
That they pass by me like the idle wind,
Which I respect not. – SHAKESPEARE.

FELLOW COUNTRY MEN AND WOMEN – I lately addressed a letter to Swing, containing certain opinions of mine, (deduced from observation, comparison, and reflection), relative to the state and condition of the children of labour in the present ill-constructed, irrational, and antagonistic disorder of human affairs: in which letter I shewed that the whole of the productive labourers, mechanics, artisans, embellishers, and others, who are not only the producers of all the wealth and all the comforts of society, but who ought to be (naturally and legitimately) the POSSESSORS of all these things, are compelled to sit down in silence, and allow their wealth (which their own hands have produced) to be abstracted from them under the name of 'law,' by a combination of murderous villains denominated kings, lords, and priests, together with their myrmidons, the masters, merchants, capitalists, and their hired assassins. This combination of miscreants has caused millions upon millions of men to be murdered in what has been termed 'honourable war,' which establishes the maxim that 'one murder makes a villain, millions the hero.' This combination has caused the death by starvation of thousands upon thousands of our fellow beings, in the midst of a superabundance of all the good things of this life, and these thousands too some of the actual producers of the very comforts and necessaries of life, of which they, the producers, had been so unjustly deprived.

Deeply weighing and examining the deplorable and helpless condition of the human slaves all over what is basely and falsely denominated the civilized world; seeing those slaves every where bending under burdens grievous to be borne, which their haughty and unfeeling tyrants would not deign to touch with one of their fingers: and taking my stand on the just principle of obtaining the greatest possible amount of good for the greatest number, with the smallest possible amount of misery; I reiterate the sentiment I formerly expressed, that KILLING, under the present circumstances, IS NOT MURDER! and, moreover, I defy the whole of the sanguinary property-mongers, with their drivelling purblind dupes, envelopped as they are in the delusive mist of fawning acquiescence, to stifle the noble sentiment of retribution that will speedily be awakened. What! shall we, then, permit ourselves to FORGET that all men are born free, all are born equal; and therefore that any attempt on the part of one or more to curtail and abridge that natural freedom and equality, is a gross violation of the laws of nature? – Never! All attempts at this violation OUGHT TO BE RESISTED; and the shivering scribes in the Pioneer are informed, that Agrarius for one WOULD resist such attempts, even unto DEATH. To put a case – If any man, or set of men, cunningly devise an abominable trick or imposture, in the form of moral or mental poison, so as to stultify the reasoning powers of the people; or, which is the same thing, introduce such a system of training as shall render the people tame and submissive, like sheep led to the slaughter; and if one of this people become surrounded by new circumstances, so as to discover an antidote for the baneful root which his fellow men had eaten, in the time of infancy (when incapable of discerning good from evil) at the hands of the priests and other nefarious jugglers, would he not be justified in administering that antidote to his fellows, nay, would he not be imperiously commanded to do so by every feeling of humanity, the first moment that his judgment should point out to him as being the proper period for affording effectual relief?

3. CRIMINALS IN ROMANCE

GEORGE BARNWELL MURDERS HIS UNCLE

[*In the previous chapter, George Barnwell has been persuaded by Milwood to commit the crime in order to show his love for her.*]

> Between the acting of a dreadful thing.
> And the first notion, all the interim is
> A fearful phantasm, or hideous dream.
> The genius and the mortal instruments
> Are then in council, and the state of man,
> Like to a little kingdom, suffers then
> The nature of an insurrection.   Old Play.

When Barnwell rushed from the apartment in which the scene narrated in the previous chapter took place, and found himself once more in the open air, his senses seemed for a time to have forsaken him. His wild demeanour, dishevelled hair, and contorted features, the darkness of the night – for it *was* night – allowed to be passed unnoticed. For some days before, the weather had been exceedingly sultry. Not a breath of wind had fanned coolness into the atmosphere, and a stifling vapour had settled over London that, formed of the accumulated clouds of smoke that had risen beyond the houses, hung like a funereal pall over the site of our mighty city. Many were the conjectures to which this had given rise. Some – and these were the majority – foreboded a return of the great Plague; others, and these were the enthusiasts, predicted the near approach of the termination of the world; whilst some – and these were right in their surmises – foretold the inhabitants that an earthquake was not far distant.

My Poor Black Bess.

Turpin Stopping the Mail on his Ride to York

When fortune, blind goodness, she fled my abode
And friends prov'd ungrateful I took to the road,
To plunder the wealthy, to aid my distress,
I bought thee to aid me, my poor black bess.

No vile whip. or spur did thy sides ever gall,
For none dids't thou need, thou would'st bound at
    my call,
For each act of kindness thou did'st me caress,
Thou wert never ungrateful my poor black bess,

When dark sable midnight its mantle had thrown,
O'er the bright face of nature how have we gone,
To fam'd Hounslow heath tho an unwelcome guest
To the minions of fortune my poor black bess.

How silent thou'st stood when a carriage' I ve sto
And their gold and jewels it's inmates have dropt,
No poor man I plunder'd oe'r did oppress,
The widow or orphan, my poor black Bess,

When Argus eyed justice did me hotly persue,
From London to York like lightening we flew,
No toll-bar could stop thee, thou the river dids't
    breast,

And in twelve hours reached it, my poor black bess

But fate darkens oe'r me despair is my lot,
The law does persue me, through a cock which I shot
To save thee poor brute thou did's do thy best'
Thou art worn out and weary. my poor black Bess.

Hark the bloodhounds approach, they never shall
    have,
A beast like thee noble, so faithful and brave
Thou must die my dumb friend. tho' it does me distress
There, there I have shot thee, my poor black Bess.

And in after ages when I'm dead and gone,
This tale will be handed from father to son,
My fate some may pity, but all will confess,
'Twas in kindness I killed thee my poor black bess.

No one can say that ingratitude dwelt,
In the honour of Turpin 'twas a vice he ne'er met,
I shall die like a man and soon be at rest,
Then farewell for ever my poor black bess.

Paul, Printer, 18, Great St. Andrew Street, 7 Dials.

This earthquake was the precursor of that which, twenty years afterwards, filled the churches with 'trembling and prayers,' and sent millions into Hyde Park, and the fields thereunto adjacent, to listen to the ministry of Whitfield, and derive consolation from the discourses of his fellow-labourers in the theological vineyard.

The night previous to the one on which our hero departed on his murderous mission, a few faint shocks had been felt. First at Hammersmith, then a meagre hamlet, containing scarcely a dozen houses; afterwards in Fleet Street, to such an extent that a few houses tottered from their foundations; and, lastly, the vibration, apparently proceeding in a south-easterly direction, passed under the bed of the river, and spent its fury upon Rotherhithe, where, according to a chronicler of the period, 'a fearful gaping of the earth took place, and swallowed up several low cottages on the marshy ground near the Thames.'

An event like this, taking place in the midst of a populous city, caused, as may be imagined, a marvellous consternation. Prayers were offered up in all places of religious worship, to deprecate the vengeance of Heaven, and avert the expected overwhelming calamity; whilst groups of anxious listeners met at the corners of every street to debate the probability of a general destruction taking place, and to prepare accordingly.

It was amidst scenes and rumours of this description that Barnwell passed; but he was too intent upon the accomplishment of his own mission to heed them more than slightly. Onwards he went over London Bridge, and down the road leading therefrom, with unabated speed. The sky appeared of a dull, leaden colour, through which not a star could be seen, to vary the monotonous, lurid hue of the heavens. The air, which, as we have previously mentioned, had remained for some days at a most heated temperature, now became agitated, and sudden gusts of wind sped like the harbingers of a hurricane over the river, and spent their fury upon the buildings beyond. Large drops of rain began to patter down on the ill-paved streets with

increasing velocity, and distant peals of thunder were heard in the distance, to break the awful silence that prevailed. Still Barnwell relaxed not his pace. His thoughts were engrossed by the contemplation of such a deed of blood as he was on the eve of committing, and fearful phantoms seemed starting up out of the darkness before him, and beckoning him onwards with wild and fantastic antics. He had now entered the precincts of Camberwell, and neither heeding the fury of the wind, the vivid flashes of the forked lightning, or the approaching sound of the thunder, pursued his way towards the Grove. His fevered brain, haunted by fearful phantasms, lent renewed energy to his limbs, and as he approached the dwelling of his revered relative, the perspiration streamed from every pore, in consequence of the haste with which he had hurried thither.

Stepping on one side, to avoid the intrusive gaze of any unwelcome passenger who might be passing at that hour, he cast his eyes towards the building in which his uncle resided. The old clock of Camberwell church at that instant struck the hour of eleven, and as the sounds of the dying hour were borne away by the gale, a loud peal of thunder shook the heavens, followed by an instantaneous blaze of light, which for a moment illumined the whole hemisphere by its transitory splendour.

Barnwell was for the instant startled by the crash that seemed to tear heaven and earth asunder; but as the changing sky again returned to its dull, leaden hue, as if it mirrored the dark thoughts that agitated his own breast, he recovered his self-possession; and, remembering that there was a private path that led to the back of the garden, he hastened towards this with a firmness of step that belied the trembling of his heart.

Unfastening a small wicket, he entered a narrow gravel path, that led downwards to the house, dividing a stately avenue of tall poplars, that interlaced their branches so closely together as to shut out all light. Stealthily creeping, like a criminal, towards the open lawn that fronted the house, he beheld a taper glimmer from the opposite room, the windows of which being open, and on a level with the grass-plot, enabled him to obtain a full view of the interior.

His uncle was reading, apparently some sacred volume, which ever and anon he would lay on one side, and burying his face in his hands, busy himself in meditation.

'Oh, Heavens!' thought Barnwell, 'I cannot – dare not, murder him thus, whilst so defenceless, and whilst so engaged! 'Tis worse than murder. I stiffen with horror at mine own impiety. What, if I resign my dreadful purpose, and fly this spot? But, whither could I go? *To-morrow!* and my employer's once friendly door will be closed against me, my name stained for ever with a damning crime, and I, an outcast. Milwood, too – aye, there's another motive. To see her whom I love – nay, 'tis more than love – the madness of desire – a fever of the soul – to see *her* poor, and in need, and to be without the power of assisting her, is more than I can bear. This night must see the damning deed performed. Take courage, then, my fainting heart, and gold shall end my woes for ever!'

He now approached the window. Cautiously and softly did he bend his steps. The casual falling of a leaf startled him from his path. He had gained the window: another moment, and the pistol would have flashed fire at his touch, but the utterance of a few words from the old man whom he was about to murder suspended his intent, and with bated breath and a beating heart Barnwell listened to the meditations of his aged relative.

'Surely,' soliloquised his uncle, 'I heard some footsteps near the window. Pshaw! it was doubtless but the pattering of the rain; some leaf, that parting from its parent stem, falls fluttering to the ground. Were I inclined to attach my faith to omens, some danger seems to threaten me. My spirits are unwontedly depressed, and fearful fantasies of bodies changed from the livid hue of death to rankling dust flit in profusion here athwart mine eyes. Oh, Death! thou strange, mysterious power; seen every day, yet never understood, save by the incommunicative dead! What art thou? Why does the extensive mind of man, that with a thought circles the earth in search of knowledge, dives to the depths below, or climbs above the stars – why does that fail, when striving to unfold thy mystery?'

Barnwell here moved aside the branches of the tree behind which he had been concealed, and again made an ineffectual attempt to pull the trigger of the pistol. Startled by the sound, the old man exclaimed in a tremulous voice as he looked towards the spot:

'Ha! a robber!'

'Nay, then,' cried Barnwell, 'there is no resource left,' and discharging the pistol as his aged uncle approached, the bullet leaped to his heart; and the heavy groan and fall that ensued, told the marksman how well the aim had been taken.

*

A quarter of an hour had elapsed since what we have above narrated had taken place. Scarcely had the winged messenger Death reached its abiding place in his uncle's heart, ere Barnwell had flown to give him succour. But this, together with accompanying repentance, had arrived too late. Recognising at a glance the form of his destroyer, the old man wept with sorrow at the discovery; and whilst Barnwell sought to assuage the blood that flowed in copious torrents from his wound, his last breath was spent in beseeching Heaven to pardon his murderer.

'Look up, once more, dear, injured relative,' exclaimed Barnwell, as he leaned over the corpse of his uncle; 'behold again your murderer in your nephew. Alas! he hears me not. He's dead! DEAD! oh! horror! and I his slayer. *I*, whom he so oft has aided. My father's only brother, killed by that father's son! The thought is madness! oh! damning crime. Worse than the guilt of Cain, for he but killed a brother; I – a father, brother, parent, all in one. Would that my tears would wipe away all memory of this deed, for fast indeed they flow.'

Pursuing useless reflections such as these, and fruitlessly bewailing the crime he had committed, Barnwell cast himself upon the inanimate form that lay before him steeped in gore, and sought to recall the vital spark that had flown for ever. Mingling his tears with the blood, he poured out bitter exclamations of remorse, and ceased not his re-

JACK SHEPPARD'S
SONGSTER.

NIX MY DOLLY!
Pals fake away.

In a box of a stone jug I was born,
Of a hempen widow the kid forlorn.
                              Fake away.
And my noble father, as I've heard say,
Was a famous merchant of capers gay,
Nix my dolly, pals, fake away,
Nix my dolly, pals, fake away.

The knucks in quod did my schoolmen play,
And put me up to the time o'day.
                              Fake away.
No dummy hunter had forks so fly,
No knuckler or cefly could fake a cly.
Nix my dolly, pals, fake away,
Nix my dolly, pals, fake away.

But my nuttiest lady one fine day,
To the beaks did her gentleman betray.
                              Fake away
And so I was bowled out at last,
And into the jug for a lag was cast.
Nix my dolly, pals, fake away,
Nix my dolly, pals, fake away.

But I slipt my darbies one fine day,
And gave to the dubsman a holliday.
                              Fake away.
And here I am, pals, merry and free,
A regular rolicking romany.
Nix my dolly, pals, fake away,
Nix my dolly, pals, fake away.

Carpenter's Daughter.

THE Carpenter's Daughter was fair and free—
Fair, fickle, and false was she,
She slighted the journeyman (meaning me)
And smiled on a gallant of high decree,
                              Degree, degree.
She smiled on a gallant of high decree.

When years rolled by she began to rue
Her love for her gentleman, (meaning you,)
" I slighted a journeyman fond," quoth she,
" But where is my gallant of high decree. ?
                              " Where, where,
" Oh! where is my gallant of high decree ?"

JOLLY NOSE.

JOLLY NOSE, the rubies that garnish thy tip
  Are dug from the mines of Canary,
And to keep up the lustre, I moisten my lip,
  With hogsheads of claret and sherry.

Jolly Nose, he who sees thee across a broad glass
  Beholds the in all thy perfection,
And, to the pale snout of a temperat ass,
  Entertains the profoundest objection.

For a big-bellied glass is the palette I use,
  And the choicest of wine is my colour,
And I find that my nose takes the mellowest hues
  The fuller I fill it—the fuller.

Jolly Nose, they are fools who say drink hurts
    the sight,
  Such dullards know nothing about it ;
'Tis better with wine to extinguish the light,
  Than live always in darkness without it.

Farewell my Scamps
and Fogles.

NOW farewell my scamps and fogles,
  Tolls and pops and all, farewell,
London—scene of all glories,
  Where I oft have come the swell.

Tyburn once I viewed refrective,
  Come old man we'll now kiss hands,
Welcome to my new perspectiv,
  Cracking cribs in other landse.

BIRT, Printer, 39, Great St. Andrew Street,
                Seven Dials.

proaches, until insensibility coming to his aid he swooned by the side of his relative.

The storm had now abated, though the wind in fitful gusts still continued to howl amidst the groves of trees, a solemn requiem to the memory of the departed. The sky cleared – the stars peeped out at intervals – and clouds in thick black masses swept across the face of night; but there Barnwell still lay, unconscious of the scene, and with his last thoughts were mingled a fearful recollection of the deed his hand had there committed.

JACK SHEPPARD'S THIRD ESCAPE FROM NEWGATE

The door of the Red-room was banded with iron, and a massive lock, whose bolt had not been withdrawn for seven years, fastened it securely: by the help of his two nails and his iron bar, in less than many minutes he wrenched off the lock, and entered a long passage that led to the chapel – his progress was here stayed by a stout door, and it was with feelings of anything but pleasure that he discovered the whole of the fastenings were upon the other side, he tried the door, but found it was strongly secured, he had but one alternative, which was to break through the wall near the bolts, and push them back – this he attempted, and found it very difficult to accomplish – the plaster had become hardened, and the wood-work being very strong, his blunt iron bar made little impression upon it, but he worked with a good heart, and had the satisfaction, after one hour's hard labour, of accomplishing his object – he passed along the passage, and when he came to the end, found a half-door, guarded by long spikes; he saw that by breaking off one of them he could easily squeeze his body through the vacancy, and thus get into the chapel – he calculated that it would take him less time by these means than by forcing the lock, he therefore twisted his bar between them, and worked it backwards and forwards until he snapped one of them in half: the broken spike he carefully possessed himself of, as he expected it would prove useful to him –

he climbed up the door, squeezed between the bars, and dropped into the chapel – he passed swiftly through it – he knew his way for here had he once listened to his condemned sermon – he hoped he should not a second time be placed in so painful a situation. He stopped not for reflections, but made his way to the entry – he knew there was a door here to stop him, and therefore was not surprised to meet with one guarded by a strong lock – it was now half-past six, and in this entry quite dark – he had no means of getting a light, and scarce the inclination if he had – he was therefore compelled to work in the dark, but his perseverance failed him not, nor did his excitement suffer him to feel fatigue – he worked manfully at it, and found his spike of good service, and after half-an-hour's labour the lock yielded to his efforts, and he found himself in an anti-room, where criminals were sometimes placed, going or returning from chapel, when their condemned sermons was preached: the room was quite dark, but he groped out the door, and passed his hands over it to discover the nature of the fastenings, his heart almost failed him on ascertaining their tremendous quality. There was a pondrous lock, with iron bars springing from it, and attached to the door: the bolts were rivetted with stout staples; the door was banded with steel and a cross bar, locked with a padlock, summed up all. To surmount these obstacles he calculated that it would take him the whole of the night, he therefore felt as if he must give up the attempt. To do this after what he had undergone in attempting to effect his escape was maddening, and he resolved to attempt breaking a hole through the wall, large enough to admit him; but he found the wall was of stone, on which his bar made not the slightest impression; it struck fire as would a flint and steel, but had no further effect in a fit of despondency he dashed the iron bar to the ground, and burst into a passionate flood of tears; in another minute his eyes were as dry as dust again, and he was upon his feet, racking his brain for some new method to overcome the opposition; he thought of breaking through the panels of the door; he tried them, but they were plated with iron; again he was at a loss; presently a new idea struck him, and he attempted to wrench the fillet from the main post of the door, and so bring box and staples with it; he commenced it; he found it practicable: he breathed his mother's name, and laboured like a horse; at last he succeeded, wrenched the fillet off, and the door was at his service; he wiped the perspiration from his forehead, and entered the succeeding room – here was another door, with strong fastenings to overcome, but he worked desperately, and with like success to the others, conquered its opposition; he was now on a lower portion of the roof; there was a flight of stone steps leading to the upper leads, over which he must pass, and he ran swiftly up them, but found an iron gate locked to intercept him; the lock and gate were too strong to force, he therefore preferred attempting to scale the wall – he descended the steps, and taking a spring, with desperate energy he succeeded in getting a hold of the top, raising himself and mounting it, jumped on to the upper leads. He now found himself on the highest part of Newgate: at this precise moment St. Paul's clock struck eight – it was moonlight, and this enabled him to see his way – he got to the end of the leads, and discovered that he must drop to those of a turner's house adjoining Newgate: he looked at his leap before he attempted it, and saw that it was a fearful height to drop – too great indeed to venture: it would be a miracle if he escaped with life, or even broken limbs, were he to attempt it without the assistance of ropes – there was no other way of descending, none other of escaping: he remembered how he had conquered such a difficulty in breaking Clerkenwell New Prison, and he recollected that he had a blanket in his cell – in a state of frenzied desperation, he determined to return and fetch it: back again did he go through every room, groping his way along, for it was quite dark in the rooms; he felt some horrid expectation of being retaken, but he was determined that they should kill him in the effort, and he would sell his life dearly: he grasped his iron bar with firmness as the idea passed through his mind. Once he stopped, for he fancied he heard voices approaching; for an instant he resolved to fly, and drop the leads at all hazards; then

again his confidence returned – he listened with more calmness, and found the voices proceeding from the other part of the prison: he went on, and at length reached the castle: he found his blanket, and his return was made with a swiftness almost inconceivable. When he was again upon the upper leads he fastened his spike firmly in the top of the wall, beating it in with his bar, he attached the blanket to it, lowered himself swiftly, and he stood on the leads of the turner's house. A trap-door was left accidentally open, he entered – he passed silently down the first flight of stairs, but in turning the bannisters his chains clanked – he heard the voice of a young woman exclaim, 'Lord! what's that?' a man in a tender voice replied, 'nothing my love, but a dog or cat.' Jack thought he heard a kiss follow the speech, but he stayed not to hear farther, but he turned back, and waited for a couple of hours. All was quiet, he again descended, just as he reached the same spot as before, the drawing-room door opened, he heard a gentleman take leave and go down stairs followed by the maid-servant with a light: he followed swiftly down, and hid himself behind an abutment at the bottom of the stairs. He heard a whispering in the passage: he heard a struggle and a kiss. 'Happy people,' thought he, 'you little think what an unhappy wretch you have near you.' The street-door opened and shut, the maid servant passed by him, smiling and setting her cap to rights as she ascended the stairs: he got into the passage when he heard her in the room above, he unfastened the door, and was once more in the streets of London: thus accomplishing one of the most hazardous and extraordinary escapes upon record.

Without considering whither he should direct his steps, he rushed up Cheapside, through back street until he reached Shoreditch; he then passed up through Hoxton, and by day-break, footsore, exhausted to extremity, and broken spirited, for the excitement over his spirits had quite deserted him, he laid himself down in a barn at Tottenham and sobbed like a child: sobbed as if his heart would break: like a sick and weary infant upon its mother's bosom, he wept himself to sleep. The sun was sinking in the heavens when a man entered the barn, his footsteps awakened Jack, who upon his entrance, sprang to his feet: the man started at beholding him, but Jack told him he was a poor fellow from the country, who had walked many miles and had laid down to rest, weary and tired: the man did not see his fetters, but exclaimed, 'God help thee, thou look'st wayworn and fatigued, sleep on, sleep on,' so saying, he left the barn – after he had left, Jack stole from the barn with the intention of getting something to eat, for he was hungry, not having tasted anything since the preceding morning; he found his legs swelled and pained by his irons so much, that he could scarce crawl: he, however, managed to get to a little shop, where he purchased a loaf – he asked the woman for a hammer, but she had not one, and he sadly left the place – he dragged slowly along, and passed a blacksmith's forge, here he resolved to hatch up a story and prevail upon the man to sell him a file – accordingly he entered, and asked him if he had one to sell: at his voice the man raised his head, ceased hammering, and stared him hard in the face. Jack repeated his request: the man threw down his hammer, and said –

'I know you: you are Jack Sheppard, and you escaped last night from Newgate.'

'I am,' returned Jack, at once, 'will you betray me?'

'I'll die first,' said the man: 'you want your irons taken off – God help me, how your legs are swelled!' the man said many other kind things, which brought tears in Jack's eyes, for he was weak and nervous from his tremendous exertions – the man rubbed Jack's legs with oil – he made him a bed, and during the day, at Jack's request, purchased him a suit of cloths in the village – early in the evening Jack determined to depart – the blacksmith refused all remuneration, but begged Jack to give him his irons, these he readily and heartily presented him with, and bidding the honest fellow a hasty farewell, he started for West End Farm: it was near daybreak when he reached. He passed a man leaning sleeping against a tree, it was Quilt Arnold, 'sleep on,' thought Jack. 'I'll not disturb you,' he gave a signal, and Escape,

who had been, ever since he heard of Jack's escape, expecting him, appeared, and swiftly admitted him. 'My mother,' were the first words Jack uttered – silently pressing his hand, Escape led him up stairs to a bed-room – he entered to see a sad sight, his mother lay upon the bed, seemingly unconscious of aught around her. Mr. Wood was kneeling at the bed-side, reading the Bible as well as his tears would permit, and Barbara, in the attitude of prayer, was on her knees at the foot – Jack stepped softly into the room, but his mother, who had heard nothing before, heard this step, knew it, and raising herself with an energy almost surprising – it was the last effort of expiring nature – her eyes flashed as her son's form met her gaze, and she exclaimed –

'Jack!'

'Mother, mother,' he said, hot tears choking his utterance.

'My boy, my dear child,' faintly articulated she. 'I see you once again, once ere I die: may the Almighty, in His infinite mercy, bless and protect you – my blessed – boy – I die – happy – bless – you all,' and with a sweet smile upon her features her spirit passed away.

'She's dead!' gasped Jack, after gazing for a moment upon her lifeless features; he staggered across the room – he pressed his hands to his forehead, the effort was too much after what he had undergone, and he fell heavily, senseless, upon the ground.

JACK SHEPPARD

First Juvenile. – I say, wasn't it well acted?

Second Juv. – I believe you. I do likes to see them sort o' robber-pieces. I wouldn't give a tizzy to see wot is call'd a moral play – they ar' so precious dull. This Jack Sheppard is worth the whole on 'em.

Third Juv. – How I should like to be among the jolly cocks; plenty to eat, drink, and spend – and every one has his *mott* too.

Fourth Juv. – Ar; shouldn't I like to be among 'em in real arnest. Wot jovial lives they seem to lead; and wot's the odds, so long as you ar' happy? Only see how such coves are handled down to posterity, I thinks it's call'd, by means of books, and plays, and pictures!

FIFTH JUV. – Blow'd if I shouldn't just like to be another *Jack Sheppard* – it only wants a little pluck to begin with. – ALL FIVE. – That's all.

THE MUMMY

The district of Spitalfields and Bethnal Green was totally unknown to Markham. Indeed, his visit upon the present occasion was the first he had ever paid to that densely populated and miserable region.

It was now midnight; and the streets were nearly deserted. The lamps, few and far between, only made darkness visible, instead of throwing a useful light upon the intricate maze of narrow thoroughfares.

Markham's object was to reach Shoreditch as soon as possible; for he knew that opposite the church there was a cab-stand where he might procure a vehicle to take him home. Emerging from Brick Lane, he crossed Church Street, and struck into that labyrinth of dirty and dangerous lanes in the vicinity of Bird-cage Walk, which we alluded to at the commencement of the preceding chapter.

He soon perceived that he had mistaken his way; and at length found himself floundering about in a long narrow street, unpaved, and here and there almost blocked up with heaps of putrescent filth. There was not a lamp in this perilous thoroughfare: no moon on high irradiated his path; – black night enveloped every thing above and below in total darkness.

Once or twice he thought he heard footsteps behind him; and then he stopped, hoping to be overtaken by some one of whom he might inquire his way. But either his ears deceived him, or else the person whose steps he heard stopped when he did.

There was not a light in any of the houses on either side; and not a sound of revelry or sorrow escaped from the ill-closed casements.

Richard was bewildered; and – to speak truly – he began to be alarmed. He remem-

bered to have read of the mysterious disappearance of persons in the east end of the metropolis, and also of certain fell deeds of crime which had been lately brought to light in the very district where he was now wandering; – and he could not help wishing that he was in some more secure and less gloomy region.

He was groping his way along, feeling with his hands against the houses to guide him, – now knee-deep in some filthy puddle, now stumbling over some heap of slimy dirt, now floundering up to his ankles in the mud, – when a heavy and crushing blow fell upon his hat from behind.

He staggered and fell against the door of a house. Almost at the same instant that door was thrust open, and two powerful arms hurled the prostrate young man down three or four steps into a passage. The person who thus ferociously attacked him leapt after him, closing the door violently behind him.

All this occupied but a couple of seconds; and though Markham was not completely stunned by the blow, he was too much stupefied by the suddenness and violence of the assault to cry out. To this circumstance he was probably indebted for his life; for the villain who had struck him no doubt conceived the blow to have been fatal; and therefore, instead of renewing the attack, he strode over Markham and entered a room into which the passage opened.

Richard's first idea was to rise and attempt an escape by the front door; but before he had time to consider it even for a moment, the murderous ruffian struck a light in the room, which, as well as a part of the passage, was immediately illuminated by a powerful glare.

Markham had been thrown upon the damp tiles with which the passage was paved, in such a manner that his head was close by the door of the room. The man who had assailed him lighted a piece of candle in a bright tin shade hanging against the wall; and the reflection produced by the metal caused the strong glare that fell so suddenly upon Richard's eyes.

Markham was about to start from his prostrate position when the interior of that room was thus abruptly revealed to him; but for a few moments the spectacle which met his sight paralyzed every limb, and rendered him breathless, speechless, and motionless with horror.

Stretched upon a shutter, which three chairs supported, was a corpse – naked, and of that blueish or livid colour which denotes the beginning of decomposition!

Near this loathsome object was a large tub full of water; and to that part of the ceiling immediately above it were affixed two large hooks, to each of which hung thick cords.

In one corner of the room were long flexible iron rods, spades, pickaxes, wooden levers, coils of thick rope, trowels, saws, hammers, huge chisels, skeleton-keys, &c.

But how great was Richard's astonishment when, glancing from the objects just described towards the villain who had hurled him into that den of horrors, his eyes were struck by the sombre and revolting countenance of the Resurrection Man.

He closed his eyes for a moment, as if he could thus banish both thought and danger.

'Now, then, Mummy,' ejaculated the Resurrection Man; 'come and hold this light while I rifle the pockets of a new subject.'

Scarcely had he uttered these words, when a low knock was heard at the front door of the house.

'D—n the thing!' cried the Resurrection Man, aloud; 'here are these fellows come for the stiff'un.'

These words struck fresh dismay into the soul of Richard Markham; for it instantly occurred to him that any friends of the Resurrection Man, who were thus craving admittance, were more likely to aid than to frustrate that villain's designs upon the life and property of a fellow-creature.

'Here, Mummy,' cried the Resurrection Man, once more; and, hastily returning into the passage, he reiterated his summons at the bottom of a staircase at the further end; 'here, Mummy, why the hell don't you come down?'

'I'm a comin', I'm a comin',' answered a cracked female voice from the top of the staircase; and in another moment an old, blear-eyed, shrivelled hag made her appearance.

She was so thin, her eyes were so sunken, her skin was so much like dirty parchment, and her entire appearance was so horrible and repulsive, that it was impossible to conceive a more appropriate and expressive nickname than the one which had been conferred upon her.

'Now come, Mummy,' said the ruffian, in a hasty whisper; 'help me to drag this fellow into the back room; there's good pickings here, and the chaps have come for the stiff'un.'

Another knock was heard at the door.

Markham, well aware that resistance was at present vain, exercised sufficient control over himself to remain motionless, with his eyes nearly closed, while the Resurrection Man and the Mummy dragged him hastily into the back room.

The Mummy turned the key in the lock, while the Resurrection Man hurried to the street door, and admitted two men into the front apartment.

One was Tom the Cracksman; the other was a rogue of the same stamp, and was known amongst his confederates in crime by the name of the Buffer. It was this man's boast that he never robbed any one without stripping him to the very skin; and as a person in a state of nudity is said to be 'in buff,' the origin of his pseudonym is easily comprehended.

'Well,' said the Cracksman, sulkily, 'you ain't at all partikler how you keep people at your door – you ain't. For twopence, I'd have sported it* with my foot.'

'Why, the old Mummy was fast asleep,' returned the Resurrection Man; 'and I was up stairs trying to awake her. But I didn't expect you till to-morrow night.'

'No; and we shouldn't have come either,' said the Cracksman, 'if there hadn't been thirty quids to earn to-night.'

'The devil there is;' cried the Resurrection Man. 'Then you ain't come for the stiff'un to-night?'

'No sich a thing; the Sawbones† that it's for don't expect it till to-morrow night; so its no use taking it. But there's t'other Sawbones, which lives down by the Middlesex Hospital,

*Burst it open.   †Surgeon.

will meet us at half-past one at the back of Shoreditch church – '

'What, to-night!' ejaculated the Resurrection Man.

'To-night – in half an hour – and with all the tools,' returned the Cracksman.

'Work for the inside of the church, he says,' added the Buffer. 'Thirty quids isn't to be sneezed at; that's ten a-piece. I'm blowed if I don't like this here resurrection business better than cracking cribs. What do you say, Tom?'

'Anythink by vay of a change; partikler as when we want a stiff'un by a certain day, and don't know in which churchyard to dive for one, we hit upon the plan of catching 'em alive in the street.'

'It was my idea, though,' exclaimed the Buffer. 'Don't you remember when we wanted a stiff'un for the wery same Sawbones which we've got to meet presently, we waited for near two hours at this house-door, and at last we caught hold of a feller that was walking so comfortable along, looking up at the moon?'

'And then I thought of holding him with his head downwards in a tub of water,' added the Cracksman, 'till he was drownded. That way don't tell no tales; – no wound on the skin – no pison in the stomach; and there ain't too much water inside neither, cos the poor devils don't swaller with their heads downwards.'

'Ah! it was a good idea,' said the Buffer; 'and now we've reduced it to a reg'lar system. Tub of water all ready on the floor – hooks and cords to hold the chaps' feet up to the ceiling; and then, my eye; there they hangs, head downwards, jest for all the world like the carcasses in the butchers' shops, if they hadn't got their clothes on.'

'And them we precious soon takes off. But I say, old feller,' said the Cracksman, turning to the Resurrection Man, who had remained silent during the colloquy between his two companions; 'what the devil are you thinking of?'

'I was thinking,' was the answer, 'that the Sawbones that you've agreed to meet to-night wants some particular body.'

'He does,' said the Cracksman; 'and the one he wants is buried in a vault.'

'Well and good,' exclaimed the Resurrection Man; 'he is too good a customer to disappoint. We must be off at once.'

The Resurrection Man did not for a moment doubt that Richard Markham had been killed by the blow which he had inflicted upon him with his life-preserver; and he therefore did not hesitate to undertake the business just proposed by his two confederates. He knew that, whatever Richard's pockets might contain, he could rely upon the *honesty* of the Mummy, who – horrible to relate – was the miscreant's own mother. Having therefore given a few instructions, in a whisper, to the old woman, he prepared to accompany the Cracksman and the Buffer.

The three worthies provided themselves with some of the long flexible rods and other implements before noticed; and the Resurrection Man took from a cupboard two boxes, each of about six inches square, and which he gave to his companions to carry. He also concealed the tin shade which held the candle, about his person; and, these preliminaries being settled, the three men left the house.

Let us now return to Richard Markham.

The moment he was deposited in the back room, and the door had closed behind the occupants of that fearful den, he started up, a prey to the most indescribable feelings of alarm and horror.

What a lurking hole of enormity – what a haunt of infamy – what a scene of desperate crime – was this in which he now found himself! A feculent smell of the decomposing corpse in the next room reached his nostrils, and produced a nauseating sensation in his stomach. And that corpse – was it the remains of one who had died a natural death, or who had been most foully murdered? He dared not answer the question which he had thus put to himself; he feared lest the solution of that mystery might prove ominous in respect to his own fate.

Oh! for the means of escape! He must fly – he must fly from that horrible sink of crime – from that human slaughter-house! But how? the door was locked – and the window was closed with a shutter. If he made the slightest noise, the ruffians in the next room would rush in and assassinate him!

But, hark! those men were talking, and he could overhear all they said. Could it be possible? The two who had just come, were going to take the third away with them upon his own revolting business! Hope returned to the bosom of the poor young man: he felt that he might yet be saved!

But – oh, horror! on what topic had the conversation turned? Those men were rejoicing in their own infernal inventions to render murder unsuspected. The object of the tub of water, and the hooks and cords upon the ceiling, were now explained. The unsuspecting individual who passed the door of that accursed dwelling by night was set upon by the murderers, dragged into the house, gagged, and suspended by his feet to these hooks, while his head hung downwards in the water. And thus he delivered up his last breath; and the wretches kept him there until decomposi-

tion commenced, that the corpse might not appear too fresh to the surgeon to whom it was to be sold!

Merciful heavens; could such things be? could atrocities of so appalling a nature be perpetrated in a great city, protected by thousands of a well-paid police? Could the voice of murder – murder effected with so much safety, cry up to heaven for vengeance through the atmosphere of London?

At length the three men went out, as before described; and Markham felt an immense weight suddenly lifted from off his mind.

Before the Resurrection Man set out upon his excursion with the Cracksman and the Buffer, he had whispered these words to the Mummy: 'While I'm gone, you can clean out the swell's pockets in the back room. He has got about four or five hundred pounds about him – so mind and take care. When you've searched his pockets, strip him, and look at his skull. I'm afraid I've fractured it, for my life-preserver came down precious heavy upon him; and he never spoke a word. If there's the wound, I must bury him to-morrow in the cellar: if not, wash him clean, and I know where to dispose of him.'

It was in obedience to these instructions that the Mummy took a candle in her hand, and proceeded to the back-room, as soon as her son and his two companions had left the house.

The horrible old woman was not afraid of the dead: her husband had been a resurrection man, and her only son followed the same business, – she was therefore too familiar with the sight of death in all its most fearful as well as its most interesting shapes to be alarmed at it. The revolting spectacle of a corpse putrid with decomposition produced no more impression upon her than the pale and beautiful remains of any lovely girl whom death had called early to the tomb, and whose form was snatched from its silent couch beneath the sod ere the finger of decay had begun its ravages. That hideous old woman considered corpses an article of commerce, and handled her wares as a trader does his merchandize. She cared no more for the sickly and fetid odour which they sent forth, than the tanner does for the smell of the tan-yard, or the scourer for the fumes of his bleaching-liquid.

The Mummy entered the back-room, holding a candle in her hand.

Markham started forward, and caught her by the wrist.

She uttered a sort of growl of savage disappointment, but gave no sign of alarm.

'Vile wretch!' exclaimed Richard; 'God has at length sent me to discover and expose your crimes!'

'Don't do me any harm – don't hurt me,' said the old woman; 'and I will do any thing you want of me.'

'Answer me,' cried Markham: 'that corpse in the other room – '

'Murdered by my son,' replied the hag.

'And the clothes? where are the clothes? They may contain some papers which may throw a light upon the name and residence of your victim.'

'Follow me – I will show you.'

The old woman turned and walked slowly out of the room. Markham went after her; for he thought that if he could discover who the unfortunate person was that had met his death in that accursed dwelling, he might be enabled to relieve his family at least from the horrors of suspense, although he should be the bearer of fatal news indeed.

The Mummy opened the door of a cupboard formed beneath the staircase, and holding forward the light, pointed to some clothes which hung upon a nail inside.

'There – take them yourself if you want them,' said the old woman; 'I won't touch them.'

With these words she drew back, but still held the candle in such a way as to throw the light into the closet.

Markham stepped forward to reach the clothes, and, in extending his hand to take them from the peg, he advanced one of his feet upon the floor of the closet.

A trap-door instantly gave way beneath his foot: he lost his balance, and fell precipitately into a subterranean excavation.

The trap-door, which moved with a spring, closed by itself above his head, and he heard the triumphant cackling laugh of the old hag, as she fastened it with a large iron bolt.

The Mummy then went and seated herself by the corpse in the front room; and, while she rocked backwards and forwards in her chair, she crooned the following song: –

The Body-Snatcher's Song

In the churchyard the body is laid,
There they inter the beautiful maid:
  'Earth to earth' is the solemn sound!
Over the sod where their daughter sleeps,
The father prays, and the mother weeps:
  'Ashes to ashes' echoes around!

Come with the axe, and come with the spade;
Come where the beautiful virgin's laid:
  Earth from earth must we take back now!
The sod is damp, and the grave is cold:
Lay the white corpse on the dark black mould,
  That the pale moonbeam may kiss its brow!

Throw back the earth, and heap up the clay;
This cold white corpse we will bear away,
  Now that the moonlight waxes dim;
For the student doth his knife prepare
To hack all over this form so fair,
  And sever the virgin limb from limb!

At morn the mother will come to pray
Over the grave where her child she lay,
  And freshest flowers thereon will spread:
And on that spot will she kneel and weep,
Nor dream that we have disturbed the sleep
  Of her who lay in that narrow bed.

We must leave the Mummy singing her horrible staves, and accompany the body-snatchers in their proceedings at Shoreditch Church.

THE STRING OF PEARLS

The Strange Customer at Sweeney Todd's

Before Fleet-street had reached its present importance, and when George the Third was young, and the two figures who used to strike the chimes at old St. Dunstan's church were in all their glory – being a great impediment to errand-boys on their progress, and a matter of gaping curiosity to country people – there stood close to the sacred edifice a small barber's shop, which was kept by a man of the name of Sweeney Todd.

How it was that he came by the name of Sweeney, as a Christian appellation, we are at a loss to conceive, but such was his name, as might be seen in extremely corpulent yellow letters over his shop window, by any who chose there to look for it.

Barbers by that time in Fleet-street had not become fashionable, and no more dreamt of calling themselves artists than of taking the tower by storm; moreover they were not, as they are now, constantly slaughtering fine fat bears, and yet, somehow people had hair on their heads just the same as they have at present, without the aid of that unctuous auxiliary. Moreover, Sweeney Todd, in common with those really primitive sort of times, did not think it at all necessary to have any waxen effigies of humanity in his window. There was no languishing young lady looking over the left shoulder in order that a profusion of auburn tresses might repose upon her lily neck, and great conquerors and great statesmen were not then, as they are now, held up to public ridicule with dabs of rouge upon their cheeks, a quantity of gunpowder scattered in for beard, and some bristles sticking on end for eyebrows.

No. Sweeney Todd was a barber of the old school, and he never thought of glorifying himself on account of any extraneous circumstance. If he had lived in Henry the Eighth's palace, it would be all the same as Henry the Eighth's dog-kennel, and he would scarcely have believed human nature to be so green as to pay an extra sixpence to be shaven and shorn in any particular locality.

A long pole painted white, with a red stripe curling spirally round it, projected into the street from his doorway, and on one of the pains of glass in his window, was presented the following couplet:—

> Easy shaving for a penny,
> As good as you will find any.

We do not put these lines forth as a specimen of the poetry of the age; they may have been the production of some young Templar; but if they were a little wanting in poetic fire, that was amply made up by the clear and precise manner in which they set forth what they intended.

The barber himself, was a long, low-jointed, ill-put-together sort of fellow, with an immense mouth, and such huge hands and feet, that he was, in his way, quite a natural curiosity; and, what was more wonderful, considering his trade, there never was seen such a head of hair as Sweeney Todd's. We know not what to compare it to; probably it came nearest to what one might suppose to be the appearance of a thick-set hedge, in which a quantity of small wire had got entangled. In truth, it was a most terrific head of hair; and as Sweeney Todd kept all his combs in it – some people said his scissors likewise – when he put his head out of the shop-door to see what sort of weather it was, he might have been mistaken for an Indian warrior with a very remarkable head-dress.

He had a short disagreeable kind of unmirthful laugh, which came in at all sorts of odd times when nobody else saw anything to laugh at at all, and which sometimes made people start again, especially when they were being shaved, and Sweeney Todd would stop short in that operation to indulge in one of those cachinatory effusions. It was evident that the remembrance of some very strange and out-of-the-way joke must occasionally flit across him, and then he gave his hyena-like laugh, but it was so short, so sudden, striking upon the ear for a moment, and then gone, that people have been known to look up to the ceiling, and on the floor, and all round them, to know from whence it had come, scarcely supposing it possible that it proceeded from mortal lips.

Mr. Todd squinted a little, to add to his charms; and so we think that by this time the reader may, in his mind's eye, see the individual whom we wish to present to him. Some thought him a careless enough, harmless fellow, with not much sense in him, and at times they almost considered he was a little cracked; but there were others who shook their heads when they spoke of him; and while they could say nothing to his prejudice, except that they certainly considered he was odd, yet, when they came to consider what a great crime and misdemeanour it really is in this world, to be odd, we shall not be surprised at the ill-odour in which Sweeney Todd was held.

But for all that he did a most thriving business, and was considered by his neighbours to be a very well-to-do sort of man, and decidedly, in city phraseology, warm.

It was so handy for the young students in the Temple to pop over to Sweeney Todd's to get their chins new rasped; so that from morning to night he drove a good business, and was evidently a thriving man.

There was only one thing that seemed in any way to detract from the great prudence of Sweeney Todd's character, and that was that he rented a large house, of which he occupied nothing but the shop and parlour, leaving the upper part entirely useless, and obstinately refusing to let it on any terms whatever.

are not many passengers in the streets, and Sweeney Todd is sitting in his shop looking keenly in the face of a boy, who stands in an attitude of trembling subjection before him.

'You will remember,' said Sweeney Todd, and he gave his countenance a most horrible twist as he spoke, 'you will remember Tobias Ragg, that you are now my apprentice, that you have of me had board, washing, and lodging, with the exception that you don't sleep here, that you take your meals at home, and that your mother, Mrs. Ragg, does your

Such was the state of things, A.D. 1785, as regarded Sweeney Todd.

The day is drawing to a close, and a small drizzling kind of rain is falling, so that there

washing, which she may very well do, being a laundress in the Temple, and making no end of money; as for lodging, you lodge here, you know, very comfortably in the shop all day.

Now, are you not a happy dog?'

'Yes, sir,' said the boy timidly.

'You will acquire a first-rate profession, quite as good as the law, which your mother tells me she would have put you to, only that a little weakness of the head-piece unqualified you. And now, Tobias, listen to me, and treasure up every word I say.'

'Yes, sir.'

'I'll cut your throat from ear to ear, if you repeat one word of what passes in this shop, or dare to make any supposition, or draw any conclusion from anything you may see, or hear, or fancy you see or hear. Now you understand me, – I'll cut your throat from ear to ear, – do you understand me?'

'Yes, sir, I won't say nothing. I wish, sir, as I may be made into veal pies at Lovett's in Bell-yard if I as much as says a vord.'

Sweeney Todd rose from his seat; and opening his huge mouth, he looked at the boy for a minute or two in silence, as if he fully intended swallowing him, but had not quite made up his mind where to begin.

'Very good,' at length he said, 'I am satisfied, I am quite satisfied; and mark me – the shop, and the shop only, is your place.'

'Yes, sir.'

'And if any customer gives you a penny, you can keep it, so that if you get enough of them you will become a rich man; only I will take care of them for you, and when I think you want them I will let you have them. Run out and see what's o'clock by St. Dunstan's.'

There was a small crowd collected opposite the church, for the figures were about to strike three-quarters past six; and among that crowd was one man who gazed with as much curiosity as anybody at the exhibition.

'Now for it!' he said, 'they are going to begin; well, that is ingenious. Look at the fellow lifting up his club and down it comes bang upon the old bell.'

The three-quarters were struck by the figures; and then the people who had loitered to see it done, many of whom had day by day looked at the same exhibition for years past, walked away, with the exception of the man who seemed so deeply interested.

He remained, and crouching at his feet was a noble-looking dog, who looked likewise up at the figures; and who, observing his master's attention to be closely fixed upon them, endeavoured to show as great an appearance of interest as he possibly could.

'What do you think of that, Hector?' said the man.

The dog gave a short low whine, and then his master proceeded, –

'There is a barber's shop opposite, so before I go any farther, as I have got to see the ladies, although it's on a very melancholy errand, for I have got to tell them that poor Mark Ingestrie is no more, and Heaven knows what poor Johanna will say – I think I should know her by his description of her, poor fellow! It grieves me to think how he used to talk about her in the long night-watches, when all was still, and not a breath of air touched a curl upon his cheek. I could almost think I saw her sometimes, as he used to tell me of her soft beaming eyes, her little gentle pouting lips, and the dimples that played about her mouth. Well, well, it's of no use grieving; he is dead and gone, poor fellow, and the salt water washes over as brave a heart as ever beat. His sweetheart, Johanna, though, shall have the string of pearls for all that; and if she cannot be Mark Ingestrie's wife in this world, she shall be rich and happy, poor young thing, while she stays in it, that is to say as happy as she can be; and she must just look forward to meeting him aloft, where there are no squalls or tempests. – And so I'll go and get shaved at once.'

He crossed the road towards Sweeney Todd's shop, and, stepping down the low doorway, he stood face to face with the odd-looking barber.

The dog gave a low growl and sniffed the air.

'Why Hector,' said his master, what's the matter? Down sir, down!'

'I have a mortal fear of dogs,' said Sweeney Todd. 'Would you mind him, sir, sitting outside the door and waiting for you, if it's all the same? Only look at him, he is going to fly at me!'

'Then you are the first person he ever touched without provocation,' said the man; 'but I suppose he don't like your looks, and I must confess I ain't much surprised at that.

I have seen a few rum-looking guys in my time, but hang me if ever I saw such a figure-head as yours. What the devil noise was that?'

'It was only me,' said Sweeney Todd; 'I laughed.'

'Laughed! do you call that a laugh? I suppose you caught it of somebody who died of it. If that's your way of laughing, I beg you won't do it any more.'

'Stop the dog! stop the dog! I can't have dogs running into my back parlour.'

'Here, Hector, here!' cried his master; 'get out!'

Most unwillingly the dog left the shop, and crouched down close to the outer door, which the barber took care to close, muttering something about a draught of air coming in, and then, turning to the apprentice boy, who was screwed up in a corner, he said, –

'Tobias, my lad, go to Leadenhall-street, and bring a small bag of the thick biscuits from Mr. Peterson's; say they are for me. Now, sir, I suppose you want to be shaved, and it is well you have come here, for there ain't a shaving-shop, although I say it, in the city of London that ever thinks of polishing anybody off as I do.'

'I tell you what it is, master barber: if you come that laugh again, I will get up and go. I don't like it, and there is an end of it.'

'Very good,' said Sweeney Todd, as he mixed up a lather. 'Who are you? where did you come from? and where are you going?'

'That's cool, at all events. Damn it! what do you mean by putting the brush in my mouth? Now, don't laugh, and since you are so fond of asking questions, just answer me one.'

'Oh, yes, of course: what is it, sir?'

'Do you know a Mr. Oakley, who lives somewhere in London, and is a spectacle-maker?'

'Yes, to be sure I do – John Oakley, the spectacle-maker, in Fore-street, and he has got a daughter named Johanna, that the young bloods call the Flower of Fore-street.'

'Ah, poor thing! do they? Now, confound you! what are you laughing at now? What do you mean by it?'

'Didn't you say, "Ah, poor thing?" Just turn your head a little to one side; that will do. You have been to sea, sir?'

'Yes, I have, and have only now lately come up the river from an Indian voyage.'

'Indeed! where can my strop be? I had it this minute. I must have laid it down somewhere. What an odd thing that I can't see it! It's very extraordinary; what can have become of it? Oh, I recollect, I took it into the parlour. Sit still, sir, I shall not be gone a moment; sit still, sir, if you please. By the by, you can amuse yourself with the *Courier*, sir, for a moment.'

Sweeney Todd walked into the back parlour and closed the door.

There was a strange sound suddenly, compounded of a rushing noise and then a heavy blow, immediately after which Sweeney Todd emerged from his parlour, and folding his arms, he looked upon *the vacant chair* where his customer had been seated, but the customer was *gone*, leaving not the slightest trace of his presence behind except his hat, and that Sweeney Todd immediately seized and thrust into a cupboard that was at one corner of the shop.

'What's that?' he said, 'what's that? I thought I heard a noise.'

'If you please, sir, I have forgot the money, and have run all the way back from St. Paul's churchyard.'

In two strides Todd reached him, and clutching him by the arm he dragged him into the farther corner of the shop, and then he stood opposite to him, glaring him full in the face with such a demoniac expression that the boy was frightfully terrified.

'Speak!' cried Todd, 'speak! and speak the truth, or your last hour has come. How long were you peeping through the door before you came in?'

'Peeping, sir?'

'Yes, peeping; don't repeat my words, but answer me at once you will find it better for you in the end.'

'I wasn't peeping, sir, at all.'

Sweeney Todd drew a long breath as he then said, in a strange, shrieking sort of manner, which he intended, no doubt, should be jocose, –

'Well, well, very well; if you did peep, what then? it's no matter; I only wanted to know, that's all; it was quite a joke, wasn't it – quite funny, though rather odd, eh? Why don't you laugh, you dog? Come, now, there is no harm done. Tell me what you thought about it at once, and we will be merry over it – very merry.'

'I don't know what you mean, sir,' said the boy, who was quite as much alarmed at Mr. Todd's mirth as he was at his anger. 'I don't know what you mean, sir; I only just come back because I hadn't any money to pay for the biscuits at Peterson's.'

'I mean nothing at all,' said Todd, suddenly turning upon his heel; 'what's that scratching at the door?'

Tobias opened the shop-door, and there stood the dog, who looked wistfully round the place, and then gave a howl which seriously alarmed the barber.

'It's the gentleman's dog, sir,' said Tobias, 'its the gentleman's dog, sir, that was looking at old St. Dunstan's clock, and came in here to be shaved, It's funny, ain't it, sir, that the dog didn't go away with his master?'

'Why don't you laugh if it's funny? Turn out the dog, Tobias; we'll have no dogs here; I hate the sight of them; turn him out – turn him out.'

'I would, sir, in a minute; but I'm afraid he wouldn't let me, somehow. Only look, sir – look; see what he is at now! did you ever see such a violent fellow, sir? why he will have down the cupboard door.'

'Stop him – stop him! the devil is in the animal! stop him I say!'

The dog was certainly getting the door open, when Sweeney Todd rushed forward to stop him! but that he was soon admonished of the danger of doing, for the dog gave him a grip of the leg, which made him give such a howl, that he precipitately retreated, and left the animal to do its pleasure. This consisted in forcing open the cupboard door, and seizing upon the hat which Sweeney Todd had thrust therein, and dashing out of the shop with it in triumph.

'The devil's in the beast,' muttered Todd, 'he's off! Tobias, you said you saw the man who owned that fiend of a cur looking at St. Dunstan's church.'

'Yes, sir, I did see him there. If you recollect, you sent me to see the time, and the figures were just going to strike three quarters past six; and before I came away, I heard him say that Mark Ingestrie was dead, and Johanna should have the string of pearls. Then I came in, and then, if you recollect, sir, he came in, and the odd thing, you know, to me, sir, is that he didn't take his dog with him, because you know, sir – '

'Because what?' shouted Todd.

'Because people generally do take their dogs with them, you know, sir; and may I be made into one of Lovett's pies, if I don't – '

'Hush some one comes; it's old Mr. Grant, from the Temple. How do you do, Mr. Grant? glad to see you looking so well, sir. It does one's heart good to see a gentleman of your years looking so fresh and hearty. Sit down, sir; a little this way, if you please. Shaved, I suppose?'

'Yes, Todd, yes. Any news?'

'No, sir, nothing stirring. Everything very quiet, sir, except the high wind. They say it blew the king's hat off yesterday, sir, and he borrowed Lord North's. Trade is dull too, sir. I suppose people won't come out to be cleaned and dressed in a mizling rain. We haven't had anybody in the shop for an hour and a half.'

'Lor' sir,' said Tobias, 'you forget the seafaring gentleman with the dog, you know, sir.'

'Ah! so I do,' said Todd. 'He went away, and I saw him get into some disturbance, I think, just at the corner of the market.'

'I wonder I didn't meet him, sir,' said Tobias, 'for I came that way; and then it's so very odd leaving his dog behind him.'

'Yes, very,' said Todd. 'Will you excuse me a moment, Mr. Grant? Tobias, my lad, I just want you to lend me a hand in the parlour.'

Tobias followed Todd very unsuspectingly into the parlour; but when they got there and the door was closed, the barber sprang upon him like an enraged tiger, and, grappling him by the throat, he gave his head such a succession of knocks against the wainscot, that Mr. Grant must have thought that some carpenter was at work. Then he tore a handful of his hair out, after which he twisted him round, and dealt him such a kick, that he was flung sprawling into a corner of the room, and then, without a word, the barber walked out again to his customer, and bolted his parlour door on the outside, leaving Tobias to digest the usage he had received at his leisure, and in the best way he could.

When he came back to Mr. Grant, he apologised for keeping him waiting, by saying, –

'It became necessary, sir, to teach my new apprentice a little bit of his business. I have left him studying it now. There is nothing like teaching young folks at once.'

'Ah!' said Mr. Grant, with a sigh, 'I know what it is to let young folks grow wild; for although I have neither chick nor child of my own, I had a sister's son to look to – a handsome, wild, harum-scarum sort of fellow, as like me as one pea is like another. I tried to make a lawyer of him, but it wouldn't do, and it's now more than two years ago he left me altogether; and yet there were some good traits about Mark.'

'Mark, sir! Did you say Mark?'

'Yes, that was his name, Mark Ingestrie. God knows what's become of him.'

'Oh!' said Sweeney Todd; and he went on lathering the chin of Mr. Grant.

*

There is a cellar of vast extent, and of dim and sepulchral aspect – some rough red tiles are laid upon the floor, and pieces of flint and large jagged stones have been hammered into the earthen walls to strengthen them; while here and there rough huge pillars made by beams of timber rise perpendicularly from the floor, and prop large flat pieces of wood against the ceiling, to support it. Here and there gleaming lights seem to be peeping out from furnaces, and there is a strange hissing, simmering sound going on, while the whole air is impregnated with a rich and savoury vapour. This is Lovett's pie manufactory beneath the pavement of Bell-yard, and at this time a night-batch of some thousands is being made for the purpose of being sent by carts the first thing in the morning all over the suburbs of London. By the earliest dawn of day a crowd of itinerant hawkers of pies would make their appearance, carrying off a large quantity to regular customers who had them daily, and no more thought of being without them, than of forbidding the milkman or the baker to call at their residences. It will be seen and understood, therefore, that the retail part of Mrs.

Lovett's business, which took place principally between the hours of twelve and one, was by no means the most important or profitable portion of a concern which was really of immense magnitude, and which brought in a large yearly income. To stand in the cellar when this immense manufacture of what, at first sight, would appear such a trivial article was carried on, and to look about as far as the eye could reach, was by no means to have a sufficient idea of the extent of the place; for there were as many doors in different directions and singular low-arched entrances to different vaults, which all appeared as black as midnight, that one might almost suppose the inhabitants of all the surrounding neighbourhood had, by common consent given up their cellars to Lovett's pie factory. There is but one miserable light, except the occasional fitful glare that comes from the ovens where the pies are stewing, hissing, and spluttering in their own luscious gravy. There is but one man, too, throughout all the place, and he is sitting on a low three-legged stool in one corner, with his head resting upon his hands, and gently rocking to and fro, as he utters scarcely audible moans. He is but lightly clad; in fact, he seems to have but little on him except a shirt and a pair of loose canvas trousers. The sleeves of the former are turned up beyond his elbows, and on his head he has a white night-cap. It seems astonishing that such a man, even with the assistance of Mrs. Lovett, could make so many pies as required in a day; but then, system does wonders, and in those cellars there are various mechanical contrivances for kneading the dough, chopping up the meat, &c., which greatly reduced the labour. But what a miserable object is that man – what a sad and soul-striken wretch he looks! His face is pale and haggard, his eyes deeply sunken; and, as he removes his hands from before his visage, and looks about him, a more perfect picture of horror could not have been found.

'I must leave to-night,' he said, in course accents – 'I must leave to-night. I know too much – my brain is full of horrors. I have not slept now for five nights, nor dare I eat anything but the raw flour. I will leave to-night if they do not watch me too closely. Oh! if I could but get into the streets – if I could but once again breathe the fresh air! Hush! what's that? I thought I heard a noise.'

He rose, and stood trembling and listening; but all was still, save the simmering and hissing of the pies, and then he resumed his seat with a deep sigh.

'All the doors fastened upon me,' he said, 'what can it mean? It's very horrible, and my heart dies within me. Six weeks only have I been here – only six weeks. I was starving before I came, Alas, alas! how much better to have starved! I should have been dead before now, and spared all this agony.'

'Skinner!' cried a voice, and it was a female one – 'Skinner, how long will the ovens be?'

'A quarter of an hour – a quarter of an hour, Mrs. Lovett. God help me!'

'What is that you say?'

'I said, God help me! – surely a man may say that without offence.'

A door slammed shut, and the miserable man was alone again.

'How strangely,' he said, 'on this night my thoughts go back to early days, and to what I once was. The pleasant scenes of my youth recur to me. I see again the ivy-mantled porch, and the pleasant village green. I hear again the merry ringing laughter of my playmates, and there, in my mind's eye, appears to me the bubbling stream, and the ancient mill, the old mansion-house, with its tall turrets, and its air of silent grandeur. I hear the music of the birds, and the winds making rough melody among the trees. 'Tis very strange that all those sights and sounds should come back to me at such a time as this, as if just to remind me what a wretch I am.'

He was silent for a few moments, during which he trembled with emotion; then he spoke again, saying –

'Thus the forms of those whom I once knew, and many of whom have gone already to the silent tomb, appear to come thronging round me. They bend their eyes momentarily upon me, and, with settled expressions, show

acutely the sympathy they feel for me. I see her, too, who first, in my bosom, lit up the flame of soft affection. I see her gliding past me like the dim vision of a dream, indistinct, but beautiful; no more than a shadow – and yet to me most palpable. What am I now – what am I now?'

He resumed his former position, with his head resting upon his hands; he rocked himself slowly to and fro, uttering those moans of a tortured spirit, which we have before noticed. But see, one of the small arch doors open in the gloom of those vaults, and a man, in a stooping posture, creeps in – a half-mask is upon his face, and he wears a cloak; but both his hands are at liberty. In one of them he carries a double-headed hammer, with a powerful handle, of about ten inches in length. He has probably come out of a darker place than the one into which he now so cautiously creeps, for he shades the light from his eyes, as if it were suddenly rather too much for him, and then he looks cautiously round the vault, until he sees the crouched-up figure of the man whose duty it is to attend the ovens. From that moment he looks at nothing else; but advances towards him, steadily and cautiously. It is evident that great secrecy is his object, for he is walking on his stocking soles only; and it is impossible to hear the slightest sounds of his footsteps. Nearer and nearer he comes, so slowly, and yet so surely, towards him, who still keeps up the low moaning sound, indicative of mental anguish. Now he is close to him, and he bends over him for a moment, with a look of fiendish malice. It is a look which, despite his mask, glances full from his eyes, and then grasping the hammer tightly, in both hands, he raises it slowly above his head, and gives it a swinging motion through the air. There is no knowing what induced the man that was crouching on the stool to rise at that moment; but he did so, and paced about with great quickness. A sudden shriek burst from his lips, as he beheld so terrific an apparition before him; but, before he could repeat the word, the hammer descended, crushing into his skull, and he fell lifeless, without a moan.

*

It wants five minutes to nine, and Mrs. Lovett's shop is filling with persons anxious to devour or to carry away one or more of the nine o'clock batch of savoury, delightful, gushing gravy pies.

Many of Mrs. Lovett's customers paid her in advance for the pies, in order that they might be quite sure of getting their orders fulfilled when the first batch should make its gracious appearance from the depths below.

'Well, Jiggs,' said one of the legal fraternity to another, 'how are you to-day, old fellow? What do you bring it in?'

'Oh! I aint very blooming. The fact is, the count and I, and a few others, made a night of it last evening; and somehow or another I don't think whiskey-and-water, half-and-half, and tripe, go well together.'

'I should wonder if they did.'

'And so I've come for a pie just to settle my stomach; you see I'm rather delicate.'

'Ah! you are just like me, young man, there,' said an elderly personage; 'I have a delicate stomach, and the slightest thing disagrees with me. A mere idea will make me quite ill.'

'Will it, really?'

'Yes; and my wife, she – '

'Oh, bother your wife! It's only five minutes to nine, don't you see? What a crowd there is, to be sure. Mrs. Lovett, you charmer, I hope you have ordered enough pies to be made to-night? You see what a lot of customers you have.'

'Oh, there will be plenty.'

'That's right. I say, don't push so; you'll be in time, I tell you; don't be pushing and driving in that sort of way – I've got ribs.'

'And so have I. Last night I didn't get a pie at all, and my old woman is in a certain condition, you see, gentlemen, and won't fancy anything but one of Lovett's veal pies; so I've come all the way from Newington to get one for – '

'Hold your row, will you? and don't push.'

'For to have the child marked with a pie on its – '

'Behind there, I say; don't be pushing a fellow as if it were half price at a theatre.'

Each moment added some new comers to the throng, and at last any strangers who had known nothing of the attractions of Mrs.

Lovett's pie-shop and had walked down Bell-yard, would have been astonished at the throng of persons there assembled – a throng that was each moment increasing in density, and becoming more and more urgent and clamorous.

*

One, two, three, four, five, six, seven, eight, nine! Yes it is nine at last. It strikes by old St. Dunstan's church clock, and in weaker strains the chronometical machine at the pie-shop echoes the sound. What excitement there is to get at the pies when they shall come! Mrs. Lovett lets down the square moveable platform that goes on pulleys in the cellar; some machinery, which only requires a handle to be turned, brings up a hundred pies in a tray. These are eagerly seized by parties who have previously paid, and such a smacking of lips ensues as never was known.

Down goes the platform for the next hundred, and a gentlemanly man says –

'Let me work the handle, Mrs. Lovett, if you please; it's too much for you I'm sure.'

'Sir, you are very kind, but I never allow anybody on this side of the counter but my own people, sir. I can turn the handle myself, sir, if you please, with the assistance of this girl. Keep your distance, sir, nobody wants your help.'

'But my dear madam, only consider your delicacy. Really you ought not to be permitted to work away like a negro slave at a winch handle. Really you ought not.'

The man who spoke thus obligingly to Mrs. Lovett, was tall and stout, and the lawyers clerks repressed the ire they otherwise would probably have given utterance to at thus finding any one quizzing their charming Mrs. Lovett.

'Sir, I tell you again that I don't want your help; keep your distance, sir, if you please.'

'Now don't get angry, fair one,' said the man. 'You don't know but I might have made you an offer before I left the shop.'

'Sir,' said Mrs. Lovett, drawing herself up and striking terror into the hearts of the limbs of the law. 'Sir! What do you want? Say what you want, and be served, sir, and then go. Do you want a pie, sir?'

'A pie? Oh, dear no, I don't want a pie. I would not eat one of the nasty things on any account. Pah!' Here the man spat on the floor. 'Oh, dear, don't ask me to eat any of your pies.'

'Shame, shame,' said several of the lawyers clerks.

'Will any gentleman who thinks it a shame, be so good as to step forward and say so a little closer?'

Everybody shrunk back upon this, instead of accepting the challenge, and Mrs. Lovett soon saw that she must, despite all the legal chivalry by which she was surrounded, fight her battles herself. With a look of vehement anger, she cried –

'Beware, sir, I am not to be trifled with. If you carry your jokes too far, you will wish that you had not found your way, sir, into this shop.'

'That, madam,' said the tall stout man, 'is not surely possible, when I have the beauty of a Mrs. Lovett to gaze upon, and render the place so exquisitely attractive; but if you will not permit me to have the pleasure of helping you up with the next batch of pies, which, after all, you may find heavier than you expect, I must leave you to do it yourself.'

'So that I am not troubled any longer by you, sir, at all,' said Mrs. Lovett, 'I don't care how heavy the next batch of pies may happen to be, sir.'

'Very good, madam.'

'Upon my word,' said a small boy, giving the side of his face a violent rub with the hope of finding the ghost of a whisker there, 'it's really too bad.'

'Ah, who's that? Let me get at him!'

'Oh, no, no, I – mean – that it's too bad of Mrs. Lovett, my dear sir. Oh, don't.'

'Oh, very good; I am satisfied. Now, madam, you see that even your dear friends here, from Lincoln's Inn – Are you from the Inn, small boy?'

'Yes, sir, if you please.'

'Very good. As I was saying, Mrs. Lovett, you now must of necessity perceive, that even your friends from the Inn, feel that your conduct is really too bad, madam.'

Mrs. Lovett was upon this so dreadfully angry, that she disdained any reply to the tall stout man, but at once she applied herself to the windlass, which worked up the little platform, upon which a whole tray of a hundred pies was wont to come up, and began to turn it with what might be called a vengeance.

How very strange it was – surely the words of the tall stout impertinent stranger were prophetic, for never before had Mrs. Lovett found what a job it was to work that handle, as upon that night. The axle creaked, and the cords and pulleys strained and wheezed, but she was a determined woman, and she worked away at it.

'I told you so, my dear madam,' said the stranger; 'it is more evidently than you can do.'

'Peace, sir.'

'I am done; work away ma'am, only don't say afterwards that I did not offer to help you, that's all.'

Indignation was swelling at the heart of Mrs Lovett, but she felt that if she wasted her breath upon the impertinent stranger, she should have none for the windlass; so setting her teeth, she fagged at it with a strength and a will that if she had not been in a right royal passion, she could not have brought to bear upon it on any account.

There was quite an awful stillness in the shop. All eyes were bent upon Mrs. Lovett, and the cavity through which the next batch of those delicious pies were coming. Those who had the good fortune to get one of the first lot, had only their appetites heightened by the luxurious feast they had partaken of, while those who had had as yet none, actually licked their lips, and snuffed up the delightful aroma from the remains of the first batch.

'Two for me, Mrs. Lovett,' cried a voice. 'One veal for me. Three porks – one pork.'

The voices grew fast and furious.

'Silence!' cried the tall stout man. 'I will engage that everybody shall be fully satisfied, and no one shall leave here without a thorough conviction that his wants in pies has been more than attended to.'

The platform could be made to stop at any stage of its upward progress, by means of a ratchet wheel and a catch, and now Mrs. Lovett paused to take breath. She attributed the unusual difficulty in working the machinery to her own weakness, contingent upon her recent immersion in the Thames.

'Sir,' she said between her clenched teeth, addressing the man who was such an eye-sore to her in the shop. 'Sir, I don't know who you are, but I hope to be able to show you when I have served these gentlemen, that even I am not to be insulted with impunity.'

'Anything you please, madam,' he replied, 'in a small way, only don't exert yourself too much.'

Mrs. Lovett flew to the windlass again, and from the manner in which she now worked at it, it was quite clear that when she had her hands free from that job, she fully intended to make good her threats against the tall stout man. The young beardless scions of the law, trembled at the idea of what might happen.

And now the tops of the pies appeared. Then they saw the rim of the large tray upon which they were, and then just as the platform itself was level with the floor of the shop, up flew tray and pies, as if something had exploded beneath them, and a tall slim man sprung upon the counter. It was the cook, who from the cellars beneath, had laid himself as flat as he could beneath the tray of pies, and so had been worked up to the shop by Mrs. Lovett!

'Gentlemen,' he cried, 'I am Mrs. Lovett's cook. The pies are made of *human flesh!*'

*

About twenty clerks rushed into Bell Yard, and there and then, to the intense surprise of the passers-by, became intensely sick. The cook, with one spring, cleared the counter, and alighted amongst the customers, and with another spring, the tall impertinent man, who had made many remarks to Mrs. Lovett of an aggravating tendency, cleared the counter likewise in the other direction, and, alighting close to Mrs. Lovett, he cried –

'Madam, you are my prisoner!'

For a moment, and only for a moment, the great – the cunning, and the redoubtable Mrs. Lovett, lost her self-possession, and, staggering back, she lurched heavily against the glass-case next to the wall, immediately behind the counter. It was only for a moment, though, that such an effect was produced upon Mrs. Lovett; and then, with a spring like an enraged tigress, she caught up a knife that was used for slipping under the pies and getting them cleanly out of the little tins, and rushed upon the tall stranger.

Yes, she rushed upon him; but for once in a way, even Mrs. Lovett had met with her match. With a dexterity, that only long practice in dealings with the more desperate portion of human nature could have taught him, the tall man closed with her, and had the knife out of her hand in a moment. He at once threw it right through the window into Bell Yard, and then, holding Mrs. Lovett in his arms, he said –

'My dear madam, you only distress yourself for nothing; all resistance is perfectly useless. Either I must take you prisoner, or you me, and I decidedly incline to the former alternative.'

The knife that had been thrown through the window was not without its object, for in a moment afterwards Mr. Crotchet made his appearance in the shop.

'All right, Crotchet,' said he who had captured Mrs. Lovett; 'first clap the bracelets on this lady.'

'Here yer is,' said Crotchet. 'Lor, mum! I had an eye on you months and months agone. How is you, mum, in yer *feelin's* this here nice evening? – Eh, mum?'

'A knife – a knife! Oh, for a knife!' cried Mrs. Lovett.

'Ex-actly, mum,' added Crotchet, as he with professional dexterity slipped the handcuffs on her wrists. 'Would you like one with a hivory handle, mum? or would anything more common do, mum?'

Mrs. Lovett fell to the floor, or rather she cast herself to it, and began voluntarily beating her head against the boards. They quickly lifted her up; and then the tall stranger turned to the cook, who, after leaping over the counter, had sat down upon a chair in a state of complete exhaustion, and he said –

'Do you know the way to Sir Richard's office, in Craven Street? He expects you there, I believe?'

'Yes, yes. But now that all is over, I feel very ill.'

'In that case, I will go with you, then. Crotchet, who have you got outside?'

'Only two of our pals, Muster Green; but it's all right, if so be as you leaves the lady to us.'

'Very well. The warrant is at Newgate, and the governor is expecting her instant arrival. You will get a coach at the corner of the yard, and be off with her at once.'

'All's right,' said Crotchet. 'I knowed as she'd be nabbed, and I had one all ready, you sees.'

'That was right, Crotchet. How amazingly quick everybody has left the shop. Why – why, what is all this?'

As the officer spoke, about half a dozen squares of glass in the shop window of the house were broken in, and a ringing shout from a dense mob that was rapidly collecting in the yard, came upon the ears of the officer. The two men whom Crotchet had mentioned, with difficulty pressed their way into the shop, and one of them cried –

'The people that were in the shop have spread the news all over the neighbourhood, and the place is getting jammed up with a mob, every one of which is mad, I think, for they talk of nothing but the tearing of Mrs. Lovett to pieces. They are pouring in from Fleet Street and Carey Street by hundreds at a time.'

VI. HEROINES

1. A GOOD DEATH

THE DAIRYMAN'S DAUGHTER

'She is a bright diamond, sir,' said the soldier, 'and will soon shine brighter than any diamond upon earth.'

We passed through lanes and fields, over hills and valleys, by open and retired paths, sometimes crossing over, and sometimes following the windings of a little brook, which gently murmured by the road side. Conversation beguiled the distance, and shortened the apparent time of our journey, till we were nearly arrived at the dairyman's cottage.

As we approached it, we became silent. Thoughts of death, eternity, and salvation, inspired by the sight of a house where a dying believer lay, filled my own mind, and, I doubt not, that of my companion also.

'No living object yet appeared, except the dairyman's dog, keeping a kind of mute watch at the door; for he did not, as formerly, bark at my approach. He seemed to partake so far of the feelings appropriate to the circumstances of the family, as not to wish to give a hasty or painful alarm. He came forward to the little wicket-gate, then looked back at the house-door, as if conscious there was sorrow within. It was as if he wanted to say, 'Tread softly over the threshold, as you enter the house of mourning; for my master's heart is full of grief.'

The soldier took my horse, and tied it up in a shed. A solemn serenity appeared to surround the whole place: it was only interrupted by the breezes passing through the large elm-trees, which stood near the house, and which my imagination indulged itself in thinking were plaintive sighs of sorrow. I gently opened the door; no one appeared, and all was still silent. The soldier followed; we came to the foot of the stairs.

'They are come,' said a voice which I knew to be the father's; 'they are come.'

He appeared at the top; I gave him my hand, and said nothing.

On entering the room above, I saw the aged mother and her son supporting the much-loved daughter and sister: the son's wife sat weeping in the window-seat, with a child on her lap; two or three persons attended in the room, to discharge any office which friendship or necessity might require.

I sat down by the bedside. The mother could not weep, but now and then sighed deeply, as she alternately looked at Elizabeth and at me. The big tear rolled down the brother's cheek, and testified an affectionate regard. The good old man stood at the foot of the bed, leaning upon the post, and unable to take his eyes off the child from whom he was so soon to part.

Elizabeth's eyes were closed, and as yet she perceived me not. But over the face, though pale, sunk, and hollow, the peace of God, which passeth all understanding, had cast a triumphant calm.

The soldier, after a short pause, silently reached out his Bible towards me, pointing with his finger at 1 Cor. xv. 55, 56, 57. I then broke silence by reading the passage: 'O death where is thy sting? O grave, where is thy victory? The sting of death is sin, and the strength of sin is the law. But thanks be to God which giveth us the victory through our Lord Jesus Christ.'

At the sound of these words her eye opened, and something like a ray of Divine light beamed on her countenance, as she said 'Victory! victory! through our Lord Jesus Christ.'

She relapsed again, taking no further notice of any one present.

'God be praised for the triumph of faith!' said I. 'Amen!' replied the soldier.

The dairyman's uplifted eye showed that the amen was in his heart, though his tongue failed to utter it.

A short struggling for breath took place in the dying young woman, which was soon over; and then I said to her,

'My dear friend, do you not feel that you are supported?'

'The Lord deals very gently with me,' she replied.

'Are not his promises now very precious to you?'

'They are all yea and amen in Christ Jesus.'

'Are you in much bodily pain?'

'So little, that I almost forget it.'

'How good the Lord is!'

'And how unworthy am I!'

'You are going to see him as he is.'

'I think – I hope – I believe that I am.'

She again fell into a short slumber.

Looking at her mother, I said, 'What a mercy to have a child so near heaven as yours is!'

'And what a mercy,' she replied, in broken accents, 'if her poor old mother might but follow her there! But, sir, it is so hard to part!'

'I hope, through grace, by faith, you will soon meet, to part no more: it will be but a little while.'

'Sir,' said the dairyman, 'that thought supports me, and the Lord's goodness makes me feel more reconciled than I was.'

'Father – mother,' said the reviving daughter, 'he is good to me – trust him, praise him evermore.'

'Sir,' added she, in a faint voice, 'I want to thank you for your kindness to me – I want to ask a favour; – you buried my sister – will you do the same for me?'

'All shall be as you wish, if God permit,' I replied.

'Thank you, sir, thank you; – I have another favour to ask – When I am gone, remember my father and mother. They are old, but I hope the good work is begun in their souls – My prayers are heard – Pray come and see them – I cannot speak much, but I want to speak for their sakes – Sir, remember them.'

The aged parents now sighed and sobbed aloud, uttering broken sentences, and gained some relief by such an expression of their feelings.

At length I said to Elizabeth, 'Do you experience any doubts or temptations on the subject of your eternal safety?'

'No sir: the Lord deals very gently with me, and gives me peace.'

'What are your views of the dark valley of death, now that you are passing through it?'

'It is *not* dark.'

'Why so?'

'My Lord is *there*, and he is my light and my salvation.'

'Have you any fears of more bodily suffering?'

'The Lord deals so gently with me, I can trust him.'

Something of a convulsion came on. When it was past, she said again and again,

'The Lord deals very gently with me. Lord, I am thine, save me – Blessed Jesus – precious Saviour – his blood cleanseth from all sin – Who shall separate? – His name is Wonderful – Thanks be to God – He giveth us the victory – I, even I, am saved – O grace, mercy, and wonder – Lord, receive my spirit! – Dear sir – dear father, mother, friends, I am going – but all is well, well, well –'

She relapsed again – We knelt down to prayer – The Lord was in the midst of us, and blessed us.

She did not again revive while I remained, nor ever speak any more words which could be understood. She slumbered for about ten hours, and at last sweetly fell asleep in the arms of that Lord who had dealt so gently with her.

I left the house an hour after she had ceased to speak. I pressed her hand as I was taking leave, and said, 'Christ is the resurrection and the life.' She gently returned the pressure, but could neither open her eyes nor utter a reply.

I never had witnessed a season so impressive as this before. It completely filled my imagination as I returned home.

'Farewell,' thought I, 'dear friend, till the morning of an eternal day shall renew our

BRADING.

E. Gover. sc

personal intercourse. Thou wast a brand plucked from the burning, that thou mightest become a star shining in the firmament of glory. I have seen thy light and thy good works, and will therefore glorify our Father which is in heaven. I have seen, in thy example, what it is to be a sinner freely saved by grace. I have learned from thee, as in a living mirror, *who* it is that begins, continues and ends the work of faith and love. Jesus is all in all: he will and shall be glorified. He won the crown, and alone deserves to wear it. May no one attempt to rob him of his glory! He saves, and saves to the uttermost. Farewell, dear sister in the Lord. Thy flesh and thy heart may fail; but God is the strength of thy heart, and shall be thy portion for ever.

*

Who can conceive or estimate the nature of that change which the soul of a believer must experience at the moment when, quitting its tabernacle of clay, it suddenly enters into the presence of God? If, even while 'we see through a glass darkly,' the views of Divine love and wisdom are so delightful to the eye of faith; what must be the glorious vision of God, when seen face to face! If it be so valued a privilege here on earth to enjoy the communion of saints, and to take sweet counsel together with our fellow travellers towards the heavenly kingdom; what shall we see and know when we finally 'come unto Mount Zion, and unto the city of the living God, the heavenly Jerusalem, and to the innumerable company of angels, to the general assembly and church of the first-born which are written in heaven, and to God the Judge of all, and to the spirits of just men made perfect, and to Jesus the Mediator of the new covenant?'

If, during the sighs and tears of a mortal pilgrimage, the consolations of the spirit are so precious, and the hope full of immortality is so animating to the soul; what heart can conceive, or what tongue utter its superior joys, when arrived at that state, where sighing and sorrow flee away, and the tears shall be wiped from every eye?

Such ideas were powerfully associated together in my imagination, as I travelled onward to the house where, in solemn preparation for the grave, lay the remains of the dairyman's daughter.

She had breathed her last shortly after the visit related in my former account. Permission was obtained, as before in the case of her sister, that I should perform the funeral service. Many pleasing yet melancholy thoughts were connected with the fulfilment of this task. I retraced the numerous and important conversations which I had held with her. But these could now no longer be maintained on earth. I reflected on the interesting and improving nature of *Christian* friendships, whether formed in palaces or in cottages; and felt thankful that I had so long enjoyed that privilege with the subject of this memorial. I then indulged a selfish sigh for a moment, on thinking that I could no longer hear the great truths of Christianity uttered by one who had drunk so deep of the waters of the river of life. But the rising murmur was checked by the animating thought: 'She is gone to eternal rest – could I wish her back again in this vale of tears?'

At that moment, the first sound of a tolling bell struck my ear. It proceeded from a village church in the valley directly beneath the ridge of a high hill, over which I had taken my way. It was Elizabeth's funeral knell.

The sound was solemn; and in ascending to the elevated spot over which I rode, it acquired a peculiar tone and character. Tolling at slow and regular intervals, (as was customary for a considerable time previous to the hour of burial,) the bell, as it were, proclaimed the blessedness of the dead who die in the Lord, and also the necessity of the living pondering these things, and laying them to heart. It seemed to say, 'Hear my warning voice, thou son of man. There is but a step between thee and death. Arise, prepare thine house, for thou shalt die, and not live.'

The scenery was in unison with that tranquil frame of mind which is most suitable for holy meditation. A rich and fruitful valley lay immediately beneath; it was adorned with corn-fields and pastures, through which a small river winded in a variety of directions, and many herds grazed upon its banks. A fine range of opposite hills, covered with grazing flocks, terminated with a bold sweep into the ocean, whose blue waves appeared at a distance beyond. Several villages, hamlets, and churches, were scattered in the valley. The noble mansions of the rich, and the lowly cottages of the poor, added their respective features to the landscape. The air was mild, and the declining sun occasioned a beautiful interchange of light and shade upon the sides of the hills. In the midst of this scene, the chief sound that arrested attention was the bell tolling for the funeral of the dairyman's daughter.

Do any of my readers inquire why I describe so minutely the circumstances of prospect and scenery which may be connected with the incidents I relate? My reply is, that the God of redemption is the God of creation likewise; and that we are taught in every part of the word of God, to unite the admiration of the beauties and wonders of nature to every other motive for devotion. When David considered the heavens, the work of God's fingers, the moon and the stars, which he has ordained, he was thereby led to the deepest humiliation of heart before his Maker. And when he viewed the sheep, and the oxen, and the beasts of the field, the fowl of the air, and the fish of the sea, he was constrained to cry out, 'O Lord, our Lord! how excellent is thy name in all the earth!'

2. IN DANGER

FATHERLESS FANNY

[*Fanny is abandoned as a child in rich clothing, with money for her upkeep.
She is left outside the school of the termagant Mrs Bridewell, who, when the money runs out, advertises her in the paper. Lord Ellencourt answers the advertisement, thinking 'Fanny', is his lost puppy; adopts Fanny, and falls in love with her.
In society life she is looked down on as an illegitimate child of unknown origin, while keeping suitors at bay with her moral purity. At this point Fanny has fallen in the hands of Lord Ballafyn, who*

imprisons her in his castle in Ireland.
Fanny has learnt that her mother died here.]

The rock was of considerable magnitude, and lofty craigs rose majestically from the solid mass that composed the base, and seemed to emulate the sky, for the clouds often rested on their summits, long after the god of day had driven them from the lower world. The ascent to this romantic promontory was made easy by a sort of natural staircase, which wound round the basement of the rock, and Fanny had soon the satisfaction of finding herself on a point so elevated, that she could see the winding coast for a considerable length of way, and on the distant waves, where the arm of the sea, that watered the shores, joined the parent ocean, she could distinguish vessels passing, their white sails glistening in the sun beam. On the other hand, a wild country with a few scattered cabins, presented a striking contrast to the richly wooded and well cultivated demesnes that skirted Ballafyn Castle, and bespoke the riches of its owner. As Fanny gazed at the dark battlements of that proud edifice, she heaved a sigh to the memory of her mother.

'Strange and unsearchable,' said she aloud, 'are the decrees of heaven, and frail mortals can only bow the head, and suffer beneath, the correcting hand of unerring wisdom. In that castle did my sainted mother breath her last sigh, and sink the victim of tyranny and oppression: and although bred an alien to every tender tie, and equally a stranger to those who would have loved, and those who would have persecuted her, the hapless off-spring of that martyred saint is now brought by force to the same spot where her mother suffered, to fall, perhaps, by the same cruelty!'

As Fanny spoke, she clasped her hands together, whilst tears of anguish chased each other down her cheek – 'On this rock,' continued she, looking around her, 'the spirit of my mother is said to walk; Oh, would to heaven that I might be permitted to behold it! Dear murdered saint! in pity listen to thy daughter's sighs; and if thou art still conscious of what is passing in this mortal vale, oh! deign to show thyself to her!'

The enthusiasm that had seized Fanny's mind, as fancy suggested the possibility of beholding the spirit of her mother, seemed to change her timid nature, and fortify her soul to meet the awful visitation she was wishing for, she cast her eyes around with an intrepid look, and seemed almost to believe that the being she apostrophised would really appear before her. No object of that description, however, met her view, and the hollow echoes of the caverns beneath her, alone answered to her voice.

The expanse of ocean – the blue ethereal vault of heaven – the grandeur of the surrounding scenery – her lonely unprotected and perilous situation, all combined to rise her soul to devotion's highest ecstacy. 'That hand,' said she, 'which shielded me through the difficulties attending my helpless and unprotected infancy, was my stay and support as I advanced towards womanhood, will still aid – will still protect me.' Oh disbelieving infidel, you, who boast of high intellectual powers, whose days are spent in contemning and ridiculing the laws of your Maker, how despicable do you appear when compared with the Christian in the hour of adversity. Few minds were more free from the influence of superstition than that of Fanny's, and at any other time or place her better judgment would reject the idea of the appearance of supernatural beings. But the discourse of Rose, the love which she bore to the memory of her persecuted mother, and her own wishes, made her in despite of reason more than cherish the idea. She now, heedless of the vicinity of Rose, began to apostrophise her mother in a louder strain, but was awakened from her delightful reverie, at last, by the loud vociferation of Rose, who, terrified at Fanny's long stay, had advanced nearer the rock, and catching the sound of the words uttered by Fanny, concluded she was conversing with some of the dreadful inhabitants of that awe-inspiring spot.

'Oh, Miss, for heaven's sake, come to me,' cried the girl, 'or I shall certainly die with terror!' – Fanny suddenly starting from her daydream which encouraged erroneous but fondly cherished thoughts – thoughts that her

reason, now resuming the empire over her mind, struggled hard to expel, and which her gentle bosom was but too well disposed again to adopt; however, she immediately descended the rock, and hastened to relieve the ill-founded fears of the frightened domestic. Rose was trembling like an aspin leaf when Fanny reached her; and it was with difficulty she persuaded her, that she had not seen nor conversed with any thing supernatural during her stay upon the haunted rock. By degrees, however, she was reconciled to the idea that had at first alarmed her, and was even brought at last, by Fanny's earnest entreaties, to promise that, if the next day was fine, she should again visit the scene that appeared to interest her so much. Their excursion was extended no farther, and Fanny, absorbed in thought, left her companion the delightful pleasure of speaking as much and upon whatever subject she pleased without contradiction, or breaking the thread of her narratives so as to give Rose a high idea of her condescension, and good nature. When they returned to the Castle, Fanny was shewn into the stately apartments she had occupied on her arrival the night before; but she entreated that she might be allowed to remain in her chamber, for she dreaded the idea of Lord Ballafyn's expected arrival, and thought, if she did not quit the precincts of her bedroom, she should at least have notice when he came, and not be liable to meet him unexpectedly.

The old woman indulged her in her request, and her meals were served to her in her chamber. The window of her closet was the favourite scene of her contemplation, for from thence she could see the distant rock, and she watched there after night fall, in spite of the remonstrances of Rose, in hopes of seeing the apparition.

The moon rose in full splendor about midnight, and reflected her brightness on the craggy summit of the rock, as well as on the undulating bosom of the restless ocean, whose waves dashed the adjacent shore. Fanny gazed for a length of time without seeing any object like the one she sought for, and she was retiring from the window to seek her pillow, when her attention was arrested by a sight that filled her bosom with an awe unfelt before that momentous period.

A tall slender figure seemed to rise suddenly from one of the projections of the mysterious rock, and standing on its summit spread out its arms towards the sea. The moon shone full upon the figure, and rendered it so distinctly visible, that Fanny could perceive the dark folds of the loose robe that enveloped it, waving occasionally to the breeze.

For awhile it seemed absorbed in contemplating the mighty waters. Then starting suddenly, as if called by some superior power, it dropped upon its knees, and raising its clasped hands to Heaven, it appeared preferring some earnest petition to the throne of mercy. Fanny's feelings were worked up to such a pitch of enthusiastic awe, whilst gazing at this strange phenomenon, that she could not have uttered a syllable, or moved from the spot, to purchase even liberty itself. Whilst she was thus lost in silent wonder, the cause of it suddenly disappeared; and although Fanny's eyes were fixed upon the figure at the moment it vanished, she was unable even to conjecture how or whither it had departed. She stood for nearly half an hour afterwards rivetted to the spot, but the vision came no more, and Rose having several times entreated her to retire to her rest, Fanny was obliged to comply.

Not a syllable did she utter to Rose of the apparition she had seen, for she well knew it would for ever interdict her from walking to the rock; which place she now felt more than ever interested in exploring; for so entirely was her mind engrossed by the desire of seeing her mother, that fear was entirely forgotten, and she felt as if she could meet the whole world of spirits, provided that beatified being were amongst them.

The next day, directly after breakfast, Fanny renewed her walk to the rock, and Rose accompanied her; the latter was now provided with a book to amuse her whilst Fanny went upon her adventurous expedition. As soon as she had left Rose seated on the stone, and engaged with her book, Fanny mounted the rock, and bent her footsteps to the very spot, as nearly as she could judge, where she had seen the figure the preceding night. All was silence and desolation, however, and she was just about to return to Rose, whose patience she was afraid of trying too severely, when she thought she heard a slight noise behind her, and turning round her head, she beheld through a fissure in the rock; the very figure that had so powerfully affected her mind the preceding night.

The form was that of a woman, and although clad in a loose robe, that seemed calculated rather to hide than display its symmetry, it was impossible not to perceive the grace that adorned its every movement. The veil that covered her head was thrown back, and displayed a face, in which the traces of sorrow had anticipated the ravages of time, and robbed it of its beauty before age authorised the theft; yet still a sweetness of expression remained more interesting than beauty itself, and although the fire of her eyes had been quenched with weeping, their languid beams were capable of penetrating the heart, exercising it to affection.

Fanny stood entranced as she gazed upon the awful vision, and scarcely daring to breathe, she waited in silent expectation of its speaking to her, She was however disappointed, for after looking some time with mournful earnestness in her face, the figure uttered a deep sigh, and waving her hand, as if forbidding Fanny to follow her, instantly disappeared.

After a considerable time had elapsed, and no sign of its returning, Fanny was obliged to leave the rock, and return with Rose to the Castle. The impression her mind had received by the wonderful sight she had seen, kept Fanny silent as she walked with Rose in her return; but when she had reached the Castle, all her thoughts were put to flight, by the news that awaited her there. Lord Ballafyn was arrived, and had been enquiring for her, and Mrs. Owen, the old housekeeper, was waiting to conduct her to his lordship, as soon as she came in.

At first Fanny refused to go with her, but on Mrs. Owen's saying that she was sure Lord Ballafyn would visit her in her bed-room, if she did not obey his summons, she was obliged to submit, and was accordingly conducted to the drawing room. She entered with evident reluctance, which Lord Ballafyn perceiving, arose to meet her, and taking her hand, said, – 'You are welcome to Ireland, my pretty lass – upon my honour you are a devilish handsome wench; pray how long have you been in keeping with my brother?' Terror had hitherto tied Fanny's tongue, but indignation now burst the bonds of silence.

'Unhand me, my lord,' said she, making a violent effort to free herself from his grasp, 'nor you, nor your base brother have any right to detain me a prisoner here, and friendless as you may think me you may find to your cost that I shall be claimed, and powerfully too, by those who will neither want the inclination nor the means to punish the violence that has been done to me.'

'Well said, my pretty little actress,' said Lord Ballafyn, placing his back against the door to prevent Fanny from escaping at it, as she saw he was meditating to do; 'upon my honour I admire my brother's taste so much, that I have half a mind to steal you from him; but perhaps you would not like the exchange, for Ross is some years younger than I am – what, I suppose he sent you away for fear jealous *Eleanor* should find out fair *Rosamond's* bower. Come now, don't pout so, my pretty prisoner, for I will not let you pass until you have paid toll.'

Fanny was almost ready to die with terror, and sinking into a chair, she sat fanning herself with her handkerchief, to keep herself from fainting.

'I cannot think,' said Lord B. 'where I have seen your face before: your features are quite familiar to me.'

As he was speaking Fanny lifted up her eyes to his face, and instantly recollected his countenance: it was that of the man who had insulted her in Hyde Park, when Mr. Hamilton released her from the persecution; and the remembrance of his former brutality added terror to the thought of being so entirely in his power.

'Upon my soul,' said his lordship, staring rudely in Fanny's face, 'I like that little vixen look of your's so well, and the air of modesty you counterfeit becomes you so much, that if you will leave Ross, and consent to live with me, I will settle a vast deal more upon you than it is in his power to do: and then if you behave well, and wheedle me prettily, who knows but you may persuade me to marry you; and that you know is what you can have no chance of with Ross. Come, I see the storm that is gathering, and I hate female hurricanes, so I will let you go to your own chamber, and you shall have four-and-twenty hours to consider of the proposal. Ross will be here in two days, so if you agree to my offer, it must be settled before he comes, and you and I must slip off until the breeze is blown over. Come, I will have a kiss, and then you shall go.'

So saying, he clasped the terrified Fanny in his arms, and almost smothered her with kisses.

Bursting from his grasp, by an effort of supernatural strength, which terror supplied her with, she escaped from further persecution, and flying to her chamber, locked herself in; then sinking on a chair, a flood of tears came to her relief, and saved her from fainting. Here she commended herself to Him, who was alone able to defeat the intentions of the wicked men into whose power she had unhappily fallen; her determination neither to be intimidated by threats, nor moved by entreaties to unlock the door became fixed, and was the only preventative which she could provide for the preservation of her honour. It was in vain that Rose, and Mrs. Owen alternately applied for admittance at her door, she resolutely refused to admit them nor would she take any of the food they brought her, because she must have opened the door to receive it,

The state of mind in which the poor girl passed that day, would be difficult to describe. Let the fair reader for a moment contemplate this interesting female, removed from that circle in which she was cherished, and beloved, torn by ruffian hands from those she held dear, and that at a time when fortune seemed to smile propitiously upon her – at a time when her little bark, which so long buffeted the tempestuous seas of life was to all appearance entering the haven of happiness – see her at such a period, placed in the hands of an unprincipled and powerful man, and surely the fear of sensibility will not be withheld; and when the darkness of night surrounded her, and she found herself without light, she could have almost compromised her other fears to have obtained a candle, but she was now left to herself, for nobody came near her, and as she was afraid to go to bed she opened her closet window, and stood watching the distant rock as the moon rose over the romantic landscape.

[*Shortly after this the figure by the rock is revealed to be Fanny's mother – not dead, but living in a nearby nunnery. They are reunited, Lord Ballafyn is defeated, committing suicide, and Fanny marries the Duke of Albemarle.*]

THE SMUGGLER KING

[*In this Gothic–nautical–domestic romance, Sir Julian Mordlington leads a double life as an aristocrat and a smuggler king.*]

It has before been shewn that Sir Julian Mordlington was a man of the most consummate and luxurious taste; and he had therefore caused the principal apartments of the tower to be fitted up in that style of elegance which has been described, and which rendered them fit for the reception of a nobleman, – black and unprepossessing as the exterior of the edifice appeared. Frequently had he conveyed the unfortunate victim of his base passions thither, and therefore had he fitted up some of the apartments especially, with every degree of elegance, – all that might captivate and lead the senses astray was to be found there. Rich hangings, silken ottomans, lofty mirrors, magnificent carpets, splendid chandeliers, chaste vases, filled with every scarce exotic that could be met with in Nature's most beautiful works. There was also a collection, in one apartment, of the most valuable paintings; and another contained a library of classic books, selected from the best authors.

The saloon which has been alluded to was a most spacious and brilliantly ornamented apartment, – one that might have vied with that of a monarch. Though all the other rooms we have mentioned were decorated with well-furnished elegance, they were inferior in point of magnificence to this. The floor was of inlaid marble, four gothic windows looked out upon the vast expansive

ocean, commanding a boundless scene. These were furnished with curtains of pink silk, the fringe of lilac and silver, with cords and tassels to correspond. The ceiling, of an octagonal form, was painted in compartments, with an allegorical representation of the seasons. The arches on the opposite sides of the room, and corresponding with the windows, were lined with white marble, and supported by pillars of the same, round which were carried rows of crystal lamps, of various colours, whose glow, when they were lighted up, was peculiarly relieved and softened by intersections of the choicest flowers, running in the same spiral manner between the lights. Alternate rows of lamps and flowers depended likewise from the cornices, and above the doors. The upper end was distinguished by a canopy to match the window curtains, and ornamented with a yet greater profusion of brilliant decorations. Tables, chairs, and stools, arranged with equal taste, and of surpassing beauty, finished the superb grandeur of the whole, and was sufficient to captivate and bewilder the most fastidious taste, and might have been mistaken for a fairy temple, or the palace of some genii, instead of the fiend in human shape to whom it belonged.

Here had the pirate-chief often (when he had steeped their senses in a delirium of sweet entrancement) triumphed over the virtue of the lovely and the innocent; – here had he wrought the destruction of many of Nature's most lovely works, and afterwards exulted in his fiend-like triumph.

It was by the brilliancy of this apartment, and the other allurements he had designed to throw out, that he hoped to delude the senses of our heroine, and to gain a conquest over her innocence, without having recourse to violence. This he resolved to endeavour to accomplish by the mockery of a marriage, performed after the mystic rites that had been established among the smugglers; and such was the vanity which he possessed, and the knowledge of his power, and that she was entirely left to his mercy, made him entertain very little doubt but that he should succeed.

Seated on the throne beneath the canopy, and surrounded by the principal portion of the crew who were at the tower, or had arrived in the Devil Skipper, Sir Julian was resting on the evening we have mentioned. The smugglers were all arrayed in the most fancy and elegant costumes, which they had for peculiar occasions like these, and altogether the scene was a most imposing one, and had more of the effect of a representation in a drama than anything else; and the imagination could scarcely perceive anything more romantic.

The lengthy table was covered with goblets of silver, and the rich decanters sparkled with the choicest of wines. Sir Julian had removed the cap from his head, and a crown, formed of all descriptions of precious stones, ornamented his brow, which glittered with dazzling brightness beneath the rays of the chandeliers that were suspended from the lofty roof. His whole appearance was in strict accordance with the scene, and could not be gazed on without astonishment, not unmixed with a feeling of admiration.

During the time that Sam Raker was gone to the apartments of Flora, the baronet had commanded that mirth should prevail; and immediately after each quaffing heartily from the contents of the goblet, Hemlock sung the following, to which all the smuggler's present lent their aid in the chorus:–

SONG.

'Old Neptune, they say, is the king of the deep,
  But that I will stoutly deny,
For a mightier king o'er its billows doth sweep,
  Who his rival doth proudly defy!
He's a king who gives freedom to all that he rules,
  No minister's tricks need they fear;
The follies of state he will leave to the fools,
  While the wide ocean-deep is his share!
    Then fill up your goblets, and loudly sing,
    Hurrah! hurrah! for the Smuggler King!

CHORUS:
    The Smuggler King! – the Smuggler King!
    Hurrah! hurrah! for the Smuggler King!

'Proudly he'll ride o'er the bright blue tide –
  No monarch so proud as he;
Gold he must have; and woe-betide
  Those who his flag shall see!
'Tis vain to oppose him in deadly fight –
  To yield he will all soon bring:

Oh, nothing can equal the power and might
  Of the dreaded Smuggler King?
  Then fill up your goblets, and loudly sing,
  Hurrah! hurrah! for the Smuggler King!
        CHORUS:
  The Smuggler King! – the Smuggler King!
  Hurrah! hurrah! for the Smuggler King!'

Every proper effect was given to the singing of this song and chorus and the applause which followed had not subsided, when Sam Raker returned to the saloon.

'How now, Sam?' demanded Sir Julian, 'where is the girl?'

Raker immediately delivered his message, to which the baronet listened with attention.

'And do you think she is really ill?' he inquired.

'Why a little so-so-like, captain,' replied the smuggler.

'Humph!' muttered the captain, 'it seems as if I am always to have my hopes deferred, and my wishes ungratified.'

'Your pardon, captain,' remarked Raker, 'but the lass no doubt is rather flurried at your arrival, and I think if you were to yield to her request, and postpone your interview with her till to-morrow, it would be likely to make a little impression upon her. I know what the fair craft is, although I am a smuggler, and leave Sam Raker alone for getting the weathergauge of them at any time,'

'You say right, Sam,' answered Sir Julian, after a pause; 'It would appear rather harsh and cruel of me to insist upon seeing her, if she is indisposed; so I will e'en take your advice, and defer my interview till the morning. This night, in the meantime, we will devote to revelry, and pass the wine-cup merrily around.'

'Then I am to say that you will expect to see the damsel to-morrow?' said Raker.

'Yes,' answered the captain, 'and deliver the message in your best style, and just let her see what intelligent and gallant fellows the Smuggler King owns for his subjects.'

'I will weigh anchor immediately, captain,' said Raker; 'and if I don't deliver my message in a manner worthy of any page, why, may I never go aloft again.'

'A very pretty page, too; ha! ha! ha!' laughed Sir Julian, when Sam Raker quitted the room, in which joke the smugglers all joined with hearty laughter.

Sam soon returned, and took his seat on the right side of the captain, beneath the throne – Will Hemlock occupying the left. The goblets were now replenished, and emptied, and replenished again, and the utmost revelry prevailed, Sir Julian setting the example. Toast followed toast, and chorus succeeded chorus, until an early hour of the following morning, when the smugglers, overpowered by the deep libations they had partaken of, staggered to rest, and Sir Julian, who was more sober than any of the rest, although he had quaffed as deeply, hastened to the gorgeous chamber which was prepared for him.

'So,' he exclaimed when he found himself alone, 'I have completely triumphed; all my enemies are removed, and here am I, in my stronghold, where no power dare molest me, and the beauteous Flora Clarendon is entirely at my disposal. Glorious triumph! Other monarchs than the Smuggler King might well envy the rich prize I possess. Her beauty inflames my passions, and her innocence but stimulated me to the consummation of all my wishes! Oh! I will shower upon her all the luxuries that wealth can produce, and if the most consummate flattery and impassioned vows can win woman's love, in a very short time I will have her heart as securely in my power as I have her person. Sir Julian Mordlington likes not a ruffian's conquest, and, therefore, by all the soft arts of which I am master, would I win her to my purpose. That would render my triumph more complete, and she must be more than woman if she be able to resist the means I will adopt to captivate her affections. If I fail it will be the first time. Wealthy maidens have yielded to my powers of fascination; damsels lovely as eastern houris have succumbed to the golden snares thrown around them by the rover of the deep; and, by old Neptune, I swear that she shall be added to my long list of conquests. The memory of her lover may, for a time, render her obstinate, and the *good* character the world has given me, and which I glory in deserving, may alarm her gentle nature; but these difficulties I do not despair of being able to surmount; and then, with his fair bride (bride, ha! ha!) how doubly proud and daring will become the much-dreaded *Smuggler King!*'

Filled with the extacy of these thoughts, Sir Julian felt not inclined to retire to his couch, and he paced the chamber, brooding in sanguine anticipation upon the *pleasures* he would shortly experience in the destruction of female innocence and purity. He thought not of the power that reigned above him, and which in a moment could thwart all his infernal plans, and level him with the dust.

[*After interminable escapes from seduction, Flora is saved from forced marriage to Mordlington by the arrival of a British man-of-war.*]

VILEROY;
OR, THE HORRORS OF
ZINDORF CASTLE

[*Caroline Mecklenburgh is being forced to marry Count Durlack in Zindorf Castle.*]

'Come,' cried the baron, 'I will parley with thee no longer. To the chapel.'

He grasped her tightly by the arm as he spoke, and hurried her forward.

Caroline did not resist further, for she saw that the looks of the brutal Roland were fixed upon her, and she dreaded being consigned to him if she persevered in a resistance, which must in the end prove useless.

'I submit to your violence,' she said, 'and put my trust in Heaven.'

The baron, without another word, conducted her hurriedly along various corridors and suites of delapidated apartments towards the castle chapel.

It seemed to Caroline as if the baron must be purposely taking her a circuitous route, in order to bewilder and confuse her knowledge of the localities of the gloomy fortress, which she had been too short a time a free inhabitant of it to explore with any chance of remembering even its principal and most striking features and internal arrangements.

They passed many apartments, which

betrayed the remains of former grandeur and magnificence; faded and torn hangings were pendant from the walls, which at one time, had, no doubt, been the pride of successful art. Massive pieces of furniture reposed in many of the rooms upon which the dust of ages seemed to have accumulated. At any other time these relics of former wealth and luxury would have afforded Caroline ample food for reflection and amusement, and would have cheated many an hour of its weariness.

Now, however, she cast but a passing glance upon these records of the annals of time, and endeavoured only to nerve her mind for the scene which she guessed was about to ensue beneath the sacred roof which was professedly reared for other purposes, than to look down upon the oppression and persecution of the innocent and virtuous.

They soon now arrived at a room which was of vast and gloomy proportions. The groined roof was lofty, and blackened with age, the windows were in several instances broken, and an universal air of devastation and neglect pervaded that old hall, which in happier and more hospitable times might have resounded with the song and the blithesome dance.

The baron, followed closely by Roland, who held a blazing torch, which threw a flickering and dancing light upon every object, conducted Caroline to the further end of this ruined hall. He took a key from his pocket, and unlocked a small door; a flight of narrow steps, upon which were the remains of a rich covering, presented themselves.

'Descend,' said the baron.

Caroline felt that it would be useless to hesitate, and she passed without a word of remonstrance through the door way.

'Roland,' said the baron, 'go before, and announce our coming.'

'This is an idle mockery,' cried Caroline.

'Peace,' cried the baron; 'aggravate not your situation by your folly. You will find this is no idle mockery; you come here to wed the Count Durlack. You depart not but as his bride.'

'Then,' said Caroline, 'my stay will be eternal!'

'Forward!' cried the baron, impatiently.

Roland at this moment opened a small door at the foot of the staircase, and holding his blazing torch high in his hand, he stood awaiting the arrival of the baron and the devoted Caroline Mecklenburgh.

The baron tightened his grasp upon Caroline's arm, as if he feared even then that the victim of his tyranny and oppression would escape him, and hurrying her down the remainder of the stairs, she in another moment found herself in the chapel of Zindorf Castle.

Roland stood by the door, and the baron, without relaxing his speed, dragged Caroline along the aisle, nor stopped till he had placed her exactly before the altar, upon which burned with a dim and sickly light, the tall candles which had been by the baron's order so hastily lighted.

With a throbbing heart, Caroline gazed around her, and in that place, once dedicated to holy purposes, she inwardly prayed to that Providence which is the guide and protector of the innocent and pure of heart, to protect her from those who sought to involve her in hopeless misery.

The greater part of the chapel was involved in darkness and obscurity for there was no light but those on the altar, and they shed but a dim radiance around the spot on which they stood.

These observations Caroline made in a moment, and then she turned her attention to two figures that were standing close to her.

The one was Count Durlack, and, dim and uncertain as the light in which he stood was, Caroline could perceive with horror, that there was an air of sneering horror, which spoke no hope or comfort to the heart of the desolate girl, who was there dragged to be coerced, if possible, into the solemnization of nuptials from which she shrunk with the most sensitive and holy horror.

The other figure was that of a priest clad in the vestments of his order. His face was completely hidden in the folds of his cassock, and, for all movement of life that he exhibited, he might have been taken for a statue.

'There must be,' thought Caroline, 'some hope of succour in the presence of this man. His sacred calling obliges him to succour the unfortunate. He cannot – he dare not become an instrument of oppression.'

A dead silence of some few moments ensued, which none seemed inclined to break. Caroline waited as calmly as she could for the first step in the fearful drama which she knew would be attempted to be acted in that building reared to the worship of the true God.

'The baroness,' said the baron, in a voice of anxiety, 'where is she?'

'She is not here,' answered the count. 'In fact, 'tis small courtesy of the noble lady to be absent from my poor nuptials, when even the blushing fair bride has arrived at the altar's foot.'

Caroline was as indignant as astonished at this audacious speech, and she immediately thought its motive must be to blind the ecclesiastic to the nature of the present proceeding; she, therefore, instantly replied: –

'If I am alluded to by the Count Durlack, I here state that I have been dragged from my chamber to this spot, and that I utterly abhor and detest the Count Durlack, and would suffer death rather than he should have the power to call me his bride. I cannot wed a murderer.'

The priest moved not, and Caroline began then, indeed, to think that she was friendless, and with nothing but her own firmness and resolution for her safeguard.

'This modest reluctance, dearest Caroline,' said the count, in the same sneering, audacious tone he had before spoken in, 'is most amiable, and most usual, on these surely interesting occasions. – Add anything you please, my lovely bride, in the same sweet strain, which only lends an additional charm to beauty and grace which must enchant all beholders.'

'Ruffian! – Accomplished villain!' cried Caroline, with indignation.

'Exactly,' sneered Durlack.

'Monster! – murderer!'

'Nay, nay, you will quite shock the holy father.'

'Oh, Heaven help me!' cried Caroline, 'and protect me, in this temple reared to thy worship, from all scorn.'

'Say "Amen," holy father,' sneered the count, in a mocking tone.

The priest shook his head slowly, but he still kept his face covered.

'Roland!' cried the baron, who had listened to this little dialogue with great and manifest impatience.

'Here,' growled Roland, advancing a pace or two, and glancing at Caroline as if he anticipated that the next order would be to offer her some personal violence, in revenge for her freedom of speech.

'Fetch the baroness,' said the baron. 'You understand? Bring her here. We wait her gracious presence.'

'We do, indeed,' said Durlack, carelessly adjusting his collar of Valenciennes lace. 'Lovers are an impatient race, and, I doubt not, my beauteous bride shares in her gentle fluttering heart, the anxieties of mine.'

Caroline disdained further reply to the count, who she saw was intent upon carrying on a mocking discourse with her, either to gratify the malignant whim of the moment, or for some sinister purpose that she knew not of. Her hopes of the interference of the priest were becoming each moment fainter and fainter, for he stirred not, nor spoke not, seemingly resolved to take no interest whatever in her fate.

The door of the chapel by which Baron Zindorf and Caroline had entered, now opened again, and Roland appeared, with a malignant smile upon his face, and holding his torch above his head.

Caroline looked anxiously at the little doorway, and in another moment she saw the form of her poor aunt appear.

The baroness paused upon the threshold of the chapel, and seemed unable, for a short space, to proceed another step.

Caroline sprang forward, and clinging round the pale and sickly-looking baroness, she exclaimed: –

'Dear aunt, do I again in this world see you? What must you not have suffered. You are looking ill, and I – I – have been the wretched cause of all that you have had to endure from –'

'Hush, Caroline. Hush!' said the baroness, in a tone of alarm. 'I – I – am better. Say nothing that – that may aggravate those who are our persecutors.'

Caroline noticed the nervous tone and trembling accents in which the baroness spoke, and a pang of anguish came across her heart, as she saw that her unfortunate relative had been completely terrified and subdued by the unwearying and violent persecution to which she had been subjected.

'Do you know, Caroline,' said the baroness, in an agitated whisper; 'do you know why you are brought here?'

'It is,' said Caroline, 'to force me into a marriage with the most odious of mankind.'

'The Count Durlack?'

'The same. The persecutor – the ruthless destroyer of my mother, and the murderer of my unfortunate father.'

'You – you will not consent?'

'Consent, aunt! How can you deem the question necessary?'

'No, no,' said the baroness, a slight flush passing across her pale features, and then leaving them paler and more haggard than before. 'I am sure you would not. And yet –'

'Yet what, aunt? Can there be the slightest mental reservation in such a case?'

'No, child, – no. But the baron, – he is violent. Oh, reflect, reflect.'

'I have, unhappily,' answered Caroline, 'had cause sufficient to reflect upon the violence of the Baron Zindorf.'

'This castle,' continued the baroness, in a tone of nervous alarm, which betrayed the shattered state of her mind. 'This castle, my dear Caroline, is a fearful place.'

'It may be so,' said Caroline,' 'if, by our fears, we make it such.'

'You – you will not wed the count?'

'Oh, aunt, aunt,' said Caroline, clasping her hands, 'do not again ask me so cruel a question. You know death were infinitely preferable.'

'Death?' said the baroness, shuddering.

'Yes, aunt, death. I do not speak idly, or in metaphor. I mean that the cruellest death would be preferable to the hateful and un-natural union proposed to me by the baron, and the – I cannot pronounce his hateful name.'

The baroness groaned, and wrung her hands in despair.

'We shall both perish,' she said, 'both perish!'

Caroline was much afflicted to perceive her aunt in so weak a state, and the persecutions of the Baron Zindorf and the Count Durlack had all failed to inflict upon her the misery she now experienced at seeing the only relative to whom she could look for advice and consolation, reduced almost to a pitiable state of mental and bodily infirmity, and ready to sink under a pressure of circum-stances which she could not control, and had not strength of mind sufficient to support herself with due calmness and resignation under.

The baron now strode with a frowning look towards the aunt and niece, who were maintaining a dialogue so unsatisfactory to each other.

The baroness trembled as he approached, and laying her hand on Caroline's arm, she said, in an alarmed whisper: –

'Hush – hush! Here is the baron. Oh, hush!'

Caroline gave a deep sigh. 'I am, indeed, alone,' she thought – 'Claudio is distant from me. The priest – the holy minister of religion, whose most sacred duty it is to protect the innocent, refuses me aid. My only relative is unable even to afford me one word of hope or consolation. I am forsaken by all but Heaven.'

'To the altar!' cried the baron. 'We waste time.'

He seized Caroline rudely by the arm, and dragged her from the door. The baroness followed with tottering steps.

'This,' said Caroline, when they arrived at the altar, 'is a mockery, as idle and wicked as it is useless.'

'You will find it is no mockery,' cried the baron.

'No earthly power,' cried Caroline, 'can compel me to wed the Count Durlack, contrary to my inclination.'

'Difficulty is the food of love,' sneered Durlack.

'Caroline Mecklenburgh,' cried the baron, 'take your place at the altar.'

'I have no place here,' said Caroline. 'To you, holy sir,' addressing the priest, 'do I appeal against this desecration of this temple of religion. I am forced here against my will.'

The priest groaned.

'Priest,' cried the baron, drawing his sword, 'to your duty!'

The priest, in a trembling voice, began to chaunt some unintelligible prayer.

Count Durlack advanced, and with the greatest effrontery, before Caroline was aware of his intention, he took hold of her hand.

'Off, villain! – off!' she cried, vehemently. 'Touch me not. There is pollution in your very presence!'

'Sweet maidenly modesty,' said Durlack, in a mocking voice, which, however, but partially concealed the passion which he was endeavouring to suppress.

'Cease priest!' cried Caroline, nerved to desperation by her situation. 'Cease your unholy exhortations. Tremble! – Do you not fear the instant vengeance of that God you are now mocking?'

The priest's voice faltered, and he dropped a small book, from which he was, or affected to be, reading.

'Ha!' cried Caroline. 'You are ashamed. You are human. – Protect me, oh, protect me.' She clung to the robe of the priest, as she spoke, and sunk on her knees at his feet, imploring his succour.

'Rise!' cried Count Durlack, in a voice of thunder, his passion overmastering his prudence, and at once dissipating the tone of cruel irony in which he had hitherto persisted in addressing Caroline.

'Save me! save me!' cried Caroline, still clinging to the priest's robe. 'You, too, my aunt; have you no word to say for her who looked up to you as a second mother for advice and protection?'

The baroness only wrung her hands and sobbed.

'Rise!' again cried the count, drawing his sword, and laying his hand heavily upon Caroline's shoulder.

'Help!' cried Caroline, 'help!' and the chapel echoed her cries.

'Confusion!' cried the baron, stamping upon the stone floor.

'Spare her! Spare her!' cried the baroness, in a tone of frenzy.

'Claudio! Claudio!' cried Caroline, in the extremity of her despair.

'Who do you call upon?' cried the baron.

'Vileroy!' shrieked Caroline; 'Vileroy! – Murderer! I call upon Vileroy!'

'He is here!' said a solemn voice.

The baron shrieked till the ancient chapel rung again, and fell heavily upon the steps of the altar.

[*Her lover Claudio rises from the altar to save her.*]

ADA, THE BETRAYED;
OR,
THE MURDER AT THE OLD SMITHY

[*The story tells of Ada's progress from a child carried from a burning smithy, to her rightful assumption of the Learmont estates and marriage. Here Ada is in the power of Gray, the evil genius who urged her uncle to murder her father in the smithy.*]

Still, however, in his heart, he quailed at the murder – the deliberate, cold-blooded murder of that innocent and beautiful girl, and he presented the ghastly appearance of a resuscitated corpse, rather than a human being who had not passed the portals of the grave. The feeling of honourable humanity was a stranger to the bosom of Jacob Gray. He did not shrink from the murder of the poor and persecuted Ada, because it was a murder – no, it was because he, Jacob Gray, had to do it, unaided and uncheered in the unholy deed, by aught save his own shivering and alarmed imagination. Jacob Gray had no compunction for the deed; his only terror arose from the fact that he could not shift its consummation on to some one else's shoulders.

He would gladly have held a light to guide the dagger of another assassin, but he did shrink from the personal danger and the personal consequences of doing it himself. He was one of those who would watch the door while the murder was doing – hold a vessel to catch the blood – anything but do the deed himself.

His little accession of strength and confidence now only arose from the fact that owing to the intervention of the circumstance of the dog, the murder was, as it were, put off for a little time; he must first dispose of the dog, then the murder itself, with all its damning train of fears and agonies, would take its former prominent place in his mind, and again would Jacob Gray tremble to his very heart's core.

Stealthily he moved his way up the staircase, his great object to ascertain if the dog was within or without the chamber of Ada.

His doubts were soon resolved, for suddenly a low growl from the faithful animal smote his ears.

Jacob Gray gave a malignant smile, as he said in a low whisper, 'The dog is outside the door.'

The growl of the hound now deepened to a louder note, and just as that again was shaping itself to a short angry bark, Jacob Gray threw up the piece of poisoned meat on to the landing on the top of the staircase.

Folding his lamp then under the lappels of his coat, Jacob Gray sat down on the staircase, with a feeling of gratification on his mind, that, in all human probability, he was at length revenged on the poor animal, whose only crime had been too much affection and fidelity towards the hand that fed and caressed him, and the voice that spoke to him in kindly tones.

All was as still as the grave after the meat had been thrown, and after several minutes of suspense, Jacob Gray began to feel anxious for some indication of the success of his scheme. Cautiously, he then ascended a step or two, and paused – no sound met his ears. A few steps more were gained – then a few more, and

finally, by stretching out his arm with the light, he could command a view of the landing-place, but he looked in vain for the dog: the animal was nowhere to be seen. Jacob Gray now stood fairly upon the landing, and peered carefully around him, with the hope of seeing the body of his foe, but such was not the case.

The open door of the outer room which led to Ada's smaller sleeping-chamber now caught his eyes, and at once afforded a clue to the retreat of the dog.

With a soft footfall that could not have possibly disturbed the lightest sleeper, Gray entered that room, and moving his hand slowly round him, so as to illuminate by turns all parts of the apartment, he saw, at length, the object of his search.

Close up to the door leading to Ada's room was the hound quite dead. The faithful creature had evidently made an effort to awaken its gentle and kind mistress, for its paws were clenched against the bottom of the door, where there was a crevice left.

For a moment Jacob Gray glanced at the fixed eyes of the dog, then spurned it from the door with his foot, as he muttered, –

'Humph! so far successful, and now for – for –'

'The murder,' he would have said, but in one moment, as if paralysed by the touch of some enchanter's wand, all his old fears returned upon him and now that there was no obstacle between him and the commission of the awful deed he meditated, he leaned against the wall for support, and the perspiration of fear rolled down his face in heavy drops, and gave his countenance an awful appearance of horror and death-like paleness.

'What – what,' he stammered, 'what if she should scream? God of Heaven, if she should scream!'

So terrified was he at the supposition that his victim might, in her death-struggle, find breath to scream, that for a moment he gave up his purpose, and retreated slowly backwards from the room.

Suddenly now the silence that reigned without was broken by the various churches striking twelve.

Gray started as the sounds met his ear.

'Twelve! twelve!' he exclaimed. 'It – it – should have been done ere this. To-morrow. The to-morrow that she looks for is come. I – I thought not 'twas so late. It must be done! it must be done!'

*

The last faint echo from the slowest clock had died away upon the midnight air, when Jacob Gray started from his position of deep attention, and placing his small lamp on one of the window sills, he drew from his breast the knife with which he intended to take the life of the hapless Ada.

'She – she surely sleeps sound,' he muttered through his clenched teeth, 'or all these clocks with their solemn and prolonged echoes must have awakened her. Yes; I – I – hope she sleeps sound. I – would not have a struggle – a struggle. Oh, no, no, not for worlds. I – can fancy her clinging to the knife and screaming – shrieking even as – as – her – father did – when he had his death wound. That would be horrible. Oh, most horrible – and yet I must kill her. I must kill her. Did she not brave me to my face? did she not tell me that she suspected me and my motives, and that no more would she keep herself immured for my sake? I – she – she did, and more than this, far more, she taunted me with. Yes – I – I am quite justified – she must die!'

The door which led into the inner chamber was in two compartments, and when Gray gently pushed against them, they both opened slightly, and the dim, sickly light of a lamp from the interior room, to his surprise, gleamed through the crevice, meeting the kindred ray of the one which Jacob Gray had placed so carefully out of the way of, as he thought, the eyes of the sleeping girl.

He crept into the room, and stood motionless for many minutes, regarding the sight that met his eyes. Seated by a small table, on which was the lamp dimly burning and near its expiration, was Ada, completely dressed, but fast asleep. Her face rested partially upon an open book, which she had evidently been reading before retiring to rest, when sleep must have come upon her unawares, and sealed her eyelids in forgetfulness.

Her long hair fell in beautiful disorder upon the table, and the one eyelash that was visible

hung upon her fair cheek wet with tears. She had been weeping, but whether from some vision that crossed her slumbers, or from lonesome and unhappy thoughts previous to dropping into that temporary oblivion of sorrow, could not be known.

Jacob Gray stood like one spell-bound by some horrible apparition, for to the wicked can there be a more horrible apparition than youth, beauty, and innocence?

'She – she sleeps,' he gasped; 'but by some strange fatality has not retired to bed. My – my task is now ten times more difficult. I – I know not what to do.'

The knife trembled in his grasp, and he shook vehemently; then, as a low murmuring sound escaped the lips of Ada, he sunk slowly down, first crouchingly, then on his knees, and lastly he grovelled on the ground at her feet in mortal agony, lest she should awaken and see him there, with those starting eyes, those livid lips, and that knife, which he came to bury in her innocent and gentle heart.

Some fearful vision was passing over the imagination of the sleeping girl. Fancy was busy in the narrow chambers of the brain, and pictured to her some scene of sorrow or terror; deep sobs burst from the breast – then she spoke, and her words thrilled through Jacob Gray, like liquid fire.

'Spare, oh, spare him!' she said; 'he is my father – Spare him; oh, spare – spare –'

She awoke not even in her agony of spirit, but wept bitterly; then the tears decreased and sobs only were heard; the vision, like a thunder-storm, was passing away, low moans succeeded, and finally all was still again.

It was, however, many minutes before Jacob Gray again rose from his crouching position of abject fear, but at length he did so, and with the glittering knife in his hand, he stood within a pace of his innocent victim.

Then arose in his mind the awful question of where should he strike? and, like a vulture, he hovered for a time over his prey, with the fatal steel uplifted, doubting where he should make the sudden swoop.

By an accidental parting of the silken curls that floated upon Ada's neck and shoulders, he saw a small portion of her breast; it was

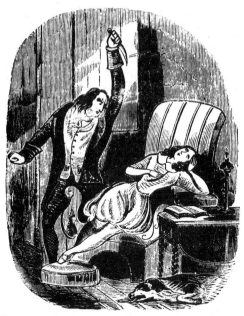

there then he determined to strike. He glanced at the blade of the knife, and he thought it long enough to reach even to her heart.

'Now – now!' he groaned through his clenched teeth. 'Now!'

The steel was uplifted; nay, it was upon the point of descending, when one heavy knock upon the outer door of the lone house echoed through the dreary pile, and arrested the arm of the murderer, while the blood rushed in terror like a gush of cold water to his heart.

There was then an awful silent pause, when again that solemn heavy knock awakened the echoes of the empty house.

Slowly, inch by inch, as if his arm worked by some machinery, Jacob Gray brought the knife by his side, and still bending over the unconscious Ada, he listened for a repetition of that knock, as if each melancholy blow was struck upon his own heart.

Again it came, and then again more rapidly, and Jacob Gray trembled so violently that he was fain to lean upon the table at which Ada slept for support.

That movement awakened Ada, and starting from her position of rest, she suddenly, with a cry of surprise, confronted the man who had sought her chamber with so fell and horrible a purpose. One glance at the knife which Jacob Gray held in his hand, and then a searching look at his face, told her all. She clasped her hands in terror as she exclaimed –

'You – you – come to kill me?'

'No – no,' stammered Gray, trying to smile, and producing his usual painful distortion of features. 'No – no – I did – not – no – no! Ada, I did not.'

'That knife?' said Ada, pointing to it as she spoke.

'The knife,' repeated Gray. 'Hark, some one knocks, Ada, at our lonely home.'

'Those looks of terror,' continued the young girl, 'those blanched cheeks, those trembling hands, all convince me that I have escaped death at your hands.'

'No; I say no,' gasped Gray.

'And my hound too,' added Ada; 'my fond, faithful dog, where is he, uncle Gray?'

'Yes; the dog,' cried Gray, eagerly catching at the hope of persuading her that it was solely to compass the destruction of the hound he had thus stolen to her room. 'I admit I did seek the dog's life; you vexed me about the animal.'

The knocking at the door sounded now more loudly than before, and the knocker was evidently plied by an impatient hand.

'Hark, hark!' cried Gray. 'Ada, hear me; whoever knocks without can be no friend of ours.'

'Indeed?' said Ada.

''Tis true; I am the only friend you have in the wide world.'

'You mean, I suppose, since you have killed my poor dog,' said Ada, pointing through the open doorway to the inanimate body of the animal.

'The dog is dead,' said Gray.

'Uncle,' replied Ada, mildly, but firmly; 'now hear me. You have broken the compact. Let those who knock so loudly for admission enter, I will not avoid them. Were they ten times my enemies they could not be more cruel than thou art.'

'Ada, you know not what you say,' cried Gray. 'They cannot be friends, and they may be foes. 'Tis light enough for me to note them from a lower window. Yes, I will see, I will see. Remain thou here, Ada. Stir not – speak not.'

'I promise nothing,' said Ada. 'You shall no longer prescribe rules of conduct for me, uncle Gray. I tell you I will promise nothing.'

Gray made an impatient gesture with his hands, and quitted the room. He repaired to a window on the ground floor, in one corner of which he had made a clear spot for the express purpose of reconnoitering the doorway, and applying his eye now close to this, he could by the dim light trace the forms of two men upon his threshold. Too well were those forms engraven on his memory. It needed not a second glance to tell him that the savage smith, Britton, and Squire Learmont, were his unwelcome and most clamorous visitors.

Now, indeed, the measure of Jacob Gray's agony appeared to be full. For a moment he completely surrendered himself to despair; and had Learmont then forced the door, he would scarcely have made an effort to escape the sword of the man of blood.

'Ha! ha!' he heard the smith say; 'I like to knock thus, it alarms poor, clever, cunning Jacob. It shatters his nerves. Oh, oh, oh!'

'Can you depend on the men you have placed at the back of the house to intercept his escape that way?' said Learmont.

'Depend upon them?' replied Britton. 'Of course. They ain't paid, and are quite sober, as you see; they are ready for any cut-throat business. Let's knock again. Oh, oh, how Jacob Gray must be shaking!'

The taunts of the smith seemed to act as a stimulant to the sickened energies of Gray. He roused himself and muttered, as he shook his clenched hand in the direction of the door –

'Indeed, Master Britton. Do not even yet make too sure of cunning Jacob Gray. He may yet prove too cunning for the sot, Britton. You think you have me so safely that you can afford to tantalize me by knocking, when a small effort of your united strength would burst yon frail door from its frailer hinges. We shall see – we shall see.'

He bounded up the staircase to the room in which he had left Ada. She was standing by the body of the dog with the lamp in her hand.

'Ada! Ada!' cried Gray; 'we are lost – lost. We shall be murdered, if you will not be guided by me.'

Ada only pointed to the dog.

Gray was thoroughly alarmed at her decisive manner, and another loud knock at the door at that moment did not tend to pacify his nervous tremors.

'There are those at the door who come purposely to seek your life!'

'*Your* life, most probably Uncle Gray.'

'Ada! Ada!' cried Gray. 'Each minute – nay, each moment is precious. There is no escape, none – none!'

'You are alarmed, Uncle Gray,' said Ada.

The perspiration of fear – intense fear, was standing upon the brow of Gray, as he felt that each fleeting moment might be his last. From exultation at the thought of still deceiving Britton and Learmont, he dropped to a state of the most trembling, abject terror.

'God of Heaven!' he cried; 'you – you will not, cannot refuse to save me!'

'Our compact is broken,' said Ada. 'I do not believe that I have so much to fear from those who seek admittance here as from him who but a few minutes since stood over me as I slept –'

'No – no!' shrieked Gray. 'It was not I –'

'It was you,' said Ada.

'I did not mean to – to kill you.'

'The knife was in your hand, uncle; you had destroyed my faithful guard; you trembled; your guilt shone forth with an unholy and hideous lustre from your eyes. Uncle Gray, God can alone see into the hearts of men, but, as I hope for heaven, and – and to meet there my dear father, whom I never knew, I do suspect you much, Uncle Gray.'

'Mercy! – Have mercy on me, Ada.'

'Ask that of Heaven.'

'In your chamber, you have clothing befitting your sex; for such an emergency as this I provided it. Go,' oh, go at once, and you may escape as a girl from those who come here to murder a boy.'

Ada glanced at the trembling man, who, with clasped hands and trembling limbs, stood before her, and then with a firm voice she said, –

'No, no, I cannot.'

With a loud crash at this moment the street-door was burst from its hinges,

Gray gave one frantic scream, and threw

himself at the feet of Ada.

'Save – oh, save my life!' he cried. 'Have mercy on me, Ada! You shall do with me as you please; I will be your slave, – will watch for you when you sleep, – tend upon you, discover your wishes ever by a look. But oh, save me – save me. I cannot – dare not die!'

Ada shuddered at the wild frantic passion of Gray. She struggled to free herself from his grasp, for he clung to her with a desperate clutch.

'Mercy! mercy!' he shrieked.

In vain she retreated backwards from him; he crawled after her on his knees, shrieking 'Mercy! mercy!'

Now Ada had gained the door of her own room, and, with loathing and horror, she tried in vain to disengage herself from Gray.

'They come! ah, they come!' suddenly cried Gray, springing to his feet. 'Now, Ada, hear the secret you pine to know!'

'The secret?' cried Ada.

'Yes, *I am your father*. These men will apprehend me for murder; but *I am your father!*'

For an instant Ada passed her hands upon her eyes; as if to shut out the hideous phantasma of a dreadful dream, and then, with a cry of exquisite anguish, she rushed through the folding doors and closed them immediately after her.

'That – that will succeed,' gasped Gray, wiping from his brow the cold perspiration that hung there in bead-like drops. 'The lie is effective; she may not believe it, but now she has not time to think. She will save me now!'

He rushed to the door of the room which led to the staircase, and in a moment locked it. Then he stood with his arms folded, and an awful demoniac smile played upon his pale and ghastly face, awaiting the issue of the next few minutes, which comprised to him the fearful question of life or death.

[*While Gray confronts his assailants, Ada escapes.*]

3. LOST

THE SORROWS OF SEDUCTION

What plaintive voice, along the midnight air,
Steals on the ear in accents of despair,
Hark! 'tis from yon emaciated form,
Chill'd in the blast and shiv'ring in the storm,
Shrunk from the public haunt's obtrusive
    light,
Veiling its woes beneath the shade of night!

Lo! a weak female, stretch'd on yonder stone,
Thus hapless weeps – unfriended and alone.

   Yet happy once, she felt a father's smile,
And grew beneath a mother's tender toil;
And, ere allur'd by love of sin to roam!
Knew the pure comforts of a virtuous home.
But, vain of beauty, fond of gaudy dress,
Her modest robes exchang'd for gay excess,
Soon flatt'ry whisper'd 'one so wise and fair
'Was lost beneath a parent's jealous care.' –
Her base deceiver watch'd the hapless hour
Unguarded virtue pli'd with subtle pow'r;
Painted the world as fill'd with ev'ry joy
Her heart could wish, unmingled with alloy,
With solemn oaths, declar'd their plighted
    hands
Should soon be join'd by wedlock's sacred
    bands.

She heard – believ'd – her simple heart was
    won –
Forsook her home – was guilty and undone!

   But where alas! is now each gay delight,
That danc'd and wanton'd in her cheated
    sight?
Her honour, friends, and *base deceiver* fled,
Where are her joys, her golden visions sped?
Swift as the passing murmurs of the wind,
All fled – but Oh! have left a sting behind.

   What would she give, ah! what, to taste
    once more
The peace she felt *in innocence* before!
A Father's blessing, and a Mother's joy,
No keen remorse to canker and annoy;
Obedient, cheerful, modest, and at ease,
Midst the glad sunshine of domestic peace!

Now – sad reverse! by pining hunger prest,
Pain racks her limbs, and anguish wrings her
    breast;
From her lov'd home, and weeping kindred
    torn,
A wretched outcast, friendless and forlorn,
Shut from the converse of the wise and good,
Doom'd through the day o'er all her woes to
    brood;
She quits, when night extends its gloomy
    shade,
Her loathsome haunt, to ply her hateful trade!

Nor this alone – the wretch must not refuse
Her hacknied smile, though spurn'd with vile
    abuse;
Submissive too, yea more – with cheerful air,
Must insults, stripes, and proud oppression
    bear!
Oh! words are poor, and language far too faint
The woes and pains of such a sin to paint!
Disease and sickness waste, with rapid stride,
Those charms so late the fruitful source of
    pride,
And vice and mis'ry, foes to youthful bloom,
Drag their sad victim to an early tomb!

Oh! ye, who proudly vain of fleeting charms,
And, mad for pleasure, rush to certain harms;
Who, deaf to reason's, deaf to virtue's voice,
Blindly prefer the flow'ry paths of vice!

Learn hence, that pleasure's but a fev'rish
    dream
Frail as the glitt'ring bubble of the stream!
Lo! deadly adders lurk beneath her flow'rs,
And mortal poison drops from all her bow'rs;
Short her delights, if once her art prevails,
But long and deep the sorrows she entails!

Yet what – if rescued from a fate so low,
From scenes so sunk in wretchedness and
    woe?
Ah! what, though riches, splendour, health,
    unite
To lull thy soul with every new delight –
Still there's a *worm* will canker and destroy
The fairest blossoms of forbidden joy!
Still shall you taste the 'wormwood and the
    gall,'
While conscience writes a curse upon them all!
Lo! keen remorse, a deadly taint shall fling
In every draught from sin's polluted spring;

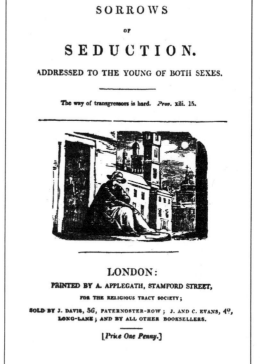

THE

SORROWS

OF

SEDUCTION.

ADDRESSED TO THE YOUNG OF BOTH SEXES.

The way of transgressors is hard. *Prov.* xiii. 15.

LONDON:

PRINTED BY A. APPLEGATH, STAMFORD STREET,

FOR THE RELIGIOUS TRACT SOCIETY;

SOLD BY J. DAVIS, 56, PATERNOSTER-ROW ; J. AND C. EVANS, 42,
LONG-LANE ; AND BY ALL OTHER BOOKSELLERS.

[*Price One Penny.*]

The mournful *future*, black with wrath
    appears,
And clouds *the present* with distracting fears;
Points to an hour beyond the darksome grave!
When vengeance strikes, nor mercy deigns to
    save!

Oh! that my pray'rs, my tears could gently
    move
Your thoughtless minds to feel *a Saviour's*
    love!
On him to fix your strength-imploring eye,
Whene'er temptation dares to venture nigh:
Then – should some lying traitor tempt to sin,
And find too strong an advocate *within*,
Soon would you feel a more than mortal arm
Stretch'd out in aid, to shield your soul from
    harm.

THE FRISKY GIRLS OF LONDON

A capital new flash chant

TUNE—*Nancy Dawson*

If you're inclined to have a treat,
Or looking out for love-joys sweet,
Stroll up the Haymarket, or Bond-street,
   Where nightly there is fun done;
If desire your mind doth teaze,
And you will pay the usual fees,
You very quickly can get ease,
   From the frisky mots of London.

The swell, all raging with love's fire,
When he a woman does require,
Selects the girl he doth admire,
   Though often he gets undone;
Though he, indeed – the truth I've said –
Is stiff with pride, he need not dread –
He's quickly made to droop his head,
   By the frisky mots of London.

The barber is a merry soul,
So with the vimen takes a stroll,
And very soon erects his pole,
   Resolved to be by none done;
With pleasure at his pole they stare,
His lather-box, and all his ware;
His pole and box suit to a hair,
   The frisky mots of London.

The jolly tar so full of glee,
Admires the tempting open C,
And very dearly likes to be
   In a port-hole where there's fun done;
Of treasure he has got a hoard,
To spend a deal he can afford,
So very soon he goes aboard
   The frisky mots of London.

The fishmonger's a frisky blade,
And, though he dearly likes a maid,
For any flat-fish, he's the blade,
   And thinks he's not by one done;
So up the Quadrant he doth plod,
The girls all follow at his nod;
They give him summut for his cod –
   The frisky mots of London.

The pawnbroker is sure to win,
The blowens he blows out with gin

So in return, they take him in,
   And vow he is by none done;
When up the spout, he 'stands alone!'
And this I'm certain you will own,
The pawnbroker's balls are very well known
   To the frisky mots of London.

Old gentleman, of sixty-four,
With lust and lechery plagued so sore,
Resolves to kiss a mot once more,
   To prove he is not undone;
No matter what his form or tan,
If he's got money please he can;
There's nothing like an old gentleman,
   To the frisky mots of London.

So, in every rank, in every stage,
Love and luxury are the rage;
But the vimen can your fire assuage
   They really are by none done;
If you a warm bath do require,
Or are stiff with cold – I'm no liar –
You soon may get as hot as fire,
   With the frisky mots of London.

HARRIET WILSON'S MEMOIRS

The next morning I received another visit from Mrs Porter, who informed me that she had just had an interview with my new lover, and had reported to him all I had desired her to say.

Since you object to meet a stranger, continued Mrs Porter, his grace desires me to say, he hopes you can keep a secret, and to inform you, that it is the Duke of Wellington, who so anxiously desires to make your acquaintance.

I have heard of his grace often, said I, in a tone of deep disappointment, for I had been indulging a kind of hope about the stranger, with the great Newfoundland dog, with whose appearance I had been so unusually struck, as to have sought for him every day, and I thought of him every hour.

His grace, Mrs Porter proceeded, only intreats to be allowed to make your acquaintance. His situation, you know, prevents the possibility of his getting regularly introduced to you.

It will never do, said I, shaking my head.

Be assured, said Mrs Porter, he is a remarkably fine-looking man, and if you are afraid of my house, promise to receive him in your own, at any hour when he may be certain to find you alone.

Well, thought I, with a sigh! I suppose he must come. I do not understand economy, and am frightened to death at debts. Argyle is going to Scotland; and I shall want a steady sort of friend, of some kind, in case a bailiff should get hold of me.

What shall I say to his grace? Mrs Porter, enquired, growing impatient.

Well, then, said I, since it must be so, tell his grace, that I will receive him to-morrow, at three; but mind, only as a common acquaintance!

Away winged Wellington's Mercury, as an old woman wings it at sixty, and most punctual to my appointment, at three, on the following day, Wellington made his appearance. He bowed first, then said –

How do you do? then thanked me for having given him permission to call on me; and then wanted to take hold of my hand.

Really, said I, withdrawing my hand; for such a renowned hero, you have very little to say for yourself.

Beautiful creature! uttered Wellington, where is Lorne?

Good gracious, said I, out of all patience at this stupidity, – what come you here for, duke!

Beautiful eye, yours! explained Wellington.

Aye man! they are greater conquerors than ever Wellington shall be; but, to be serious, I understood you came here to try to make yourself agreeable?

What, child! do you think that I have nothing better to do, than to make speeches to please ladies? said Wellington.

Après avoir depeuplé la terre vous devez faire tout pour la repeupler, I replied.

You should see me where I shine, Wellington observed, laughing.

Where's that, in God's name?

In a field of battle, answered the hero.

Battez vous donc, et qu'un autre me fasse la cour! said I.

But love scenes, or even love quarrels, seldom tend to amuse the reader, so, to be brief, what was a mere man, even though it were the handsome duke of Argyle, to a Wellington!!!

*

Wellington was now my constant visitor: – a most unentertaining one, Heaven knows! and, in the evenings, when he wore his broad red ribbon, he looked very like a rat catcher.

Do you know, said I, to him, one day, do you know the world talks about hanging you?

Eh? said Wellington.

They say you will be hanged, in spite of all your brother Wellesley can say in your defence.

Ha!! said Wellington, very seriously, what paper did you read?

AN AMAZON

[*The Prince of Wales is 'entertained' while his desk is searched for proof that Sir Richard Stamford is a child of George III and a Quakeress, Anna Lightfoot.*]

About thirty-five years previously to the date mentioned at the opening of this tale, a certain Letitia Fluke was born in a miserable attic in Lukner's Lane, St Giles's. As she grew up, she became remarkable for the beauty of her person, the masculine energy of her character, and the profligacy of her morals. Seduced by Rann, the celebrated highwayman who bore the *sobriquet* of 'Sixteen-String Jack,' she lived with him as his mistress for some time; and being endowed with extraordinary intelligence, she taught herself not only the rudiments of a good education, but likewise acquired the facility of expressing herself with grammatical accuracy and conversational elegance. After passing through various gradations, she married Sir John Lade, a wealthy and amorous baronet who was old enough to be her grandfather; and, on becoming Lady Letitia Lade she soon wheedled herself into that sort of society at the West End which may be described as 'not over particular.' Her great personal beauty, splendid figure, easy virtue, and proficiency in all the sports of the field rendered her a special favourite with the dashing noblemen and gentlemen about town; and her reputation as a huntress was second only to that of her friend Tim Meagles as a hunter. She rode exquisitely – was always one of the foremost in at the death – and could leap a five-barred gate or practise any of the most daring feats characteristic of steeple-chasing.

This lady was it whom Meagles had brought with him to the Prince's room on the present occasion. She was however dressed in male attire, which became her admirably; and had it not been for the fulness of her bosom, she might have been taken by a stranger for a man; though, as a matter of course, it would have been a man of beardless face and of rather effeminate appearance. As it was, she looked like a modern Diana the Huntress: for she had spurs upon her boots and carried a riding-whip in her hand – and her form,

though robust and vigorous, was admirably symmetrical, while all her movements were characterised by a graceful ease. Nothing could exceed the elegance of her costume. The hat, with its broad brim, set off her handsome countenance to the greatest advantage; and when she removed it on entering the chamber, her magnificent black hair showered in a myriad glossy ringlets over her broad and sloping shoulders. The blue frock-coat, braided most elaborately in front, fitted close to her form, developing the contours of her

swelling hips, and giving a wasp-like appearance to the waist; while the grey small-clothes and the polished hessian-boots, with their tassels and spurs, completed an attire at once tasteful and becoming. Being tall in stature, Lady Letitia had a masculine air, and enacted the part of 'the man' to perfection – the robust proportions and straightness of her limbs, with the solid firmness of the flesh, giving a fulness of shape to her entire person and rendering ample justice to the excellent 'fit' of her garments.

Having admitted his disguised companion into the royal bed-chamber, Tim Meagles closed and locked the door by which they had thus entered; and bursting into a hearty laugh as he approached the couch, he exclaimed, 'My dear Prince, you seem to stare at my friend here, as if you had never seen him in all your life.'

'And who the devil is it?' demanded his Royal Highness, sitting up in bed, while his countenance wore an expression which showed that he was half inclined to be angry. 'Why! by heavens – 'tis a woman,' he exclaimed, as Letitia advanced towards him: then, his features expanding into a smile, he said, 'Ah! my beautiful huntress – I recognise you now! Well, I suppose Meagles has brought you to breakfast with me – and this is an unexpected pleasure.'

'Your Royal Highness is very kind thus to receive me,' returned Letitia, her smile revealing a set of large but brilliant teeth. 'It was not my fault – Meagles would insist upon bringing me – and your Royal Highness knows what a harum-scarum fellow he is.'

'Egad! I was quite sure that you would be welcome,' exclaimed Meagles, taking up a foil from the table and making a sham thrust at her ladyship. 'Only conceive,' he added, turning towards the Prince, who was surveying with gloating eyes the fine form of the huntress; – 'I met our fair friend here as she was coming from her morning's ride –'

'I was just about to put up my horse in the stables in King Street,' interrupted Lady Letitia: 'for I went out alone for a good scamper at daybreak – and when I came back, there was not a groom nor even a body in attendance to take the animal from me.'

'Well – and I offered to unsaddle him for you,' said Meagles.

'But I did it for myself while you were thinking about it,' responded the lady, as she gave her friend a real lash with her riding-whip in acknowledgement of the sham thrust he had made at her.

'Don't spare him!' cried the Prince, laughing heartily as Tim Meagles vainly cut a caper to avoid the blow. 'But had I anticipated the pleasure of your company, my dear Letitia, I would have risen to receive you. Indeed, I ordered Germain not to make his appearance with breakfast until eleven, though I knew that Meagles would be here at ten – because I had resolved to take a bath in the interim.'

'Treat me just as if I were one of your own sex,' exclaimed the lady; 'and have your bath, by all means. Here – I will give you your dressing-gown and slippers,' she continued, throwing the former upon the bed and placing the latter in a convenient position on the carpet by the side of the couch.

'And you mean me to rise in your presence?' asked the Prince, laughingly.

'Why not?' demanded Letitia. 'You do not suppose that I shall go home and tell the baronet that I have had the honour of assisting at the toilette of his Royal Highness the Prince of Wales?'

'Egad! you are quite capable of telling your husband anything,' exclaimed Meagles, putting on a pair of boxing-gloves and attacking an imaginary antagonist in a most scientific fashion.

'You are very brave in buffetting the empty air, Tim,' said Lady Letitia: 'but if you really want some one to spar with you, I don't mind gratifying you in that way;' – and as she thus spoke, the Amazon threw down her riding-whip, and thrust her hands into a pair of pugilistic gloves.

'This is excellent!' cried the Prince, leaping from his couch, and putting on the figured silk dressing-gown and the embroidered morocco slippers which the lady had placed within his reach.

But while he was thus employed, the huntress had turned her back towards him, inasmuch as she had commenced a regular sparring match with Tim Meagles, who very complacently allowed her to buffet him about to her heart's content – though, had he chosen to exercise his skill in the art of self-defence, she would never have had a chance of even hitting him a single blow.

Presently Tim Meagles began to retreat rapidly – then he darted aside with an abrupt movement – then he leapt and capered all about the room in order to weary his fair antagonist – both of them highly enjoying the sport, while the Prince of Wales was equally amused as a spectator. At last, the humorous Meagles put an end to the fun by suddenly dealing Lady Letitia a blow on the forehead, which knocked her flat down upon her back; but she rose laughing heartily, and throwing aside the gloves, declared that she had had enough of boxing for the present occasion.

'Now we'll take a little drop of brandy, my brave Amazonian friend,' exclaimed Meagles; and filling a couple of wine-glasses, he handed one to Lady Letitia, who tossed off the contents without winking. 'By the bye, I quite forgot you, my dear Prince,' observed Tim, turning towards his Royal Highness. 'Shall I pour out a thimbleful?'

'No – not at present, Meagles,' was the reply. 'I have had my hock and soda-water, and a dram to sink it – and I therefore think that I shall be able to manage very well until after breakfast. But now for my bath,' added the Prince, gathering his ample dressing-gown round his somewhat portly form, and descending from the dais.

'I envy your Royal Highness the possession of a bathing-room contiguous to your sleeping chamber,' said Lady Letitia. 'I must positively make Sir John have one fitted up for me,' she added, exchanging a rapid glance of intelligence with Meagles.

'Have you ever seen my bath-room?' inquired the Prince.

'Only as I catch a glimpse of it now through the half-open door,' responded the Amazon. 'Your Royal Highness must recollect that this is the first time I have had the honour of being admitted to your private apartments.'

'And it need not be the last,' observed George, bending upon her a significant look: for although he had known the lady for two or three years, she had never struck him as being so handsome as she appeared on the present occasion.

'Excellent!' cried the huntress, laughing. 'The Prince is paying me compliments!'

'Compliments? No – I am telling you truths,' said George.

'Do you persist in forgetting that I am a gentleman for the nonce?' – and again she laughed.

'There, now!' cried Meagles, who had been pretending to be very busy in examining the lock of one of the Prince's rifles for the last two or three minutes; 'I knew that your Royal Highness would not be displeased with me bringing Lady Letitia hither this morning?'

'Displeased!' ejaculated George: 'I am delighted! But will you inspect my bath-room before I enter it?' he asked, turning again towards the lovely Amazon.

'Before you enter it?' repeated the lady, as if she had not heard aright. 'Why should you stand upon any such ceremony with me? I cannot succeed in persuading you to forget that my attire is unsuited to my sex'

'It becomes you admirably, at all events,' observed the Prince, advancing close up to the huntress, who was leaning negligently against the toilette-table: then, proffering her his hand, he said, 'Permit me to show you my bath-room.'

'Oh! with much pleasure,' exclaimed Lady Letitia. 'It will perhaps afford me a hint for the establishment of some humble imitation at my own town residence.'

Thus speaking, the Amazon accompanied the Prince into the adjacent chamber; and when he closed the door behind him, she affected not to perceive the incident.

'Well, upon my word, your Royal Highness possesses a perfect oriental bathing-room,' she observed, throwing herself on one of the voluptuous ottomans and surveying the place in a leisurely and altogether unembarrassed manner: 'it is really a delightful scene – exquisitely fitted up – and evincing in every detail that fine taste for which your Royal Highness is so justly celebrated.'

'I am pleased that you admire my bath-room,' said the Prince, seating himself by her side. 'Can you not for the moment fancy that you are in some apartment attached to the harem of a Turkish palace?'

'Never having been in the Mussulman's country, I cannot precisely make so free with my imagination,' answered the huntress, in a lively tone. 'At the same time, from all I have read, I could, without a very large stretch of the fancy, conceive your Royal Highness to be a Sultan in *deshabillée*,' she added, with a significant glance at the Prince's figured silk dressing-gown and embroidered red morocco slippers.

'I am perfectly willing that you should entertain such a belief, on condition that you permit me to exercise my fancy with regard to yourself,' exclaimed George, his eyes wandering over the form of the huntress.

'Oh! certainly – I cannot have the least objection,' she cried, – 'especially after having compared you to the Grand Turk. And now tell me, pray, for what you are inclined to take me?'

'For my Sultana of an hour,' responded the Prince, throwing his arms round Lady Letitia's neck.

'You are determined to make me feel that I am a woman, in spite of my male attire,' she exclaimed, laughing.

We must however leave the Prince and the huntress in the bath-room, and return to Mr Meagles, who at the moment when they were quitting the bed-chamber, was to all appearances very busily engaged in examining the miscellaneous articles strewed upon the central table.

Nor did he desist from his occupation as soon as he found himself alone: for he thought it probable that the Prince might return to fetch something, or to give him instructions relative to the exclusion of any one who might seek admission to the bed-chamber. He accordingly remained at the table, and began to examine the indecent French prints, which he had not seen before, as they had only arrived on the previous day. They were not however much to his taste; for Tim Meagles was too ardent and impassioned a votary at the shrine of Venus to need any stimulant of the kind for the purpose of exciting his imagination. Besides, he had a certain important object in view, and which engrossed' his thoughts: he therefore turned the prints over in a listless manner, and very shortly passed from them to the inspection of the fire-arms. These he scrutinized with less abstraction of mind – for there were several new fowling-pieces and pistols which he had not seen before.

But when about a quarter of an hour had elapsed Tim Meagles suddenly raised his eyes, looked around him and then listened. All was still; and then the next instant the Amazon's clear, merry, musical laugh ringing from the bath-room, met Meagles' ears. A cloud swept over his countenance: for Tim Meagles, although he had long been on terms of the most tender intimacy with her, was for a moment annoyed at himself for having purposely brought her to Carlton House on the present occasion with the view of throwing her into the arms of the Prince.

But this feeling of jealousy was as evanescent as, under the circumstances, it was absurd; and it was instantaneously succeeded by a lively satisfaction, as he thought to himself, 'She has played her cards admirably – and she will succeed in engrossing the Prince's attention during the half-hour that I enjoined her to be sure and keep him engaged!'

Thus rejoicing in the success of a pre-arranged stratagem, Tim Meagles advanced to the royal couch, and took from beneath the pillow a long, thin gold chain to which a key of very peculiar workmanship was attached.

He then approached the writing-desk to which we have already alluded; and having carefully opened it, proceeded to examine several small packets of papers, which were tied round with pink riband, and bore endorsements indicative of the various matters to which they respectively referred. But while thus occupied, he more than once cast an anxious look towards the door of the bath-room: – his apprehensions were not however verified by any sudden interruption on the part of the Prince.

His search in the two compartments of the desk lasted for upwards of ten minutes, there being numerous packets of papers, which he examined one after the other until nearly the whole were thus disposed of – and still he had not lighted on the particular parcel which he sought. He now began to fear that it might not be in the desk at all: – and yet he knew full well that the Prince kept every document of an important or private nature there. But, as it frequently happens in such cases, the very last packet which Tim Meagles drew from the desk bore the endorsement that he had hitherto so vainly sought; and having secured this little parcel about his person, he re-arranged all the others – locked the desk – and restored the key to its place of concealment under the pillow of the couch.

For a few moments a smile of triumph played upon the lips of Tim Meagles: but it almost immediately yielded to that calm, free-and-easy, and independent expression which was the natural characteristic of his features. Drawing a large arm-chair close to the fire, he deposited himself indolently in the luxurious seat, and lighted a cigar.

In a few minutes the door of the bath-room opened, and Lady Letitia came forth, followed by the Prince. Not a blush appeared upon her cheek – not the slightest embarrassment marked her manner, as she emerged from the bathing-room: but Meagles turned an arch look upon the Prince, exclaiming, 'Well, are you displeased with me for having brought our Amazonian friend this morning?'

'Hold your tongue, Tim,' cried the lady, laughing. 'Ah! I thought I smelt the delightful flavour of the weed. I will keep you company with a cigar, while the Prince dresses himself – and then for breakfast. I already feel as hungry as a hunter.'

'Or a huntress – which?' observed Meagles.

'Both,' replied Lady Letitia, throwing herself upon a chair opposite to her humorous friend: then, taking an elegant ivory case from the pocket of her frock-coat, she drew forth a little Spanish cigarette, which she lighted by the aid of Meagles' full-flavoured Havannah.

'And so you smoke, Letitia – do you?' asked the Prince.

'Your Royal Highness sees that I can manage a cigarette,' responded the huntress, – 'but barely a cigar. And as for tobacco – I mean as it is smoked in a pipe – pah! – the idea makes me feel –'

'Not sick,' interjected Meagles; 'but only as if you would spoil your beautiful teeth. It's all vanity on your part, my beauty! – and if it wasn't for the teeth you'd be smoking the strongest Cavendish, I know!'

The huntress laughed, and then gave Tim a tap on the cheek, which compliment he returned by means of a somewhat hard smack upon the lady's back; whereupon she dealt him so sound a box on the ears that all the blood in his body seemed in a moment to rise into his cheeks and stagnate there. But the next instant he burst out laughing, and the Prince as well as the Amazon herself shared in the merriment.

A quarter of an hour was thus whiled away by means of smoking, jesting, and chattering; and in the interval the Prince of Wales had made such improvements in his toilette that he now appeared in an elegant *deshabillée*. Germain shortly afterwards entered the room, bearing a large silver tray containing the breakfast-things; – and although he observed Lady Letitia and instantly recognised her, he nevertheless affected to take no more notice of her presence than if she were a phantom visible only to the Prince and Meagles. For Germain was a very discreet Frenchman: otherwise he would not have long held the post of *valet intime*, or rather 'confidential gentleman,' about the person of the Prince of Wales.

An elegant breakfast was now served up, and to which both Lady Letitia and Tim Meagles did ample justice; but George had indulged overnight too liberally in curaçoa-punch to be able to eat with any degree of appetite in the morning.

'You don't seem to be peckish, my dear Prince,' observed Meagles as he committed a second and very desperate assault upon a cold partridge pie.

'You made the punch too strong last night, Tim,' answered his Royal Highness.

'Not a bit of it!' cried Meagles. 'By the bye, my dear Prince,' he continued, turning towards his Royal Highness, 'I missed you from a quarter to six to nearly half-past ten last evening –'

'And you are very likely to miss me for precisely the same period *this* evening, Mr

Meagles,' interrupted the Prince, suddenly assuming a tone that had just sufficient haughtiness in it to serve as a tacit intimation that the subject was not to be dwelt upon.

'Then, instead of taking an early dinner with your Royal Highness, I shall fasten myself upon the hospitality of our Amazonian friend here,' remarked Meagles, who understood the hint to abandon the delicate topic which he had touched upon, but who did not choose to appear disconcerted by the reproof that he had received.

'But I shall expect you at midnight, Tim,' exclaimed the Prince, resuming his familiarity of manner as suddenly and as easily as he had thrown it aside for a momentary purpose: besides, it would not at all have suited his views to quarrel with an agent who was invaluable to him. 'You and I shall be alone together to-night, Tim,' he continued: 'and then I will explain to you a little service that I require at your hands.'

'Well, I don't mind promising to be here at midnight,' said Meagles, who never chose to let it appear that he was servile in his attendance upon the Prince, or that he was a mere toad-eater constantly ready at the beck and call of his illustrious patron. 'And now,' he exclaimed, pushing away his plate, 'we will have a drop of kirchwasser after this famous breakfast.'

Thus speaking, he filled three liqueur-glasses with the potent cordial; and Lady Letitia tossed off her dram with as much real *gusto* as her two companions.

Shortly afterwards the Amazon and Tim Meagles took their departure by the private staircase; and the Prince of Wales rang the bell to desire the attendance of his secretary with the morning's newspapers and letters.

A DERELICT FROM THE REGENCY COURT

This unfortunate woman [Mary Anne Pearce], who, for many years past had been the terror of beadles, watchmen, publicans, & police-officers, expired on Monday night at her lodging, a miserable attic, in the house No. 8,

Charles-street, Drury-lane. She was twice taken to the station-house in Covent-garden on Sunday last for disorderly conduct, and discharged by Mr Thomas, the superintendent, for at least the hundredth time. On being discharged for the last time, she addressed Mr Thomas, saying, 'I have given you a great deal of trouble, Sir, but I shall not give you much more. It is almost over with me.' Mr Thomas observing that she appeared faint and ill, advised her to go home and go to bed, & she left the station promising to follow his advice. But the ruling passion of her life, the love of gin overcame her resolution, for it appeared that instead of returning to her lodging, she found out some of her favourite haunts, and became again intoxicated. In this state she reached her home, where she was put to bed, and about midnight the owner of the house came to the station and gave information that the unfortunate woman was either dead or dying. Mr Thomas immediately went to the house, supposing that she might have met with some ill-treatment, but on his arrival there at midnight, he found that she had been dead about ten minutes, having expired from a general decay of nature, brought on by her addiction to gin, and the miserable life she had led. For the last 15 years she had been a constant visitor at every police-office in London, & by far the greater portion of that time she has lived in prison. Her excess, under the influence of liquor, occurred so frequently, that the evening of the day on which she was discharged from prison generally found her there again. Her conduct in confinement formed a singular contrast to her behaviour on obtaining her discharge. In prison, where of course she had no opportunity of indulging in her favourite beverage, she conducted herself with so much decency and propriety, that Mr Nodder, the governor of Tothill-fields gaol, usually appointed her to watch over the female prisoners in the capacity of matron, and he has often declared that he could not have selected a more fit person, and he always regretted, for her own sake, when the expiration of the term of her imprisonment took place. Her appearance on quitting prison was extremely decent, but the first use which she made of her liberty, was a visit to the gin-shop, and in half an hour after she might be seen staggering through the streets, followed by a crowd of idlers, plaguing and annoying the wretched woman. To avoid them she generally took refuge in a public-house, where she would demand more drink, & if refused, her first act was to smash the windows, and destroy every thing that came within her reach. Those outrages of course led to her apprehension, but, being a powerful woman she seldom resigned her liberty without a struggle, in which her captors generally received some token of her prowess; and in the days of her strength the old watchman were so fearful of encountering her Ladyship single handed, that they seldom presumed to approach her unless in a body, and even then they were frequently obliged to resort to a stratagem before they could effectually secure her. The unfortunate woman, although reduced to the lowest state of misery and prostitution, was once the dashing chere amie of Lord Barrymore, with whom for a period she enjoyed all the luxuries and gaieties of life, living in a splendid house, and riding in her carriage. When this connexion terminated, his Lordship provided her with a husband in the person of one of his servants, named Pearce, on whom it is said he settled a yearly sum. The visions, however, of her former splendour haunted the unhappy woman, and her marriage with Pearce, produced continual bickerings and unhappiness, and finally led her to adopt the miserable course of life the irregularities of which obtained for her so much notoriety.

KATE ELMORE DEFENDS HERSELF

[*In this incident from* Eliza Grimwood (*c. 1838*) *the stereotype of the attempted rape of a young girl by a cynical aristocrat has a strong flavour of authenticity.*]

Kate Elmore, as has been previously said, was at this time but a few months over thirteen. She was a fair-haired, blue-eyed girl; tall, and intelligent enough to look a year or two older: but she was not too young to excite the pity of Lord Rakemore when his passions were concerned. After evil had been done, he was not backward in making reparation so far as money could repair; but a strong animal nature, and long indulged habits of a sensual kind, had rendered him callous to all appeals of humanity.

'It must be done,' said he to Mrs Bruin for the tenth time, as she still objected.

'Then you must take her to the castle,' replied the old woman. 'I shall try and persuade her to go with you. If you promise her new dresses, and all that sort of thing, you may get her to go; for she is as full of pride as an egg is full of meat.'

Kate knew no reason why they should want to deprive her of life; but neither Bluebeard nor the giants who lived in castles, and of whom she had read, gave particular reasons for killing their victims; and that old Grimwood intended to kill Eliza she had no doubt. Neither could she doubt that they intended to kill her – what else could they mean?

Such thoughts as these passed through her head as she watched the first motion that they would make towards the room door; she watched that first motion, to be ready to flee up stairs to get out at the window.

Lord Rakemore counted money – heavy pieces of money, into Mrs Bruin's hand, and the latter put them into a cup in her cupboard. When she shut the cupboard door she came towards that which opened into the room; and Kate, snatching up her cloak and still retaining the knife, rushed to the stairs.

Mrs Bruin lifted the latch of the bed-room door, and tried to push it up. The table and chairs prevented her.

Kate lifted the latch of the door which opened from the bottom step of the stair; but found the door locked, and the key out.

Mrs Bruin put all her strength to the door, and pushed back the chairs and tables far enough to get in her head; and with the light which entered with her head, she saw Kate standing by the staircase.

She put her shoulders to that which opposed her, again pushed with all her might, but she only made an additional inch of opening.

Kate tried the bedroom window, but it was fastened down by a screw. She tried to unscrew it; and Mrs Bruin dared her to do so. This made her the more determined to persevere, but her fingers were too nervous or the screw was too fast; she could not turn it.

Lord Rakemore came to Mrs Bruin's assistance and both put their shoulders to the door. They opened it four inches; and that only because of the breaking one of the chair feet.

Kate saw that the table and the chairs formed a line from the bedstead to the door, and that, as the bedstead was close to the wall, they must crush the chairs to pieces or break the door before they could enter; and, in the mean time, she tried to break the windows. The glass rattled down, but the panes were small, and the frame was tough wrought iron. It withstood all her efforts, – and there were shutters outside.

Mrs Bruin in a violent tone ordered her to take the chairs from behind the door; and at the same time with Lord Rakemore's powerful shoulders and her own, broke part of another chair, and made an opening wide enough to admit herself edgeways.

Kate grasped the knife firmly and screamed.

Lord Rakemore in a soothing voice prayed her to be quiet, and to put the knife down.

Mrs Bruin knew by Kate's terror and violence that she must have been listening to what was said; and that now she must be prevented at all hazards from getting back to her friends and companions.

Lord Rakemore put in his arm and drew away one of the chairs. Then opened the door wide and took in the lighted candle; begging Kate at the same time to be quiet, as no one would harm her.

Kate kept Mrs Bruin off by flourishing the knife.

Mrs Bruin said that now since it was so his lordship might do with her and to her what he pleased; and in that very room too; she would not prevent him.

Lord Rakemore spoke soothingly, but assured Kate they would soon take the knife from her if she did not put it down.

Kate retreated to the farthest corner of the room; and, standing with her back in it and her face outward, kept them at bay with the knife.

Mrs Bruin again told her that for this violent conduct with the knife, as also for her screams, she would let Lord Rakemore do what he chose to her, and if he took her life, she, Mrs Bruin, would not prevent him.

Kate needed no such assurance, she believed that all along.

Lord Rakemore said, 'Lay hold of her; she won't do any harm with it.'

Kate said, 'Won't I though? I'll cut the first of ye that touches me, as deep as the knife will go!'

Mrs Bruin, enraged, said, 'I'll see whether you will or not, you impudent slut!' and at the same moment rushed forward to seize the arm which held the knife. She missed it in her passion, and caught Kate by the hair of the head.

Kate screamed.

Mrs Bruin dragged her from the corner with great force, and as she did so gave a shriek, let go her hold, and staggered backwards to the bedside.

Kate had fulfilled her threat to cut as deep as the knife would go. It had gone from beneath the breast to the back bone, and was drawn out ready to go into the next one that came within its reach.

Mrs Bruin groaned. The blood rushed inwards from the wound; and she fell on the floor dead.

Lord Rakemore stood confounded, and was only able to beg Kate to put the knife down.

Kate stood crouching into the corner with the blooded weapon in her hand, and told him to keep off.

He hurriedly retreated and shut the outer door behind him. The moment he had done so Kate's eyes caught sight of the bleeding corpse she had made. The distorted features filled her with *horror*, and she shook as if paralytic. The knife fell from her hand; she sunk down in the corner, and felt as if she dreamt some hateful dream from which she struggled to awake, but could not.
[*Rakemore fastens the murder on Kate's father.*]

NANCY DAWSON

A very scarce and celebrated out-and-out flash ditty, As sung at the Coal Hole

Air – *The Pretty Girls of London*

Nancy Dawson was a —
And in that town were many more;
And when the sailors went on shore,
    Law! they asked for Nancy Dawson!
For she was such a sprightly lass,
All other mots she did surpass;
Show her your staff, she'd wag her —
    'All right,' says Nancy Dawson.

The jolly tar so stout and bold,
Who o'er the sea for months had roll'd,
Come home with rare galore of gold,
    Would fly to Nancy Dawson.
When he lugged out his marlingspike,
'My eye,' says Nancy, "tis what I like,
So let us quick the bargain strike
    Aboard the Nancy Dawson.'

The tall, the short, the old, the young,
No matter, so they were well hung,
The port holes open free were flung,
    Of frisky Nancy Dawson.
Upon her beam-ends she would lay,
And her full broadside would display,
Then cried, 'My lads, come, fire away,
    Spank into Nancy Dawson.'

Such battering she'd received, 'tis true,
And still a vessel fair to view;
The tars, full loaded, ever flew
    For an action with Nancy Dawson.

The midshipman, then went to work,
He was as hungry as a Turk,
Her duff she up and down did jerk,
    Did frisky Nancy Dawson.
The lieutenant of the ship came by,
'As quick as you can, mate,' he did cry,
'I'm bursting now to have a shy
    At the craft of Nancy Dawson.'

The lieutenant so strong and gay,
Then stepp'd on board and fired away;
Such courage he did then display
    He well pleased Nancy Dawson.
Then passed the rare old commodore,
Who for ten years hadn't had a —
Vowed that he would have a bore
    At frisky Nancy Dawson.

The commodore was hot and strong,
His member it was stout and long,
He made sad mess the works among
    Of pretty Nancy Dawson.
'Hold off,' she cried, but on he jogged.
'If I leave off may I be flogged,
Until your vessel's water-logged.'
    'O dear,' says Nancy Dawson.

For full an hour he drove away,
While Nancy, panting, there did lay,
And ever since that fatal day,
    Done up is Nancy Dawson.
So all fair crafts, who lust afford,
Your little port-holes careful hoard,
Ne'er take a commodore on board,
    Like frisky Nancy Dawson.

For fourteen-pounders she cared not,
For bomb-shells, or for good grape shot,
So long as she good ramming got,
    'All right,' says Nancy Dawson.

The Royal George to England came,
With tars aboard of gallant fame,
Who all, with courage in a flame,
    Steer'd off to Nancy Dawson.
When all the crew had bored her straight,
With their good marlingspikes so great,
'I'll take the admiral to make weight,
    On board', says Nancy Dawson.

The tall black cook with her made free,
One day beneath the apple tree,
And gave her pinches three times three;
    'Bore on,' said Nancy Dawson.
A midshipman then came in view,
So out his little dirk he drew,
And cried out, 'Shipmate, after you,
    For a turn at Nancy Dawson.'

4. WHITE SLAVES

THE DISTRESSED SEMPSTRESS

Air – *Jenny Jones*

A great number of those young women (after twelve hours hard labour) being without friends are compelled to walk the streets at night, in order to make out a miserable existence.

You gentles of England, I pray give attention
Unto those few lines, I'm going to relate,

Concerning the sempstress, I'm going to
   mention,
Who long time has been, in a sad wretched
   state,
Laboriously toiling, both night, noon, and
   morning,
For a wretched subsistance, now mark what I
   say,
Quite unprotected, forlorn, and dejected,
For sixpence, eightpence, or tenpence a day.

The wages that's paid to the hard working
   sempstress
Keeps them in wretchedness, sorrow, and
   debt,
They scarcely can earn, a temporary subsist-
   ance,
Which causes the beauty of Britain to fret,
From daylight till dark, she works brisk at
   her needle,
The fruits of her labour, is all she desires,
Pay her, her rights, and she never will
   murmer,
Justice and mercy is all she requires.

The sempstress, for charity, never was crav-
   ing,
The sweat of her fingers, is her sole delight,
There once was a time, she could live and be
   saving,
But long on her labours, there has been a
   blight,
Come forward you nobles, and grant them
   assistance
Give them employ, and a fair price them pay,
And then you will find, the poor hard working
   sempstress,
From honour and virtue will not go astray.

To shew them compassion pray quickly be
   stirring,
In delay, there is danger, there's no time to
   spare,
Their heads they are drooping, come forward
   and cheer them,
The pride of the world is o'er whelmed with
   care,
Old England's considered, for honour and
   virtue,
And beauty the glory and pride of the world,
Nor be not hesitating, but boldly step
   forward,
Suppression and tyranny, far away hurl.

MISERRIMA!!!

[*G. W. M. Reynolds describes the plight
of a sempstress in London.*]

We now come to a sad episode in our history –
and yet one in which there is perhaps less
romance and more truth than in any scene
yet depicted.

   We have already warned our reader that
he will have to accompany us amidst appalling scenes of vice and wretchedness: – we are
now about to introduce him to one of destitution and suffering – of powerful struggle and
unavailing toil – whose details are so very
sad, that we have been able to find no better
heading for our chapter than *miserrima*, or
'very miserable things.'

   The reader will remember that we have
brought our narrative, in preceding chapters,
up to the end of 1838: – we must now go back
for a period of two years, in order to commence the harrowing details of our present
episode.

   In one of the low dark rooms of a gloomy
house in a court leading out of Golden Lane,
St Luke's, a young girl of seventeen sate at
work. It was about nine o'clock in the evening; and a single candle lighted the miserable
chamber, which was almost completely de-
nuded of furniture. The cold wind of December whistled through the ill-closed casement
and the broken panes, over which thin paper
had been pasted to repel the biting chill. A
small deal table, two common chairs, and a
mattress were all the articles of furniture
which this wretched room contained. A door
at the end opposite the window opened into
another smaller chamber: and this latter one
was furnished with nothing, save an old
mattress. There were no blankets – no cover-
lids in either room. The occupants had no
other covering at night than their own clothes;
– and those clothes – God knows they were
thin, worn, and scanty enough!

   Not a spark of fire burned in the grate; –
and yet that front room in which the young
girl was seated was as cold as the nave of a
vast cathedral in the depth of winter.

The reader has perhaps experienced that icy chill which seems to strike to the very marrow of the bones, when entering a huge stone edifice: – the cold which prevailed in that room, and in which the young creature was at work with her needle, was more intense – more penetrating – more bitter – more frost-like than even that icy chill!

Miserable and cheerless was that chamber: the dull light of the candle only served to render its nakedness the more apparent, without relieving it of any of its gloom. And as the cold draught from the wretched casement caused the flame of that candle to flicker and oscillate, the poor girl was compelled to seat herself between the window and the table, to protect her light from the wind. Thus, the chilling December blast blew upon the back of the young sempstress, whose clothing was so thin and scant – so very scant!

The sempstress was, as we have before said, about seventeen years of age. She was very beautiful; and her features, although pale with want, and wan with care and long vigils, were pleasing and agreeable. The cast of her countenance was purely Grecian – the shape of her head eminently classical – and her form was of a perfect and symmetrical mould. Although clothed in the most scanty and wretched manner, she was singularly neat and clean in her appearance; and her air and demeanour were far above her humble occupation and her impoverished condition.

She had, indeed, seen better days! Reared in the lap of luxury by fond, but too indulgent parents, her education had been of a high order; and thus her qualifications were rather calculated to embellish her in prosperity than to prove of use to her in adversity. She had lost her mother at the age of twelve; and her father – kind and fond, and proud of his only child – had sought to make her shine in that sphere which she had then appeared destined to adorn. But misfortunes came upon them like a thunderbolt: and when poverty – grim poverty stared them in the face – this poor girl had no resource, save her needle! Now and then her father earned a trifle in the City, by making out accounts or copying deeds; – but sorrow and ill-health had almost entirely incapacitated him from labour or occupation of any kind; – and his young and affectionate daughter was compelled to toil from sun-rise until a late hour in the night to earn even a pittance.

One after another, all their little comforts, in the shape of furniture and clothing, disappeared; and after vainly endeavouring to maintain a humble lodging in a cheap but respectable neighbourhood, poverty compelled them to take refuge in that dark, narrow, filthy court leading out of Golden Lane.

Such was the sad fate of Mr Monroe and his daughter Ellen.

At the time when we introduce the latter to our readers, her father was absent in the City. He had a little occupation in a counting-house, which was to last three days, which kept him hard at work from nine in the morning till eleven at night, and for which he was to receive a pittance so small we dare not mention its amount! This is how it was: – an official assignee belonging to the Bankruptcy Court had some heavy accounts to make up by a certain day: he was consequently compelled to employ an accountant to aid him; the accountant employed a petty scrivener to make out the balance-sheet; and the petty scrivener employed Monroe to ease him of a portion of the toil. It is therefore plain that Monroe was not to receive much for his three days' labour.

And so Ellen was compelled to toil and work, and work and toil – to rise early, and go to bed late – so late that she had scarcely fallen asleep, worn out with fatigue, when it appeared time to get up again; – and thus the roses forsook her cheeks – and her health suffered – and her head ached – and her eyes grew dim – and her limbs were stiff with the chill!

And so she worked and toiled, and toiled and worked.

We said it was about nine o'clock in the evening.

Ellen's fingers were almost paralysed with cold and labour; and yet the work which she had in her hands must be done that night; else no supper then – and no breakfast on the morrow; for on the shelf in that cheerless chamber there was not a morsel of bread!

And for sixteen hours had that poor girl fasted already; for she had eaten a crust at five in the morning, when she had risen from her hard cold couch 'in the back chamber. She had left the larger portion of the bread that then remained, for her father; and she had assured him that she had a few halfpence to purchase more for herself – but she had therein deceived him! Ah! how noble and generous was that deception; – and how often – how very often did that poor girl practise it!

Ellen had risen at five that morning to embroider a silk shawl with eighty flowers. She had calculated upon finishing it by eight in the evening; but although she had worked, and worked, and worked hour after hour, without ceasing, save for a moment at long intervals to rest her aching head and stretch her cramped fingers, eight had struck – and nine had struck also – and still the blossoms were not all embroidered.

It was a quarter to ten when the last stitch was put into the last flower.

But then the poor creature could not rest: – not to her was it allowed to repose after that severe day of toil! She was hungry – she was faint – her stomach was sick for want of food; and at eleven her father would come home, hungry, faint, and sick at stomach also!

Rising from her chair – every limb stiff, cramped, and aching with cold and weariness – the poor creature put on her modest straw bonnet with a faded riband, and her thin wretched shawl, to take home her work.

Her employer dwelt upon Finsbury Pavement; and as it was now late, the poor girl was compelled to hasten as fast as her aching limbs would carry her.

The shop to which she repaired was brilliant with lamps and gas-lights. Articles of great variety and large value were piled in the windows, on the counters, on the shelves. Upwards of twenty young men were busily employed in serving the customers. The proprietor of that establishment was at that moment entertaining a party of friends up stairs, at a champagne supper!

The young girl walked timidly into the vast magazine of fashions, and, with downcast eyes, advanced towards an elderly woman who was sitting at a counter at the farther end of the shop. To this female did she present the shawl.

'A pretty time of night to come!' murmured the shopwoman. 'This ought to have been done by three or four o'clock.'

'I have worked since five this morning, without ceasing,' answered Ellen: 'and I could not finish it before.'

'Ah! I see,' exclaimed the shopwoman, turning the shawl over, and examining it critically; 'there are fifty or sixty flowers, I see.'

'Eighty,' said Ellen; 'I was ordered to embroider that number.'

'Well Miss – and is there so much difference between sixty and eighty?'

'Difference, ma'am!' ejaculated the young girl, the tears starting into her eyes; 'the difference is more than four hours' work!'

'Very likely, very likely, Miss. And how much do you expect for this?'

'I must leave it entirely to you, ma'am.'

The poor girl spoke deferentially to this cold-hearted woman, in order to make her generous. Oh! poverty renders even the innocence of seventeen selfish, mundane, and calculating!

'Oh! you leave it to me, do you?' said the woman, turning the shawl over and over, and scrutinising it in all points; but she could not discover a single fault in Ellen's work. 'You leave it to me? Well, it isn't so badly done – very tolerably for a girl of your age and inexperience! I presume,' she added, thrusting her hand into the till under the counter, and drawing forth sixpence, 'I presume that this is sufficient.'

'Madam,' said Ellen, bursting into tears, 'I have worked nearly seventeen hours at that shawl –'

She could say no more: her voice was lost in sobs.

'Come, come,' cried the shopwoman harshly, 'no whimpering here! Take up your money, if you like it – and if you don't, leave it. Only decide one way or another, and make haste!'

Ellen took up the sixpence, wiped her eyes, and hastily turned to leave the shop.

'Do you not want any more work?' demanded the shopwoman abruptly.

The fact was that the poor girl worked well, and did not 'shirk' labour; and the woman knew that it was the interest of her master to retain that young creature's services.

Those words, 'Do you not want any more work?' reminded Ellen that she and her father must live – that they could not starve! She accordingly turned towards that uncouth female once more, and received another shawl, to embroider in the same manner, and at the same price!

Eighty blossoms for sixpence!

Sixteen hours' work for sixpence!!

A farthing and a half per hour!!!

The young girl returned to the dirty court in Golden Lane, after purchasing some food, coarse and cheap, on her way home.

On the ground-floor of a house in the same court dwelt an old woman – one of those old women who are the moral sewers of great towns – the sinks towards which flow all the impurities of the human passions. One of those abominable hags was she who dishonour the sanctity of old age. She had hideous wrinkles upon her face; and as she stretched out her huge, dry, and bony hand, and tapped the young girl upon the shoulder, as the latter hurried past her door, the very touch seemed to chill the maiden even through her clothes.

Ellen turned abruptly around, and shuddered – she scarcely knew why – when she found herself confronting that old hag by the dim lustre of the lights which shone through the windows in the narrow court.

That old woman, who was the widow of crime, assumed as pleasant an aspect as her horrible countenance would allow her to put on, and addressed the timid maiden in a strain which the latter scarcely comprehended. All that Ellen could understand was that the old woman suspected how hardly she toiled and how badly she was paid, and offered to point out a more pleasant and profitable mode of earning money.

Without precisely knowing why, Ellen shrank from the contact of that hideous old hag, and trembled at the words which issued from the crone's mouth.

'You do not answer me,' said the wretch. 'Well, well; when you have no bread to eat – no work – no money to pay your rent – and nothing but the workhouse before you, you will think better of it and come to me.'

Thus saying, the old hag turned abruptly into her own den, the door of which she banged violently.

With her heart fluttering like a little bird in its cage, poor Ellen hastened to her own miserable abode.

She placed the food upon the table, but would not touch it until her father should return. She longed for a spark of fire, for she was so cold and so wretched – and even in warm weather misery makes one shiver! But that room was as cold as an ice-house – and the unhappiness of that poor girl was a burden almost too heavy for her to bear.

She sate down, and thought. Oh! how poignant is meditation in such a condition as hers. Her prospects were utterly black and hopeless.

When she and her father had first taken those lodgings, she had obtained work from a 'middle-woman.' This middle-woman was one who contracted with great drapery and upholstery firms to do their needle-work at certain low rates. The middle-woman had to live, and was therefore compelled to make a decent profit upon her work. So she gave it out to poor creatures like Ellen Monroe, and got it done for next to nothing.

Thus for some weeks had Ellen made shirts – with the collars, wristbands, and fronts all well stitched – for four-pence the shirt.

And it took her twelve hours, without intermission, to make a shirt: and it cost her a penny for needles and thread, and candle.

She therefore had three-pence for herself!

Twelve hours' unwearied toil for three-pence!!

One farthing an hour!!!

Sometimes she had made dissecting-trousers, which were sold to the medical students at the hospitals; and for those she was paid two-pence half-penny each.

It occupied her eight hours to make one pair of those trousers!

At length the middle-woman had recommended her to the linen-draper's establishment on Finsbury Pavement; and there she was told that she might have plenty of work, and be well paid.

Well paid!

At the rate of a farthing and a half per hour!

Oh! it was a mockery – a hideous mockery, to give that young creature gay flowers and blossoms to work – she, who was working her own winding-sheet!

She sate, shivering with the cold, awaiting her father's return. Ever and anon the words of that old crone who had addressed her in the court, rang in her ears. What could she mean? How could she – stern in her own wretchedness herself, and perhaps stern to the wretchedness of others – how could that old hag possess the means of teaching her a pleasant and profitable mode of earning money? The soul of Ellen was purity itself – although she dwelt in the low, obscene, filthy, and disreputable neighbourhood. She seemed like a solitary lily in the midst of a black morass swarming with reptiles!

The words of the old woman were therefore unintelligible to that fair young creature of seventeen: – and yet she intuitively reproached herself for pondering upon them. Oh! mysterious influence of an all-wise and all-seeing Providence, that thus furnishes warnings against dangers yet unseen!

She tried to avert her thoughts from the contemplation of her own misery, and of the tempting offer made to her by the wrinkled harridan in the adjoining house; and so she busied herself with thinking of the condition of the other lodgers in the same tenement which she and her father inhabited. She then perceived that there were others in the world as wretched and as badly off as herself; but, in contradiction to the detestable maxim of Rochefoucauld – she found no consolation in this conviction.

In the attics were Irish families, whose children ran all day, half naked, about the court and lane, paddling with their poor cold bare feet in the puddle or the snow, and apparently thriving in dirt, hunger, and privation. Ellen and her father occupied the two rooms on the second floor. On the first floor, in the front room, lived two families – an elderly man and woman, with their grown-up sons and daughters; and with one of those sons were a wife and young children.

Eleven souls thus herded together, without shame, in a room eighteen feet wide! These eleven human beings, dwelling in so swine-like a manner, existed upon twenty-five shillings a week, the joint earnings of all of them who were able to work. In the back chamber on the same floor was a tailor, with a paralytic wife and a complete tribe of children. This poor wretch worked for a celebrated 'Clothing Mart,' and sometimes toiled for twenty hours a-day – never less than seventeen, Sunday included – to earn – what?

Eight shillings a week.

He made mackintoshes at the rate of one shilling and three-pence each; and he could make one each day. But then he had to find needles and thread; and the cost of these, together with candles, amounted to nine-pence a week.

He thus had eight shillings remaining for himself, after working like a slave, without recreation or rest, even upon the sabbath, seventeen hours every day.

A week contains a hundred and sixty-eight hours.

And he worked a hundred and nineteen hours each week!

And earned eight shillings!!

A decimal more than three farthings an hour!!!

On the ground floor of the house the tenants were no better off. In the front room dwelt a poor costermonger, or hawker of fruit, who earned upon an average seven shillings a week, out of which he was compelled to pay one shilling to treat the policeman upon the beat where he took his stand. His wife did a little washing, and perhaps earned eighteen-pence. And that was all this poor couple with four children had to subsist upon. The back room on the ground floor was occupied by the landlady of the house. She paid twelve shillings a week for rent and taxes, and let the various rooms for an aggregate of twenty-one shillings. She thus had nine shillings to live upon, supposing that every one of her lodgers paid her – which was never the case.

Poor Ellen, in reflecting in this manner upon the condition of her neighbours, found herself surrounded on all sides by misery. Misery was above – misery below: misery was on the right and on the left. Misery was the genius of that dwelling, and of every other in that court. Misery was the cold and speechless companion of the young girl as she sate in that icy chamber: misery spread her meal, and made her bed, and was her chambermaid at morning and at night!

Eleven o'clock struck by St Luke's church; and Mr Monroe returned to his wretched abode. It had begun to rain shortly after Ellen had returned home; and the old man was wet to the skin.

'Oh! my dear father!' exclaimed the poor girl, 'you are wet, and there is not a morsel of fire in the grate!'

'And I have no money, dearest,' returned the heart-broken father, pressing his thin lips upon the forehead of his daughter. 'But I am not cold, Nell – I am not cold!'

Without uttering a word, Ellen hastened out of the room, and begged a few sticks from one lodger, and a little coal from another. It would shame the affluent great, did they know how ready are the miserable – miserable poor to assist each other!

With her delicate taper fingers – with those little white hands which seemed never made to do menial service, the young girl laid the fire; and when she saw the flame blazing cheerfully up the chimney, she turned towards the old man – and smiled!

She would not for worlds have begged any thing for herself – but for her father – oh! she would have submitted to any degradation!

And then for a moment a gleam of something like happiness stole upon that hitherto mournful scene, as the father and daughter partook of their frugal – very frugal and sparing meal together.

As soon as it was concluded, Ellen rose, kissed her parent affectionately, wished him 'good night,' and retired into her own miserable, cold, and naked chamber.

She extinguished her candle in a few moments, to induce her father to believe that she had sought repose; but when she knew that the old man was asleep, she lighted the candle once more, and seated herself upon the old mattress, to embroider a few blossoms upon the silk which had been confided to her at the establishment in Finsbury.

From the neighbouring houses the sounds of boisterous revelry fell upon her ears. She was too young and inexperienced to know that this mirth emanated from persons perhaps as miserable as herself, and that they were only drowning care in liquor, instead of encountering their miseries face to face. The din of that hilarity and those shouts of laughter, therefore made her sad.

Presently that noise grew fainter and fainter; and at length it altogether ceased. The clock of St Luke's church struck one; and all was then silent around.

A lovely moon rode high in the heavens; the rain had ceased, and the night was beautiful – but bitter, bitter cold.

Wearied with toil, the young maiden threw down her work, and, opening the casement, looked forth from her wretched chamber. The gentle breeze, though bearing on its wing the chill of ice, refreshed her; and as she gazed upwards to the moon, she wondered within herself whether the spirit of her departed mother was permitted to look down upon her from the empyrean palaces on high. Tears – large tears trickled down her cheeks; and she was too much overcome by her feelings even to pray.

While she was thus endeavouring to divert her thoughts from the appalling miseries of earth to the transcendant glories of heaven, she was diverted from her mournful reverie by the sound of a window opening in a neighbouring house; and in a few moments violent sobs fell upon her ears. Those sobs, evidently coming from a female bosom, were so acute, so heart-rending, so full of anguish, that Ellen was herself overcome with grief. At length those indications of extreme woe ceased gradually, and then these words – 'Oh my God! what will become of my starving babes!' fell upon Ellen's ears. She was about to inquire into the cause of that profound affliction, when the voice of a man was heard to exclaim gruffly, 'Come – let's have no more of this gammon: we must all go to the workus in the morning – that's all!' And then the window was closed violently.

The workhouse! That word sounded like a

fearful knell upon Ellen's ears. Oh! for hours and hours together had that poor girl meditated upon the sad condition of her father and herself, until she had traced, in imagination, their melancholy career up to the very door of the workhouse. And there she had stopped: she dared think no more – or she would have gone mad, raving mad! For she had heard of the horrors of those asylums for the poor; and she knew that she should be separated from her father on the day when their stern destinies should drive them to that much-dreaded refuge. And to part from him – from the parent whom she loved so tenderly, and who loved her so well; – no – death were far preferable!

The workhouse! How was it that the idea of this fearful home – more dreaded than the prison, less formidable than the grave – had taken so strong a hold upon the poor girl's mind? Because the former tenant of the miserable room which now was hers had passed thence to the workhouse: but ere she went away, she left behind her a record of her feelings in anticipation of that removal to the pauper's home!

Impelled by an influence which she could not control – that species of impulse which urges the timid one to gaze upon the corpse of the dead, even while shuddering at the aspect of death – Ellen closed the window, and read for the hundredth time the following lines, which were pencilled in a neat hand upon the whitewashed wall of the naked chamber: –

'I Had a Tender Mother Once.'

I had a tender mother once,
  Whose eyes so sad and mild
Beamed tearfully yet kindly on
  Her little orphan child.
A father's care I never knew;
  But in that mother dear,
Was centred every thing to love,
  To cherish, and revere!

I loved her with that fervent love
  Which daughters only know;
And often o'er my little head
  Her bitter tears would flow.
Perhaps she knew that death approached
  To snatch her from my side;
And on one gloomy winter day
  This tender mother died.

They laid her in the pauper's ground,
  And hurried o'er the prayer:
It nearly broke my heart to think
  That they should place her there.
And now it seems I see her still
  Within her snowy shroud;
And in the dark and silent night
  My spirit weeps aloud.

I know not how the years have passed
  Since my poor mother died;
But I too have an orphan girl,
  That grows up by my side.
O God! thou know'st I do not crave
  To eat the bread of sloth:
I labour hard both day and night,
  To earn enough for both!

But though I starve myself for her,
  Yet hunger wastes her form: –
My God! and must that darling child
  Soon feed the loathsome worm?
'T is vain – for I can work no more –
  My eyes with toil are dim;
My fingers seem all paralyzed,
  And stiff is every limb!

And now there is but one resource;
  The pauper's dreaded doom!
To hasten to the workhouse, and
  There find a living tomb.
I know that they will separate
  My darling child from me;
And though 't will break our hearts, yet both
  Must bow to that decree!

Henceforth our tears must fall apart,
  Nor flow together more;
And from to-day our prayers may not
  Be mingled as before!
O God! is this the Christian creed,
  So merciful and mild?
The daughter from the mother snatched,
  The mother from her child!

Ah! we shall ne'er be blessed again
  Till death has closed our eyes,
And we meet in the pauper's ground
  Where my poor mother lies.
Though sad this chamber, it is bright
  To what must be our doom;
The portal of the workhouse is
  The entrance of the tomb!

Ellen read these lines till her eyes were dim with tears. She then retired to her wretched couch; and she slept through sheer fatigue. But dreams of hunger and of cold filled up her slumbers; – and yet those dreams were light beside the waking pangs which realised the visions!

The young maiden slept for three hours, and then arose, unrefreshed, and paler than she was on the preceding day. It was dark: the moon had gone down; and some time would yet elapse ere the dawn. Ellen washed herself in water upon which the ice floated; and the cold piercing breeze of the morning whistled through the window upon her fair and delicate form.

As soon as she was dressed, she lighted her candle and crept gently into her father's room. The old man slept soundly. Ellen flung his clothes over her arm, took his boots up in her hand, and stole noiselessly back to her own chamber. She then brushed those garments, and cleaned those boots, all bespattered with thick mud as they were; and this task – so hard for her delicate and diminutive hands – she performed with the most heart-felt satisfaction.

As soon as this occupation was finished, she sate down once more to work.

Thus that poor girl knew no rest!

THE FACTORY GIRL

PRICE 1*d.* – *The profits arising therefrom to go towards forwarding the TEN HOURS BILL!!!*

Who is she with pallid face?
That slowly moves with languid pace,
Her limbs bespeak her wearied frame
She seems in suff'ring, grief, and pain!
'A little child' – with list'ning ear,
Approach'd me with a falling tear
    And said – 'tis Jane the Factory Girl!

I took her by her little hand –
Though from fatigue, she scarce could stand,
I tried to soothe her tender grief
By friendship's pow'r to give relief;
And ask'd in accents most sincere
What caus'd the anguish so severe?
    Of Jane – the Village Factory Girl!

She answer'd! near that little wood,
Once liv'd my mother – kind – and good:
My father died upon that morn,
When I unhappily was born:

And now one only sister dear
Is left – the broken heart to cheer
    Of Jane – the Orphan Factory Girl!

Oh! Sir! we work from morning's light
Till darkness settles at the night:
No rest we know – no parents come
To welcome our return to home,
We call on Heaven to bless our cot
For earthly friends have all forgot
    The poor neglected Factory Girl!

The overlooker – many a time,
Without a fault – without a crime,
Has beat me with such savage might
That scarce could I reach home at night:
Oh! then I've wept in anguish deep,
And blest those parents now asleep
    Who lov'd Jane, the Factory Girl!

Oh! yes! upon their lowly bier
Oft have I shed a mournful tear!
And wish'd that I alas could sleep
No more to suffer, nor to weep:
But soon I feel that welcome death
Will claim the last – the parting breath
    Of Jane, the wretched Factory Girl!

She cast her eyes with wildness round,
Then sunk exhausted on the ground:
I clasp'd the sufferer to my breast,
But she – poor girl – was now at rest!!
No cruel tyrant now could place
A tear upon the snowy face
    Of Jane, the lifeless Factory Girl!

Ye! who alone on Gold are bent,
Blush! at the Murder'd Innocent,
Let not Old England's glorious pride
Be stain'd by black Infanticide!!
But let Humanity's bright Ray
Protect from greedy Tyrant's sway
    The poor defenceless Factory Girl!

5. MUSIC HALL HEROINE

VILLIKINS AND HIS DINAH

In London's fair city a merchant did dwell,
He had but one daughter, an unkimmon nice
young gal.
Her name it was Dinah – just sixteen years
old, –
With a wery large fortin in *soap* and in gold.
      Singing, too ral li, &c.

Now as Dinah was a-valking in the garden
one day,
Her papa he comed to her, and thus he did
say: –
'Go, dress yourself, Dinah, in gorgeous array, –
For I've got you an husband, both gallant
and gay.'
      Singing, too ral li, &c.

'Oh, papa, oh, papa, I've not made up my
mind,
And to marry just yet I'm not quite inclined;
And all my large fortin I'll gladly give o'er,
If you'll let me be single just one year or
more.'
      Singing, too ral li, &c.

'Go, go, boldest daughter,' the parient replied,
'If you won't consent for to be this young
man's bride,
I'll give all your large fortin to the nearest of
kin,
And you shan't reap the benefit of one single
pin.'
      Singing, too ral li, &c.

As Villikins was a-valking in the Garden one
day,
He spied his dear Dinah lying dead upon the
clay –
And a cup of cold pisin was a-lying by her side,
And a billet-dux to say that for Villikins she
died!
      Singing, too ral li, &c.

He kissed her cold corpis a thousand times
o'er;
He called her his Dinah, though she was no
more –
And swallowed up the pisin like a lovier so
brave,
And Villikins and his Dinah are buried in one
grave.
      Singing, too ral li, &c.

MORAL.

Now all ye young ladies, take heed to what I
say,
And never, not by no means, your guv'ners
disobey;
Now all ye young men mind whom ye cast
your eyes on,
Think of Villikins and his Dinah, and the cup
of cold pisin.
      Singing, too ral li, &c.

12TH EDITION.
VILIKENS AND HIS DINAH.

MR F. ROBSON,
THE WANDERING MINSTREL,
ROYAL OLYMPIC THEATRE
JOHN BARNARD.
LONDON CAMPBELL RANSFORD AC° 53 NEW BOND ST

6. PENNY VALENTINES

A. PARK, LONDON.

If the devil step'd, old lady, from his regions just below,
He couldn't find a picture like the one before me now:
No doubt you know the gentleman, a sable one is he,
And he's said to be Papa of all the lies that yet might be.
Your eyes are false, your nose is false, and falser still your tongue,
Your breast is false, your heart is false, as ever poet sung ;
And if disgust did not prevail, upon my present will
I could speak of something villainous, and yet more filthy still.

How shalt my faithful heart confess,
Or humble words like mine express,
Unchanging love and true?
O could I once my heart declare,
Or half the warm affection share
My bosom feels for you.

Printed & Published by J. WRIGLEY, 25, Miller-st., Manchester.

Then would you anxious be to join,
Your destiny, my love, with mine ;
Consent thou, then, with me to prove
The joys of friendship and of love.

7. DOMESTIC ROMANCE

LILIAS GRANGER,
OR PRACTICAL ROMANCE

[*All the* Family Herald *values of domestic virtue in opposition to romantic fantasy come neatly through this short story.*]

> Her face was fairer than face of earth;
> What is the thing to liken it to?
> A lily just dipp'd in the summer dew –
> Parian marble – snow's first fall?
> Her brow was fairer than each and all.
> —L. E. L.

'Why! Lily, Lily dearest, you are quite demented. There you have sat, for the last three hours, with your nose obstinately buried between the leaves of that trashy novel, and not one word have you vouchsafed me during the whole blessed time. Now, don't open your eyes with such a bewildered stare, as though you had just awoke from a century's sleep, like the enchanted princess in a fairy tale; but – there, that's right – drop your book: and now that you are fairly aroused, I will proceed. Would you believe it, that provoking Madame Bernard has sent me *such* a hat. But stop! you shall see it; for one might as well attempt to describe the mechanism of a steam-engine.' And tripping across the room, the lively girl lifted the hat from the floor, where she had thrown it half an hour before in a fit of disgust; and elevating it upon the tips of her fingers, broke into a peal of laughter, which had nearly wakened an echo in the heart of her languid cousin, who, however, only smiled faintly, and exclaimed in silvery and half-impatient tones, 'What will you have me do, dear Helen? You cannot expect me to reduce to anything like symmetry that overgrown mass of feathers and flowers.'

'Feathers and flowers! aye, and ribbons, lace, silk, satin, and I know not what beside. Why, it is a perfect parterre, a dish of salmagundi. Reduce it to symmetry! Alas! my unsophisticated cousin, don't you see that it is perfectly hopeless? No,' – throwing down the hat, and sinking into a chair – 'no; I did not call you from dream-land to discuss the perfections of this "miracle of beauty," as madame poetically styles it, but to plan another after my own heart. What say you, *ma belle*, to a pale primrose satin, with a brim just deep enough to cast a soft glow upon the face – a low crown, encircled with a half wreath of blush-roses, or *white ones*, rather, with just the slightest tinge of pink in the heart? As for the veil, let me see. Brussels are quite the *ton*, yet I very much admire these. Why, Lily! Lilias Granger, you have not heard one word I have been saying. How provoking! you are actually reading that book again. As I live, your eyes are brimming with tears. Poor Lily! you are utterly ruined – ruined for life. Pity your father had not foreseen it when he allowed you to grow up wild in an out-of-the-way country place, under the guardianship of an old woman, who considered all books alike, the bible and cookery-book excepted. Had he lived to have seen you safely married, all might have been well. But now that you are left an heiress to the care of my father, who, good man! never cares for anything besides his banking interests, I foresee the result. You will meet with some mysterious adventurer, with whom you will fall in love, and elope, merely on account

of the romance of such an adventure. The consequences of such a course are well portrayed in your favourite fictions.'

'You are wrong, Helen; such will never be my fate. My heart has a guardian talisman, which will for ever close its portals against the unknown and worthless adventurer. It is pride. No, no, dear Helen, it is pleasant, I will own, to dream over a tale of true love, pleasant even to fancy one's self the heroine, blest with the deathless love of a pure and manly heart, and loving in return, oh, how devotedly! in spite of want, and wretchedness, and shame – pleasant to live, in the compass of an hour, a whole long life, darkened with many sorrows, it is true, and yet who would live always in life's sunshine? Yet in this working and every-day world how bitter would be the reality!'

'Bitter, indeed! far more so than you imagine; for you, Lily, look on life through a treacherous medium. Cousin Frank says –'

But what cousin Frank said was left entirely to conjecture, for rap, tap, tap – the knuckles of some one outside were applied in no very gentle manner to the door; and before Helen could recover her breath from the unfinished sentence, the veritable Frank himself appeared being incited thereto, as he said, by the sound of his own name pronounced in a key rather elevated.

With a cordial 'good afternoon' to Lilias, and a slight nod to 'cousin Nell,' he threw himself on a luxuriously stuffed 'chaise lounge,' and desired to know the grounds of the dispute, as he perceived that he had just come in time to act as arbitrator.

'Yes, just in time, for once, cousin Frank; were it not so, I would read you a lecture on etiquette for presuming to enter our boudoir without a bidding. But I will spare you for the present, as I am in need of your assistance. I have been trying to convince Lily that her love of fiction will finally destroy her happiness; and that a girl who spends her days in romantic and illusory dreams may finally realise them in her own experience, bereft of all their sunshine, and embittered by the repinings of a heart unable to distinguish false happiness from true. Am I not right?'

'Yes, right in all but prophesying so dark a

fate for our own Lilias. No, wild Nell, that can never be while we have power to protect her. Is it not so?'

Helen bit her lips with vexation at this unlooked for reply, while Lily raised her eyes, with a half-triumphant smile, to the face of her champion; but they fell again beneath his earnest gaze, while a crimson flush stole up over her blue-veined temples at the thought that she could even need such defence.

For five long minutes Helen sat in pouting silence, while Frank Sherwood gave a humourous and most *apropos* description of a runaway match. Then, what could ail the girl? Starting up, she scattered with a sudden toss the gilded paper she had been industriously 'macadamising' all over the floor; and with a burst of laughter, which seemed almost hysterical in its violence, took sudden possession of the hand that rested on her cousin's chair; and with a few whispered words, dragged her unwilling captive from the room. Was she mad? Lilias thought it highly probable, as she sat with her large dilating eyes of sunny blue fixed on the door through which they had vanished. A half-smile curled her lips – those lips so like those of early childhood in their bright coral hue, and the dimples that nestled so roguishly just where their clear red melted away into the peach-bloom of the cheek. But we will leave her enshrined in a flood of rosy light which streamed in at the western window, tinting her graceful ringlets with flickering gold, and revealing her exquisite form in full relief against the crimson cushions of the *fauteuil*. We will leave her to her own reflections; and bitter they were, if one might judge from the sadness that weighed down the lids of her violet eyes, and half-effaced those floating and child-like dimples. In the meantime, we will give our readers some slight knowledge of the *dramatis personae* of our story.

Helen Granger was the daughter of an opulent banker, who flourished some time during the past century in that queen of cities, New York. Losing her mother in infancy, she might possibly have become that most intolerable of all earthly torments, a spoiled child, had not a widowed sister of her departed mother bequeathed, with her latest breath,

her orphan son to the fatherly kindness of Mr Granger. The little stranger thus became the recipient of half the caresses and sugar-plums with which Helen might otherwise have been surfeited; for, like Dame Fortune, our nurses have not always our best interests at heart in the bestowal of their favours. The children grew up together the best friends in the world, the boy's prudent and habitual thoughtfulness tempering and restraining the wild and impetuous spirit of the merry girl, and her sunny buoyancy charming away the many evils to which his greater sensitiveness exposed him. Their friendship still continued when, as they grew older, the boy went out into the world; and Helen, tied, as she affirmed, for six mortal hours daily to the piano, and buried deep in all the mysteries of French and Italian, met him less often.

When Lilias, after the death of her father, was taken home by Mr Granger – for, as the good man often said, 'though Nature had blessed him with but one child, his friends were determined that he should never suffer from the oversight' – when, therefore, in compliance with his brother's last request, Lilias was taken home, the two cousins admitted her at once into their confidence, and the domestic duet – as the ever merry Helen observed – became a trio.

PART II.

'Oh, Jupiter! how weary are my spirits.'
— SHAKESPEARE.
'Good night. How can such good night be?'
— SHELLEY.

'Are you never coming, lazy Lily? Why, in the name of all dilatory damsels, do you linger so long over your toilette? Here poor Frank has been waiting this half-hour, twisting the buttons off his best coat, I doubt not, in a frenzy of impatience.'

'Coming – coming, Nelly,' said Lilias, as she slowly descended the stairs and joined her cousin and Frank Sherwood in the hall below. 'I ask Mr Sherwood's pardon for the detention; but in truth dear Helen, I hardly care to attend the opera to-night. I feel unusually sad; I could almost believe that some terrible misfortune is even now hanging over my head.'

'Nonsense!' interrupted Helen. 'Away with such insane fancies! You must go. It would be cruel to remain at home, for you look unusually lovely to-night. Does she not, cousin Frank?'

'She never looks otherwise to me,' was the reply, in tones so low, that they only reached the ear of Lilias; while Helen continued: – 'If your gloomy thoughts so much heighten the lustre of your charms, 'tis a thousand pities they don't visit you every day. It would save you fifty per cent. in millinery and knick-knacks.' And, with a gay laugh, the wild girl ran down the steps, and sprang into the carriage before her more tardy companions had reached the *pavé*.

The curtain rose that night on a wildly rugged scene – a mountain pass in Italy; and Lilias found, in the reckless bravery of the dark eyed and swarthy brigands, something so near akin to her own chivalrous and romantic emotions, that her whole soul became absorbed in the shifting scene before her, and the soft nothings of the courtly beaux who thronged their box fell unheeded and almost unheard upon her ear. It was not until the curtain fell after the fourth act that she raised her jewelled opera-glass to take the range of the surrounding boxes. 'Where are the Sinclairs?' inquired she, after a momentary glance, turning to a gentleman who stood behind her. 'One as much expects to see the musicians' seats in the orchestra vacant as their place in yonder box.'

'They are indeed fixtures for one-half the year,' was the laughing reply; 'but the remaining six months they spend in the country, making amends, by a course of starving, pinching economy, for the otherwise ruinous expenses of their city life. Being at one time in the vicinity of their country residence, I determined to give them a call *en passant*, and accordingly made all due inquiries as to the whereabouts of Sinclair Lodge. Remarkably euphonious name, is it not? Being directed to a dilapidated farm-house, I ascended the steps, not without many misgivings; and raising the rusty old-fashioned knocker, I gave a peal that was answered, after a long delay, by a filthy housemaid, guiltless of shoe or stocking. On inquiring if the young ladies were at home, she answered, in a drawling tone, 'No, they aren't!' which information I took the liberty to disbelieve, the sudden opening of the door having afforded me a glimpse of Miss Mary herself shuffling through a side-door, in a *dishabille* anything but becoming. Since then I have made it a part of my religion to refrain from dropping in on families in the chrysalis state. Strange – is it not, Miss Granger? – that a family like the Sinclairs, who might live happily in their own station of life, will render themselves miserable, by striving for what is beyond their attainment.'

'Strange indeed,' said Lilias with a sigh. 'Yet how many thus mistake the aim of their existence?'

'And thereby make themselves ridiculous, as does that foreign-looking fellow, who has been staring at you so boldly for the last hour.'

'Where?' And following the glance of her companion, Lilias saw indeed a pair of large dark eyes fixed upon her with an intensity which sent the blood to her brow. The next moment she drew quietly back within the shadow of the curtains, calmly replying, 'Doubtless he mistakes me for another.'

One by one the loungers withdrew, and Lilias at last found leisure to peep from her shadowed nook at the gentleman who had been so sneeringly introduced to her notice. She readily pronounced him a stranger; for though from time to time he conversed with the gentlemen around him, it was with a coldly ceremonious air, all unlike the unguarded familiarity of friendly intercourse; yet, excepting the moustache that shaded his short curved upper lip, there was nothing in his appearance that indicated foreign extraction. The strong light of a chandelier fell full on the raven curls that lay clustered in a mass of glancing light and shadow around his brow – that brow so broad and pale, with its 'fringed lakes of an unfathomed darkness couched below.' And Lilias gazed on that calm proud face till all other sights faded out; and wrapped in a delicious dream, she was only roused by the thrice-repeated question of her cousin, 'What *are* we to do?'

'Do about what?' asked Lilias, half-alarmed at the despairing tone in which the inquiry was made.

'Do about what!' reiterated Helen. 'How can you ask? Or, as you seem so perfectly at ease, perhaps I might better merely ask your ladyship *who* is to escort us to our carriage?'

'Who! Why, where is Frank?' And Lilias saw, for the first time, that the house was fast thinning, and they were entirely alone.

'You are too provoking, Lily. I myself heard Frank tell you, that having an unavoidable engagement, he could remain with us only an hour; and now you very calmly ask where he is.'

'I assure you, Helen, that I did not hear him; and why, if he was obliged to go, did he not request some one to see us safely home?'

'So he would have done, had I permitted it; but foolishly forgetting it was club-night, I depended on the politeness of our usual retinue of beaux. But see, Lilias, they are extinguishing the lights; we must not remain here. Come, let us trust for once to good luck and sharp elbows; and fortune, perchance, may send us a beau. Hasten! hasten!' And passing her arm through that of Lilias, they quitted the box; and passing through a side-door, plunged at once into the crowd. Now following in the wake of some burly individual, and now yielding to the pressure of the throng, they passed along, till above the heads of the multitude might be caught brief glimpses of the star-lit sky; and even the sinking heart of Lilias grew light as the chill air from the entrance passed across her brow.

Another moment, and they were safe; but just then the horses attached to a carriage in waiting grew restive; and plunging violently, drove the frightened multitude back, with a wild cry, through the portal.

Torn from her cousin's side, Lilias was borne back like a feather on the tide, till breathless, and crushed by the pressure, she was thrown against one of the supporting pillars of the entrance hall. The sick giddiness that precedes a swoon crept over her, her brain reeled and a flood of fiery motes swam before her eyes. Another moment and she would have sunk helplessly down to be trodden under foot; but a strong arm upheld

her, while a deep voice whispered in her ear, 'You have lost your companion, lady, let me assist you to seek for her.' Lilias tried to reply but the words died away in a convulsive sob, and a quick shower of tears rained over her glittering and snowy robe. Without another word, the stranger of the opera – for it was he, who like a guardian angel, came to rescue the helpless girl – drew her hand within his arm, and sternly desiring the crowd to give way, led her at once to the entrance, where, under the protection of her father, she encountered Helen returning to seek for her cousin. With a whispered 'Good night!' the stranger pressed a card into the trembling hand of his companion, and, turning away, vanished in the crowd.

'Are you safe, dear Lily?' said Helen, as she wound her arm round her cousin. 'And who was that stranger who so kindly protected you? – But no matter now – you look pale, Lily – you tremble: support her to the carriage, dear father.'

Once more at home, poor Lilias gave way to the emotions so long controuled, and replied only with hysterical sobs to her cousin's repeated inquiries. Convinced that she only needed rest, Helen at last reluctantly lighted her night-lamp, and with a murmured 'Good night!' and an invocation of pleasant visions, left her alone.

But no pleasant visions brightened poor Lily's slumbers that weary night; but wild and stormy phantoms flitted round; while amid the visible darkness ever gleamed that one calm face, like a newly-risen star in her life's horizon.

PART III.

Lean on me, love!
Oh! such a bridal-night befits not such a bride!
*　　*　　*　　*　　but if truth*
And tenderness, can pay thee back for comfort,
Thou shalt ne'er regret the time.
　　　　　　– BRIDAL NIGHT.

It was the eve of a delicious day in May, one of those May-days so very rare in our chilly climates, when the noon-day sun has enough of fervour to make the denizens of cities long 'to hear the babbling of brooks,' and the whispering of Heaven's free winds amid the opening leaves: – one of those days whose evenings are so welcome, so like a pleasant dream, when the very air seems fraught with a soft and dewy hush; and leaning from the open casement, we hold communion with the far-off burning stars; when the spiritual wakens within us, and points to a world beyond – a shadowy and mysterious world to the 'child of clay,' for the veil is over our eyes – we see through a glass darkly.

It was on such an eve that Lilias Granger sat at her open window; her graceful head rested on the casement, and her large sad eyes, whose shadowy lashes were heavy with tears, fixed on the moon that hung, a tremulous crescent of silver, in the azure heavens. 'Alas, dear Helen!' she murmured half aloud, as though her thoughts had found a voice unwittingly. 'Alas, dear Helen! three short months ago, had you known how sadly true your idle prophecy might prove, you would have sought to check the current of my fate. But now it is too late. And yet you were wrong; you said I should wed a poor and worthless man, and poor he is indeed, but worthless – oh, never!' Raising from the floor an open letter which had fallen from her grasp, she read from its pages, in a low, sad tone, the following: –

'Ah, Lilias, I blush to tear you from your pleasant home, to share the loneliness of my humble life. Why did we ever meet? Why are you so lovely, that the life unblessed by the sunshine of your smile would be a living curse? Is it my fault, that, like the serpent in Eden, I have come to blight your fairest flowers? Is it my fault, that we met on that terrible yet blessed night, when I found you, like a drooping lily indeed, fainting, and alone in the crowd? Could I do less than protect you? And when for one moment I held you in my arms, and felt the throbbing of your heart against mine, was I made of sterner stuff than other men, that I could go away and lose the memory of that sweet face for ever? Oh no! by all the happiness of our after meetings no! And yet, dearest one, when I look forward to the uncertain future, and think perchance my love may cast a shadow over all your coming hours, I tremble. Oh!

pause and reflect on all your love for me; and then, if you will trust me, come. Till then, good night!   'HENRY FORSYTHE'

For a long time Lilias sat with her head bent down, and the tears starting between the slender fingers pressed upon her eyes; and then, rising like one imbued with sudden courage, she folded an ample shawl about her, and tying on a deep veiled bonnet, with trembling fingers she silently unclosed her door, and stole out into the corridor. For a moment she paused at her cousin's door, and laying her hand upon the latch, seemed about to enter, but turning away again, with a burst of violent sorrow that shook her slight frame like an aspen, she hurried on with one small hand pressed closely on her lips, to stifle her sob-like breathings. Gliding down the broad and winding staircase, she stood the next moment beneath the light in the hall below, trembling like the guilty truant thing she was. Sinking against the wall, she threw back her bonnet as if for freer air, while her pale features writhed with a restless pain, like one in life's last agony. A little while, and the iron tongues of a hundred bells pealed out the hour of midnight, and with one last sad lingering look on all she left for ever behind her, she drew her veil around her, and unclasping the outer door, stole out into the clear star light. A dark figure sprang toward her, and sinking into his arms, she awoke only to find herself borne along with the speed of light over the rough pavement, while a manly voice whispered words of hope to her sinking heart.

'You will protect me, will you not?' murmured Lily, as she gazed into the noble face that bent above her.

'With my life,' was the reply; 'and oh my own Lily, may you never repent that you have left all which made your life like a fairy dream for one who has nothing but a heart to bestow.'

'And is not such a heart worth all earth's perishing possessions?' said Lilias. 'Is not love worth more than all the pomp and power of life? – Love the only divine spark that still lingers unquenched in our fallen world!'

'You are right, dear Lily. Love is the only satisfying principle in our nature. But come, dear one, here is the chapel; a moment more, and you will be mine – mine for ever!'

A little while and the two stood before the altar, when the light of a single lamp shed a dim halo round the white robed priest, while all beyond lay in deepest shadow. The beautiful and touching service of the Church of England commenced, and upon the stillness of the night came, in the full deep tones of manhood, 'I, Henry, take thee, Lilias, to be my wedded wife,' and the heart of the young girl grew firm beneath the thrill of those solemn words; and gazing up at the truthful eyes which were thenceforward to be the twin stars of her destiny, a sudden joy awoke in her heart that lent a calm truthfulness to her voice as she repeated her portion of the holy rite. The last prayer had ascended – the last blessing was invoked, and turning away from the altar, Lilias remarked for the first time the presence of two muffled figures, who stood together in the shade of the pulpit.

'Who are they?' she asked, as leaning on the arm of her husband, she entered again the little vestry-room.

'They are the witnesses,' replied Henry Forsythe, as with a darkened brow he conducted his lovely bride to a seat, and flinging himself beside her, bent his brow upon his hand like one in troubled thought.

'Let us go,' said Lilias, after a moment's silence. 'Do you fear, dear Henry, to take me to your lowly home? Do you think I shall remember, with little repinings, the luxuries I have left behind?'

'No, dearest Lily, I do not doubt you: I only grieve that you trust me too fondly. What will you say when I confess that I have basely deceived you? Can you, will you forgive me?' and sinking on his knees before his bewildered bride, he raised his hands, and the next moment the raven curls, the moustache and disguising whiskers fell at her feet, while the poor girl sank forward like one death stricken into the arms of *cousin Frank*. A merry laugh came like a burst of music through the open door, and Helen Granger, with her fair face but half visible, beneath the innumerable veils and hoods that formed her disguises, crept softly into the room, followed closely by her father. Frank Sherwood lifted not his eyes from the face that lay in the shadow of its sunny curls upon his arm; but checking, with a stern whisper, the mirth of his thoughtless cousin, he continued, with trembling hands, to shed over the gleaming brow the cool drops that still lingered in the baptismal font.

'Forgive me, dear Frank,' said Helen, as she knelt beside him, 'but who could avoid laughing at your abrupt confession. Poor Lily! why! it was enough to frighten any woman living into a syncope. But hist! she revives,' and Lilias, with a shivering sigh, like one who wakes from an unpleasant dream, unclosed her eyes. For a moment her gaze lingered wildly on the familiar and beloved faces that watched around her; then, as a new light awoke like a sunbeam in her heart with a fervent 'thank God,' she raised her brimming eyes to the face of her husband, and whispered, 'Oh, Frank, 'twas a cruel deception!'

'Cruel indeed,' replied Frank Sherwood; 'but I pray God "the end may sanctify the means." Think, my Lily, if I had been in truth what I seemed to you, how wretched might have been your after life; for the man who, with a base premeditation, could steal the heart of an innocent girl, and drag her from a luxurious and happy home to the dark realities of a life of penury and wretchedness, is a heartless and cowardly villain. There was a deep rooted and deforming weed in the garden of your heart, the offspring of a misguided education, and beneath its baleful influence your fancy reared a glittering and *illusory world*, which closed your eyes to the happiness of the *real*. Dearly as I loved you, Lily, and with all my numerous perfections and appliances to boot, I could never have won your heart (and Frank gazed with a provoking smile into the sweet face of his wife), had I not wooed in the garb of a nameless adventurer. But forgive us, my own Lily, for all the sorrow we have brought you, and God grant this may be our last experiment in "Practical Romance." '

8. THE QUEEN

THE QUEEN, OR THE POPE?

THE SONG OF THE BRITISH PROTESTANT

Will Briton's sons desert the faith,
   For which their fathers' died?
Or, led by priests, be cringing slaves,
   To please the Pontiff's pride?
Oh! Cranmer, Hooper, Ridley, lend
   Thy sturdy bravery!
Luther! the mighty genius send,
   And wake dull lethargy!

CHORUS

Oh, no! then rally round the Throne,
   Be to your Country true;
Or else the hungry Pope of Rome.
   Will snatch that Throne from you.

Will Albion's high nobility,
   Succumb to Popish wiles?
And will her gallant gentry
   Be duped by Jesuit smiles?
Deserted shall her people cry.
   For liberty, in vain!
And shall dark Popery's hatred yoke
   Be cast on them again?

               Oh, no &c.

Unless our minds are fettered,
   Unless our reason's gone,
We'll join to free our Country,
   We'll rally for the Throne!
We'll meet the Romish scemers,
   On truth's broad, sacred field;
And with the 'bible in our hands,'
   We'll make the Pontiff yieald.

               Oh, no &c.

The tiger is blood-thirsty yet,
   The modern fox is sly;
The Pope, he the thinks of England's
   And rolls his greedy eye.
Oh; think of freedom's choicest sons

Who in this dungeon lie
Oh! think of Antonina doomed,
   In cruel chains to die,

               Oh, no &c.

Before the noble lion's rage
   As wolves and tigers flee,
So awed by true Religion's might,
   The Pope shall conquered be,
As springeth up the bended oak,
   More proudly to the sky,
So Luther's faith, though bent awhile,
   Shall raise its head on high.

               Oh, no &c.

But should the friends of Popery dare,
   To aid her with their power,
The fate of scarlet Rome itself,
   Is settled from that hour,
A Protestant, and dauntless band,
   Men of another race,
Will tear Rome's banner down, & rear
   Victoria in its place.

They'll burst apart the gates of sin,
   Her dungeons of dispair;
And give to nations struggling now
   Religion, 'free as air.'

Then struggle against Popery,
   And posterity shall tell,
How we saw through Popish liberty,
   How Pio Nono fell;
And to England's friends and foemen,
   It shall joyfully be shown,
How God preserved our country,
   Our faith, our State, our throne.

Then rally, rally Protestants,
   Be to your country true,
And liberty in soul mind,
   Shall flourish long for you.

Petticoats for Ever,
AND
GOD BLESS THE QUEEN.

KITTY.—Well, Mother Joan, what do you think of our young Queen? I am told she is going to do wonders, and all in favour of the women.

JOAN.—Well, I am very glad of it; the men have had their turn long enough; and I heard she's going to pass a new Act of Parliament, for my old man told me that a man told him, that he heard another man say, that another man read it in the Newspaper; so sit down and have a cup of chatterwater and I will tell you all about it—All married men are to allow their wives one pint of beer and one glass of gin every day and as much tea and snuff as they like; or be compelled to sleep under the bed for a week.

KITTY.—So I've heard; and I know that all women, married or single, are to have a roving commission, to go where they like, do as they like, and work when they like, provided they do not disgrace themselves, but behave in a becoming manner; and all women in Great Britain, Little Britain, and all other great and little places, shall have, (if they can get it) a gallon of cream of the valley each to drink health to the Queen, may she live long, have a happy reign, a good husband, and lots of pretty children.

JOAN.—That's capital, Mother, what do you call 'em? It's the best Act I ever heard of.

KITTY.—But that's not all, for there will be a Parliament of women, all reg'lar rum'uns, besides Mother Mouthalmighty, Prime Minister; Mrs. Kitty, Cock o' the Walk, Chanceseller at the Checquers; Mrs. Tickle-breeches, Privy Door-keeper; Mrs. Neverout, Home Secretary; and Miss Gadabout, Foreign Secretary.

JOAN.—That's right, we'll settle the men, and let them know that Petticoats are master.

KITTY.—Every man who strikes his wife shall be tied to the leg of the bedstead till he begs his wife's pardon; all single women, under thirty years of age, having neither crooked legs nor snaggle teeth, are invited to join the Guard of Honour; and any one having more than six children at a birth is to be promoted to the rank of Staff Serjeant; and if he don't do a husband's duty as he ought to do, and conform to every clause in the new Act, make him drink his tea without sugar, till he dies.

Come all you fair maidens and list while I sing
The new laws of England and your young Queen;
For great alterations there'll certainly be,
And Petticoat now will be master you'll see.

So maids, wives, and widows, all merrily sing
Petticoats for ever! and God bless the Queen.

Now all married men I'd have you look out,
Or Petticoats will put you all to the rout;
For the women have got the right side of the Queen,
And success to the Petticoats wherever they've been.

Our Parliament Women, I'll tell you quite flat,
Will do the men brown, what think you of that?
They will pass their own Acts, and have their own way,
And send all molly cuddles to Botany Bay.

So all you young girls who are out of your teens,
When it comes to your turn you'll all be made Queens;
If you marry a spoony then give him hard thumps,
And we'll let him know he's turn'd up Queen of Trumps.

Printed for T. Moore.

THE CORONATION.

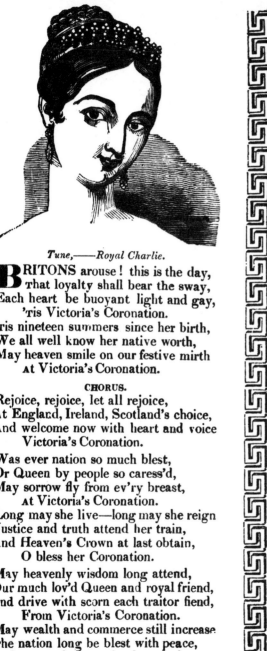

Tune,——Royal Charlie.

BRITONS arouse ! this is the day,
That loyalty shall bear the sway,
Each heart be buoyant light and gay,
   'Tis Victoria's Coronation.
'Tis nineteen summers since her birth,
We all well know her native worth,
May heaven smile on our festive mirth
   At Victoria's Coronation.

CHORUS.

Rejoice, rejoice, let all rejoice,
At England, Ireland, Scotland's choice,
And welcome now with heart and voice
   Victoria's Coronation.

Was ever nation so much blest,
Or Queen by people so caress'd,
May sorrow fly from ev'ry breast,
   At Victoria's Coronation.
Long may she live—long may she reign
Justice and truth attend her train,
And Heaven's Crown at last obtain,
   O bless her Coronation.

May heavenly wisdom long attend,
Our much lov'd Queen and royal friend,
And drive with scorn each traitor fiend,
   From Victoria's Coronation.
May wealth and commerce still increase
The nation long be blest with peace,
And care and sorrow be decreas'd,
   Thro' Victoria's Coronation.

The sons of France may boast they're free
And say they gain'd true liberty,
But still they're not so blest as we,
   At Victoria's Coronation.
When Philip's son to France does steer,
He'll say how Britons does revere,
Likewise how bravely they did cheer,
   At Victoria's Coronation.

What praise is due to her who rear'd,
A Queen to England so endear'd,
May her name by Britons be rever'd,
   At Victoria's Coronation.
Tho' Victoria does the sceptre sway,
Her parent may she still obey,
Each British heart will shout huzza
   at Victoria's Coronation.

May health her youthful brow adorn,
And may the children yet unborn,
Rejoice upon this happy morn,
   Of Victoria's Coronation.
E'er she resigns all earthly things,
Be mother to a line of Kings,
Whose virtues rare such love may bring
   As Victoria's Coronation.

J. Catnach. Printer. 2, & 3, Monmouth-Court,
7 Dials.

CORONATION
HANDKERCHIEF.

The Consequences of having Kings, and Priests, and Lords.
No. 2.

This day, Thursday, the 8th of September, 1831, there is to be a spectacle in Westminster, called the Coronation of the King and the Queen. In relation to former spectacles of the kind, this is to be an abridgment. There is to be no foot procession from the Hall to the Abbey,—no banquet,—no play-thing-champion to challenge opposition to the King's title. But even this is to cost fifty thousand pounds: while that sum of money would keep alive a thousand families for a year, that are now perishing from want, occasioned by that species of taxation which has raised this fifty thousand pounds, and which so squanders a thousand other fifty thousand pounds every year.

This coronation is an entire mummery, and a disgrace to the growing knowledge of the present time; but it is the consequence of having kings, and priests, and lords. Its meaning is nothing more than to grease the King's body, and the Queen's head, with a little oil,—to put a tinselled bauble on each of their heads, and some playthings in their hands,—to sing a song,—to say a prayer,—and to say *God save the King and Queen*, and to mean *God damn the people*. It is a festival, at which the king, the priests, and the lords, celebrate their triumph over a conquered and degraded people,—pledge themselves to a mutual support of their earthly trinity in unity,—and send the bill of fifty thousand pounds to the people, to be paid by them for their own degradation, because the king, and priests, and lords are up, and the people are down.

One argument, raised by shallow minds, for the utility of such a spectacle, is, that it makes good for trade. It is a narrow view. The good is a very partial, momentary good, that arises from universal evil. If you draw any thing from the community, such as taxes are drawn, you cannot again diffuse it. If the attempt were made to raise a million in taxes, and to spread back that million from whence it had been taken, it could not be done; there would be the loss of all the time, and all the expense of the parties collect-

ing and distributing beside the laying idle of the money. But when we know that our kings, our priests, and our lords, have the motive to collect the taxes, but not the motive to send them back as far as they can, we can see clearly what the mass of the people lose by having kings, and priests, and lords.

Another set-off question is, are kings, and priests, and lords, useful as legislators, and as administerers of law? I answer no. And my argument is this:—That which would be useful in law, and in administration of law, for the people, can be best judged of by the people,—be best furnished in delegation by the people,—which delegation should never cease to be identified with the interests of the people, by responsibility, by frequent election, and as respectable servants, valued and placed in trust.

Now, the interest of kings, and priests, and lords is a distinct interest from that of the people; it is a thing conquered from the people. It consults not the people. It produces nothing toward the common good; but it detracts its most lavish subsistence from the scanty means of the people.—The means of the people are crippled by the burden which the king, the priests, and the lords are upon them; and as they are the more crippled, these kings, these priests, and these lords become the more rapacious, until want produces convulsions, and anarchy breaks up the wicked system.

To suppose that there would be any defect in human society, if there were no kings, no priests, no lords, is an erroneous supposition. All the enjoyments of life arise from the productions of human labour; and these will be all the stronger, and all the better, as they are more diffused, and as they are left, as far as desired, in the hands that produce them. Even a single queen-bee would be a nuisance and an evil in human society. They who labour should be the masters. They who superintend the arrangements of society, should be the appointed and salaried servants of the master producers. This is the rationale of society, and this will lead us all to exclaim, DOWN WITH KINGS, WITH PRIESTS, AND WITH LORDS.

RICHARD CARLILE.

PRINTED AND PUBLISHED BY R. CARLILE, 62, FLEET STREET—PRICE THREE-PENCE.

PRINCE ALBERT, IN ENGLAND.

Paul, Printer, 22, Brick Lane, Spitalfields.

☞ Shops and Travellers supplied.

I am a German just arrived,
  With you for to be mingling,
My passage it was paid,
  From Germany to England;
To wed your bloomiug Queen,
  For better or worse I take her,
My father is a duke,
  And I'm a sausage maker.

CHORUS.

Here I am in rags and jags,
  Come from the land of all dirt,
I married England's Queen.
  My name it is young Albert.

I am a cousin to the Queen,
  And our mothers they are cronies,
My father lives at home,
  And deals in nice polonies :
Lots of sour crout and brooms.
  For money he'll be giving,
And by working very nard,
  He gets a tidy living.

He said to me one day.
  We poor long time have tarried,
And I will shut up shop,
  My son when you get married.
He gave me eighteen-pence,
  And twenty pounds of sausage,
Saying off to England go,
  And that will pay your passage

That was not quite enough,
  And father had no riches
So mother pawn'd her gown,
  And father sold his breeches,
My brother sold his boots,
  Cause he on me was doating,
So from Germany I came,
  To England a courting.

You Englishmen are rich,
  Or I am much mistaken,
You have good bread and beer,
  With mutton, beef, and bacon:
While father's folks at home,
  Live all the week on cabbage,
And on a Sunday they will dine,
  On sour crout and sausage.

Your Queen loves me right well,
  And says too long she has tarried,
She is going to buy me a pair
  Of boots now we are married ;
A handsome coat and shirt,
  For she's got lots of riches,
A four and ninepenny tile,
  And a slashing pair of breeches.

She's going to buy me a sword,
  Cause she said her mother told her,
She is going to give me a horse,
  And make me a Waterloo soldier;
She'll give me lots of money to spend
  But save it up I'd rather,
And send a crown a week,
  To Germany to father.

She says now we are wed,
  I must not dare to tease her,
But strive both day and night,
  All e'er I can to please her,
I told her I would do
  For her all I was able,
And when she had a son
  I would sit and rock the cradle.

THE QUEEN'S MARRIAGE – AN ASTROLOGER'S VIEW

In reference to the subject of the Queen's Marriage, respecting which you consulted me some time ago, I am almost pursuaded that it will never take place. The aspects of the house of marriage lead to something very different from marriage with a German Prince younger than herself. If it does take place, it will be a most unfortunate marriage – a marriage, in fact, which will be virtually broken very soon after, to the shame and discomfiture of many parties. The sun is evidently oriental, and leads to an early marriage, but with a person considerably older than herself, for Jupiter is in the meridian; yet curious enough, the sun is in very bad aspect to Saturn, which is unfavourable to marriage altogether! I will not be at all surprised if the marriage, though apparently fixed and resolved upon, never takes place.

A DESCRIPTIVE LIST OF
THE ROYAL NUPTIAL CEREMONIES.

Containing an account of the Queen's Wedding Dress, and the Dresses of her 12 Bridemaids; a description of the Marriage Presents; Portraits of Her Majesty and the King Consort; a Pedigree of Prince Albert; a description of the Chapel Royal, and the interior of the Palaces; the preparations for the Banquet, &c., &c., &c.

ROCESSION.

rocession of the Bridegroom.
Drums and trumpets.
Serjeant Trumpeter.
Master of the Ceremonies.
room's Gent. of Honour and 2 Heralds.
Majesty's Her Majesty's
hamberlain. Lord Chamberlain.

THE BRIDEGROOM.

ted by their Serene Highnesses the of Saxe Coburg and Gotha, and the rince of Saxe Coburg and Gotha.
ntering the Chapel, the drums and s will file off without the door, and degroom will be conducted to the seat d for him on the left of the altar. His es will occupy seats near the Prince, of the Ceremonies and the officers of degroom will stand near. The Lord erlain and the Vice Chamberlain will turn to Her Majesty.

Procession of the Bride.
Drums and trumpets.
Serjeant Trumpeter.
Knight Marshal.
Pursuivants.
Heralds.
Pages of Honour.
ery in Waiting. Clerk Marshal.
m in Waiting. Lord in Waiting.
roller of H. M.'s Comptroller of H. M.'s
ousehold. Household.
d Steward of H. M.'s Household.
y King of Clarencieux King of
Arms. Arms.
Privy Seal. Lord Pres. of Council.
erjeants Two Serjeants
mon. Ld. Chancellor. at Arms.
r Gentleman Usher Quarterly Waiter.
. Usher. Gent. Usher.
Garter King of Arms.
Earl Marshal.
ncess Sophia-Matilda of Gloucester.
Princess Mary of Cambridge.
Princess Augusta of Cambridge.
Prince George of Cambridge.
Duchess of Cambridge.
Duchess of Kent.
Duchess of Gloucester.
Princess Augusta.
Duke of Cambridge.
Duke of Sussex.
hamberlain. Lord Chamberlain.
ord of State borne by Ld. Melbourne.

EXPLANATION OF THE FIGURES IN THE ENGRAVING. 1, *Her Most Gracious Majesty*; 2, *His Royal Highness Prince Albert*; 3, *the Archbishop of Canterbury and the Bishop of London*; 4, *Duke of Sussex*; 5, *Duke of Kent*; 6, *Duchess of Sutherland, Mistress of Robes*; 7, *Lady A. Paget*; 8, *Lady F. E. Cowper*; 9, *Lady E. West*; 10, *Lady M. A. Grimston*; 11, *Lady C. A. Lennox*; 12, *Lady I. Hay*; 13, *Lady J. H. Bouverie*; 14, *Lord Albemarle, Master of Horse*; 15, *Duke of Saxe Coburg and Gotha*; 16, *Duke of Cambridge*; 17, *Duke of Sussex*; 18, *Groom of the Robes*; 19, *Lord Melbourne*; 20, *Lord J. Russell*; 21, *Lord Normanby*; 22, *the Gallery*.

THE QUEEN.

Her Majesty's train borne by the following 12 un-married ladies.

Lady A. Paget Lady S. F. C. Villiers.
F. E. Cowper. E. West.
M. A. F. Grimston. E. C. Paget.
C. A. G. Lennox. E. A. G. Howard.
I. Hay. C. L. Stanhope.
J. H. Bouverie. M. C. Howard.
Groom of the Robes.
Master of the Horse. Mistress of Robes.
Ladies of the Bedchamber;
March. Normanby. Duchess of Bedford.
Countess Charlemont. Countess of Sandwich.
Lady Lyttelton. Countess Burlington.
Lady Portman. Lady Barham.
Maids of Honour:
Hon Harriet Pitt.
Hon. A. Murray. Hon. C. Cox.
H. Anson. M. Paget.
H. Lister. S. M. Cavendish.
Women of the Bedchamber;
Lady H. Clive. Viscountess Forbes.
Lady C. Copley. Lady C. Barrington.
Mrs. Brand. Lady Gardiner.
Hon. Mrs. Campbell.
Capt. of the Yeo. of Capt. of Band Gentle.
the Guard. Gold Stick. at Arms.
Keeper of the Privy Purse.
Six Gents. at Arms.
Six Yeomen of the Guard to close Procession.

On arriving at the entrance of the Chapel the drums and trumpets will file off.

The Gentlemen at Arms will remain outside Chapel door during the Ceremony.

The Yeomen of the Guard will remain at the foot of the staircase.

The respective persons will then be conducted to the seats prepared for them.

The Princes and Princesses of the Blood Royal will have seats on the Haut-Pas.

The Ladies attending on the Queen will sit near Her Majesty.

The Queen

On reaching the Haut-Pas, will take her seat in the Chair of State, on the right of the altar.

On the conclusion of the Ceremony, the Procession will return, that of the Bridegroom preceding, but His Royal Highness will conduct Her Majesty in the return.

The Knights of the several orders present at the Solemnity, will wear their respective Collars, with white Rosettes.

GOD SAVE THE QUEEN.

THE PROCESSION, &c.

The Chapel.—The chapel has undergone considerable improvement. Arrangements have been made so as to accommodate about 500 of the nobility. There has also been a part devoted to the use of the Foreign Ministers. The members of the Royal Family will assemble on each side the altar, and the space in the middle will be reservdd for the illustrious couple and their attendants. The altar will be lined with velvet, and richly hung with drapery, over the communion-table will be a rich display of communion-plate. State chairs and devotional stools of the most tasteful description will be placed for the use of her Majesty and the King Consort, and the floor will be covered with a rich carpet of purple and gold.

HER MOST GRACIOUS MAJESTY, QUEEN VICTORIA
Born May 24, 1819.

Her Majesty's Bridal Dress is made of white satin, with a broad flounce the most expensive ever produced. The dresses and jewels of the bride and her bridesmaids will cost upwards of a million money.

Buckingham Palace.—Her Majesty, the Duchess of Kent, the bridesmaids, or train-bearers, twelve in number, and the Officers of State, will assemble in Buckingham Palace, and go in procession to the garden entrance of St. James's Palace, by which her Majesty will proceed up the grand stair-case to the Queen's closet or council chamber, where she will remain till the order of procession is arranged in front of the throne, of which she will receive due notice from the Lord Chamberlain.

The Ante Throne-Room.—The procession of the bridegroom will here assemble, and be duly placed by the officers of the Earl Marshal. The folding-doors between these rooms will be kept closed till all be in readiness.

The Throne-Room.—Here the members of the Royal Family, the great Officers of State, and such persons as are to accompany her Majesty to the chapel, will assemble, and take their proper places.

The Procession.—Prince Albert's portion of the procession will move first, preceded by the Lord and Deputy Chamberlain, who will conduct his Royal Highness to the chapel. The Lord and Deputy Chamberlain will then return to the Queen, and her Majesty's procession will then advance, preceded bp music, and guided by the Earl Marshal.

In Queen Anne's Drawing-room, raised seats have been erected, which will be covered with crimson cloth. The Guard Chamber has seats erected in it, and will be hung with ancient tapestry. In the Armoury there are seats erected. The Colonnade leading to the chapel has had seats erected in it, capable of accommodating 360 persons, which will be covered with crimson cloth; there have been three extensive sky-lights introduced into the roof, and large windows have been opened in the back of the inclosure. The whole course, from the Throne-room to the door of the chapel, will be covered with a rich carpet of a most beautiful and expensive pattern. It is calculated that there will be accommodation for 1200 persons, on the staircase and in the chambers.

The Conclusion of the Ceremony. At the conclusion of the ceremony, which will be performed by the Archbishop of Canterbury and the Bishop of London, at a given signal, the Park and Tower guns will fire a salute. Her Majesty and the King Consort will then take their seats in state chairs, on each side the altar, receiving the congratulations of the illustrious groups by whom they will be surrounded. The procession will then re-form, and the illustrious couple will return to the Palace, the spectotors all standing. On the return to the Throne-room the attestation of the royal marriage will take place. For this portion of the ceremonial a new table has been made, of exquisite workmanship.

In the evening there will be a splendid banquet given in the Banquet-room, fitted up by George IV., in St. James's Palace, to all the members of her Majesty's Household. Covers for about one hundred and thirty persons will be laid. All the public offices will be illuminated, and extensive preparations are being made by all classes for a general illumination; and it is expected, from the general love and esteem in which her Majesty and her Royal Consort are held, that the illumination will be one of the most splendid ever witnessed.

His Royal Highness the Duke of Sussex will give her Majesty away. The Duke of Cumberland will not be present; but their Royal Highnesses the Duke and Duchess of Cambridge, Prince George of Cambridge, and the two Princesses, the Princess Augusta, Princess Sophia, of Gloucester, and other members of the Royal Family, will join in the procession.

A drawing-room will be held in the evening, at which her Majesty will receive the congratulations of her subjects, including the Lord Mayor and Common Councilmen, the Universities of Cambridge and Oxford, and other public bodies, as well as the Foreign Ministers.

Throughout the kingdom preparations are in progress for celebrating the evenr in a becoming manner, and there will not be a town or village in which there will not be rejoicing. White favours will be generally worn.

The Royal Bridecake that has been provided for the occasion, is one of the most costly description; it weighs three hundred pounds. It has been prepared by Mr. J. C. Mawditt, First Yeoman Confectioner to the Queen.

THE ROYAL BRIDAL CHAMBERS.

The suite of private apartments that have been prepared at Buckingham Palace, for the reception of her Majesty and her Royal Consort, are on the north wing, overlooking the Palace Gardens and Grosvenor Place. They extend from end to end of that range of the building, and have been remodelled and fitted up, under the direction of the Lord Chamberlain. Three hundred men have been employed upon the decorations. The prevailing ground colour is a maiden's blush, with milk-white mountings throughout the suite, the cornices, ornamented ceilings, and mouldings of the architraves to the windows and doors are all of burnished gold. The following is a correct outline of the arrangement of the rooms.

North Wing—Garden Front.

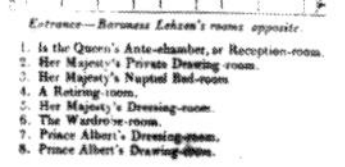

Entrance—Baroness Lehzen's rooms opposite.

1. Is the Queen's Ante-chamber, or Reception-room.
2. Her Majesty's Private Drawing-room.
3. Her Majesty's Nuptial Bed-room.
4. A Retiring-room.
5. Her Majesty's Dressing-room.
6. The Wardrobe-room.
7. Prince Albert's Dressing-room.
8. Prince Albert's Drawing-room.

PEDIGREE OF PRINCE ALBERT.

Saxe Coburg Gotha.—Reigning Duke—Ernest born January 2, 1784, succeeded his father Francis Duke of Saxe Saalfeld Coburg, on December, 9. 1806, in that duchy, created by the second convention of Paris Prince Lichtenburg, and by the convention of November 12, 1826, Duke of Saxe Coburg Gotha. His Highness married July 31, 1817, Louisa, daughter of Augustus, Duke of Saxe Gotha Altenburg (from whom he is separated) and has issue—

Ernest, hereditary prince, born June 21, 1818.

Albert, born August 26, 1819.

Brothers and Sisters of the Duke.—Ferdinand George, born March 28, 1785, lieutenant-field-marshall in the Austrian service, and proprietare of the 8th regiment of hussars; married January 2, 1816, Maria, daughter of Prince Francis Joseph, of Kohary, born July 3, 1797, and has issue—

Ferdinand, born October 29, 1816; married to the Queen of Portugal.

Augustus, born June 16, 1818.

Leopold, born January 31, 1824.

Victoria, born February 14, 1822.

Leopold George, born December 16, 1790; espoused May, 2, 1816, Her Royal Highness Princess Charlotte of Wales, only daughter of His Majesty, King George IV. of Great Britain and Ireland. The lamented Princess died November 6, 1817.—King of the Belgians.

Sophia Frederica, born, August 19, 1778; married February 22, 1804, to Count Emanuel de Mensdorf, chamber-lain to the Emperor, major-general in the Austrian service, and governor of the fortress of Mentz.

Juliana Henrietta, born September 23, 1781; married February 26, 1796, to the Grand-Duke Constantine of Russia, from whom Her Highness was separated, April 2, 1820.

Victoria Maria Louisa, born August 17, 1786, married December 21, 1804, to Enrich Charles, Prince of Leinenghen, by whom (who died July 4, 1814) she has issue—

Charles Frederick, born September 15, 1804, present Prince Leinenghen; married February 13, 1829, Maria, daughter of the late count Maximilian of Klebelsberg.

Anne Feodorowna, born December 7, 1807; married February 8, 1828, to Ernest Christian Charles, present Prince of Hohenlohe-Langenburg.

Her Highness espoused, secondly, July 11, 1818, His Royal Highness Edward Duke of Kent, fourth son of King George III, of Great Britain; by whom (who died January 23, 1820) she has an only child, QUEEN ALEXANDRINA VICTORIA, BORN MAY 24, 1819.

Mother of the Duke. — Duchess-dowager Augusta Caroline, daughter of Henry XXIV., Prince of Reuss Eberedorf born January 19, 1737, married June 13, 1777.

TITLES FOR PRINCE ALBERT.

Among other matters of speculation connected with Prince Albert, is the title of the dukedom which will be conferred upon him, if indeed he be so ill advised as to accept of a British peerage. Some title already dignified by having belonged to a royal persouage would probably be selected; but care should be taken lest one be chosen which, though supposed to be extinct, does in fact belong to some living individual; and the possibility of such a mistake is shown by the following instances, which are not generally known. In 1706, Queen Anne created the Electoral Prince of Hanover (afterwards King George the second), Baron of Tewkesbury Viscount Northallerton, Earl of Milford Haven, and Marquis and Duke of Cambridge, to hold to him and the heirs male of his body. In 1717, Frederick Lewis, eldest son of the Prince of Wales, was made Duke of Gloucester; and in 1726, he was created Baron Snawdon, Viscount Launceston, Earl of Eltham, Marquis of Ely, and Duke of Edinburgh. The limitation of all those honors being "to him and the heirs male of his body." They were inherited by his son, Prince George, afterwards King George III. It has been supposed that the dukedoms of Cambridge, Gloucester, and Edinburgh, and all other dignities above-mentioned, became so completely lost in the regal dignity on the accession of King George the second and third, as to be utterly extinct; and upon this presumption similar titles were conferred upon various branches of the royal family.

As George III. was the heir male of George II., and as George IV. and William IV. were the heirs male of George III., all the honors in question would have devolved upon those personages, under the limitations in the patents, so that there could have been no question on the subject; but on the accession of Queen Victoria, the sovereign and the heir male of the bodies of George II. and George III. were for the first time different individuals; and it consequently appears that the dukedoms of Cambridge, Gloucester, and Edinburgh, the Marquisates of Ely and Cambridge the Earldoms of Milford Haven and Eltham, the Viscounties of Northallerton and Launceston, and the Baronies of Tewkesbury and Snawdon, have devolved upon the King of Hanover, as heir male of his father and great-grandfather, to whom they were granted by the patents of 1766, 1717, and 1726. The dictum of Lord Hale, and other authorities, seem decisive upon the point. By the common law, whatever the King acquire on coming to the crown, vests in a politic capacity; but what he possessed before his accession, or inherits from a collateral ancestor after his accession, vests in a natural capacity: hence the honours a king may have possessed before his accession remain in their original state; and when the heir to whom they were limited is a different person from the sovereign, they will necessarily descend to such heir, instead of being (as is erroneously supposed) destroyed by their union with the royal dignity.

There are, however, several royal titles which would be fitting for Prince Albert, and to which no one has any pretensions. York, Kent, and Clarence, in England—Albany, Strathearn, and Saint Andrew, in Scotland—Ulster and Dublin in Ireland—afford a sufficient choice; and most of those names are rich in historical associations. "Kendal" has been suggested, apparently because it was the earldom of Prince George of Denmark; but it ought not to be chosen, for though it formed part of the honours of the great Duke of Bedford, brother of Henry the Fifth, and afterwards of the Beauforts, Dukes of

PRINCE ALBERT, OF SAXE COBURG.
Born August, 26, 1819.

Somerset—was given to John de Foix, a Gascon—next as a Barony to Prince Rupert—was the dukedom to which an infant son of James Duke of York was nominated in 1666, and was afterwards granted to Prince George of Denmark; the name lost all its lustre by being conferred upon Madame de Schulenberg, mistress of George the First, who was created Duchess of Munster in Ireland and Duchess of Kendal in England by her Royal lover. It has since born the title of a Barony granted to sir James Lowther, Earl of Lonsdale; but it became extinct on his death in 1802.

The manner in which Prince Albert's peerage should be limited is deserving of consideration. If in the usual terms, to the "heirs male of his body," his honours might eventually descend to those for whom they were never designed—namely, to the sons of any other marriage, on the failure of male issue by this; and such a contingency shows the propriety of Prince Leopold's not having a peerage with a limitation of that description. The most judicious plan seems to limit Prince Albert's honours to the second son of his marriage with Queen Victoria; for the eldest son will be the Duke of Cornwall at his birth, and will of course be soon after created Prince of Wales.

The Royal Nuptial Banquet.

THE

Royal Banquet.

Tune—"Rule Britannia."

Sound, sound the music, lo! appears
Arrayed in Royal robes so grand,
Victoria comes midst loyal cheers,
And to Prince Albert gives her hand.

CHORUS.

Then let nought but mirth and gaiety around us be seen,
For this is the marriage of England's Queen.

Behold what wealth and rank are seen,
Bedecked with dazzling diamonds bright
They come to hail our King and Queen,
With loyalty and pure delight.

Well may such general joy prevail,
When England's monarch does appear,
The Royal Banquet will not fail
To show good feeling and good cheer.

The richly laden table see,
What honours crown the Royal state,
In their good wishes all agree,
Long live our Queen and Consort great.

In every part of Britain wide,
Let every loyal heart prepare,
And drink, with heartfelt joy and pride,
Health to our Queen and Consort dear.

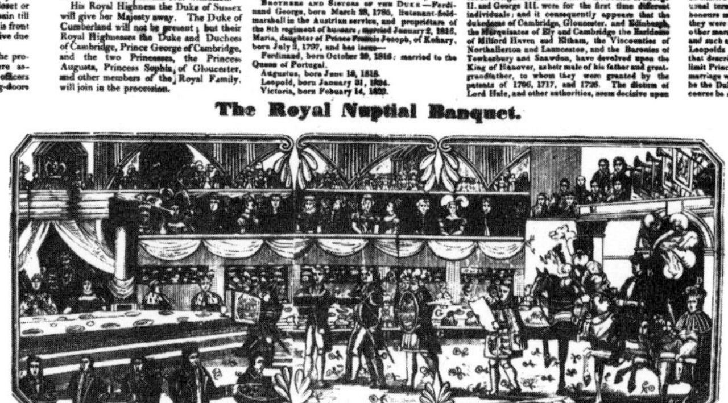

Let all who hear my loyal strain
Join their good wishes with my song,
And sing with yonder splendid train,
May the happy pair live long.

EXPLANATION OF THE FIGURES IN THE ENGRAVING.

A A. Her Most Gracious Majesty the Queen and the King Consort, Prince Albert of Saxe Coburg and Gotha.

B. The Hereditary Grand Champion of England.

C. His Lordship the Lord Chamberlain.

D. His Lordship the Deputy Lord Chamberlain.

F. The Grand and Noble Herald of England.

G. Two Esquires carrying the Lance and Shield of the Grand Champion.

H. The Grand Macebearer, and the Knight of the Gold Stick.

I. His Lordship the Master of the Horse.

K. The Royal Trumpeters.

Paul and Co., Printers, 2 and 3, Monmouth Court, Seven Dials.

VICTORIA

The Star of England.

AIR.—" The Roast Beef of old England."

SEE the glory of England how beauti-
ously bright,
Like the star of the morning all beaming
with light,   (sight,
As the sun in its splendour she gladdens our

CHORUS.

Long life to the pride of Old England,
  The pride of our Nations the Queen.

The nuptial torch's lighted the sacred rites
done,
Victoria and Albert they now are made one
May love crown their bliss and care ever
shun,
The glory and pride of Old England,
  The pride of our Nations the Queen

May she govern with justice, & mercy at-
tend,   (friend,
And merrit oppress'd may she allways be-
To the rights of her people her ear may
she lend.
Then we'll bless the pride of Old England
  The glory of England the Queen

Blessings attend her for the pardon she
gave,
The scepter of mercy she extended to save,
The Chartist, from death & an untimely
grave,
Did the mercyfull Queen of Old England,
  Old England's Virtuous Queen.

Of that pious deed after ages will tell,
And each loyal bosom with gratitude swell
On the fame of her virtues with rapture
they dwell,
And revere the great name of Victoria,
  The glory of England the Queen.

To the corn bill she is a staunch friend.
To support it her power will lend,
No doubt it will pass in the end.
For the welfare and glory of England.
  The pride of our Nation's the Queen.

She shall live in our hearts and be dear to
our souls,   to pole,
And her fame be resounded from pole un-
Till ages to come in eternity roll.
Her fame shall not die in Old England.
  The pride of our Nation's the Queen.

Long life to Prince Albert, be wisdom his
guide,
May honour and justice attend by his side
May jove shower blessings on him and his
bride.
The glorious Queen of Old England.
  The pride of England the Queen.

May the wealth of all nation's be laid at
their feet,
And Tyrany tremble & shake in his seat,
We the foes of Old England like Britons
defeat,
For the glory and honour of England,
  The pride of our Nation's the Queen,

Long live victoria, long may she reign,
Our rights to uphold may she never disdain
May commerce & plenty yet flourish again.
And blossom afresh in Old England.
  The pride of our Nation's the Queen.

Printed by H. PAUL, 22, Brick Lane, Spitalfields, London.

NOTES TO THE ANTHOLOGY

I. WORK AND ENTERTAINMENT

1. RURAL (*pages 95–106*)

Cobbett and the Sand-Hill
William Cobbett, 'Rural Rides', *Cobbett's Register*, 5 October 1827, cols. 19–24. Written on Friday 27 September 1827 at Odiham.
 Canning was appointed Prime Minister in April 1827 but died the following year. The Six Acts were passed in 1819 and were an attempt to suppress cheap periodicals and public meetings.

Man crossing a natural bridge
Woodcut by Thomas Bewick, from *A History of British Birds*, vol. 2, 1804.

The Life of Swing
In this pamphlet, anonymous but attributed to Richard Carlile, which was produced at the time of the 'Captain Swing' rick burning and machine breaking (1830), Swing tells how he is driven into ever-increasing destitution by the avarice of landlords and the tithes demanded by the church. It was first sold in Carlile's shop by an ingenious dial and chute method whereby the seller was unseen. Vizetelli, when trying to buy a copy, received a harmless compilation of newspaper reports: see Vizetelli, *Glances Back*, 1869; see also E. J. Hobsbawm and G. Rudé, *Captain Swing*, Penguin University Books, 1973.

£150 Reward
Broadsheet, 25.5 x 31 cm.

Rural Sports at Northfleet
Pierce Egan Sr, *Pierce Egan's Book of Sports*, 1832, pp. 259–66.
 Northfleet, twenty-eight miles (three shillings return) by steamer downriver from London, was one of several popular recreation centres frequented by both city people and locals.

Wrekington Hiring
Author unknown, probably written *c*. 1820. Printed in *A Collection of Songs Comic, Satiric and Descriptive, Chiefly in the Newcastle Dialect*, Newcastle upon Tyne 1827; also frequently found in broadsheet form, from which this is taken. Hiring fairs were annual, often biennial, events.
 Wrekington: Wreckenton, County Durham. King pit caller: man who summoned miners to the King pit, which was closed in the 1830s. Whag: chunk. Pepper-cyek: thick gingerbread. Scranchim: thin gingerbread. Lonnen: lane. A heet: urging on. Hitchy: bouncing. Laith: unwilling. Lyem: lame. Bonk an' byen: lusty and strong. In the south: in the souse (?) – tipsy. Other difficulties come from the phonetic spelling. Gyep: gape. Yell: ale.

Trial of George Loveless
George Loveless, *Victims of Whiggery*, 1837, pp. 6–7.
 George Loveless was the leader of the 'Tolpuddle Martyrs' – six agricultural labourers who took an illegal oath to a 'lodge' while seeking higher wages (their pay was seven shillings a week). They were convicted on 18 March 1834 and sentenced to seven years' deportation. In spite of massive protest and a trade-union procession in London it was two years before they were returned to England.

The Plowman's Ditty
Probably a middle-class propaganda sheet, but no imprint or date.

Daft Watty's Ramble to Carlisle
A good example of the alternating song and 'patter' provided by many balladsellers. This is from a Newcastle chapbook *c*. 1820. Most verbal problems are due only to phonetic spelling.
 Codling: nesting. Brock: badger. Duds: clothes. Forbye: except. Trapan: trap.

2. MINING (*pages 106–11*)

Labourers Wanted
Broadsheet, 25 x 20 cm.

The Collier's Rant
This version of this traditional mining song comes from *The Coal-Hole Companion*, 1844, but it had already appeared in J. Ritson, *Northumberland Garland; or Newcastle Nightingale*, 1793, and has since appeared in A. L. Lloyd, *Come all ye Bold Miners*, 1952, and elsewhere. Miners believed digging too deep brought one to Hell.
 Low: lamp. Driving the drift: cutting a tunnel between coal seams. Putting the tram: pushing the waggon. Shin-splints: wooden leg-protectors. Beak: nose. Hoggar: stacking gate. Marrow: mate.

A Bang-up Collier's Letter to His Sweetheart
A rare broadsheet making use of parallels between the sexual act and the position of the miner who often had to labour half naked because of the heat.
 Corf: coal-basket. Tram: chassis on which corf rode. Mother-gate: main tunnel. Pillar: vertical section of coal left in to support roof. Thready: weak. Thrust: roof-fall. Sark: shirt. Happ'd up: covered, enfolded. Sump: dig down, as in sinking a shaft. Hack: pick used especially for breaking stone and sinking work. Full: fill, fulfil. Jud:

a measure of coal, usually as much as a strong man could hew in a shift. Hence 'full your jud' would imply 'give you full measure'. Mal: sledgehammer. Bank: surface, the top of the shaft.

Collier Lass
Broadsheet, c. 1838. 9.5 x 24 cm.

Brave Collier Lads
An anonymous broadsheet of 1838. Mining scene, Thomas Bewick (1797).

The Colliery Union
Broadsheet printed by Henderson of North Shields, 1844. Celebrates successful Durham colliery strike, 1844. W. P. Roberts, union leader, and editor of *Miners' Monthly Magazine* (1844–5). William Beesley, his assistant. See M. Vicinus, *The Industrial Muse*, 1974, ch. 2.

Haswell Cages
Haswell is a small colliery town in County Durham. The ballad, published c. 1839, 'is an early specimen of that painstaking factual coal-dust and cast-iron manner that was to characterise so much mine, workshop and foundry poetry in later years', A. L. Lloyd, *Folk Song in England*, 1967, pp. 350–53. This also prints the music. Screen: where coal is sorted from other matter. Keeker: check-weighman. Corves: baskets.

3. WEAVING (pages 111–14)

Jone O'Grinfilt
An undated broadsheet, attributed to Joseph Lees and Joseph Coupe. See Harland, *Ballads and Songs of Lancashire*, pp. 162–75, Vicinus, pp. 49–52.
Originated in the period of extreme hardship after Waterloo. The strongest of a family of ballads with the same hero, all descended from an earlier and very popular song about a simple weaver who forsakes his looms to seek better fortune in the Napoleonic Wars. The present example exists in many broadside and orally transmitted versions: it appears in Mrs Gaskell's novel *Mary Barton* as 'The Oldham

Weaver'. Hand-weaving scene by James Catnach, c. 1826.
Clugs: clogs. Brossen: broken. Clem: starve. Picked o'er: worked a loom. Fast: stuck. Tit: pony. Wick: living. Bout: without.

Cotton Spinners from Manchester
Broadsheet offered by unemployed weavers, c. 1836. 25 x 18 cm.

Bury New Loom
Discussion and music in Lloyd, *Folk Song in England*, pp. 319–20; also see Vicinus, pp. 40–44. Lloyd notes earlier examples of the sexualizing of work tools which goes back to magic and fertility rites.
New Loom: Dobbie Handloom popular during the Napoleonic War. Lams: foot treadles moving the jacks. Jacks: levers that raise the harness holding the warp. Heald: loops, making up harness, through which the warp threads pass. Lathe: supporting stand on loom. Reiving: raiding. Pickers: attachments to upper end of picking stick which thrusts shuttle through the warp. Foreloom-post: front overhanging portion of loom.

The Weaver and the Factory Maid
An anonymous broadsheet, c. 1825.

4. MACHINERY (pages 114–26)

The Need for Machinery
Harriet Martineau, *The Rioters*, F. Houlston, Wellington, 1827, pp. 36–9. Issued as a tract distributed against machine-breaking; re-issued 1842. See R. K. Webb, *Harriet Martineau*, 1960, p. 99.

A Factory Victim
The Poor Man's Advocate, 23 June 1832, p. 177, an unstamped paper, edited by John Doherty and then James Turner, a leading force behind the 1833 Factory Act, which limited children's work to eight hours a day.
For a medical practitioner's view of factory conditions see P. Gaskell, *Artisans and Machinery*, 1836, which influenced Engels.

The Factory Lad
The Factory Lad: or, The Life of Simon Smike, c. 1838, pp. 35–6, 144–6. *Simon Smike* was one of several fictional works dealing with the privations of factory life, including John Walker's fine play *The Factory Lad*, Surrey Theatre, 1834, and Frances Trollope's novel, *Michael Armstrong, the Factory Boy*, 1840. *Simon Smike* was loosely based on John Brown's *A Memoir of Robert Blincoe*, published in Carlile's *The Lion*, 25 September 1827 to 22 February 1828; Manchester, 1832: this is a factual account of cruelties suffered in Litton Mill, Derbyshire, 1803–13. Compare with William Dodd's fraudulent *A Narrative of the Experience and Sufferings of W. D.*, 1841, which deceived Lord Ashley.

Steam at Sheffield
From Ebenezer Elliott, *Steam at Sheffield*, 1835, sections ii, iii, vi, vii.

The New London Railway
Anonymous broadsheet. Commercial railways began with the Stockton and Darlington Railway, opened 1826; by 1845 over 33 million passengers a year were carried. Pub. Sunderland [1845?].

Railway Exhibition
Advertisement, 1834.

The Productions of All Nations!!!
Broadsheet, 1851, 38 x 50 cm.

The Exhibition Opened
The Working Man's Friend and Family Instructor, 17 May 1851, pp. 187–9.
The Great Exhibition was opened by Queen Victoria on 1 May 1851 in Hyde Park. Prince Albert, who had become President of the Society of Arts in 1847, had played a vital part in organizing the exhibition which was intended as a survey of human progress in the arts and manufactures of a world of peaceful nations. The Crystal Palace was designed by Sir Joseph Paxton (1801-65).

A Reverie about the Crystal Palace
By Martin Tupper (1810–89). Broadsheet, 1851.

5. DOMESTIC (*pages 126–33*)

The Pawnshop Bleezin'
J. P. Robson, *Bards of the Tyne*, 1849. On the burning down of Mrs Trotter's pawnshop, The Side, Newcastle, 1849.

A Hint to Husbands & Wives
Broadsheet, 1832, 20 x 25 cm.

A Comical and Diverting Dialogue
Broadsheet, c. 1830, 24 x 38 cm.

Pauper's Drive
An anonymous undated broadsheet.

The Workhouse and the Rich
G. W. M. Reynolds, *Mysteries of London*, 1845, vol. I, pp. 179–80.

The Rural Police
Penny Satirist (22 August 1840), p. 1. Borough police were established in 1835; County police, 1839–40.

Song
Ebenezer Elliott, *Corn-Law Rhymes*, 1831. Elliott was an influential campaigner against duty on cheap imported corn; this was repealed in 1846.

The Charter
Joseph Radford, *The Northern Star*, 2 January 1841.
The Chartist movement began in 1836 with the aim of parliamentary reform. Its six points' charter (universal manhood suffrage, secret ballot, equal electoral districts, annual parliaments, abolition of property rights for M.P.s and payment of M.P.s) was presented to parliament three times (1839, 1842 and 1848) each time accompanied by a huge petition and each time rejected by parliament out of hand. *The Northern Star* was founded by Feargus O'Connor in Leeds in 1837 and was the leading advocate of chartism.

New Poor Law Bill in Force
The New Poor Law (1834) deliberately made parish relief unattractive. Outdoor relief was abolished and workhouse conditions were hard. The sexes were segregated.

To the West
Henry Russell, *The Far West, c. 1859*, pp. 13–14. A popular song, by Charles Mackay, from an entertainment depicting the life of the emigrant. By 1850, 280, 843 British emigrated each year.

6. SPORT (*pages 133–45*)

Great Fight for the Championship between Spring and Langan
Broadsheet, 37 x 51 cm.

Great Battle between Spring, and Langan
Broadsheet. Tom Spring (real name Thomas Winter) was Champion of England, 1824–5; John Langan was Champion of Ireland. Spring beat Langan again five months later at Chichester. Pierce Egan, supplement to *Bell's Weekly Dispatch*, 11 January 1824.

Boxing – another View
Poor Man's Guardian, 19 November 1831.

Mr Bayley and Club against Mary-la-bonne
Pierce Egan's Book of Sports, 1832, pp. 347–8.

Blackburn Mick
Broadsheet published by Harkness in Preston. Pedestrianism was popular from the late eighteenth century; often performed at fairs.

Bullbaiting
The Factory Lad: or, The Life of Samuel Smike, pp. 132–3. Bullbaiting was outlawed in 1835 but remained popular into the 1850s.

The Bonny Gray
An undated, anonymous broadsheet. Lord Derby: Edward, 12th Earl, who died in 1834. Jim Ward: Liverpool boxer and innkeeper. Cockfighting was ineffectively outlawed in 1849. Another version, with melody, is in Lloyd, *Come All Ye Bold Miners*, pp. 36, 125.

Wednesbury Cocking
An anonymous, undated broadsheet.

The Derby Foot-Ball Play
Penny Magazine, no. 450, 6 April 1839, pp. 131–2.

Snowball the Fastest Greyhound in England
Pierce Egan's Book of Sports, 1832, pp. 389–90.

7. LOW LIFE IN LONDON (*pages 145–151*)

Life in London
Pierce Egan Sr, *Life in London*, 1821, pp. 22–4, 286–90. The slums around Seven Dials, London, were a 'tourist attraction' for young bloods, including the Prince Regent, especially after Egan's account.
Slang: Flue-faker: chimney sweep. Scran: bread. Cove: man, chap. Duce: twopence. Heavy wet: malt liquor, especially porter and stout. Flash of lightning: a glass of gin. Scholard: scholar. Blunt: money. Downy: an artful fellow. Ogles: eyes. Beaks were out on the nose: the constables were prowling around. Mollisher: woman (a thief's mistress). Crib: place, public house. Office: signal, hint. Double shuffle: a hornpipe step in which each foot is shuffled, rapidly and neatly, twice in succession. Out-and-outer: a very determined, unscrupulous fellow. Back slums: residential area for criminals and near criminals. Bosky: mildly drunk. Max: gin. Mud-lark: a man who scavenges in gutters. Gammon: to trick, deceive. Chaff: to banter, lightly rail at. Mug: ply with drink. Spooney: sentimentally in love, foolishly amorous. Ken: house. Mungo: Negro. Three sheets in the wind: drunk. Barnacles: spectacles. Rattler: cab.

Life in Liverpool
Playbill illustrating Egan's influence outside London. 29 x 38 cm.

The Literary Dustman
W. T. Moncrieff, *Songbook*, 1834. 'The Literary Dustman' was made popular by George Walbourne in W. T. Moncrieff's dramatization, *Tom and Jerry* (Adelphi, 1821). It became representative of the

'March of Intellect' and a probable model for Dickens's Mr Boffin. Grisi: Giulia Grisi (1812–69), celebrated soprano. Sin Stephen's College: the old House of Commons, destroyed 1834.

Funeral of Tom and Jerry
Broadsheet, c. 1828. 37 x 50 cm.

II. RELIGION

1. FAITH (*pages 153–6*)

The Great Assize
Broadsheet originally posted at Richmond next to the theatre by Rowland Hill in 1774. Constantly reprinted during the nineteenth century. 29 x 38 cm.

Messenger of Mortality
Broadsheet, c. 1838. 29 x 38 cm.

The Sun of Righteousness
Broadsheet, c. 1840. 37 x 50 cm.

The Stages of Life
Broadsheet, c. 1825. 38 x 50 cm.

2. TRACTS (*pages 157–61*)

On the Advantages of Reading
F. E. Trueman, *Cottager's Monthly Visitor* (1821), pp. 168–70.

The Tract Distributor
An extract from an undated, anonymous, tract *The Soldier*.

Nature and Grace
An anonymous, undated tract.

The Broken Sabbath
An anonymous tract, c. 1840.

3. CONTROVERSY (*pages 161–6*)

Who is Abaddon?
Christian Corrector, 7 March 1832, pp. 370–71. Woodcut, Catnach, n.d.

The Dexterous Fornicator
Anonymous, *Crimes of the Clergy*, 1823, pp. 35–7.

The Gospel According to Richard Carlile
Richard Carlile, *The Gospel According to Richard Carlile*, 1827, pp.

11–13. Carlile (1790–1843) was a dedicated champion of Freethought and the liberty of the press.

The Promotion of Priestianity
G. Cruikshank, *A Slap at the Church* (10 March 1832).

The Church is Our Guide
Roman Catholic broadsheet. 19 x 25 cm.

Beware of the Pope!!
Anti-Catholic broadsheet. 19 x 25 cm. Against Papal aggression [1850?].

Warning
Anonymous northern broadsheet, n.d. 18 x 21 cm.

4. POLITICAL (*pages 167–71*)

Protestantism versus Socialism
Penny Satirist (7 March 1840) p. 1.

Methodist Call to Resist Subversion
Jonathon Crowther and Jabez Bunting, *Address of the Conference*, 7 August 1819, pp. 1–2.

Owen's Religion
Robert Owen, *The New Religion*, 1830, pp. 10–11.

A Chartist Sermon
Rev. J. R. Stephens, *The Political Pulpit*, nos. iv and v, 1839, pp. 29–31.
 John Rayner Stephens (1805–79), a radical Methodist, was imprisoned in 1839–40 for sedition. This sermon was preached in the market-place of Newcastle-under-Lyme on 3 March 1838, the congregation being too large for any available church.

The Charter the People's Hope
Broadsheet, 1842. 37 x 50 cm. P.R.O., H.O. 45. OS 242.

III. ADMONITORY

1. DISEASE AND CLEANLINESS (*pages 173–7*)

The Cholera
Christian Corrector, 7 March 1832.
 England and Wales suffered

cholera epidemics 1831–2 and 1848–9. The latter killed 53,293 persons.

Has Death (in a Rage)
Broadsheet, 1832. 12 x 15.5 cm.

Alarming Visitation of Divine Providence
Anonymous, *An Affectionate Address to the Inhabitants of Newcastle and Gateshead*, Newcastle upon Tyne, 1832 (extract).

Hints to Working People about Clothing
Manchester and Salford Sanitary Association, Tract 5, Manchester, 1843 (extract).

Cleanliness
Broadsheet, undated. 18 x 23 cm.

Soap
Family Economist, 1850, pp. 15–16.

2. TEMPERANCE (*pages 177–86*)

A Labourer's Home
Mary Gillies, *Howitt's Journal*, 1847, pp. 61–4.

The Drunkard's Coat of Arms
Broadsheet, undated. 25.5 x 19.5 cm.

A Sermon on Malt
Temperance broadsheet, undated. 14 x 22 cm.

Temperance Thermometer
London Journal, I, 1845, p. 31.

Pins A-Piece
Henry Anderton, *Temperance Songs*, Todmorden, 1836, p. 9.
 Anderton (1808–55) was a working-class pioneer of the Temperance movement. See Brian Harrison, *Drink and the Victorians*, 1971, pp. 127–8.

Sam Weller Signs the Pledge
G. W. M. Reynolds, 'Noctes Pickwickianae', *The Teetotaller*, 1841, pp. 7–8.
 The young author who wrote *Pickwick Abroad* (1838) was Reynolds himself. In the original version of Weller's song he drinks

brandy. Isaac van Amburgh: celebrated American animal trainer (1805–65).

3. THE ART OF LIFE (*pages 186–8*)

The Art of Life
Eliza Cook's Journal, 14 December 1850, pp. 103–4.
  Possibly by Samuel Smiles. The phrase was made popular in this context as the title of a poem by Ebenezer Elliott, Smiles's friend, the 'Corn Law Poet'.

The Importance of Punctuality
Broadsheet, n.d. 24 x 18 cm.

A Thermometer
Broadsheet, n.d. 10.5 x 16 cm.

4. BE SOMETHING (*pages 188–94*)

Be Something
Family Economist, 1850, p. 17.

The Carpenter's Boy
Anonymous, *Working Man's Friend*, 2 March 1850, pp. 264–6.
  America had a significant influence on English 'self-help' movements, especially through the example of Benjamin Franklin.

Gerald Massey
Eliza Cook's Journal, 12 April 1851, pp. 372–4.
  This is by Samuel Smiles who later reprinted it, abbreviated, as a preface to Massey's *Poems and Ballads*, 1854. Smiles was a regular contributor to *Eliza Cook's Journal*, and by 1851 he was writing as much as half of the prose in each issue. He left the periodical in 1854, when Cook gave up the editorship. In this, *The People's* and *Howitt's Journal* he advocated the virtues of discipline and enterprise that he was to make famous in *Self-Help*, 1859. See *The Autobiography of Samuel Smiles*, ed. C. McKay, 1905, pp. 160–65. Ebenezer Elliott (1781–1848): a largely self-educated poet and Radical, in the iron trade. David Nicoll (1820–91): once a tailor, M.P. and inventor. Samuel Bamford (1788–

1872): once a weaver, became a writer and Radical leader. Frances Davis, the 'Belfast Man' (1810–85): weaver, poet and editor. De Jean: not traced.

IV. FABLES

1. TALES (*pages 195–227*)

Wonderful Adventures of the Seven Champions of Christendom
Original by R. Johnson, published *c.* 1597. This chapbook form, W. and T. Fordyce, Newcastle, *c.* 1838.

Letters of the Black Dwarf
(Thomas) Jonathon Wooler, *The Black Dwarf*, 13 June 1821, pp. 845–50.
  Wooler spent eighteen months in Warwick gaol for taking part in electing Sir Charles Wolsey 'legislatorial attorney' for Birmingham in 1819, at the height of the agitation for parliamentary reform. Castlereagh was Foreign Secretary and Leader of the House of Commons 1812–22, Eldon was Lord High Chancellor 1801, almost continuously until 1827.

King Death and the Knight of the Silver Shield
Broadsheet, undated. 9 x 20 cm.

Richard the Lion King Meets a Lion
Thomas Archer, *Richard of England*, 1842, pp. 386–94.
  Besides telling of the adventures of Richard in Europe and during the Middle East Crusades, the book tells how Eustace de Vere, who is half Norman, proves his valour and overcomes the prejudice of the Saxon Oswald against a Norman marrying his daughter, Alena.
  Archer was also a popular dramatist.

Herman is Initiated into the 'Order of Benevolence'
The Red Cross Warrior; or, the Spirit of the Night, 1843, pp. 135–8.

The Fatal Book Opened!
Broadsheet, n.d. 19 x 25 cm.

The Demon of Sicily
Edward Montague, *The Demon of Sicily*, *c.* 1840, pp. 6–10.

Wonderful Adventures of Mr O'Flynn
Broadsheet, n.d. 18 x 21 cm.

Varney, the Vampyre
James Malcolm Rymer, *Varney, the Vampyre; or, the Feast of Blood*, 1846, pp. 1–11.
  In the course of the story Flora is found not to have been harmed, and Varney emerges as a sympathetic character plagued by his vampirism. After various adventures, including some that took place in the seventeenth century according to Varney, he ends his life down Vesuvius. See Montague Summers, *The Vampire*, 1928.

The Vampire!
Undated playbill, Pettingell Collection, University of Kent.

Novels and Romances
John Cassell (?), *Working Man's Friend*, II, 8 June 1850, p. 289.

2. WONDERS (*pages 227–34*)

The Mermaid
The Mirror, 9 November 1832, pp. 17–19.

Three Beautiful Albini Children
Undated broadsheet, Sheffield Public Library. 19 x 33 cm.

Miraculous Circumstance
Broadsheet. 19 x 25 cm.

The Dreamer's Companion
Penny-issues, *c.* 1838. 12.5 x 18.5 cm.

For the Good of the Public!!
Broadsheet. 22 x 27 cm.

The Significance of Dreams
The Royal Dream Book, *c.* 1830, pp. 4–5.

The Origins of Holloway's Ointment
From 'Mr Holloway', *Penny Satirist*, 22 January 1839, pp. 1–2.

Sonnet to the Memory of Old Parr

Written by a 'Lady from Nottingham' who had been miraculously cured of a grievous disease by Parr's Life Pills. *Northern Star*, December 1841, p. 2.

According to *Old Parr's Last Will and Testament* Thomas Parr lived to the 'almost incredible' age of 152 before dying as a direct consequence of bad medical aid. His grave contained the recipe by which 'by ye grace of Almighty God' he had achieved his longevity. Another of Ingram's handouts claimed that Parr could fulfil the promise of 120 years' life contained in Genesis 6, v. 3 (*The Life and Times of Thomas Parr*, c. 1841).

Parr's Life Pills
Advertising broadsheet, n.d. 13 x 27 cm.

3. SPECTACLE (*pages 234–42*)

Mr Pickwick and the Blood-Stained Bandit
'Bos', *The Penny Pickwick*, 1839, pp. 55–7.

The Fiend's Frying Pan
Etching by George Cruikshank, 1 September 1832. 37 x 28 cm.

Hughes's Mammoth Theatre
Advertising pamphlet, 1845. 24 x 30 cm.

Astley's Grand Spectacle Extraordinary
On Astleys, see Dickens, *Sketches by Boz* (1837), ch. xi. *Mazeppa* was based on Byron's poem (1819).

De Original Jim Crow
T. D. Rice, from the *Jim Crow Songster* (1840). For 'Jim Crow', see note in next column.

Baggy Nanny; or, the Pitman's Frolic
Robert Emery (1794–1838), in Fordyce, *Newcastle Song Book*, 1842.

Celebrates the performances of the violinist Nicolo Paganini who visited Newcastle 9–11 September 1833.

Thrang: hale, hearty. Sair: sore. Hinny: a term of endearment.

Bowdykite: abusive name for precocious child.

Jim Crow's Songster
Song-book cover, 21.5 x 20 cm.

'Jim Crow', a comic black, introduced from America into England by T. D. Rice in 1836, quickly became, like Sam Weller, a figure of folk-myth.

4. POLITICAL SHOWMAN (*pages 242–7*)

The Boa Desolator, or Legitimate Vampire
William Hone and George Cruikshank, *Political Showman*, 1821, pp. 27–9.
The Vampire is the State.

Grand Political Pantomime
G. A. à Beckett and R. Seymour, *Figaro in London*, 31 December 1831, pp. 13–14.

The basis of pantomime was magical transformations under the wand of the good fairy. Here the shifting of political stance before the 1832 Reform Bill is satirized as pantomime, which also was often satirical. See David Mayer, *Harlequin in His Element*, Cambridge, Mass., 1969. Vagabonds: Burdett, Hobhouse, Grey, Brougham supported reform against Eldon, Wetherall, Howe (Queen's Chamberlain), Wharncliffe. William: William IV.

Lord John Russell's Committee
Pamphlet for the South Devon election lost by Russell in 1835.

Totnes Parrot: Jasper Parrot, M.P. for Totnes. Church Trick: proposal to disestablish the Church of Ireland. Transformation Trick: Russell's support of the Reform Act. Tithe Trick: Proposal to abolish tithes.

Republics and Monarchies
Broadsheet on politics in dramatic form, 1832. Note the pro-American sentiments. Public Record Office, H.O. 64/18. 37 x 50 cm.

Manchester and Salford Elections
Broadsheet in newspaper form.

Manchester Public Library, 1835. 27x 40 cm.

V. CRIME

1. MURDER GALLERY (*pages 248–58*)

Cruel Murder
Broadsheet, n.d. 21 x 36 cm.

John Thurtell, Executed for the Murder of Weare: A Newspaper Report
Pierce Egan Sr, *Bell's Life in London*, 9 January 1824, p. 16.

John Thurtell (1794–1824) was hanged at Hertford for the murder of William Weare, a solicitor, whom Thurtell accused of cheating him at cards.

Pierce Egan had two interviews with Thurtell while the latter was under sentence of death, and published *Recollections of John Thurtell*, 1824.

Maria Marten
From actors' manuscript in Pettingell College, University of Canterbury.

The play was based on the real-life murder of Maria Marten by William Corder at the Red Barn in Suffolk on 18 May 1827. The murder aroused considerable interest when it was discovered some months later because of the extraordinary incidents associated with it. For instance, the body was found when a search was made at the Red Barn at the instigation of Maria's mother who, it was claimed, repeatedly dreamed that her daughter lay buried there. Flats: painted scenes sliding along grooves. L.C. etc.: stage positions. Picture: tableau. Hurry: rapid music. Mad: disturbed music.

A Horrible Murder
Broadsheet, n.d. 26 x 37.5 cm.

God's Revenge Against Murder
Ostensibly religious penny periodical, 1833–4. 20 x 27 cm.

James Greenacre, Executed for the Murder of Hannah Brown
'Old Barrister', *Newgate Calendar*, Derby, c. 1840, pp. 310–16.

Trial of Good
Broadsheet, 26 x 37.5 cm.

Daniel Good, a London coach-man, killed Jane Jones, his lover, in 1842, sawed the body into pieces and buried them in a stable.

The Sorrowful Lamentation of James Bloomfield Rush
An undated, anonymous broad-sheet.

On 28 November 1848, Rush, a tenant farmer on the estate of Isaac Jermy, shot and killed Jermy and his son and wounded the son's wife and the housemaid. This followed several disputes that Rush had had with his landlord after the succession of Jermy to the family property in 1838. Jermy's right of possession had been disputed and Rush had sided with John Larner, one of the claimants, who had taken forcible possession of Stanfield Hall in September 1838 but was expelled by the military.

2. ATTITUDES *(pages 258–64)*

Licentiousness of the Press
Livesey's *Moral Reformer*, iii, 1833, pp. 63–4.

Mary White
Broadsheet, undated. 21.5 x 38.5 cm.

On the Pursuit, Apprehension and Execution of Good
Editorial, *Cleave's Gazette of Variety*, 14 May 1842, p. 2, quoted from *The Spectator*, 1 May 1842.

Daniel Good, the Monster Murderer!!!
Unidentified penny Sunday news-paper cutting, John Johnson Collection.

Saved by Castlereagh
Thomas Frost, *Paul the Poacher*, 1848, pp. 131–4.

Thomas Frost (1821–92), a char-tist and journalist, took the plot for *Paul the Poacher* from William Clarke's *Three Courses and a Dessert*, 1830, but infused the story of a poacher who accidentally kills the gamekeeper with strong Radical feeling.

Killing No Murder
George Petrie, *Man*, 10 August 1834, p. 2.

Continued debate begun by pamphlet of the same name pub-lished in 1657, advising assassina-tion of Oliver Cromwell.

3. CRIMINALS IN ROMANCE *(pages 264–87)*

George Barnwell Murders His Uncle
George Barnwell, 1840, pp. 213–16.
Lillo's popular drama, *The London Merchant*, 1731, was based on an obscure Shropshire criminal cele-brated in ballad from about 1650. Lillo used the story to express the middle-class values of industry and chastity in scriptural terms. Per-formed annually in London until 1819, and a favourite with travel-ling troupes and amateur actors (including Dickens's Mr Pumble-chook), Lillo's portrayal of crime in apocalyptic terms continued.

My Poor Black Bess
Broadsheet. 19 x 25 cm.

Jack Sheppard's Songster
Broadsheet, c. 1840. Songs (first three Ainsworth's) in J. B. Buckstone, *Jack Sheppard* (1839).

Jack Sheppard's Third Escape from Newgate
Anonymous, *The Life and Adven-tures of Jack Sheppard*, c. 1840, pp. 273–8.

Jack Sheppard was hanged for theft at Tyburn in 1724, aged twenty-two. He entered popular mythology because of his three extraordinary escapes from New-gate prison. A Jack Sheppard craze followed the success of Ainsworth's novel.

Jack Sheppard
Penny Satirist, 14 December 1839.

The Mummy
G. W. M. Reynolds, *The Mysteries of London*, 1845, I, pp. 122–5.

This episode shows the 'hero' (a girl in disguise) caught up in the trade of dead bodies for dissection practised by 'resurrection men'. The drowning method shown here had been used by Bishop and May,

executed in 1831. The 'hero' escapes.

The String of Pearls
T. P. Prest, *The String of Pearls*, 1848, pp. 1–7, 58–9, 491–5.

The story may have been partly suggested by an article in *The Tell-Tale* of 1825 but the idea was not new – Catnach had been gaoled in 1818 for a ballad about a cannibalistic butcher. The story went through later penny-issue versions, and Dibdin Pitt's play *The String of Pearls*, Britannia, Hoxton, 1847, was the first of several popular dramatizations.

VI. HEROINES

1. A GOOD DEATH *(pages 289–92)*

The Dairyman's Daughter
Legh Richmond, 'The Dairyman's Daughter', *The Annals of the Poor*, Religious Tract Society, c. 1830, pp. 82–91.

The Reverend Legh Richmond's 'The Dairyman's Daughter' sold over two million copies in eighteen years and was the most popular of scores of accounts of 'dying in the Lord' which have fictional counterparts in the deaths of Little Nell and Paul Dombey in Dickens's novels.

The tract consists of letters the Reverend Richmond sent to conversations he held with Eliza-beth W—, the dairyman's daugh-ter, and a former servant, and includes the funeral services he conducted for both and musings on their deaths. It was violently attacked for its complacent piety in *Blackwood's Edinburgh Maga-zine*, December 1822.

2. IN DANGER *(pages 292–310)*

Fatherless Fanny
Anonymous, *Fatherless Fanny; or, the Little Mendicant*, 1819, pp. 322–30.

The Smuggler King
T. P. Prest, *The Smuggler King*, 1844, pp. 316–19.

Vileroy; or, The Horrors of Zindorf Castle

T. P. Prest, *Vileroy; or, The Horrors of Zindorf Castle*, 1844, pp. 239–45.

Ada, the Betrayed
James Malcolm Rymer, *Ada, the Betrayed; or, the Murder at the Old Smithy*, 1847, pp. 69–74.
James Malcolm Rymer, an intelligent and versatile writer, could manipulate the clichés of Gothic melodrama with a detachment that borders on the camp. *Ada, the Betrayed* is his best-known novel.

3. LOST (*pages 310–22*)

The Sorrows of Seduction
For detailed survey of the trade see Bracebridge Hemyng, 'Prostitution in London' in H. Mayhew, *London Labour and the London Poor*, extra volume, 1862, pp. 210–69.

The Frisky Girls of London
The Coal Hole Companion, c. 1844, pp. 50–51.

Harriet Wilson's Memoirs
Harriet Wilson, *Memoirs*, penny-issue edition, n.d., pp. 29–30.
Harriet Wilson was one of the most celebrated Regency courtesans. Before publishing her memoirs in 1838 she offered to remove passages referring to specific people – at a price. This is reputed to have occasioned the Duke of Wellington's reply, 'Publish and be damned'.

An Amazon
G. W. M. Reynolds, *The Mysteries of the Court of London*, vol. 1, 1849, pp. 56–60.
This is from Reynolds's widely popular exposé of the corruption of the Regency court. A penny weekly serial, *The Mysteries of the Court of London*, ran from 1849 to 1856.

A Derelict from the Regency Court
Anonymous broadsheet, *The Extraordinary Life and Death of Mary Pearce*, c. 1836.

Kate Elmore Defends Herself
Anonymous, *Eliza Grimwood: A Legend of the Waterloo Road*, c. 1838, pp. 25–7.

Nancy Dawson
The Coal Hole Companion, c. 1844, pp. 21–5.

4. WHITE SLAVES (*pages 322–30*)

The Distressed Sempstress
An anonymous undated broadsheet.

Miserrima!!!
G. W. M. Reynolds, *The Mysteries of London*, vol. 1, 1845, pp. 167–71.

The Factory Girl
Robert Dibb, broadsheet, dedicated to John Wood, M.P. for Preston. Published 1846 [?]; the Ten Hours Bill passed in 1847.

5. MUSIC HALL HEROINE (*page 331*)

Villikins and His Dinah
Anonymous, *The Modern Comic Songster*, 1846. Sung by Frederick Robson at the Grecian Saloon and Olympic Tavern, in the 1840s.

6. PENNY VALENTINES (*page 332*)

Valentines were originally folded papers with names from which you picked your lover as by lot. The O.E.D. records the modern sense of a letter or card occurring in 1821: a transitional form may have been a folded sheet so designed that you received a love message according to the way you opened it (there is an example in the British Museum, pressmark 1881 c. 351). By the 1840s cheap stationers blossomed with printed valentines in early February.

7. DOMESTIC ROMANCE (*pages 332–8*)

Lilias Granger, or Practical Romance
Family Herald, III, 23 August 1845.

8. THE QUEEN (*pages 339–46*)

The Queen, or the Pope?
Broadsheet, c. 1850. 25 x 19 cm.

Petticoats for Ever
Broadsheet, c. 1837. 19 x 25 cm.

The Coronation
Broadsheet, c. 1837. 19 x 25.5 cm.

Coronation Handkerchief
Broadsheet. A Radical protest against public spending on the Coronation. P.R.O., H.O. 64.18. 39 x 55 cm.

Prince Albert, in England
Broadsheet, n.d. 19 x 25 cm.

The Queen's Marriage – an Astrologer's View
The Penny Satirist, 21 December 1839, p. 1.

Descriptive List of the Royal Nuptial Ceremonies
Broadsheet, 1840. 48 x 61.5 cm.

Victoria the Star of England
Broadsheet. 19 x 24 cm.

BIBLIOGRAPHY

The Major Libraries Used

Birmingham Public Library
Bodleian Library, Oxford (*esp. John Johnson Collection*)
British Museum Library, Blooms-bury and Colindale, London
Brushmakers, National Society of, Watford (*Archives*)
Cambridge Folk Museum
Cambridge University Library (*esp. Madden Collection of Ballads*)

Canterbury Public Library (*esp. Courtenay Collection*)
Chetham's Library, Manchester
Friends House Library, London
Harvard University Library
Kent University Library, Canterbury
London University Library (*esp. Goldsmith's Collection*)
Manchester Public Library
Methodist Archives, London

New York Public Library (*esp. Sterling Collection*)
Public Record Office, London
Reading University Library (*esp. Museum of English Rural Life*)
St Bride's Printing Library, London
Sheffield University Library
Victoria and Albert Museum, London (*esp. Enthoven Theatre Collection*)
Yale University Library

SELECT BIBLIOGRAPHY OF CHEAP LITERATURE, LITERACY, AND THE SOCIAL BACKGROUND

(Place of publication London unless otherwise stated)

List of Headings
Advertising
Almanacks
Art and Popular Iconography
Astrology
Ballads, Broadsheets, Street Literature
Crime
Fiction and Chapbooks
Folklore and Superstition
'Life in London'
Literacy
Melodrama
Music Hall and Popular Entertainment
Newspapers
Peterloo
Poetry, Working-Class and Northern
Printing and Illustration
Religion and Tracts
Social Background 1: General
Social Background 2: Autobiography and Biography
Sport
Time

Advertising
(See also *Ballads* and *Printing*)
Burn, J. D.: *The Language of the Walls*, 1855 (Unrecognized, pioneer study of effects of advertising and mass print)
de Vries, L.: *Victorian Advertisements*, 1968 (Uncritically arranged, and mainly middle class, but good reproductions)
Knight, C., ed.: 'Advertisements', in *London*, vol. V, 1843, pp. 33–48 (Closely observed contemporary account)
'Literary Policeman': 'The Battle of the Posters', *Howitt's Journal*, I, 1847, pp. 54–5 (Attractive short piece on posters and daydreaming)
Rickards, M.: *The Rise and Fall of the Poster*, Newton Abbot 1973 (General, illustrated survey)
Sampson, H.: *A History of Advertising*, 1874 (Main Victorian study)
Smith, W.: *Advertise. How? When?*

Where?, 1863 (Handbook of advice)
Turner, E. S.: *The Shocking History of Advertising*, 1952 (Entertaining)

Almanacks
[Anon.]: 'English Almanacks', *London Magazine*, ser. 3, II, December 1828, pp. 591–601
Dick, J.: *On the Improvement of Knowledge by the S.D.U.K.* (n.d.) (Praises *British Almanack*)
Grobel, M.: *The Society for the Diffusion of Useful Knowledge*, M.A. Thesis, University of London 1933, esp. II, app. VI, p. v (The only thorough study of the Society, which paid particular attention to countering popular almanacks)
Heywood, A., Junior: *Three Papers on English Almanacks*, Manchester 1904 (Almanacks from Lilly to late nineteenth century. Useful)

Nicholson, M.: 'English Almanacks and the New Astrology', *Annals of Science*, IV, 1939, pp. 19–26 (Mainly eighteenth century, but relevant background material)

Art and Popular Iconography
(See also *Printing*)
Fletcher, G. S.: *Popular Art in England*, 1962 (Short, general study)
Gallo, Max: *The Poster in History*, New York, 1974 (Mainly later, but useful for wider perspective)
George, M. D.: *Hogarth to Cruikshank: Social Change in Graphic Satire*, 1962 (Well-illustrated survey by topics)
Gombrich, E. H.: 'Imagery and Art in the Romantic Period' in *Meditations on a Hobby Horse*, 1963 (On caricature)
Gorman, J.: *Banner Bright*, Allen Lane, 1973 (On working-class banners, illustrated)
Hackwood, F. W.: *William Hone*, 1912 (Standard biography)
Hall, S. and P. Whannel, eds.: *The Popular Arts*, 1964 (Mostly modern, but stimulating theory)
James, L.: 'An Artist in Time: George Cruikshank in Three Eras', *Princeton U.L. Chronicle*, XXV, 1973–4
Jones, B.: *The Unsophisticated Arts*, 1951 (Excellent general discussion)
Klingender, F. D.: *Art and the Industrial Revolution*, rev. 1968 (Influential study of impact of industry on nineteenth-century cultural sensibilities)
Leeson, R. A.: *United We Stand*, Bath 1971 (The history of working-class emblems)
Marx, E. and M. Lambert: *English Popular and Traditional Art*, 1951 (Including plaster casts, fairground painting, etc.)
Panofsky, E.: *Studies in Iconology*, New York, 1962
— *Meaning in the Visual Arts*, Harmondsworth 1970 (Earlier in concern, but with many insights relevant to nineteenth century)
Rennert, J.: *A Hundred Years of Circus Posters*, New York 1974, London 1975 (Stunning multinational collection)
Rickwood, E. (ed.): *Radical Squibs and Loyal Ripostes*, Bath 1971

(Reproduction of Hone's pamphlets and replies to them: useful introduction)

Astrology
(See also *Almanacks*, *Time*)
[Anon.]: *The Dreamer's Companion; or Universal Interpreter of Dreams*, c. 1832.
[Anon.]: *The Familiar Astrologer*, 1831
[Napoleon attrib., tr. H. Kirchenhofer]: *The Book of Fate, formerly in the Possession of Napoleon*, 14th ed., 1822 (Many versions)
[Nixon attrib.]: *The Wonderful Prophecies of Robert Nixon*, 1714 and constantly reprinted in early nineteenth century (Read by Dickens's Sam Weller)
— [Astrology], articles in *Penny Dispatch*, 4, 11, 18 September 1842 (Explains method for general reader)
— *The Straggling Astrologer; or Magazine of Celestial Intelligence*, 1824 (Typical of many fortune-telling periodicals)

Ballads, Broadsheets, Street Literature (See also *Poetry*, *Working-Class and Northern*)
Allan, T. O. G.: *Allan's Illustrated Edition of Tyneside Songs*, Newcastle 1881 (Indispensable collection, with introductions to the authors)
Bell, J. (ed.): *Rhymes of the Northern Bards*, Newcastle 1812
Berry, W. T. and G. Buday: 'Nineteenth Century Broadsheets', *Penrose Annual* 49, 1955, pp. 28–30
Bronson, B. H.: *The Ballad as Song*, Los Angeles 1969 (Important study linking words and music)
Buchan, D.: *The Ballad and the Folk*, 1971 (Emphatic and scholarly work on border ballads and the impact of print on oral traditions)
Collison, R.: *The Story of Street Literature*, 1973 (Lengthy excerpts; uneven commentary)
Crawhall, H.: *A Bewk o' Newcassel Songs*, 1888
Harland, J.: *Ballads and Songs of Lancashire*, 1865 (Important collection, good notes)
Henderson, W.: *Victorian Street

Ballads*, 1937
Hindley, C.: *The Catnach Press*, 1869
— *Curiosities of Street Literature*, 1871
— *The Life and Times of James Catnach*, 1867 (Hindley's work is the foundation of all subsequent research in Victorian street literature)
Hindley, C., Junior: *The History of the Catnach Press*, 1887 (Extensive reprinting from original blocks)
Holloway, J.: 'Cherry Girls and Crafty Maidens', 'Broadside Verse Traditions', 'The Irish Ballads', *The Listener*, 83, May–June 1970, pp. 680–86, 710–14, 744–8 (Broadcast talks, with reprinted examples of ballads discussed)
Ingledew, C. D. J. (ed.): *The Ballads and Songs of Yorkshire*, 1860
Jewett, L. (ed.): *The Ballads and Songs of Derbyshire*, 1867
Kidson, F. and M. Neal: *English Folk Song and Dance*, Cambridge 1915 (Useful section on broadsheet ballad)
Laws, G. Malcolm: *The British Literary Ballad*, Carbondale, Ill. 1971 (The use of the popular ballad by middle-class writers)
Lloyd, A. L.: *Folk Song in England*, 1967 (Good discussion of ballad in its social context by one both a singer and a scholar)
— *Come all ye Bold Miners*, 1952 (Fine collection of colliery songs, with notes)
Mackerness, E. D.: *A Social History of English Music*, 1964 (Useful study of the place of music in society)
Mayhew, H: *London Labour and the London Poor*, I, 1851, pp. 227–61 (The natural history of the ballad singer. Fascinating)
Muir, W.: *Living with Ballads*, 1951 (Growing up with song and dance in Scotland – of much wider relevance)
Nettel, R.: *Music in the Five Towns*, 1956 (Close study of growth of choral societies in northern societies, mainly later)
Pinto, V. de Sola and A. E. Rodway: *The Common Muse*, 1957 (Still the most stimulating general anthology of broadsheet ballads: good introduction)

Pulling, C.: *They Were Singing*, 1952 (General survey)

Robson, J. P.: *Bards of the Tyne*, 1849 (Includes much original material)

Shepard, L.: *The Broadside Ballad*, 1962

— *The History of Street Literature*, 1973

— *John Pitt: Ballad Printer of Seven Dials*, 1969 (The book on Pitt is the best sustained study)

Smith, C. M.: *The Little World of London*, 1886 (Much-quoted chapter on London broadsheet traffic)

Crime

Altick, R.: *Victorian Studies in Scarlet*, New York 1970 (Entertaining account of nineteenth-century preoccupation with crime)

Curtis, J.: *An Authentic History . . . Maria Marten*, 1828 (As interesting for Curtis's absorption in the event as for the crime itself)

De Quincey, T.: 'On Murder, considered as one of the Fine Arts', *Blackwood's Magazine*, XXI, 1827 (Three papers that move, through irony, to grotesque and sinister comedy: illustrates some complex attitudes behind interest in crime)

Hollingsworth, K.: *The Newgate Novel, 1830–1847*, Detroit 1963 (Study of middle-class criminal novels by Bulwer *et al.*)

Newton, H. C.: *Crime and the Drama*, 1927 (Shows how crime was taken up on the stage)

'Pelham, Camden' (ed.): *The New Newgate Calendar*, 1841 (One of several registers of criminal histories)

Fiction and Chapbooks

(For a full bibliography, see James, L., below)

(See also *Ballads*)

Cruse, A.: *The Englishman and his Books in the early Nineteenth Century*, 1930 (Outdated but still useful; mainly on middle-class light reading)

Dalziel, M.: *Popular Fiction a Hundred Years Ago*, 1957 (Includes discussion of moral status of cheap fiction and such topics as the heroines)

Davidson, W.: *Halfpenny Chapbooks*, Newcastle 1972

Dixon, J. H.: 'The Literature of the Lower Orders', *Daily News*, 26 October, 7 November, 9 November 1847 (Largely disapproving)

Frost, T.: *Forty Years' Recollections*, 1880 (Frost wrote some 'penny dreadfuls')

Haining, P. (ed.): *The Penny Dreadful*, 1975 (Anthology, introduction, bibliography)

Hunter, J. V. B.: 'George Reynolds', *Book Handbook*, IV, 1947, pp. 225–36 (On 'the most popular writer of his day')

James, L.: *Fiction for the Working Man*, Harmondsworth 1974 (Includes a much fuller bibliography than can be given here)

Jay, F.: *Peeps into the Past*, supp. to *Spare Moments*, 1918–19 (Useful bibliographies by enthusiastic amateur)

Leavis, Q. D.: *Fiction and the Reading Public*, 1932 (A pioneering survey that raised a continuing debate about the moral tendencies of mass literature)

Neuberg, V. S.: *The Penny Histories*, 1968 (Lively and illustrated account of chapbook trade)

— *Chapbook Bibliography* (Standard bibliography for studies of street literature)

Summers, A. J. M. M.-A.: *Gothic Bibliography*, 1940 (Uneven but still useful bibliography of sensational fiction)

— *Gothic Quest*, 1941 (On Gothic novel)

Taylor, J. T.: *Early Opposition to the English Novel*, New York 1943 (Neglected study of moral controversy surrounding early novels)

Turner, E. S.: *Boys will be Boys*, rev. 1957 (Includes spirited account of penny-issue fiction)

Watt, W. W.: *Shilling Shockers of the Gothic School*, Cambridge, Mass. 1932 (Short, useful introduction to Gothic chapbooks)

Folklore and Superstition

(See also *Social Background*)

[Anon.]: 'Popular Superstition', *Working Man's Friend*, VI, 1851, pp. 176–9 (Disapproving)

Bamford, S.: *Walks in South Lancashire*, 1844, pp. 205–10

Blakeborough, R.: *Wit, Character, Folklore and Customs of the North Riding of Yorkshire*, 1898 (Especially pp. 67–93, 126–209)

Brigg, K. M.: *A Dictionary of British Folk Tales*, Part A, Indiana 1970; Part B, London 1971 (The standard work on this: fascinating)

Burne, C. S. (ed.): *Shropshire Folklore*, 1883

Colquhoun, J. C.: *A History of Magic, Witchcraft and Animal Magnetism*, 1851 (Written on the borderland between magic and science)

Harland, J. and T. T. Wilkinson: *Lancashire Folk Lore*, 1867

— *Lancashire Legends, Traditions, Pageants, Sports &c.*, 1873 (Both are important source-books)

Hole, C.: *Witchcraft in England*, 1945 (Entertainingly written)

Hone, W. (ed.): *The Every-day Book*, 1826–7

— *The Table Book*, 1827–8 (Useful rag-bags of entertaining information; indexed)

Hunt, R.: *Popular Romances of the West of England*, 1881; New York 1916 (Collected in 1820s when wandering 'droll-tellers' still roamed Devon and Cornwall)

Nicholson, J.: *Folk Lore of East Yorkshire*, 1890

Porter, E.: *Cambridgeshire Customs and Folklore*, 1969

Sternberg, T.: *The Dialect and Folklore of Northamptonshire*, 1851

'Life in London'

[Anon]: *Real Life in London*, 1821–2 (Less dash, more facts, than Egan's work)

Egan, P., Sr: *Life in London*, 1820–21 (Highly influential in the development of urban literature, though almost unreadable today)

Hindley, C.: *The True History of Tom and Jerry*, 1888

Nicholson, R. (ed.): *The Town*, 1839–42 (Journal of the 'man-about-town')

Reid, J. C.: *Bucks and Bruisers*, 1971 (Carefully researched account of Pierce Egan, his writings and sporting milieu)

Smith, J. T.: *Vagabondia*, 1817 (Pre-Egan account of London beggars)

Literacy
(See also *Social Background*)
Altick, R. D.: *The English Common Reader 1800–1900*, Chicago 1957 (Basic study of subject, factual and readable)
Arnold, M.: *Culture and Anarchy*, 1869 (Later, but cannot be ignored in any discussion of mass literacy)
Bailey, S.: *Essay on the Formation and Publication of Opinions*, 1821 (Utilitarian statement on 'march of knowledge')
Berelson, B. and M. Janowitz (eds.): *Reader in Public Opinion and Communication*, Glencoe, rev. 1953 (Becoming outdated, but still a useful primer on sociological perspectives)
Cipolla, C. M.: *Literacy and the Development of the West*, Harmondsworth 1969
Cooper, T.: 'The Press and the People', *Leicestershire Movement*, I, 13 April 1850 (Plea for working-class educated literature)
Goldstrom, J. M.: *The Social Context of Education 1808–70*, 1972 (Shows how education was used as a socially conditioning agent)
Goody, H. and I. Watt (eds.): *Literacy and Traditional Societies*, Cambridge 1968 (Anthology of both general and specific relevance)
Halloran, J. D.: *Control or Consent?*, 1963 (Introduction to social implications of mass communications)
Harrison, J. F. C.: *Living and Learning 1790–1960*, 1961 (Education in the total social milieu: excellent survey)
Lowenthal, L.: *Literature, Popular Culture and Society*, Englewood Cliffs, New Jersey 1961 (Includes chapter on nineteenth-century debate)
McLuhan, M.: *The Gutenberg Galaxy*, Toronto 1962 (Stimulating conjectures about the effects of print on society)
Merryweather, M.: *Experiences of Factory Life*, 1862 (Includes account of educating mill-girls)
— 'On the Advantages of Reading', *Cottager's Monthly Visitor*, April 1821, pp. 168–70 (The Church of England case)
Quinlan, M. J.: *Victorian Prelude*, New York 1941 (Background to religious and social developments)
Reisman, D.: 'The Oral and Written Traditions', in E. Carpenter and M. McLuhan (eds.), *Explorations in Communication*, Boston 1960 (Highly quotable essay on the social effects of reading ability)
Webb, R. K.: *The British Working Class Reader 1770–1848*, 1955 (Standard study)
— 'Working Class Readers in Early Victorian England', *English Historical Review*, 65, 1950, pp. 33–5

Melodrama
(See also *Music Hall and Popular Entertainment*)
Barker, C.: 'The Chartists, Theatre, Reform and Research', *Theatre Quarterly*, I, October–December 1971, pp. 3–10 (hereafter *T.Q.*) (Links popular drama and radicalism)
Bentley, E.: *The Life of the Drama*, 1965 (Important section on melodrama)
Booth, M.: *English Melodrama*, 1965 (Good general introduction)
Crawford, A. L.: *Sam and Sallie*, 1933 (Fictionalized account of the Lanes of the Britannia, Hoxton, and East End Theatre)
Dickens, C.: 'The Amusements of the People', *Household Words*, I, 1850, pp. 13–15, 57–60 (A patronizing tone cannot hide Dickens's sympathetic fascination)
— 'Private Theatricals', in *Sketches by 'Boz'*, 1837
Disher, W. D.: *Blood and Thunder* 1949
— *Melodrama*, 1954 (Both stimulating, but ill-documented)
Egan, P., Sr: *Life of an Actor*, 1825 (Factually based account of actor's progress to success)
Fitzball, E.: *Thirty-five Years of a Dramatic Author's Life*, 1859 (Lively autobiography of prolific dramatic hack and inventor of stage effects)
Grant, J.: 'Penny Theatres' in *Sketches in London*, 1838, pp. 161–92 (Important first-hand witness)
Last, J. M.: 'Andrew Ducrow' in *T.Q.*, pp. 37–9 (On the most famous of equestrian actors)
Nicholson, W.: *The Struggle for a Free Stage in London*, Boston 1906 (The war on the Licensing Act and its social implications)
Nicoll, A.: *A History of English Drama, Vol. IV, 1800–1850*, 1955 (The standard survey)
[Parliamentary Papers]: *House of Commons S.C. Report on Dramatic Literature*, 1831–2 (Includes evidence by actors and managers)
Rahill, F.: *The World of Melodrama*, Penn. State U.P., 1967 (Includes English, American and French situations)
Rowell, G.: *The Victorian Theatre*, 1956 (Scholarly history)
Siddons, H.: *Practical Illustrations of Rhetorical Gestures*, 1822 (Fascinating handbook for actors, with illustrations of how to express different emotions)
Speaight, G.: *Juvenile Drama*, 1946 (Toy theatres are an important source of information about Victorian drama: this is the standard history)
Sypher, W.: 'The Aesthetic of Revolution: the Marxist Melodrama', *Kenyon Review*, X, Summer 1968, pp. 431–44 (Melodrama as the central nineteenth-century mode)
Trewin, J. C.: *The Pomping Folk in the Nineteenth Century*, 1968 (The lives of travelling actors, from contemporary accounts)
Trussler, S.: 'A Chronology of Early Melodrama', *T.Q.*, pp. 19–22
Warwick, L.: *Theatre Un-Royal*, Northampton 1974 (Drama and society in a provincial town)
Winter, M. H.: *Le Théâtre du Merveilleux*, Paris 1962 (Studies the element of wonder in nineteenth-century theatre)

Music Hall and Popular Entertainment
Briggs, A.: *Mass Entertainment*, Melbourne 1960
Davison, P. (ed.): *Songs of the British Music Hall*, New York 1971 (Songs with music and introduction)

Disher, M. W.: *Victorian Song*, 1955 (Surveys varied range of subjects)

Frost, T.: *The Old Showmen*, 1874 (On fairground performers)

McKechnie, S.: *Popular Entertainments through the Ages*, 1931

Mander, R. and J. Nicholson: *British Music Hall*, 1965 (History)

Mellor, G. J.: *The Northern Music Hall*, Newcastle 1970

Miller, D. P.: *The Life of a Showman*, 1849 (Lively autobiography)

Robson, J. P.: *The Life and Adventures of . . . Billy Purvis*, Newcastle 1849 (Purvis was the most famous clown of the North of England)

Sanger, 'Lord' G.: *Seventy Years a Showman*, 1910 (Good impression of circus life)

Scott, H.: *The Early Doors*, 1946 (Unpretentious but well informed)

Thackeray, W. M.: *The History of Pendennis*, 1849–50

— *The Newcomes*, 1854–5 (Good vivid pictures of music halls, of the more genteel caste)

Wilson, A. E.: *East End Entertainment*, 1954

Newspapers

Aspinal, A.: 'The Circulation of Newspapers in the Nineteenth Century', *R.E.S.*, XXII, January 1946, pp. 29–43

Bourne, H. R. F.: *English Newspapers*, 1887 (Survey)

Briggs, A.: 'Press and Public in Early Nineteenth Century Birmingham', *Dugdale Society Occasional Papers* no. 8, 1950, 21ff. (Important case-study of development of local press)

Campbell, T. C.: *The Battle of the Press*, 1899 (Examines Carlile's war with the Stamp Office and the Censor, often from Carlile's own documents)

Collet, C. D.: *History of the Taxes on Knowledge*, 1890 (On Stamp Act and opposition to it)

Grant, J.: *The Newspaper Press*, 1871–2 (Grant worked in Fleet Street)

Guest, J.: 'A Free Press, and How it became Free', in W. Hutton, *History of Birmingham*, 6th ed., Birmingham 1861, pp. 494–506 (A radical view, by a veteran of the fight)

Hatton, J.: *Journalistic London*, 1882 (The newspaper world)

Herd, H.: *The March of Journalism*, 1952 (Survey of reporters' profession)

Hollis, P.: *The Pauper Press*, 1970 (Densely documented study of the unstamped press and its implications)

Kellett, E. E.: 'The Press' in G. M. Young, ed., *Early Victorian England*, 1934

Morison, S.: *The English Newspaper*, Cambridge 1932 (Basic study)

— *A Catalogue of . . . John Bell and . . . John Browne Bell*, 1931 (Studies two major forces in Victorian journalism)

[Parliamentary Papers]: *House of Commons, S.C. on Newspaper Stamps*, 1851, xvii (Details of circulation and readership)

Read, D.: *Press and People, 1790–1850*, 1961 (Examines social impact of press in selected areas)

Routledge, J.: *Chapters in the History of Popular Progress*, 1876 (Includes struggle for freedom from Stamp Act)

Smith, W. A.: *Shepherd Smith the Universalist*, 1892 (Life of J. E. Smith, a bizarre mystic and journalist, whose enterprises included the successful *Penny Satirist*)

Thompson, D.: 'La presse de la classe ouvrière anglaise', in J. Godechot, ed., *La Presse ouvrière, 1819–1850*, Paris 1966 (Important study of the radical press at this period)

Wadsworth, A. P.: *Newspaper Circulation, 1800–1954*, Manchester 1955

Watts, W. H.: *My Private Notebook*, 1862 (A reporter's account of his trade, and its relation to the literature of the day)

Wickwar, W. H.: *The Struggle for the Freedom of the Press*, 1928 (Covers the period following the 1819 Seditious Publications Act)

Wiener, J.: *Unstamped British Periodicals, 1830–1836*, 1970 (Outstanding detective work in tracing ephemera)

— *The War of the Unstamped*, Ithaca 1969 (Readable and scholarly)

Wiles, R. M.: *Freshest Advices:*

English Provincial Newspapers in England, Columbus, Ohio 1965 (Standard study of important area of journalism)

Peterloo

House, H.: *All in Due Time*, 1955, pp. 46–67 (Why Peterloo is humanly interesting)

Read, D.: *Peterloo and its Background*, Manchester 1958 (Peterloo in context)

Walmsley, R.: *Peterloo*, 1968 (New material, though few new conclusions)

Poetry, Working-Class and Northern

(For fuller bibliography, see Vicinus, M., below)

Andrews, W.: *North Country Poets*, 1888 (Anthology with notes)

Briggs, A.: 'Ebenezer Elliott', *Cambridgeshire Journal*, III, 1950, pp. 686–95

Brown, S.: *Ebenezer Elliott*, University of Leicester Victorian Studies Handlists, no. 3, 1971 (Bibliography)

Burland, J.: *Poems on Various Subjects*, 1865 (Chartist poet)

Carlyle, T.: 'Corn Law Rhymes', *Edinburgh Review*, LV, July 1832, pp. 338–61 (On Elliott)

Collins, P.: *Thomas Cooper the Chartist*, Nottingham 1969 (Wide-ranging Byron lecture)

Cooper, T.: *Poetical Works*, 1877 (Includes 'Purgatory of Suicides')

Elliott, E.: *Poems*, 1840 (See in particular 'The Splendid Village')

Heaton, W.: *The Flowers of Calder Dale*, Halifax 1848

Hull, G.: *The Poets and Poetry of Blackburn*, Blackburn 1902

Kovalev, Y. V. (ed.): *An Anthology of Chartist Verse*, Moscow 1956 (The most complete available anthology of this: introduction translated from Russian in *Victorian Studies*, II, 1958, pp. 117–38)

Massey, G.: *Poems and Ballads*, 1854 (For a short account of his life, see above, pp. 191–4)

Mather, J.: *The Songs of Joseph Mather*, Sheffield 1862 (Astringent radical verse from the turn of the century)

Millhouse, R.: *The Destinies of Man*, 1832–4 (Example of ambitious verse epic)

Prince, J. C.: *Hours with the Muses*, Manchester 1841 (Only moments of poetic achievement)

Ridings, E.: *The Village Festival*, Manchester 1848 (Rural nostalgia)

Southey, R.: *Lives of the Uneducated Poets*, 1835 (Middle-class view, sympathetic)

Thompson, W.: 'The Politics of Poets', *Chartists Circular*, Glasgow, 42, 11 July 1846, p. 170 (Radical perspectives)

Vicinus, M.: 'The Study of Nineteenth Century British Working Class Poetry', in L. Kampf and P. Lauter, eds., *The Politics of Literature*, New York 1970, 1972, pp. 322–53

— 'Working Class Voices in an Industrial Town', in H. J. Dyos and M. Wolff, eds., *The Victorian City*, 1973, ii, pp. 739–62

— *The Industrial Muse*, 1974 (Standard survey of Victorian working-class poetry; full bibliography)

Wilson, T.: *Pitman's Pay and Other Poems*, 1872 (Includes important verse descriptions of miners' work conditions)

Printing and Illustration
(See also *Art*)

Bewick, T.: *A Memoir*, Newcastle 1862 (Vivid glimpse of Bewick's personality)

Catling, T.: *My Life's Pilgrimage*, 1911 (Autobiography including details of working for the popular publisher E. Lloyd)

Chambers, W.: *A Memoir of Robert Chambers*, 2nd ed., Edinburgh 1872

— *The Story of a Long and Busy Life*, Edinburgh 1882 (Progress from humble beginnings to becoming major publishers largely through success in cheap literature)

Jackson, M.: *The Pictorial Press*, 1885

Knight, C.: *The Old Printer and the Modern Press*, 1854

— *Passages in a Working Life*, 1864 (Knight was an important figure in cheap publishing both for his technical expertise and his crusading educational spirit)

Lewis, J.: *The Anatomy of Printing*, 1971

— *Printed Ephemera*, Ipswich 1962 (The latter is a valuable anthology of English and American items; paperback edition 1969)

'Old Printer' (J. Farlow Wilson): *A Few Personal Recollections*, 1896 (Fragmentary but fascinating personal view of cheap printing scene)

Pike, G. Holden: *John Cassell*, 1894 (Life of leading temperance worker and publisher for the working classes)

Plant, M.: *The English Book Trade*, 1939 (Useful technical history)

Savage, W.: *A Dictionary of the Art of Printing*, 1841

Twyman, M.: *Printing 1770–1970*, 1970 (Useful history: anthology of printed ephemera somewhat overcrowded)

Wood, R.: *Victorian Delights*, 1967 (Well-reproduced file of West Hartlepool printer in nineteenth century; full of social and typographical interest)

Wroot, W. E.: 'William Milner of Halifax', *Bookman*, March 1897, pp. 169–75 (On leading cheap publisher in north, with details of his best-sellers)

Religion and Tracts

Armytage, W. H. G.: *Heavens Below*, 1961 (Utopian movements)

Balleine, G. R.: *Past Finding Out*, 1956 (Sympathetic account of prophetic movements)

Chadwick, W. O.: *The Victorian Church*, 1970 (Scholarly history)

Gay, J. D.: *The Geography of Religion in England*, 1971 (Uneven but suggestive survey of distribution of religious sects in England)

Green, S. G.: *The Story of the Religious Tract Society*, 1899 (Best account of major distributor of tracts)

Halévy, E., transl. E. I. Watkins and D. A. Barker: *A History of the English People in 1815*, 1912, Bk. III. (The study of the place of religion in popular politics here started a continuing debate)

Harrison, B.: 'Religion and Recreation in Nineteenth Century England', *Past and Present*, no. 38, December 1967, pp. 98–125 (On the moral regulation of sports and pastimes)

Harrison, J. F. C.: *Robert Owen and the Owenites in Britain and America*, 1969 (Goes beyond Owen in evaluating utopian movements and spirit of the age)

Himmelfarb, G.: 'Postscript on Halévy', in her *Victorian Minds*, 1968, pp. 292–9 (Succinct account of debate on political significance of Methodism, including what protagonists *don't* say to each other)

Hobsbawm, E. J.: *Primitive Rebels*, 1959 (Seminal work on motivation of working-class radicals)

Hopkins, M. A.: *Hannah More and Her Circle*, 1947 (On leading tract writer and publisher)

Inglis, K. S.: *Churches and the Working Classes in Victorian England*, 1963 (Standard study)

Owen, R.: *An Address to the Inhabitants of New Lanark*, 2nd ed., 1816 (Owen at his most explicit and hopeful)

Rogers, P. G.: *The Battle of Bossenden Wood*, 1961 (Standard account of 'Sir William Courtenay')

Spinney, G. H.: 'Cheap Repository Tract: Hazard and Marshall Edition', *The Library*, ser. 4, XX, 1939, pp. 295–340

Thomas, K.: *Religion and the Decline of Magic*, 1971 (Too early for this anthology, but a brilliant study affecting later studies in religion and society)

Townsend, W. J., H. B. Workman and G. Eayrs (eds.): *A New History of Methodism*, 1909 (Standard history)

Wearmouth, R.: *Methodism and the Working Class Movements of England 1800–1850*, 1934 (Argues case for political importance of religious nonconformity)

Social Background 1: General
(See also *Folklore, Literacy, Religion*)

Aspin, C.: *Lancashire, the First Industrial Society*, Helmshore 1969 (Written with extensive use of local records and autobiographies)

Briggs, A.: 'The Language of Class in Early Victorian England' in A. Briggs and J. Saville, eds.,

Essays in Labour History 1886–1923, 1960 (On the evolution of the concepts 'middle' and then 'working' class)

Chesney, K.: *The Victorian Underworld*, 1972 (Lively account for general reader)

Cobbett, W.: *Rural Rides*, 1830; G. Woodcock, ed., Harmondsworth 1967 (Classic of both history and literature)

Cole, G. D. H. and Raymond Postgate: *The Common People 1746–1946*, rev. 1942 (Readable and informed survey)

Cole, G. D. H.: *Chartist Portraits*, 1941

— *The Life of William Cobbett*, 3rd ed. 1947 (Standard biography)

— *A Short History of the British Working-Class Movement 1789–1947*, 1948

Coleman, T.: *The Railway Navvies*, rev. Harmondsworth 1968 (Highly readable account of the labourers who changed the face of England in two decades)

Dyos, H. J. (ed.): *The Study of Urban History*, 1968 (Includes exploration of the sensibility of urban communities)

Dyos, H. J. and M. Wolff (eds.): *The Victorian City*, 1973 (Includes chapters on aspects of working-class culture in the towns)

Engels, F.: *The Condition of the Working Class in England*, 1892 (Still fresh, humane and indignant)

Francis, J.: *A History of the English Railway, 1820–1845*, 1851

Frow, R., L. Frow and M. Katanka: *Strikes*, 1971 (Documents of significant agitations, including Luddites and Tolpuddle Martyrs)

Fuller, M. D.: *West Country Friendly Societies*, Reading 1964

Gosden, P. H. J.: *The Friendly Societies of England*, Manchester 1961 (The standard survey, but to be supplemented by such local studies as M. D. Fuller's, above)

Harrison, B.: *Drink and the Victorians*, 1971 (Of interest beyond the immediate subject, teetotalism, as a study of the Victorian temper)

Head, Sir G.: *Home Tour through the Manufacturing Districts of England in ... 1835*, 1836

Hobsbawm, E. J.: *Labouring Men*, 1964 (Empathetic scholarship)

Hobsbawm, E. J. and G. Rudé: *Captain Swing*, Harmondsworth 1973 (Standard work on the 'Swing' rural disturbances)

Hollis, P. (ed.): *Class and Conflict in Nineteenth Century England*, 1973 (Anthology of readings)

Howitt, W.: *The Rural Life of England*, 1838 (Amateur but useful survey; emphasizes the decline of country customs in nineteenth century)

'A Journeyman Engineer' (Thomas Wright): *Some Customs and Habits of the Working Class*, 1867 (Includes drinking habits, theatre-going, and popular medicine)

Knight, C.: *London*, 1841–4 (From drains to almanacks, from architecture to authors)

Laslett, P.: *The World We Have Lost*, rev. 1970 (Largely early, but illuminating study of the societies behind the Victorian age)

Lawson, J.: *Letters to the Young on Progress in Pudsey*, Stanningley 1887 (Vivid reminiscences of early decades of the century)

Leifchild, J. R.: *Our Coal and Coal-Pits*, 1853 (Notes reading habits and superstitions of colliers, but to be used with caution)

Levine, G.: *The Emergence of Victorian Consciousness*, New York 1967 (Perceptive anthology of Victorian writing arranged to show 'the Spirit of the Age')

Ludlow, J. M. and L. Jones: *The Progress of the Working Classes 1832–1867*, 1867 (Christian Socialist critique of working-class culture, including reading habits, singing and sport)

Mayhew, H.: *London Labour and the London Poor*, 1851–64 (Unflagging research without condescension into life of the Victorian underprivileged)

Mayhew, H.: *The Unknown Mayhew*, E. P. Thompson and E. Yeo, eds., Harmondsworth 1973 (Mayhew's uncollected journalism)

Miller, T.: *Our Old Town*, 1857 (Slightly sentimentalized reminiscences of early nineteenth-century Gainsborough)

Peel, F.: *The Spen Valley: Past and Present*, Heckmondwike 1893 (Includes background to Plug riots of 1842)

Pimlott, R.: *Recreations*, 1968 (Profusely illustrated)

Pinchbeck, I.: *Women Workers and the Industrial Revolution, 1750–1850*, 1930

Scruton, W.: *Pen and Pencil Pictures of Old Bradford*, Bradford 1889 (Particularly good on early theatre in Bradford)

Sigsworth, E. M. and T. J. Wyke: 'A Study of Victorian Prostitution and Venereal Disease', in M. Vicinus (ed.), *Suffer and be Still*, Bloomington 1972, pp. 77–91 (Usefully outlines important issues)

Thompson, D. (ed.): *The Early Chartists*, 1971 (Excellent anthology of Chartist literature from autobiography to handbills)

Thompson, E. P.: *The Making of the English Working Class*, 1963, rev. Harmondsworth 1969 (Seminal in-depth study from Radical angle)

Ward, J. T.: *The Factory Movement, 1830–1855*, Newton Abbot 1962

Ward, J. T. (ed.): *Popular Movements 1830–1850*, 1970 (Useful collection of essays)

Williams, R.: *The Long Revolution*, Harmondsworth 1965 (How English class system has evolved through gradual change)

— *The Country and the City*, 1973 (Especially chs. 15–17 on town and country life)

Social Background 2: Autobiography and Biography

Adams, W. E.: *Memoirs of a Social Atom*, 1903 (Adams was born in Cheltenham, 1832. His autobiography includes vivid accounts of rural customs, and, briefly, his reading of 'penny dreadfuls')

Andrews, W. and J. Gutteridge: *Master and Artisan in Victorian England*, 1969 (Diary and biography: Andrews achieved wealth; Gutteridge remained an impoverished ribbon-weaver. Mostly later)

Bamford, S., W. H. Challoner (ed.): *Autobiography*, 1967 (Combines *Early Days*, 1849 and *Passages in* the *Life of a Radical*, 1844. With Cobbett's *Rural Rides*, the high point of nineteenth-century working-class literary achievement)

Barker, J., J. T. Barker (ed.): *Life*, 1880 (Barker was both a religious journalist and a remarkable one-man publishing enterprise)

Blincoe, R.: *A Memoir of Robert Blincoe*, Manchester 1832 (Derbyshire factory atrocities: Factory Act propaganda)

Brierley, B.: *Home Memories and Recollections*, Manchester 1886 (Mostly later: life in Manchester by dialect writer)

Burn, J. D.: *Autobiography of a Beggar Boy*, 1855 (Courageous childhood of one of the poor who escaped to respectability)

Burnett, J. (ed.): *Useful Toil*, 1974 (Excellent collection of working-class autobiographies; bibliography)

Cooper, T.: *Life*, 1871 (The vivid childhood reminiscences of Lincolnshire stand out best in this Chartist autobiography)

Everett, J.: *The Walls End Miner*, 1835 (Methodist memoir of William Crister)

Heaton, W.: *The Old Soldier: together with a Sketch of the Author's Life*, 1872

Holyoake, G. J.: *The Life and Character of Richard Carlile*, 1849
— *The Life and Character of Henry Hetherington*, 1849
— *Sixty Years of an Agitator's Life*, 1892 (Important documents concerning both working-class organization and cheap literature)

Jackson, T.: *Recollections of my own Life and Times*, 1873 (Autobiography of important Methodist leader, including childhood reminiscences of village life)

Linton, W. J.: *Memories*, 1895 (Engraver associated with popular literature)
— *James Watson: a Memoir*, 1879 (Working-class organizer and publisher)

Lovett, W.: *Life and Struggles*, 1876 (A working man 'in pursuit of Bread, Knowledge and Freedom')

Neff, F.: *Victorian Working Women: an Historical and Literary*

Study of Women in British Industries and Professions, 1832–1850, 1929

'Old Potter' (C. Shore): *When I was a Child*, 1903 (Vivid account of self-education under difficulties, and of life in the potteries)

Pearce, J. (ed.): *The Life and Teaching of Joseph Livesey*, 1873 (Includes autobiographical memoir of teetotal leader)

Place, F.: *Autobiography*, 1972

Reitzel, W. (ed.): *William Cobbett: the Progress of a Ploughboy to a Seat in Parliament*, 1933 (Anthology of autobiographical passages)

Smith, C. M.: *A Working Man's Way in the World*, 1857 (Life of printer: full of interest for history of printing)

Somerville, A.: *Autobiography of a Working Man*, 1848 (Self-education)

Wallas, G.: *The Life of Francis Place 1771–1851*, 1925

Wedgwood, H. A.: *People of the Potteries*, Bath 1970 (Vivid anecdotes of Staffordshire people and events, including pot-seller caught unwittingly in Peterloo)

Williams, Gwyn A.: *Rowland Detrosier*, New York 1965 (Life of working-class leader)

Sport

Alexander, S.: *St Giles' Fair 1830–1914*, Ruskin College History Workshop Pamphlet 2, Oxford 1970 (Excellent local history)

Alken, H.: *The National Sports of Great Britain*, 1832

Arlott, J., ed.: *Oxford Companion to Games and Sports*, 1975

Aspin, J.: *Ancient Customs, Sports and Pastimes of the English*, 1832 (Mostly early)

Bowen, R.: *Cricket*, 1970 (Attempt to be the definitive history, but thin on localized knowledge)

Egan, P., Sr: *Boxiana*, 1812, 1818, 1821, n.s. 1825, 1829
— *Pierce Egan's Book of Sports*, 1832 (Mannered style but enthusiastic expertise)

Elias, N. and E. Dunning: 'Folk Football', in E. Dunning (ed.), *The Sociology of Sport*, 1971, pp. 116–32 (Examines the ritual origins)

Ford, J.: *Prize-Fighting*, 1971 (Scholarly)

Hackwood, F. W.: *Old English Sports*, 1907 (Mainly early)

Harrison, B.: See above, 'Religion and Recreation' under *Religion*

Hazlitt, W.: 'The Fight', 1822 (Vivid Romantic movement perspective on boxing struggle; the future murderer Thurtell appears as 'Tom Turtle')

Higginson, A. H.: *British and American Sporting Authors*, 1951 (Useful references)

Hole, C.: *English Sports and Pastimes*, 1948 (Readable general introduction)

James, C. L. R.: *Beyond a Boundary*, 1963 (Brilliant if idiosyncratic study of cricket as art and social force)

Leibling, A. J.: *The Sweet Science*, 1956 (On boxing; enthusiastic)

Litt, W.: *Wrestliana*, Whitehaven 1823 (Not to be compared with *Boxiana*, but useful)

Malcolmson, R. W.: *Popular Recreations in English Society 1700–1850*, 1973 (Scholarly study extensively using local records; most useful on earlier period)

Marples, M.: *A History of Football*, 1954

Mitford, M. R.: 'A Country Cricket Match', in *Our Village*, 1824–32

Smith, H.: *Festivals, Games and Amusements, Ancient and Modern*, 1831 (Largely antiquarian interest)

Strutt, J., ed. W. Hone: *The Sports and Pastimes of the People of England*, 1838 (Updates Strutt's basic study: illustrated and indexed)

Turner, E. S.: *All Heaven in a Rage*, 1964 (Popular but informed account of opposition to cruel sports in England)

Walvin, J.: *The People's Game*, 1973 (History of football)

Warner, P. F. (ed.): *Imperial Cricket*, 1912 (History illustrated)

Time

Buckley, J. H.: *The Triumph of Time*, Cambridge, Mass. 1967 (Stimulating study of changing time concepts in nineteenth century)

Durkheim, E. R.: *The Elementary Forms of Religious Life*, 1915 (Classic sociological text on the way religion affects social perspectives, including time)

Kermode, F.: *The Sense of an Ending*, 1967 (How time-sense dictates fictional forms)

Leach, E. R.: 'Two Essays concerning the Symbolic Representation of Time', in his *Rethinking Anthropology*, 1961 (Moves on from Durkheim to suggest how we create structures which give social meaning to time)

Thompson, E. P.: 'Time, Work-discipline and Industrial Capitalism', *Past and Present*, no. 29, December 1964, pp. 50–62 (Brilliant and densely documented essay on industrialism and time)

Whistler, L.: *The English Festivals*, 1947

Wright, A. R., ed. T. E. Jones: *British Calendar Customs*, 1936–40 (Useful reference)

INDEX

The following are listed under main headings:
ALMANACKS; BROADSHEETS AND
CHAPBOOKS; CRIMINALS; EMBLEMS;
PERIODICALS; PLAYBILLS; POSTERS AND
HANDBILLS; SONGBOOKS; TRACTS.
Figures in italics indicate reproduced material.